Writing First

PRACTICE IN CONTEXT

WITH READINGS

Writing First

PRACTICE IN CONTEXT

WITH READINGS

Laurie G. Kirszner

University of the Sciences in Philadelphia

Stephen R. Mandell

Drexel University

Bedford/St. Martin's

Boston ■ New York

For Bedford/St. Martin's

Developmental Editor: Talvi Laev
Senior Project Editor: Michael Weber
Senior Production Supervisor: Dennis J. Conroy
Marketing Manager: Brian Wheel
Editorial Assistant: Belinda Delpêche
Art Director: Lucy Krikorian
Text and Cover Design: Wanda Kossak and Wanda Lubelska
Photo Research: Inge King
Cover Photos: top, left to right: Bob Daemmrich/Stock, Boston; David Wells/
    The Image Works; Gary Conner/PhotoEdit; Paul Barton/The Stock Market;
    bottom, left to right: Bob Mahoney/The Image Works; David Young-Wolff/
    PhotoEdit; David Weintraub/Photo Researchers; T. Stewart/The Stock Market
Composition: Monotype Composition Company, Inc.
Printing and Binding: R. R. Donnelly & Sons Co.

President: Charles H. Christensen
Editorial Director: Joan E. Feinberg
Editor in Chief: Nancy Perry
Director of Editing, Design, and Production: Marcia Cohen
Managing Editor: Erica T. Appel

Library of Congress Catalog Card Number: 99-62230

5 4 3 2
f e

For information, contact: Bedford/St. Martin's, 75 Arlington Street, Boston,
MA 02116   (617-426-7440)

ISBN: 0-312-19380-7

Acknowledgments

Picture acknowledgements
    Unit openers: *Unit 1:* Paul Barton/The Stock Market; *Unit 2:* Bob Mahoney/
The Image Works; *Unit 3:* Gary Conner/PhotoEdit; *Unit 4:* Bob Daemmrich/Stock,
Boston; *Unit 5:* T. Stewart/The Stock Market; *Unit 6:* David Young-Wolff/PhotoEdit;
Unit 7: David Weintraub/Photo Researchers; *Unit 8:* David Wells/The Image Works.

Acknowledgments and copyrights are continued at the back of the book on pages
585–86, which constitute an extension of the copyright page.

Preface for Instructors

In college, writing comes first. As soon as students set foot in a classroom, they are asked to write—to take notes, to complete assignments, and to pass exams. But writing is also crucial outside the classroom, because it empowers students for life, enabling them to participate more fully in their communities and their workplaces. As our years in the classroom have taught us, students begin to value writing skills only when they see how mastering these skills transforms the writing they do every day at home, in school, and on the job.

For this reason, *Writing First: Practice in Context* puts writing first. When we wrote an earlier edition of this text, we called it *Windows on Writing* because we believed it could open windows for students by helping them gain confidence and skill as writers. Now that we have revised the text, we have come to realize that the original title, although accurate, did not really communicate what we have always seen as the book's central premise. We believe that the new title is consistent with our priorities as teachers as well as with the two central realities of writing in college—that writing comes first, and that students learn writing skills best in the context of their own writing.

In *Writing First,* writing is first chronologically: the book begins with thorough coverage of the writing process, and most chapters begin with writing prompts. Writing is also first in importance: extensive writing practice is central to the grammar chapters as well as to the writing process chapters. In addition to an abundance of practices and drills, each grammar chapter includes a unique three-step sequence of writing and editing prompts (Writing First/Flashback/Revising and Editing) that guides students in applying the chapter's concepts to a piece of their own writing. By moving from their own writing to workbook-style mastery exercises and back to their own work, students learn more effectively and more purposefully.

We wrote this book for adults—our own interested, concerned, hardworking students—and we tailored the book's approach and content to them. We have avoided exercises that present writing as a seemingly dull, pointless, and artificial activity, and we have chosen fresh, contemporary examples, writing assignments, and student passages. In the book's style and tone, we try to show respect for our audience (as well as for our subject matter), and we try to talk *to* our students, not at or down to them.

Our chief goal is still a simple one: to develop a text that will motivate students to improve their writing for college and everyday life, and that can give them the tools they need to do so. By practicing these skills in the context of their own writing, students will come to see writing as something at which they can succeed. We have tried to design a text flexible enough to complement a variety of teaching styles and to meet the needs of individual students. Most of all, we have tried to write a text that respects its audience—that treats college students as adults who can take responsibility for their own learning and for their development as writers.

Organization

Writing First: Practice in Context has a flexible organization that lets instructors teach various topics in the order that works best for them and their students. The book is divided into three sections: "Writing Paragraphs and Essays," "Revising and Editing Your Writing," and "Becoming a Critical Reader." The first section provides a comprehensive discussion of the writing process. The second section presents a thorough review of sentence skills, grammar, punctuation, mechanics, and spelling. The third section introduces students to critical reading skills and includes nineteen professional essays, each illustrating a particular pattern of development. Finally, two appendixes—Appendix A, "Writing Paragraphs and Essays for Exams," and Appendix B, "Writing a Research Paper"— provide help with skills that students will need in other courses. Appendix B gives a brief overview of the research process, illustrates and explains MLA documentation style, and includes an annotated, fully documented student research paper.

Features

Central to *Writing First* is our "student writing first" philosophy, supported by innovative features designed to make students' writing practice meaningful, productive, and enjoyable.

The text's process approach guides students step-by-step through the writing process, providing comprehensive coverage in a flexible format. Eleven chapters on paragraph development (Units 1 and 2) feature many examples of student and professional writing, with separate chapters on each method of paragraph development, giving instructors flexibility in planning the course. A comprehensive treatment of essay writing (Unit 3) starts with Chapter 12, "Writing an Essay"; Chapter 13, "Introductions and Conclusions," offers guidance rarely found in developmental writing texts. In Chapter 14, "Patterns of Essay Development," each pattern is illustrated by a student essay.

Unique "practice in context" activities let students apply each new concept to their own writing. Most chapters begin with a *Writing First* activity that asks students to write a response to a specific prompt. Then, a series of *Flashback* exercises encourages students to practice skills introduced in the chapter in the context of their Writing First response. At the end of the chapter, a *Revising and Editing* activity guides students through a final look at their Writing First responses.

Writing First **makes information easy to find and use.** The engaging full-color design supports the text's pedagogy and helps students find information quickly. *Focus boxes* highlight key concepts and important information, *quick-reference corner tabs* make the book easy to navigate, and *marginal cross-references* to other parts of the text help students find and review key information. *Writing Tips* in the margins provide additional information, address common problem areas, and make connections between academic and everyday writing situations. *Computer Tips* give helpful advice for students writing with computers.

Both native and nonnative writers get the grammar help they need. Thorough, accessible grammar explanations are complemented by clear, helpful examples. Chapter 30, "Grammar and Usage Issues for ESL Writers," discusses concerns of special interest to nonnative writers. *ESL Tips* in the *Instructor's Annotated Edition* guide instructors in helping ESL students get the most out of the text.

Each chapter offers numerous opportunities for practice and review. Easy-to-grade *Practices* following each section of each chapter form a strand of workbook-style mastery exercises that let students hone specific skills. (These Practices can supplement or replace the Writing First strand, depending on an instructor's preference.) *Visual writing prompts* in many of the essay assignments serve as additional sources of inspiration for writing. *Self-Assessment Checklists* in the paragraph and essay chapters show students how to revise and edit their own writing. Three kinds of *Chapter Review* activities provide additional practice opportunities: an *Editing Practice* featuring a passage of student writing gives students an opportunity to edit to eliminate a specific writing problem; *Collaborative Activities* offer creative options for student-centered classroom learning; and a *Review Checklist* recaps the main points of each chapter for quick review. Finally, *Answers to Odd-Numbered Exercises* at the end of the book let students check their own work as they practice and review.

Writing First **helps students make the connection between reading and writing.** Chapter 35, "Reading Critically," guides students step by step through the reading process and includes a sample annotated reading. Chapter 36, "Readings for Writers," contains nineteen professional readings that illustrate the patterns of development covered in the paragraph and essay chapters of the book. Questions following each reading test comprehension, help build vocabulary skills, and offer topics for student writing.

Writing First **respects students as serious writers.** The text has more student writing than any other developmental textbook: numerous paragraph-length examples as well as thirty-three complete essays provide realistic models. *Student Voices* in the margins evoke the experiences of actual students working to master the topic at hand. The tone and level of explanatory material, as well as the subject matter of examples and exercises, acknowledge the diverse interests, ages, and experiences of developmental writers.

Two appendixes cover skills that students can also use in other courses. Appendix A, "Writing Paragraphs and Essays for Exams," gives students practical strategies they can use in a variety of subject areas. Appendix B, "Writing a Research Paper," teaches students the basics of researching and writing a paper and citing and documenting sources. The chapter includes an annotated sample student paper in MLA style.

Ancillaries

Writing First is accompanied by a comprehensive teaching support package that includes the following items:

- The *Instructor's Annotated Edition* includes answers to the Practice exercises as well as numerous teaching tips and ESL tips in the margins.
- *Classroom Resources for Instructors Using* **Writing First** includes helpful teaching suggestions, sample syllabi, and additional teaching materials.
- *Background Readings for Instructors Using* **Writing First** offers more than two dozen professional articles on topics of interest to developmental writing instructors, accompanied by suggestions for practical applications to the classroom.
- **Exercise Central,** the largest collection of grammar exercises available with any writing text, includes multiple-exercise sets on every grammar topic to give students all the practice they need. This software can be accessed via the World Wide Web at <bedfordstmartins.com/composition/exercises>.
- *Exercises and Tests to Accompany* **Writing First** contains grammar exercises and diagnostic and mastery tests (including material from Exercise Central) in a book with perforated pages that allow instructors to copy the material and distribute it to students.
- *Interactive Writing Software to Accompany* **Writing First** supports students as they work on paragraph and essay assignments. This software is available for Windows and Macintosh platforms.
- *Transparency Masters to Accompany* **Writing First,** including editable student writing samples from the text, are available as a printed package and as files downloadable from the Web site.
- The *Writing First* Web site <http://bedfordstmartins.com/writingfirst> offers downloadable teaching aids and links to other useful materials.

Acknowledgments

In our work on *Writing First,* we have benefited from the help of a great many people.

Franklin E. Horowitz of Teachers College, Columbia University, drafted an early version of Chapter 30, "Grammar and Usage Issues for ESL Writers," and his linguist's insight continues to inform that chapter. Linda Stine and Linda Stengle of Lincoln University devoted energy and vision to the preparation of *Classroom Resources for Instructors.* Linda

Mason Austin of McLennan Community College drew on her extensive teaching experience to contribute teaching tips and ESL tips to the *Instructor's Annotated Edition.* Susan Bernstein's work on the compilation and annotation of *Background Readings for Instructors* reflects her deep commitment to scholarship and teaching. We are very grateful for their contributions.

We thank Judith Lechner for her work on Exercise Central and the accompanying exercise book, and we appreciate Joanne Diaz's last-minute help with *Background Readings.*

Writing First could not exist without our students, whose words appear on almost every page of the book, whether in sample sentences, paragraphs, and essays, or as Student Voices. Our thanks go to Lis Bare, Kevin Bey, Dan Brody, Susan Burkhart, Michelle Cooper, Daniel Corey, Shannon Cornell, Mark Cotharn, Sutapa Das, Megan Davia, Demetrius Davis, Andrea DeMarco, Kim DiPialo, Jerry Doyle, Ann Duong, Thaddeus Eddy, Mohamad Faisal, John Fleeger, Richard Greene, Linda Grossman, Monica Han, Catherine Hartman, Beth Haurin, Russ Hightower, Keith Jackson, Panhej Jolanpretra, Willa Kincaid, Nicholas Kinlaw, Serge Komanawski, Meredith Krall, Peter Likus, George Lin, Jennifer Loucks, Dan Lynn, Krishna Mahajan, Toni-Ann Marro, Felicia May, Jeremy McDonald, Matt McDonald, Michael McManus, Timothy E. Miles, Kelly Miller, Kristin Miller, Hiro Nakamura, Miniinah Neal, Samantha Nguyen, Karoline Ozols, Nirav Patel, Doreen Queenan, James Ramos, Linda Richards, Cheri Rodriguez, Allison Rogers, Christina Rose, Terry Simons, Todd Slunt, Rizwana Syed, Deborah Ulrich, Lisa Van Hoboken, Jason Varghese, Jason Walsh, Jen Weber, Scott Weckerly, Kristin Whitehead, Janice Williams, Teren Williams, Tom Woller, Alisha Woolery, Mai Yoshikawa, and Jessica Zimmerman.

Instructors throughout the country have contributed suggestions and encouragement at various stages of the book's development. For their collegial support, we thank Alan Ainsworth, Houston Community College–Central; Sheila Allen, Harford Community College; Linda Mason Austin, McLennan Community College; Sandra Barnhill, South Plains College; Jan Barshis, Harold Washington College; Wendy G. Beckett, Cuesta Community College; Tamara Brawner, Thomas College; Marcia Bronstein, Montgomery College; Della A. Burt-Bradley, Harold Washington College; Debra O. Callen, Harold Washington College; Jessica Carroll, Miami-Dade Community College–Wolfson; Lawrence Checkett, St. Charles County Community College; David Critchett, Community College of Rhode Island; Rocco Ditello, Broward Community College; David Elias, Eastern Kentucky University; Jennifer Ferguson, Cazenovia College; Eddye S. Gallagher, Tarrant County College–Northeast; Sandy B. Gittleson, CUNY–Hostos Community College; Jennifer Handley, Skagit Valley College; Judy Hathcock, Amarillo College; Paula Hillis, Idaho State University; Jennifer C. James, Montgomery College; Caroline Klingensmith, Rio Hondo College; Martha F. Krupa, Valencia Community College–East; Teresa Kynell, Northern Michigan University; Eleanor Latham, Central Oregon Community College; Patricia A. Malinowski, Finger Lakes Community College; Laurell Meredith, Napa Valley College; Mary Ann Merz, Oklahoma City Community College; Ron Miazga, Kalamazoo Valley College; Gary Mitchner, Sinclair Community College; Mercy E. Moore, Broward Community College; Kathryn Coad Narramore, CUNY–Hunter College; Sue Haynes Pine, Florida Community College–Jacksonville;

Merlene Purkiss, Miami-Dade Community College; Shirley Rawlston, Tarrant County College; Melinda Reichelt, University of Toledo; Kelly Rupp, Redlands Community College; Sara Lee Sanderson, Miami-Dade Community College–Kendall; John Silva, CUNY–La Guardia Community College; Kent Smead, Minneapolis Community and Technical College; Linda J. Stine, Lincoln University; Joyce Stoffers, Southwestern Oklahoma State University; John Thornburg, San Jacinto Community College–Central; Janet K. Turk, Lamar University; Paige Wilson, Pasadena City College; Carla R. Witcher, Montgomery College; and Alfred J. Zucker, Los Angeles Valley College.

At Bedford/St. Martin's, we thank Chuck Christensen, president of Bedford/St. Martin's, and Joan Feinberg, editorial director, who believed in this project and gave us support and encouragement from the outset. We thank Nancy Perry, editor in chief and our longtime friend, who continues to earn our respect as well as our affection. We also thank Belinda Delpêche, editorial assistant, for helping with numerous tasks, big and small; Erica Appel, managing editor, and Michael Weber, senior project editor, for guiding the book ably through production; and Lucy Krikorian, art director, for overseeing the beautiful and innovative design. Thanks also go to Dennis Conroy, senior production supervisor; Karen Melton, director of marketing; and Brian Wheel, marketing manager. Our biggest thanks go to our editor, the amazing Talvi Laev, who made sure every *i* was dotted and every *t* was crossed. Her incredibly high standards and attention to detail kept the project on track as she encouraged us to make this book as good as it could possibly be.

We are grateful, too, for the continued support of our families—Mark, Adam, and Rebecca Kirszner and Demi, David, and Sarah Mandell. We thank them here for services rendered. Finally, we are grateful for the survival and growth of the writing partnership we entered into in 1975, when we were graduate students. We had no idea then of the wonderful places our collaborative efforts would take us. Now, we know.

Laurie G. Kirszner
Stephen R. Mandell

Contents

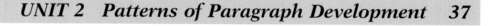

UNIT 2   *Patterns of Paragraph Development*   37

UNIT 3   *Focus on Essays*   101

REVISING AND EDITING YOUR WRITING   195

UNIT 7 *Understanding Punctuation, Mechanics, and Spelling* *419*

BECOMING A CRITICAL READER   479

UNIT 8   *Reading Essays   479*

A Student's Guide to Using Writing First

What *Writing First* Can Do for You

As you look through *Writing First*, you may be wondering, "What can this book do for me?" To answer this question, you might start by thinking about the title. It's no secret that writing will be very important in most of the courses you take in college. Whether you write lab reports or English papers, midterms or final exams, your ability to organize your thoughts and express them in writing will affect how well you do. In other words, succeeding at writing is the first step toward succeeding in college. Even more important, writing is a key to success outside the classroom. On the job and in everyday life, if you can express yourself clearly and effectively, you will stand a better chance of achieving your goals and influencing the world around you.

Whether you write as a student, as an employee, as a parent, or as a concerned citizen, your writing almost always has a specific purpose. When you write an essay, a memo, a letter, or a research paper, you are writing not just to complete an exercise but to give other people information or to tell them your ideas or opinions. That is why, in this book, we don't ask you simply to do grammar exercises and fill in blanks; in each chapter, we also ask you to apply the skills you are learning to a piece of your own writing.

As teachers—and former students—we know how demanding college can be and how hard it is to juggle assignments with work and family responsibilities. We also know that you don't want to waste your time or money. That is why in *Writing First* we make information easy to find and use and provide many different features to help you become a better writer.

The following sections describe the key features of *Writing First*. If you take the time now to familiarize yourself with these features, you will be able to use the book more effectively later on.

How *Writing First* Makes Information Easy to Find and Use

Brief table of contents   Inside the front cover is a brief table of contents that summarizes the topics covered in this book. The brief contents can help you find a particular chapter quickly.

Detailed table of contents   The table of contents that starts on page xi provides a detailed breakdown of the book's topics. Use this table of contents to find a specific part of a particular chapter.

Index   The index, which appears at the back of the book starting on page 587, lets you find all the available information about a particular topic. The topics appear in alphabetical order, so, for example, if you wanted to find out how to use commas, you would find the *C* section and look up the word *comma*. (If the page number following a word is **bold-faced**, then on that page you can find a definition of the word.)

List of Self-Assessment Checklists   On page xxviii is a list of checklists designed to help you write, revise, and fine-tune the paragraphs and essays you write. Use this list to find the checklist that is most useful for the particular writing assignment you are working on.

A handy cross-referencing system   Often, an *italicized marginal cross-reference* will point you to another section of the book (for example, "See 28A and 28B"). At the tops of most pages of *Writing First*, you'll find *quick-reference corner tabs* consisting of green-and-blue boxes, each containing a number and a letter. This information tells you which chapter you have turned to and which section of that chapter you are looking at. Together, the cross-references and the tabs help you find information quickly. For example, if a note in the text suggested, "See 10A for more on classification," you could use the tabs to locate section 10A.

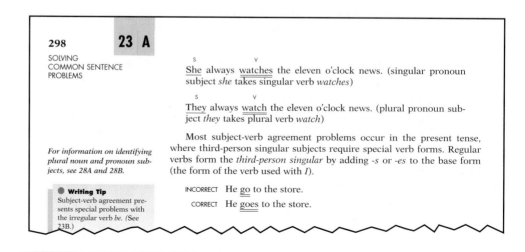

How *Writing First* Can Help You Become a Better Writer

Preview boxes   Each chapter starts with a list of key terms and concepts that will be discussed in the chapter. Looking at these boxes before you skim the chapter will help you get an overview of the chapter.

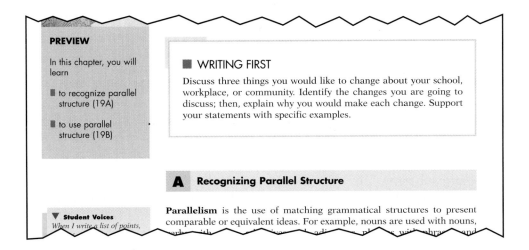

Writing First activities   Most chapters include a three-part writing activity that helps you apply specific skills to your own writing. Each chapter starts with a *Writing First* exercise that asks you to write about a particular topic. Throughout the chapter, *Flashback* exercises help you analyze your Writing First response so you can identify and correct specific writing problems. Finally, a *Revising and Editing* exercise asks you to fine-tune your writing. (See, for example, pages 197, 198, and 204 in Chapter 15.)

Focus boxes   Throughout the book, boxes with the word *Focus* in a red banner highlight useful information, identify key points, and explain difficult concepts.

FOCUS *There Is* and *There Are*

In a sentence that begins with *there is* or *there are*, the subject comes after the form of the verb *be*. (*There* can never be the subject.)

$$\overset{\text{v}}{\text{There are}} \quad \text{nine} \underset{\text{s}}{\underline{\text{justices}}} \text{ on the Supreme Court.}$$

$$\overset{\text{v}}{\text{There is}} \quad \text{one} \underset{\text{s}}{\underline{\text{chief justice}}} \text{ presiding over the Court.}$$

Self-Assessment Checklists   Chapters 1, 3–12, and 14 include Self-Assessment Checklists that give you a handy way to check your work and

measure your progress. Use these checklists to revise your writing before
you hand it in.

☑ SELF-ASSESSMENT CHECKLIST:

Writing an Exemplification Paragraph

Unity

☐ Does your topic sentence focus on an idea that can be developed in a single paragraph?

☐ Is your topic sentence specifically worded?

☐ Does your topic sentence clearly express what the rest of the paragraph is about?

☐ Do all your examples support your topic sentence?

Marginal notes In the margins of *Writing First,* you'll find several
kinds of notes that give you additional information in an easy-to-read format. *Writing Tips* offer practical information and helpful hints, including
definitions and examples. **Computer Tips** help you make effective use of
your computer as you write. *Student Voices* present the words of real students telling what works and doesn't work for them when they write.

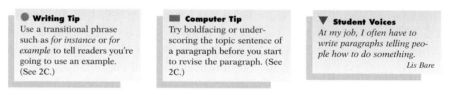

● **Writing Tip**
Use a transitional phrase such as *for instance* or *for example* to tell readers you're going to use an example. (See 2C.)

■ **Computer Tip**
Try boldfacing or underscoring the topic sentence of a paragraph before you start to revise the paragraph. (See 2C.)

▼ **Student Voices**
At my job, I often have to write paragraphs telling people how to do something.
Lis Bare

Review Checklists Each chapter ends with a summary of the most
important information in the chapter. Use these checklists to review material for quizzes or to remind yourself of the main points in the chapter
you've been studying.

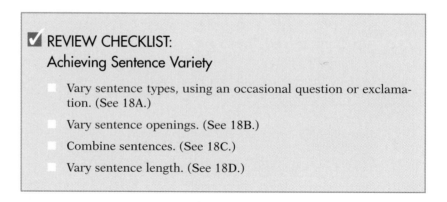

☑ REVIEW CHECKLIST:

Achieving Sentence Variety

☐ Vary sentence types, using an occasional question or exclamation. (See 18A.)

☐ Vary sentence openings. (See 18B.)

☐ Combine sentences. (See 18C.)

☐ Vary sentence length. (See 18D.)

Answers to Odd-Numbered Exercises Starting on page 577, you'll find
answers for some of the Practice items in the book. When you need to
study a topic independently or when your instructor has you complete a
Practice but not hand it in, you can consult these answers to see if you're
on the right track.

How *Writing First* Can Help You Succeed in Other Courses

In a sense, this whole book is all about succeeding in other courses. After all, as we said earlier, writing is the key to success in college. But *Writing First* also includes sections (at the end of the book) that you may find especially useful in courses you take later on in college. We have designed these sections so you can use them either on your own or with your instructor's help.

Appendix A, "Writing Paragraphs and Essays for Exams"   This practical guide shows you how to study effectively for written exams and how to write successful answers to essay questions when you are under time pressure.

Appendix B, "Writing a Research Paper"   This appendix gives a short overview of the research process and shows how to document sources and create a list of works cited. A student paper complete with helpful marginal notes is also included.

List of correction symbols   The chart inside the back cover lists marks that many instructors use when evaluating and marking student papers. Becoming familiar with these symbols will help you get the most out of your instructor's comments on your work.

Self-Assessment Checklists for Writing Paragraphs and Essays

Units 1–3 of *Writing First* include a number of Self-Assessment Checklists designed to help you write, revise, and fine-tune your paragraphs and essays. You can use these checklists both in your writing course and in other courses that include written assignments. The following list shows the page number for each checklist.

UNIT ONE

Focus on Paragraphs

1

Writing a Paragraph

Writing is not just something you do in school to complete an assignment and get a grade; writing is a life skill. If you can write clearly, you can express your ideas convincingly to others—not only in school but also on the job and in the community. Writing tasks take many different forms. As a student, you might be asked to write a single paragraph, an essay exam, a short paper, or a long research paper. At work, you might need to write a memo, a proposal, or a report. In your daily life as a citizen of your community, you might write a letter asking for information, explaining a problem, or complaining about a service. Writing is important. If you can write, you can communicate; if you can communicate effectively, your writing will get a response.

This chapter takes you through the process of writing a **paragraph**, a group of related sentences that develop one central idea. A paragraph can be part of a longer piece of writing, as it is in an essay, or it can stand alone, as it does in a one-paragraph classroom exercise or an exam answer. Because paragraphs play a part in almost every writing task, learning to write a paragraph is an important step in becoming a competent writer.

PREVIEW

In this chapter, you will learn

- to focus on your assignment, purpose, and audience (1A)

- to use invention strategies (1B)

- to select and arrange ideas (1C)

- to draft a paragraph (1D)

- to revise a paragraph (1E)

A Focusing on Your Assignment, Purpose, and Audience

Before you begin any writing task, you need to figure out what the task involves. In college, a writing task usually begins with an assignment. Instead of plunging in headfirst and starting to write, take time to consider some questions about your assignment (*what* you are expected to write), your purpose (*why* you are writing), and your audience (*for whom* you are writing). Finding out the answers to these questions at this point will save you time in the long run.

▼ **Student Voices**
As soon as I get a writing assignment, I choose a time to set aside distractions and concentrate on my paper.
Jason Varghese

Questions about Assignment, Purpose, and Audience

Assignment
- What is your assignment?
- Do you have a word or page limit?

(continued on the following page)

3

(continued from the previous page)

- When is your assignment due?
- Will you be expected to complete your assignment at home or in class?
- Will you be expected to work on your own or with others?
- Will you be allowed to revise after you hand in your assignment?

Purpose

- Are you expected to express your personal reactions—for example, to tell how you feel about a piece of music or a news event?
- Are you expected to present information—for example, to answer an exam question, describe a process in a lab report, or summarize a story or essay you have read?
- Are you expected to argue for or against a position on a controversial issue?

Audience

- Who will read your paper—just your instructor, or other students, too?
- Do you have an audience beyond the classroom—for example, your supervisor or your landlord?
- How much will your readers know about your topic?
- Will your readers expect you to use formal or informal language?

◆ PRACTICE 1-1

Each of the following writing tasks has a different audience and purpose. Think about how you would approach each task. (The above Questions about Assignment, Purpose, and Audience can help you decide on the best strategy.) On the lines following each task, write some notes about your approach. Discuss your responses with your class or in a small group.

1. For the other students in your writing class, describe your best or worst educational experience.

   _____

   _____

   _____

   _____

2. For the instructor of an introductory psychology course, discuss how early educational experiences can affect a student's performance throughout his or her schooling.

   _____

   _____

   _____

   _____

3. Write a short letter to your community's school board in which you try to convince members to make two or three specific changes that you believe would improve the schools you attended or those your children might attend.

_____

_____

_____

_____

4. Write a letter to a work supervisor—either past or current—telling what you appreciate about his or her management style and how it has helped you develop as an employee.

_____

_____

_____

_____

B   Using Invention Strategies

Once you know what, why, and for whom you are writing, you can begin to experiment with different invention strategies. **Invention**—sometimes called *prewriting* or *discovery*—is the process of finding material to write about. This process is different for every writer. You may be the kind of person who is comfortable with a systematic, structured approach, or you may prefer a more relaxed, less structured way of finding ideas.

Erica Quintos, a student in an introductory composition course, was given the following assignment.

Write a paragraph on the topic of your personal heroes.

Before she drafted her paragraph, Erica used a variety of invention strategies to come up with ideas. The pages that follow illustrate the four strategies she used: *freewriting, brainstorming, clustering,* and *journal writing.* When you write, you try each strategy to see which ones work best for you.

Freewriting

When you **freewrite**, you write for a set period of time—perhaps five minutes—without stopping, even if what you are writing doesn't seem to have a point or a direction. Your goal is to relax and let ideas flow. You can freewrite without a topic in mind, but sometimes you will focus your attention on a topic. This strategy is called **focused freewriting**.

When you finish freewriting, read what you have written, and underline any ideas you think you might be able to use. If you find an idea you want to explore further, freewrite again, using that idea as a starting point.

> ▼ **Student Voices**
> *I get ideas by looking at all angles of a topic—personal, social, religious, political. If I have trouble finding something to write about, I ask other people for ideas.*
> Monica Han

> ■ **Computer Tip**
> Try doing "invisible freewriting" by turning off your monitor and writing without looking at the screen. When you have finished, turn on the monitor to see what you have written.

Here is an example of Erica's focused freewriting on the topic of personal heroes.

Heroes? Didn't I already do this — in fifth grade? My hero (heroine?) was Lucretia Mott, the abolitionist. Maybe write about her now — but can't remember much — just that she was a Quaker and lived in Philadelphia. Not much to start with. Maybe a sports hero — but not exactly heroes except Dr. J. — he did a lot for the community — spoke at school once. I don't know much about sports — maybe TV stars? Cartoon characters? Bugs Bunny always outsmarted Elmer Fudd. My little sister wanted to be She-Ra — the action figure came with a sword, a shield, & a comb. Not my hero — my hero — I used to think Mike Schmidt was pretty impressive (why?) but not really a hero. Now it's athletes again — again — who else? Not Charles Barkley — he said people shouldn't think of him as a role model — but I forget why. I keep thinking of athletes. Who isn't an athlete? Ben Franklin — I named one of my dolls after him (why?). This is a lot harder than I thought — & why am I thinking about people who were my heroes when I was a kid? I need some heroes for now.

Freewriting

◆ **PRACTICE 1-2**

Reread Erica's freewriting on the topic of personal heroes. If you were advising her, what ideas would you suggest she explore further? Write your suggestions here.

_____

_____

_____

_____

_____

_____

_____

_____

_____

_____

◆ **PRACTICE 1-3**

Freewrite about any two of the following topics. Use a blank sheet of paper for each topic, and freewrite on each topic for *at least five minutes without stopping.* If you have trouble thinking of something to write, keep recopying the last word you have written until something else comes to mind. When you have finished each freewriting exercise, reread what you have written. Underline any ideas that you might use if you were writing a paper about that topic.

Your personal heroes	Holidays
Unhealthy diets	A problem facing your
Work pressures or pleasures	community
Things that annoy you	People who have influenced you
A problem at your school or	Learning a new language
workplace	A recent news story
Telling lies	A problem facing young people
An overrated movie	Your ideal work environment

◆ **PRACTICE 1-4**

Reread the freewriting you did for Practice 1-3. Which topic suggested the most interesting ideas? Choose one idea, and use it as a starting point for a focused freewriting exercise.

Brainstorming

When you **brainstorm**, you record all the ideas about your topic that come to mind. Unlike freewriting, brainstorming is often scattered all over the page. You don't have to use complete sentences; single words or phrases are fine. You can underline, star, or box important points. You can also ask questions, list points, and draw arrows to connect ideas.

An example of Erica's brainstorming on the topic of personal heroes appears on the following page.

▼ **Student Voices**
I get ideas by brainstorming to see which topics I have the most information about. If I get stuck, I ask my friends or look through magazines.
Jennifer Loucks

FOCUS **Brainstorming**

Sometimes your instructor may ask you and another student to brainstorm together. At other times, the class might brainstorm as a group as your instructor writes ideas on the board that the class can later evaluate. However you brainstorm, your goal is the same: to come up with as much material on your topic as you can.

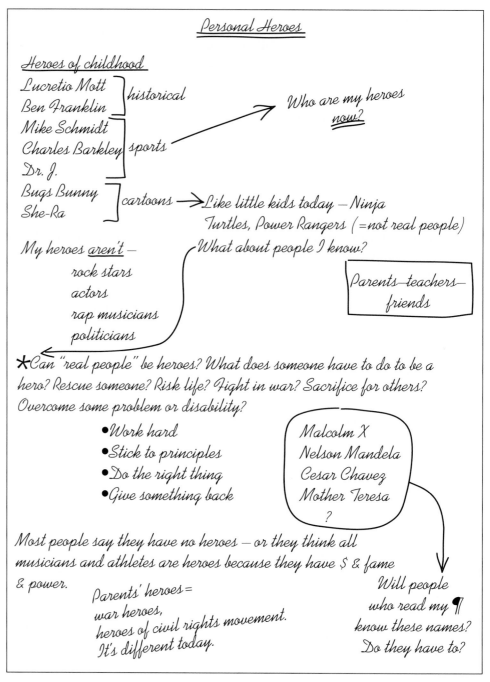

Brainstorming

◆ PRACTICE 1-5

Reread Erica's brainstorming on the subject of personal heroes. How is it similar to her freewriting on the same subject (page 6)? How is it different? If you were advising Erica, which ideas would you suggest that she cross out as she continues to explore her subject? Write your suggestions on the lines that follow.

_____

_____

_____

_____

_____

_____

_____

_____

◆ PRACTICE 1-6

Practice brainstorming on one of the topics you used for freewriting in Practice 1-3. Use a separate _unlined_ page for each topic. Write quickly, without worrying about using complete sentences. Try writing on different parts of the page, making lists, and drawing arrows to connect related ideas. When you have finished, look over what you have written. Which ideas are the most interesting? Did you come up with any new ideas as you brainstormed that you did not discover while freewriting?

◆ PRACTICE 1-7

Working as a class or in a group of three or four students, practice _collaborative brainstorming_. First, agree as a group on a topic for brainstorming. (Your instructor may choose a topic for you.) Next, choose one person to write down ideas on a blank sheet of paper or on the board. (If your group is large enough, you might choose two people to write down ideas and have them compare notes at the end of the brainstorming session.) Then, discuss the topic informally, with each member contributing at least one idea. After fifteen minutes or so, review the ideas that have been written down. As a group, try to identify interesting connections among ideas and suggest ideas that might be explored further.

Clustering

Some writers like to use visual invention strategies. **Clustering**, sometimes called _mapping_, is one such strategy. When you cluster, you begin by writing your topic in the center of a sheet of paper. Then you branch out, drawing lines from the center to the corners of the page, and becoming more specific as you move farther out from the center. When you finish your first cluster exercise, you can cluster again on a new sheet of paper, this time beginning with a topic from one of the branches. Sometimes, one branch of your exercise will give you all the material you need; at other times, you may decide to write about ideas from several branches.

An example of Erica's clustering on the topic of personal heroes appears below.

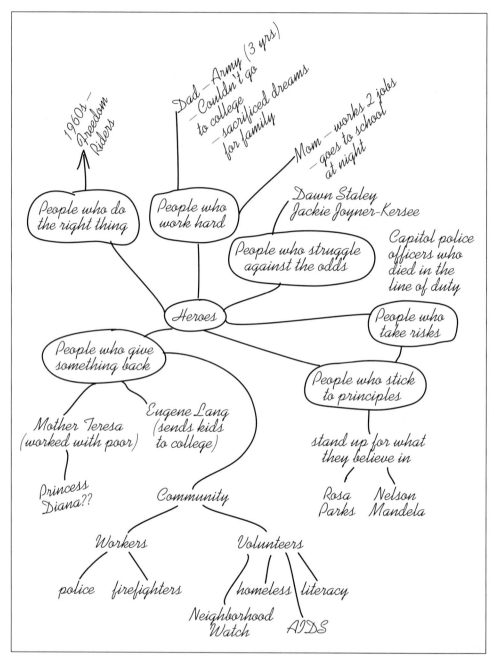

Clustering

◆ PRACTICE 1-8

Reread Erica's clustering on the subject of personal heroes. How is it similar to her brainstorming on the same subject (page 8)? How is it different? If you were advising Erica, which branch of the cluster diagram would you say seems most promising? Why? Can you add any branches? Write your suggestions on the lines on the next page. Then discuss them with your class or in a small group.

_____

_____

_____

_____

◆ **PRACTICE 1-9**

Practice clustering on the topic you used when you practiced freewriting and brainstorming. Begin by writing your topic in the center of a blank sheet of unlined paper. Circle the topic, and then branch out with specific ideas and examples, continuing to the edge of the page if you can. When you have finished, look over what you have written. What are the most interesting items in your cluster diagram? Which branches seem most promising as the basis for further writing? What new ideas have you come up with that your freewriting and brainstorming did not suggest?

Journal Writing

A **journal** is an informal record of your thoughts and ideas. In a journal, you can reflect, question, summarize, or even complain. When you are actively involved in a writing project, your journal is a place where you note ideas to write about, and think on paper about your assignment. Here you can try to resolve a problem, restart a stalled project, argue with yourself about your topic, or critique a draft. You can also try out different versions of sentences, keep track of details or examples, or keep a record of potentially useful things you read or observe.

Once you have started making regular entries in a journal, take the time every week or so to go back and reread what you have written. You may find material you want to explore in further journal entries — or even an idea for a paper.

> ■ **Computer Tip**
> Try keeping a journal on your computer by making entries at set times every day — when you check your e-mail, for example.

FOCUS **Journals**

Here are some subjects you can write about in your journal.

- ■ _Your school work_   Of course, you can use your journal to explore ideas for writing assignments. Your journal can also be a place where you think about what you have learned, ask questions about things you're having trouble understanding, and examine new ideas and new ways of seeing the world. Writing regularly in a journal about what you're studying in school can even help you become a better student.

- ■ _Your job_   In your journal, you can record job-related triumphs and frustrations, work through conflicts with coworkers, or note how you handled problems on the job. Reading over these

(continued on the following page)

(continued from the previous page)

entries can help you understand your strengths and weaknesses and become a more effective employee. As an added bonus, you may discover work-related topics to write about in school.

■ *Your ideas about current events* Expressing your opinions in the privacy of your journal can be a good way to explore complex ideas or just let off steam. Your entries may spur you to write letters to your local or school newspaper or to public officials—and even to become involved in community projects or political activities.

■ *Your impressions of what you see around you* Many professional and amateur writers carry their notebooks or journals with them everywhere so they can record any interesting or unusual or funny things they observe in the course of their daily lives. Rather than relying on memory, they jot down images of memorable people, places, or events as soon as possible after they observe them. If you get into the habit of recording such impressions, you can later incorporate them into stories or other pieces of writing.

■ *Aspects of your personal life* Although you may not want to record the intimate details of your life if your instructor will collect your journal, such entries are the most common of all in a private journal. Writing about relationships with family and friends, personal problems, hopes and dreams—all the details of your life—can help you reach a better understanding of yourself and others.

Here is an example of Erica's journal entry on the topic of personal heroes.

It's been really hard to figure out who my heroes are, or even what a hero is. Heroes are different when you're a kid. Who your heroes are probably has a lot to do with what you like — what music, TV shows, books, sports, etc. Now that I'm older, maybe I need more female heroes because I'm female. Maybe my heroes have to be people I could become, people who are like me. Or maybe they have to be people who <u>aren't</u> like me but people I wish I could be, male or female. The main thing is that heroes don't have to be important or famous. They can be ordinary people who do something out of the ordinary. But they actually have to <u>do</u> something. I keep coming back to this idea of a hero being someone who sticks to principles, speaks out, works hard, etc. I've read about plenty of people like this, and I even know some of them. That's what I should write about. I don't want my paragraph to be just a list of names that people who read it might not recognize. I want to explain the qualities that I think make someone a hero. Then I'll worry about adding examples.

Journal Entry

◆ **PRACTICE 1-10**

Buy a notebook to use as a journal. (Your instructor may require a specific size and format, particularly if journals are going to be collected at some point.) Set a time to write for fifteen minutes or so in your journal—during your lunch break, for example, or before you go to bed. Make entries daily or several times a week, depending on your schedule and your instructor's suggestions.

C **Selecting and Arranging Ideas**

When you think you have enough material to write about, you can move on to the next stage of the writing process: finding a main idea to develop into a paragraph and selecting and organizing the details that will support that idea most effectively.

Finding an Idea to Develop

Begin by taking stock of what you have on paper. As you read through your freewriting, brainstorming, clustering, and journal entries, look for your **main idea**—the central point that your material seems to support. A sentence that states this main idea and gives your paragraph its focus is called the paragraph's **topic sentence**.

Erica Quintos thought her notes could support the idea that her heroes have one thing in common: they take action. She stated this idea in a sentence.

My heroes are people who take action.

> ● **Writing Tip**
> If at any stage in the writing process you run out of ideas, return to the invention strategies you found most helpful and use them to find more material.

Choosing Supporting Material

After you identify your main idea, review your notes again. This time, look for material (specific details, facts, and examples) that provides **support** for your main idea. Write or type the topic sentence that states this main idea at the top of a blank page. As you review your notes, list all the supporting points you think you might be able to use.

Erica chose the following points from her notes to support her paragraph's main idea.

```
      Main idea: My heroes are people who take action.
```

- Heroes work hard.
- Heroes stick to principles.
- Heroes give something back to the community.
- Heroes take risks.
- Heroes are not just important or famous people.
- Heroes could be ordinary people--people I know.
- Heroes stand up for what they believe in.

1 C

● **Writing Tip**
You can arrange your points
in time order, in spatial
order, or in sequential order.
(See 2C.)

Ordering Supporting Material

Once you have made a list of points you can use, arrange them in the order in which you plan to present them, as Erica did in the following list.

        Main idea: My heroes are people who take action.

- Heroes can be ordinary people or famous ones.
  --Mom (hard-working)
  --Nelson Mandela (sticks to principles)
- Heroes stand up for what they believe in.
- Heroes take risks.
- Heroes give something back to the community.

◆ PRACTICE 1-11

In Practices 1-3, 1-6, and 1-9, you practiced freewriting, brainstorming, and clustering. Now, you are ready to write a paragraph about your topic. Look over the invention exercises you have done, and try to find one main idea that your material can support. Write a sentence that expresses this idea on the following lines.

_____

_____

_____

Now, reread your invention exercises, and list the points you believe will support your main idea most effectively. Also, list any new points you think of.

_____

_____

_____

_____

_____

_____

_____

Look over the material you listed above, making sure each point supports your main idea. Cross out any points that do not belong. Arrange the remaining points here in the order in which you plan to write about them.

1. _____

2. _____

3. _____

4. _____

5. _____

6. _____

7. _____

D   Drafting Your Paragraph

Once you have found a main idea for your paragraph, identified the points you will discuss, and arranged them in the order in which you plan to write about them, you are ready to write a first draft. In a first draft, your goal is to get your ideas down on paper. Begin with a topic sentence stating your paragraph's main idea. Then, keeping an eye on the list of points you plan to discuss, write or type without worrying about correct wording, spelling, or punctuation. If a new idea—one that is not on your list—occurs to you, write it down. Don't worry about where (or whether) it fits. Your goal is not to produce a perfect piece of writing but simply to create a working draft. When you revise, you will have a chance to rethink ideas and rework sentences.

Because you will revise this draft—add or cross out words and phrases, reorder ideas and details, clarify connections between ideas, and rephrase—you should leave plenty of room for rewriting. Leave wide margins, write on every other line, and leave extra space in places where you might need to add material. Feel free to be messy and to cross out; remember, the only person who will see this draft is you.

When you have finished your draft, don't start tearing it apart right away. Take a break and think about something—anything—else. Then return to your draft, and read it with a fresh eye.

Here is a draft of Erica's paragraph on the topic of personal heroes.

> **Computer Tip**
> If you're typing your draft on a computer, use large type and triple-space between lines to make the draft easier to edit.

My Heroes

My heroes are people who take action. Some of my heroes are famous people, and others are people I know. They work hard, sometimes at more than one job, like my mom. They struggle against the odds. They stick to their principles. Nelson Mandela is a good example of this. They stand up for what they believe in. They take risks. And they give something back to their communities. I think this last quality is really the most important. Some people work with charities, and others are active in their communities in other ways. They do these things even though they don't have to do them. That makes them heroes to me.

Draft

◆ PRACTICE 1-12

Reread Erica's draft paragraph about personal heroes. If you were advising Erica, what would you suggest that she change in the draft? What might she add? What might she cross out? Write your suggestions on the following lines. Then, discuss your ideas with your class or in a small group.

_____

_____

_____

_____

◆ PRACTICE 1-13

Using the material you came up with for Practice 1-11, draft a paragraph about your topic that states your main idea and supports it with specific points. Be sure to leave wide margins; if you like, leave every other line blank. (If you type your draft, you can triple-space.) When you are finished, give your paragraph a title.

E   Revising Your Paragraph

Revision is the process of reseeing, rethinking, reevaluating, and rewriting your work. Revision involves much more than substituting one word for another or correcting a comma here and there. Often it means moving sentences, adding words and phrases, and even changing the direction or emphasis of your ideas. To get the most out of the revision process, begin by carefully rereading your draft with a critical eye.

▼ **Student Voices**
When I revise, I look to see if everything flows and if there are any out-of-place ideas, weird sentences, or odd words.
                Felicia May

☑ SELF-ASSESSMENT CHECKLIST:
Revising Your Paragraph

- Have you stated your main idea clearly in your topic sentence?

- Do you have enough material to support your paragraph's main idea, or do you need to look back at your notes or try another invention strategy to find additional supporting material?

- Do you need to explain anything more fully or clearly?

- Do you need to add more examples or details?

- Should you cross out any examples or details?

- Does every sentence say what you mean?

- Can you combine any sentences to make your writing smoother?

- Should you move any sentences?

- Are all your words necessary, or can you cut some?

- Should you change any words?

After Erica drafted the paragraph on page 15 by hand, she typed it, triple-spacing to allow room for handwritten changes. Guided by the Self-Assessment Checklist on page 16, she then revised her paragraph.

My Heroes

My heroes are people who take action, *instead of waiting for others to act.* Some of my heroes are famous people, ~~and~~ *but many* others are people I know. They work hard, sometimes at more than one job, like my mom *, who also goes to school at night.* They *like Olympic athlete Jackie Joyner-Kersee, who competed despite severe asthma.* struggle against the odds. They stick to their principles, *like Nelson Mandela, Rosa Parks, and Cesar Chavez—* ~~Nelson Mandela is a good example of this. They~~ *and they* stand up *, like the two Capitol police officers who died trying to protect others and like the police officers and firefighters who work in my neighborhood.* for what they believe in. They take risks, ~~And they~~ give *A New York City businessman named Eugene Lang did this when he set up the I Have a Dream Foundation to send all the graduates of his elementary school to college.* something back to their communities. ~~I think this last~~ *Most important, heroes* ~~quality is really the most important. Some people work~~ ~~with charities, and others are active in their~~ communities *Mother Teresa gave something back every day.* ~~in other ways.~~ They do these things even though they don't have to do them, *and that* ~~That~~ makes them heroes to me.

The real heroes of my community are volunteers. They work without pay in food banks and soup kitchens. They participate in Neighborhood Watch, and they tutor in literacy programs. They volunteer to be Big Brothers and Big Sisters, work in the schools, deliver meals to the elderly, and care for AIDS babies.

Revised Draft

When she revised, Erica didn't worry about being neat. She crossed out, added material, and made major changes in her words, sentences, and ideas. For instance, she added more examples of heroic figures, both famous and familiar, and she expanded her paragraph to explain what she meant by "give something back" and why she felt this was so important. The final typed version of her paragraph appears on the following page.

My Heroes

My heroes are people who take action instead of waiting for others to act. Some of my heroes are famous people, but many others are people I know. They work hard, sometimes at more than one job, like my mom (who also goes to school at night). They struggle against the odds, like Olympic athlete Jackie Joyner-Kersee, who competed despite severe asthma. They stick to their principles, and they stand up for what they believe in--like Nelson Mandela, Rosa Parks, and Cesar Chavez. They take risks, like the two Capitol police officers who died trying to protect others and like the police officers and firefighters who work in my neighborhood. Most important, heroes give something back to their communities. A New York City businessman named Eugene Lang did this when he set up the I Have a Dream Foundation to send all the graduates of his elementary school to college. Mother Teresa gave something back every day. The heroes of my community are the volunteers. They work without pay in food banks and soup kitchens. They participate in Neighborhood Watch, and they tutor in literacy programs. They volunteer to be Big Brothers and Big Sisters, work in the schools, deliver meals to the elderly, and care for AIDS babies. They do these things even though they don't have to do them, and that makes them heroes to me.

FOCUS Editing

Don't confuse revision with editing. Revision involves serious rewriting and rearranging, and it can be hard work. Editing comes after revision.

When you **edit**, you concentrate on the surface features of your writing, checking for clarity and for correct grammar, punctuation, mechanics, and spelling. You proofread carefully for typographical errors that a computer spell checker may not identify.

Although editing is a lot less comprehensive than revision, it is a vital last step in the writing process. Many readers will not take you seriously if you have made grammatical or mechanical errors in your work, and correctness goes a long way toward establishing your competence and authority with your audience.

◆ PRACTICE 1-14

Reread the final draft of Erica's paragraph about heroes (above), and compare it with her draft (page 15). What kinds of changes did she make?

Which do you think are her most effective changes? Why? Note your thoughts on the lines below. Then, with your class or in a small group, discuss your reaction to the revised paragraph.

_____

_____

_____

_____

◆ PRACTICE 1-15

Use the Self-Assessment Checklist on page 16 to evaluate the paragraph you drafted for Practice 1-13. What additions can you make to support your main idea more fully? Should anything be crossed out because it doesn't support your main idea? Can anything be stated more clearly? On the lines below, list some of the changes you might make in your draft.

_____

_____

_____

_____

Now, revise your draft. Cross out unnecessary material and material you want to rewrite, and add new and rewritten material between the lines and in the margins. After you finish your revision, edit your paragraph, checking grammar, punctuation, mechanics, and spelling—and look carefully for typos. When you are satisfied with your paragraph, type or print out a clean copy, and hold it for the Writing First exercise that opens Chapter 2.

☑ REVIEW CHECKLIST:
Writing a Paragraph

- Before you start to write, consider your assignment, purpose, and audience. (See 1A.)

- Use invention strategies—freewriting, brainstorming, clustering, and journal writing—to find ideas. (See 1B.)

- Select ideas from your notes, and arrange them in a logical order. (See 1C.)

- Write a first draft. (See 1D.)

- Revise your draft. (See 1E.)

- Edit your draft. (See 1E.)

2

Fine-Tuning Your Paragraph

PREVIEW

In this chapter, you will learn

■ to write unified paragraphs (2A)

■ to write well-developed paragraphs (2B)

■ to write coherent paragraphs (2C)

▼ **Student Voices**
The biggest problem I have is making sure my paragraphs make sense.
Terry Simons

■ **WRITING FIRST**

Copy the final draft of the passage that you wrote and revised in Chapter 1 onto a separate sheet of paper. You will continue to work on your paragraph as you go through this chapter.

A   Writing Unified Paragraphs

A paragraph is **unified** when it focuses on a single **main idea**. Many paragraphs express this central idea in a **topic sentence**. Because it states the main idea, the topic sentence is usually the most general sentence in a paragraph. The other sentences are more specific because they give further information about the main idea.

Stating the Topic Sentence

An effective topic sentence should present an idea that you can discuss in a single paragraph. If your topic sentence is too broad, you will not be able to discuss it in just one paragraph. If your topic sentence is too narrow, you will not be able to think of much to say about it.

TOPIC SENTENCE TOO BROAD	Students with jobs have special needs.
TOPIC SENTENCE TOO NARROW	The tutoring center closes at 5 p.m.
EFFECTIVE TOPIC SENTENCE	Many campus facilities do not meet the needs of students who work.

20

FOCUS **Topic Sentences**

There is a difference between a **topic** and a **topic sentence**. The *topic* is what a paragraph is about; the *topic sentence* is a complete sentence that states the paragraph's main idea.

Topic	Topic Sentence
Television violence	Violent television shows have a negative effect on my younger brothers.
Animal testing	One reason not to buy products tested on animals is that most animal testing is unnecessary.
Heroes	My heroes are people who take action instead of waiting for others to act.

● **Writing Tip**
Although a topic sentence can appear anywhere in a paragraph, it's a good idea to put it at the beginning. The topic sentence at the beginning will immediately tell your readers what you are writing about; it will also keep you on track as you write.

Revising Paragraphs for Unity

A paragraph lacks **unity** when its sentences do not focus on its main idea. You can correct this problem by rereading your paragraphs and rewriting or deleting sentences that do not support the main idea stated in the topic sentence.

Paragraph Not Unified

The changing economic picture has led many people to move away from the rural Pennsylvania community where I was raised. Over the years, farmland has become more and more expensive. Years ago, a family could buy each of its children twenty-five acres on which they could start farming. Today, the price of land is so high that the average farmer cannot afford to buy this amount of land. I am tired of seeing my friends move away. After I graduate, I intend to return to my town and get a job there. Even though many factories have moved out of the area, I think I can get a job. My uncle owns a hardware store, and he told me that after I graduate, he will teach me the business. I think I can contribute something to the business and to the town.

Topic sentence

■ **Computer Tip**
Try boldfacing or underscoring the topic sentence of a paragraph before you start to revise the paragraph.

The preceding paragraph is not unified. After presenting one reason why people are moving away, the writer abandons his paragraph's main idea and starts to complain about his friends and discuss his future plans. The rest of the paragraph consists of digressions that do not support the paragraph's topic sentence.

Paragraph Unified

The changing economic picture has led many people to move away from the rural Pennsylvania community where I was raised. Over the years, farmland has become more and more expensive. Years ago, a family could buy each of its children twenty-five acres on which they could start farming. Today, the price of land is so high that the average farmer cannot afford to buy this amount of land, and those who choose not to farm have few alternatives. They just cannot get good jobs anymore. Factories have moved out of the area and have taken

Topic sentence

with them the jobs that many young people got after high school. As a result, many eighteen-year-olds have no choice but to move to Pittsburgh to find employment.

The paragraph is now unified. It discusses only what the topic sentence promises: the reasons why people have moved away from the writer's hometown.

◆ PRACTICE 2-1

Decide whether the following statements could be effective topic sentences for paragraphs. If a sentence is too broad, write "too broad" in the blank following the sentence. If the sentence is too narrow, write "too narrow" in the blank. If the sentence is an effective topic sentence, write "OK" in the blank.

> **Example:** Thanksgiving always falls on the fourth Thursday in
>
> November. ___*too narrow*___

1. Computers are changing the world. _____

2. There are five computer terminals in the campus library. _____

3. The computer I use at work makes my job easier. _____

4. Soccer is not as popular in the United States as it is in Europe.

   _____

5. Americans enjoy watching many types of sporting events on television.

   _____

6. There is one quality that distinguishes a good coach from a mediocre

   one. _____

7. Vegetarianism is a healthy way of life. _____

8. Uncooked spinach has fourteen times as much iron as steak does.

   _____

9. Fast-food restaurants are finally beginning to respond to the growing

   number of customers who are vegetarians. _____

10. There are many different kinds of cars to choose from. _____

◆ PRACTICE 2-2

The following paragraphs are not unified because not every sentence clearly relates to or supports the topic sentence. Cross out the sentence or sentences in each paragraph that do not belong.

1. The one possession I could not live without is my car. In addition to attending school full time, I hold down two part-time jobs that are many

miles from each other, from where I live, and from school. Even though my car is almost twelve years old and has close to 120,000 miles on it, I couldn't manage without it. I'm thinking about buying a new car, and I always check the classified ads, but I haven't found anything I want that I can afford. If my old car breaks down, I guess I'll have to, though. I couldn't live without my portable tape recorder because I use it to record all the class lectures I attend. Then I can play them back while I'm driving or during my breaks at work. Three nights a week and on weekends, I work as a counselor at a home for teenagers with problems, and my other job is in the tire department at Sam's. Without my car, I'd be lost.

2. Studies conducted by Dr. Leonard Eron over the last thirty years suggest that the more television violence children are exposed to, the more aggressive they are as teenagers and adults. In 1960, Eron questioned parents about how they treated their children at home, including how much television their children watched. There is more violence on television today than there was then. Ten years later, he interviewed these families again and discovered that whether teenage sons were aggressive depended less on how they had been treated by their parents than on how much violent television programming they had watched as children. Returning in 1990, he found that these same young men, now in their thirties, were still more likely to be aggressive and to commit crimes. Researchers estimate that a child today is likely to watch 100,000 violent acts on television before finishing elementary school.

3. Libraries today hold a lot more than just books. Of course, books still outnumber anything else on the shelves, but more and more libraries are expanding to include other specialized services. For example, many libraries now offer extensive collections of tapes and compact discs, ranging from classical music to jazz to country to rock. Many have also increased their holdings of videotapes, both instructional programs and popular recent and vintage movies. However, most people probably still get more movies from video stores than from libraries. In addition, the children's section often has games and toys young patrons can play with in the library or even check out. Most important, libraries are offering more and more computerized data services, which can provide much more detailed and up-to-date information than printed sources. These expanding nonprint sources are the wave of the future for even the smallest libraries and will allow patrons access to much more information than books or magazines ever could. People who don't know how to use a computer are going to be out of luck.

■ WRITING FIRST: Flashback

Look back at the paragraph you wrote for the Writing First exercise on page 20. Does your paragraph have a topic sentence? If it does, write that sentence on the lines below. If necessary, revise the topic sentence so that it clearly states the main idea of the paragraph. (If your paragraph does not have a topic sentence, write one

(continued on the following page)

(continued from the previous page)
below.) Finally, review your paragraph for unity and cross out any
sentences that do not support the topic sentence.

_____

_____

_____

B Writing Well-Developed Paragraphs

A paragraph is **well developed** when it contains enough details, facts, and
examples to support the topic sentence. Keep in mind, however, that
although a long paragraph offers room for development, length alone does
not guarantee that a paragraph is developed enough. A paragraph is well
developed only when it includes both *enough* support and the appropriate
kind of support.

Supporting the Topic Sentence

To determine the amount and kind of support you need, ask yourself two
questions:

1. *How complicated is your main idea?* A complicated main idea will need
   more explanation than a relatively simple one.
2. *How much do your readers know about your main idea?* If readers have
   eaten a lot of food prepared by your school's food service facilities, you
   do not need to give many examples to convince them that the food is
   bad. If, on the other hand, your readers are not familiar with the food
   at your school, you have to supply several examples and perhaps even
   definitions (what is "anything goes stew," for example?) to support
   your point.

FOCUS Developing Paragraphs

A paragraph that leaves too many questions unanswered, too many
claims unsupported, or too many ideas unillustrated or unexplained
will not be effective. By adding details, facts, and examples, you can
turn a relatively unconvincing paragraph into an interesting and
persuasive one.

Revising Paragraphs for Development

A paragraph is not well developed when it lacks the support readers need to understand or accept its main idea. You can correct this problem by looking for unsupported generalizations and supplying the details and examples you need to support them.

Undeveloped Paragraph

> Although pit bulls were originally bred to fight, they can actually make good pets. Today, many people are afraid of pit bulls. These dogs are sometimes mistreated. As a result, they become more aggressive. For this reason, they are misunderstood and persecuted. In fact, some cities have taken action against them. But pit bulls do not deserve their bad reputation. Contrary to popular opinion, they can make good pets.

The preceding paragraph is not well developed. It contains a series of general statements that leave the writer's points unclear and therefore do not provide adequate support for the main idea.

Well-Developed Paragraph

> Although pit bulls were originally bred to fight, they can actually make good pets. It is true that their powerful jaws, short muscular legs, and large teeth are ideally suited to fighting, and they were used extensively for this purpose in the rural South and Southwest. It is also true that some pit bulls—especially males—can be aggressive toward other dogs. However, most pit bulls like human beings and are quite friendly. Owners report that pit bulls are affectionate, loyal, and good with children. When pit bulls behave viciously, it is usually because they have been mistreated. As a recent newspaper article pointed out, the number of reported bites by pit bulls is no greater than the number of bites by other breeds. In fact, some dogs, such as cocker spaniels, bite much more frequently. The problem is that whenever a pit bull attacks a person, the incident is reported in the paper. As you can see, pit bulls do not deserve their reputation. With a little bit of tender, loving care, a pit bull can be a welcome addition to any family.

The paragraph is now well developed. General statements are clarified by examples or details. As a result, readers are more likely to accept the idea that pit bulls can make good pets.

Computer Tip

Hit the Enter or Return key after your topic sentence and after each sentence that follows it. By highlighting each detail and example, you can evaluate the amount and kind of support you have used.

◆ PRACTICE 2-3

The following two paragraphs are not well developed. On the lines that follow each paragraph, write three questions or suggestions that might help the writer develop his or her ideas more fully.

1. Other than my parents, the biggest influence on my life was probably my Aunt Sylva. When I was little, she used to baby-sit for me every day, and she always found interesting and educational things for us to do, either at home or on trips downtown. She had lived in Mexico City for many years, and I always admired her exotic looks. As a teenager, I tried to copy the way she walked, talked, and even dressed. Even today, I often

think of her when I catch myself putting on the sort of outfit she might have worn. Tragically, she died just before my eighteenth birthday.

_____

_____

_____

2. Computerized special effects have made a big difference in movies over the last ten years. Science fiction films are more spectacular than ever, and filmmakers are able to take moviegoers to places they've never been before. New special-effects techniques can also create fierce monsters, more terrifying than anything seen on the screen before. Other effects have been used in comedies to create hilarious visual gags. It's likely that the future will bring even more impressive effects for the enjoyment of movie audiences.

_____

_____

_____

■ WRITING FIRST: Flashback

Look back at the paragraph you wrote for the Writing First exercise on page 20. Is your paragraph well developed? On the lines below, list the examples and details that you used to support your main idea. Then, list suggestions for revision, noting the kinds of examples and details you might add.

Examples and details:

_____

_____

_____

_____

_____

Suggestions for revision:

_____

_____

_____

_____

_____

C   Writing Coherent Paragraphs

A paragraph is **coherent** if all its sentences are arranged in a clear, logical order. You can make a paragraph coherent by arranging details logically and by supplying transitional words and phrases that show the connections between sentences.

Arranging Details Logically

In general, you can arrange the details in a paragraph according to *time order, spatial order,* or *sequential order.*

Paragraphs that are arranged in **time order** present events chronologically—often in the exact order in which they occurred. Stories, historical accounts, and instructions are generally arranged in time order.

The following paragraph presents events in time order. The words *before, once, then, finally,* and *after* indicate the sequence of events in the paragraph.

> In 1856, my great-great-great-grandparents, Anne and Charles McGinley, came to the United States to start a new life. Before they left Ireland, their English landlords had raised the taxes on their land so high that my ancestors could not afford to pay them. It took them three years to save the money for passage. Once they had saved the money, they had to look for a ship that was willing to take them. Then my great-great-great-grandparents were on their way. They and their ten children spent four long months on a small ship. Storms, strong tides, and damaged sails made the trip longer than it should have been. Finally, in November of 1856, they saw land, and two days later they sailed into New York Harbor. After they were admitted to the United States, they took a train to Baltimore, Maryland, where some cousins lived.

Paragraphs that are arranged in **spatial order** present details in the order in which they are observed—top to bottom, near to far, or right to left, for example. Spatial order is central to paragraphs that tell what a person, place, animal, or object looks like (and perhaps what it sounds, smells, tastes, and feels like).

The following paragraph presents events in spatial order. Notice how the phrases *directly in front of, next to, behind, in between, on top of, inside,* and *in the center of* help establish the order—far to near—in which readers will view the details of the scene.

> The day I arrived at the Amish school I knew it was unlike any other school I had seen before. A long, tree-lined dirt road led to the small wooden schoolhouse. Directly in front of the school was a line of bicycles and metal scooters. A small baseball diamond had been carved into the dirt in the yard next to the schoolhouse. Behind the school, two little outhouses stood next to each other with a green water pump in between. The schoolhouse itself was a small one-story structure. White paint curled off its clapboard siding, and a short steeple, holding a brass bell, sat firmly on top of the roof. Inside the open door, a long line of black hats hung on pegs. In the center of the small schoolhouse was an iron potbellied stove surrounded by the children's desks.

Paragraphs that are arranged in **sequential order** present ideas in a logical sequence—from least important to most important, general to specific, or most familiar to least familiar, for example. Writers often build suspense by presenting the least important idea first and then leading up to the most important one.

The following paragraph presents ideas in sequential order. Here, the phrases *the first rule, an even sillier rule,* and *the most ridiculous rule* establish the order in which the rules are presented—from least to most silly—and help readers move from one point to another.

My high school had three rules that were silly at best and ridiculous at worst. The first rule was that only seniors could go outside the school building for lunch. In spite of this rule, many students went outside to eat because the cafeteria was not big enough to accommodate all the school's students at the same time. Understanding the problem, the teachers and the principal looked the other way as long as we returned to school before the lunch period was over. An even sillier rule was that we had to attend 95 percent of the classes for every course. This rule meant that a person could miss only about six days of class every semester. Naturally, this rule was never enforced because if it had been, half the students would have failed. The most ridiculous rule, however, was that students could not throw their hats into the air during graduation. At one point in the past—no one seems to know when—a parent had complained that a falling hat could poke someone in the eye. As a result, graduating classes were told that under no circumstance could they throw their hats. Naturally, on graduation day we did what every previous graduating class had done—ignored the rule and threw our hats into the air.

◆ PRACTICE 2-4

Read each of the following topic sentences carefully. If you were writing a paragraph introduced by the sentence, how would you arrange the supporting details—in time order, spatial order, or sequential order? Write your answer in the blank following the topic sentence.

Example: It is important to keep several things in mind when shopping for a new stereo. *sequential order*

1. My first week at my new job began badly but ended better than I ever could have expected. _____

2. People would get along better if everyone practiced a few important rules of common courtesy. _____

3. My son's bedroom reflects his many different interests and hobbies. _____

4. The Mustangs are a stronger team than the Bobcats for three reasons. _____

5. Babies develop in amazing ways during the first three months of life. _____

6. When you interview for a job, keep in mind that most employers look for the same qualities in a prospective employee. _____

7. Dressing for success means looking your best from the hair on your head to the shoes on your feet. _____

8. I had always felt safe in my neighborhood until last year, when something happened that changed my attitude completely. _____

9. To protect yourself on campus after dark, you should always take the following precautions. _____

10. The new Southern Trust Bank in Gaston is one of the ugliest buildings in town. _____

Using Transitional Words and Phrases

Within a paragraph, **transitional words and phrases** often indicate the relationships among sentences. By establishing the time order, spatial order, and sequential order of the ideas in a paragraph, these words and expressions enable readers to see the connections among ideas.

Transitional Words and Phrases

Words and Phrases That Signal Time Order

after	later
afterward	next
at first	now
before	soon
earlier	then
finally	dates (for example, "In June")

Words and Phrases That Signal Spatial Order

above	in front	on the right
behind	near	on top
below	next to	over
beside	on the bottom	under
in back	on the left	

Words and Phrases That Signal Sequential Order

although	not only . . . but also
consequently	one . . . another
equally important	on the one hand . . . on the other hand
first . . . second . . . third	similarly
furthermore	the least important
in addition	the most important
last	therefore
next	

■ **Computer Tip**
Keep a list of transitional words and phrases in a separate file. When you revise, consult this file to see if you've used the most appropriate transitions.

Revising Paragraphs for Coherence

Because transitional words and phrases establish **coherence**, a paragraph without them will be difficult to understand. You can correct this problem by including in your paragraph all the words and phrases that are needed to link the ideas in the paragraph.

Paragraph without Transitional Words and Phrases

During his lifetime, Jim Thorpe faced many obstacles. Thorpe was born in 1888 in Indian territory, the son of an Irish father and a Native American mother. He was sent to the Carlisle Indian School in Pennsylvania. "Pop" Warner, the legendary coach at Carlisle, discovered Thorpe when he saw him jump more than six feet while he was wearing street clothes. Thorpe became a star on the Carlisle track team and a substitute on the football team. Thorpe left Carlisle to play baseball for two seasons in the newly formed East Carolina minor league. Thorpe returned to Carlisle, played football, and was named to the All-American team. Thorpe went to the 1912 Olympic games in Stockholm, where he won two gold medals. King Gustav V of Sweden said to him, "Sir, you are the greatest athlete in the world." Thorpe's career took a dramatic turn for the worse when a sportswriter who had seen him play baseball in North Carolina exposed him as a professional. The Amateur Athletic Union stripped him of his records and medals. The International Olympic Committee returned Thorpe's Olympic medals to his family.

The above paragraph is not coherent because it does not include the transitional words and phrases needed to establish how the events relate to one another.

Paragraph with Transitional Words and Phrases

During his lifetime, Jim Thorpe faced many obstacles. Thorpe was born in 1888 in Indian territory, the son of an Irish father and a Native American mother. In 1904, he was sent to the Carlisle Indian School in Pennsylvania. The next year, "Pop" Warner, the legendary coach at Carlisle, discovered Thorpe when he saw him jump more than six feet while he was wearing street clothes. Almost immediately, Thorpe became a star on the Carlisle track team and a substitute on the football team. Thorpe left Carlisle in 1909 to play baseball for two seasons in the newly formed East Carolina minor league. In 1911, Thorpe returned to Carlisle, played football, and was named to the All-American team. Thorpe's most notable achievement came at the 1912 Olympic games in Stockholm, where he won two gold medals. At the games, King Gustav V of Sweden said to him, "Sir, you are the greatest athlete in the world." The next year, however, Thorpe's career took a dramatic turn for the worse when a sportswriter who had seen him play baseball in North Carolina exposed him as a professional. As a result, the Amateur Athletic Union stripped him of his records and medals. After years of appeals, the International Olympic Committee returned Thorpe's Olympic medals to his family in 1982, more than thirty years after his death.

The paragraph is now coherent. It contains transitional words and phrases —*almost immediately, the next year,* and *after years of appeals,* for example—that establish the relationships among key events in Thorpe's life.

◆ PRACTICE 2-5

Underline the transitional words and phrases in each of the following paragraphs. Then decide what order—time order, spatial order, or sequential order—the writer has chosen for arranging details in each paragraph. Write your answers in the blanks provided.

1. Alarmed that teenage girls today get only half as much exercise as boys, researchers are trying to find out why. One reason, they say, is the amount of television girls watch. But this is not an adequate explanation because boys generally watch as much television as girls do. A more important reason is that many girls do not have available to them the sorts of organized athletic programs that are available to boys. Furthermore, because both parents often work now, girls are more likely to have responsibilities at home that leave them less free time than boys have to pursue physical activity. Most important, though, may be the lingering attitude that boys aren't attracted to girls who are athletic. Being "feminine," for many girls, means avoiding anything that might mess up their hair or make them sweat. Unless these habits and attitudes change, the current generation of teenage girls may grow into a generation of women plagued by serious health problems.

Order: _____

2. The high school I attended is unusual because, instead of being a single building, it is actually a campus consisting of six separate buildings located on a small hill. The front building, which faces the street, houses administrative offices, the library, and the cafeteria. Beside the administration building is a large structure that contains the gym, a swimming pool, and rehearsal rooms for band and chorus. In back of the administration building is a parallel building where English and foreign language classes are held. Behind this is a large grassy space flanked by two buildings that run at right angles to the English building. The building on the right is for social studies and business courses, and the building on the left is for math and the sciences. At the far end of the grassy space is a small A-frame building containing the art studio and the shop. Between the buildings are covered cement walkways. Changing classes requires going from building to building, and this is usually a nice break—except in the dead of winter, when people freeze as they pass from class to class.

Order: _____

3. The Caribbean island of Puerto Rico has a complex history. Before the 1400s, the island's inhabitants for centuries were the native Arawak Indians. In 1493, Christopher Columbus and his crew were the earliest Europeans to reach the island. Fifteen years later, Ponce de Leon conquered the island for Spain, and the Spanish subjected the Arawaks to virtual slavery to develop a sugar industry. Finally, these native people were annihilated completely, slaughtered by the sword and by European diseases to which they had no immunity. The Arawaks were soon replaced by African slaves as a European plantation culture flourished. In 1898, after the Spanish-American War, the island was ceded to the United States. The next year, the United States designated Puerto Rico a colony under an American governor. Later, in 1917, Puerto Ricans were granted U.S. citizenship, and the country became a U.S. commonwealth in 1952. Since then, Puerto

Ricans have debated this status, with some arguing for statehood and others for independence. For now, the island remains a commonwealth, and its citizens share most of the rights and obligations of U.S. citizenship.

Order: _____

■ WRITING FIRST: Flashback

Look back at the paragraph you wrote for the Writing First exercise on page 20. Are all its sentences arranged in a logical order? Is this order time, spatial, or sequential? List below the transitional words and phrases that signal this order to readers.

_____   _____

_____   _____

_____   _____

_____   _____

_____

■ WRITING FIRST: Revising and Editing

Review the work you did for the Flashback exercises on pages 23, 26, and on this page, and revise your paragraph for unity, development, and coherence.

CHAPTER REVIEW

◆ EDITING PRACTICE

Read the following paragraphs, and evaluate each in terms of its unity, development, and coherence. First, underline each topic sentence. Then, cross out any sentences that do not support the topic sentence. Add transitional words and phrases where needed. Finally, discuss in class whether additional details and examples could be added to each paragraph.

1.   In 1979, a series of mechanical and human errors

    in Unit 2 of the nuclear generating plant at Three Mile

    Island, near Harrisburg, Pennsylvania, caused an accident that profoundly affected the nuclear power industry. A combination of stuck valves, human error, and poor decisions caused a partial meltdown of the reactor core. Large amounts of radioactive gases were released into the atmosphere. The governor of Pennsylvania immediately evacuated pregnant women from the area. People panicked and left their homes. The nuclear regulatory agency claimed that the situation was not really dangerous and that the released gases were not a health threat, but activists and local residents disputed this. The reactor itself remained unusable for more than ten years. Massive demonstrations followed the accident, including a rally of more than 200,000 people in New York City. Some people came because the day was nice. By the mid-1980s, new construction of nuclear power plants in the United States had stopped.

2.   A survey of cigarette commercials shows how tobacco companies have consistently encouraged people to continue smoking. One of the earliest television ads showed two boxes of cigarettes dancing to an advertising jingle. The approach in this ad was simple: create an entertaining commercial, and people will buy your product. Many people liked these ads. Other commercials were more subtle. Some were aimed at specific audiences. Marlboro commercials, with the rugged Marlboro man, targeted men. Virginia Slims made an overt pitch to women by saying, "You've come a long way, baby!" Salem, a mentholated cigarette, showed rural scenes and targeted people who liked the freshness of the outdoors. Kent, with its "micronite filter," appealed to those who were health conscious by claiming that Kent contained less tar and nicotine than any other brand. This claim was not entirely true. Other brands had less tar and nicotine. Cigarette companies responded to the national decline in smoking by directing advertising at the less well

educated. Camel introduced the cartoon character Joe Camel, which was aimed at teenagers and young adults. Merit and other high-tar and high-nicotine cigarettes used commercials that were specifically directed at minorities.

3.   Cities created police forces for a number of reasons. The first reason was status: after the Civil War, it became a status symbol for cities to have a uniformed police force. A police force provided a large number of political jobs. Politicians were able to promise jobs to people who would work to support them. Police forces made people feel safe. Police officers helped visitors find their way. They took in lost children and sometimes fed the homeless. They directed traffic, enforced health ordinances, and provided a series of other services. Police officers kept order. Without a visible, uniformed police force, criminals would have made life in nineteenth-century cities unbearable.

◆ COLLABORATIVE ACTIVITIES

1. Working in a group, list the reasons why students decide to attend your school. After working together to arrange these reasons from least to most important, create a topic sentence that states the main idea suggested by these reasons. Finally, work on your own to draft a paragraph in which you discuss the factors that lead students to attend your school.

2. In a newspaper or magazine, find an illustration or photograph that includes a lot of visual details. Write a paragraph describing what you see in the photograph so that readers will be able to "see" it almost as clearly as you can. Decide on a specific spatial order—top to bottom, left to right, clockwise from the center, or another arrangement that makes sense to you. Use that spatial order to organize the details in your draft paragraph. Finally, trade paragraphs with another student and offer suggestions that could improve his or her paragraph.

3. Bring to class a paragraph from a newspaper or a magazine. Working in a group, decide whether each paragraph is unified, well developed, and coherent. If it is not, try as a group to rewrite the paragraph to make it more effective.

✔ REVIEW CHECKLIST:
Fine-Tuning Your Paragraph

- A paragraph is unified when it focuses on a single main idea, which is often stated in a topic sentence at the beginning of the paragraph. (See 2A.)

- A topic sentence can be placed anywhere in a paragraph, but often it is the paragraph's first sentence. (See 2A.)

- A paragraph is well developed when it contains enough details and examples to support the main idea. (See 2B.)

- A paragraph is coherent if its sentences are arranged in a clear, logical order and it includes all necessary transitional words and phrases. (See 2C.)

UNIT TWO

Patterns of Paragraph Development

C H A P T E R

3

Exemplification

PREVIEW

In this chapter, you
will learn to write
an exemplification
paragraph.

■ **WRITING FIRST**

Write a paragraph in which you discuss two or three accomplishments of which you are proud. Identify the accomplishments in
your topic sentence.

In Chapters 1 and 2, you learned how to write paragraphs. In Chapters 3
through 11, you will become acquainted with the options you have for
organizing ideas within paragraphs. As you write, you will see that your
ideas tend to develop in ways that reflect how your mind works to make
sense of information and communicate it to others: you give examples, tell
what happened, describe physical characteristics, explain how something
operates, identify causes or predict effects, identify similarities and differences, classify information into categories, define, or persuade. These
methods of arranging ideas correspond to specific patterns of paragraph
(and essay) development: *exemplification, narration, description, process,
cause and effect, comparison and contrast, classification, definition,* and
argument. Recognizing these patterns and understanding how they help
you organize your ideas will help you become a more confident writer.

▼ **Student Voices**
*Examples, examples: my
instructor is always telling
me to use more examples.*
Nicholas Kinlaw

A Understanding Exemplification

Exemplification is writing that explains a general statement with one or
more specific examples. In an **exemplification paragraph**, you use examples to illustrate and explain the point you are making in the topic sentence.
To be effective, examples must be *appropriate* (that is, they must support or
explain your point), and they must be *specific* (that is, they must be precise). Because an example is a piece of information that supports the paragraph's main idea, it is always more specific than the topic sentence.

● **Writing Tip**
Use a transitional phrase
such as *for instance* or *for
example* to tell readers you're
going to use an example.
(See 2C.)

39

You can use a number of short examples to support your topic sentence, or, if one example is particularly vivid or compelling, you can use a single extended example. Thus, a single paragraph may contain either a series of short examples or one extended example. The following paragraph about the 1969 Woodstock festival uses a number of short examples.

Topic sentence

Series of short examples

> In most respects, after all, Woodstock was a disaster. To begin with, it rained and rained for weeks before the festival, and then, of course, it rained during the festival. The promoters lost weeks of preparation time when the site had to be switched twice. They rented Yasgur's field less than a month before the concert. The stage wasn't finished, and the sound system was stitched together perilously close to the start of the show. As soon as the festival opened, the water- and food-delivery arrangements broke down, the gates and fences disintegrated, and tens of thousands of new bodies kept pouring in. (One powerful lure was the rumor that the revered Bob Dylan was going to perform; he wasn't.) In response to an emergency appeal for volunteers, fifty doctors were flown in. The Air Force brought in food on Huey helicopters, and the Women's Community Center in Monticello sent thirty thousand sandwiches. One kid was killed as he was run over by a tractor, one died of appendicitis, and another died of a drug overdose.
>
> Hal Espen, "The Woodstock Wars"

● **Writing Tip**
Many everyday tasks call for exemplification. In a letter to your local paper, you might give examples of quality-of-life improvements that need to be made in your neighborhood.

The writer of this paragraph piles on a series of examples, one after the other, to support his paragraph's main idea. Each example gives a specific illustration of how Woodstock was a disaster: it rained, the promoters had to switch sites, water and food were not delivered as planned, and so on.

The following paragraph uses a single extended example to support its main idea—that fear can move people to take action.

Topic sentence

Single extended example

> Sometimes, fear can be a great motivator. Once, when I was in high school, I tried out for a part in the school play. I was surprised and thrilled when I was given one of the leads. Never for a moment, however, did I consider how long my part was or how hard I would have to work to memorize it. All I could think of was how much attention I was getting from my friends. I even ignored the warnings of the play's director, who told me I would be in trouble if I did not begin to memorize my lines. The reality of my situation finally sank in during our first dress rehearsal when I stumbled all over my lines and the rest of the cast laughed at me. That night, and for the two weeks leading up to the play, I spent hours going over my lines. Miraculously, I got through the first night of the play without missing (at least obviously missing) many of my lines. As a result of that experience, I learned two things: first, that I could do almost anything if I was frightened enough, and second, that I would never try out for another play.
>
> Jerry Doyle (student)

Here, a single extended example supports the topic sentence. Often, a personal experience like this one can be an interesting and powerful way of illustrating your ideas for your readers.

Exemplification

The number of examples you need depends on the idea in your topic sentence. If the topic sentence is somewhat general, you may need several examples to illustrate it. If the topic sentence is specific, a single example explained in detail may be all you need.

B **Writing an Exemplification Paragraph**

◆ PRACTICE 3-1

Read this exemplification paragraph; then, follow the instructions below.

                    Youthful Style?

     As a teenager in the late 1960s and early 1970s, I
was always pretty tolerant of radical clothing styles,
but more and more today I find myself asking, "Why do
these kids want to look so weird?" For example, I do not
understand why a boy would wear a baseball cap backwards
on his head. To me, this just looks weird, like something
a person would do and then talk in a really stupid voice
to make his friends laugh. Under the backward cap, the boy
probably has his hair in a buzz cut, except for one long
strand of hair reaching halfway down his back. I can't
imagine who thought up this hairstyle, unless it was an ex-
monk. Furthermore, every boy I see today seems to be wearing a T-shirt that looks ten sizes too big for him and
comes down below his knees, or, if not that, he's got all
his clothes on inside out or backwards or both! Then there
are the girls. Since when did it become stylish to wear
your underwear on top of your regular clothes? Who decided
that it was attractive to combine a white T-shirt and a
long, sheer, flowing skirt with a pair of huge black jack-
boots? I'm so confused. It all just makes me nostalgic for
the days of frayed bell-bottoms, tie-dyed tank tops,
strands of hippie beads, and headbands circling heads of
long, stringy hair.

                          Willa Kincaid (student)

1. Underline the topic sentence of the paragraph.

2. List the specific examples the writer uses to support her topic sentence. The first example has been listed for you.

boys wearing baseball caps backward _____

_____

_____

_____

_____

_____

3. Circle the transitions that the writer uses to connect ideas in the paragraph.

◆ PRACTICE 3-2

Following are four possible topic sentences for exemplification paragraphs. List three supporting examples for each topic sentence. For example, if you were writing a paragraph about how difficult the first week of your new job was, you could mention waking up early, getting to know your coworkers, and learning new routines.

1. I have a number of reasons for liking my neighborhood.

_____

_____

_____

2. Summer jobs provide valuable opportunities for young people by allowing them to develop their interests and test their abilities.

_____

_____

_____

3. Some rules and regulations are unfair.

_____

_____

_____

4. Many television programs insult their audiences.

_____

_____

_____

◆ PRACTICE 3-3

Choose one of the topics below (or one of your own choice) as the subject of an exemplification paragraph. Then, on a separate sheet of paper, use one or more of the invention strategies described in 1B to think of as many examples as you can for the topic you have chosen.

Effective (or ineffective) politicians	Aerobic training
Qualities that make a song popular	Terrible dates
Successful movies	Racial conflicts
Challenges that students face	Role models
Why people watch soap operas	Rude behavior
Unattractive clothing styles	Politicians
Peer pressure	Acts of bravery
The benefits of cooperation	Difficult jobs

◆ PRACTICE 3-4

Review your notes from Practice 3-3, and list the examples that can help you develop a paragraph on the topic you have chosen.

_____

_____

_____

_____

◆ PRACTICE 3-5

Reread your list of examples from Practice 3-4. Now, draft a topic sentence that introduces your topic and communicates the main idea your paragraph will discuss.

_____

_____

◆ PRACTICE 3-6

Arrange the examples you listed in Practice 3-4 in a logical order—for example, from most important to least important, or from specific to general.

1. _____

2. _____

3. _____

4. _____

◆ **PRACTICE 3-7**

On a separate sheet of paper, write your exemplification paragraph. Then, using the Self-Assessment Checklist below, revise your paragraph for unity, development, and coherence.

◆ **PRACTICE 3-8**

On a separate sheet of paper, write a final, edited draft of your exemplification paragraph.

■ WRITING FIRST: Revising and Editing

Look back at your response to the Writing First exercise on page 39, and evaluate it for unity, development, and coherence. Then, prepare a final, edited draft of your paragraph.

☑ SELF-ASSESSMENT CHECKLIST:
Writing an Exemplification Paragraph

Unity

☐ Does your topic sentence focus on an idea that can be developed in a single paragraph?

☐ Is your topic sentence specifically worded?

☐ Does your topic sentence clearly express what the rest of the paragraph is about?

☐ Do all your examples support your topic sentence?

Development

☐ Do you have enough examples?

☐ Do you need to find examples that more clearly support your topic sentence?

☐ Should you use one of the invention strategies discussed in 1B to come up with more ideas?

Coherence

☐ Are your examples arranged in a logical order?

☐ Do you need to add transitional words or phrases?

CHAPTER

4

Narration

PREVIEW

In this chapter, you will learn to write a narrative paragraph.

■ WRITING FIRST

Write a paragraph in which you tell about an incident that was a turning point in your life—for example, a death in your family, the birth of a child, or your entering college. Make sure your topic sentence clearly states how the incident affected your life.

A Understanding Narration

Narration is writing that tells a story. In a **narrative paragraph**, you relate a sequence of events. A narrative paragraph usually has a topic sentence that tells readers what the point of the paragraph is—that is, why you are telling this particular story. The rest of the paragraph develops this point, with ideas arranged in time order.

In the following paragraph, Vietnam veteran and writer Ron Kovic tells how he celebrated his birthday when he was a child.

> When the Fourth of July came, there were fireworks going off all over the neighborhood. It was the most exciting time of year for me next to Christmas. Being born on the exact same day as my country I thought was really great. I was so proud. And every Fourth of July, I had a birthday party and all my friends would come over with birthday presents and we'd put on silly hats and blow these horns my dad brought home from the A&P. We'd eat lots of ice cream and watermelon and I'd open up all the presents and blow out the candles on the big red, white, and blue birthday cake and then we'd all sing "Happy Birthday" and "I'm a Yankee Doodle Dandy." At night everyone would pile into Bobby's mother's old car and we'd go down to the drive-in, where we'd watch the fireworks display. Before the movie started, we'd all get out and sit up on the roof of the car with our blankets wrapped

> ▼ **Student Voices**
> *When I write narratives, I get to tell my own story.*
> *Miniinah Neal*

Topic sentence

Events presented in time order

> ● **Writing Tip**
> Because narrative paragraphs tell what happened, they often rely on transitional words and phrases that indicate time. (See 2C.)

45

around us watching the rockets and Roman candles going up and exploding into fountains of rainbow colors, and later after Mrs. Zimmer dropped me off, I'd lie on my bed feeling a little sad that it all had to end so soon. As I closed my eyes I could still hear strings of firecrackers and cherry bombs going off all over the neighborhood.

Ron Kovic, *Born on the Fourth of July*

In this paragraph, all events and activities are related to the topic sentence, and transitional words and phrases—*at night, later,* and *as I closed my eyes*—clearly identify the order in which the events occurred.

FOCUS **Narrative**

Not all narrative paragraphs have topic sentences. Sometimes a writer uses a narrative just to tell an interesting story, not to make a point. Even so, the events in the paragraph all contribute to a single idea—that an experience was exciting or unusual, for example.

● **Writing Tip**
Many everyday writing tasks call for narration. In a complaint letter, you might summarize in chronological order the problems you had with a particular product.

B **Writing a Narrative Paragraph**

◆ **PRACTICE 4-1**

Read this narrative paragraph; then, follow the instructions on page 47.

                The Trip to a Brand-New Life

    When I was seven, my family took a trip that changed
our entire lives--the trip to America. Leaving our native
Vietnam illegally, we first traveled three days in a small
boat with about fifty other people. We soon ran out of
food and supplies, and I thought we would never make it,
but at last we reached Malaysia. The people who met us on
shore led us to a campsite where there were hundreds of
other Vietnamese refugees. For nine months, my family stayed
there, living in a shelter consisting of logs covered with
thick plastic. During this time, we were called in to present our situation to representatives from a variety of
countries so they could process our documents and decide
whether to accept us as immigrants. We were among the fortunate ones accepted by the United States. Next, we were
transferred to a camp in the Philippines where the houses
were more stable and the floors were cement instead of
dirt. For three months, we continued to study English;
then, the happy moment came when we learned that we would
be leaving for America. A few days later, we were headed

for New York, changing planes in several countries before reaching our destination. As the last plane landed, I was overwhelmed by the realization that my family and I had finally reached the end of our dreams. I knew that my first step on the ground would lead me to a new future and a completely new life. I was scared, but I did not hesitate.

Ann Duong (student)

1. Underline the topic sentence of the paragraph.

2. List below the major events of the narrative. The first event has been listed for you.

The family left Vietnam and spent three days on the water.

_____

_____

_____

_____

_____

3. Reread the narrative, circling the transitional words and phrases the writer uses to link events in time.

◆ PRACTICE 4-2

Following are four possible topic sentences for narrative paragraphs. After each topic sentence, list four events you could include in a narrative paragraph to support the main idea. For example, if you were telling about a barbecue that turned into a disaster, you could tell about burning the hamburgers, spilling the soda, and forgetting to buy paper plates.

1. One event made me realize that I was no longer as young as I thought.

_____

_____

_____

_____

2. The first time I _____, I got more than I bargained for.

_____

_____

_____

_____

3. Even though the accident lasted only a few seconds, it seemed to last much longer.

_____

_____

_____

_____

4. I remember one particular news event very clearly.

_____

_____

_____

_____

◆ PRACTICE 4-3

Choose one of the topics below (or one of your own choice) as the subject of a narrative paragraph. On a separate sheet of paper, use one or more of the invention strategies described in 1-B to recall details about the topic you have chosen.

A difficult choice	An embarrassing situation
A frightening situation	A memorable holiday
A time of rejection	A sudden understanding
A triumph	Something funny a friend did
An act of violence	An unexpected failure
A lesson learned	A conflict with authority
Your happiest moment	An event that changed your life
An instance of injustice	An important decision

◆ PRACTICE 4-4

List the events you recalled in Practice 4-3 that can help you develop a narrative paragraph on the topic you have chosen.

_____

_____

_____

_____

_____

_____

◆ PRACTICE 4-5

Reread your list of events from Practice 4-4. Then, draft a topic sentence that introduces your topic and communicates the main idea your paragraph will discuss.

_____

_____

_____

◆ PRACTICE 4-6

Write down the events you listed in Practice 4-4 in the order in which they occurred.

1. _____

2. _____

3. _____

4. _____

5. _____

◆ PRACTICE 4-7

On a separate sheet of paper, write your narrative paragraph. Then, using the Self-Assessment Checklist on page 50, revise your paragraph for unity, development, and coherence.

◆ PRACTICE 4-8

On a separate sheet of paper, write a final, edited draft of your narrative paragraph.

■ WRITING FIRST: Revising and Editing

Look back at your response to the Writing First exercise on page 45, and evaluate it for unity, development, and coherence. Then, prepare a final, edited draft of your paragraph.

☑ SELF-ASSESSMENT CHECKLIST:
Writing a Narrative Paragraph

Unity

☐ Does your topic sentence focus on an idea that can be developed in a single paragraph?

☐ Is your topic sentence specific enough?

☐ Do you need to revise the topic sentence so that it takes into account all the events you discuss?

☐ Do all details and events support your topic sentence?

Development

☐ Should you add more events or details to make your narrative clearer or livelier?

☐ Should you use one of the invention strategies discussed in 1B to come up with more ideas?

Coherence

☐ Does your narrative proceed clearly from an earlier time to a later time?

☐ Do you need to add transitional words or phrases?

5

Description

■ WRITING FIRST

Write a paragraph in which you describe a person you encounter every day—for example, a street vendor, a bus driver, or a worker in your school cafeteria. Before you begin writing, decide what general impression you want to convey about the person you are describing.

A Understanding Description

Description is writing that paints a word picture of a person, place, or thing. You use description when you want readers to see what you see, hear what you hear, smell what you smell, taste what you taste, and feel what you feel. In a **descriptive paragraph**, the words you use help to create a single **dominant impression**—the mood or feeling that you want to communicate to your readers. All the sentences in the paragraph should reinforce this dominant impression.

   In general, there are two kinds of descriptive paragraphs: *objective* and *subjective*. Writers use **objective description** to describe something precisely without conveying their own emotions. This kind of description is used in technical or scientific writing but can also be used in other kinds of writing. In the following paragraph, the writer uses precise language and specific details to describe a scene to readers, but her writing does not indicate whether the scene has any special meaning for her.

   Just south of Delaware Bay, where the land juts out and curves down the east coast, is a small town called Bethany Beach, Delaware. Each summer, the population of this little resort town swells from a few hundred to several thousand. <u>One look at the beach at Bethany shows the effect of construction on the shoreline.</u> On the Atlantic side of Bethany, the white beach slopes gradually up from the ocean. In back of the beach are low rippling dunes that gradually blend into higher mounds of sand that have been planted with several types of beach grass and stubby green shrubs. The town council hoped that these plants would stabilize the dune structure and stop the erosion that threatens the beach every time there is a storm. Arching over the dunes are narrow gray boardwalks that protect the fragile dunes from the human traffic that eventually would destroy them. Behind the dunes, however, nature seems to stop. As far as you can see down the coast, the land has been divided into sandy plots, each with its own beach house or apartment. The gentle flow of the beach has been interrupted by geometrical structures of shining glass and weathered gray wood.

Kim DiPialo (student)

Because the writer's purpose is to help readers picture the scene she describes, her description is primarily objective. The topic sentence presents the main idea of the paragraph. Then, the writer describes the beach, the dunes, and finally the area behind the dunes. Transitional words and phrases identify the spatial relationships—*in back of the beach, arching over the dunes*, and *behind the dunes*—that connect various parts of the description. Details such as *stubby green shrubs, narrow gray boardwalks*, and *weathered gray wood* give readers a clear picture of the scene.

Writers use **subjective description** to convey their feelings and emotions about a person, place, or thing. In addition to conveying impressions, subjective descriptions contain specific details, just as objective descriptions do. In the following paragraph, the writer describes impressions of an object that has strong emotional associations for her.

Once in a long while, four times so far for me, my mother brings out the metal tube that holds her medical diploma. On the tube are gold circles crossed with seven red lines each—"joy" ideographs in abstract. There are also little flowers that look like gears for a gold machine. According to the scraps of labels with Chinese and American addresses, stamps, and postmarks, the family airmailed the can from Hong Kong in 1950. It got crushed in the middle, and whoever tried to peel the labels off stopped because the red and gold paint came off too, leaving silver scratches that rust. Somebody tried to pry the end off before discovering that the tube pulls apart. When I open it, the smell of China flies out, a thousand-year-old bat flying heavy-headed out of the Chinese caverns where bats are as white as dust, a smell that comes from long ago, far back in the brain. Crates from Canton, Hong Kong, Singapore, and Taiwan have that smell too, only stronger because they are more recently come from the Chinese.

Maxine Hong Kingston, *The Woman Warrior*

In this paragraph, the topic sentence states the main idea of the paragraph. Transitional words and phrases convey the spatial relationships—*on the tube, in the middle*—that connect various aspects of the description. The

---

Writing Tip

Many everyday writing tasks call for description. At work, you might write a memo describing a piece of equipment you would like your department to purchase.

Writing Tip

Descriptive paragraphs often use transitional words and phrases that signal spatial order. (See 2C.)

Writing Tip

Descriptions often use language that conveys sensory details—that tells what something looks, smells, sounds, tastes, or feels like (*a blue sky, a musty smell*).

paragraph conveys the writer's emotional responses to the object she describes—for example, she tells how she imagines "the smell of China" flying out of the tube like "a thousand-year-old bat." In addition, the paragraph contains specific details that give readers a clear picture of the tube.

FOCUS Description

Most descriptive paragraphs mix objective and subjective description. Although one kind of description may dominate, the other will probably be present as well. Whether objective or subjective description is dominant depends on the writer's purpose and audience.

B Writing a Descriptive Paragraph

◆ PRACTICE 5-1

Read this descriptive paragraph; then, follow the instructions on the next page.

Camaro Joe

When I was growing up, my older sister Roxanne invariably managed to come up with the greasiest lowlifes for boyfriends, generally characterized by their lip-snarling, cigarette-smoke-trailing, "I-just-might-die-tomorrow-and-I-might-as-well-take-someone-with-me" attitude. Usually named Mitch or Jake, these guys would hoist my delicate sister onto the backs of their black, chrome-laden motorcycles and tear off in a cloud of dirt and exhaust fumes. I particularly remember the one we called Camaro Joe, Roxanne's boyfriend the summer I was twelve. When he first squealed into our driveway in a sputtering dirty-gold Camaro with a thumping stereo that shook the trees, we knew my sister had picked another winner. Joe's cowboy boots swung from his car onto the gravel of our driveway, and we watched as he launched his massive beer belly from the low seat. His waddle up to the house reminded me of a penguin. Joe was short and stocky with beady black eyes and a thin, fuzzy mustache. He wore his black hair slicked back with grease, and a Camel cigarette hung from his lower lip as if it had

been glued there. Like any good Neanderthal, he communi-
cated mostly in grunts. My father eventually laid down the
law and insisted that Roxanne stop seeing Joe, and, much to
Dad's satisfaction, she did. Of course, it wasn't long
before Joe was replaced by another Mitch--or was it Jake?

Susan Burkhart (student)

1. Underline the topic sentence of the paragraph.

2. In a few words, summarize the dominant impression the writer wants
   to give of her subject, Camaro Joe.

   _____

   _____

3. What are some of the details the writer uses to create this dominant
   impression? The first detail has been listed for you.

   drives a dirty Camaro _____

   _____

   _____

   _____

   _____

   _____

◆ PRACTICE 5-2

Each of the four topic sentences below states a possible dominant impression for a paragraph. After each topic sentence, list three details that could
help convey this dominant impression. For example, to support the idea
that sitting in front of a fireplace is a good way to spend a winter's night,
you could describe the crackling of the fire, the pine scent of the smoke,
and the changing colors of the flames.

1. After the rainstorm, everything in the city seemed clean and new.

   _____

   _____

   _____

2. The bus was at least twenty years old and looked shabby.

   _____

   _____

   _____

3. I could see the toll that living on the streets had taken on him.

_____

_____

_____

4. One of the most interesting stores I've seen sells used (or, as they say, "recycled") clothing.

_____

_____

_____

◆ PRACTICE 5-3

Choose one of the topics below (or one of your own choice) as the subject of a descriptive paragraph. On a separate sheet of paper, use one or more of the invention strategies described in 1B to come up with specific details about the topic you have chosen. If you can, observe your subject directly and write down your observations.

A favorite place from childhood
A place you felt trapped in
A quiet spot on campus
An unusual-looking person
A place you find depressing
A family member or friend
A neighborhood character
A work of art
A treasured possession

Your workplace
A favorite article of clothing
An interesting object found in nature
A pet
A place you find frightening
Your car or truck
A scenic spot

◆ PRACTICE 5-4

List the details you came up with in Practice 5-3 that can best help you develop a descriptive paragraph on the topic you have chosen.

_____

_____

_____

_____

_____

_____

_____

◆ PRACTICE 5-5

Reread your list of details from Practice 5-4. Then, draft a topic sentence that summarizes the dominant impression you want to convey in your paragraph.

_____

_____

◆ PRACTICE 5-6

Arrange the details you listed in Practice 5-4 in a logical spatial order. You might arrange them in the order in which you are looking at them—for example, from left to right, near to far, or top to bottom.

1. _____

2. _____

3. _____

4. _____

5. _____

6. _____

7. _____

◆ PRACTICE 5-7

On a separate sheet of paper, write your descriptive paragraph. Then, using the Self-Assessment Checklist on page 57, revise your paragraph for unity, development, and coherence.

◆ PRACTICE 5-8

On a separate sheet of paper, write a final, edited draft of your descriptive paragraph.

■ WRITING FIRST: Revising and Editing

Look back at your response to the Writing First exercise on page 51, and evaluate it for unity, development, and coherence. Then, prepare a final, edited draft of your paragraph.

☑ SELF-ASSESSMENT CHECKLIST:
Writing a Descriptive Paragraph

Unity

☐ Does your topic sentence indicate the dominant impression you want to create?

☐ Do all the details support your topic sentence?

☐ Are all the details consistent with the dominant impression you want to convey?

Development

☐ Do you need to include more objective description to make your subject clear?

☐ Do you need to add more subjective description to express your feelings about your subject?

☐ Should you use one of the invention strategies discussed in 1B to come up with more ideas?

Coherence

☐ Are your details arranged in a logical order?

☐ Do you need to add transitional words or phrases?

6

Process

PREVIEW

In this chapter, you will learn how to write a process paragraph.

■ WRITING FIRST

Write a paragraph in which you describe a process that is familiar to you but may not be familiar to others—for example, how to plan a wedding, how to change the washer in a faucet, or how to set up a budget. Include clear transitions to help your readers understand how each step of your process relates to the next.

A Understanding Process

A **process** is a series of steps (usually in chronological order) that leads to a particular result. In a **process paragraph**, you explain how something works or tell how to do something. The topic sentence of your paragraph should identify the process (for example, "Frying chicken is easy" or "The typical job interview has three distinct phases"). The rest of the paragraph should discuss the steps in the process, one by one, in the order in which they occur.

In general, there are two kinds of process paragraphs: *process explanations* and *instructions*. In a **process explanation**, the writer's purpose is simply to help readers understand a process, not perform it. The following paragraph is a process explanation.

> **▼ Student Voices**
> *At my job, I often have to write paragraphs telling people how to do something.*
> *Lis Bare*

Topic sentence

Stage 1

Stage 2

Once asleep, we go through four distinct stages. The first stage of sleep is marked by an easing of muscle tension and a change in brain-wave activity. This transitional stage is especially light and typically lasts about twenty minutes, during which time you may be easily awakened. In stage two, brain waves slow and slumber grows deeper. Even with the eyes taped open, we are quite literally blind during this phase and would be incapable of seeing anything—even a hand passing over the face—since the eye-brain connection has been shut off. More than half of the time devoted solely to sleep is spent in stage two, and no dreaming occurs. Stages three and four are marked by even slower brain waves, but the deepest sleep occurs in stage four. Mysteriously, the highest levels of the body's growth hormone are released during this sleep stage. After cycling back for a few minutes of stage-two sleep, dreaming begins. The first dream phase, lasting only a few minutes, is the shortest of the night. When dreaming is over, the sleeper retraces all the stages back to lighter sleep and then repeats the deep-sleep stages back to dreaming.

Stages 3 and 4

Mark McCuchen, *The Compass in Your Nose and*
Other Astonishing Facts about Humans

The topic sentence identifies the process, and the rest of the paragraph presents the steps in strict chronological order. Throughout the paragraph, transitional words and phrases—*the first stage*, *in stage two*, and *stages three and four*—clearly identify individual steps in the process.

Other process paragraphs present **instructions**. Here, the writer's purpose is to give readers the information they need to perform a task or activity. The following paragraph gives instructions for checking a pair of in-line skates before beginning to skate.

Now that you are the proud owner of in-lines, you must be sure your skates are fine-tuned and road-worthy, so before you roll, be sure to do the following. First, sit down and place your blades between your legs, wheels facing up. Make certain they are clean so you won't get dirty. Next, wiggle each wheel, making certain there is no lateral play (side-to-side). If bolts are loose, tighten them with the Allen, socket, or crescent wrench supplied by the manufacturer. Then, spin each wheel so they all spin smoothly and evenly. Feel and listen for any grinding. If this occurs, the bearings may need to be cleaned or replaced. After checking the wheels, look at your brake. Some stoppers screw on, while others have bolts on the side or through the center. Jiggle the stopper, and if it's loose, tighten it. If it is worn, replace it. It is best to replace your brake before you start to wear it down to the metal, or you might strip the threads of the bolt and have to saw off the brake, a time-consuming and difficult process. Finally, check your laces or buckles for any wear and tear. Properly serviced, a pair of skates will have a long life span and allow you to roll more easily and smoothly.

Topic sentence

Step 1

Step 2

Step 3

Step 4

Step 5

Joel Rappelfeld, *The Complete Blader*

Because the writer of this process paragraph expects readers to follow his instructions, he addresses them directly, using commands to tell them what to do (for instance, "Sit down and place your blades between your legs"). He uses clear transitional words and expressions—*next*, *then*, *after checking the wheels*—to help readers know the exact sequence in which the steps are to be performed. He even includes cautions and reminders ("Make certain they are clean so you won't get dirty") and explains the purpose for some steps, such as replacing a worn brake.

● **Writing Tip**
Many everyday writing tasks call for outlining a process. At home, you might write a set of instructions telling your family members what to do in case of a fire.

FOCUS **Process**

Like narrative paragraphs, process paragraphs present a sequence of events. Unlike narrative paragraphs, however, process paragraphs describe a sequence that occurs—or should occur—in exactly the same way every time.

B **Writing a Process Paragraph**

◆ PRACTICE 6-1

Read this process paragraph; then, follow the instructions on page 61.

An Order of Fries

I had always enjoyed the french fries at McDonald's and other fast-food restaurants, but I never realized just how much work goes into making them until I worked at a potato processing plant in Hermiston, Oregon. The process begins with freshly dug potatoes being shoveled from trucks onto conveyor belts leading into the plant. During this stage, workers must sort out any rocks that may have been dug up with the potatoes because these could severely damage the automated peelers. After the potatoes have gone through the peelers, they travel on a conveyor belt through the "trim line." Here, workers cut out any bad spots, being careful not to waste potatoes by trimming too much. Next, the potatoes are sliced in automated cutters and then fried for about a minute. After this, they continue along a conveyor belt to the "wet line." Here, workers again look for bad spots, discarding any rotten pieces. At this point, the potatoes go to a second set of fryers for three minutes before being moved to subzero freezers for ten minutes. Then it's on to the "frozen line" for a final inspection. The inspected fries are weighed by machines and then sealed into five-pound plastic packages, which are weighed again by workers who also check that the packages are properly sealed. The bags are then packed into boxes and made ready for shipment to various McDonald's and other restaurants across the western United States. This process goes on continuously, twenty-four hours a day, to bring us consumers the tasty french fries we all enjoy so much.

Cheri Rodriguez (student)

1. Underline the topic sentence of the paragraph.

2. Is this a process explanation or instructions?_____

   How do you know?_____

3. List the steps in the process. The first step has been listed for you.

   *The potatoes are unloaded, and the rocks are sorted out.*____

   _____

   _____

   _____

   _____

   _____

   _____

◆ PRACTICE 6-2

Following are four possible topic sentences for process paragraphs. After each topic sentence, list three or four steps that explain the process the sentence identifies. For example, if you were explaining the process of getting a job, you could list preparing a résumé, looking at the classified ads, writing a job application letter, and going on an interview. Make sure each step follows logically from the one that precedes it.

1. There are four major steps in the process of making the perfect sandwich.

   a. _____

   b. _____

   c. _____

   d. _____

2. Recycling is easy if you follow these steps.

   a. _____

   b. _____

   c. _____

   d. _____

3. Before you begin any fitness program, you should take the time to set up a workout routine.

   a. _____

   b. _____

c. _____

d. _____

4. Discouraging unwanted attention from a coworker is a delicate process.

a. _____

b. _____

c. _____

d. _____

◆ **PRACTICE 6-3**

Choose one of the topics below (or one of your own choice) as the subject of a process paragraph. On a separate sheet of paper, use one or more of the invention strategies described in 1B to come up with as many steps as you can for the topic you have chosen.

How to do a popular dance	A specific car or household repair
A daily workplace task	The stages of a puppy's development
Strategies for winning a particular game	A baby's first six weeks
How to create a popular hairstyle	Running a computer program
Planning an event	A process involved in a hobby
Your typical work or school day	The stages of a relationship
A scientific process	A simple medical procedure
A process you have observed in nature	Painting a room

◆ **PRACTICE 6-4**

List the steps you wrote in Practice 6-3 that can best help you develop a process paragraph on the topic you have chosen. (You may come up with more steps than you can actually use. Later, you will select the ones that are the most important.)

_____   _____

_____   _____

_____   _____

_____   _____

_____   _____

◆ PRACTICE 6-5

Reread your list of steps from Practice 6-4. Then, draft a topic sentence that identifies the process you will discuss and communicates the point you will make about it.

_____

_____

_____

◆ PRACTICE 6-6

Choose the most important steps you listed in Practice 6-4. Then, write them down in chronological (time) order, moving from the first step to the last.

1. _____   4. _____

2. _____   5. _____

3. _____   6. _____

◆ PRACTICE 6-7

On a separate sheet of paper, write your process paragraph. Then, using the Self-Assessment Checklist on page 64, revise your paragraph for unity, development, and coherence.

◆ PRACTICE 6-8

On a separate sheet of paper, write a final, edited draft of your process paragraph.

■ WRITING FIRST: Revising and Editing

Look back at your response to the Writing First exercise on page 58, and evaluate it for unity, development, and coherence. Then, prepare a final, edited draft of your paragraph.

☑ SELF-ASSESSMENT CHECKLIST:
Writing a Process Paragraph

Unity

- [ ] Does your topic sentence identify the process you will discuss and the main point you will make about it?

- [ ] Is your topic sentence specifically worded?

- [ ] Have you eliminated information that doesn't relate directly to the process or that might confuse readers?

Development

- [ ] Have you included all the steps that readers need to know in order to understand the process?

- [ ] Do you need to explain any steps in greater detail?

- [ ] Should you use one of the invention strategies discussed in 1B to help you come up with more ideas?

Coherence

- [ ] Do you need to rearrange any steps?

- [ ] Do you need to add transitional words or phrases?

Cause and Effect

■ WRITING FIRST

Write a paragraph in which you describe the effect of a particular electronic gadget on your life or the life of your family—for example, the effect of a coffeemaker, a pager, a cell phone, or a VCR. Be sure that your topic sentence identifies the piece of equipment and that the rest of the paragraph discusses its impact.

A   Understanding Cause and Effect

A **cause** is what makes a particular thing happen. An **effect** is what results from a particular situation, activity, or behavior. You write **cause-and-effect paragraphs** when your purpose is to help readers understand why something happened or is happening, or when you want to show readers how one thing affects something else. You can also use cause-and-effect writing to predict future events.

The main difficulty you may have when planning a cause-and-effect paragraph is making sure that a **causal relationship** exists—that one event caused another event and did not just precede it in time. Another problem is considering all possible causes and effects, not just the most obvious or most important ones. As you write, assess the importance of the causes or effects you discuss; don't make a particular cause or effect seem more significant than it actually is, just to strengthen your case.

The following paragraph identifies causes.

> ▼ **Student Voices**
> *The most interesting paragraph I ever wrote was about how something my high school chemistry teacher said caused me to go to college.*
> *Janice Williams*

      Newspapers are folding. Paper costs are high, but loss of literate readers is much higher. Forty-five percent of adult citizens do not read newspapers. Only 10 percent abstain by choice. The rest have been excluded by their inability to read. Even the most distinguished daily papers are now written at an estimated tenth-grade level. Magazines

Topic sentence: effect

First (minor) cause: paper costs

Second (major) cause: illiteracy

such as the *Nation, New Republic, Time, Newsweek,* and the *National Review* are written at a minimum of twelfth-grade level. Circulation battles represent a competition for the largest piece of a diminished pie. Enlargement of that pie does not yet seem to have occurred to those who enter these increasingly unhappy competitions. The only successful major paper to be launched in the last decade, *USA Today,* relies on a simplistic lexicon, large headlines, color photographs, and fanciful weather maps that seek to duplicate the instant entertainment on TV.

Jonathan Kozol, *Illiterate America*

The topic sentence identifies the effect the paragraph will discuss. After mentioning one relatively minor cause of the problem (the cost of paper), the paragraph goes on to analyze the primary cause of the problem—illiteracy.

The next paragraph discusses effects.

● **Writing Tip**
Many everyday writing tasks call for discussing causes and effects. At work, you might write a memo describing the effects a new procedure might have on your job performance.

Topic sentence: cause

Professional athletes are sometimes severely disadvantaged by trainers whose job it is to keep them in action. The more famous the athlete, the greater the risk that he or she may be subjected to extreme medical measures when injury strikes. The star baseball player whose arm is sore because of a torn muscle or tissue damage may need sustained rest more than anything else. But his team is battling for a place in the World Series; so the trainer or team doctor, called upon to work his magic, reaches for a strong dose of butazolidine or other powerful pain suppressants. Presto, the pain disappears! The pitcher takes his place on the mound and does superbly. That could be the last game, however, in which he is able to throw a ball with full strength. The drugs didn't repair torn muscle or cause the damaged tissue to heal. What they did was to mask the pain, enabling the pitcher to throw hard, further damaging the torn muscle. Little wonder that so many star athletes are cut down in their prime, more the victims of overzealous treatment of their injuries than of the injuries themselves.

First effect: pain disappears

Second effect: muscle damaged further

Norman Cousins,
"Pain Is Not the Ultimate Enemy"

The topic sentence identifies the cause of the problem the paragraph will consider. The paragraph then goes on to discuss two effects—the second more important than the first—of the trainer's actions.

For more on commonly confused words, see 34E.

FOCUS	Cause and Effect

Be careful not to confuse the words *affect* and *effect*. *Affect* is a verb meaning "to influence." *Effect* can be a verb meaning "to bring about" or a noun meaning "result."

B Writing a Cause-and-Effect Paragraph

◆ PRACTICE 7-1

Read this cause-and-effect paragraph; then, follow the instructions below.

```
                    The Ultimate High

       Some people associate running only with panting,
sweating, and plain and simple torture, but for me and
other experienced runners the effect of running is pure and
utter pleasure. When I run, it may look as though I'm in
agony, with my gaping mouth, soaked brow, and constantly
contracting leg muscles. In fact, however, my daily half-
hour run represents a time of complete physical and mental
relaxation. As I begin my run, my lungs escape the stuffy
atmosphere of my job and school and are immediately
refreshed by the clean, open air. The daily tensions built
up in my body ease as my muscles stretch and pump, releas-
ing all feelings of anger or frustration. I mentally dive
into my run and feel as though I am lifting my feet from
the pavement and ascending into the air. My mind wanders
toward the outer limits of my imagination, and I seem to
float, daydreaming about wherever my thoughts take me. I
take pride in the salty perspiration that trickles down my
face and body, signifying my effort and ambition. After I
complete my run and cool down with long, deep breaths, my
body tingles slightly and feels energized, as if I had just
come off a roller coaster. I am more alert, my concentra-
tion is sharper, and my state of mind is relaxed and
peaceful. I feel alive. Beginning runners who initially
experience soreness and fatigue rather than this kind of
"high" should be patient. As the body builds up strength
and tolerance, they will no longer equate running with pain
but rather with relief from tension and with greater emo-
tional well-being.

                              Scott Weckerly (student)
```

1. Underline the topic sentence of the paragraph.

2. Does this paragraph deal mainly with the causes or the effects of run-

   ning? _____ How do you know?_____

   _____

3. List some of the effects the writer describes. The first effect has been
   listed for you.

His lungs are refreshed with clean air.

_____

_____

_____

_____

_____

◆ **PRACTICE 7-2**

Following are four possible topic sentences for cause-and-effect paragraphs. After each topic sentence, list the effects that could result from the cause identified in the topic sentence. For example, if you were writing a paragraph about the effects of excessive drinking on campus, you could list low grades, health problems, and property damage.

1. Studying at the last minute can cause a number of problems.

_____

_____

_____

2. Learning a second language has many advantages.

_____

_____

_____

3. Giving up smoking can have some important benefits.

_____

_____

_____

4. Not knowing how to read can have negative effects on a person's daily life.

_____

_____

_____

◆ **PRACTICE 7-3**

List three causes that could support each of the following topic sentences.

1. The causes of teenage smoking are easy to identify.

_____

_____

_____

2. Chronic unemployment can have many causes.

_____

_____

_____

3. Why is college tuition so high?

_____

_____

_____

4. Athletes' exorbitant salaries can be explained by the principle of supply and demand.

_____

_____

_____

5. People maintain high credit-card bills for a variety of reasons.

_____

_____

_____

◆ PRACTICE 7-4

Choose one of the topics below (or one of your own choice) as the subject of a paragraph that examines causes or effects. Then, on a separate sheet of paper, use one or more of the invention strategies described in 1B to think of as many causes or effects as you can for the topic you have chosen.

Why a current television show or movie is popular
Some causes (or effects) of stress
Why so many Americans do not vote
The effects of treating others with respect
Why teenagers (or adults) drink
Some reasons relationships break up
The effects of a particular medication or medical treatment
How becoming a vegetarian might change your life
The beneficial effects of running (or some other kind of physical exercise)
Why a particular sport is so popular
How an important person in your life influenced you

Why some people find writing so difficult

Effects of a new baby on a household

The major reasons that high school or college students drop out of
school

How managers can get the best (or the worst) from their employees

*For more on creating a cluster
diagram, see 1B.*

◆ PRACTICE 7-5

Review your notes from Practice 7-4, and create a cluster diagram. Write
the topic you have chosen in the center of the page, and draw arrows
branching out to various specific causes or effects.

◆ PRACTICE 7-6

Choose two to four causes or effects from the cluster diagram you made in
Practice 7-5, and list them here.

_____

_____

_____

_____

◆ PRACTICE 7-7

Reread your list of causes or effects from Practice 7-6. Then, draft a topic
sentence that introduces your topic and communicates the point you will
make about it.

_____

_____

◆ PRACTICE 7-8

List the causes or effects you will discuss in your paragraph, arranging
them in an effective order—for example, from least to most important.

1. _____

2. _____

3. _____

4. _____

5. _____

◆ PRACTICE 7-9

On a separate sheet of paper, write your cause-and-effect paragraph. Then,
using the Self-Assessment Checklist on page 71, revise your paragraph for
unity, development, and coherence.

◆ **PRACTICE 7-10**

On a separate sheet of paper, write a final, edited draft of your cause-and-effect paragraph.

■ WRITING FIRST: Revising and Editing

Look back at your response to the Writing First exercise on page 65, and evaluate it for unity, development, and coherence. Then, prepare a final, edited draft of your paragraph.

☑ SELF-ASSESSMENT CHECKLIST:
Writing a Cause-and-Effect Paragraph

Unity

  Does your topic sentence clearly identify the causes or effects on which your paragraph will focus?

  Does all your information relate directly to the causes or effects you are discussing?

  Should you revise your topic sentence to reflect additional ideas?

Development

  Do you need to add other important causes or effects?

  Does your audience need more information about any causes or effects you have included?

  Should you use one of the invention strategies discussed in 1B to come up with more ideas?

Coherence

  Are your causes and effects arranged in a logical order?

  Do you need to add transitional words or phrases?

8

Comparison and Contrast

■ **WRITING FIRST**

Write a paragraph in which you compare or contrast two places that you know well. Be sure your topic sentence indicates whether you are focusing on similarities or differences.

A   **Understanding Comparison and Contrast**

A **comparison** tells how two things are similar. A **contrast** tells how they are different. A **comparison-and-contrast paragraph** can do either or both.

In general, you can organize information in a comparison-and-contrast paragraph in two ways. In a **subject-by-subject** arrangement, you first discuss all your points about one subject and then discuss all your points about the other subject. A subject-by-subject arrangement can have the following structure.

Subject-by-subject arrangement

    Subject A _____

        Point 1 _____

        Point 2 _____

        Point 3 _____

        Point 4 _____

    Subject B _____

        Point 1 _____

        Point 2 _____

        Point 3 _____

        Point 4 _____

The following paragraph is an example of a subject-by-subject comparison.

Topic sentence

Subject 1 (women's conversations)

<u>First, it is important to note that men and women regard conversation quite differently.</u> For women it is a passion, a sport, an activity even more important to life than eating because it doesn't involve weight gain. The first sign of closeness among women is when they find themselves engaging in endless, secretless rounds of conversation with one another. And as soon as a woman begins to relax and feel comfortable in a relationship with a man, she tries to have that type of conversation with him as well. However, the first sign that a man is feeling close to a woman is when he admits that he'd rather she please quiet down so he can hear the TV. A man who feels truly intimate with a woman often reserves for her and her alone the precious gift of one-word answers. Everyone knows that the surest way to spot a successful long-term relationship is to look around a restaurant for the table where no one is talking. Ah . . . now *that's* real love.

Subject 2 (men's conversations)

Merrill Markoe, *Men, Women, and Conversation*

This paragraph begins with a topic sentence that states the main idea of the paragraph and indicates that the paragraph will focus on differences between men and women. The writer then discusses each subject separately. The transition *however* signals the writer's shift from one subject to the other.

The other way to organize information in a comparison-and-contrast paragraph is a **point-by-point** arrangement, in which you discuss each point for *both* subjects before going on to the next point. A point-by-point arrangement can have the following structure.

> **Writing Tip**
> Many everyday writing tasks call for comparison and contrast. At work, you might write a paragraph comparing the qualifications of two people applying for the same job.

> **Writing Tip**
> Comparison-and-contrast paragraphs often rely on transitions that identify similarities and differences. (See 2C.)

Point-by-point arrangement

Point 1 _____

    Subject A _____

    Subject B _____

Point 2 _____

    Subject A _____

    Subject B _____

Point 3 _____

    Subject A _____

    Subject B _____

Point 4 _____

    Subject A _____

    Subject B _____

The following paragraph is an example of a point-by-point comparison.

Topic sentence

Point 1

<u>After a short time in England, I began to understand why the English see Americans as loud and ill-mannered.</u> Americans are open and confident; the English are reserved and modest. Americans frequently spend money blatantly; the English spend money quietly. For example, when Americans tip a doorman at a hotel, they hand him the money in

Point 2

Point 3

Point 4

full view. When the English perform the same act, they fold the bill and slip it into the person's hand. Americans seem to swagger when they walk; the English walk deliberately—to get from one place to another. Finally, and perhaps most irritating to the English, Americans frequently call people they have just met by their first names. Most English people will call someone by his or her first name only after they have been asked to.

Beth Haurin (student)

Like a subject-by-subject comparison, this point-by-point comparison begins with a topic sentence that states the main idea of the paragraph and indicates that the paragraph will concentrate on differences between the English and Americans. The rest of the paragraph applies the same four points of contrast, one at a time—first to Americans and then to the English. In addition, it gives an example of one of the points—spending money. Shifts from one subject to another are signaled by the words *Americans* and *the English*.

FOCUS **Comparison**

Before you can compare and contrast two things, there has to be a **basis of comparison**—that is, the things have to share some significant characteristic. For example, both people and chimpanzees are mammals, and both live in social groups. Without at least one common element, there would be no basis for comparison.

B **Writing a Comparison-and-Contrast Paragraph**

◆ **PRACTICE 8-1**

Read this comparison-and-contrast paragraph; then, follow the instructions below.

Comparing the British and
American Education Systems

The British system of education is common not only in England but in countries all over the world that were once British colonies. It differs from the American system in a number of ways. First, most American children have only one year of kindergarten, beginning at age five. Under the British system, children begin kindergarten at age four and then go on to another year of more advanced kindergarten

called "preparatory" or "prep," which is comparable to
American first grade. Starting in seventh grade, most American students study basic subjects separately, devoting a
semester to algebra, for example, and another semester to
geometry. However, under the British system, algebra, geometry, and trigonometry are taught together in a single
course that is then repeated at a higher level every term.
Also, in American high schools some classes, particularly
electives, may include sophomores, juniors, and seniors.
In schools run according to the British system, students
at different levels, or "forms," are not mixed in classes;
each form attends all its classes together. Finally, American students generally graduate after their twelfth year
of school, and senior year is just another year of course
work. British students, on the other hand, finish everything they need to learn in secondary school during the
first term of their eleventh year of school. During the
second term, they study for comprehensive final exams that
cover everything they have learned for the last three and a
half years. These exams, which include three separate tests
for every subject, are taken during the final term.

Lisa Van Hoboken (student)

1. Underline the topic sentence of the paragraph.

2. Does this paragraph deal mainly with similarities or differences?
_____ How do you know? _____

_____

3. Is this paragraph organized subject by subject or point by point?
_____ How do you know? _____

_____

4. List some of the contrasts the writer describes. The first contrast has been listed for you.

   American students start kindergarten at age five, while students in

   British schools start kindergarten at age four.

   _____

   _____

   _____

   _____

   _____

   _____

◆ **PRACTICE 8-2**

Following are four possible topic sentences. List three similarities or differences for the two subjects being considered in the topic sentence. For example, if you were writing a paragraph comparing health care provided by a local clinic to health care provided by a private physician, you could discuss cost, the length of waiting time, the quality of care, and the frequency of follow-up visits.

1. My mother (or father) and I are very much alike.

_____

_____

_____

2. Home-cooked meals are much better than fast food.

_____

_____

_____

3. My friends and I have similar views on

_____

_____

_____

4. Two of my college instructors have very different teaching styles.

_____

_____

_____

◆ **PRACTICE 8-3**

Choose one of the topics below (or one of your own choice) as the subject of a paragraph exploring similarities or differences. On a separate sheet of paper, use one or more of the invention strategies described in 1B to think of as many similarities and differences as you can for the topic you have chosen. (If you use clustering, create a separate cluster diagram for each subject.)

Two popular television or radio talk-show hosts
Two related styles of music, such as reggae and dance hall
A common perception of something versus its reality
How you act in two different situations (home and work, for example) or with two different sets of people (such as your family and your friends)
Two ads for similar products directed at different audiences

Two different bosses

Men's and women's attitudes toward dating, shopping, or conversation

Your goals when you were a child versus your goals today

Smokers versus nonsmokers

Two competing consumer goods, such as two car models, two computer systems, or two types of food

Two relatives who have very different personalities

Two different types of pets

Two generations' attitudes toward a particular issue or subject (for example, how people in their forties and people in their teens view religion or politics)

◆ PRACTICE 8-4

Review your notes from Practice 8-3 and decide whether to focus on similarities or differences. On the following lines, list the similarities or differences that can help you develop a comparison-and-contrast paragraph on the topic you have selected.

_____

_____

_____

_____

_____

◆ PRACTICE 8-5

Reread your list of similarities or differences from Practice 8-4. Then, draft a topic sentence that introduces your two subjects and suggests your purpose for comparing or contrasting them.

_____

_____

◆ PRACTICE 8-6

In the space below, outline a plan for your paragraph. If you plan to use a subject-by-subject arrangement, decide which subject you will discuss first and which you will discuss second. If you plan to use a point-by-point arrangement, decide on the order in which you will present your points—for example, from least important to most important.

Subject-by-subject arrangement

Subject A _____

Point 1 _____

Point 2 _____

Point 3 _____

Point 4 _____

Subject B _____
  Point 1 _____
  Point 2 _____
  Point 3 _____
  Point 4 _____

Point-by-point arrangement
  Point 1 _____
    Subject A _____
    Subject B _____
  Point 2 _____
    Subject A _____
    Subject B _____
  Point 3 _____
    Subject A _____
    Subject B _____
  Point 4 _____
    Subject A _____
    Subject B _____

◆ PRACTICE 8-7

On a separate sheet of paper, write your comparison-and-contrast paragraph. Then, using the Self-Assessment Checklist on page 79, revise your paragraph for unity, development, and coherence.

◆ PRACTICE 8-8

On a separate sheet of paper, write a final, edited draft of your comparison-and-contrast paragraph.

■ WRITING FIRST: Revising and Editing

Look back at your response to the Writing First exercise on page 72, and evaluate it for unity, development, and coherence. Then, prepare a final, edited draft of your paragraph.

☑ SELF-ASSESSMENT CHECKLIST:
Writing a Comparison-and-Contrast Paragraph

Unity

- Does your topic sentence indicate whether you are stressing similarities or differences?

- Does all your information relate directly to the similarities or differences between your two subjects?

- Do you need to revise your topic sentence?

Development

- Is there a basis of comparison between your two subjects?

- Do you need to include more similarities? More differences?

- Do you need to use one of the invention strategies discussed in 1B to help you come up with more ideas?

Coherence

- Have you used a subject-by-subject or a point-by-point arrangement?

- Would arranging points in a different order be more effective?

- If your paragraph is a subject-by-subject comparison, have you treated the points for the second subject in the same order as the points for the first subject?

- Do you need to add any transitional words or phrases?

9

Classification

PREVIEW

In this chapter, you will learn to write a classification paragraph.

■ **WRITING FIRST**

Write a paragraph in which you discuss the various kinds of members of a particular group. You might discuss types of sports fans (for example, baseball, football, and hockey fans) or the kinds of students in your former high school (for example, high achievers, average achievers, and those who just don't seem to care).

A Understanding Classification

Classification is the activity of sorting items (people, things, ideas) into categories. A given kind of information can be classified in more than one way. For instance, animals can be classified by their species as well as by their behavioral traits—aggressiveness, docility, friendliness, and so on. Cars can be classified by cost as well as by type—sedan, convertible, and so on. In a **classification paragraph**, you tell readers how a collection of items can be sorted into categories. Each of the groups into which you classify information must be *distinct:* an item cannot fit into more than one group. For example, you would not classify novels into mysteries, romance novels, and paperbacks because a mystery or romance novel could also be a paperback.

The topic sentence of a classification paragraph identifies the subject (the group of items being discussed) and the categories into which items will be sorted. The rest of the paragraph considers the categories in the order in which they are mentioned in the topic sentence. The following is an example of a classification paragraph.

I can classify my friends into three categories: those who know what they want out of life, those who don't have a clue, and those who are searching for goals. In the first category are those who know what they want; they are the most mature. They know exactly what they want to do for the rest of their lives. Although these friends will most likely be successful, they are the most boring. In the second category are those who don't have a clue; they are the most immature. They seem to live for the minute and don't think much about the future. If there is a party the night before a big test, they will go to the party and then try to study when they get back. Although these friends can be a bad influence, they are the most fun. In the third category are those who are searching for goals; they are somewhere between the other two when it comes to maturity. They do not know exactly what they want to do with their lives, but they realize that they should be trying to find a goal. Although these friends can sometimes be unpredictable, they are by far the most interesting.

Daniel Corey (student)

Topic sentence
Category 1

Category 2

Category 3

The topic sentence clearly identifies the paragraph's subject—friends—and the three categories into which individual friends will be sorted. The rest of the paragraph discusses each category, one at a time. The shift from one category to another is signaled by the transitional phrases *the first category*, *the second category*, and *the third category*.

● **Writing Tip**
Classification paragraphs often use transitional words and phrases that emphasize categories (for example, *the first type, the second type,* and *the last type*).

FOCUS Classification

Before you can classify information, you must choose a **basis for classification**—the quality that your selected items have in common. For example, instructors can be classified according to their teaching ability, and computers can be classified according to their speed at processing information.

B Writing a Classification Paragraph

◆ **PRACTICE 9-1**

Read this classification paragraph; then follow the instructions below.

● **Writing Tip**
Many everyday writing tasks call for classification. For your local library's book sale, you might write a flyer classifying books according to subject and grade level.

Baldness

There are three basic categories of balding men. Most common are men who lose hair beginning at the crowns of their heads. Some men's hair remains very thin in this area without falling out completely, so just a bit of the scalp shows through. Other men, however, do lose the hair completely to reveal a circle of bare scalp, often so shiny that it appears polished. The circle usually increases in circumference as time goes by. Second most common are men with receding hairlines. In most such cases, the hairline recedes only from the sides of the forehead, often leaving enough hair at the front to disguise the loss at the sides. Depending on the shape of his head, his facial features, and the texture of his hair, a man's appearance can actually be improved by a slightly receding hairline. Least common are the unlucky men who suffer from both these patterns of baldness at once. The balding crown expands as the hairline recedes, often leaving just a tuft of hair at the front and a fringe around the sides and back. In an attempt to hide their condition, some of these men grow the hair on one side of their heads and carefully plaster it over the scalp to resemble normal hair parted on the side. Others choose to celebrate their condition by shaving their heads, which is generally necessary if a man is to be completely bald; oddly enough, it is very uncommon for a man to lose the hair at the sides and around the back of his head.

Peter Likus (student)

1. Underline the topic sentence of the paragraph.

2. What is the subject of the paragraph? _____
   What three categories of the subject does the writer describe?

   _____

   _____

   _____

3. Circle the phrases the writer uses to introduce each of the categories.

◆ PRACTICE 9-2

Classify the following groups of items into categories.

1. All the items on your desk

   _____   _____

   _____   _____

   _____   _____

   _____   _____

2. Television sitcoms

_____   _____

_____   _____

_____   _____

3. Your friends

_____   _____

_____   _____

_____   _____

4. The various parts of a piece of equipment you use for a course or on the job

_____   _____

_____   _____

_____   _____

◆ PRACTICE 9-3

Choose one of the topics below (or one of your own choice) as the subject of a classification paragraph. On a separate sheet of paper, use one or more of the invention strategies described in 1B to classify the members of the group you have chosen into as many categories as possible.

Your friends	Radio stations
Drivers	Popular music
Commuters on public trans- portation	Diets or fitness routines
	Sports fans
Television game shows	Talk shows
Employees or bosses	Teachers
Parents or children	Dates
Shoppers, Laundromat users, or fast-food customers	Popular magazines

◆ PRACTICE 9-4

Review the information you came up with in Practice 9-3. On the following lines, list three or four categories you can develop in your paragraph.

Category 1: _____

Category 2: _____

Category 3: _____

Category 4: _____

◆ PRACTICE 9-5

Reread the list you made in Practice 9-4. Then, draft a topic sentence that introduces your subject and the categories you will discuss.

_____

_____

_____

◆ PRACTICE 9-6

List the points for your classification paragraph below in the order in which you will discuss them.

1. _____   5. _____

2. _____   6. _____

3. _____   7. _____

4. _____   8. _____

◆ PRACTICE 9-7

On a separate sheet of paper, write your classification paragraph. Then, using the Self-Assessment Checklist on page 85, revise your paragraph for unity, development, and coherence.

◆ PRACTICE 9-8

On a separate sheet of paper, write a final, edited draft of your classification paragraph.

■ WRITING FIRST: Revising and Editing

Look back at your response to the Writing First exercise on page 80, and evaluate it for unity, development, and coherence. Then, prepare a final, edited draft of your paragraph.

☑ SELF-ASSESSMENT CHECKLIST:
Writing a Classification Paragraph

Unity

- [ ] Does all your information support your topic sentence or relate to your subject and its categories?

- [ ] Do you need to revise your topic sentence to accommodate additional information?

Development

- [ ] Do you have a basis for classification?

- [ ] Do you need to include additional categories?

- [ ] Do you need to include more examples or more specific information for any category?

- [ ] Do you need to use one of the invention strategies discussed in 1B to help you come up with more ideas?

Coherence

- [ ] Do you need to rearrange categories (or details within categories)?

- [ ] Do you need to add transitional words or phrases?

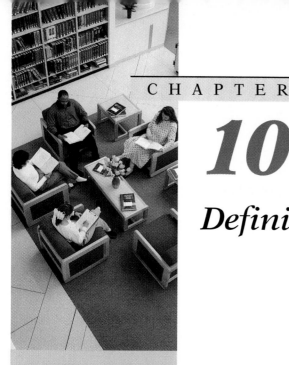

10

Definition

PREVIEW

In this chapter, you will learn to write a definition paragraph.

■ WRITING FIRST

Write a paragraph in which you define a positive personal trait—for example, *loyalty* or *bravery*. Include an example or two to develop your definition.

A Understanding Definition

A **definition** explains what a term means. When you want your readers to know exactly how you are using a certain term or an unfamiliar concept, you use definition.

When most people think of definitions, they think of the one- or two-sentence **formal definitions** they see in a dictionary. These definitions have a three-part structure that includes the term to be defined, the general class to which the term belongs, and the things that make the term different from all other terms in that class.

Term	Class	Differentiation
A pineapple	is a tropical fruit	that has large swordlike leaves and yellow edible fruit.
Basketball	is a game	played between two teams in which the object is to put a ball through an elevated basket on the opponent's side of a rectangular court.

A single-sentence formal definition may not be enough to define an abstract concept (*envy* or *democracy*, for example), a technical term, or a complex subject. In such cases, you may need to expand this definition by writing a **definition paragraph**. A definition paragraph usually includes the three components of a formal definition, but it does not follow a particular pattern of development. It may define a term or concept by using examples, by outlining a process, or by using any of the other patterns discussed in this text. A definition paragraph may even define a term by using **negation**, telling what the term is not—for example, that a bicycle is *not* a motorized vehicle.

In a definition paragraph, the topic sentence identifies the term to be defined (and may briefly define it as well). The rest of the paragraph develops the definition by means of one or more of the patterns of development. The following paragraph defines what it means to be a traveler.

For more on patterns of paragraph development, see page 39.

How do you know if you are a traveler? What are the tell-tale signs? As with most compulsions, such as being a gambler, a kleptomaniac, or a writer, the obvious proof is that you can't stop. If you are hooked, you are hooked. One sure sign of travelers is their relationship to maps. I cannot say how much of my life I have spent looking at maps, but there is no map I won't stare at and study. I love to measure each detail with my thumb, to see how far I have come, how far I've yet to go. I love maps the way stamp collectors love stamps—not for their usefulness but rather for the sheer beauty of the object itself. I love to look at a map, even if it is a map of Mars, and figure out where I am going and how I am going to get there, what route I will take. I imagine what adventures might await me even though I know the journey is never what we plan for; it's what happens between the lines.

Mary Morris, *Nothing to Declare*

Topic sentence

Series of examples

● Writing Tip
Many everyday writing tasks call for definition. For a study group at your place of worship, you might write short definitions of terms such as *morality, goodness,* and *repentance.*

The topic sentence, in the form of a question, presents the term that the paragraph will define. The rest of the paragraph defines the term and uses several short examples to establish that the writer is indeed a traveler.

The following paragraph defines a piece of equipment from the field of gymnastics—the pommel horse.

The pommel horse is of ancient origin. The Romans used it for the very practical purpose of training soldiers to mount horses. Some suggest it was used even earlier, by the bull dancers of Minoan Crete. Jumping over the bulls by doing springs off the animals' horns, these dancers surely must have practiced on something a little tamer than a live bull. Today, the pommel horse events are less exciting. The gymnast performs intricate leg-swinging movements while supporting his weight on his hands, which are either grasping the pommels or lying flat on the leather of the horse. As he swings his legs so that one follows, or "shadows," the other, the gymnast demonstrates strength, balance, and timing. Exercises such as single or double leg circles and scissors must be done continuously and in both directions. The pommel horse is difficult to master and not a favorite among gymnasts; they call it "the beast."

Ford Hovis, *The Sports Encyclopedia*

Topic sentence

History and background: comparison and contrast

Explanation of current function: process

Here, the writer defines a specialized object in terms of its background and its current function, using comparison and contrast and process.

> ### FOCUS Definition
>
> In general, avoid including a dictionary or encyclopedia definition in your definition paragraph. After all, readers can look up a term themselves. Your definition paragraph should show how you define a term—not how a dictionary does.

B Writing a Definition Paragraph

◆ PRACTICE 10-1

Read this definition paragraph; then, follow the instructions on page 89.

The Agony Called Writer's Block

Have you ever sat staring at a blank notebook page or piece of typing paper or computer screen, searching your brain for words and ideas, fidgeting with frustration, and longing to be anywhere else? If so, you probably want to know more about writer's block. Writer's block is a condition that afflicts ten out of ten writers at least sometime during their lives. It is, simply stated, the inability to start a piece of writing. For novelists and other creative writers, writer's block can be a disaster. Remember Jack Nicholson as a novelist in Stephen King's The Shining typing over and over again "All work and no play makes Jack a dull boy"--just before he goes after his family with a butcher knife? For nonprofessionals, writer's block almost always involves a writing assignment of some kind, such as a paper for school or a report for work. After all, people rarely feel blocked when they are writing simply for pleasure. Sometimes writer's block is caused by poor preparation. The writer has not allowed enough time to think and make notes that will pave the way for the actual writing of a draft. However, even prepared writers with many ideas already on paper can experience the freeze of writer's block. It's comparable to being tongue-tied, only this kind of writer's block is more like being brain-tied. All the ideas keep bouncing around but won't settle into any order, and the writer can't think of what to say first. When the agony of writer's block strikes, often the only cure is to give up and find another time to start.

Thaddeus Eddy (student)

1. Underline the topic sentence of the paragraph.

2. What is the subject of this definition?_____

3. What is the writer's one-sentence definition of the subject?

_____

4. List some of the specific information the writer uses to define his subject. The first piece of information has been listed for you.

It is a disaster for creative writers like the Jack Nicholson character in

The Shining.

_____

_____

_____

5. What patterns of development does the writer use in his definition? List them here.

_____

_____

_____

◆ PRACTICE 10-2

Following are four possible topic sentences for definition paragraphs. Each topic sentence includes an underlined word. In the space provided, write two possible patterns of development that you could use to expand a definition of the underlined word. For example, you could define the word *feminist* by giving examples or by telling a story.

1. During the football game, the quarterback showed a great deal of courage.

   Possible strategy: _____

   Possible strategy: _____

2. Loyalty is one of the chief characteristics of golden retrievers.

   Possible strategy: _____

   Possible strategy: _____

3. Thirty years after President Johnson's Great Society initiative, we have yet to eliminate poverty in the United States.

   Possible strategy: _____

   Possible strategy: _____

4. The problem with movies today is that they are just too <u>violent</u>.

Possible strategy: _____

Possible strategy: _____

◆ PRACTICE 10-3

Choose one of the topics below (or one of your own choice) as the subject of a definition paragraph. On a separate sheet of paper, freewrite or brainstorm about the topic you have chosen. Name it, describe it, give examples of it, tell how it works, explain its purpose, consider its history or future, compare it to other similar things; in short, do whatever works best for defining your specific subject.

> A negative quality, such as envy or dishonesty
> An ideal, such as the ideal friend or the ideal politician
> A type of person, such as a worrier or a show-off
> A social concept, such as equality, opportunity, or discrimination
> A strategic play in a particular sport or game
> A hobby you pursue or an activity associated with that hobby
> A technical term or a specific piece of equipment you use in your job
> An object (such as an article of clothing) that is important to your
>   culture or religion
> A basic concept in a course you are taking
> A particular style of music or dancing
> A controversial subject whose definition not all people agree on, such
>   as affirmative action or date rape

◆ PRACTICE 10-4

Review your notes from Practice 10-3, focusing on the most important ideas. On the following lines, list the details that you think you can use to develop a definition paragraph.

_____

_____

_____

_____

_____

_____

_____

_____

◆ PRACTICE 10-5

Reread your notes from Practice 10-4. Then, draft a topic sentence that summarizes the main point you want to make about the term you are going to define.

_____

_____

_____

◆ PRACTICE 10-6

List the ideas you will discuss in your paragraph, arranging them in an effective order.

1. _____

2. _____

3. _____

4. _____

5. _____

◆ PRACTICE 10-7

On a separate sheet of paper, write your definition paragraph. Then, using the Self-Assessment Checklist on page 92, revise your paragraph for unity, development, and coherence.

◆ PRACTICE 10-8

On a separate sheet of paper, write a final, edited draft of your definition paragraph.

■ WRITING FIRST: Revising and Editing

Look back at your response to the Writing First exercise on page 86, and evaluate it for unity, development, and coherence. Then, prepare a final, edited draft of your paragraph.

> ☑ SELF-ASSESSMENT CHECKLIST:
> Writing a Definition Paragraph
>
> *Unity*
>
> ☐ Does all your information support your topic sentence?
>
> ☐ Do you need to revise your topic sentence to include any additional information?
>
> *Development*
>
> ☐ Is your subject defined clearly?
>
> ☐ Do you make your points effectively?
>
> ☐ Do you need to include more information about your subject?
>
> ☐ Do you need to use one or more of the invention strategies discussed in 1B to come up with more ideas?
>
> ☐ Would a different pattern of development be more effective?
>
> *Coherence*
>
> ☐ Would arranging the information in a different order make it clearer or more interesting to readers?
>
> ☐ Do you need to add transitional words or phrases?

11

Argument

PREVIEW

In this chapter, you will learn to write an argument paragraph.

■ WRITING FIRST

Write a paragraph in which you argue for or against one of the following policies.

■ Requiring AIDS testing for all health-care workers
■ Offering single-sex math and science courses
■ Eliminating laws requiring seatbelt use
■ Banning the sale of all tobacco products in the United States
■ Requiring every gun owner to pass a test of his or her expertise in handling a gun

Include examples from your experience or from your reading to support your position.

A   Understanding Argument

An **argument** defends a particular position on a debatable subject. When you write an **argument paragraph**, your purpose is to persuade readers that your position has merit. The topic sentence states your position; in the rest of the paragraph, you support your position with **evidence**—*facts*, *examples*, and references to the opinions of *authorities*. If your evidence is effective and your reasoning is sound, the paragraph is likely to lead to a conclusion that readers will accept.

A **fact** is information that can be verified as objectively true. For example, it is a fact that A comes before G in the alphabet and that Mark McGwire set a new home-run record in 1998. If you make the point that students are less prepared for college today than they were twenty years ago, you should support it with facts—for example, by citing SAT scores and college dropout rates. Avoid sweeping statements that are not supported by facts from encyclopedias, newspapers, or other reliable

▼ **Student Voices**
In high school, I wrote a paragraph arguing against censorship. I liked having a chance to write about something I'm really interested in.
              Dan Lynn

sources. If you use unsupported statements, readers will question your position.

An **example** is a specific illustration of a general statement. To be convincing, an example should relate clearly to your point and should be typical, not exceptional. For example, to support the point that the quality of life in your neighborhood has improved recently, you could discuss new businesses that have opened and new neighbors who have spent a lot of time and money improving their properties.

An **authority** is someone who is generally recognized as an expert on a particular subject. The opinion of an authority supporting your view on a subject can be very persuasive. For example, if you wanted to show that the use of seatbelts together with airbags can save thousands of lives each year, you could quote Ralph Nader, an expert on automobile safety. Because Nader is an acknowledged authority, his opinion carries a great deal of weight. Remember, however, that a person who is an expert in one field is not necessarily an expert in another field. For instance, a radio personality's opinion about television violence would have less value than that of someone who has spent most of his or her professional life studying media violence.

The following paragraph argues against the use of Astroturf surfaces in sports stadiums.

> ● **Writing Tip**
> Using *should* or *should not* in the topic sentence of your argument makes your position clear.

Topic sentence

Facts and examples

Authority

Conclusion

Sports stadiums built during the 1960s and 1970s use Astroturf because it requires little maintenance and creates a uniform playing surface. But recently it has become clear that Astroturf has caused so many injuries that it should be eliminated from all pro sports stadiums. Anyone who follows baseball or football knows that Astroturf causes many knee and ankle injuries. The main reason for this situation is that it does not absorb impact the way a natural grass surface does. Astroturf is a layer of rough artificial grass on top of a layer of padding. Beneath these layers is a cement pad. Players who fall on Astroturf or, in the case of football, are thrown down onto it, risk serious injury. The New York Giants, for example, lost tight end Mark Bavaro to knee injuries caused by his falling onto his knees on the artificial surface of the Meadowlands Stadium. And the Astroturf surface in Philadelphia's Veterans Stadium, long known by players to be the worst in the country, has caused the Eagles to lose a number of key players. As sports columnist Bill Lyon points out, when you sit in the stands of Veterans Stadium, you can see the gaps where sections of the Astroturf do not meet properly. When a player catches a foot in these gaps, the result can be a painful sprain or worse. The situations in Philadelphia and New Jersey are not unique. You can see the same problems in every stadium that has an Astroturf playing surface. For this reason, players, owners, and fans should insist that stadiums remove Astroturf and restore natural grass surfaces.

Toni-Ann Marro (student)

> ● **Writing Tip**
> Argument paragraphs often use transitions such as *the first reason, the second reason,* and *therefore* to signal the sequence of ideas. (See 2C.)

The paragraph begins with a sentence that provides some background. The topic sentence then states the main idea—the writer's position. After explaining what Astroturf is, the paragraph presents facts, examples, and a statement by an authority. The paragraph ends with a conclusion based on the evidence presented. Throughout the paragraph, transitional words and phrases—*the main reason, for example,* and *for this reason*—lead readers through the argument.

● **Writing Tip**
Many everyday tasks call for argumentation. In a letter to your local school board, you might argue against raising class size in the elementary school.

FOCUS **Argument**

In addition to presenting evidence to support your argument, you need to consider the effect of your argument on your audience. Before you write, try to determine whether your readers are likely to be hostile, friendly, or neutral to your position. Let your analysis of your audience determine the approach you use.

For example, if you suspect your audience may not be receptive to your position, you might mention their possible objections in your topic sentence before stating your position. In your paragraph, you can **refute** (argue against) those objections.

> While some people may argue that students won't get a well-rounded education [possible objection], limiting course requirements will actually benefit most community college students [position].

In cases where you expect your audience to disagree with you, consider saving your topic sentence for the end of your paragraph so you can lead up to it gradually.

B   Writing an Argument Paragraph

◆ PRACTICE 11-1

Read this argument paragraph; then, follow the instructions on page 96.

> Did Popeye Watch Too Many Violent Cartoons?
>
> My four-year-old son recently talked about a television character who was "killed." Since our children are not allowed to watch violent television programs, I wondered what he had seen and decided that monitoring the cartoons he watches might be a good idea. Surprisingly, nearly all of them, from Daffy Duck to Power Rangers, contain some sort of violence. Popeye cartoons, which were childhood favorites of mine, are among the worst. In one episode, Bluto is smashed over the head with a telephone pole, and Popeye is thrown into wet cement and then freed when his head is drilled with a pile driver. In another, Olive is beaten up for spurning Bluto's amorous attentions. At a time when children and teenagers are assaulting and even killing others for clothes, bicycles, and money, I believe it is time to consider limiting the amount of violence in children's programs. Just as superior programs such as Sesame Street have favorable effects because they teach children useful skills and positive values, violent

programs must also have some effect on impressionable
minds. When violence is depicted as a legitimate means of
settling disputes, for example, children learn to turn to
violence as an answer. Of course, cartoons are not entirely
to blame, and other factors, such as home life and even
medical conditions, can lead to violence among children.
Nonetheless, concerned parents should pay more attention to
the "harmless" programming aimed at children, limit their
children's access to such programming, and lobby networks
and local stations to provide more positive, less violent
programs for children.

Tom Woller (student)

1. Underline the topic sentence of the paragraph. Why do you think the writer places the topic sentence where he does?

_____

_____

_____

2. What is the controversial subject that the writer is dealing with?

_____

What is the writer's position on the subject?

_____

3. List some of the evidence the writer uses to support his position. The first piece of evidence has been listed for you.

Most cartoons contain violence (examples from Popeye).

_____

_____

_____

4. List the kinds of evidence (facts, examples, or authorities) the writer uses to support his position.

_____

_____

_____

5. What other kinds of evidence could the writer have used?

_____

_____

_____

_____

◆ PRACTICE 11-2

Following are four statements that could serve as topic sentences for argument paragraphs. For each statement, list three or four pieces of evidence that could support the statement. For example, if you were arguing in support of laws requiring motorcycle riders to wear safety helmets, you could list accident statistics, state laws, and statements by state troopers and emergency room physicians.

1. Television and radio talk shows undermine our ability to think clearly.

_____

_____

_____

_____

2. Sexual harassment is a big problem in the workplace.

_____

_____

_____

_____

3. Every individual should have the right to end his or her own life.

_____

_____

_____

_____

4. The freedom of speech guaranteed by the Constitution should not include hate speech.

_____

_____

_____

_____

◆ PRACTICE 11-3

Choose one of the topics below (or one of your own choice) as the subject of an argument paragraph. Then, on a separate sheet of paper, use one or more of the invention strategies described in 1B to focus on a specific issue to discuss in an argument paragraph.

An issue related to your school

Grading policies   Course offerings
Required courses   Student activity fees

Entrance requirements The physical condition of classrooms
Attendance policies   Child-care facilities

A community issue

The need for a traffic signal, a youth center, or something else you
  think would benefit your community
An action you think local officials should take, such as changing
  school hours, cleaning up a public eyesore, or improving a specific
  service
A new law you would like to see enacted
A current law you would like to see repealed
A controversy you have been following in the news

◆ PRACTICE 11-4

Once you have chosen an issue in Practice 11-3, write a journal entry
about your position on the issue. Consider the following questions: Why
do you feel the way you do? Do many people share your views or are you
in the minority? What specific actions do you think should be taken? What
objections are likely to be raised against your position? How would you
respond to these objections?

◆ PRACTICE 11-5

Review your notes from Practice 11-4 and choose the ideas that best support your position. List these ideas below. (You may also want to list the
strongest objections to your position.)

_____

_____

_____

_____

_____

◆ PRACTICE 11-6

Draft a one-sentence topic sentence that clearly expresses the position you
will take in your paragraph.

_____

_____

◆ PRACTICE 11-7

In the space provided, arrange the ideas that support your position in an
order that you think will be convincing to your audience.

1. _____

2. _____

3. _____

4. _____

5. _____

◆ PRACTICE 11-8

On a separate sheet of paper, write your argument paragraph. Then, using the Self-Assessment Checklist below, revise your paragraph for unity, development, and coherence.

◆ PRACTICE 11-9

On a separate sheet of paper, write a final, edited draft of your argument paragraph.

■ WRITING FIRST: Revising and Editing

Look back at your response to the Writing First exercise on page 93, and evaluate it for unity, development, and coherence. Then, prepare a final, edited draft of your paragraph.

☑ SELF-ASSESSMENT CHECKLIST:
Writing an Argument Paragraph

Unity

☐ Does your topic sentence clearly state your position?

☐ Is all your information directly related to your position?

☐ Do you need to revise your topic sentence to accommodate new ideas?

Development

☐ Do you need more facts or other evidence to convince your audience to accept your position?

☐ Do you need to use one or more of the invention strategies discussed in 1B to come up with more ideas?

Coherence

☐ Would arranging ideas in a different order make your argument more convincing to readers?

☐ Do you need to add transitional words or phrases?

UNIT THREE

Focus on Essays

12

Writing an Essay

Most of the writing you do in school will be longer than a paragraph. Often, you will be asked to write an **essay**—a group of paragraphs on a single subject. When you write an essay, you follow the same process you do when you write a paragraph: you move from invention to selecting and arranging ideas and then to drafting, revising, and editing. Chapters 12 through 14 will show you how to apply the paragraph skills you learned in Chapters 1 through 11 to writing essays.

A Understanding Essay Structure

Like paragraphs, essays are unified by a single main idea. In a paragraph, the **topic sentence** presents the main idea, and the rest of the paragraph **supports** the main idea.

Paragraph

> The **topic sentence** states the main idea of the paragraph.
>
> **Support** develops the main idea with details, facts, and examples.

Many essays have a **thesis-and-support** structure. The first paragraph begins with opening remarks and closes with a **thesis statement**, which presents the main idea. The body of the essay is made up of several paragraphs that **support** the thesis with details, facts, and examples. Each of these paragraphs begins with a topic sentence that states the paragraph's main idea. The last paragraph, which may restate the thesis, offers the writer's concluding thoughts on the subject.

PREVIEW

In this chapter, you will learn

- to understand essay structure (12A)

- to decide on a topic (12B)

- to use invention strategies (12C)

- to state a thesis (12D)

- to arrange ideas (12E)

- to draft an essay (12F)

- to revise and edit your essay (12G)

For a discussion of writing paragraphs, see Chapter 1.

● **Writing Tip**
Many writing situations outside of school require more than a paragraph. The skills you learn in this chapter can also be applied to these writing tasks.

103

12 A

Essay

Opening remarks introduce the subject to be discussed.

The **thesis statement** presents the main idea of the essay in the last sentence of the first paragraph.

Introductory paragraph

Topic sentence (first main point)

Support (details, facts, examples)

Topic sentence (second main point)

Support (details, facts, examples)

Body paragraphs

Topic sentence (third main point)

Support (details, facts, examples)

The **restatement of the thesis** summarizes the essay's main idea.

Closing remarks present the writer's last thoughts on the subject.

Concluding paragraph

Paragraphs and essays are structurally very similar. In fact, a paragraph is in many ways like a miniature essay. Consider the following paragraph.

Topic sentence
Point 1

Several strategies can help smokers stop smoking. The first and easiest strategy is substituting something for the cigarette that they've gotten used to holding. Some people use a pencil, a straw, or a coin, but almost any small object will work. Next, people who quit smoking generally substitute something for the stimulation they get from cigarettes. They might chew a strongly flavored sugarless gum, for example, or take fast, short breaths, or do anything that gives a physical jolt to the system. A third strategy is to change habits associated with smoking. For instance, people who associate smoking with drinking coffee might temporarily switch to tea or another beverage with caffeine. Finally, most people who successfully quit smoking prepare themselves to resist temptation in moments of stress or discomfort. Rather than reaching for a cigarette, they have another sort of treat ready for themselves. These four antismoking strategies have worked for many ex-smokers, who recommend them highly.

Point 2

Point 3

Point 4

Concluding thoughts

If the paragraph were rewritten as an essay, the paragraph's topic sentence could become the essay's thesis statement, and each of the paragraph's supporting points could become a topic sentence for one of the essay's body paragraphs. The sentence in which the writer states the paragraph's concluding thoughts could become the restatement of the essay's thesis.

> ● **Writing Tip**
> Knowing how paragraphs and essays are similar can help you develop your ideas as you move from writing paragraphs to writing essays.

Opening remarks

Thesis statement   Several strategies can help smokers stop smoking.

Introductory paragraph

Topic sentence   The first and easiest strategy is substituting something for the cigarette that they've gotten used to holding.

Support (details, facts, examples)

Body paragraphs

Topic sentence   Next, people who quit smoking need to substitute something for the stimulation they get from smoking.

Support (details, facts, examples)

Topic sentence   A third strategy is to change habits associated with smoking.

Support (details, facts, examples)

Body paragraphs

Topic sentence   Finally, most people who successfully quit smoking prepare themselves to resist temptation in moments of stress or discomfort.

Support (details, facts, examples)

Restatement of the thesis   These four antismoking strategies have worked for many ex-smokers, who recommend them highly.

Concluding paragraph

Closing remarks

◆ PRACTICE 12-1

Following is a completed essay developed from the preceding diagram. After you have finished reading the essay, answer the questions that follow it, comparing the original paragraph on page 104 to the essay. Discuss your answers with your class or writing group.

Introductory paragraph

More and more smokers today are aware of the serious risks smoking poses both for themselves and for the nonsmokers around them. Many of them would like to quit but just don't think they can. However, several strategies can help smokers achieve this goal.

Body paragraphs

The first and easiest strategy is substituting something for the cigarette that they've gotten used to holding. Some people use a pencil, a straw, or a coin. I have a friend who started using a Japanese fan. There are even special products available to keep people's hands busy, such as worry beads and small rubber balls. Almost any small object will work as long as it is satisfactory for the individual.

Next, people who quit smoking need to substitute something for the stimulation they get from cigarettes. They might chew a strongly flavored sugarless gum, for example, or take fast, short breaths. Other people splash their faces with ice cold water or do some light exercise. Some even claim that standing on their heads has helped. The point is to find something that gives a physical jolt to the system.

A third strategy is to change habits associated with smoking. For example, people who associate cigarettes with drinking coffee might temporarily switch to tea or another beverage with caffeine, while people who generally smoke while on the telephone might try using e-mail instead of making long-distance calls. Unfortunately, some smoking-associated activities are difficult to eliminate. People who associate smoking with being in their cars obviously can't give up driving. The point, though, is to alter as many habits as possible to eliminate times when one would normally reach for a cigarette.

Finally, most people who successfully quit smoking prepare themselves to resist temptation in moments of stress or discomfort. Rather than reaching for a cigarette, they have another sort of treat ready for themselves. Some people, understandably, choose candy or sweets of some kind, but these are not the best alternatives, for obvious reasons. A better idea is to use the money saved by not buying cigarettes to purchase something to pamper oneself with, such as expensive cologne or a personal CD player.

Body paragraphs

No one would say that it's easy to quit smoking, but this fact shouldn't keep people from recognizing that they can kick the habit. These four antismoking strategies have worked for many ex-smokers, who recommend them highly.

Concluding paragraph

1. How was the opening sentence of the original paragraph expanded into the essay's introductory paragraph?

_____

_____

2. How was the first point developed?

_____

_____

3. How was the second point developed?

_____

_____

4. How was the third point developed?

_____

_____

5. How was the fourth point developed?

_____

_____

6. How was the paragraph's closing sentence expanded into the essay's concluding paragraph?

_____

_____

B   Deciding on a Topic

Most of the essays you write in college begin as a **topic** suggested by an assignment your instructor gives you. The following topics are typical of those you may be asked to write about.

Discuss some things you would change about this school.

What can college students do to improve the environment?

Describe an activity you do outside school that supplements your education.

Because these assignments are so general, responding to any of them would be difficult if not impossible. What specific things would you change? Exactly what might college students do to improve the environment? Which activity should you write about? Answering these questions will help you narrow these assignments until they are specific enough to write about.

Assignment	Topic
Discuss some things you would change about this school.	Three things I would change to improve the quality of life at Jackson County Community College
What can college students do to improve the environment?	The campus recycling project
Describe an activity you do outside school that supplements your education.	The advantages of having a part-time job in college

◆ PRACTICE 12-2

Decide whether the following topics are narrow enough for an essay of four or five paragraphs. If a topic is suitable, write "OK" in the blank. If it is not, write in the blank a version of the same topic that is narrow enough for a brief essay.

Examples: Successful strategies for quitting smoking _____*OK*_____

Horror movies _____*1950s Japanese monster movies*_____

1. Violence in American public schools _____

   _____

2. Ways to improve your study skills _____

   _____

3. Using pets as therapy for nursing-home patients_____

   _____

4. Teachers _____

_____

5. Safe ways to lose weight _____

_____

6. Clothing styles _____

_____

7. Parent-child relationships _____

_____

8. Reasons children lie to their parents _____

_____

9. College education _____

_____

10. Television's impact on children _____

_____

C Using Invention Strategies

Before you start writing about a topic, ask yourself some questions to get a sense of your assignment, your purpose, and your audience. Once you have done this, you are ready to narrow your topic and decide on a workable thesis. Sometimes, ideas may come to you easily. More often, you will have to use one or more **invention strategies** such as *freewriting* or *brainstorming* to come up with ideas about your topic and narrow your focus.

For a discussion of purpose and audience, see 1A.

For a discussion of invention strategies, see 1B.

Freewriting

When you **freewrite**, you write (or type) for a fixed period of time without stopping. When you engage in **focused freewriting**, you write with a specific topic in mind, read what you have written, and choose the ideas you think you can use. Following is an example of focused freewriting by a student, Kevin Coleman, on the topic *the advantages of having a part-time job in college*.

```
    Working in college. I never really wanted to work,
but my parents told me that I'd have to pick up some of
my expenses. I got a student loan, but it didn't cover
everything--movies, food, etc. I began working during
my second semester. I had a bunch of part-time jobs.
Waiter. Library. Pizza truck. Some were fun--others were
```

■ **Computer Tip**
Keep your invention mate-
rial separate from your first
draft by saving it in a separate file.

pretty bad. I hated driving that truck. But there were
some advantages. One was that I didn't have to ask my
parents for money all the time. That made them happy.
Paid half of my tuition. Working also made me happy. I
began to feel independent. Yeah--My Declaration of Independence. I saw that if things got tough, I could make
it. (Not a bad thing to know about yourself.) I wonder
if my parents knew this all along. Or is this something
that just happened? Maybe working taught me some lessons
that I didn't learn in school. I guess I'll never know.
It's not like I can really ask them. I'm running out of
things to say. The end.

◆ PRACTICE 12-3

Reread Kevin Coleman's freewriting. If you were advising Kevin, which
ideas would you suggest that he explore further? Why? Write your answers
below.

_____

_____

_____

_____

◆ PRACTICE 12-4

Choose two of the topics listed in Practice 12-2, and freewrite about them
on a separate sheet of paper. For which of the topics did you come up with
the most interesting ideas? On the lines below, write the ideas you would
like to develop further and explain why.

_____

_____

_____

_____

Brainstorming

When you **brainstorm** (either individually or with others), you write (or
type) all you can think of about a particular topic. After you have recorded
as much material as you can, you look over your notes to figure out where
your ideas seem to be going. Here are Kevin Coleman's brainstorming
notes on the advantages of part-time jobs for college students.

```
             Advantages of a Part-Time Job

Working ever since my second year of college
Bad jobs
      Waiter--library--pizza truck driver (good tips)
```

```
Gained confidence
Helped pay tuition
Got independence
Bought lots of clothes
Bought photography supplies
Got a lot of satisfaction
Felt like an adult--had my own money
Brother going to college next year
Sometimes not enough time
Final exams--papers
Not enough free time
Did grades suffer? Did social life?
Always found time
Things you learn
        Responsibility
        Business
        About independence, survival skills
```

◆ PRACTICE 12-5

Brainstorm about the two topics you wrote about in Practice 12-4. What ideas did you get from your brainstorming that you did not get from freewriting? Write your response on the following lines.

_____

_____

_____

D   **Stating Your Thesis**

After you have gathered information about your topic, you can decide what you want to say about it. By choosing and rejecting ideas and by identifying connections among the ideas you keep, you can decide on the point you want your essay to make. You can then express this point in a **thesis statement**: a single sentence that clearly expresses your essay's main idea.

▼ **Student Voices**
I always try to make sure I have a strong thesis that will accurately represent my ideas.
Demetrius Davis

Topic	Thesis Statement
Three things I would change about Jackson County Community College	If I could change three things to improve Jackson County Community College, I would expand the food choices, decrease class size in first-year courses, and ship some of my classmates to the North Pole.
The campus recycling project	The recycling project recently begun on our campus should be promoted more actively.

Like a topic sentence, a thesis statement tells readers what to expect. An effective thesis statement has two important characteristics.

1. *An effective thesis statement makes a point about a topic or takes a stand on an issue; for this reason, it must do more than state a fact or announce what you plan to write about.*

STATEMENT OF FACT	Many college students work.
ANNOUNCEMENT	In this essay, I would like to present my opinion about whether college students should work.
EFFECTIVE THESIS STATEMENT	A part-time job is a valuable part of any college student's education.

A statement of fact is not an effective thesis statement because it takes no position and gives you nothing to develop in your essay. For example, how much can you say about the *fact* that many college students work? Likewise, an announcement of what you plan to discuss gives readers no indication of the position you will take on your topic. An effective thesis statement takes a stand. It could say, for example, that a part-time job is a valuable part of a college education.

2. *An effective thesis statement is clearly worded and specific.*

VAGUE THESIS STATEMENT	Television commercials aren't like real life.
EFFECTIVE THESIS STATEMENT	Television commercials do not accurately portray women or minorities.

The vague statement above says little about the ideas that the essay will discuss or how it will present those ideas. It does not say, for example, *why* television commercials aren't realistic. The effective thesis statement is more focused. It tells readers that the essay will give examples of television commercials that present unrealistic portrayals of women and minorities.

FOCUS **Stating Your Thesis**

Keep in mind that at this stage of the writing process, your thesis statement is *tentative*. You will almost certainly change this tentative thesis statement as you write and revise your essay.

◆ **PRACTICE 12-6**

In the space provided, indicate whether each of the following items is a fact (F), an announcement (A), a vague statement (VS), or an effective thesis (ET).

Examples

My commute between home and school takes more than an hour each

way. _____F____

I don't like my commute between home and school. __vs____

1. Students who must commute a long distance to school are at a disad-

   vantage compared to students who live close by. _____

2. In this paper, I will discuss cheating and why students shouldn't cheat.

   _____

3. Any school can establish specific policies that will discourage students

   from cheating. _____

4. Cheating is a problem for both students and teachers. _____

5. Television commercials are designed to sell products. _____

6. I would like to explain why some television commercials are funny.

   _____

7. Single parents have a rough time. _____

8. An article in the newspaper says that young people are starting to

   abuse alcohol and drugs at earlier ages than in the past. _____

9. Alcohol and drug abuse are major problems in our society. _____

10. Families can use several strategies to help children avoid alcohol and

    drugs. _____

◆ PRACTICE 12-7

Look at the two topics you freewrote and brainstormed about in Practices
12-4 and 12-5, and choose the topic you like better. After reviewing your
freewriting and brainstorming notes, draft a thesis statement for this topic
on the lines below.

_____

_____

E   **Arranging Ideas**

Once you have decided on a thesis statement, look over your freewriting
and brainstorming notes to find the points that best support your
thesis. Then, make a list of these points. Here is Kevin Coleman's list of

12 E

supporting points about the advantages of part-time jobs for college students.

> **Computer Tip**
> Try making an outline by first typing a list of words and phrases and then re-arranging them until the order makes sense.

```
Job makes parents happy
Job gives satisfaction
Job provides an income
Able to buy photography supplies
Don't have to ask parents for money
Paid half of my tuition
Feel like an adult
Buy clothing
Brother going to college next year
Gained confidence
```

> **Computer Tip**
> Indent items in your outline with the Tab key to show how they are related.

After you have selected the points you think will best support your thesis, arrange them in the order in which you will discuss them (for example, from general to specific, or from least important to most important). This orderly list of points can serve as a rough outline to guide you as you write. Kevin listed his points in the following order.

```
Job provides steady income
   Buy clothing
   Able to buy photography supplies
Job helps pay tuition
   Makes parents happy
   Brother going to college next year
   Paid half of my tuition
Job gives satisfaction
   Feel like an adult
   Gained confidence
```

◆ PRACTICE 12-8

Write the thesis statement you drafted in Practice 12-7 on the lines provided.

_____

_____

Now, review your freewriting and brainstorming notes, and list the points you plan to use to support your thesis statement.

_____

_____

_____

_____

_____

Finally, arrange these points in an order in which you could write about them. Cross out any points that do not support your thesis statement.

1. _____

2. _____

3. _____

4. _____

5. _____

F Drafting Your Essay

After you have developed a thesis for your essay and have arranged your points in the order in which you will discuss them, you are ready to draft your essay. At this stage of the writing process, you should not worry about spelling or grammar or about composing a "perfect" introduction or conclusion. Your main goal is to get your ideas down so you can react to them. Remember that the draft you are writing will be revised, so leave lots of room for your changes: write on every other line, and triple-space if you are typing. Follow your rough outline, but don't hesitate to depart from it if you think of new points or if your ideas take an interesting or unexpected turn.

For a discussion of introductions and conclusions, see Chapter 13.

As you write, remember that your essay's final structure will be determined by the concept of **thesis and support**—that is, it will state a thesis and support it with examples or reasons. Because this structure enables you to present your ideas clearly and persuasively, it will be central to much of the writing you do in college. Regardless of the specific **pattern of development** you use to structure a particular essay, each of your essays should follow this basic structure. Here is a diagram of how a thesis-and-support essay about part-time jobs in college might look.

For a discussion of thesis and support, see 12A.

For a discussion of patterns of essay development, see Chapter 14.

Essay

Opening remarks

Thesis statement   A part-time job is a valuable part of any college student's education.

Introductory paragraph

Topic sentence   The first reason to work is that a part-time job provides a steady income.

Support   (details, facts, examples)

Body paragraphs

Topic sentence   Another reason for working is that a part-time job helps pay tuition.

Support   (details, facts, examples)

Body paragraphs

Topic sentence   A third reason to work is that a part-time job gives satisfaction.

Support   (details, facts, examples)

Restatement of the thesis

Concluding paragraph

Closing remarks

Each topic sentence in the thesis-and-support essay developed from this diagram focuses on one part of the thesis—one reason for working. In addition, the topic sentences link the paragraphs in the essay by using transitional expressions ("The first reason . . . Another reason . . . A third reason . . .") and repeated words and ideas from the thesis statement ("part-time job"). These topic sentences not only reinforce the thesis but also remind readers about the main point of the essay.

Here is a first draft of Kevin Coleman's essay.

```
                        Working

        Ever since I began college, I have been working.
While some of my friends sat around wasting time, I have
managed to hold down several part-time jobs. I have
gained a lot by working. A part-time job is a valuable
part of any college student's education.
        The first reason to work is that a job provides
income. I've had a number of part-time jobs, and I
didn't like them all, but they did have their uses. When
I want to buy books or clothes, I usually can. If an
unexpected expense comes up, I can usually increase my
hours so I can earn more. Last year, for example, I
unexpectedly had to buy supplies for a photography
course I was taking.
```

Another reason for working is that a job helps pay tuition. Both my parents work, and they are able to make ends meet. My mother is a teacher, and my father works for an insurance company. Their jobs are demanding, and they are usually tired at the end of the day. Even so, they don't have the money to pay all my tuition. My brother will be going to college next year, and they have to save for him. Every summer, I try to earn enough money to pay part of my tuition. The jobs I hold during the year pay for most of my weekly expenses. This past year, I was able to pay almost half my tuition and almost all of my living expenses.

The third reason for working is that a job gives me satisfaction. By working, I feel that I am earning the respect of my parents. I am not a drain on the family, and I set a good example for my brother. I would feel horrible if I had to run to my parents every time I needed money. I would also feel like a kid, not an adult. By working, I am developing the confidence I will need when I graduate and enter the work force. Because I have been able to earn my own way, I know I can support myself no matter what happens.

I would advise any student to consider getting a part-time job. Working supplements income and helps pay tuition, and it also provides a great deal of satisfaction.

◆ PRACTICE 12-9

Reread Kevin Coleman's first draft. What changes would you suggest he make? What might he add? What might he delete? Write your suggestions on the lines below.

_____

_____

_____

_____

_____

◆ PRACTICE 12-10

On a separate sheet of paper, write a draft of an essay about the topic you chose in Practice 12-7. Be sure to include the thesis statement you drafted in Practice 12-8 as well as your list of points.

● **Writing Tip**
Most writers see revising
and editing as distinct activities. First, they revise (several times, if necessary), and
then they edit.

G Revising and Editing Your Essay

When you **revise** your essay, you follow the same general procedure you
do for a paragraph: you resee, rethink, reevaluate, and rewrite your work.
Some of the changes you make—such as adding, deleting, or rearranging
several sentences or even a whole paragraph—will be major. Others will
be small—for example, adding or deleting words or phrases. Before you
begin revising, put your paper aside for a time. This "cooling-off" period
allows you to put some distance between yourself and what you have written so you can view your draft more objectively. When you begin to revise,
feel free to write directly on your draft: draw arrows, underline, cross out,
and write above lines and in the margins.

When you **edit** your essay, you check grammar and sentence structure.
Then, you look at punctuation, mechanics, and spelling.

As you revise and edit, think carefully about the questions in the two
Self-Assessment Checklists that follow.

■ **Computer Tip**
Revise and edit on a hard
copy of your essay before
you type in your changes.

■ **Computer Tip**
When you remove material
from your draft, move it to
the end of the draft or to a
separate file. Don't delete it
until you're sure you don't
need it.

*For a discussion of how to
write paragraphs that are unified, well developed, and coherent, see Chapter 2.*

☑ **SELF-ASSESSMENT CHECKLIST:**
Revising Your Essay

    ☐ Does your essay have an introduction, a body, and a conclusion?

    ☐ Does your essay have a clearly worded thesis statement?

    ☐ Does your thesis statement make a point about your topic?

    ☐ Does each body paragraph have a topic sentence?

    ☐ Does each topic sentence reinforce the thesis?

    ☐ Does each body paragraph contain enough details, facts, or
       examples to support the topic sentence?

    ☐ Are the body paragraphs unified, well developed, and coherent?

    ☐ Do you restate your thesis or summarize your main points in
       your conclusion?

    ☐ Have you varied sentence type, structure, and length? (See
       Chapter 18.)

    ☐ Have you used effective parallel structure in your sentences?
       (See Chapter 19.)

☑ **SELF-ASSESSMENT CHECKLIST:**
Editing Your Essay

Editing for Common Sentence Problems

    ☐ Have you avoided run-ons and comma splices? (See Chapter 21.)

(continued on the following page)

(continued from the previous page)

☐ Have you avoided sentence fragments? (See Chapter 22.)

☐ Do your subjects and verbs agree? (See Chapter 23.) Have you avoided illogical shifts? (See Chapter 24.)

☐ Have you avoided dangling modifiers? (See Chapter 25.)

Editing for Grammar

☐ Are your verb forms and verb tenses correct? (See Chapters 26 and 27.)

☐ Have you used nouns and pronouns correctly? (See Chapter 28.)

☐ Have you used adjectives and adverbs correctly? (See Chapter 29.)

Editing for Punctuation, Mechanics, and Spelling

☐ Have you used commas correctly? (See Chapter 31.)

☐ Have you used apostrophes correctly? (See Chapter 32.)

☐ Have you used capital letters where they are required? (See Chapter 33.)

☐ Have you used quotation marks correctly where they are needed? (See Chapter 33.)

☐ Have you spelled every word correctly? (See Chapter 34.)

■ **Computer Tip**
Use the Search function to find spelling errors that you commonly make (but that the spell checker won't catch)—using *there* instead of *their,* for example.

As he typed the first draft of his essay about the advantages of having a part-time job in college, Kevin triple-spaced to make his revision process easier. Here is his draft, with his handwritten revision and editing changes.

```
                          Working

        Ever since I began college, I have been working.

While some of my friends sat around wasting time, I have
          Even though there have been times when I wished I didn't have to work,
managed to hold down several part-time jobs. ^I have
                              can be
gained a lot by working. A part-time job ^is a valuable

part of any college student's education ; I know it has been for me.

        The first reason to work is that a job provides
a steady source of money for day-to-day expenses.
income. ^I've had a number of part-time jobs, and I
                              Because I have a steady salary, when
didn't like them all, but they did have their uses. When
                              ^
I want to buy books or clothes, I usually can. If an

unexpected expense comes up, I can usually increase my
```

Even though my parents have never said anything to me, I know that paying my tuition is a hardship for them.

hours so I can earn more. Last year, for example, I unexpectedly had to buy supplies for a photography course I was taking. *At first I thought I would have to drop the course because I couldn't afford the supplies. After talking to my boss, however, I was able to arrange to work a few extra hours and earn enough to buy the supplies I needed.*

Another reason for working is that a job helps pay tuition. Both my parents work, and they are able to make ends meet. ~~My mother is a teacher, and my father works for an insurance company. Their jobs are demanding, and they are usually tired at the end of the day. Even so,~~ *But even with loans, we* ~~they~~ don't have the money to pay all my tuition. ~~My~~ *In addition, my* brother will be going to college next year, and they have to save for him. Every summer, I try to earn enough money to pay part of my tuition. ~~The jobs I hold during the year pay for most of my weekly expenses.~~ This past year, I was able to pay almost half my tuition ~~and almost all of my living expenses.~~

The *most important* ~~third~~ reason for working is that a job gives me satisfaction. By working, I feel that I am earning the respect of my parents. I am not a drain on the family, and I set a good example for my brother. I would feel horrible if I had to run to my parents every time I needed money. I would also feel like a kid, not an adult. By working, I am *also* developing the confidence I will need when I graduate and enter the work force. Because I have been able to pay my own way *so far*, I know I can support myself no matter what happens.

I would advise any student to consider getting a part-time job. Working ~~supplements~~ *not only provides needed* income and helps pay tuition, ~~and it~~ *but* also ~~provides a great deal of~~ *offers* satisfaction. *In my case, a job has given me the insight and the confidence I will need to succeed after I graduate.*

◆ PRACTICE 12-11

What material did Kevin Coleman add to his draft? What did he delete? Why did he make these changes? Write your answers on the following lines.

_____

_____

_____

_____

When his major revisions were complete, Kevin proofread his essay to be sure he had not missed any errors. The final revised and edited version of his essay appears below.

```
                    Working

    Ever since I began college, I have been working.
While some of my friends sat around wasting time, I have
managed to hold down several part-time jobs. Even though
there have been times when I wished I didn't have to
work, I have gained a lot by working. A part-time job
can be a valuable part of any college student's educa-
tion; I know it has been for me.

    The first reason to work is that a job provides a
steady source of income for day-to-day expenses. I've
had a number of part-time jobs, and even though I didn't
like them all, they did have their uses. Because I have
a steady salary, when I want to buy books or an item of
clothing, I usually can. If an unexpected expense comes
up, I can usually increase my hours so I can earn more.
Last year, for example, I unexpectedly had to buy sup-
plies for a photography course I was taking. At first,
I thought I would have to drop the course because I
couldn't afford the supplies. After talking to my boss,
however, I was able to arrange to work a few extra
hours and earn enough to buy the supplies I needed.

    Another reason for working is that a job helps pay
tuition. Even though my parents have never said anything
to me, I know that paying my tuition is a hardship for
them. Both my parents work, and they are able to make
ends meet. But even with loans, they don't have the
money to pay all my tuition. In addition, my brother
will be going to college next year, and they have to
save for him. Every summer I try to earn enough money
to pay part of my tuition. This past year, I was able
to pay almost half my tuition.
```

The most important reason for working is that a job gives me satisfaction. By working, I feel that I am earning the respect of my parents. I am not a drain on the family, and I set a good example for my brother. I would feel horrible if I had to run to my parents every time I needed money. I would also feel like a kid, not an adult. Furthermore, by working, I am developing the confidence I will need when I graduate and enter the work force. Because I have been able to pay my own way so far, I know I can support myself no matter what happens.

I would advise any student to consider getting a part-time job. Working not only provides needed income and helps pay tuition but also offers satisfaction. In my case, a job has given me the insight and the confidence I will need to succeed after I graduate.

◆ PRACTICE 12-12

Reread the final draft of Kevin Coleman's essay. Do you think this draft is an improvement over the previous one? What other changes could Kevin have made? Write your ideas here.

_____

_____

_____

_____

_____

◆ PRACTICE 12-13

Using the Self-Assessment Checklist for revising your essay on page 118 as a guide, evaluate the essay you wrote for Practice 12-10. What points can you add to support your thesis more fully? What points can you delete? Can any ideas be stated more clearly? (You may want to get feedback by exchanging essays with another student.) On the following lines, describe any changes you think you should make to your draft.

_____

_____

_____

_____

_____

◆ PRACTICE 12-14

Revise and edit the draft of your essay, writing in new material between the lines or in the margins. Edit this revised draft, using the Self-Assessment Checklist for revising your essay on page 118 to help you find errors in grammar, sentence structure, punctuation, mechanics, and spelling.

◆ PRACTICE 12-15

Prepare a final draft of your essay.

CHAPTER REVIEW

◆ EDITING PRACTICE

After reading the following student essay, write an appropriate thesis statement on the lines provided. (Make sure your thesis statement clearly communicates the essay's main idea. Then, fill in the topic sentences for the second, third, and fourth paragraphs. Finally, restate the thesis in different words in your conclusion.

```
              Preparing for a Job Interview
       I have read a lot of books that give advice on how to
do well on a job interview. Some recommend practicing your
handshake, and others suggest rehearsing answers to typical
questions. This advice is useful, but not many books tell
how to get mentally prepared for an interview. [Thesis
statement:] _____
_____
_____

       [Topic sentence for the second paragraph:] _____
_____
_____

Feeling good about how I look is important, so I usually
wear a jacket and tie to an interview. Even if you will
not be dressing this formally on the job, try to make a
good first impression. For this reason, you should never
come to an interview dressed in jeans or shorts. Still, you
```

should be careful not to overdress. For example, wearing a suit or a dressy dress to an interview at a fast-food restaurant might make you feel good, but it could also make you look as if you do not really want to work in a casual setting.

[Topic sentence for the third paragraph:] _____

_____

_____

Going on an interview is a little like getting ready to participate in an important sporting event. You have to go in with the right attitude. If you think you are not going to be successful, chances are that you will not be. So before I go on any interview, I spend some time building my confidence. I tell myself that I can do the job and that I will do well in the interview. By the time I get to the interview, I am convinced that I am the right person for the job.

[Topic sentence for the fourth paragraph:] _____

_____

_____

Most people go to an interview knowing little or nothing about the job. They expect the interviewer to tell them what they will have to do. Once, an interviewer told me that he likes a person who has taken the time to do his or her homework. Since that time, I have always done some research before I go on an interview--even for a part-time job. (Most of the time, my research is nothing more than a call to a person who has a job where I want to work.) This kind of research really pays off. At my last interview, for example, I was able to talk in specific terms about the job's duties and indicate which shift I would prefer. The interviewer must have been impressed because she offered me the job on the spot.

[Restatement of thesis in the conclusion:] _____

_____

Of course, following my suggestions will not guarantee that
you get a job. You still have to do well at the interview
itself. Even so, getting mentally prepared for the interview will give you an advantage over others who do almost
nothing before they walk in the door.

◆ COLLABORATIVE ACTIVITIES

1. On your own, find a paragraph in a magazine or a newspaper about a controversial issue that interests you. Working in a group, select the best paragraph. Choose three points about the issue discussed that you could develop in a short essay, and then brainstorm about these points. Finally, write a statement that could serve as the thesis for an essay.

2. Working in a group, come up with thesis statements suitable for essays on three of the following topics.

Professional sports	Workfare
The Internet	Political corruption
Vegetarians	College entrance exams
Parenthood	Handguns
Honesty	Managed care

3. Exchange your group's three thesis statements with those of another group. Choose the best one of the other group's thesis statements. A member of each group can then read the thesis statement to the class and explain the group's choice.

For information on stating a thesis, see 12D.

☑ REVIEW CHECKLIST:
Writing an Essay

- Most essays have a thesis and support structure: the thesis statement presents the main idea, and the body paragraphs support the thesis. (See 12A.)

- Begin by deciding on a topic. (See 12B.)

- Use invention strategies to narrow your focus and find ideas to write about. (See 12C.)

- Develop an effective thesis statement. (See 12D.)

(continued on the following page)

(continued from the previous page)

- List the points that best support your thesis, and arrange them in the order in which you plan to discuss them. (See 12E.)

- As you write your first draft, make sure your essay has a thesis-and-support structure. (See 12F.)

- Revise your essay. (See 12G.)

- Edit the final draft of your essay. (See 12G.)

13

Introductions and Conclusions

PREVIEW

In this chapter, you will learn

■ to write an introduction (13A)

■ to choose a title (13A)

■ to write a conclusion (13B)

■ **WRITING FIRST**

Copy the introduction and the conclusion of the essay you wrote for Chapter 12 onto a separate page. As you go through this chapter, you will continue to work on these paragraphs.

When you draft an essay, you usually concentrate on the **body** because it is the largest single section, and because it is the section in which you develop your ideas. A well-constructed essay, however, is more than a series of body paragraphs. It also includes an **introduction** and a **conclusion**, both of which contribute to the overall effectiveness of your writing.

A Introductions

An introduction is the first thing people see when they read your essay. If your introduction is interesting and effective, it is likely to draw readers into your essay. If it is not, readers may get bored and stop reading.

Your introduction should prepare readers for your essay by giving them the information they need to follow your discussion. For this reason, the introduction usually includes a **thesis statement** that presents the main idea of your essay. This statement usually appears at the end of the introductory paragraph, but it can also appear earlier.

Your introduction should make people want to read further. To arouse readers' interest, you can begin with a narrative or a question or even a quotation. Understanding your options can help you write varied and interesting introductions. (In each of the following examples, the thesis statement is underlined.)

▼ **Student Voices**
When I write an introduction, I try to start with something that will surprise my readers.

Kelly Miller

● **Writing Tip**
The introduction performs many functions; therefore, it should be a full paragraph.

FOCUS Introductions

Don't begin your essays by announcing what you plan to write about. Avoid unnecessary statements like "This essay is about . . .," "Today I will talk about . . .," or "In my essay I will discuss. . . ." Instead, start with an introduction that flows naturally into the rest of your essay.

Beginning with a Direct Approach

Often, the best way to open an essay is by presenting a few opening remarks and then listing the points you will discuss in your essay. This straightforward approach moves readers directly to the central concerns of your essay. (Once you feel comfortable with this strategy, you can experiment with other approaches.)

> In 1994, the Republicans won a majority in both the House and the Senate for the first time in forty years. After their victory, there was quite a bit of finger pointing and discussion in the Democratic Party. Some thought the defeat of President Clinton's health-care bill was to blame. Others said that so many Democrats lost because the party was out of touch with the voters. Certainly, both these issues were important, but even more important were taxes, welfare, and anxiety about the national debt.

> Serge Komanawski (student)

Beginning with a Narrative

You can begin an essay with a narrative drawn from your own experience or from a current news event. If your story is interesting, it will involve readers almost immediately. Notice how the narrative in the following introduction sets the stage for an argument in favor of animal testing. (Also note that this introductory paragraph does not include a thesis statement. Because the writer considers his thesis to be controversial, he does not state it until his conclusion.)

> In a desperate—and successful—attempt to save the life of a dying man, woman, child, or infant sometime in the next few months, surgeons will implant another heart or liver from a baboon or perhaps even a pig into a human body. Then, two things will happen. Doctors will decide whether the recipient will use the animal organ as a "bridge," until a human organ can be located for transplant, or if the patient will keep the animal organ as a permanent transplant. Second, animal-rights activists will picket the hospital where the medical miracle took place.

> Richard Pothier, "Animal Tests Saved My Life"

Beginning with a Question (or a Series of Questions)

Using one or more questions at the beginning of your essay is an effective introductory strategy. Because readers expect you to answer the questions in your essay, they will want to read further. Notice how two questions in the following introduction catch the reader's eye.

> Imagine this scene: A child is sitting under a Christmas tree opening her presents. She laughs and claps her hands as she gets a doll, a pair of shoes, and a sweater. What could spoil this picture? What information could cause the child's parents to feel guilt? The answer is this: <u>that children from developing countries probably worked long hours in substandard conditions so this American child could receive her gifts.</u>

Megan Davia (student)

Beginning with a Definition

A definition at the beginning of your essay can give valuable information to readers. Such information can explain a confusing concept or clarify a complicated idea, as the following paragraph demonstrates.

> The term *good parent* is not easy to define. Some things about being a good parent are obvious—keeping your children safe, taking them to the dentist for regular checkups, helping them with their homework, being there for them when they want to talk, and staying up at night with them when they are sick, for example. Other things are not so obvious, however. I found this out last year when I became a volunteer at my daughter's middle school. <u>Up until that time, I never would have dreamed that one morning a week could do so much to improve my daughter's attitude toward school.</u>

Russ Hightower (student)

FOCUS   **Beginning with a Definition**

Don't introduce a definition with a tired opening phrase such as "According to *Webster's* . . ." or "*The American Heritage Dictionary* defines . . ."

Beginning with a Background Statement

A background statement can provide an overview of a subject and set the stage for the discussion to follow. It can also—as the following introduction illustrates—help prepare readers for a surprising or controversial thesis statement.

English is the most widely spoken language in the history of our planet, used in some way by at least one out of every seven human beings around the globe. Half of the world's books are written in English, and the majority of international telephone calls are made in English. English is the language of over sixty percent of the world's radio programs, many of them beamed, ironically, by the Russians, who know that to win friends and influence nations, they're best off using English. More than seventy percent of international mail is written and addressed in English, and eighty percent of all computer text is stored in English. English has acquired the largest vocabulary of all the world's languages, perhaps as many as two million words, and has generated one of the noblest bodies of literature in the annals of the human race. Nonetheless, it is now time to face the fact that English is a crazy language.

Richard Lederer, "English Is a Crazy Language"

Beginning with a Quotation

An appropriate saying or an interesting piece of dialogue can immediately draw readers into your essay. Notice how the quotation below creates interest and leads smoothly and logically into the thesis statement at the end of the introduction.

According to the comedian Jerry Seinfeld, "When you're single, you are the dictator of your own life. . . . When you're married, you are part of a vast decision-making body." In other words, before you can do anything, you have to discuss it with someone else. These words kept going through my mind as I thought about asking my girlfriend to marry me. The more I thought about Seinfeld's words, the more I hesitated. I never suspected that I would pay a price for my indecision.

Dan Brody (student)

FOCUS Titles

Every essay you write should have a **title**. Like an introduction, a title should suggest the subject of your essay and make people want to read further. Before you choose a title, be sure to reread your paper (especially your thesis statement).

■ A title can be a straightforward announcement.

How Your Body Works

■ A title can be a question.

Is a Tree Worth a Life?

(continued on the following page)

(continued from the previous page)

■ A title can be an announcement of a controversial position.

The Case against Animal Testing

■ A title can establish a personal connection with readers.

Animal Tests Saved My Life

■ A title can offer an unusual perspective.

Showering with Your Dog

■ A title can be a paraphrase or quotation of a familiar saying or a quotation from your essay itself.

An Offer I Couldn't Refuse

My Absolutely Worst Day Ever

Just Do It

■ A title can relate to the method of development used in the essay.

Three Ways to Make Your Neighborhood Better (exemplification)

The Rise and Fall of Doo-Wop (narrative)

My Grandfather (description)

How to Write an Effective Résumé (process)

Why the Titanic Sank (cause and effect)

Four-Year vs. Two-Year Colleges (comparison and contrast)

Types of Sports Fans (classification)

What It Means to Be Happy (definition)

Let's Stop Persecuting Smokers (argument)

■ WRITING FIRST: Flashback

Look back at your response to the Writing First exercise on page 127. Evaluate your introduction. Does it prepare readers for the essay to follow? Does it include a thesis statement? Is it likely to interest readers? On a separate sheet of paper, draft a different opening paragraph using one of the options presented in 13A. Be

(continued on the following page)

(continued from the previous page) sure to include a clear thesis statement. In the space provided, indicate the kind of introduction you have drafted.

After you have finished drafting a new introduction, think of a new title that will attract your readers' attention. (Use one of the options listed in the Focus box on page 130.) In the space provided, indicate the option you used, and write your new title.

Option used for new introduction: _____

New title: _____

Option used for new title: _____

B   Conclusions

Because your **conclusion** is the last thing readers see, they often judge your entire essay by the effectiveness of the conclusion. For this reason, conclusions should be planned, drafted, and revised with care. Like an introduction, a conclusion is usually a full paragraph.

Your conclusion should give readers a sense of completion. One way you can accomplish this is by restating the essay's thesis. Keep in mind, however, that a conclusion is more than a word-for-word restatement of the thesis. If you return to your thesis here, you should summarize it, expand on it, and make some general concluding remarks; then, end with a sentence that readers will remember.

FOCUS   Essay Exams

In essay exams, when time is limited, a one-sentence restatement of your thesis is often enough for a conclusion. Likewise, an in-class essay exam may require just a one- or two-sentence introduction. (See Appendix A, "Writing Paragraphs and Essays for Exams.")

Here are some options you can experiment with when you write your conclusions.

Concluding with a Restatement of Your Thesis

This no-nonsense conclusion reinforces your essay's most important ideas by restating your thesis in different words and reviewing the main points of the discussion.

In 1994, voters' concerns about high taxes, increased welfare costs, and the huge national debt helped propel the Republicans into the House and the Senate. Republican candidates used these issues to exploit the public's distrust of government. For their part, voters did not seem to care that taxes were not as high as they were in the 1960s and 1970s, that welfare costs were a small part of federal spending, or that the national debt was lower than it had been just two years before.

Serge Komanawski (student)

Concluding with a Narrative

A narrative conclusion can bring an event discussed in the essay to a logical, satisfying close. The following conclusion uses a narrative to tie up the essay's loose ends.

After twenty years, the tree began to bear. Although Grandfather complained about how much he lost because pollen never reached the poor part of town, because at the market he had to haggle over the price of avocados, he loved that tree. It grew, as did his family, and when he died, all his sons standing on each other's shoulders, oldest to youngest, could not reach the highest branches. The wind could move the branches, but the trunk, thicker than any waist, hugged the ground.

Gary Soto, "The Grandfather"

Concluding with a Question (or a Series of Questions)

By ending with a question, you leave readers with something to think about. The question should build on the thesis statement and not introduce any new issues. Notice how the conclusion below asks a series of questions before restating the essay's thesis.

Why is it that when the sun or the moon or the stars are out, they are visible, but when the lights are out, they are invisible, and that when I wind up my watch, I start it, but when I wind up this essay, I shall end it? English is a crazy language.

Richard Lederer, "English Is a Crazy Language"

FOCUS **Conclusions**

Overused phrases that announce your essay is coming to a close—for example, *in summary* or *in conclusion*—are unnecessary and can be annoying. Try to avoid them. Also avoid words and phrases that weaken your readers' confidence in you, such as "I may not be an expert," "at least that's my opinion," and "I could be wrong, but . . ."

Concluding with a Prediction

This type of conclusion not only sums up the thesis but also looks to the future. The following conclusion uses this technique to paint a troubling picture of the future of American cities.

> On that little street were the ghosts of the people who brought me into being and the flesh-and-blood kids who will be my children's companions in the twenty-first century. You could tell by their eyes that they couldn't figure out why I was there. They were accustomed to being ignored, even by the people who had once populated their rooms. And as long as that continues, our cities will burst and burn, burst and burn, over and over again.
>
> Anna Quindlen, "The Old Block"

Concluding with a Recommendation

Once you think you have convinced readers that a problem exists, you can make recommendations in your conclusion about how the problem should be solved. Notice how the following paragraph makes a series of recommendations about a cancer drug made from the Pacific yew tree.

> Every effort should be made to ensure that the yew tree is made available for the continued research and development of taxol. Environmental groups, the timber industry, and the Forest Service must recognize that the most important value of the Pacific yew is as a treatment for cancer. At the same time, its harvest can be managed in a way that allows for the production of taxol without endangering the continual survival of the yew tree.
>
> Sally Thane Christensen, "Is a Tree Worth a Life?"

Concluding with a Quotation

▼ **Student Voices**
I like to end my essays with a quotation from the book I'm writing about.
Meredith Krall

Frequently, a well-chosen quotation—even a brief one—can add a lot to your essay. In some cases, a quotation can add authority to your ideas. In others, as in the following paragraph, the quotation can reinforce the main point of the essay.

> It was 4:25 a.m. when the ambulance arrived to take the body of Miss Genovese. It drove off. "Then," a solemn police detective said, "the people came out."
>
> Martin Gansberg, "Thirty-Eight Who Saw Murder Didn't Call the Police"

FOCUS **Introductions and Conclusions**

The content of your introduction and conclusion depends on the points you make in the body of your essay. For this reason, you

(continued on the following page)

(continued from the previous page)
should draft the body paragraphs before you spend much time writing the introduction or conclusion. Once you see the direction in which your essay has developed, you can revise your introduction and conclusion so they are consistent in tone and content with the rest of your essay.

■ WRITING FIRST: Flashback

Look back at your response to the Writing First exercise on page 127. Evaluate your conclusion. Is it suitable for your topic and thesis? Does it bring your essay to a clear and satisfying close that will leave a strong impression on readers? On a separate sheet of paper, try drafting a different concluding paragraph using one of the options presented in 13B. In the space provided, indicate what kind of conclusion you have drafted.

Option used for new conclusion: _____

■ WRITING FIRST: Revising and Editing

Reread your responses to the Flashback exercise above and the one on page 131. Are the new paragraphs you wrote more effective than the introduction and conclusion you recopied for the Writing First exercise on page 127? If so, substitute them for the opening and closing paragraphs of the essay you wrote in Chapter 12.

CHAPTER REVIEW

◆ **EDITING PRACTICE**

The following student essay has an undeveloped introduction and conclusion. Decide what introductory and concluding strategies would be most appropriate for the essay, and, on a separate sheet of paper, rewrite both the introduction and the conclusion to make them more effective. Finally, try to think of an interesting title for the essay.

Geraldine Ferraro's life shows how someone who comes from a poor background can make a difference.

Geraldine Ferraro came from humble beginnings. Her father was an Italian immigrant who died when she was eight years old. Her mother supported the family by sewing beads on women's clothes. After graduating from college, Ferraro taught elementary school, worked as a legal secretary, and eventually graduated from law school.

Throughout the 1960s, Ferraro raised a family and practiced law on a part-time basis. Her cousin, who was a district attorney in Queens, New York, helped her get a job as an assistant district attorney. In 1978, when the congressional representative in her district retired, Ferraro ran for his seat and won. While in the House of Representatives, she worked tirelessly for the people in her district, and, as a result, she was reelected in 1980 and 1982. Because of her hard work and her involvement in party affairs, she was named chair of the Democratic National Committee in 1984.

At the 1984 Democratic National Convention, Ferraro was asked to be Walter Mondale's running mate. By accepting the nomination, Ferraro became the first woman to become a vice-presidential candidate from a major party. Ferraro was chosen for at least two reasons. First, she was a smart, aggressive campaigner. In addition, she could help the Democratic Party appeal to women, Catholics, and blue-collar workers. Throughout the campaign, she handled herself with dignity, responding well to attacks questioning her ability to lead. Although the Democrats were defeated, Ferraro's nomination established once and for all that women were a major force in American politics.

As Geraldine Ferraro's life shows, someone who comes from a poor family can work hard and make a difference.

◆ COLLABORATIVE ACTIVITIES

1. Bring into class several copies of an essay you wrote for another class. Have each person in your group comment on your essay's introduction and conclusion. Revise the introduction and conclusion in response to your classmates' suggestions.

2. Find a magazine or newspaper article that interests you. Cut off the introduction and conclusion and bring the body of the article to class. Ask your group to decide on the best strategy for introducing and concluding the article. Then, collaborate on writing new opening and closing paragraphs and an interesting title.

3. Working in a group, think of interesting and appropriate titles for essays on each of the following topics. Try to use as many of the different options outlined in the Focus box on page 130 as you can.

The high salaries of sports figures

The evils of gambling

The need for regular exercise

The joys of living in the city (or in the country)

The rights of gun owners

Gadgets that make life easier

Job interviews

Buying a car

Celebrating the holidays

Parents (or being a parent)

☑ REVIEW CHECKLIST:
Introductions and Conclusions

- The introduction of your essay should prepare readers for the ideas to follow and should include a thesis statement. It should also create interest. (See 13A.) You can begin an essay with any of the following.

A direct approach	A definition
A narrative	A background statement
A question	A quotation

- Your title should suggest the subject of your essay and make people want to read further. (See 13A.)

- The conclusion of your essay should restate the thesis and make some general concluding remarks. (See 13B.) You can conclude an essay with any of the following.

A restatement of the thesis	A prediction
A narrative	A recommendation
A question	A quotation

14

Patterns of Essay Development

As you learned in Chapters 3 through 11, writers have a variety of options for developing ideas within a paragraph. These options include *exemplification, narration, description, process, cause and effect, comparison and contrast, classification, definition,* and *argument.* When you write an essay, you can use these same strategies to organize your material.

In your college courses, different assignments and writing situations call for different patterns of essay development. For instance, if an exam question asked you to compare two systems of government, you would use *comparison and contrast* to structure your essay. If your lab manual asked you to explain the stages of a particular chemical reaction, you would use *process.* If an English composition assignment asked you to tell about a childhood experience, you would use *narration.* If a section of a research paper on environmental pollution called for examples of dangerous waste disposal practices, you would use *exemplification.*

Each section in this chapter defines and explains one pattern of essay development, gives examples of how it is used in typical college writing assignments, provides several options for organizing an essay, and includes a list of useful transitions. A student essay illustrates each pattern, and a list of writing topics and a Self-Assessment Checklist give you opportunities for practice and review.

As you move through this chapter, you may want to look back at Chapters 3–11, which explain and illustrate the various patterns of paragraph development.

A   Exemplification

For information on writing an exemplification paragraph, see Chapter 3.

Exemplification illustrates a general statement with specific examples that support it. An exemplification essay uses specific examples to support a thesis.

FOCUS **Topics for Exemplification**

The wording of your assignment may suggest exemplification—for example, by asking you to *illustrate* or to *give examples*.

Topic/Assignment

Education   Should children be taught only in their native languages or in English as well? Support your answer with an example of one student or one class.

Literature   Does *Othello* have to end tragically? Illustrate your position with references to specific characters.

Composition   Discuss the worst job you ever had. Include plenty of specific examples to support your thesis.

Thesis Statement

The success of students in a bilingual third-grade class suggests the value of teaching elementary-school students in English as well as in their native languages.

Each of the three major characters in *Othello* contributes to the play's tragic ending.

My summer job at a fast-food restaurant was my all-time worst job because of the endless stream of rude customers, the many boring and repetitive tasks I had to perform, and my manager's insensitive treatment of employees.

● **Writing Tip**
Many everyday writing tasks call for exemplification. In a parent committee report for your child's day-care center, you might present examples of environmental hazards in the school building.

In an exemplification essay, each body paragraph can present a single example or discuss several examples.

Options for Organizing Exemplification Essays

One Example per Paragraph	**Several Related Examples per Paragraph**
¶1 Introduction	¶1 Introduction
¶2 First example	¶2 First group of examples
¶3 Second example	¶3 Second group of examples
¶4 Third example	¶4 Third group of examples
¶5 Conclusion	¶5 Conclusion

All the examples you select should relate to your thesis, and your essay's topic sentences should make clear just how each example supports the thesis statement. In addition, transitional words and phrases should introduce each example and indicate the relationship between one example and another.

Also	In addition	The most impor-
Besides	Moreover	tant example
For example	One example . . .	The next example
For instance	Another example	
Furthermore	Specifically	

The following student essay, "Fighting Fire with Fire Safety Educa-tion" by Timothy E. Miles, uses a series of examples to illustrate the need to educate children about fire safety. Some paragraphs group several brief examples together; others develop a single example. Notice how Timothy uses clear topic sentences and helpful transitions to introduce his ex-amples and link them to one another.

Fighting Fire with Fire Safety Education

Since young children suffer more fire-related injuries and fatalities than most others do, fire safety education must be introduced at an early age. This can be done both by parents and by local fire departments. Fire safety for children is an ongoing concern, and adults must take the responsibility for educating and protecting them. `1`

What should small children be taught? First, they should understand what matches are and what the conse-quences of playing with them can be. They should be taught that matches are not toys and that they can cause great damage. Children should also be taught how to avoid contact burns from stove burners, hot liquids, and electrical appliances. `2`

Another essential part of fire safety education for children is learning how to extinguish fires once they have started. Many children are burned by their own clothing. The chance of injury can be prevented if they are taught how to "Stop, Drop, and Roll." One way of teaching this is for the adult to cut out a "flame" from paper and tape it lightly to the child. When the child actually stops, drops, and rolls on the ground, the "flame" will fall off, thereby "extinguishing" the "fire." `3`

Exit drills in the home can also save lives. These drills need to include information such as how to crawl low to escape smoke, how to feel for hot doors, and how `4` to place towels or clothing under doors to stop smoke from coming into a room. (Children should also understand that smoke and fumes, not the fire itself, cause most deaths.) The need for a meeting place where all family members can be accounted for is perhaps the most important thing to emphasize.

Making sure children know the fire department phone number is another way to reduce fire-related injuries and deaths. It is very important that children know the correct number because not all areas have a 911 system. The numbers of all emergency services should be posted near each phone. Children should know how to dial these numbers and should know the address from which they are calling. To practice reporting a fire, a child can use a toy phone, with an adult assuming the role of the operator.

Finally, children should be aware of what firefighters look like in their equipment. Some children, particularly very young ones, are afraid of firefighters because of their unfamiliar appearance. During a visit to any local firehouse, children can meet firefighters who can answer questions and demonstrate and explain their equipment and gear.

Of course, educating children is not enough in itself to ensure fire safety; parents and other adults must also educate themselves about what to do (and what not to do) if a fire actually occurs. For example, do not hide or go back into a fire for any reason. Have a meeting place where family members can be accounted for. Do not try to put out a fire; instead, have someone notify the fire department immediately. Also, adults should take the responsibility for getting children involved in fire prevention. Many children learn best by example. Handouts, displays, and videotapes are especially helpful. Demonstration and practice of exit drills in the home and of "Stop, Drop, and Roll" are also useful, particularly during special fire hazard periods such as Halloween and Christmas. Participating in drawing escape plans and making inspections of the home for potential problems also make children feel they are helping. In fact, children can sometimes see things that adults overlook.

By keeping these points in mind, children and their parents can join together to avoid potential disaster. If family members learn about fire safety and if they practice and review what they have learned on a regular basis, lives will be saved.

◆ **PRACTICE 14-1**

1. Underline the thesis of "Fighting Fire with Fire Safety Education."
   Restate it below in your own words.

   _____

   _____

2. (a) List the examples Tim uses to support his thesis. (b) Which examples does he group together? Why? (c) Which examples does he
   develop in paragraphs of their own? Why?

   _____

   _____

   _____

   _____

   _____

   _____

   _____

   _____

   _____

   _____

   _____

3. Underline the transitional words in each topic sentence that serve this
   purpose. How do Tim's topic sentences link paragraphs to one another?

   _____

   _____

4. Is the straightforward introduction effective? How else might Tim have
   opened his essay?

   _____

   _____

5. Is the conclusion effective? How else could Tim have ended his essay?

   _____

   _____

6. What is this essay's greatest strength? What is its greatest weakness?

Strength: _____

Weakness: _____

◆ PRACTICE 14-2

Following the writing process outlined in Chapter 12, write an exemplification essay on one of the following topics.

> Advantages (or disadvantages) of starting college right after high
>   school
> The three best things ever invented
> Who (or what) should appear on U.S. postage stamps? Why?
> Advantages (or disadvantages) of being a young parent
> Athletes who really are role models
> Four items (or qualities) students need to survive in college
> What messages do various rap artists send to listeners?

◆ PRACTICE 14-3

On a separate sheet of paper, explain how this advertisement appeals to its target audience. Is it effective? Why or why not? Begin by identifying the ad, the product it promotes, and the audience you think it hopes to reach. Then, state your thesis. After briefly describing the ad, give examples to support your thesis.

☑ SELF-ASSESSMENT CHECKLIST:
Writing an Exemplification Essay

- Does your introduction give readers a clear idea of what to expect? If not, revise your introduction to clarify your essay's goals.

- Does your essay include a clearly stated thesis? If not, revise your thesis statement to clarify your essay's main idea.

- Do all your examples support your thesis? Eliminate any irrelevant examples.

- Do you have enough examples to support your thesis? Add examples where necessary.

- Is each example clearly related to the essay's thesis? If not, reword your topic sentences to clarify the connection.

- Are your examples arranged logically? Rearrange them if necessary.

- Do transitional words and phrases clearly link your examples to one another? Add transitions where necessary.

- Does your conclusion sum up the main idea of your essay? If not, revise the conclusion to make this idea clear to readers.

- What problems did you experience in writing your essay? What would you do differently next time?

B Narration

For information on writing a narrative paragraph, see Chapter 4.

Narration tells a story, generally presenting a series of events in chronological (time) order, moving from beginning to end. A narrative essay can tell a personal story, or it can recount a recent or historical event or a fictional story.

FOCUS Topics for Narration

Sometimes, the wording of your assignment may suggest narration. For example, you may be asked to *tell*, *trace*, *summarize*, or *recount*.

Topic/Assignment	Thesis Statement
Composition Tell about a time when you had to show courage even though you were afraid.	Sometimes a person can exhibit great courage despite being afraid.

(continued on the following page)

● **Writing Tip**
Many everyday writing tasks call for narration. In a job application letter, you might summarize your previous work experience.

(continued from the previous page)

Topic/Assignment	Thesis Statement
American history Summarize the events that occurred during President Franklin Delano Roosevelt's first one hundred days in office.	Although many thought they were extreme, the measures enacted by Roosevelt during his first one hundred days in office were necessary to fight the effects of the economic depression.
Political science Trace the development of the Mississippi Freedom Democratic Party.	As the Mississippi Freedom Democratic Party developed, it found a voice that spoke for equality and justice.

When you write a narrative essay, you can present one event or several in each paragraph of your essay.

Options for Organizing Narrative Essays

One Event per Paragraph	Several Events per Paragraph
¶1 Introduction	¶1 Introduction
¶2 First event	¶2 First group of events
¶3 Second event	¶3 Second group of events
¶4 Third event	¶4 Third group of events
¶5 Conclusion	¶5 Conclusion

Sometimes, to add interest to your narrative, you may choose not to use exact chronological order. For example, you might begin with the end of your story and then move back to the beginning to trace the events that led to this outcome. Carefully worded topic sentences and clear transitional words and phrases will help readers follow your narrative.

FOCUS **Transitions for Narration**

After	First . . . Second . . .	Now
As soon as	Third	Soon
At the same time	Immediately	Then
Before	Later	Two days later
Earlier	Meanwhile	
Finally	Next	

The following student essay, "Swing Shift" by Mark Cotharn, is a narrative that relates the events of a day in the life of a police officer. Notice that Mark uses present tense to make his dramatic, emotional story more immediate. (Paragraph 3, which moves back in time to summarize events that occurred earlier in the week, uses past tense.) Transitional words and phrases help link events in chronological order, and the mention of specific days and times also helps keep readers on track.

Swing Shift

I'm home, safe within familiar walls. Surrounded by my wife and children, I sit at my kitchen table drinking a cold beer, trying to wake up. 1

Today is Thursday, and I've got to pull myself together long enough for one more shift. It's eleven o'clock in the morning, and I've got one hour to prepare mentally for work. This was such a crazy week, I'm not sure if I can. 2

Monday it was the guy on Weeping Willow who was cut up like a side of beef by two parolees. Later that evening, there was that seventeen-year-old boy who was stabbed to death by his friend. Tuesday brought a father angry at me for giving his kid a citation. The kid didn't tell his old man I threw a bag of dope away, to give him a second chance. Wednesday was the triple gangland execution on Holley. I will never forget the way Teto Gomez looked with most of his head gone or the way his brains decorated the yellow rose bush. But the worst part of that case was doing CPR on Robert Berassa, who had been shot fourteen times. He was wearing a white T-shirt that was turning crimson. Every time I compressed on his chest, my shirt turned crimson, too. It was too late; Robert was dead. 3

I finish my beer and make my way to the station. Only God can know what the day's events will bring, but I really hope it won't be much. 4

After a short briefing, I begin my shift on patrol. Within minutes, I find myself in pursuit of an armed robbery suspect carrying several handguns and some dynamite. I chase him through the city for almost twelve minutes, at speeds exceeding a hundred miles per hour, before his van quits running and comes to a stop. 5

I stop my unit behind his van. Then, with shotgun in hand, I make my way to approximately twenty feet away from his door. I repeat commands for him to put his hands up, but he won't listen to me. Instead, he opens his door and charges me. I see that he has something in his hand, but I can't tell what it is. I hear two loud booms. The suspect falls to the ground in a pool of blood. Confused, I feel the rotorwash of a helicopter twenty feet over my head and hear the wail of approaching police cars. Still, I don't understand why the suspect dropped so suddenly until I see smoke rising from 6 the barrel of my shotgun. The suspect is dead, clutching a stick of dynamite.

Unable to let go of my professionalism in public, I detach myself from all emotions or feelings. Many fellow officers come to me and call me Stud, Killer, Ice Man, Exterminator; others come to me and congratulate me on a job well done. 7

Heading back to the station, I turn off the radio and listen to the silence of my thoughts. I know when I get there I will be read my rights and interviewed like a common crook. What did I do wrong? 8

As I expected, I'm met at the door by a shooting team from Internal Affairs. These guys are serious about their job. If the team can find a reason to convict me, they will. The interrogation is lengthy; I'm exhausted. Twelve hours or so have gone by, and the questions are still coming. I recognize the interrogation technique because it's the same one I use. 9

It's three o'clock in the morning. The shooting team is done with me, and I'm headed out the door for home when my chief tells me to go upstairs and talk to the department shrink. Why? I don't need a shrink; I need sleep. 10

The shrink is asking me stupid questions like "How do you feel?" and "Are you going to be OK?" What am I supposed to say? No? I tell her I'm just fine and that I'll be back to work in two days. 11

Finally, on my way home, alone in my car, I come to. My palms sweat; my chest constricts; my pulse hammers. My mind races back to the intersection of Citrus and Arrow. I can see his face; he's laughing at me. I hear two crisp booms and see him fall. 12

◆ PRACTICE 14-4

1. What is the thesis of "Swing Shift"? Restate the thesis in your own words.

_____

_____

2. Underline the specific transitional words and phrases and the references to days and times that Mark uses to link events in chronological order.

3. Where does Mark mention specific days and times?

_____

_____

_____

4. What specific events and situations support Mark's thesis? List as many as you can.

_____

_____

_____

5. Do you think Mark's essay should have a longer, more fully developed opening paragraph, or do you like the introduction he has? Why?

_____

_____

_____

6. Do you think Mark's conclusion should summarize the events his essay discusses, or is his conclusion effective? Why?

_____

_____

_____

7. What is this essay's greatest strength? What is its greatest weakness?

Strength: _____

Weakness: _____

◆ PRACTICE 14-5

Following the writing process outlined in Chapter 12, write a narrative essay on one of the following topics.

An ideal day
The plot summary of a terrible book or movie
An event you wish had never happened
Your first confrontation with authority
An important historical event
A day everything went wrong

◆ PRACTICE 14-6

On a separate sheet of paper, write a narrative essay that tells the story behind the picture on the following page.

Scene from a movie from the early 1900s in which the heroine narrowly escapes from a variety of perilous situations.

☑ SELF-ASSESSMENT CHECKLIST:
Writing a Narrative Essay

- Does your introduction make your purpose clear to readers? Does it set the scene and introduce important characters? Develop your opening paragraph further if you need to.

- Does your essay include an explicitly stated thesis? Does it need one? If necessary, revise your essay to make its main idea clear.

- Have you included all the specific events you need? Add material if necessary.

- Do you discuss any irrelevant events? If necessary, revise your essay to eliminate irrelevant material.

- Are all the events you discuss logically connected to your thesis statement? If necessary, revise your essay to clarify the relationship of each event to your essay's main idea.

- Are the events you discuss arranged in clear chronological order? Rearrange events if necessary to reflect the order in which they occurred.

- Do topic sentences and transitional words and phrases make the sequence of events clear? Revise if necessary to clarify this sequence.

(continued on the following page)

> *(continued from the previous page)*
>
> ☐ Does your conclusion remind readers why you have told them your story? If necessary, revise your conclusion to make your purpose clear.
>
> ☐ What problems did you experience in writing your essay? What would you do differently next time?

C Description

For information on writing a descriptive paragraph, see Chapter 5.

Description tells what something looks, sounds, smells, tastes, or feels like. A descriptive essay uses details to give readers a clear, vivid picture of a person, place, or object.

● **Writing Tip**
Many everday writing tasks call for description. In a statement to your insurance company after an automobile accident, you might describe damage to your car.

FOCUS Topics for Description

Sometimes your assignment suggests description. For example, it may ask you to *describe* or to *tell what an object looks like*.

Topic/Assignment	Thesis Statement
Composition Describe a room that was important to you when you were a child.	Pink-and-white striped wallpaper, tall shelves of cuddly stuffed animals, and the smell of Oreos dominated the bedroom I shared with my sister.
Scientific writing Describe a piece of scientific equipment.	The mass spectrometer is a complex instrument, but every part is ideally suited to its purpose.
Art history Choose one modern painting and describe its visual elements.	The strange images crowded together in Picasso's *Guernica* suggest the senselessness of war.

When you plan a descriptive essay, focus on selecting details that help your readers see what you see. Your goal is to create a single **dominant impression**, a central theme or idea to which all the details relate. This dominant impression unifies the description and gives readers an overall sense of what the person, object, or scene looks like (and perhaps what it sounds, smells, tastes, or feels like). Sometimes—but not always—your details will support a thesis, making a point about the subject you are describing.

You can arrange details in many different ways. For example, you can move from least to most important details (or vice versa). You can also move from top to bottom (or from bottom to top or side to side)—or from far to near (or near to far). Each of your essay's body paragraphs may focus on one key characteristic or on several related descriptive details.

Options for Organizing Descriptive Essays

Least to Most Important	Top to Bottom	Far to Near
¶1 Introduction	¶1 Introduction	¶1 Introduction
¶2 Least important details	¶2 Details at top	¶2 Distant details
¶3 More important details	¶3 Details in middle	¶3 Closer details
¶4 Most important details	¶4 Details on bottom	¶4 Closest details
¶5 Conclusion	¶5 Conclusion	¶5 Conclusion

When you describe a person, object, or scene, you can use **objective description**, reporting only what your senses of sight, sound, smell, taste, and touch tell you ("The columns were two feet tall and made of white marble"). You can also use **subjective description**, conveying your attitude or your feelings about what you observe ("The columns were tall and powerful looking, and their marble surface seemed as smooth as a glacier"). Many essays combine the two kinds of description.

Descriptive writing, particularly subjective description, is frequently enriched by *figures of speech*—language that creates special or unusual effects.

- A **simile** uses *like* or *as* to compare two unlike things.

  Her smile was like sunshine.

- A **metaphor** compares two unlike things without using *like* or *as*.

  The fog comes / on little cat feet. (Carl Sandburg)

- **Personification** suggests a comparison between a nonliving thing and a person by giving the nonliving thing human traits.

  The wind howled.

As you write, use transitional words and expressions to guide readers through your description. (Many of these transitions are prepositions or other words and phrases that indicate location or distance.)

The following student essay, "African Violet" by Alisha Woolery, uses description to create a portrait of a family member. By combining subjective and objective description and using specific visual details, Alisha conveys a vivid impression of her great-grandmother as physically frail yet emotionally spirited.

African Violet

The black-and-white picture of my great-grand-parents is a picture I often bring into my mind when I have decided to look at the "big picture" of life and think all the "deep thoughts." I see their faces, etched into the contrasting grays, so young, so hopeful for their new lives together. My mind then shifts to a more recent picture of my great-grandma with her small, frail body, which in the end gave her more pain than she could handle. I often question the justice of aging, but I also realize, perhaps in not so many words, how much she taught me about life and death--and about everything in between. 1

My great-grandfather died when I was quite young, and I have only a faint memory of riding his foot like a horse while he recited "Banbury Cross." I have to create an image of him from my relatives' fond memories. Fortunately, however, I knew my great-grandma well, and the conversations we had are among my favorite memories of her. I particularly recall her telling me one of the numerous stories of her youth. 2

"One time I was getting to be about sixteen years old, and there was this boy who asked me on a picnic." Her eyes brightened as she told her story. "He was older than me, and he had a horse and buggy! And Whoowee! That was really something." 3

The look of astonishment on my face must have been apparent because we laughed until I thought we would 4 keel over. There she was, ninety years old, with absolutely no teeth, telling me how hot this boy who'd asked her out was. It was then I realized that the eyes looking out from her aging face were the same brown eyes that had flirted with boys, had fallen in love, and had seen her children and her children's children's children. She had years of experience, and I had very little, but on that warm summer evening, as we sat in her living room, her story bridged the gap between generations.

Besides my great-grandma's love of telling stories about her life to others, her one true passion was her plants. She loved them all, but her favorites were small plants with dark green leaves and purple blossoms: African violets. I didn't inherit her green thumb, so the miracles she worked with plants were a constant wonder to me. Stems and leaves seemed to flourish under her gentle touch. Plants were her pride and joy, and until she was in her mid-eighties you could still see her, on hands and knees, digging around in the dirt in her front yard.

No, Grandma didn't resign herself to age and let life pass her by; she rode it for all it was worth. This enthusiasm was also apparent in her driving. The woman was a traffic hazard, not because she poked along as so many older folks do but because she was a speed demon! Poised for action, Grandma strapped herself into her brown 1972 Nova and sped out toward destinations unknown, with one foot on the gas and the other on the brake. (I am sure she followed the basic traffic laws most of the time, or at least I think so.)

I suppose by all laws of nature, her driving escapades should have done her in, but Grandma died a peaceful death with quiet resolution and acceptance. In fact, she probably had a better outlook on the whole thing than anyone else in the family. She was the closest person to me to die, so it was especially difficult for me to accept that our talks were simply over. I was fifteen at the time and wrote a poem entitled "African Violet," expressing the idea that I didn't feel it was time for her to leave me.

It wasn't until recently that I realized that even by her dying, Grandma was continuing to teach me about life. I saw how bravely she dealt with the increasing pain in her legs as her body deteriorated and how, when she took her last breath, it came as almost a relief to her. I had never thought about death in this way, and she made me question many things about life that I had never truly thought about.

The memories of my great-grandma are very important 9
to me, and sometimes it scares me when a detail escapes
my mind because remembering our time together and what
I've learned from her is all I have left of her. It is
virtually impossible to communicate the impact she has
had on me. The only way I feel I can repay her is by
telling about her ideas and stories, keeping her memory
alive in a legacy of wisdom and laughter.

◆ PRACTICE 14-7

1. What dominant impression of her great-grandmother does Alisha convey to readers?

_____

_____

2. List the specific visual details Alisha uses to convey her essay's dominant impression. What other details could she have included?

_____

_____

_____

_____

3. What determines the order in which details are presented in this essay? How else might Alisha have arranged details?

_____

_____

_____

4. Is this essay primarily a subjective or an objective description?

_____

5. What is this essay's greatest strength? What is its greatest weakness?

Strength: _____

Weakness: _____

◆ PRACTICE 14-8

Following the writing process outlined in Chapter 12, write a descriptive essay on one of the following topics.

An abandoned building   A street, road, or highway
Your supervisor   A painting

A person or character who makes you laugh (or frightens you)	A historical site or monument An advertisement

◆ PRACTICE 14-9

On a separate sheet of paper, write a real-estate brochure for the house pictured here, using your imagination to describe its setting, exterior, and interior in detail. Your goal in this descriptive essay is to provide enough positive details to interest a prospective buyer.

☑ SELF-ASSESSMENT CHECKLIST:
Writing a Descriptive Essay

☐ Does your introduction identify the subject of your description and convey your essay's dominant impression? Revise your introduction if necessary to clarify your essay's focus.

☐ Do you describe every significant aspect of your subject in detail? If necessary, add specific visual details to create a more complete, more vivid picture.

☐ Do all the details in your essay support your dominant impression? Eliminate any irrelevant details.

☐ Are your details arranged logically within paragraphs? Rearrange them if necessary.

(continued on the following page)

14 D

(continued from the previous page)

☐ Do topic sentences and transitional words and phrases move readers smoothly from one part of your subject to another? Reword topic sentences and add transitions where necessary.

☐ Does your conclusion leave readers with a clear sense of your essay's purpose? Revise if necessary to reinforce the dominant impression you want your description to convey.

☐ What problems did you experience in writing your essay? What would you do differently next time?

D **Process**

For information on writing a process paragraph, see Chapter 6.

A **process** is a series of chronological steps that produces a particular result. Process essays explain the steps in a procedure, telling how something is (or was) done. A process essay can be organized as either a *process explanation* or a set of *instructions*.

FOCUS **Topics for Process**

● **Writing Tip**
Many everyday writing tasks describe a process. In a training manual for new employees at your place of work, you might explain how to operate a piece of equipment or what to do in an emergency.

The wording of your assignment may suggest process. For example, you may be asked to *explain a process*, *give instructions*, *give directions*, or *give a step-by-step account*.

Topic/Assignment	Thesis Statement
American government Explain the process by which a bill becomes a law.	The process by which a bill becomes a law is long and complex, involving numerous revisions and a great deal of compromise.
Pharmacy practice Summarize the procedure for conducting a clinical trial of a new drug.	To ensure that drugs are safe and effective, scientists follow strict procedural guidelines for testing and evaluating them.
Technical writing Write a set of instructions for applying for a student internship in a state agency.	The process of applying for an internship requires that students follow a few important steps.

If your purpose is just to help readers understand a process, you will write a process explanation. **Process explanations**, like the first two examples in the Focus box above, often use present tense verbs ("Once a bill *is* introduced in Congress" or "A scientist first *submits* a funding application") to explain how a procedure is generally carried out. However, when a process explanation describes a specific procedure that was completed in the past, it uses past tense verbs ("The next thing I *did*").

If your purpose is to enable readers to actually perform the steps in a process, you will write instructions. **Instructions**, like the last example in the Focus box on page 156, always use present tense verbs in the form of commands to tell readers what to do ("First, *meet* with your adviser"). Whichever kind of process essay you write, you can either devote a full paragraph to each step of the process or group a series of minor steps together in a single paragraph.

Options for Organizing Process Essays

One Step per Paragraph	**Several Steps per Paragraph**
¶1 Introduction	¶1 Introduction
¶2 First step in process	¶2 First group of steps
¶3 Second step in process	¶3 Second group of steps
¶4 Third step in process	¶4 Third group of steps
¶5 Conclusion	¶5 Conclusion

As you write your process essay, discuss each step in the order in which it is performed, making sure your topic sentences clearly identify the function of each step or group of steps. If you are writing instructions, be sure to include any warnings or reminders you believe are necessary.

Transitions are extremely important in process essays because they enable readers to follow the sequence of steps in the process and, if necessary, to perform the process themselves.

FOCUS **Transitions for Process**

After that	Next	Then
As	Now	The next step
As soon as	Once	When
At the same time	Soon	While
Finally	Subsequently	
Immediately	The first (second,	
Later	third) step	
Meanwhile	The last step	

The following student essay, Mai Yoshikawa's "Under Water," explains the process of scuba diving. Because Mai did not think her readers would be likely to have the opportunity to try scuba diving, she did not write her essay in the form of instructions. Instead, she wrote a process explanation, using present tense verbs. Notice how clear transitions move readers smoothly through the steps of the process.

Under Water

For most people, their first scuba-diving experience in the ocean does not turn out to be a very good one, and so it was with me. Because I rushed to see the beauty of the seascape, I wasted oxygen and didn't pay much attention to the instructor. Unexpected dangers lie under water, and most first-time divers, like me, are unaware of the risk they are taking when they enter this other world. Now, as a more experienced diver, I have learned that I need to protect myself from trouble by having the right equipment and knowing how to use it well.

To ensure a safe dive, you need some basic equipment: an air tank, fins, snorkel, mask, life vest, weight belt, gloves, regulator, pressure and depth gauges, and, occasionally, a wetsuit. The weight belt maintains the diver's neutral buoyancy; therefore, the number of weights a person carries will vary. While I am floating under water, the weight belt and the air pressure work together to enable me to stay at a certain depth without moving up and down. The lighter the diver, the more weights he or she needs. The nylon socks keep my fins from slipping and help me avoid foot injuries. The pressure and depth gauges are connected to the tank where I can easily reach them and check to make sure the numbers on the two instruments correspond. The gauges are set to notify me how deep I can swim with the amount of oxygen left in my tank. Once I get all this equipment and check it, I plan the day's activities and routes with the instructor. The instructor, at that point, becomes my "buddy."

In order to reduce the risk of accidents, a thorough, careful equipment check must be done. If there are more than two divers, each person pairs up with another person. Usually someone who has had a lot of experience and knows the significance of the inspection, such as an assistant instructor or the owner of the dive shop, is available to help the amateur divers get set up.

Using the buddy system is extremely important. I check my partner's equipment and make sure every part is in gear, and she checks mine as well. I make sure that the mask fits my buddy's face and that no hair is caught in the rubber lining because any space will allow water to enter. I pull the string on her life vest, examine the jacket as the air inflates, and listen to make sure it holds the air with no leak. Next, I place the regulator in my mouth, and I try breathing for a

1

2

3

4

while as the oxygen from the tank flows into me each
time I inhale. Finally, I open the valve of the tank to
its fullest so that my partner will get enough oxygen as
she dives.

As I check to make sure my equipment is working, I 5
get tense and nervous, thinking about possible accidents
that, in the worst situation, could kill me. Once this
serious phase is finished, however, I am ready for the
main event of the day. Usually, the group dive lasts for
two or three separate periods, each consisting of
approximately twenty to forty minutes. Changing diving
spots after every swim gives me the opportunity to enjoy
different scenery. On lucky days, I can see rare, enor-
mous fish that I never dreamt of viewing except on the
television screen. In most cases, the instructors give
us permission to feed these fish.

Scuba diving is an exciting, breathtaking sport, no 6
matter how many times I experience it. I have learned
that I have to be very careful and responsible about the
actions I take both before and after I enter the water.
But once I start swimming deep into the ocean, I feel
so small, yet so free. The fear and panic disappear from
my mind with the bubbles of oxygen that flow out from
my regulator with my very own, short-winded human breath
as it echoes in my ears.

◆ PRACTICE 14-10

1. List the steps in the process of scuba diving. Does the writer present
   them in strict chronological order?

   _____

   _____

   _____

2. What identifies Mai's essay as a process explanation rather than a set
   of instructions?

   _____

   _____

3. Underline some of the transitional words and phrases that link the
   steps in the process. Are any other transitions needed?

   _____

   _____

4. Does Mai's essay have an explicitly stated thesis? Express the essay's thesis in your own words.

_____

_____

_____

_____

5. Why does Mai open her essay with a negative experience? Is this an effective opening strategy?

_____

_____

_____

_____

_____

_____

6. What is the essay's greatest strength? What is its greatest weakness?

Strength: _____

Weakness: _____

◆ PRACTICE 14-11

Following the writing process outlined in Chapter 12, write a process essay on one of the following topics. (Note: Before you begin, decide whether a process explanation or a set of instructions will be more appropriate for your purpose.)

College registration
Finding an apartment
Applying for a job
Getting dressed for a costume
  party

A do-it-yourself project that
  didn't get done
Your own writing process
A self-improvement program
  (past, present, or future)

◆ PRACTICE 14-12

Examine the two humorous cartoons by Rube Goldberg that appear on page 161. The first cartoon illustrates a ridiculously complex way of performing a simple task: moth extermination. The caption below the cartoon lists the steps in the process.

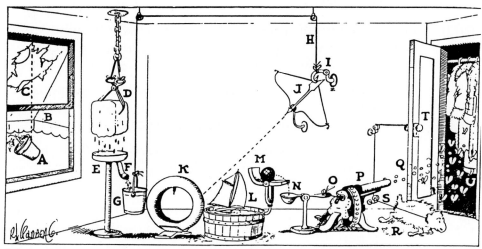

THE PROFESSOR EMERGES FROM THE GOOFY BOOTH WITH A DEVICE FOR THE EXTERMINATION OF MOTHS.
START SINGING. LADY UPSTAIRS, WHEN SUFFICIENTLY ANNOYED, THROWS FLOWER POT(A) THROUGH AWNING(B). HOLE(C) ALLOWS SUN TO COME THROUGH AND MELT CAKE OF ICE(D). WATER DRIPS INTO PAN(E) RUNNING THROUGH PIPE(F) INTO PAIL(G). WEIGHT OF PAIL CAUSES CORD(H) TO RELEASE HOOK(I) AND ALLOW ARROW(J) TO SHOOT INTO TIRE (K). ESCAPING AIR BLOWS AGAINST TOY SAILBOAT(L) DRIVING IT AGAINST LEVER(M) AND CAUSING BALL TO ROLL INTO SPOON(N) AND PULL STRING(O) WHICH SETS OFF MACHINE GUN(P) DISCHARGING CAMPHOR BALLS(Q). REPORT OF GUN FRIGHTENS LAMB(R) WHICH RUNS AND PULLS CORD(S), OPENING CLOSET DOOR(T). AS MOTHS(U) FLY OUT TO EAT WOOL FROM LAMB'S BACK THEY ARE KILLED BY THE BARRAGE OF MOTH BALLS.
IF ANY OF THE MOTHS ESCAPE AND THERE IS DANGER OF THEIR RETURNING, YOU CAN FOOL THEM BY MOVING.

Rube Goldberg™ © *Rube Goldberg Inc. Distributed by United Media.*

Here is another Rube Goldberg cartoon, this one without a caption. Write an essay based on this cartoon, giving a set of instructions for how to operate an automated back scratcher. Then, rewrite your set of instructions as a process explanation.

Rube Goldberg™ © *Rube Goldberg Inc. Distributed by United Media.*

☑ SELF-ASSESSMENT CHECKLIST:
Writing a Process Essay

☐ Does your introduction identify the process you will discuss and indicate its purpose? Revise your introduction if necessary to clarify your purpose.

☐ Is your essay a process explanation or a set of instructions? If your strategy is not appropriate for your essay's purpose, rewrite the essay using a different strategy.

☐ Does your thesis statement present an overview of the process? If not, revise the statement to make it as clear and specific as you can.

☐ Do you include every important step in the process? If not, add steps that will help readers understand (or perform) the process.

☐ Are all the steps you present necessary? Delete any irrelevant or unimportant ones.

☐ Are the steps in the process presented in strict chronological order? Rearrange any that are out of order.

☐ Are individual steps grouped logically into paragraphs? If not, revise to make each paragraph unified.

☐ Do topic sentences clearly identify major stages in the process? Do they clarify the function of each step or group of steps? Revise topic sentences as necessary.

☐ Do transitional words and phrases clarify the relationship between steps? If necessary, add transitions to make connections clear.

☐ Have you included all necessary warnings or reminders? Add cautions or clarifications as needed.

☐ Does your conclusion effectively sum up your process? Revise as necessary to clarify your purpose.

☐ What problems did you experience in writing your essay? What would you do differently next time?

E Cause and Effect

For information on writing a cause-and-effect paragraph, see Chapter 7.

A **cause** makes something happen; an **effect** is a result of a particular cause or event. Cause-and-effect essays identify causes or predict effects; sometimes they do both.

The wording of your assignment may suggest cause and effect. For example, the assignment may ask you to *explain why*, *predict the outcome*, *list contributing factors*, *discuss the consequences*, or tell what *caused* something else or how something is *affected* by something else.

Topic/Assignment	Thesis Statement
Women's studies What factors contributed to the rise of the women's movement in the 1970s?	The women's movement had its origins in the peace and civil rights movements of the 1960s.
Public health Discuss the possible long-term effects of smoking.	In addition to its physical effects, smoking may also have long-term social and emotional consequences.
Media and society How has television affected the lives of those who have grown up with it?	Television has created a generation of people who learn differently from those in previous generations.

● **Writing Tip**
Many everyday writing tasks involve discussing causes and effects. In a letter to your community's zoning board, you might discuss possible consequences of building a road, mall, or multiplex.

A cause-and-effect essay can focus on causes or on effects. When you write about causes, be sure to examine *all* pertinent causes. Focus on the cause you consider the most important, and don't forget to consider other causes that may be relevant to your topic. Similarly, when you write about effects, consider *all* significant effects of a particular cause, not just the first few that you think of.

If your focus is on finding causes, as it is in the first assignment in the Focus box above, your introductory paragraph should identify the effect (the women's movement). If your focus is on predicting effects, as it is in the second and third assignments listed above, begin by identifying the cause (smoking, television). In the body of your essay, you can devote a full paragraph to each cause (or effect), or you can group several related causes (or effects) together in each paragraph.

▼ **Student Voices**
I like writing about real-life situations. My essay about binge drinking on college campuses allowed me to express my views about underage drinking and also learn how widespread it is.
Jennifer Loucks

● **Writing Tip**
Be careful not to confuse *affect* (usually a verb) and *effect* (usually a noun) in your cause-and-effect essays. (See 34E.)

Options for Organizing Cause-and-Effect Essays

Identifying Causes	**Predicting Effects**
¶1 Introduction (identifies effect)	¶1 Introduction (identifies cause)
¶2 First cause	¶2 First effect
¶3 Second cause	¶3 Second effect
¶4 Third (and most important) cause	¶4 Third (and most important) effect
¶5 Conclusion	¶5 Conclusion

Transitions are important in cause-and-effect essays because they establish causal connections, telling readers that A caused B and not the other way around. They also make it clear that events have a *causal* relationship (A *caused* B) and not just a *sequential* one (A *preceded* B). Remember, when one event follows another, the second is not necessarily the result of the first.

FOCUS **Transitions for Cause and Effect**

Accordingly	For this reason	The most impor-
Another cause	Since	tant cause
Another effect	So	The most impor-
As a result	The first (second,	tant effect
Because	third) cause	Therefore
Consequently	The first (second,	
For	third) effect	

The following student essay, "How My Parents' Separation Changed My Life" by Andrea DeMarco, examines the effects of a significant event on the author and her family. Andrea begins by identifying the cause—the separation—and then goes on to explain its specific effects on her family and on herself. Notice how transitional words and phrases make Andrea's causal connections clear to her readers.

How My Parents' Separation Changed My Life

Until I was ten, I lived the perfect all-American 1
life with my perfect all-American family. I lived in a
suburb of Albany, New York, with my parents, my sister
and brother, and our dog Daisy. We had a Ping-Pong table
in the basement, a barbecue in the backyard, and two
cars in the garage. My Dad and Mom were high-school
teachers, and every summer we took a family vacation.
Then, it all changed.

One day, just before Halloween, when my sister was 2
twelve and my brother was fourteen (Daisy was seven),
our parents called us into the kitchen for a family conference. We didn't think anything was wrong at first;
they were always calling these annoying meetings. We
figured it was time for us to plan a vacation, talk
about household chores, or be nagged to clean our rooms.
As soon as we sat down, though, we knew this was different. We could tell Mom had been crying, and Dad's
voice cracked when he told us the news. They were sepa-
rating--they called it a "trial separation"--and Dad was
moving out of our house.

3

I hardly remember what else we talked about that day. But I do remember how things changed right after that. Every Halloween we'd always had a big jack-o'-lantern on our front porch. Dad used to spend hours at the kitchen table cutting out the eyes, nose, and mouth and hollowing out the insides. That Halloween, because he didn't live with us, things were different. Mom bought a pumpkin, and I guess she was planning to carve it up. But she never did, and we never mentioned it. It sat on the kitchen counter for a couple of weeks, getting soft and wrinkled, and then it just disappeared. I suppose Mom threw it out.

4

Other holidays were also different because Mom and Dad weren't living together. Our first Thanksgiving without Dad was pathetic. I don't even want to talk about it. Christmas was different, too. We spent Christmas Eve with Dad and our relatives on his side, and Christmas Day with Mom and her family. Of course, we got twice as many presents as usual. I realize now that both our parents were trying to make up for the pain of the separation. The worst part came when I opened my big present from Mom: Barbie's Dream House. This was something I'd always wanted. Even at ten, I knew how hard it must have been for Mom to afford it. The trouble was, I'd gotten the same thing from Dad the night before.

5

The worst effect of my parents' separation on all three of us was not the big events but the disruption in our everyday lives. Dinner used to be a family time, a chance to talk about our day and make plans. But after Dad left, Mom seemed to stop eating. Sometimes she'd just have coffee while we ate, and sometimes she wouldn't eat at all. She'd microwave some frozen thing for us or heat up soup or cook some hot dogs. We didn't care--after all, now she let us watch TV while we ate--but we did notice.

6

Other parts of our routine changed, too. Because Dad didn't live with us anymore, we had to spend every Saturday and every Wednesday night at his place, no matter what else we had planned. Usually he'd take us to dinner at McDonald's on Wednesdays, and then we'd go back to his place and do our homework or watch TV. That wasn't too bad. Saturdays were a lot worse. We really wanted to be home, hanging out with our friends in our own rooms in our own house. Instead, we had to do some planned activity with Dad, like go to a movie or a hockey game.

7

My parents were separated for only eight months, but it seemed like forever. By the end of the school year, they'd somehow worked things out, and Dad was back home again. That June, at a family conference around the kitchen table, we made our summer vacation plans. We decided on Williamsburg, Virginia, the all-American vacation destination. So things were back to normal, but I wasn't, and I'm still not. Now, eight years later, my mother and father are OK, but I still worry they'll split up again. And I worry about my own future husband and how I'll ever be sure he's the one I'll stay married to. As a result of what happened in my own family, it's hard for me to believe any relationship is forever.

◆ PRACTICE 14-13

1. What is Andrea's thesis? Does she state it? If so, where?

_____

_____

_____

_____

2. What specific effects of her parents' separation does Andrea identify?

_____

_____

_____

3. Underline the transitional words and phrases that make the causal connections in Andrea's essay clear to her readers.

4. Is Andrea's relatively long concluding paragraph effective? Why or why not? Do you think it should be shortened or divided into two paragraphs?

_____

_____

_____

5. Is Andrea's straightforward title effective, or should she have used a more creative or eye-catching title? Can you suggest an alternative?

_____

_____

6. What is this essay's greatest strength? What is its greatest weakness?

Strength: _____

Weakness: _____

◆ PRACTICE 14-14

Following the writing process outlined in Chapter 12, write a cause-and-effect essay on one of the following topics.

> Why a certain academic subject (or household chore) has always been your least favorite
>
> Why you voted a certain way in a recent election (or why you didn't vote)
>
> How your life would be different if you stopped—or started—smoking
>
> How a particular invention (for example, the pager) has changed your life
>
> How inheriting a million dollars would change your life
>
> How having a child would change (or has changed) your life
>
> How a particular season (or day of the week) affects your mood

◆ PRACTICE 14-15

How might the accident pictured here have happened? Imagine factors that might have caused the accident. Discuss them in detail on a separate sheet of paper, moving from the least to the most important cause. In your thesis statement, explain how the accident could have been prevented.

☑ SELF-ASSESSMENT CHECKLIST:
Writing a Cause-and-Effect Essay

- Does your introduction identify the particular causes or effects on which your essay will focus? Revise your introduction if necessary to zero in on your topic.

(continued on the following page)

(continued from the previous page)

- Does your essay focus on causes or effects? Does your thesis statement convey this emphasis to readers? If not, revise your thesis statement to identify the key causes or effects that you will emphasize.

- Do you identify all causes or effects relevant to your topic? If not, revise to include all significant causes or effects.

- Do you discuss any irrelevant causes or effects? If necessary, revise to eliminate them.

- Which cause or effect is most important? Arrange causes or effects to indicate their relative importance.

- Does each body paragraph identify and explain one particular cause or effect (or several closely related causes or effects)? Revise where necessary to unify each body paragraph.

- Do your topic sentences and transitional words and phrases make causal connections clear? If not, revise to clarify the relationships among individual causes or effects and between the causes or effects you discuss and your thesis.

- Does your conclusion reinforce the causal relationships you discuss? Revise to make your emphasis clearer.

- What problems did you experience in writing your essay? What would you do differently next time?

F Comparison and Contrast

For information on writing a comparison-and-contrast paragraph, see Chapter 8.

Comparison identifies similarities; **contrast** identifies differences. Comparison-and-contrast essays explain how two things are alike or how they are different; sometimes, they discuss both similarities and differences.

When you organize a comparison-and-contrast essay, you can choose either a *point-by-point* or a *subject-by-subject* arrangement. A **point-by-point** comparison alternates between the two subjects you are comparing or contrasting, moving back and forth from one subject to the other. A

● **Writing Tip**
Many everyday writing tasks call for comparison and contrast. In a report to your supervisor at work, you might compare the merits of two procedures or two suppliers.

FOCUS Topics for Comparison and Contrast

The wording of your assignment may suggest comparison and contrast—for example, by asking you to *compare*, *contrast*, *discuss similarities*, or *identify differences*.

(continued on the following page)

(continued from the previous page)

Topic/Assignment	Thesis Statement
Philosophy What basic similarities do you find in the beliefs of Henry David Thoreau and Martin Luther King Jr.?	Although King was more politically active, both he and Thoreau strongly supported the idea of civil disobedience.
Nutrition How do the diets of native Japanese and Japanese Americans differ?	As they become more and more assimilated, Japanese Americans consume more fats than their Japanese counterparts do.
Literature Contrast the two sisters in Alice Walker's short story "Everyday Use."	Unlike Maggie, Dee—her more successful, better-educated sister—has rejected her family's heritage.

subject-by-subject comparison treats its two subjects separately, first fully discussing one subject and then moving on to consider the other subject. In both kinds of comparison-and-contrast essays, the same points of comparison and contrast are applied to the two subjects.

● **Writing Tip**
In a comparison, your points must match up. If you discuss the appearance and behavior of one dog breed, you should discuss the same two points for the other breeds you're writing about.

Options for Organizing Comparison-and-Contrast Essays

Point-by-Point Comparison	Subject-by-Subject Comparison
¶1 Introduction (identifies subjects to be compared or contrasted)	¶1 Introduction (identifies subjects to be compared or contrasted)
¶2 First point of similarity or difference discussed for both subjects	¶¶2–3 First subject discussed (points of similarity or difference discussed)
¶3 Second point of similarity or difference discussed for both subjects	¶¶4–5 Second subject discussed (points of similarity or difference discussed in same order as for first subject)
¶4 Third point of similarity or difference discussed for both subjects	
¶5 Conclusion	¶6 Conclusion

The transitional words and phrases you use in a comparison-and-contrast essay tell readers whether you are focusing on similarities or differences. Transitions also help move readers through your essay from one subject to the other and from one point of similarity or difference to the next.

FOCUS **Transitions for Comparison and Contrast**

Although	Likewise
But	Nevertheless
Even though	On the contrary
However	On the one hand . . . On the other hand
In comparison	Similarly
In contrast	Unlike
Like	Whereas

The following student essay, "Jason Vorhees, Meet Count Dracula" by Cheri Rodriguez, contrasts two well-known horror movie characters. A point-by-point comparison, Cheri's essay alternates between her two subjects, treating the same points in the same order for each. Notice that topic sentences identify the subject under discussion in each paragraph and clearly signal shifts from one subject to the next.

Jason Vorhees, Meet Count Dracula

Many people like being scared, and horror movies are the best form of entertainment for accomplishing this. In fact, horror movies have gone to extremes to terrify those who watch them. What was considered frightening fifty or sixty years ago seems mild compared to the horror movies of today, whose main characters are violent and vicious. This difference becomes obvious when we contrast early depictions of Count Dracula with the popular contemporary character Jason Vorhees. 1

Count Dracula, a popular character in the 1930s, was an aristocratic man with dark eyes, pale skin, and dark hair. He wore black suits with white shirts and bow ties. A floor-length black cape with a stiff collar set off his attire and made him look like a true count. Tall, slender, and rather handsome, Count Dracula spoke with a strong foreign accent that made him seem mysterious and distinguished. His movements were graceful and elegant; his pale countenance was meant to strike fear in those who saw him. His dark hair and bluish tinted lips added to his formidable appearance. Still, Dracula was usually polite and charming, even to his victims. 2

The appearance of Jason Vorhees, the villain in the _Friday the Thirteenth_ movies, is strikingly different from Count Dracula's. Jason's face is horribly deformed, so he hides it behind a hockey mask, which is removed only when he wants to frighten a victim or when it is accidentally torn off his face by someone. He's bald, with a few ugly bumps on his head, and he dresses in a 3 dark, long-sleeved shirt, blue jeans, and boots. Unlike Count Dracula, Jason is stocky and ugly. He never utters a word. He moves with a lumbering gait that is neither graceful nor elegant. As a horror movie character, he is gruesome to look at, even with his face covered (as it is most of the time).

As a vampire, Dracula sought out victims so that he could feed on their blood. The lust for blood was a driving force that he could not control, and he attacked people out of a need to survive. Every night, in the form of a bat, he sought out his victims. Most of the time he had a particular victim in mind, and the audience was kept in suspense, wondering if Dracula would claim his victim or be stopped by the hero of the movie. 4

Unlike Dracula, Jason Vorhees is a psychotic killer who attacks his victims just for the thrill of it. He's never particular about who his victims are, and if there are five people staying in a cabin in the woods for the weekend, he'll attack all of them. Usually one person out of the group survives, and the audience tries to guess who will make it out alive. 5

In their time, the Dracula movies were suspenseful and frightening. Count Dracula's intended victim was usually a beautiful young woman who reminded him of someone he had known centuries before. Dracula's goal throughout each movie was to drink the heroine's blood and make her one of the "undead" like himself so that she could live with him for eternity. His ability to change into a bat and appear in the room of his victim would cause the audience to shiver. The sight of him sinking his fangs into his victim's throat would bring gasps of horror from viewers. Nevertheless, the Dracula movies were more suspenseful than they were violent. Few scenes were bloody (except those in which he bit his victim on the throat). I doubt if the Dracula movies would give today's audiences nightmares or make them afraid of the dark. Viewers know that there are no vampires and that they have nothing to fear from bats after leaving the theater. 6

Jason is a much more frightening character than Dracula ever was. Most of the time he carries a weapon with him, whether it is a knife, a hatchet, or a sledgehammer. If he doesn't have a weapon, he will use anything within his reach. He appears at the most unexpected times and manages to annihilate most of his victims in one evening. Jason's methods of attacking his prey bring screams of horror and revulsion from the audience. Almost every scene includes an act of 7

violence. These movies have no real plot; Jason just
goes around killing people. At the beginning of each
movie, Jason is revived--no matter how he was destroyed
in the preceding movie. The violence is very graphic,
and these movies are not for the squeamish or weak-
stomached.

Both horror movies and the characters they depict
have changed dramatically over the years. The main characters are more gruesome than they used to be, and the
movies contain much more graphic violence than before.
Although the old movie characters seem corny and old-
fashioned to some people, I prefer an evil but elegant
villain in a long black cape to an ugly, inarticulate
brute in a hockey mask.

8

◆ PRACTICE 14-16

1. Does Cheri's opening paragraph identify the subjects she will discuss?
   Will she focus on similarities or on differences?

   _____

   _____

2. Cheri's essay is a point-by-point comparison. What three points does
   she discuss for each of her two subjects?

   _____

   _____

3. Underline some transitional words and phrases Cheri uses to move
   readers from one subject (Dracula) to the other (Jason).

4. Reread Cheri's topic sentences. What information does each contribute
   to the essay?

   _____

   _____

   _____

   _____

5. Which kind of horror film character does Cheri prefer? Why? Where
   does she make her preference clear to readers?

   _____

   _____

6. What is this essay's greatest strength? What is its greatest weakness?

   Strength: _____

   Weakness: _____

◆ PRACTICE 14-17

Following the writing process outlined in Chapter 12, write a comparison-and-contrast essay on one of the following topics.

Two movie heroes
How you expect your life to be different from the lives of your parents
Men's and women's ideas about their body images
A healthy diet and an unhealthy diet
Risk-takers and people who play it safe
E-mail and regular mail
Country and city living (or you can compare suburban living with either)

◆ PRACTICE 14-18

On a separate sheet of paper, write an essay in which you compare these two photographs, considering both what the monuments look like and their emotional impact on you.

Iwo Jima memorial statue at Arlington National Cemetery.

Vietnam Veterans Memorial in Washington, D.C.

☑ SELF-ASSESSMENT CHECKLIST:
Writing a Comparison-and-Contrast Essay

◻ Does your introduction identify the subjects you will compare and contrast? If not, revise to make the focus of your essay clear.

◻ Does your essay focus on similarities or on differences? If necessary, revise your thesis statement to make your emphasis clear.

◻ Have you discussed all significant points of comparison or contrast that apply to your two subjects? Develop your discussion further if necessary.

◻ Are any points insignificant or irrelevant? If necessary, revise to eliminate any points of comparison or contrast that do not support your thesis.

◻ Have you treated the same points for both of your two subjects? Revise if necessary to make your discussion balanced.

◻ Is your essay a point-by-point comparison or a subject-by-subject comparison? If necessary, revise to make your organization consistent with one of these two options.

◻ Does each topic sentence clearly identify the subject and the point of comparison or contrast being discussed? If necessary, revise topic sentences to clarify each paragraph's focus.

◻ Do transitional words and phrases move readers from one subject or point to another? Add transitions where necessary.

◻ Does your conclusion sum up the major similarities or differences between your two subjects? If not, revise to reinforce your essay's focus.

◻ What problems did you experience during the process of writing your essay? What would you do differently next time?

G   Classification

For information on writing a classification paragraph, see Chapter 9.

Classification is the act of sorting items into appropriate categories. Classification essays divide a whole into parts and sort various items into categories.

As a rule, each paragraph of a classification essay examines a separate category—a different part of the whole. For example, a paragraph could focus on one kind of course in the college curriculum, one component of the blood, or one type of child. Within each paragraph, you discuss the individual items that you have assigned to a particular category—for example, accounting courses, red blood cells, or gifted students. If you consider some categories less important than others, you may decide to

● **Writing Tip**
Many everyday writing tasks
call for classification. If you
coach a youth sports team,
you might write a recruit-
ment flyer classifying player
requirements by age, grade,
and level of experience.

FOCUS **Topics for Classification**

The wording of your assignment may suggest classification. For example, you may be asked to consider *kinds*, *types*, *categories*, *components*, *segments*, or *parts* of a whole.

Topic/Assignment	Thesis Statement
Business What kinds of courses are most useful for students planning to run their own businesses?	Courses dealing with accounting, management, interpersonal communication, and computer science offer the most useful skills for future business owners.
Biology List the components of the blood, and explain the function of each.	Red blood cells, white blood cells, platelets, and plasma have very distinct functions.
Education Classify elementary school children according to their academic needs.	The elementary school population includes special-needs students, students with reading and math skills at or near grade level, and academically gifted students.

discuss those minor categories together in a single paragraph, devoting full paragraphs only to the most significant categories.

Options for Organizing Classification Essays

One Category in Each Paragraph

¶1 Introduction (identifies whole and its major categories)
¶2 First category
¶3 Second category
¶4 Third category

¶5 Conclusion

Major Categories in Separate Paragraphs; Minor Categories Grouped Together

¶1 Introduction (identifies whole and its major categories)
¶2 Minor categories
¶3 First major category
¶4 Second (and most important) major category
¶5 Conclusion

In a classification essay, topic sentences clarify the connection between the whole and its individual categories. Transitional words and phrases signal movement from one category to the next and may also tell readers which categories you consider most and least important.

FOCUS **Transitions for Classification**

One kind . . .	The first (second,	The most impor-
Another kind	third) category	tant component
The final type	The last group	The next part

The following student essay, "Sports Fans Are in a Class by Themselves" by Deborah Ulrich, classifies sports fans into three different categories on the basis of the degree of their involvement in sports. Notice that Deborah discusses one category in each of her body paragraphs, using clear topic sentences to identify and define each kind of fan and relate each category to the group as a whole.

Sports Fans Are in a Class by Themselves

To say that all sports fans are alike would be as   1
inaccurate as saying that the seasons never change and
are exactly the same all year round. Sports fans are
such a diverse group of people that they cannot be
forced into a single category. Just as each season
brings a change in climate, so it brings various sports
activities. No matter what the season or the sporting
event, however, there are three basic types of sports
fans: dedicated, semidedicated, and totally uninterested.

Dedicated sports fans prepare weeks ahead of time   2
for the big game. If they plan on attending the sporting
event, dedicated sports fans buy their tickets months
before the actual game date. They, like the letter car-
rier, do not let rain, sleet, snow, or blazing sun stand
in the way of their passion. They come prepared to with-
stand all of the elements of Mother Nature, determined
to cheer their team to victory. If they plan to view
the game at home, they check the television thoroughly
in advance to make sure it is in perfect working order.
They also clearly circle the date, time, and channel of
the event, in red ink, in TV Guide so they will not
forget the game. All the necessities, such as popcorn,
chips, and beverages, are already stocked away in the
cupboards and labeled "Do Not Touch!" (Remember, whatever you do, do not even whisper while the game is on.
In the view of the dedicated sports fan, anything you
have to say can wait until the game is over.)

Semidedicated sports fans are different. These fans   3
are not terribly upset if tickets to the game are sold
out. After all, it's only a game; if they happen to be
at home, they will watch it on television, and if not,
they will find out from their buddies who won. Sure,

they want their team to win, but semidedicated fans understand that someone has to win and someone has to lose. To them, a sport is not a passion but a leisurely form of entertainment.

At the opposite end of the spectrum from dedicated sports fans are the totally uninterested sports fans. These are people who are usually conned or forced into going along to a sporting event with someone who is really interested in the game. After about an hour of viewing, totally uninterested fans will say, "What sport did you say this is?" and will begin to get more interested in the people around them than in those on the field or court. These fans are very easy to detect because they are the ones who know more about the location of the restroom and snack bar than about the score of the game. You might say that they are the movers and shakers of the game because they are constantly up and out of their seats, disturbing everyone else's view of the game. And yes, they are the first to make a mad dash for home when the long ordeal has finally drawn to an end.

For dedicated fans, sporting events are almost always interesting. For semidedicated fans, too, sporting events can be interesting; if they aren't, sometimes just watching the people around them can be as much fun as watching the game itself. Just ask the totally uninterested fans. They know.

◆ **PRACTICE 14-19**

1. What three categories of sports fans does Deborah discuss in her essay?

_____

_____

2. Is Deborah's treatment of the three categories similar? Does she make the same points about each kind of fan?

_____

_____

_____

_____

_____

3. How do Deborah's topic sentences move readers from one category to the next? How do they link the three categories?

_____

_____

_____

_____

_____

4. What is Deborah's thesis?

_____

_____

_____

_____

5. Deborah's introduction and conclusion are straightforward. Is this direct strategy effective, or should she have used a more creative opening or closing strategy—for example, a quotation or an anecdote?

_____

_____

_____

_____

6. What is this essay's greatest strength? What is its greatest weakness?

Strength: _____

Weakness: _____

◆ **PRACTICE 14-20**

Following the writing process outlined in Chapter 12, write a classification essay on one of the following topics.

Types of teachers	Traits of oldest children, middle
Work-related stress	children, and youngest children
Ways to lose (or gain) weight	Stereotypes
Things that hang on your walls	Kinds of junk food

◆ **PRACTICE 14-21**

On a separate sheet of paper, write a classification essay based on the following photograph. The categories you create can classify the fruit according to origin, uses, or some other system.

☑ SELF-ASSESSMENT CHECKLIST:
Writing a Classification Essay

- Does your introduction give readers an overview of the subject you will discuss? If necessary, revise to clarify the subject of your classification.

- What categories does your essay discuss? Does your thesis statement identify these categories? If not, revise your thesis statement to clarify your essay's focus.

- Does each body paragraph discuss a single category or a related group of minor categories? If not, revise to create unified paragraphs.

- Are any categories insignificant or irrelevant? Revise to eliminate any categories that are not central to your essay's purpose.

- Does each topic sentence identify and define the category or categories the paragraph discusses? If necessary, revise topic sentences to clarify the focus of each paragraph.

- Do topic sentences clearly show the relationship between the individual categories and the whole? If necessary, revise to clarify these relationships.

- Have you treated each major category similarly and with equal thoroughness? If not, revise to make your discussion balanced.

- Do transitional words and phrases clearly lead readers from one category to the next? If not, revise to make your essay flow more smoothly.

- Does your conclusion review the major categories your essay discusses? If necessary, revise to sum up the categories and their relationships to one another.

- What problems did you experience in writing your essay? What would you do differently next time?

14 H

*For information on writing a
definition paragraph, see
Chapter 10.*

H | **Definition**

Definition explains the meaning of a term or concept. A definition essay presents an *extended definition*, using other patterns of development to move beyond a simple dictionary definition.

● **Writing Tip**
Many everyday writing tasks
call for definition. In a letter
of complaint to a neighborhood business, you might
define what you mean by
terms like *excessive noise*
and *rude behavior.*

FOCUS | **Topics for Definition**

The wording of your assignment may suggest definition. For example, you may be asked to *define* or *explain,* or to answer the question *What is x?* or *What does x mean?*

Topic/Assignment	Thesis Statement
Art Explain the meaning of the term *performance art.*	Unlike more conventional forms of art, *performance art* extends beyond the canvas.
Biology What did Darwin mean by *natural selection?*	*Natural selection,* popularly known as "survival of the fittest," is a good deal more complicated than most people think.
Psychology What is *attention deficit disorder?*	*Attention deficit disorder* (ADD), once narrowly defined as a childhood problem, is now known to affect adults as well as children.

As the above thesis statements suggest, definition essays can be developed in various ways. For example, you can define something by telling how it occurred (narration), by describing its appearance (description), by giving a series of examples (exemplification), by telling how it operates

---

Options for Organizing Definition Essays

Single Pattern of Development	**Combination of Several Different Patterns of Development**
¶1 Introduction (identifies term to be defined)	¶1 Introduction (identifies term to be defined)
¶2 Definition by example	¶2 Definition by description
¶3 Additional examples	¶3 Definition by example
¶4 Additional examples	¶4 Definition by comparison and contrast
¶5 Conclusion	¶5 Conclusion

(process), by telling how it is similar to or different from something else (comparison and contrast), or by discussing its parts (classification). Some definition essays use a single pattern of development; others combine several patterns of development, perhaps using a different one in each paragraph.

The kinds of transitions used in a definition essay depend on the specific pattern or patterns of development in the essay. (In addition to the transitional words and expressions listed in the following Focus box, you may also use those appropriate for the particular patterns you use to develop your definition essay. These transitions are listed in Focus boxes throughout this chapter.)

FOCUS Transitions for Definition

Also	One characteristic . . . Another
For example	characteristic
In addition	One way . . . Another way
In particular	Specifically
Like	

The following student essay, "Street Smart" by Kristin Whitehead, defines the term *street smart*. In the essay's introduction, Kristin defines her term briefly; in the essay's body paragraphs, she expands her definition. Notice that the topic sentences of Kristin's three body paragraphs repeat a key phrase to remind readers of the essay's focus.

Street Smart

I grew up in a big city, so I was practically born   1
street smart. I learned the hard way how to act and
what to do, and so did my friends. To us, street smart
meant having common sense. We wanted to be cool, but we
needed to be safe, too. Now I go to college in a big
city, and I realize that not everyone here grew up the
way I did. Lots of students are from suburbs or rural
areas, and they are either terrified of the city or
totally ignorant of city life. The few suburban or rural
kids who are willing to venture downtown all have one
thing in common: they are not street smart.

For me, being street smart means knowing how to   2
protect my possessions. Friends of mine who aren't used
to city life insist on wearing all their jewelry when
they go downtown. I think this is asking for trouble,
and I know better. I always tuck my chain under my shirt
and leave my gold earrings home. Another thing that surprises me is how some of my friends wave their money
around. They always seem to be standing on the street,
trying to count their change or stuff dollars into their

wallet. Street-smart people make sure to put their money safely away in their pockets or purses before they leave a store. A street-smart person will also carry a back-pack, a purse strapped across the chest, or no purse at all. A person who is not street smart carries a purse loosely over one shoulder or dangles it by its handle. Again, these people are asking for trouble.

Being street smart also means protecting myself. It means being aware of my surroundings at all times and looking as if I am. A lot of times I've been downtown with people who kept stopping on the street to talk about where they should go next or walking up and down the same street over and over again. A street-smart per-son would never do this. It's important for me that I look as if I know where I'm going at all times, even if I don't. Whenever possible, I decide on a destination in advance, and I make sure I know how to get there. Even if I'm not completely sure where I'm headed, I make sure my body language conveys my confidence in my ability to reach my destination.

Finally, being street smart means protecting my life. A street-smart person does not walk alone, espe-cially after dark, in an unfamiliar neighborhood. A street-smart person does not ask strangers for direc-tions; when lost, he or she asks a shopkeeper for help. A street-smart person takes main streets instead of side streets. When faced with danger or the threat of danger, a street-smart person knows when to run, when to scream, and when to give up money or possessions to avoid violence.

So how does someone get to be street smart? Some people think it is a gift, but I think it is something one can learn. Probably the best way to learn how to be street smart is to hang out with people who know where they are going.

◆ **PRACTICE 14-22**

1. In your own words, define the term *street smart*. Why does this term require more than a one-sentence definition?

_____

_____

_____

2. Where does Kristin use examples to develop her definition? Where does she use comparison and contrast?

_____

_____

_____

_____

3. What phrase does Kristin repeat in the topic sentences of her three body paragraphs?

_____

4. Kristin's introduction explains how she and her friends are different from some of her college classmates. In what ways is this an effective opening strategy?

_____

_____

_____

5. Kristin's conclusion is quite a bit shorter than her other paragraphs. What, if anything, should she add to this paragraph?

_____

_____

_____

6. What is this essay's greatest strength? What is its greatest weakness?

Strength: _____

Weakness: _____

◆ PRACTICE 14-23

Following the writing process outlined in Chapter 12, write a definition essay on one of the following topics.

Fear	Success
Upward mobility	Responsibility
Peer pressure	Procrastination
Competition	

◆ PRACTICE 14-24

On a separate sheet of paper, write an essay in which you define *family*. In what ways do the family groups shown on the following page fit or not fit into your definition?

☑ SELF-ASSESSMENT CHECKLIST:
Writing a Definition Essay

- Does your introduction identify the term that your essay defines and briefly define it? If not, revise to make the scope of your essay clear.

- Does your thesis statement indicate why you are defining the term? If not, revise to clarify your purpose.

- What pattern or patterns of development do you use to develop your definition? Try exploring other options.

- Do topic sentences clearly introduce the different aspects of your definition? If necessary, revise to clarify the relationships between paragraphs.

- Are all your ideas clearly related to the term you are defining? If not, revise to eliminate any irrelevant ideas.

- Do transitional words and phrases clearly link your ideas? If necessary, add transitions to help guide readers through your essay.

- Does your conclusion sum up your essay's main points? Does it remind readers why you are defining the term? If necessary, revise to make your conclusion consistent with the rest of your essay.

- What problems did you experience in writing your essay? What would you do differently next time?

For more on the patterns of development, see Chapters 3–11.

I   Argument

Argument takes a stand on one side of a debatable issue. An argument essay uses different kinds of evidence—facts, examples, and expert opinion—to persuade readers to accept a position.

For information on writing an argument paragraph, see Chapter 11.

FOCUS   Topics for Argument

The wording of your assignment may suggest argument. For example, you may be asked to *debate, argue, consider, give your opinion, take a position,* or *take a stand.*

(continued on the following page)

● Writing Tip
Many everyday writing tasks call for argument. In a letter to the editor of a newspaper, you might take a stand on a political, social, economic, religious, or environmental issue affecting your family or community.

(continued from the previous page)

Topic/Assignment	Thesis Statement
Composition Explain your position on the debate about national health care.	A system of national health care should be developed, assuming both taxpayers and the government are prepared to pay for it.
American history Do you believe that General Lee was responsible for the South's defeat at the Battle of Gettysburg? Why or why not?	Because Lee refused to listen to the advice given to him by General Longstreet, he is largely responsible for the South's defeat at the Battle of Gettysburg.
Ethics In your opinion, should physician-assisted suicide be legalized?	Although many people think physician-assisted suicide should remain illegal, I believe it should be legal in certain situations.

An argument essay can be organized *inductively* or *deductively*. An **inductive argument** moves from the specific to the general—that is, from a group of specific observations to a general conclusion based on these observations. An inductive argument responding to the first of the three topics in the Focus box above, for example, could begin with a series of observations about the value of national health care and end with the conclusion that national health care makes sense if it can be paid for.

A **deductive argument** moves from the general to the specific. A deductive argument begins with a **major premise** (a general statement that the writer believes his or her audience will accept) and then moves to a **minor premise** (a specific instance of the belief stated in the major premise). It ends with a **conclusion** that follows from the two premises. For example, an essay that responds to the last topic in the Focus box above could begin with the major premise that all terminally ill patients who are in great pain should be given access to physician-assisted suicide. It could then go on to state and explain the minor premise that a particular patient is both terminally ill and in great pain, offering facts, examples, and the opinions of authorities to support this premise. The essay could conclude that this patient should, therefore, be allowed the option of physician-assisted suicide. In this way, the deductive argument goes through three steps.

MAJOR PREMISE All terminally ill patients who are in great pain should be allowed to choose physician-assisted suicide.

MINOR PREMISE John Lacca is a terminally ill patient who is in great pain.

CONCLUSION Therefore, John Lacca should be allowed to choose physician-assisted suicide.

Before you present your argument, think about whether your readers will be hostile, neutral, or in agreement with your thesis. Once you understand your audience, you can decide which arguments to use.

As you write your argument essay, begin each paragraph with a topic sentence that clearly relates the discussion to the previous paragraph or to your thesis statement. Throughout your essay, try to include specific examples that will make your arguments persuasive. Keep in mind that arguments that rely just on generalizations are not as convincing as those that include vivid details and pointed examples. Finally, strive for a balanced, moderate tone, and avoid name-calling or personal attacks.

In addition to presenting your case, you should also briefly identify arguments *against* your position and **refute** them (that is, prove them false) by identifying factual errors or errors in logic. If an opposing argument is particularly strong, concede its strength—but try to point out some weakness as well. Dealing with the opposing point of view in this manner will help you overcome any objections your audience might have and will establish you as a fair and reasonable person.

Options for Organizing Argument Essays

Induction	**Deduction**
¶1 Introduction	¶1 Introduction
¶2 First set of observations	¶2 Major premise stated and explained
¶3 Second set of observations	¶3 Minor premise stated and explained
¶4 Third set of observations	¶4 Evidence supporting minor premise presented
¶5 Identification and refutation of opposing arguments	¶5 Opposing arguments identified and refuted
¶6 Conclusion	¶6 Conclusion

Transitions are extremely important in argument essays because they not only signal the movement from one part of the argument to another but also relate specific points to each other and to the thesis statement.

FOCUS **Transitions for Argument**

Accordingly	Granted	Of course
Admittedly	However	On the one hand
Although	In conclusion	. . . On the other
Because	Indeed	hand
But	In fact	Since
Certainly	In summary	Therefore
Consequently	Moreover	Thus
Despite	Nevertheless	To be sure
Even so	Nonetheless	Truly

The following student paper, "Why Isn't Pete Rose in the Hall of Fame?" by John Fleeger, is an argument essay. John takes a strong stand, and he supports his thesis with specific facts and examples. The deductive argument that underlies John's essay moves from the major premise ("Qualified players who do not violate major-league rules should be inducted into the Hall of Fame") to the minor premise ("Pete Rose is a qualified player who did not violate major-league rules") to the conclusion ("Therefore, Pete Rose should be inducted into the Hall of Fame").

Why Isn't Pete Rose in the Hall of Fame?

The year 1992 was the first year Pete Rose would have been eligible for the National Baseball Hall of Fame. Not only was he not elected, his name did not even appear on the ballot. Why? Has he not established himself as the all-time best hitter in baseball? Was he not a member of two championship teams with the Cincinnati Reds and one with the Philadelphia Phillies? Did he not help build the foundation for the 1990 championship Reds team? Has he not set or tied several major-league and team records during his career? The answer to all of these questions is yes. His dedication to and enthusiasm for the game of baseball earned him the nickname "Charlie Hustle" but not his rightful place in the Hall of Fame. This situation is unfair and should be changed.

In the late summer of 1989, Pete Rose was banned from professional baseball. The legal agreement reached between major-league officials and Pete Rose does not offer any evidence that Rose bet on any baseball games, and Rose himself does not say that he did. Despite the lack of any confirmation, A. Bartlett Giamatti, Commissioner of Baseball at that time, publicly declared that Rose bet not only on baseball but also on his own team. Betting on baseball is a violation of major-league rules and is punishable by lifetime banishment from baseball. This was the sentence Pete Rose received.

In 1991, the Hall of Fame Committee along with Fay Vincent, who was then Commissioner of Baseball, decided that as long as a player is banned from baseball, he is ineligible for Hall of Fame selection. This action was taken just a few weeks before Rose's name could have been placed on the ballot, and many believe that Vincent encouraged it specifically to make sure Rose could not be considered for selection. Several of the baseball writers who voted for the Hall of Fame candidates voiced their disapproval of this policy by writing in Rose's name on the ballot. Unfortunately, write-in votes are not counted.

Rose's only hope of making the Hall of Fame depends on his being readmitted to baseball. The commissioner would have to review Rose's application and approve his reinstatement. Chances are not good, however, that the commissioner would reinstate Rose. Therefore, Rose

1

2

3

4

will probably have to wait for a commissioner who is sympathetic to his situation before he applies for re-instatement.

Meanwhile, on the strength of circumstantial evidence and the testimony of convicted felons, baseball has convicted Pete Rose of betting on baseball. He has admitted to betting on horse races and football games but denies ever betting on the sport he loves. He has also admitted that his gambling was a problem and that he has spent time in counseling. Why is a player who once gambled any worse than the many players who have tested positive for drugs? Those players are suspended from the game for a period of time and are given one or more chances to recover and return to the major league. Why are gamblers not treated the same way as drug abusers?   5

Many people mistakenly believe that Pete Rose went to prison for betting on baseball and that, for this reason, he should be kept out of the Hall of Fame. The fact is, however, that Rose went to prison for tax-law violations. He failed to pay income tax on his gambling winnings and on the money he made at baseball-card shows. Even so, when has the Hall of Fame ever been reserved for perfect people? Babe Ruth was an adulterer and a serious drinker, but he still holds a place in the Hall. Mickey Mantle and Willie Mays were barred from baseball for being employees of an Atlantic City casino (an obvious gambling connection), but even this decision was eventually overturned.   6

I have met Pete Rose, and, granted, he does not have the greatest personality, but his personal short-comings are no reason to keep him out of the Hall of Fame. His contributions to the game and his accomplishments as a player more than qualify him to occupy a place beside the greats of the game. Baseball should, in all fairness, let Pete Rose return to the game and allow him to take his rightful place in the Hall of Fame.   7

◆ PRACTICE 14-25

1. What position does John take in his essay?

_____

_____

2. List the facts and examples John uses to support his thesis. Can you think of any that he doesn't mention?

_____

_____

_____

_____

_____

_____

3. Underline the transitional words and phrases John uses to move his argument along. Does he need to add any transitions? If so, where?

_____

_____

4. John's opening paragraph includes a series of questions he does not expect his readers to answer. Is this an effective opening strategy? Why or why not?

_____

_____

5. In his conclusion, John mentions Pete Rose's personal shortcomings. Do you think this is a good idea? Why or why not?

_____

_____

_____

6. Where does John address opposing arguments? What other arguments should he have addressed?

_____

_____

_____

7. What is this essay's greatest strength? What is its greatest weakness?

Strength: _____

Weakness: _____

◆ PRACTICE 14-26

Following the writing process outlined in Chapter 12, write an argument essay on one of the following topics.

The United States should (or should not) have an "open-door" immigration policy, with no restrictions.

Parents should (or should not) be permitted to use government vouchers to pay private school tuition.

Public school students should (or should not) be required to wear uniforms.

College financial aid should (or should not) be based solely on need.

Health-care workers should (or should not) be subject to mandatory HIV tests.

Government funds should (or should not) be used to support the arts.

Public high schools should (or should not) be permitted to distribute condoms to students.

◆ PRACTICE 14-27

Many people criticize television talk shows, arguing that they have a negative impact on viewers and serve no useful purpose. Can you argue that despite scenes like the one below, talk shows do have value? Or do you agree with the critics? Take one position or the other, and write an argument essay supporting your position with specific references to talk shows you have watched.

During the taping of a Geraldo Rivera television show segment on November 3, 1988, a dispute erupted between two panelists, and a number of audience members stormed the stage.

☑ SELF-ASSESSMENT CHECKLIST:
Writing an Argument Essay

- Does your introduction present the issue you will discuss and clearly state your position? If necessary, revise to clarify your purpose.

- Is your topic debatable? Make sure you take a position on an issue that really has two sides.

(continued on the following page)

(continued from the previous page)

☐ Does your thesis statement clearly express the stand you take on the issue? If necessary, revise to clarify your position.

☐ Are your readers likely to be hostile, neutral, or in agreement with your position? Be sure you consider your audience's expectations when choosing the points you will make.

☐ Is your essay an inductive argument or a deductive argument? If necessary, revise the structure of your argument so it conforms to the requirements of the option you have chosen.

☐ Have you addressed the major arguments against your position? Identify any additional opposing arguments, and refute them if you can.

☐ Do you have enough evidence to support your points? If not, add facts, examples, and the opinions of authorities if necessary.

☐ Do all your points clearly support your position? If not, revise to eliminate any points that are not directly related to your argument.

☐ Do transitional words and phrases help readers follow the logic of your argument? Add transitions if necessary.

☐ Does your conclusion follow logically from the points you have made in your essay? If necessary, revise so your concluding paragraph summarizes and reinforces your main points.

☐ What problems did you experience in writing your essay? What would you do differently next time?

✔ **REVIEW CHECKLIST:**
Patterns of Essay Development

☐ Exemplification essays use specific examples to support a thesis. (See 14A.)

☐ Narrative essays tell a story by presenting a series of events in chronological order. (See 14B.)

☐ Descriptive essays use details to give readers a clear, vivid picture of a person, place, or object. (See 14C.)

☐ Process essays explain the steps in a procedure, telling how something is (or was) done. (See 14D.)

☐ Cause-and-effect essays identify causes or predict effects. (See 14E.)

(continued on the following page)

(continued from the previous page)

- Comparison-and-contrast essays explain how two things are alike or how they are different. (See 14F.)

- Classification essays divide a whole into parts and sort various items into categories. (See 14G.)

- Definition essays use various patterns of development to present an extended definition. (See 14H.)

- Argument essays take a stand on a debatable issue, using evidence to persuade readers to accept a position. (See 14I.)

UNIT FOUR

Writing Effective Sentences

15

Writing Simple Sentences

■ WRITING FIRST

Write about a person with whom you would like to trade places. What is this person like? What appeals to you about this person's life?

A **sentence** is a group of words that expresses a complete thought. Every sentence includes a <u>subject</u> and a <u>verb</u>.

A   Identifying Subjects

The **subject** of a sentence tells who or what is being talked about in the sentence.

<u>Derek Walcott</u> won the 1992 Nobel Prize in literature.

<u>St. Lucia</u> is an island in the Caribbean.

Every sentence includes a subject. This subject can be a noun or a pronoun. A **noun** names a person, place, or thing—*Derek Walcott, St. Lucia.* A **pronoun** takes the place of a noun—*I, you, he, she, it, we, they.*

The subject of a simple sentence can be *singular* or *plural*. A **singular subject** is one person, place, or thing *(Derek Walcott, St. Lucia, he).*

A **plural subject** is more than one person, place, or thing *(poems, islands, they).*

Walcott's <u>poems</u> are studied in college courses.

A plural subject that joins two subjects with *and* is called a **compound subject**.

<u>St. Lucia and Trinidad</u> are Caribbean islands.

PREVIEW

In this chapter, you will learn

■ to identify a sentence's subject (15A)

■ to identify prepositions and prepositional phrases (15B)

■ to distinguish a prepositional phrase from a subject (15B)

■ to identify a sentence's verb (15C)

For information on subject-verb agreement with compound subjects, see 23A.

● **Writing Tip**
Sometimes an *-ing* word can be a singular subject: *Reading is fundamental.*

197

◆ PRACTICE 15-1

Underline the subject of each sentence in the paragraph below.

Example: The poet's <u>parents</u> were both teachers.

(1) Derek Walcott was born in 1930. (2) His ancestors came from Africa, the Netherlands, and England. (3) Walcott's early years were spent on the Caribbean island of St. Lucia. (4) Writing poetry occupied much of his time. (5) His early poems were published in Trinidad. (6) He later studied in Jamaica and in New York and founded the Trinidad Theatre Workshop. (7) Walcott eventually gained wide recognition as a poet. (8) He was a visiting lecturer at Harvard in 1981. (9) In 1990, the renowned poet published *Omeros*. (10) This long poem about classical Greek heroes is set in the West Indies. (11) In 1992, the sixty-two-year-old Caribbean poet was honored with a Nobel Prize. (12) Walcott and Paul Simon later collaborated on *The Capeman*, a Broadway musical.

■ WRITING FIRST: Flashback

Look back at your response to the Writing First exercise on page 197. Underline the subject of each of your sentences. Then, list all of those subjects on the lines below.

_____   _____

_____   _____

_____   _____

_____   _____

| **B** | **Identifying Prepositional Phrases** |

A **phrase** is a group of words that lacks a subject or a verb or both and therefore cannot stand alone as a sentence. A **prepositional phrase** consists of a **preposition** (a word such as *on, to, in,* or *with*) and its **object** (a noun or pronoun).

Frequently Used Prepositions

about	behind	except	off	toward
above	below	for	on	under
across	beneath	from	onto	underneath
after	beside	in	out	until
against	between	inside	outside	up
along	beyond	into	over	upon
among	by	like	through	with
around	despite	near	throughout	within
at	during	of	to	without
before				

Preposition	+	Object	=	Prepositional phrase
on		the stage		on the stage
to		Nia's house		to Nia's house
in		my new car		in my new car
with		them		with them

A prepositional phrase modifies another word or word group in the sentence.

The girl with long red hair was first in line. *(With long red hair* modifies the noun *girl.)*

Ken met his future wife at Ted's house. *(At Ted's house* modifies the verb *met.)*

Because the object of a preposition is a noun or a pronoun, you may sometimes think it is the subject of a sentence. However, the object of a preposition can never be the subject of a sentence. To identify a sentence's subject, cross out each prepositional phrase.

The cost ~~of the repairs~~ was astronomical.

~~At the end of the novel, after an exciting chase,~~ the lovers flee ~~to Mexico.~~

Once the prepositional phrases have been crossed out, the subject of each sentence is clear.

◆ PRACTICE 15-2

Each of the following sentences includes at least one prepositional phrase. To identify each sentence's subject, begin by crossing out each prepositional phrase. Then, underline the subject of the sentence.

Example: ~~In twentieth-century presidential elections,~~ third-party candidates have attracted many voters.

(1) With more than 27 percent of the vote, Theodore Roosevelt was the strongest third-party presidential candidate in history. (2) In the 1912 race with Democrat Woodrow Wilson and Republican William H. Taft,

> ● **Writing Tip**
> Prepositions are often combined with other words to form familiar expressions. (See 30L.)

> ▼ **Student Voices**
> *When I revise, I cover prepositional phrases with my finger so I can check to make sure subjects and verbs match.*
> Samantha Nguyen

Roosevelt ran second to Wilson. (3) Other candidates on the ballot were Socialist Eugene V. Debs and Eugene W. Chafin of the Prohibition Party. (4) Until Roosevelt, no third-party candidate had won a significant number of votes. (5) However, some candidates of other parties made strong showings after 1912. (6) For example, Robert M. LaFollette of the Progressive Party won about 16 percent of the vote in the 1924 race. (7) In 1968, with more than 13 percent of the popular vote, American Independent Party candidate George C. Wallace placed third behind Republican Richard M. Nixon and Democrat Hubert H. Humphrey. (8) In 1980, John B. Anderson, an Independent, challenged Republican Ronald Reagan and Democrat Jimmy Carter and got 6.6 percent of the vote. (9) With nearly 19 percent of the popular vote, Independent Ross Perot ran a strong race against Democrat Bill Clinton and Republican George Bush in 1992. (10) During the twentieth century, the two-party system of the United States has remained intact despite many challenges by third-party candidates.

■ WRITING FIRST: Flashback

Look back at your response to the Writing First exercise on page 197. Can you identify any prepositional phrases? List as many as you can on the lines below.

_____

_____

_____

_____

C Identifying Verbs

In addition to its subject, every sentence also includes a verb. The **verb** tells what the subject does or connects the subject to words that describe or rename it. Without a verb, a sentence is not complete.

Action Verbs

An **action verb** tells what the subject does, did, or will do.

Nomar Garciaparra <u>plays</u> baseball.

Renee <u>will drive</u> to Tampa on Friday.

Amelia Earhart <u>flew</u> across the Atlantic.

Action verbs can also show mental and emotional actions.

Travis always <u>worries</u> about his job.

Note that a sentence may have more than one action verb.

He <u>hit</u> the ball, <u>threw</u> down his bat, and <u>ran</u> toward first base.

Linking Verbs

Not all verbs tell what the subject does. A **linking** verb does not show action. Instead, it connects the subject to a word or words that describe or rename it. The linking verb tells what the subject is (or what it was, will be, or seems to be).

A googolplex <u>is</u> an extremely large number.

Many linking verbs, like *is*, are forms of the verb *be*. Other linking verbs refer to the senses (*look, feel*, and so on).

The photocopy <u>looks</u> blurry.

Some students <u>feel</u> anxious about the future.

Frequently Used Linking Verbs

act	feel	seem
appear	get	smell
be (am, is, are,	grow	sound
was, were)	look	taste
become	remain	turn

◆ PRACTICE 15-3

Underline the verbs in each sentence twice. Remember that a verb can be an action verb or a linking verb.

Example: Emily <u>looked</u> pale.

(1) Ann Radcliffe wrote *The Mysteries of Udolpho,* an eighteenth-

century Gothic novel. (2) The novel tells the story of Emily St. Aubert.

(3) Emily is intelligent and talented. (4) However, she seems remarkably

naive. (5) She often feels weak and faint. (6) Emily loves a noble but dull young man named Valancourt. (7) She lives with her foster uncle Montoni, the novel's villain. (8) Montoni appears alarmingly evil. (9) As the story progresses, Montoni frightens Emily. (10) After Montoni's death, however, Emily and Valancourt are happy.

Helping Verbs

Many verbs are made up of more than one word. The verb in the following sentence consists of two words.

Minh <u>must make</u> a decision about his future.

In this sentence, *make* is the **main verb**, and *must* is a **helping verb**.

FOCUS **Helping Verbs**

Helping verbs include forms of *be, have,* and *do* as well as the words *must, will, can, could, may, might, should,* and *would.* Some helping verbs, like forms of *be* and *have,* combine with main verbs to give information about when the action occurs. Forms of *do* combine with main verbs to form questions and negative statements. Still other helping verbs indicate willingness *(can),* possibility *(may),* necessity *(should),* obligation *(must),* and so on.

A sentence's **complete verb** is made up of a main verb plus any helping verbs that accompany it. In the following sentences, the complete verb is underlined twice, and the helping verbs are checkmarked.

<blockquote>
● **Writing Tip**
Sometimes, other words can come between the parts of a complete verb.
</blockquote>

  Minh <u>should have gone</u> earlier.

  <u>Did</u> Minh <u>ask</u> the right questions?

  Minh <u>will work</u> hard.

  Minh <u>can</u> really <u>succeed</u>.

For information on past participles, see Chapter 27.

FOCUS Helping Verbs with Participles

Present participles, such as *thinking*, and many irregular **past participles**, such as *gone,* cannot stand alone as main verbs in a sentence. They need a helping verb to make them complete.

INCORRECT   Minh gone to the library.

CORRECT   Minh <u>has gone</u> to the library.

◆ PRACTICE 15-4

The verbs in the sentences that follow consist of a main verb and one or more helping verbs. In each sentence, underline the complete verb twice, and put a check mark above the helping verb(s).

Example: The Salk polio vaccine <u>was given</u> to more than a million schoolchildren in 1954.

(1) By the 1950s, parents had become terrified of polio. (2) For years, it had puzzled doctors and researchers. (3) Thousands had become ill each year in the United States alone. (4) Children should have been playing happily. (5) Instead, they would get very sick. (6) Polio was sometimes called infantile paralysis. (7) In fact, it did cause paralysis in children and in adults as well. (8) Some patients could breathe only with the help of machines called iron lungs. (9) Others would remain in wheelchairs for life. (10) By 1960, Jonas Salk's vaccine had reduced the incidence of polio in the United States by more than 90 percent.

■ WRITING FIRST: Flashback

Look back at your response to the Writing First exercise on page 197. In each sentence, underline the complete verb twice, and put a check mark above each helping verb. Then, write the helping verbs on the lines below.

_____ _____ _____ _____

_____ _____ _____ _____

> ■ WRITING FIRST: Revising and Editing
>
> Look back at your response to the Writing First exercise on page 197. Circle every action verb. Then, try to replace some of them with different action verbs that express more precisely what the subject of each sentence is, was, or will be doing. For example, you might replace *makes* with *builds* or *creates*.

CHAPTER REVIEW

◆ EDITING PRACTICE

Read the following student passage. Underline the subject of each sentence once, and underline the complete verb of each sentence twice. If you have trouble locating the subject, try crossing out the prepositional phrases. The first sentence has been done for you.

Escape to Freedom

~~On April 14, 1979, at 10 p.m.~~, my <u>family</u> <u><u>left</u></u> Vietnam. My mother had hidden gold and jewelry in water pipes. Now we could use these unconfiscated items. We could buy seats on a fishing boat. Then we could escape to freedom. The trip was extremely dangerous. Forty-two people drifted aimlessly on the water. We drifted for four days and five nights on the Pacific Ocean. At last, on the 18th of April, we saw land. We stopped at Natuna Besar, Indonesia, for three days. Then, on the 21st, we came to Sedanau, another island of Indonesia. After a stay of one month, we traveled to Tanjungpinang, Indonesia. We stayed there for three and a half months. Life in the refugee camp was not luxurious. Living space was very limited. Food was scarce. Luckily, my father had once been a captain in the army. As a result, our family was quickly resettled to the United States.

◆ **COLLABORATIVE ACTIVITIES**

1. Fold a sheet of paper in half vertically. Working in a group of three or four students, spend two minutes listing as many nouns as you can in the column to the left of the fold. When your time is up, exchange papers with another group of students. Limiting yourselves to five minutes, write an appropriate action verb beside each noun. Each noun will now be the subject of a short sentence.

2. Choose five short sentences from those you wrote for Collaborative Activity 1. Again working in a group, create more fully developed sentences. First, expand each subject by adding words or prepositional phrases that give more information about the subject. (For example, you could expand *boat* to *the small, leaky boat with the red sail.*) Then expand each sentence further, adding ideas after the verb. (For example, the sentence *The boat bounced* could become *The small, leaky boat with the red sail bounced helplessly on the water.*)

3. Collaborate in a group of three or four students to write one original sentence for each of the linking verbs listed on page 201. When you have finished, exchange papers with another group. Now, try to add words and phrases to the other group's sentences to make them more interesting.

☑ REVIEW CHECKLIST:
Writing Simple Sentences

- A sentence expresses a complete thought. The subject tells who or what is being talked about in the sentence. (See 15A.)

- Prepositions connect words and groups of words in a sentence. They are combined with nouns or pronouns to form prepositional phrases. (See 15B.)

- The object of a preposition cannot be the subject of a sentence. (See 15B.)

- An action verb tells what the subject does, did, or will do. (See 15C.)

- A linking verb connects the subject to a word or words that describe or rename it. (See 15C.)

- Many verbs are made up of more than one word. The complete verb in a sentence includes the main verb plus any helping verbs. (See 15C.)

16

Writing Compound Sentences

PREVIEW

In this chapter, you will learn

■ to form compound sentences with coordinating conjunctions (16A)

■ to form compound sentences with semicolons (16B)

■ to form compound sentences with conjunctive adverbs (16C)

● **Writing Tip**
The subject of a simple sentence can be singular or plural. (See 15A.)

■ WRITING FIRST

Imagine that you have invented a new product, such as Velcro, the zipper, aluminum foil, Scotch tape, the safety pin, the paper clip, the rubber band, or Styrofoam. Begin by identifying this new product. Then, describe what it looks like. Finally, give examples of its possible uses to an audience who has never heard of it before.

A | **Forming Compound Sentences with Coordinating Conjunctions**

A simple sentence includes a subject and a verb.

European <u>immigrants</u> <u>arrived</u> at Ellis Island.

Asian <u>immigrants</u> <u>arrived</u> at Angel Island.

Two simple sentences can be joined into one **compound sentence** with a **coordinating conjunction** preceded by a comma.

European immigrants arrived at Ellis Island, <u>but</u> Asian immigrants arrived at Angel Island.

Coordinating Conjunctions

and	for	or	yet
but	nor	so	

Coordinating conjunctions join ideas of equal importance. They describe the relationship between two ideas and show how and why the ideas are connected. Different coordinating conjunctions have different meanings.

- If you want to indicate addition, use *and*.

  He acts like a child, <u>and</u> people think he is cute.

- If you want to indicate contrast or contradiction, use *but* or *yet*.

  He acts like a child, <u>but</u> he is an adult.

  He acts like a child, <u>yet</u> he longs to be taken seriously.

- If you want to indicate a cause-effect relationship, use *so* or *for*.

  He acts like a child, <u>so</u> we treat him like one.

  He acts like a child, <u>for</u> he craves attention.

- If you want to present alternatives, use *or*.

  He acts like a child, <u>or</u> he is ignored.

- If you want to eliminate alternatives, use *nor*.

  He does not act like a child, <u>nor</u> does he look like one.

> ● **Writing Tip**
> When a compound sentence is formed with *nor*, the verb comes before the subject in the second part of the compound sentence.

FOCUS **Punctuating with Coordinating Conjunctions**

When you use a coordinating conjunction to link two short sentences into a single compound sentence, always put a comma before the coordinating conjunction.

Either we will stand in line all night, or we will go home now.

We can stand in line all night, or we can go home now.

However, don't use a comma before a coordinating conjunction unless it links two *complete sentences*.

INCORRECT   We can stand in line all night, or go home now.

CORRECT   We can stand in line all night or go home now.

◆ PRACTICE 16-1

Fill in the coordinating conjunction—*and, but, for, nor, or, so,* or *yet*—that most logically links the two parts of each compound sentence. Remember to insert a comma before each coordinating conjunction.

Example: Fairy tales have been told by many people around the world, *but* the stories by two German brothers may be the most famous.

(1) Jakob and Wilhelm Grimm lived in the nineteenth century _____ they wrote many well-known fairy tales. (2) Most people think fondly of

fairy tales _____ the Brothers Grimm wrote many unpleasant and violent stories. (3) In their best-known works, children are abused ____ endings are not always happy. (4) Either innocent children are brutally punished for no reason _____ they are neglected. (5) For example, in "Hansel and Gretel," the stepmother mistreats the children _____ their father abandons them in the woods. (6) In this story, the events are horrifying _____ the ending is still happy. (7) The children outwit the evil adults _____ they escape unharmed. (8) Apparently, they are not injured physically ____ are they harmed emotionally. (9) Nevertheless, their story can hardly be called pleasant ____ it remains a story of child abuse and neglect.

◆ PRACTICE 16-2

Add coordinating conjunctions to combine these sentences where necessary to relate one idea to another. Remember to put a comma before each coordinating conjunction you add.

Example: Years ago, few Americans lived to be one hundred/ ~~Today,~~ *, but today,* there are more than 32,000 centenarians.

(1) Most people assume that diet, exercise, and family history account for centenarians' long lives. (2) This is not necessarily true. (3) Recently, a study was conducted in Georgia that showed surprising common traits among centenarians. (4) They did not necessarily avoid tobacco and alcohol. (5) They did not eat low-fat diets. (6) In fact, they ate relatively large amounts of fat, cholesterol, and sugar. (7) Diet could not explain their long lives. (8) They did, however, share four key survival characteristics. (9) First, all of the centenarians were optimistic about life. (10) All of them were positive thinkers. (11) They were also involved in religious life and had deep religious faith. (12) In addition, all the centenarians had continued to lead physically active lives. (13) They remained mobile even as elderly people. (14) Finally, all were able to adapt to loss. (15) They had all experienced the deaths of friends, spouses, or children. (16) They were able to get on with their lives.

■ WRITING FIRST: Flashback

Look back at your response to the Writing First exercise on page 206. If you see any compound sentences, bracket them. If you see any pairs of simple sentences that could be combined, rewrite them on the lines below, joining them with appropriate coordinating conjunctions to create compound sentences.

1. _____

_____

2. _____

_____

3. _____

_____

Be sure each of your compound sentences includes a comma before the coordinating conjunction.

B Forming Compound Sentences with Semicolons

You can also create a **compound sentence** by joining two simple sentences with a *semicolon*.

> The AIDS quilt contains thousands of panels; each panel is shaped like a coffin.

A semicolon generally connects independent clauses whose ideas are closely linked.

▼ **Student Voices**
My sentences are usually too long and have more than one idea, so I try to use semicolons.
Matt McDonald

FOCUS Using Semicolons to Join Sentences

Remember that a semicolon can only join two *complete sentences*. A semicolon cannot join a sentence and a fragment.

┌──────────── FRAGMENT ────────────┐
INCORRECT Because thousands are dying of AIDS; more research is clearly needed.

CORRECT Thousands are dying of AIDS; more research is clearly needed.

For information on avoiding sentence fragments, see Chapter 22.

◆ **PRACTICE 16-3**

Each of the following sentences can be linked with a semicolon to another short sentence to form a compound sentence. In each case, add a semicolon; then, complete the compound sentence with another sentence.

Example: My brother is addicted to fast food *; he eats it every day.*

1. Fast-food restaurants have become an American institution _____

   _____

2. Families eat at these restaurants_____

   _____

3. Many teenagers work there_____

   _____

4. McDonald's is known for its hamburgers_____

   _____

5. KFC is famous for its fried chicken_____

   _____

6. Taco Bell serves Mexican-style food_____

   _____

7. Pizza Hut specializes in pizza_____

   _____

8. Many fast-food restaurants offer some low-fat menu items _____

   _____

9. Some offer recyclable packaging_____

   _____

10. Some even have playgrounds_____

    _____

■ WRITING FIRST: Flashback

Look back at your response to the Writing First exercise on page 206. Do you see any pairs of sentences that you could connect with semicolons? If so, link each pair with a semicolon on the following lines.

(continued on the following page)

(continued from the previous page)

_____

_____

_____

_____

C   Forming Compound Sentences with Conjunctive Adverbs

Another way to combine two sentences into one **compound sentence** is with a **conjunctive adverb**. When a conjunctive adverb joins two sentences, a semicolon always comes *before* the conjunctive adverb, and a comma always comes *after* it.

> Some college students receive grants; <u>however</u>, others must take out loans.

● **Writing Tip**
When a coordinating conjunction links two sentences, use a comma, not a semicolon, before the coordinating conjunction. (See 16A.)

Frequently Used Conjunctive Adverbs

also	instead	still
besides	meanwhile	then
consequently	moreover	therefore
furthermore	nevertheless	thus
however	otherwise	

The addition of a conjunctive adverb makes the connection between ideas in a sentence more precise than it would be if the ideas were linked with a semicolon alone. Different conjunctive adverbs convey different meanings.

- Some conjunctive adverbs signal addition *(also, besides, furthermore, moreover).*

    > I have a lot on my mind; <u>also</u>, I have a lot of things to do.

- Some conjunctive adverbs make causal connections *(therefore, consequently, thus).*

    > I have a lot on my mind; <u>therefore</u>, I need to concentrate.

- Some conjunctive adverbs indicate contradiction or contrast *(nevertheless, however, still).*

    > I have a lot on my mind; <u>nevertheless</u>, I must try to relax.

■ Some conjunctive adverbs present alternatives.

> I have a lot on my mind; <u>otherwise</u>, I could relax.
>
> I will try not to think; <u>instead</u>, I will relax.

■ Some conjunctive adverbs indicate time sequence.

> I have a lot on my mind; <u>meanwhile</u>, I still have work to do.

> **FOCUS** **Transitional Expressions**
>
> Like conjunctive adverbs, **transitional expressions** can link two
> simple sentences into one compound sentence.
>
> > He had a miserable time at the party; <u>in addition</u>, he drank
> > too much.
>
> The transitional expression is preceded by a semicolon and followed
> by a comma.

Frequently Used Transitional Expressions

as a result	in comparison
at the same time	in fact
for example	on the contrary
for instance	on the other hand
in addition	that is

◆ **PRACTICE 16-4**

Add semicolons and commas where required to set off conjunctive adverbs
or transitional expressions that join two sentences.

Example: Fire has always been a threat to big cities ; however , the
threat has lessened over the years.

(1) The United States has a long history of disastrous fires in
addition it has a long history of innovations in fire safety. (2) A major
fire destroyed much of Boston in 1653 as a result each house was
required to have a ladder and a fire bucket. (3) City governments became
more concerned about fires therefore volunteer fire companies were
started in the eighteenth century. (4) Fire hydrants were installed in

Boston, Philadelphia, and New York in the early nineteenth century however hydrants sometimes froze. (5) Other innovations were clearly needed consequently fire alarm boxes and steam-powered fire engines were developed. (6) These developments helped nevertheless fires of disastrous proportions still plagued American cities.

◆ PRACTICE 16-5

Consulting the list of conjunctive adverbs on page 211 and the list of transitional expressions on page 212, choose a word or expression that logically connects each pair of sentences below into one compound sentence. Be sure to punctuate appropriately.

Example: Every year since 1927, *Time* has designated a Man of the

Year, ~~The~~ Man of the Year has not always been a man.
; however, the

(1) *Time* selects the Man of the Year to honor the person who has most influenced the previous year's events. The choice is often a prominent politician. (2) In the 1920s and 1930s, world leaders were often chosen. Franklin Delano Roosevelt was chosen twice and Ethiopia's Haile Selassie once. (3) In 1936, the Man of the Year was not a head of state. It was Wallis Warfield Simpson, the woman for whom King Edward VIII of England abdicated the throne. (4) During the war years, Hitler, Stalin, Churchill, and Roosevelt were all chosen. Stalin was featured twice. (5) Occasionally, the Man of the Year was not an individual. In 1950, it was The American Fighting Man. (6) In 1956, The Hungarian Freedom Fighter was Man of the Year. In 1966, *Time* editors chose The Young Generation. (7) Only a few individual women have been selected. Queen Elizabeth II was featured in 1952 and Corazon Aquino in 1986. (8) In 1975, American Women were honored as a group. The Man of the Year has nearly always been male. (9) Very few people of color have been designated Man of the Year. Martin Luther King Jr. was honored in 1963. (10) The Man of the Year has almost always been one or more human beings. The Computer was selected in 1982 and Endangered Earth in 1988.

◆ PRACTICE 16-6

Using the specified topics and conjunctive adverbs or transitional expressions, create five compound sentences. Be sure to punctuate appropriately.

Example:
Topic: fad diets
Transitional expression: for example

People are always falling for fad diets; for example, some people eat only

pineapple to lose weight.

1. *Topic:* laws to protect people with disabilities
   Transitional expression: in addition

   _____

   _____

2. *Topic:* gay men and lesbians as adoptive parents
   Conjunctive adverb: however

   _____

   _____

3. *Topic:* prayer in public schools
   Conjunctive adverb: therefore

   _____

   _____

4. *Topic:* high-school proms
   Conjunctive adverb: also

   _____

   _____

5. *Topic:* course requirements at your school
   Conjunctive adverb: instead

   _____

   _____

■ WRITING FIRST: Flashback

Look back at your response to the Writing First exercise on page 206. Have you used any conjunctive adverbs or transitional expressions to link sentences? If so, check to make sure that you have punctuated them correctly and that you haven't incorrectly joined any fragments to sentences. Next, check to see that you have used

(continued on the following page)

(continued from the previous page)

the word or expression that best shows the relationship between the ideas in the two sentences.

■ WRITING FIRST: Revising and Editing

Look back at your response to the Writing First exercise on page 206. Underline each compound sentence you find. Have you used the coordinating conjunction, conjunctive adverb, or transitional expression that best conveys your meaning? Have you punctuated these sentences correctly? Look for other pairs of sentences that you could combine into compound sentences. (Use your responses to the Flashback exercises on pages 209, 210, and 214 to help you revise your sentences.) When you have finished, look over a piece of writing you have done in response to another assignment, and try combining some simple sentences into compound sentences.

CHAPTER REVIEW

◆ EDITING PRACTICE

Read the following student essay. Then, revise it by linking pairs of sentences where appropriate with a coordinating conjunction, a semicolon, or a semicolon followed by either a conjunctive adverb or a transitional expression. Remember to put commas before coordinating conjunctions and to use semicolons and commas correctly with conjunctive adverbs. The first two sentences have been combined for you.

My Father's Life

My grandparents were born in Ukraine, *but they* ~~They~~ raised my father in western Pennsylvania. The ninth of their ten children, he had a life I cannot begin to imagine. To me, he is my big, strong, powerful Daddy. In reality, he is a child of poverty.

My grandfather worked for the American Car Foundry. The family lived in a company house. They shopped at the company store. In 1934, my grandfather was laid off. He went to work for the government digging sewer lines. At that time, the family was on relief. Every week, they were entitled to get food rations. My father would go to pick up the food. They desperately needed the prunes, beans, flour, margarine, and other things.

For years, my father wore his brothers' hand-me-down clothes. He wore thrift-shop shoes with cardboard over the holes in the soles. He was often hungry. He would sometimes sit by the side of the railroad tracks, waiting for the engineer to throw him an orange. My father would do any job to earn a quarter. Once, for example, he weeded a mile-long row of tomato plants. He was paid twenty-five cents and a pack of Necco wafers. (Twenty-five cents was a lot of money during the Depression.)

My father saved his pennies. Eventually, he was able to buy a used bicycle for two dollars. He dropped out of school at fourteen and got a job. The family badly needed his income. He woke up every day at 4 a.m. and rode his bike to his job at a meatpacking plant. He worked for fifty cents a day.

In 1943, at the age of seventeen, my father joined the U.S. Navy. He discovered a new world. For the first time in his life, he had enough to eat. He was always first in line at the mess hall. He went back for seconds and thirds before anyone else. After the war ended in 1945, he was discharged from the Navy. He went to work in a meat market in New York City. The only trade he knew was the meat business. Three years later, he had saved enough to open his own store, Pete's Quality Meats.

◆ COLLABORATIVE ACTIVITIES

1. Working in a small group, pair each of the short sentences in the left-hand column that follows with a sentence in the right-hand column to create ten compound sentences. Use as many different coordinating conjunctions as you can to connect ideas. Be sure each coordinating conjunction you choose conveys a logical relationship between ideas;

and remember to put a comma before each one. You may use some of the listed sentences more than once. *Note:* Many different combinations—some serious and factually accurate, some humorous—are possible.

Some dogs wear little sweaters.
Pit bulls are raised to fight.
Bonobos are pygmy chimpanzees.
Many people fear Dobermans.
Leopards have spots.
Dalmations can live in firehouses.
Horses can wear blankets.
All mules are sterile.
Great Danes are huge dogs.
Parrots can often speak.

Many are named Hamlet.
They live in groups.
One even sings Christmas carols.
They can wear bandanas.
They can play Frisbee.
Many live in equatorial Zaire.
Some people think they are gentle.
They don't get cold in winter.
They are half horse and half donkey.
They can be unpredictable.

2. Work in a group of three or four students to create a cast of five characters for a movie, a television pilot, or a music video. Working individually, write five brief descriptive sentences—one about each character. Then, exchange papers with another student. Add a coordinating conjunction to each sentence on the list to create five new sentences.

Example

ORIGINAL SENTENCE   Mark is a handsome heartthrob.

NEW SENTENCE   Mark is a handsome heartthrob, but he has green dreadlocks.

Next, select the three characters who sound most interesting. Write additional descriptive sentences about those characters, using compound sentences whenever possible. Your new sentences can provide information about the characters' relationships with one another as well as about their personalities and physical traits.

☑ REVIEW CHECKLIST:
Writing Compound Sentences

☐ A compound sentence is made up of two parts, and each part has a subject and a verb. (See 16A.)

☐ A coordinating conjunction—*and, but, for, nor, or, so,* or *yet*— can join the two parts of a compound sentence. A comma always comes before the coordinating conjunction. (See 16A.)

☐ A semicolon can join two complete sentences into one compound sentence. (See 16B.)

☐ A conjunctive adverb or transitional expression can also join two complete sentences into one compound sentence. When it joins two sentences, a conjunctive adverb or transitional expression is always preceded by a semicolon and followed by a comma. (See 16C.)

17

Writing Complex Sentences

PREVIEW

In this chapter, you will learn

▇ to use subordinating conjunctions to form complex sentences (17A)

▇ to use relative pronouns to form complex sentences (17B)

▇ **WRITING FIRST**

Describe something that you believe needs to be changed—for example, a rule, a law, a policy, a situation, or a custom. First, identify what you think needs to be changed; then, explain why you think a change is necessary.

A **clause** is a group of words that contains a subject and a verb. An **independent clause** can stand alone as a sentence.

The French sculptor Auguste Rodin caused controversy.

A **dependent clause** cannot stand alone because it needs other words to complete it.

INCORRECT   Because his nude figures shocked many viewers.

In the following sentence, the independent clause completes the idea in the dependent clause. The result is a **complex sentence**, a sentence that consists of one independent clause along with one or more dependent clauses.

┌─── DEPENDENT CLAUSE ───┐ ┌─ INDEPENDENT CLAUSE ─┐
Because his nude figures shocked many viewers, the French sculptor Auguste Rodin caused controversy.

A   Forming Complex Sentences with Subordinating Conjunctions

Subordinating conjunctions—words like *although* and *because*—can be used to join two simple sentences by making one sentence a dependent clause. The result is a complex sentence in which the subordinating conjunction shows the relationship between the ideas in the two clauses it links.

TWO SENTENCES   He was stripped of his title for refusing to be inducted into the army. Many people consider Muhammad Ali a hero.

COMBINED
COMPLEX SENTENCE   Although he was stripped of his title for refusing to be inducted into the army, many people consider Muhammad Ali a hero. (complex sentence)

Frequently Used Subordinating Conjunctions

after	even if	now that	that	where
although	even	once	though	whereas
as	though	provided	till	wherever
as if	if	rather than	unless	whether
as though	if only	since	until	which
because	in order	so that	when	while
before	that	than	whenever	

Different subordinating conjunctions express different relationships between dependent and independent clauses.

Relationship between clauses	Subordinating conjunction	Example
Time	after, before, since, until, when, whenever, while	When the whale surfaced, Ahab threw his harpoon.
Reason or cause	as, because	Scientists scaled back the project because the government cut funds.
Result or effect	in order that, so, so that	So that students' math scores will improve, many schools have instituted special programs.
Condition	even if, if, unless	The rain forest could disappear unless steps are taken immediately.
Contrast	although, even though, though	Although Edison had almost no formal education, he was a productive inventor.
Location	where, wherever	Pittsburgh was built where the Allegheny and Monongahela Rivers meet.

FOCUS **Punctuating with Subordinating Conjunctions**

Place a comma after the dependent clause when it comes *before* the independent clause in the sentence. Do not use a comma when the dependent clause comes *after* the independent idea in the sentence.

┌─────────── DEPENDENT CLAUSE ───────────┐ ┌─── INDEPENDENT CLAUSE ───┐
<u>Although</u> she wore the scarlet letter, Hester carried herself
proudly.

┌──── INDEPENDENT CLAUSE ────┐ ┌──────── DEPENDENT CLAUSE ────────┐
Hester carried herself proudly <u>although</u> she wore the scarlet
letter.

● **Writing Tip**
A clause that begins with a subordinating conjunction does not express a complete thought. Used by itself, it is a sentence fragment. (See 22C.)

◆ **PRACTICE 17-1**

Write an appropriate subordinating conjunction in each blank in the sentences below. Look at the list of subordinating conjunctions on page 219 to make sure you choose a conjunction that establishes the proper relationship between ideas. (The required punctuation has been provided.)

Example: Eugene V. Debs, the son of Alsatian immigrants, grew up in Terre Haute, Indiana, _*where*_ he was born in 1855.

(1) _____ Debs left school at age fourteen, he held various jobs for the railroad. (2) _____ he was intelligent and hard-working, he became the grand secretary of the Brotherhood of Locomotive Firemen. (3) By 1877, Debs had become interested in the social conditions of railroad workers. (4) _____ he had once defended the union, Debs now criticized its policies. (5) _____ he did not have much money, he resigned his position with the union and formed the American Railway Union (ARU). (6) _____ violence occurred during a strike called by the union, Debs went to jail for six months. (7) Debs had always supported the Democratic Party _____ he organized the Social Democratic Party of America in 1897. (8) Debs was nominated as the Socialist Labor Party's presidential candidate five times. (9) _____ he completed a difficult campaign in 1912, he received 900,000 votes (6 percent of the total), the largest vote ever for a socialist presidential candidate. (10) Debs

remained a popular labor leader his entire life _____ he was jailed for giving a speech denouncing America's entry into World War I.

◆ PRACTICE 17-2

Form one complex sentence by combining each of the following pairs of sentences. Use a subordinating conjunction from the list on page 219 to clarify the relationship between the dependent and independent clauses in each sentence. Make sure you include a comma where one is required.

Example: Orville and Wilbur Wright built the first powered plane/
although they
~~They~~ had no formal training as engineers.
                 ^

1. Professional midwives are used widely in Europe. In the United States, they usually practice independently only in areas where there are few doctors.

2. John Deere constructed his first steel plow in 1837. A new era began in prairie agriculture.

3. Stephen Crane powerfully describes battles in *The Red Badge of Courage*. He never experienced a war.

4. Elvis Presley died suddenly in 1977. Thousands of his fans gathered in front of his mansion.

5. Jonas Salk developed the first polio vaccine in the 1950s. The incidence of polio began to decline rapidly in the United States.

6. The salaries of baseball players rose dramatically in the 1980s. Some sportswriters predicted that fans would stop attending games.

7. The gunpowder manufacturers the Du Ponts arrived in Rhode Island from France in 1800. American gunpowder was expensive and inferior to the kind manufactured by the French.

8. Margaret Sanger opened her first birth-control clinic in America in 1916. She was arrested and sentenced to thirty days in jail.

9. Thaddeus Stevens thought plantation land should be distributed to freed slaves. He disagreed with Lincoln's peace terms for the South.

10. Steven Spielberg directed some of the most popular movies of all time. He didn't win an Academy Award until *Schindler's List*.

■ **WRITING FIRST: Flashback**

Look back at your response to the Writing First exercise on page 218. Identify two pairs of sentences that could be combined with subordinating conjunctions. On the lines below, combine each pair into a complex sentence. Check to make sure you have punctuated your new sentences correctly.

_____

_____

_____

_____

B **Forming Complex Sentences with Relative Pronouns**

A **relative pronoun** (*who, that, which,* and so on) introduces a **dependent clause** that describes a noun or pronoun in the sentence.

■ **Computer Tip**
Using the word-processing function that shows the average length of sentences, compare your first and final drafts to see if your sentences have become more complex.

Relative Pronouns			
that	which	whoever	whomever
what	who	whom	whose

Nadine Gordimer, who won the Nobel Prize in literature in 1991, comes from South Africa.

Many words that are slang eventually become part of the language.

Transistors, which were invented in 1948, have replaced vacuum tubes in radios and televisions.

FOCUS **Using *Who, Which,* and *That***

■ *Who* refers to people.

He is the man who bought the car.

(continued on the following page)

(continued from the previous page)

■ *Which* refers to things.

> Years of effort produced the Hubble telescope, <u>which</u> is very powerful.

■ *That* refers to things or to groups of people.

> The subject <u>that</u> we discussed was how to increase sales.

> The Rockies were the team <u>that</u> won.

Like subordinating conjunctions, relative pronouns can join two sentences by making one sentence a dependent clause. The result is a complex sentence in which the relative pronoun shows the relationship between the ideas in the two clauses it links.

● **Writing Tip**
A clause that contains a relative pronoun does not by itself express a complete thought; it is therefore a fragment. (See 22C.)

TWO SENTENCES   The African Company was an all-black acting troop. It performed Shakespeare's plays in the early 1820s.

COMBINED   The African Company was an all-black acting troop <u>that</u> performed Shakespeare's plays in the early 1820s. (complex sentence)

For information on punctuating who, which, *and* that, *see 31D.*

FOCUS   **Punctuating with Relative Pronouns**

In general, commas are used to set off a dependent clause introduced by *which*. Commas are not used to set off a dependent clause introduced by *that*. Depending on its meaning in a sentence, a dependent clause introduced by *who* is sometimes but not always set off by commas. For more on commas, see 31D.

◆ **PRACTICE 17-3**

Combine each of the following pairs of sentences into one complex sentence, using the relative pronoun that follows each pair.

Example: The United States is frightening to many Japanese. It is seen as a place where everyone owns or carries a gun. (which)

The United States, which is seen as a place where everyone owns or

carries a gun, is frightening to many Japanese.

1. This image is reinforced by a television show.
   It started several years ago. (that)

_____

_____

_____

2. On Sunday nights, viewers tune in to see Hyota overcome his latest disaster.
He is a Japanese traveler trying to survive in America. (who)

_____

_____

_____

3. One Sunday, Hyota was wandering through the streets, looking for someone to help him.
They were full of people. (which)

_____

_____

_____

4. His questions were misunderstood.
They were halfway between English and Japanese. (which)

_____

_____

_____

5. This television program is very popular.
It teaches American street expressions to Japanese viewers. (which)

_____

_____

_____

6. Most Japanese learn English in high school by reading formal passages from textbooks.
The textbooks are designed to get them into universities. (that)

_____

_____

_____

7. The English they learn is of little use in the real world.
It is not enough to protect them from street hustlers. (which)

_____

_____

_____

8. Some Japanese have been killed or injured in the United States.
They could not understand spoken English. (who)

_____

_____

_____

9. For example, a sixteen-year-old Japanese exchange student was shot.
He did not understand the command _freeze_. (who)

_____

_____

_____

10. This case has led many Japanese to learn "usable English."
It will help them when they travel to the United States. (that)

_____

_____

_____

■ WRITING FIRST: Flashback

Look back at your response to the Writing First exercise on page 218. Identify two sentences that could be combined with a relative pronoun. (If you cannot find two appropriate sentences, write two new ones.) On the lines below, write the new complex sentence.

_____

_____

_____

_____

■ WRITING FIRST: Revising and Editing

Look back at your response to the Writing First exercise on page 218. Correct any errors in your use of subordinating conjunctions and relative pronouns. When you have finished, look over a piece of writing you have done in response to another assignment, and try combining some sentences into complex sentences.

CHAPTER REVIEW

◆ **EDITING PRACTICE**

Read the following student essay, and revise it by using subordinating conjunctions or relative pronouns to combine pairs of short sentences. Be sure to punctuate correctly. The first sentence has been revised for you.

My Life in Haiti

My father and mother lived in Haiti/ *although* I was born in the United States. My father and his brother opened a small business in Haiti. I was a baby. I grew up in Haiti. I experienced the culture as a native, not a foreigner. My friends were all Haitian. They wanted only to play soccer. I tried to teach them baseball and football. Before I learned to speak English, I spoke only the Haitian Creole dialect. I was a toddler. I went to New York to visit my grandmother. One day I was thirsty. I asked her in Creole for a glass of water. At the same time, I pointed to the refrigerator. My grandmother had no idea what I meant. She spoke only English. I finally had to point to a glass so she would know what I wanted.

In Haiti, I developed close relationships with the neighbors. They lived on our street. They never shut their doors. I was constantly walking in and out of their houses. Whenever I opened my mouth, one of them fed me some candy or a bowl of curried goat stew. Dina was an elderly Cuban woman. She was like a grandmother to me. She encouraged me to eat. She thought I was too skinny. Lita, another neighbor, was an excellent storyteller. She would tell my friends and me tales of voodoo. We were afraid to walk home. Her stories terrified us. We could not wait to hear more.

When I was twelve, my life in Haiti ended. My father died of cancer. He had been sick for a year. My mother and

I could have stayed in Haiti. She decided to return to her parents in New York. She sold her share of the business to my uncle. We needed the money. Sometimes, my mind wanders back to those days. My life in Haiti is over. I will never forget the people I knew and loved there.

◆ COLLABORATIVE ACTIVITIES

1. Working in a group of four students, make a list of four or five of your favorite recording artists. Divide into pairs, and with your partner, write two sentences describing each artist. Next, use subordinating conjunctions or relative pronouns to combine each pair of sentences into one complex sentence. With your group, discuss how the ideas in each sentence are related, and make sure you have used the subordinating conjunction or relative pronoun that best conveys this relationship.

   Example: Many of Bob Marley's songs celebrate the lives of Jamaicans. He achieved worldwide recognition.

   Although many of Bob Marley's songs celebrate the lives of Jamaicans, he achieved worldwide recognition.

2. Imagine that you and the members of your group live in a neighborhood where workers are repairing underground power lines. As they work, the workers talk loudly and use foul language. Write a letter of complaint to the power company in which you explain that the workers' behavior is offensive to you and to your children. Tell the company that you want the offensive behavior to end. Write the first draft of your letter in simple sentences. After you have written this draft, work as a group to combine as many sentences as you can with subordinating conjunctions and relative pronouns.

3. Assume you are in a competition to determine which collaborative group in your class is best at writing complex sentences. Working in a group, prepare a letter to your instructor in which you present the strengths of your group. Be sure to use a subordinating conjunction or relative pronoun in each of the sentences in your letter.

   Next, as a class, evaluate the letters from the groups. Choose the letter that most successfully convinces you that its group is best.

✔ REVIEW CHECKLIST:
Writing Complex Sentences

   When an independent clause is joined with a dependent clause, the result is a complex sentence. (See 17A.)

(continued on the following page)

(continued from the previous page)

- Subordinating conjunctions—such as *although, after, when, while,* and *because*—can join two sentences into one complex sentence. (See 17A.)

- Always use a comma after a dependent clause when it comes before the independent clause in the sentence. Do not use a comma when the dependent clause follows the independent clause. (See 17A.)

- A relative pronoun introduces a dependent clause that describes a noun or pronoun in a sentence. Relative pronouns can join two sentences into one complex sentence. (See 17B.)

- When you link two sentences with a relative pronoun, use a comma before *which;* do not use a comma before *that. Who* is sometimes preceded by a comma.

18

Achieving Sentence Variety

PREVIEW

In this chapter, you will learn

■ to vary sentence types (18A)

■ to vary sentence openings (18B)

■ to experiment with different ways of combining sentences (18C)

■ to vary sentence length (18D)

■ WRITING FIRST

Plan a time capsule that your children will open when they are adults. What items would you include? How would you expect each item to communicate to your children what you and your world were like?

In Chapters 15 through 17, you learned to write simple, compound, and complex sentences. Now, you are ready to focus on varying the form and length of the sentences you use. A passage of varied sentences flows more smoothly, is easier to read and understand, and is more interesting than one in which all the sentences are the same length and begin with the subject.

A Varying Sentence Types

Most English sentences are **statements**. Others are **questions** or **exclamations**. As you explore your options for increasing sentence variety, try to experiment with all three types of sentences.

In the following paragraph, a question and an exclamation add variety to the original.

In less than twenty years, the image of African Americans in television sitcoms seemed to change dramatically, reflecting the changing status of black men and women in American society. But had anything really changed? In *Beulah,* the 1950 sitcom that was the first to star an African-American woman, the title character was a maid. Her friends were portrayed as irresponsible and not very smart. *Amos 'n' Andy,* which also appeared in the 1950s, continued these negative stereotypes

● **Writing Tip**
When you write instructions, you can also use **commands** —statements that address readers directly: *Now, unplug the appliance.* (See 14D and 36D.)

Question

229

18 A

Exclamation

of black characters. In 1968, with the civil rights movement at its height, the NBC comedy hit *Julia* portrayed a black woman in a much more favorable light. A widowed nurse, raising a small boy on her own, Julia was a dedicated professional and a patient and devoted mother. The image of the African American was certainly more positive, but the character was no more balanced or three-dimensional than earlier black characters had been. Julia was not an object of ridicule; instead, she was a saint!

◆ PRACTICE 18-1

Revise the following passage by changing one of the statements into a question and one of the statements into an exclamation.

Example: Many people wonder about the relationship between smoking and weight loss. (statement)

Is there a relationship between smoking and weight loss? (question)

(1) A recent study shows that Americans are getting fatter every year. (2) On average, adult Americans today are eight pounds heavier than they were ten years ago. (3) Several factors are responsible for this trend. (4) First, Americans are increasingly less active than they have been in the past. (5) In addition, most Americans consume too many high-calorie fast-food meals. (6) Finally, experts believe that the decline in the number of Americans who smoke has contributed to this national weight gain. (7) Ex-smokers often replace cigarettes with food, and because nicotine raises the rate at which the body burns calories, smokers burn calories somewhat more slowly after they quit. (8) Therefore, people who quit smoking almost can't help but gain weight. (9) This is certainly a dilemma.

● **Writing Tip**
A statement ends with a period, a question ends with a question mark, and an exclamation ends with an exclamation point.

● **Writing Tip**
Exclamations are widely used in informal, personal writing and in dialogue to suggest emotional intensity and convey emphasis. They are used less often in formal writing.

■ WRITING FIRST: Flashback

Look back at your response to the Writing First exercise on page 229. What questions does your paragraph answer? Write one or two on the lines below.

Question 1: _____

_____

(continued on the following page)

(continued from the previous page)

Question 2: _____

_____

If you can, add one of these questions to your paragraph.

If you think an exclamation would be an appropriate addition to your paragraph, suggest one below.

Exclamation: _____

_____

Where in your paragraph could you add this exclamation?

B   Varying Sentence Openings

Varying the way you begin your sentences is another way of adding life to your writing. If you always begin your sentences with the subject, your writing is likely to seem dull and repetitive, as the writing in the paragraph below does.

> Scientists have been observing a disturbing phenomenon. The population of frogs, toads, and salamanders has been declining. This decline was first noticed in the mid-1980s. Some reports blamed chemical pollution. Some biologists began to suspect that a fungal disease was killing these amphibians. The most plausible explanation seems to be that the amphibians' eggs are threatened by solar radiation. This radiation penetrates the thinned ozone layer, which used to shield them from the sun's rays.

Beginning with Adverbs

Instead of opening every sentence with the subject, try beginning with one or more **adverbs**, as the following paragraph illustrates.

> Scientists have been observing a disturbing phenomenon. <u>Gradually but steadily</u>, the population of frogs, toads, and salamanders has been declining. This decline was first noticed in the mid-1980s. Some reports blamed chemical pollution. Some biologists began to suspect that a fungal disease was killing these amphibians. <u>However</u>, the most plausible explanation seems to be that the amphibians' eggs are threatened by solar radiation. This radiation penetrates the thinned ozone layer, which used to shield them from the sun's rays.

▼ **Student Voices**
To vary my sentences, I make sure I start them with different words.
          Krishna Mahajan

■ **Computer Tip**
Use the Search or Find command to locate every use of *The, This,* and *It* at the beginning of a sentence. Then, revise if necessary to vary sentence openings.

● **Writing Tip**
Adverbs are words—such as *tightly* or *quickly*—that describe or identify other words (verbs, adjectives, or other adverbs). (See Chapter 29.)

● **Writing Tip**
Place a comma after an adverb or a prepositional phrase that opens a sentence. (See 31B.)

● **Writing Tip**
Frequently used prepositions include *after, at, before, by, for, from, in, into, near, of, on, over, through, to, under, until,* and *with.* (See 15B.)

Beginning with Prepositional Phrases

You can also begin some sentences with prepositional phrases. A **prepositional phrase** (such as *along the river* or *near the diner*) is made up of a preposition and its object.

> In recent years, scientists have been observing a disturbing phenomenon. Gradually but steadily, the population of frogs, toads, and salamanders has been declining. This decline was first noticed in the mid-1980s. At first, some reports blamed chemical pollution. After a while, some biologists began to suspect that a fungal disease was killing these amphibians. However, the most plausible explanation seems to be that the amphibians' eggs are threatened by solar radiation. This radiation penetrates the thinned ozone layer, which used to shield them from the sun's rays.

FOCUS **Sentence Openings**

Note that in addition to adding variety, adverbs and prepositional phrases at the beginnings of sentences can also function as transitions, joining the sentences smoothly into a paragraph. (See 2C.)

■ **Computer Tip**
Keep a list of possible sentence openings (adverbs and prepositional phrases, for example) in a separate file. Refer to this file to find different ways to begin sentences.

◆ PRACTICE 18-2

Several sentences in the following passage contain prepositional phrases and adverbs that could be moved to the beginnings of sentences. Revise the passage to vary the sentence openings by moving prepositional phrases to the beginnings of three sentences and moving adverbs to the beginnings of three other sentences. Be sure to place a comma after these prepositional phrases and adverbs.

Example: *In hotels, safety*
~~Safety~~ is a top priority ~~in hotels~~.

(1) A disaster struck Kansas City in 1981, tragically killing more than one hundred people. (2) Partygoers were dancing in the crowded lobby of a new hotel, the Hyatt Regency. (3) The dancers suddenly heard a very loud cracking sound. (4) Two suspended walkways above them were packed with observers stomping heavily in time to the music. (5) The dancers watched in horror as the walkways began to crash into the lobby. (6) The top walkway broke loose from the ceiling and crashed into a second walkway beneath it. (7) Both concrete walkways then collapsed with a loud roar into the hotel's crowded lobby bar. (8) People who had

been having a good time only moments before now screamed hysterically as they watched others die horrible deaths. (9) It was certainly a scene the survivors would not soon forget.

◆ PRACTICE 18-3

Listed below are three adverbs and three prepositional phrases. In the passage that follows, add one of these words or phrases to the beginning of each sentence in order to vary the sentence openings. Be sure your additions connect ideas clearly and logically. Remember to add commas where they are needed.

Occasionally	Sadly
For example	In fact
With their screams and chants	Of course

Example: ~~Pro~~ *Sadly, pro* football players face great danger.

(1) Professional football is one of the most popular sports in the country; it is also one of the most dangerous. (2) Bob Utley and Darryl Stingley are now paraplegics because of injuries they suffered on the field, and the disabled list increases each season.

(3) The league has established new rules to make the game safer, and some of these have cut down on serious injuries. (4) A player cannot tackle a kicker after he has kicked the ball, and a player cannot tackle a quarterback after he has thrown the ball or a runner after he has gone out of bounds. (5) These precautions, however, do not always protect players. (6) Players still tackle other players in violation of the rules because they are angry and frustrated or even as a calculated strategy. (7) One coach is rumored to have placed bounties on rival players. (8) A team member collects by putting the opposing players out of commission for the entire game.

(9) The fans also share the blame for the violence of football. (10) They encourage players to hit harder or play with more intensity. (11) They believe their team should do anything to win. (12) The unfortunate fact is that as football becomes more dangerous to players, it becomes more popular with fans.

■ **WRITING FIRST: Flashback**

Look back at your response to the Writing First exercise on page 229. Identify one sentence that you could revise by beginning it with an adverb and one that could open with a prepositional phrase. Write the revised sentences on the lines below.

1. _____ , _____

           (Adverb)   (Original sentence)

    _____

2. _____ , _____

   (Prepositional phrase)   (Original sentence)

    _____

C **Combining Sentences**

For information on forming compound sentences, see Chapter 16. For information on forming complex sentences, see Chapter 17.

Another way to achieve sentence variety is to experiment with different ways of combining sentences. You have already learned to combine simple sentences to create compound sentences (Chapter 16) and complex sentences (Chapter 17). You can also combine short, choppy sentences with *present participles, past participles, compounds,* or *appositives.* These different techniques will help you create varied, interesting sentences.

Using Present Participles

The **present participle** is the *-ing* form of a verb: *using, carrying.* You can use a present participle to combine two sentences.

For more on present participles, see 25A.

> TWO SENTENCES Duke Ellington composed more than a thousand songs. He worked hard to establish his reputation as a musician.

> COMBINED <u>Composing</u> more than a thousand songs, Duke Ellington worked hard to establish his reputation as a musician. (present participle)

● **Writing Tip**

Place a comma after a phrase introduced by a present or past participle.

When the sentences are combined, the present participle *(composing)* introduces a phrase that describes the sentence's subject *(Duke Ellington).*

Using Past Participles

For more on past participles, see 25B; for a list of irregular past participles, see 27B.

Past participles of verbs are usually formed with *-ed (carried)* or *-d (used),* but there are also many irregular past participle forms *(known, written).* Two sentences can often be combined when one of them contains a past participle.

TWO SENTENCES   Nogales is located on the border between Arizona and Mexico. It is a bilingual city.

COMBINED   <u>Located</u> on the border between Arizona and Mexico, Nogales is a bilingual city. (past participle)

When the sentences are combined, the past participle *(located)* introduces a phrase that describes the sentence's subject *(Nogales)*.

● **Writing Tip**
Make sure that modifiers introduced by past or present participles clearly refer to the words they describe. (See 25C and 25D.)

◆ PRACTICE 18-4

Use a present participle to combine each of the following pairs of sentences into a single sentence. Eliminate any unnecessary words, and use a comma to set off each phrase introduced by a present participle. When you are finished, underline the present participle in each new sentence.

Example: Moviegoers accepted Chaplin unquestioningly. They saw his early characters as representations of the common man.

<u>Accepting</u> Chaplin unquestioningly, moviegoers saw his early characters

as representations of the common man.

or

<u>Seeing</u> his early characters as representations of the common man,

moviegoers accepted Chaplin unquestioningly.

1. Charlie Chaplin grew up in the slums of London. He held various jobs and played small parts in vaudeville shows.

2. Chaplin arrived in Hollywood in 1910. He was soon discovered by the director Mack Sennett.

3. Chaplin turned to writing and directing. He made his first famous film, *The Tramp*.

4. Chaplin wore baggy pants and a sad expression. He often appeared in his "little tramp" role.

5. Chaplin moved from silent to talking pictures. He made *City Lights* and *Modern Times*.

_____

_____

6. Chaplin wanted to satirize Nazi Germany. He directed and starred in *The Great Dictator*.

_____

_____

7. Anticommunist crusaders criticized him for his politics and his personal behavior. They attacked Chaplin in the 1950s.

_____

_____

8. Chaplin left Hollywood. He settled in England.

_____

_____

◆ PRACTICE 18-5

Use a past participle to combine each of the following pairs of sentences into a single sentence. Eliminate any unnecessary words, and use a comma to set off each phrase introduced by a past participle. When you are finished, underline the past participle in each new sentence.

Example: Langston Hughes was born in Missouri. He was a major American writer.

Born in Missouri, Langston Hughes was a major American writer.

1. Hughes was interested in writing even in his high school days. He published his first poem in 1921.

_____

_____

_____

2. Hughes was troubled by the treatment of African Americans. He wrote poems about their lives.

_____

_____

3. Hughes was convinced that African-American music could be translated into poetry. He wrote his first book of poems, *The Weary Blues*.

_____

_____

_____

4. Hughes was celebrated by both white and black critics. He was praised for the freshness of his language and verse.

_____

_____

_____

5. Hughes was known primarily as a poet. He also collaborated on several plays and published a novel and a collection of stories.

_____

_____

_____

6. Hughes was inspired by the people of Harlem. He did some of his most important work after moving there.

_____

_____

_____

7. Hughes was determined to convey his ideas to a wide audience. He wrote columns for several newspapers.

_____

_____

_____

8. Hughes was also interested in black history. He wrote *The First Book of Negroes* (1952) and *Famous American Negroes* (1954).

_____

_____

_____

Using Compound Subjects or Compound Verbs

A **compound subject** consists of two nouns or pronouns, usually joined by *and;* a **compound verb** consists of two verbs, usually joined by *and.*

TWO SENTENCES   Elijah McCoy was an African-American inventor. Garrett Morgan was also an African-American inventor.

COMBINED   <u>Elijah McCoy and Garrett Morgan</u> were African-American inventors. (compound subject)

Writing Tip
Remember that a compound subject joined by *and* takes a plural verb. (See 23A.)

TWO SENTENCES	Robert Redford starred in *All the President's Men* in 1976. He directed *Quiz Show* in 1994.
COMBINED	Robert Redford <u>starred</u> in *All the President's Men* in 1976 <u>and directed</u> *Quiz Show* in 1994. (compound verb)

◆ PRACTICE 18-6

Combine each of the following pairs of sentences into one sentence by creating a compound subject or a compound verb.

Example: The NCAA Presidents Commission wants to reform college athletic programs. It has recommended a number of measures for doing so.

(1) These college presidents want to improve the academic performance of college athletes. Their supporters also want to improve the academic performance of college athletes. (2) Their first proposal raises the number of required core courses for entering freshmen. It increases the SAT scores necessary for admittance. (3) A second proposal requires athletes to earn a certain number of credits every year. It mandates a similar advancement in an athlete's grade point average. (4) Many athletic directors see the changes as unfair. They are resisting them. (5) Many Big East coaches believe standardized test scores are biased. They want their use in screening student athletes banned. (6) Some coaches also fear that the new rules will force many athletes to choose easy majors. Other opponents fear the same thing. (7) According to supporters, however, many athletes under the current system fail to advance academically. They often finish their eligibility fifty or more hours short of graduation. (8) The new rules, they say, give student athletes a fair chance. They also keep them on the graduation track. (9) In the supporters' view, poor supervision by athletic directors is to be blamed for the poor performance of student athletes. Lack of support for academic excellence is also to blame.

Using Appositives

An **appositive** is a word or word group that identifies or renames a noun or pronoun. Using an appositive is often a good way to combine two sentences about the same subject.

TWO SENTENCES   C. J. Walker was the first American woman to become a self-made millionaire. She marketed a line of hair-care products for black women.

COMBINED   C. J. Walker, <u>the first American woman to become a self-made millionaire,</u> marketed a line of hair-care products for black women. (appositive)

Notice that an appositive can also come at the beginning or at the end of a sentence.

<u>The first American woman to become a self-made millionaire,</u> C. J. Walker marketed a line of hair-care products for black women.

Several books have been written about C. J. Walker, <u>the first American woman to become a self-made millionaire.</u>

◆ PRACTICE 18-7

Use appositives to combine each of the following pairs of sentences into one sentence. Three of your sentences should have the appositive at the beginning, three should have the appositive in the middle, and three should have the appositive at the end. Be sure to use commas appropriately.

Example: Alfred Hitchcock *, a film and television director,* was born in 1899 and died in 1980. ~~He was a film and television director.~~

(1) Alfred Hitchcock's first big success came in 1935 with *The Thirty-Nine Steps.* It was a thriller about an innocent man mistaken for a criminal. (2) His next big English-made hit brought many offers from Hollywood. It was *The Lady Vanishes.* (3) His first Hollywood film was the suspense classic *Rebecca.* It was a 1940 film version of a popular novel by Daphne du Maurier. (4) *Spellbound* was one of his odder movies of the 1940s. It is the story of the amnesiac head of a psychiatric hospital and includes a surreal dream sequence by Salvador Dali. (5) His most controversial film was *Psycho.* It stars Anthony Perkins as the mentally unstable proprietor of the Bates Motel, as well as his own "mother." (6) Audiences in 1960 were truly shocked by *Psycho's* infamous depiction of a woman's bloody murder in a shower. This is a scene that represents brilliant use of sound and editing. (7) Hitchcock was a well-known television personality as well as a film director. He hosted two successful series in the late 1950s and the early 1960s. (8) His hefty profile and deep voice were trademarks of the early television shows. They are still

recognizable in reruns to viewers today. (9) Hitchcock was one of the great masters of film technique. He made movies admired by both popular audiences and academic critics.

■ **WRITING FIRST: Flashback**

Look back at your response to the Writing First exercise on page 229. Underline two or three pairs of sentences that you think could be combined. On the lines below, combine each pair of sentences into a single sentence, using one of the methods discussed in 18C. Use a different method for each pair of sentences.

1. _____

   _____

2. _____

   _____

3. _____

   _____

D **Varying Sentence Length**

A paragraph of short, choppy sentences—or a paragraph of long, rambling ones—is usually monotonous. By mixing long and short sentences, perhaps following a string of several long sentences with a relatively brief one, you create a more interesting paragraph.

In the following paragraph, the sentences are all quite short, and the result is a dull passage.

> The world's first drive-in movie theater opened on June 6, 1933, in Camden, New Jersey. Automobiles became more popular. Drive-ins did too. By the 1950s, there were more than four thousand drive-ins in the United States. Over the years, the high cost of land hurt drive-ins. So did the rising popularity of television. Now, they have been replaced by the multiplex and the VCR. There are no drive-ins at all in Alaska. There are none in Rhode Island or Delaware either. New Jersey's last drive-in closed in 1991.

The revised paragraph that appears below is more interesting because it mixes long and short sentences.

> The world's first drive-in movie theater opened on June 6, 1933, in Camden, New Jersey. As automobiles became more popular, drive-ins

■ **Computer Tip**

Some word-processing programs can tell you how long your average sentence is and how many words are in your shortest and longest sentences. Use this feature to help you vary sentence length.

did too, and by the 1950s, there were more than four thousand drive-ins in the United States. Today, there are fewer than a thousand. Over the years, the high cost of land, combined with the rising popularity of television, hurt drive-ins. Now, they have been replaced by the multiplex and the VCR. There are no drive-ins at all in Alaska, Rhode Island, or Delaware, and New Jersey's last drive-in closed in 1991.

To increase sentence variety, the writer first combined some of the original paragraph's short sentences and then added a new short sentence ("Today, there are fewer than a thousand") for emphasis after a long one.

◆ **PRACTICE 18-8**

The following passage contains a series of short, choppy sentences. Revise it so that it mixes long and short sentences. Be sure to use commas and other punctuation appropriately.

Example: Kente cloth has special significance for many African Americans, *but many* ~~Many~~ white people do not understand this significance.

(1) Kente cloth is made in western Africa. (2) It is produced primarily by the Ashanti people. (3) It has been worn for hundreds of years by African royalty. (4) They consider it a sign of power and status. (5) Many African Americans wear kente cloth. (6) They see it as a link to their heritage. (7) Each motif or pattern on the cloth has a name. (8) Each color has a special significance. (9) For example, red and yellow suggest a long and healthy life. (10) Green and white suggest a good harvest. (11) African women may wear kente cloth as a dress or head wrap. (12) African-American women, like men, usually wear strips of cloth around their shoulders. (13) Men and women of African descent wear kente cloth as a sign of black pride.

■ WRITING FIRST: Flashback

Look back at your response to the Writing First exercise on page 229. Count the number of words in each sentence, and write the results on the following lines.

(continued on the following page)

18 D

(continued from the previous page)

Sentence 1 _____   Sentence 6 _____

Sentence 2 _____   Sentence 7 _____

Sentence 3 _____   Sentence 8 _____

Sentence 4 _____   Sentence 9 _____

Sentence 5 _____   Sentence 10 _____

Now, write a new short sentence to follow your longest sentence.

New sentence: _____

_____

_____

▼ **Student Voices**

My sentences don't always flow, so when I'm proofreading a first draft, I try to add transitions and smooth out each sentence.

Kristin Miller

■ **Computer Tip**

Using the word-processing function that shows the average length of sentences, compare your first and final drafts to see if your sentences have become longer and more complex.

■ WRITING FIRST: Revising and Editing

Look back at your response to the Writing First exercise on page 229. Using any strategies from this chapter that seem appropriate, revise your writing so that your sentences are varied, interesting, and smoothly connected. (Refer to your responses to the Flashback exercises on pages 230, 234, 240, and 241 as needed.) When you are finished, revise the sentences in an assignment you have completed for another course.

CHAPTER REVIEW

◆ **EDITING PRACTICE**

Many of the sentences in the student essay that follows begin with the subject—*my dad, he,* and *my father,* for example. Using the revision strategies illustrated in this chapter, revise the passage so its sentences are varied, interesting, and smoothly connected. The first two sentences have been edited for you.

Golf Course Management

My father ,is a golf course superintendent, He works

long hours in winter and longer hours in summer. Many

people consider the career of a golf course superintendent a recreational, low-stress occupation with many advantages, such as idle winters and frequent opportunities to play golf. In fact, I am often asked the question, "What does your dad do in the winter?" My response is that his job is demanding all year long.

My father arrives at work about 5:30 a.m. during the summer. He gets much of his work done in the early morning hours. He keeps his crew at work until two or three in the afternoon. During this time, they groom the course. They also fertilize the greens and fairways.

My dad usually returns home during the summer between 4 and 7 p.m. It depends on how much he and his crew are able to accomplish. He sometimes returns to work after dinner for an hour or two in order to irrigate. He avoids most irrigation during the daytime. (Members would be quite upset if he turned on the irrigation system during their golf games.)

Summer hours are often long and tiring for a golf course superintendent because most of the responsibility falls on his shoulders. His crew is able to maintain the course, but they lack the specific training and education of a certified golf course superintendent. My dad has a four-year college degree, as most superintendents do. He knows all about horticulture, soils, and drainage. He has also studied fertilizing techniques and chemistry. He also knows how to diagnose diseases occurring in grass and trees. He knows how to apply the safest, most effective treatments. He also controls nuisances such as water algae and harmful insects. These insects permeate the grass and trees and, if not stopped, will kill them.

The workload decreases considerably as the weather turns colder. A golf course superintendent still has plenty to keep him occupied. For instance, he does paperwork. He supervises the year-round employees. He attends seminars. These seminars are designed to help golf course superintendents. They provide important information about the latest improvements in turf management. Superintendents also find out about current treatments. They learn about fertilizers too. Many golf course superintendents attend these conferences. Educators and suppliers from around the world also attend.

My father enjoys working as a golf course superintendent. He doesn't mind the long hours and stress this job entails. It does bother him when people don't take his job seriously or think it is merely a part-time job for a person who likes to play golf.

◆ **COLLABORATIVE ACTIVITIES**

Read the following list of sentences.

Many well-known African-American writers left the United States in the years following World War II.

Many went to Paris.

Richard Wright was a novelist.

He wrote *Native Son* and *Black Boy*.

He wrote *Uncle Tom's Children*.

He left the United States for Paris in 1947.

James Baldwin wrote *Another Country, The Fire Next Time,* and *Giovanni's Room.*

He also wrote essays.

He came to Paris in 1948.

Chester Himes was a detective story writer.

He arrived in Paris in 1953.

William Gardner Smith was a novelist and journalist.

He also left the United States for Paris.

These expatriates found Paris more hospitable than America.

They also found it less racist.

1. Working in a small group, add to the list one related sentence that is a question or an exclamation. Begin one or more of the sentences on the list with an adverb or with a prepositional phrase.

2. Continuing to work in your group, combine sentences on the list to create a varied and interesting paragraph. Use the strategies illustrated in 18C as a guide.

3. When your group's revisions are complete, trade paragraphs with another group and further edit the other group's paragraph to improve sentence variety.

☑ REVIEW CHECKLIST:
Achieving Sentence Variety

☐ Vary sentence types, using an occasional question or exclamation. (See 18A.)

☐ Vary sentence openings. (See 18B.)

☐ Combine sentences. (See 18C.)

☐ Vary sentence length. (See 18D.)

Using Parallelism

■ **WRITING FIRST**

Discuss three things you would like to change about your school, workplace, or community. Identify the changes you are going to discuss; then, explain why you would make each change. Support your statements with specific examples.

A Recognizing Parallel Structure

▼ **Student Voices**
When I write a list of points, reasons, examples, or arguments, I have to remind myself to use parallel structure.

Michelle Cooper

Parallelism is the use of matching grammatical structures to present comparable or equivalent ideas. For example, nouns are used with nouns, verbs with verbs, adjectives with adjectives, phrases with phrases, and clauses with clauses.

> Casey is a <u>snowboarder</u>, not a <u>skier</u>. (two nouns)
>
> We saw the ducks <u>fly</u>, <u>swim</u>, and <u>fish</u>. (three verbs)
>
> The road of life is <u>long</u>, <u>bumpy</u>, and <u>steep</u>. (three adjectives)
>
> <u>Making the team</u> was one thing; <u>staying on it</u> was another. (two phrases)

FOCUS Parallel Structure

The more complicated your ideas, the more you need parallelism. By repeating certain structural patterns, you emphasize connections between ideas and make your writing easier to read.

My, what big eyes you have, grandma! My, what big ears you have! My, what big teeth you have! (three independent clauses)

Faulty parallelism occurs when different grammatical patterns are used to present comparable or equivalent ideas. For example, look at how awkward and wordy the sentences that follow are compared to the sentences above and on page 246.

Casey is a snowboarder, but skiing is not something that interests him.

We saw the ducks fly, and some swam, while others were fishing.

The road of life is long, has a lot of bumps, and climbs steeply.

Making the team was one thing, but she was worried about staying on the team.

My, what big eyes you have, Grandma! And you do have big ears. Your teeth are also quite large.

To correct faulty parallelism, reword all your comparable points so that they use matching grammatical forms.

◆ **PRACTICE 19-1**

In the following sentences, decide whether the underlined words are parallel. If so, write *P* in the blank. If not, rewrite the sentences to make them parallel.

Examples: As a shopper, I <u>insist on quality</u>, <u>expect good service</u>, and <u>seek out value</u>. ___*P*___

For me, <u>getting an A on a math test</u> is harder than <u>~~when I swim~~ ten</u> ^*swimming*^

<u>miles</u>. _____

1. People today are <u>working more</u> and <u>playing less</u>. _____

2. Some smokers say that they smoke cigarettes to help <u>wake themselves up</u>, <u>give themselves a break</u>, and <u>also so that they can keep themselves going</u>. _____

3. They also admit that cigarettes are <u>expensive</u>, <u>smelly</u>, and <u>have dangers</u>. _____

4. Surfing the Internet can be <u>addictive</u> and <u>hypnotic</u>. _____

5. <u>Being happy in life</u> is more important to me than <u>that I make a lot of money</u>. _____

6. The team <u>lost the game</u> even though the quarterback <u>played his best</u>.

_____

7. Judges must <u>care about justice</u>, <u>uphold the laws</u>, and <u>they should treat defendants fairly</u>. ____

8. <u>According to the newspaper, the economy is getting stronger</u>. <u>According to my wallet, the economy is getting weaker</u>. ____

9. <u>Love is blind</u>, but <u>the feeling of hate is blinder</u>. ____

10. To succeed, <u>set realistic goals</u>, <u>work toward them diligently</u>, and <u>you must also believe in yourself</u>. ____

B Using Parallel Structure

As you have seen, parallel structure enables you to emphasize the relationship among comparable or equivalent ideas. Therefore, parallel structure is especially important for *paired items, comparisons,* and *items in a series.*

Paired Items

Use parallel structure when you connect ideas with a coordinating conjunction—*and, but, for, nor, or, so,* and *yet.*

> George believes in <u>doing a good job</u> and <u>minding his own business</u>.
> You can <u>pay me now</u> or <u>pay me later</u>.

Also use parallel structure for paired items joined by correlative conjunctions, like *both . . . and, not only . . . but also, either . . . or, neither . . . nor,* and *rather . . . than.*

> Jan is both <u>artistically talented</u> and <u>mechanically inclined</u>.
> The group's new recording not only <u>has a great dance beat</u> but also <u>has thought-provoking lyrics</u>.
> I'd rather <u>eat one worm by itself</u> than <u>eat twenty with ice cream</u>.

Comparisons Formed with *Than* or *As*

Because they present two items as equivalent, comparisons formed with *than* or *as* require parallel structure.

> <u>Working hard</u> is more important than <u>being lucky</u>.
> She cares about <u>her patients</u> as much as <u>she cares about her family</u>.

Items in a Series

Items in a series—words, phrases, or clauses—are expressed in parallel terms.

Increased demand, high factory output, and a strong dollar help the economy.

She is a champion because she stays in excellent physical condition, puts in long hours of practice, and has an intense desire to win.

◆ PRACTICE 19-2

Fill in the blanks in the following sentences with parallel words, phrases, or clauses of your own that make sense in context.

Example: A good teacher ___*knows the subject*___ and

respects the students.

1. Before a test, I am both _____ and _____.

2. My ideal mate is _____, _____, and _____.

3. Next semester I will either _____

   or _____.

4. I define success more as _____

   than as _____.

5. Rich people _____, but poor people _____

   _____.

6. I have noticed that some _____,

   while other _____.

7. To advance in a job, you must _____, _____, and

   _____.

8. Three reasons to go to college are _____, _____,

   and _____.

9. _____ is more important to me than _____

   _____.

10. I enjoy _____ more than _____.

◆ PRACTICE 19-3

Rewrite the following sentences to achieve parallel structure.

Example: California's San Gabriel Valley is close to mountains, and beaches and deserts are nearby.

California's San Gabriel Valley is close to mountains, beaches, and

deserts.

1. Pasadena and Claremont are major cities in the valley. So is Pomona.

_____

_____

2. Pasadena offers the famous Rose Bowl stadium, and the Norton Simon Museum and the historic Wrigley house are also there.

_____

_____

3. Watching the big Tournament of Roses Parade is more exciting than it is to view the Macy's Thanksgiving parade.

_____

_____

4. You can watch from the crowded parade route. The comfort of your living room is also a possibility.

_____

_____

5. Judges rate the rose-covered floats on their originality, what artistic merit they have, and the overall impact they make.

_____

_____

6. Some people enjoy the parade more than going to the Rose Bowl game.

_____

_____

7. The Rose Bowl game is not only America's oldest collegiate championship but also the bowl game that is the country's most popular.

_____

_____

8. Held every fall in Pomona, the Los Angeles County Fair offers carnival rides, popular performers are presented, and there are agricultural shows included.

_____

_____

9. Visitors come to play challenging skill games, and they also can enjoy various ethnic foods.

_____

_____

10. The starting gate was introduced at the valley's Santa Anita Race Track, and so was electrical timing, as well as the photo finish.

_____

_____

■ WRITING FIRST: Flashback

Look back at your response to the Writing First exercise on page 246. On the lines below, rewrite three sentences from your response, and then revise them as follows. (1) In one sentence, use a coordinating conjunction such as *and* or *but;* (2) in another sentence, make a comparison using *than* or *as;* (3) in a third sentence, present items in a series. When you have finished, check to make sure you have used parallel structure in each sentence.

1. _____

_____

_____

_____

2. _____

_____

_____

_____

3. _____

_____

_____

_____

■ WRITING FIRST: Revising and Editing

Look back at your response to the Writing First exercise on page 246. Underline any pairs (or series) of words, phrases, or clauses you encounter. Then, add parallel constructions where you can to emphasize a relationship or increase clarity. When you are finished, do the same for another assignment you are currently working on.

CHAPTER REVIEW

◆ **EDITING PRACTICE**

Read the following student essay, into which examples of faulty parallelism have been introduced. Identify the sentences you think need to be corrected, and make the changes required to achieve parallelism. In addition, supply all words necessary for clarity, grammar, and sense, adding punctuation as needed. The first sentence has been edited for you.

Questionable Heroes

Heroes are people who are looked up to for their out-
standing achievements and their personal qualities *admirable* ~~are also admired~~. Earlier generations looked up to heroes who played a part in their country's history, who contributed some-thing to society, and they also liked people who showed moral or intellectual superiority. These heroes included the colonial Americans who established this country. The abolitionists who brought an end to slavery, and the sol-diers because they served their country in time of war, were also included. Most young people today, however, do not understand the real definition of a hero. They find their heroes not in books or in history, but television is the place they look. Not only do they admire rock perform-ers, but also athletes and movie stars are admired by them.

The heroes of today are recognized not for their hon-esty or leadership, but they are liked for the entertain-ment they provide. How can big-name celebrities like Arnold Schwarzenegger, Madonna, and Michael Jordan compare to gen-uine heroes like George Washington, Thomas Jefferson, or Martin Luther King Jr.? The answer is that they do not. Washington helped the thirteen colonies gain their indepen-dence from Great Britain, and the Declaration of Indepen-dence was drafted by Jefferson. In addition; Martin Luther King Jr. risked his life to achieve equal rights. By contrast, the people who are on the covers of magazines today are honored only because of their looks or they can toss a football. Sadly, many of today's heroes are admired not because of anything they have actually done, but people admire them because of the image they project.

Fictional characters have always served as role models for children. Early American heroes like Johnny Appleseed and Molly Pitcher were brave and also acted generously. Compare these figures to Bart Simpson and Beavis and Butthead, cartoon characters who have brought the concept of heroism to a new low. Their crude behavior, their lack of interest in school, and the fact that they have questionable values make their attraction a mystery. Sold-out Halloween masks of these crude characters, however, are proof of their great popularity.

Clearly, the stature of heroes has diminished over time. The forgotten heroes of the past who represented honesty, loyalty, and leadership have been replaced by individuals who are sarcastic and cynical. They are also juvenile. Heroes like George Washington, Thomas Jefferson, and Martin Luther King Jr. stand much higher than the slick media creations of today.

◆ COLLABORATIVE ACTIVITIES

1. Working in a group, list three or four qualities that you associate with each word in the following pairs.

   Brothers/sisters
   Teachers/students
   Parents/children
   City/country
   Baseball/football
   The Internet/television
   Work/play

2. Write a compound sentence comparing each of the above pairs of words. Use a coordinating conjunction to join the clauses, and make sure each sentence uses clear parallel structure, mentions both words, and includes the qualities you listed for the words in Collaborative Activity 1.

3. Choose the three best sentences your group has written for Collaborative Activity 2. Assign one student from each group to write these sentences on the board so the entire class can read them. The class can then decide which sentences use parallelism most effectively.

☑ **REVIEW CHECKLIST:**
Using Parallelism

- Use matching grammatical structures to present comparable or equivalent ideas. (See 19A.)

- Use parallel constructions with paired items. (See 19B.)

- Use parallel constructions in comparisons formed with *than* or *as*. (See 19B.)

- Use parallel constructions for items in a series. (See 19B.)

20

Using Words Effectively

PREVIEW

In this chapter, you will learn

■ to choose exact words (20A)

■ to use concise language (20B)

■ to avoid clichés (20C)

■ to use similes and metaphors (20D)

■ to avoid sexist language (20E)

■ **WRITING FIRST**

Describe your dream house. What would it look like? What things would it contain? Discuss some of the qualities your dream house would have. Be as specific as possible.

A Choosing Exact Words

Good writing involves more than writing grammatically correct sentences and clear paragraphs. It also requires choosing words that convey your ideas with precision and clarity—that is, words that are *specific* and *concrete*.

Specific words refer to particular people, places, things, or ideas, while **general** words refer to entire classes or groups. Statements that contain specific words are generally more vivid than ones that contain only generalities. Each of the following sentences contains a word that gives little precise information.

> While walking in the woods, I saw an <u>animal</u>.
>
> <u>Someone</u> decided to run for Congress.
>
> <u>Weapons</u> are responsible for many murders.
>
> Denise bought new <u>clothes</u>.
>
> I enjoyed my <u>meal</u>.
>
> Darrell had always wanted a <u>classic car</u>.

Specific words make the following revised sentences clearer and more precise.

> While walking in the woods, I saw a <u>baby skunk</u>.
>
> <u>Rebecca</u> decided to run for Congress.

255

Saturday night specials are responsible for many murders.

Denise bought a new blue vest.

I enjoyed my pepperoni pizza a lot.

Darrell has always wanted a black 1957 Chevy convertible.

Concrete words appeal to your senses by naming things you can see, hear, taste, feel, and smell—for example, *orange, blaring, salty, rough,* and *pungent.* **Abstract** words, on the other hand, refer to ideas or qualities you cannot perceive with the senses—*happiness* or *truth,* for example. Although both concrete and abstract words are important, concrete words enrich your writing because they convey a clearer picture to readers.

FOCUS **Choosing Exact Words**

One way to strengthen your writing is to avoid **utility words**— vague words like *good, nice,* or *great* that some writers use instead of taking the time to think of more precise words. For example, when you say the ocean looked *pretty,* do you really mean that it *sparkled, glistened, rippled, foamed, surged,* or *billowed?*

◆ **PRACTICE 20-1**

In the following passage, the writer describes an old store in the town of Nameless, Tennessee. Underline the specific, concrete words in the passage that help you experience the scene the writer describes. The first sentence has been done for you.

(1) The old store, lighted only by three fifty-watt bulbs, smelled of coal oil and baking bread. (2) In the middle of the rectangular room, where the oak floor sagged a little, stood an iron stove. (3) To the right was a wooden table with an unfinished game of checkers and a stool made from an apple-tree stump. (4) On shelves around the walls sat earthen jugs with corncob stoppers, a few canned goods, and some of the two thousand old clocks and clockworks Thurmond Watts owned. (5) Only one was ticking; the others he just looked at.

William Least Heat Moon, *Blue Highways*

◆ **PRACTICE 20-2**

Here are five general words. In the blank beside each, write a more specific word. Use the more specific word in a sentence of your own.

Example: talked _chattered_ _____

All through dinner, my six-year-old chattered excitedly about his first day

of school.

1. car _____

_____

_____

2. walk _____

_____

_____

3. big _____

_____

_____

4. animal _____

_____

_____

5. clothing _____

_____

_____

◆ PRACTICE 20-3

The following paragraph is a vaguely worded letter of application for a job. Choose a job that you might want to apply for. As you rewrite the paragraph on a separate page, substitute specific language for the vague language of the original, and add details where necessary. Start by making the first sentence, which identifies the job, more specific: for example, "I would like to apply for the dental technician position you advertised in today's *Post*." Go on to include specific information about your background and qualifications, expanding the original paragraph into a three-paragraph letter.

I would like to apply for the position you advertised in today's paper. I graduated from high school and am currently attending college. I have taken several courses that have prepared me to fulfill the duties the position requires. I also have several personal qualities that I think you would find important in a person holding this position. In addition, I have had certain experiences that qualify me for such a job. I would appreciate the opportunity to meet with you to discuss your needs as an employer. Thank you.

■ **WRITING FIRST: Flashback**

Look back at your response to the Writing First exercise on page 255. Find several general or abstract words, and write those words on the lines below. For each word, substitute another word that is more specific or concrete.

General or abstract words

_____

_____

_____

Specific or concrete alternatives

_____

_____

_____

B   Using Concise Language

Concise writing comes right to the point and says what it has to say in as few words as possible. Too often, however, writers construct wordy sentences full of empty phrases that add nothing to meaning. A good way to test a sentence for nonessential words is to see if crossing out the words affects its meaning.

> The flower was red ~~in color~~.

If the sentence's meaning does not change, you can assume the sentence is better off without the extra words.

WORDY	Due to the fact that I was tired, I missed my first class.
CONCISE	Because I was tired, I missed my first class.
WORDY	In order to follow the plot, you must make an outline.
CONCISE	To follow the plot, you must make an outline.

FOCUS   **Using Concise Language**

The following phrases add nothing to a sentence. You can usually delete or condense them with no loss of meaning.

Wordy	Concise
It is clear that	(delete)
It is a fact that	(delete)
The reason is that	Because
It is my opinion that	I think/I believe
Due to the fact that	Because

(continued on the following page)

(continued from the previous page)

Wordy	Concise
Despite the fact that	Although
At the present time	Today/Currently
At that time	Then
In most cases	Usually
In order to	To
In the final analysis	Finally
Subsequent to	After

Repetition also adds words to your writing. Although repetition can be used effectively—for example, to emphasize important ideas—unnecessary repetition should be eliminated.

> My instructor told me the book was <u>old-fashioned and outdated</u>.

> The <u>terrible tragedy</u> of the fire could have been avoided with a smoke detector.

The repeated phrases in the two sentences above add nothing. (An old-fashioned book *is* outdated; a tragedy is *always* terrible.) Notice how easily these sentences can be edited to eliminate unnecessary repetition.

> My instructor told me the book was ~~old-fashioned and~~ outdated.

> The ~~terrible~~ tragedy of the fire could have been avoided with a smoke detector.

◆ PRACTICE 20-4

To make the following sentences more concise, eliminate any unnecessary repetition, and edit wordy expressions.

Example: ~~It is a fact that many~~ *Many* grown-up children have trouble getting their parents, ~~their mother and father,~~ to treat them as adults.

(1) Adult children can become frustrated due to the fact that their parents seem to treat them as if they were not capable of making their own decisions by themselves. (2) For example, some parents constantly criticize all the time and offer unwanted advice that their children do not desire to hear. (3) When this happens, the children may begin to whine childishly and in a juvenile manner or even throw a temper tantrum despite the fact that such behavior only reinforces their parents' attitude. (4) In most cases, there are better ways to improve one's parents' behavior for the better. (5) In order to get parents to stop being critical, an

adult child might turn the tables and encourage his or her parents to have a discussion and talk about their own childhoods. (6) The child can then point out any similarities between the parents' behavior then in the past and his or her behavior now in the present. (7) Another thing adult children might also do is to explain that while they value their parents' opinion, they are still going to make their own decisions. (8) Finally, an adult child should not sit by idly doing nothing when family stories are being told or related. (9) Despite the fact that parents may have been telling these stories the same way for years and years, the child may have a very different perspective on the event. (10) Expressing and talking about this different perspective can help an adult child define his or her position in the family in a new way that is different from the old way.

◆ PRACTICE 20-5

The following passage is wordy. Cross out any unnecessary words, and make any revisions that may be needed.

> **Example:** Psychologist Marcia Morris began to study flirting when she was ~~a student studying~~ in graduate school.

(1) It is Marcia Morris's own opinion that in all species the female makes the original choice of mate. (2) First, a female originally chooses the male that interests her. (3) Subsequent to this, she begins to send signals to show that he may approach. (4) Morris wanted to learn what signals women send to let men know they are interested. (5) She and her assistants visited singles bars to observe and to record their observations of what they saw.

(6) To attract a man, they found, women in most of the cases glance at him first and then smile in a friendly way. (7) After they turn away so they are no longer looking at the man, they may toss their heads, flip their hair, or laugh. (8) A woman may also sway side to side with the music being played, which typically in most cases leads the man to request a dance. (9) In the final analysis, Morris's studies show that a

woman's ability to get a man to talk to her depends less on her looks and whether she is beautiful than on her flirting skills. (10) One of Morris's assistants used the techniques their research uncovered and bragged boastfully that it never took her more than ten minutes to attract a man's attention.

■ WRITING FIRST: Flashback

Look back at your response to the Writing First exercise on page 255. Identify a sentence that contains unnecessary repetition. Rewrite the sentence on the lines below, editing it so it is more concise.

_____

_____

C   Avoiding Clichés

One way of making your writing more effective is to avoid **clichés**, expressions that have been used so often they have lost their original impact. Writers tend to plug in such ready-made phrases—for example, "easier said than done," "last but not least," and "work like a dog"—without giving them much thought, but these worn-out expressions deaden writing and do little to create interest.

When you identify a cliché in your writing, replace it with a direct statement—or, if possible, substitute a fresher expression.

CLICHÉ   When school was over, she felt <u>free as a bird</u>.

REVISED   When school was over, she felt like a bird that had just escaped from its cage.

CLICHÉ   These days, you have to be <u>sick as a dog</u> before you are admitted to a hospital.

REVISED   These days, you have to be seriously ill before you are admitted to a hospital.

> ■ **Computer Tip**
> Many grammar-checking programs flag clichés and wordy constructions. Remember, however, that although a grammar checker may highlight possible trouble spots, you, not the computer, must make the final judgment.

◆ PRACTICE 20-6

Cross out any clichés in the following sentences, and either substitute a fresher expression or restate the idea in more direct language.

Example: Lottery winners often think they will be ~~free as a bird~~ for
the rest of their lives.   *free of financial worries*

(1) Many people think that a million-dollar lottery jackpot allows the winner to stop working like a dog and start living high on the hog. (2) All things considered, however, the reality for lottery winners is quite different. (3) For one thing, lottery winners who hit the jackpot do not receive their winnings all at once; instead, payments—$50,000—are usually spread out over twenty years. (4) Of that $50,000 a year, close to $20,000 goes to taxes and anything else the lucky stiff owes the government, such as student loans. (5) Next come relatives and friends with their hands out, leaving winners between a rock and a hard place. (6) They can either cough up gifts and loans or wave bye-bye to many of their loved ones. (7) Adding insult to injury, many lottery winners have lost their jobs because employers thought that once they were "millionaires," they no longer needed to draw a salary. (8) Many lottery winners wind up way over their heads in debt within a few years. (9) In their hour of need, many would like to sell their future payments to companies that offer lump-sum payments of forty to forty-five cents on the dollar. (10) This is easier said than done, however, because most state lotteries won't allow winners to sell their winnings.

■ WRITING FIRST: Flashback

Look back at your response to the Writing First exercise on page 255. If you have used any clichés, list them below, and edit them so they are more direct. If possible, think of a more original way of expressing the idea.

Cliché   *Revised*

_____   _____

_____   _____

_____   _____

_____   _____

D   **Using Similes and Metaphors**

A **simile** is a comparison of two unlike things that uses *like* or *as*.

His arm hung at his side <u>like</u> a broken shutter.

He was <u>as</u> content <u>as</u> a cat napping on a windowsill.

A **metaphor** is a comparison of two unlike things that does *not* use *like* or *as*.

Invaders from another world, dandelions conquered my garden.

He was a beast of burden, carrying cement from sunrise to sunset.

Experienced writers know that similes and metaphors can add fresh and memorable touches to their writing. The force of similes and metaphors comes from the surprise of seeing two seemingly unlike things being compared and, as a result, seeing a hidden or unnoticed similarity between them. Used in moderation, similes and metaphors can enhance your writing.

> ● **Writing Tip**
> Both similes and metaphors compare two *dissimilar* things. If the items being compared are *alike,* the result is a statement of fact—*Your boat is like my boat*—not a simile or metaphor.

◆ **PRACTICE 20-7**

Underline the similes and metaphors in the following sentences. Above the similes write *S*, and above the metaphors write *M*.

                                          M

Example: My workload is <u>a pit it seems I'll never climb out of.</u>

1. Her heart was as fragile as a newly laid egg.

2. My boss's words were a cold shower, bringing me back to reality.

3. It rained so heavily that the atmosphere was like the inside of a jellyfish.

4. Selena's singing career was a skyrocket just waiting to be lit.

5. Looking like a lopsided wedding cake, the old white house seemed about to topple over.

◆ **PRACTICE 20-8**

Use your imagination to complete each of the following by creating three appropriate similes.

Example: A boring class is like *toast without jam.*

                                            a straitjacket.

                                            a bedtime story.

1. A good friend is like _____

_____

_____

2. A thunderstorm is like _____

_____

_____

3. Falling in love is like _____

_____

_____

◆ PRACTICE 20-9

Think of a person you know well. Using that person as your subject, fill in each of the following blanks to create metaphors. Try to complete each metaphor with more than a single word, as in the example.

Example: If ___*my baby sister*___ were an animal, ___*she*___ would be ___*a curious little kitten.*___

1. If _____ were an animal, _____ would be _____

_____

2. If _____ were a food, _____ would be _____

_____

3. If _____ were a means of transportation, _____ would be

_____

4. If _____ were a natural phenomenon, _____ would be _____

_____

5. If _____ were a toy, _____ would be _____

_____

■ WRITING FIRST: Flashback

Look back at your response to the Writing First exercise on page 255. Find two sentences that could be enriched with a simile or a metaphor. Add a simile to one sentence and a metaphor to the other.

(continued on the following page)

(continued from the previous page)

1. _____

_____

2. _____

_____

E　Avoiding Sexist Language

Sexist language refers to men and women in derogatory or insulting terms. Sexist language is not just words like *hunk, bimbo,* or *babe,* which many people find objectionable. It can also be words or phrases that unnecessarily call attention to gender or that suggest a job or profession is exclusively male or female when it actually is not. It is also considered sexist to give information about a woman—for example, her marital status— that you would not offer about a man.

Usually, you can avoid sexist usage by being sensitive and using a little common sense. For every sexist usage, there is almost always an acceptable nonsexist alternative.

Sexist	*Nonsexist*
man, mankind	humanity, humankind, human race
businessman	executive, business person
fireman, policeman, mailman	fire fighter, police officer, letter carrier
male nurse, woman engineer	nurse, engineer
congressman	member of Congress, representative
stewardess, steward	flight attendant
man and wife	man and woman, husband and wife
manmade	synthetic
chairman	chair, chairperson
anchorwoman, anchorman	anchor

> ● **Writing Tip**
> In addition to avoiding sexist language, avoid potentially offensive references to a person's age, physical condition, or sexual orientation.

FOCUS　Avoiding Sexist Language

Don't use *he* when your subject could be either male or female.

Everyone should complete <u>his</u> assignment by next week.

(continued on the following page)

> ▪ **Computer Tip**
> Use the Find or Search feature of your word processor to check uses of *he*. If you have used the word in a sexist manner, correct the problem.

20 E

> *(continued from the previous page)*
> You can correct this problem in three ways.
>
> ■ Use *he or she* or *his or her*.
>
>   Everyone should complete <u>his or her</u> assignment by next week.
>
> ■ Use plural forms.
>
>   Students should complete <u>their</u> assignment by next week.
>
> ■ Eliminate the pronoun.
>
>   Everyone should complete <u>the</u> assignment by next week.

◆ **PRACTICE 20-10**

Edit the following sentences to eliminate sexist language.

1. Many people today would like to see more policemen patrolling the streets.

2. A doctor should be honest with his patients.

3. The attorneys representing the plaintiff are Geraldo Diaz and Mrs. Barbara Wilkerson.

4. Chris Fox is the female mayor of Port London, Maine.

5. Travel to other planets will be a significant step for man.

■ WRITING FIRST: Flashback

Look back at your response to the Writing First exercise on page 255. Have you used any words or phrases that unnecessarily call attention to gender? Have you used *he* to refer to both genders when your subject could be either male or female? Rewrite on the lines below any sentences in which these problems occur. Then, cross out the sexist language and substitute acceptable nonsexist alternatives.

_____

_____

_____

_____

■ WRITING FIRST: Revising and Editing

Look back at your response to the Writing First exercise on page
255. Revise the paragraph, making sure your language is as exact
and concise as possible. In addition, be sure you have avoided using
clichés or sexist expressions. When you have finished, do the same
for another writing assignment you are currently working on.

CHAPTER REVIEW

◆ EDITING PRACTICE

Read the following student essay carefully, and then revise it, making sure
your revision is as concise as possible and uses exact words and specific,
concrete language. In addition, eliminate sexist language and clichés. If
you can, add an occasional simile or metaphor to increase the impact of
the essay. Finally, underline any expressions that seem particularly fresh
and original. The first sentence has been edited for you.

A Day at the Pool

It all begins on a ~~nice~~ *bright* summer day as we carry

our neatly packed pool equipment from the car and head to

the pool. We walk across the bumpy, gravel-covered parking

lot with our arms piled high with a pretty beach bag, a

gaily striped beach chair, colored beach towels, and an

interesting drinking cup. We make it through the entrance

and walk into the ladies' locker room. The walls are lined

with lockers, and past the lockers is a metal door held

open by a wooden wedge. Walking through the doorway, we

proceed to our usual spot in the shaded grass area. This

is where we spend our day socializing with other "pool

princesses" and checking out the hunks.

As I sit, I hear the sounds of children crying and

laughing and of parents bellowing at them. Suddenly, the

noises cease at the sound of a loud, high-pitched whistle.

All eyes are on the female lifeguard. She's dressed in a nice bathing suit covered by a tank top with an unusual design on the front. She's wearing black Ray-Ban sunglasses, and she holds a silver whistle in her mouth. She sits on her high wooden platform and raises her hand, pointing her finger at the accused. Then, as quickly as the silence began, it ceases.

Due to the fact I am hungry, I go to the snack bar. I am enticed by the scent of freshly popped popcorn, the tantalizing aroma of spicy fries, and the equally tempting smell of hamburgers. The choice is difficult. I finally decide on a bright banana-yellow popsicle. It tastes good and takes care of my thirst. I turn and come face to face with a small child. His cheeks are red from overexposure to the burning rays of the sun. His nose is a white painted triangle, and his eyes are illuminated as he converses with his mother about purchasing more goodies from the snack bar. Slithering around him, I head back to the safety of my towel.

Reaching my chair, I look down to see a strange toddler sitting as quiet as a mouse. He seems to have claimed my seat as his own. He looks up and smiles as drool slides out of the corner of his mouth. As he rises and waddles off, his wet diaper sags around his knees. I discover that he has left his mark on my chair. At this point, I decide it is time to go home.

We gather our belongings and head for the car. Again we pass through the metal door, down the hallway of lockers, out the exit to the parking lot, and across the gravel parking lot to our car. After we load our trunk, we get into the car only to find that the air is so hot and thick. As I sit in the hot car, I wonder whether it makes sense to go through all this trouble just to spend a couple of hours at the pool.

◆ **COLLABORATIVE ACTIVITIES**

1. Bring in two or three paragraphs of description from a romance novel, a western novel, or a mystery novel. Working in a group, choose one paragraph that seems to need clearer, more concise language.

2. As a group, revise the paragraph you chose for Collaborative Activity 1, making it as clear and concise as possible and eliminating any clichés or sexist language.

3. Exchange your revised paragraph from Collaborative Activity 2 with another group, and check the other group's revisions. Make any additional changes you think your paragraph needs.

☑ REVIEW CHECKLIST:
Using Words Effectively

☐ Specific words refer to particular people, places, things, or ideas. General words refer to entire classes or groups. Concrete words refer to things you can see, hear, taste, feel, and smell. Abstract words refer to ideas or qualities that cannot be perceived with the senses. (See 20A.)

☐ Concise writing comes right to the point and says what it has to say in the fewest possible words. (See 20B.)

☐ Avoid clichés (overused expressions). (See 20C.)

☐ A simile is a comparison that uses *like* or *as*. A metaphor is a comparison that does not use *like* or *as*. (See 20D.)

☐ Avoid sexist language. (See 20E.)

UNIT FIVE

Solving Common Sentence Problems

21

Run-Ons and Comma Splices

PREVIEW

In this chapter, you will learn

■ to recognize run-on sentences and comma splices (21A)

■ to correct run-ons and comma splices in five different ways (21B)

■ **WRITING FIRST**

What is the purpose of college—to give students a general education, or to prepare them for specific jobs? Support your opinion with examples.

A Recognizing Run-Ons and Comma Splices

A **run-on sentence** is an error that occurs when two sentences (independent clauses) are joined without punctuation.

> RUN-ON More and more students are earning high school equivalency diplomas the value of these diplomas is currently under debate.

A **comma splice** is an error that occurs when two sentences are joined with just a comma.

> COMMA SPLICE More and more students are earning high school equivalency diplomas, the value of these diplomas is currently under debate.

● **Writing Tip**
A comma can join two sentences only when it is followed by a coordinating conjunction. (See 16A.)

◆ PRACTICE 21-1

Some of the sentences in the following passage are correct, but others are run-on sentences or comma splices. In the answer space after each sentence, write *C* if the sentence is correct, *RO* if it is a run-on, and *CS* if it is a comma splice.

Example: "Race movies" had all-black casts, they were intended for African-American audiences. ___*CS*___

273

(1) In 1919, African-American director Oscar Micheaux filmed *Within Our Gates* this movie examined black life in Chicago. _____ (2) The film included scenes of violence, it even depicted two lynchings. _____ (3) It also treated interracial relationships white censors banned it. _____ (4) Race riots had occurred in Chicago that year, the censors feared violence. _____ (5) Micheaux appealed to the board they agreed to the film's release in Chicago. _____ (6) The movie was shown, twelve hundred feet of film were omitted. _____ (7) Micheaux later made many low-budget movies, but few survive today. _____ (8) Some are musicals others are melodramas. _____ (9) Few are socially conscious films like *Within Our Gates*. _____ (10) One, *Body and Soul*, was Paul Robeson's first film. _____ (11) Micheaux died in 1951. _____ (12) In 1990, an uncut version of *Within Our Gates* was discovered in Madrid, it was shown in Chicago for the first time in 1992. _____

■ **Computer Tip**
Grammar checkers sometimes identify a sentence as a run-on or comma splice simply because it's long. Such a sentence is a run-on or comma splice only if it contains two independent clauses joined without punctuation or with just a comma. (See 21B.)

■ **WRITING FIRST: Flashback**

Look back at your response to the Writing First exercise on page 273. Do you see any run-ons or comma splices? If so, put brackets around them.

▼ **Student Voices**
My high school teachers said I wrote run-ons, so I started writing really short sentences. Now my sentences are too choppy. I need to find another way to revise.
                    Richard Greene

B   Correcting Run-Ons and Comma Splices

You can correct a run-on sentence or comma splice in five different ways.

1. Create two separate sentences. If two ideas are of equal importance but not closely related, create two separate sentences.

INCORRECT Muslims fast for a period of thirty days this period is called Ramadan. (run-on)

INCORRECT Muslims fast for a period of thirty days, this period is called Ramadan. (comma splice)

CORRECT Muslims fast for a period of thirty days. This period is called Ramadan. (two separate sentences)

For more on connecting ideas with a coordinating conjunction, see 16A.

2. Connect ideas with a comma followed by a coordinating conjunction. If two ideas are of equal importance and you want to indicate a particular relationship between them—for example, cause and effect or contrast—use a comma followed by an appropriate coordinating conjunction.

INCORRECT   The Emancipation Proclamation freed U.S. slaves in 1863 slaves in Texas were not officially freed until June 19, 1865 ("Juneteenth"). (run-on)

INCORRECT   The Emancipation Proclamation freed U.S. slaves in 1863, slaves in Texas were not officially freed until June 19, 1865 ("Juneteenth"). (comma splice)

CORRECT   The Emancipation Proclamation freed U.S. slaves in 1863, but slaves in Texas were not officially freed until June 19, 1865 ("Juneteenth"). (ideas connected with a comma followed by a coordinating conjunction)

3. Connect ideas with a semicolon. If you want to indicate a particularly close connection—or a strong contrast—between two ideas, use a semicolon.

For more on connecting ideas with a semicolon, see 16B.

INCORRECT   In ancient times, the swastika was a symbol of good luck after 1935, it became the official emblem of the Nazi party. (run-on)

INCORRECT   In ancient times, the swastika was a symbol of good luck, after 1935, it became the official emblem of the Nazi party. (comma splice)

CORRECT   In ancient times, the swastika was a symbol of good luck; after 1935, it became the official emblem of the Nazi party. (ideas connected with a semicolon)

4. Connect ideas with a semicolon and a conjunctive adverb or transitional expression. To show a specific relationship between two closely related ideas, add a conjunctive adverb or transitional expression after the semicolon.

INCORRECT   *Titanic* is more than just an adventure story it is really a love story. (run-on)

INCORRECT   *Titanic* is more than just an adventure story, it is really a love story. (comma splice)

CORRECT   *Titanic* is more than just an adventure story; in fact, it is really a love story. (ideas connected with a semicolon and a transitional expression)

> ● **Writing Tip**
> Conjunctive adverbs include words such as *however* and *therefore*; transitional expressions include *in fact, as a result,* and *for example*. (See 16C.)

FOCUS   **Run-Ons and Comma Splices with Conjunctive Adverbs or Transitional Expressions**

Run-on sentences and comma splices often occur when a conjunctive adverb or transitional expression joins two sentences *without the required punctuation.*

INCORRECT   Some students have computers, microwaves, and refrigerators in their dorm rooms as a result, electrical circuits are overloaded. (run-on)

(continued on the following page)

> *(continued from the previous page)*
>
> INCORRECT Some students have computers, microwaves, and refrigerators in their dorm rooms, as a result, electrical circuits are overloaded. (comma splice)
>
> To correct this kind of run-on or comma splice, simply add the missing semicolon.
>
> CORRECT Some students have computers, microwaves, and refrigerators in their dorm rooms; as a result, electrical circuits are overloaded.

● **Writing Tip**
When you use a relative pronoun to correct a run-on or comma splice, the relative pronoun takes the place of another pronoun in the sentence.

For more on connecting ideas with a subordinating conjunction or relative pronoun, see Chapter 17.

5. Connect ideas with a subordinating conjunction or relative pronoun. When one idea is dependent on another, you can turn the dependent idea into a dependent clause by adding a subordinating conjunction or a relative pronoun *(who, which, or that).*

INCORRECT Horace Mann was the first president of Antioch College he encouraged the development of students' social consciences. (run-on)

INCORRECT Horace Mann was the first president of Antioch College, he encouraged the development of students' social consciences. (comma splice)

CORRECT When Horace Mann was the first president of Antioch College, he encouraged the development of students' social consciences. (ideas connected by a subordinating conjunction)

CORRECT Horace Mann, who was the first president of Antioch College, encouraged the development of students' social consciences. (ideas connected by a relative pronoun)

◆ PRACTICE 21-2

Correct each of the following run-on sentences and comma splices by creating two separate sentences, by connecting ideas with a comma followed by a coordinating conjunction, by connecting ideas with a semicolon, or by connecting ideas with a semicolon and a conjunctive adverb or transitional expression. Be sure punctuation is correct. Remember to put a semicolon before, and a comma after, each conjunctive adverb or transitional expression.

Example: Some people believe chronic sex offenders should be given therapy ; however , others believe they should be executed.

1. Nursing offers job security and high pay, therefore many people are choosing nursing as a career.

2. Anne Boleyn was the second wife of Henry VIII her daughter was Elizabeth I.

3. The Democratic Republic of the Congo was previously known as Zaire before that it was the Belgian Congo.

4. Housewife Jean Nidetch started Weight Watchers in 1961 in 1978 she sold the company for $100 million.

5. Millions of Jews were killed during the Holocaust, in addition Catholics, Gypsies, homosexuals, and other "undesirables" were killed.

6. Sojourner Truth was born a slave however she became a leading abolitionist and feminist.

7. First-generation Japanese Americans are called nisei second-generation Japanese Americans are called sansei.

8. Oliver Wendell Holmes Jr. was a Supreme Court Justice, his father was a physician and writer.

9. Père Noel is another name for Santa Claus, he is also known as Father Christmas and St. Nicholas.

10. Latin is one classical language Greek is another.

◆ PRACTICE 21-3

Use the list of subordinating conjunctions on page 219 and the list of relative pronouns on page 222 to correct the following run-on sentences and comma splices. Be sure to add correct punctuation where necessary.

Examples: Harlem was rural until the nineteenth century *, when* improved transportation linked it to lower Manhattan.

The community *, which* was soon home to people escaping the crowds of New York City, ~~it~~ became a fashionable suburb.

(1) Harlem was populated mostly by European immigrants at the turn of the century, it saw an influx of African Americans beginning in 1910. (2) This migration from the South continued for several decades Harlem became one of the largest African-American communities in the United States. (3) Many African-American artists and writers settled in

Harlem during the 1920s, this led to a flowering of African-American art. (4) This "Harlem Renaissance" was an important era in American literary history it is not even mentioned in some textbooks. (5) Scholars of the era recognize the great works produced then, they point to writers such as Langston Hughes and Countee Cullen and sculptors such as Henry Tanner and Sargent Johnson. (6) Zora Neale Hurston moved to Harlem from her native Florida in 1925, she began work there on her famous book of African-American folklore. (7) Harlem was an exciting place in the 1920s people from all over the city went there to hear jazz and to dance. (8) The white playwright Eugene O'Neill went to Harlem to audition actors for his play *The Emperor Jones* it made an international star of the great Paul Robeson. (9) Contemporary African-American artists know about the Harlem Renaissance, it is still not familiar to others. (10) The Great Depression occurred in the 1930s it led to the end of the Harlem Renaissance.

◆ PRACTICE 21-4

Correct each run-on sentence and comma splice in the following passage in the way that best indicates the relationship between ideas. Be sure punctuation is appropriate.

> **Example:** Coney Island was once a bustling seaside resort , but it has declined considerably in recent years.

In the late nineteenth century, Coney Island was famous, in fact, it was legendary. Every summer, it was crowded, people mailed hundreds of thousands of postcards from the resort on some days. Coney Island was considered exotic and exciting, it even boasted a hotel shaped like an elephant. Some people saw Coney Island as seedy, others thought it was a wonderful, magical place. It had beaches, hotels, racetracks, and a stadium however by the turn of the century, it was best known for three amusement parks. These parks were Luna Park, Steeplechase, and Dreamland. Gaslight was still the norm in New York, a million electric lights lit Luna Park. Steeplechase offered many rides, its main attraction was a two-mile ride on mechanical horses. At Dreamland, people could see a submarine, in addition, they could travel through an Eskimo village or visit Lilliputia, with its three hundred midgets. Today, the old Coney Island no longer exists. Fire destroyed Dreamland in 1911, Luna Park burned down in 1946. In 1964, Steeplechase closed. The once-grand Coney Island is gone, still its beach and its boardwalk endure. Its famous roller coaster, the Cyclone, still exists, its giant Ferris wheel, the Wonder Wheel, keeps on turning. Maybe someday the old Coney Island will be reborn.

■ WRITING FIRST: Flashback

For each run-on or comma splice you identified in the Flashback exercise on page 274, write two possible corrected versions here.

_____

_____

_____

_____

_____

_____

■ WRITING FIRST: Revising and Editing

Look back at your responses to the Writing First exercise on page 273 and the Flashback exercises on page 274 and above. For each run-on sentence and comma splice you found, choose the revision that best conveys your meaning and work it into your writing. If you do not find any run-ons or comma splices in your own writing, work with a classmate to correct his or her writing, or edit the work you did for another assignment.

CHAPTER REVIEW

◆ EDITING PRACTICE

Read the following student essay, into which sentence errors have been introduced. Then, revise it by eliminating run-on sentences and comma splices and carefully correcting them to indicate the relationships between ideas. Be sure punctuation is correct. The first error has been corrected for you.

Blood Sports

Since the time of ancient Rome, citizens have rushed to the stadium to see battles. <u>While</u> Christians fought lions in ancient times, today athletes fight each other. Society may have evolved morally to some degree, I believe only our laws keep us from behaving like the ancient Romans. The craving for blood is still evident, for example, football and hockey fans still yell "Kill him!" and "Rip their faces off!"

I played "barbaric" sports for ten years. My parents encouraged my athletic career they got me started in sports early on. Between the ages of ten and seventeen, I was very active in martial arts, for four years, I played high school football. As a young child, I competed in karate tournaments I received many injuries. I broke my nose three times, I also broke my hand twice and my foot once. As a competitor, I enjoyed the thrill of battle, however I feared serious injury. Eventually, I gave up karate, instead I concentrated on football.

Extreme force was very important in high school foot-ball. I played defense, I often hurt my opponents. Once, I hit a quarterback in his hip with my helmet the blow knocked him to the ground. They carried him off the field, and my team's fans went berserk. For weeks, people congrat-ulated me still I felt uncomfortable. I now believe playing

sports requires a great deal of physical aggressiveness and
pain. I accept this as part of the game I just don't want
to play anymore.

◆ **COLLABORATIVE ACTIVITIES**

1. Find an interesting passage from a newspaper or magazine article.
   Working in a small group, recopy a few paragraphs onto a separate
   sheet of paper, creating run-ons and comma splices. Exchange exercises with another group.

2. Work in a small group to correct each run-on and comma splice in an
   exercise prepared by another group of students. When you have finished, return the exercise to the group that created it.

3. Continuing to work with members of your group, evaluate the other
   group's work on your exercise, comparing it to the original newspaper
   or magazine passage. Pay particular attention to punctuation. Where
   the students' version differs from the original, decide whether their
   version is incorrect or whether it represents an acceptable (or even
   superior) alternative to the original.

☑ REVIEW CHECKLIST:
Run-Ons and Comma Splices

> A run-on sentence is an error that occurs when two sentences
> are joined without punctuation. (See 21A.)

> A comma splice is an error that occurs when two sentences are
> joined with just a comma. (See 21A.)

> Correct a run-on or comma splice by creating two separate
> sentences, by connecting ideas with a comma followed by a
> coordinating conjunction, by connecting ideas with a semi-
> colon, by connecting ideas with a semicolon and a conjunctive
> adverb or transitional expression, or by connecting ideas with
> a subordinating conjunction or relative pronoun. (See 21B.)

22

Sentence Fragments

■ **WRITING FIRST**

Explain how you and your family celebrate your favorite holiday. Describe some typical activities and foods, supplying enough details to give your readers a sense of why you enjoy this holiday so much.

A **sentence fragment** is an incomplete sentence. Every sentence must include at least one subject and one verb, and every sentence must express a complete thought. If a group of words does not do *all* these things, it is a fragment and not a sentence—even if it begins with a capital letter and ends with a period.

A Recognizing Sentence Fragments

> ● **Writing Tip**
> You may see sentence fragments used in advertisements and other informal writing, but fragments are not acceptable in college writing.

The following complete sentence includes both a subject and a verb and expresses a complete idea.

> SENTENCE The <u>actors</u> in the play *Into the Woods* <u>were</u> ethnically diverse.

The following are not complete sentences.

> FRAGMENT The actors in the play *Into the Woods.*
>
> FRAGMENT Were ethnically diverse.

> **Teaching Tip**
> Remind students that although sentence fragments are often used in informal writing (particularly advertising), they aren't acceptable in college writing.

The first group of words, "The actors in the play *Into the Woods,*" has no verb: What *point* is being made about the actors in the play? The second group of words, "Were ethnically diverse," has no subject: *What* was ethnically diverse? Because a sentence must have both a subject and a verb and express a complete thought, these two examples are fragments.

FOCUS Identifying Sentence Fragments

Sentence fragments almost always appear in paragraphs and longer passages, right beside complete sentences.

┌─── COMPLETE SENTENCE ───┐ ┌──────── FRAGMENT ────────┐
Celia took two electives. Computer Science 320 and Spanish
101.

The fragment above does not have a verb. The complete sentence, however, has both a subject *(Celia)* and a verb *(took)*.

Often, you can correct a sentence fragment by attaching it to a nearby sentence that supplies the missing words.

Celia took two electives, Computer Science 320 and Spanish 101.

▼ **Student Voices**
Thinking of a sentence fragment as a piece of a sentence helps me remember that the fragment needs to be attached to a whole sentence.
Keith Jackson

◆ PRACTICE 22-1

In the following passage, some of the numbered groups of words are missing a subject, a verb, or both. Identify each fragment by labeling it *F*. Attach each fragment to a nearby word group to create a complete new sentence. Finally, rewrite the entire passage, using complete sentences, on the lines provided.

Example: Martha Grimes, Ruth Rendell, and Deborah Crombie write detective novels. _____ Set in England. _*F*_

Martha Grimes, Ruth Rendell, and Deborah Crombie write detective novels

set in England.

(1) Sara Paretsky writes detective novels. _____ (2) Such as *Burn Marks* and *Guardian Angel.* _____ (3) These novels are about V. I. Warshawski. _____ (4) A private detective. _____ (5) V. I. lives and works in Chicago. _____ (6) The Windy City. _____ (7) Every day as a detective. _____ (8) V. I. takes risks. _____ (9) V. I. is tough. _____ (10) She is also a woman. _____

Rewrite:

_____

_____

_____

_____

■ **WRITING FIRST: Flashback**

Look back at your response to the Writing First exercise on page 282. Do all your sentences seem complete? If you think any are not complete, copy them here.

_____

_____

_____

_____

B Correcting Phrase Fragments

Every sentence must include a subject and a verb. A **phrase** is a group of words that is missing a subject or a verb or both. When you punctuate a phrase as if it were a sentence, you create a fragment.

	┌─── FRAG ───┐
INCORRECT	The librarian recommended *The Children.* A book about the civil rights movement.

To correct a phrase fragment, attach it to the sentence that contains the missing subject or verb.

CORRECT	The librarian recommended *The Children,* a book about the civil rights movement.

Another way to correct a phrase fragment is to add the missing subject or verb.

CORRECT	The librarian recommended *The Children.* This book is about the civil rights movement.

The kinds of phrases that are most often written as sentence fragments are *appositives, prepositional phrases, participial phrases,* and *infinitive phrases.*

Appositive Fragments

For more on appositives, see 18C.

An **appositive** identifies or renames a noun or a pronoun. An appositive cannot stand alone as a sentence. To correct an appositive fragment, attach it to the sentence that contains the words the appositive identifies.

	┌─── FRAG ───┐
INCORRECT	He decorated the room in his favorite colors. Brown and black.

CORRECT   He decorated the room in his favorite colors, brown and black.

Sometimes *such as, for example,* or *for instance* introduces an appositive. Even if an appositive is introduced by one of these expressions, it is still a fragment.

INCORRECT   A good diet should include high-fiber foods. Such as ⌐FRAG⌐ leafy vegetables, fruits, beans, and whole-grain bread.

CORRECT   A good diet should include high-fiber foods, such as leafy vegetables, fruits, beans, and whole-grain bread.

Prepositional Phrase Fragments

A **prepositional phrase** consists of a preposition and its object. A prepositional phrase cannot stand alone as a sentence. To correct a prepositional phrase fragment, attach it to a nearby sentence.

For more on prepositional phrases, see 15B.

INCORRECT   She promised to stand by him. In sickness and in health.

CORRECT   She promised to stand by him in sickness and in health.

Participial Phrase Fragments

The verb in a sentence must be a **complete verb**. Present participles and past participles are not complete verbs.

A **present participle**, such as *looking*, is not a complete verb because it cannot stand alone without a **helping verb**, such as *is, are, was,* or *were*. When you use a present participle without a helping verb, you create a fragment.

For more on complete verbs and helping verbs, see 15C.

FRAGMENT   Looking for trouble.

One way to correct this fragment is to add a subject and a helping verb.

CORRECT   They were looking for trouble.

● **Writing Tip**
A pronoun, such as *he* or *they*, can be the subject of a sentence. (See 15A.)

Another way to correct the fragment is to attach it to a nearby sentence.

INCORRECT   The twins spent most of the day outside. Looking for trouble.

CORRECT   The twins spent most of the day outside looking for trouble.

● **Writing Tip**
Avoid creating dangling modifiers with participles such as *looking*. (See 25C.)

Most irregular **past participles**, such as *hidden*, cannot stand alone in a sentence without a helping verb *(is hidden, was hidden, has hidden, had hidden)*. When you use one of these past participles without a helping verb, you create a fragment.

For more on past participles, see Chapter 27. For more on using participles as modifiers, see Chapter 25.

FRAGMENT   Hidden behind the sofa pillow.

One way to correct this fragment is to add a subject and a helping verb.

CORRECT   The gerbil was hidden behind the sofa pillow.

Another way to correct the fragment is to attach it to a nearby sentence.

INCORRECT   We finally found the gerbil. Hidden behind the sofa pillow.

CORRECT   We finally found the gerbil, hidden behind the sofa pillow.

Infinitive Phrase Fragments

An **infinitive** consists of *to* plus the base form of the verb *(to be, to go, to write)*. An infinitive phrase *(to be free, to go home, to write a novel)* cannot stand alone as a sentence because it does not include a complete verb. (An infinitive is not a complete verb.) You can correct an infinitive phrase fragment by adding a subject and a complete verb.

INCORRECT   Eric studied for years. To become a systems analyst.

CORRECT   Eric studied for years to become a systems analyst.

Another solution is to attach the fragment to a nearby sentence.

INCORRECT   He graduated first in his class. With many honors.

CORRECT   He graduated first in his class, with many honors.

◆ PRACTICE 22-2

Each of the following items is a fragment because it lacks a subject or a verb or both. Correct each fragment by adding any words needed to turn the fragment into a complete sentence.

Example: Setting behind the clouds.

The sun was setting behind the clouds.

or

The sun sank from the sky, setting behind the clouds.

1. To write plays about the Chinese-American experience. _____

_____

2. Been worried about money for a long time. _____

_____

3. The worst week of my life._____

_____

4. Trying to decide where to live. _____

_____

5. Chosen to play the lead in *A Raisin in the Sun*. _____

_____

6. Behind door number 3. _____

_____

7. Always complaining about the lab manual. _____

_____

8. Fallen from the heating ducts. _____

_____

9. A difficult career decision. _____

_____

10. Wondering which job to take. _____

_____

11. Getting away with murder. _____

_____

12. In less than a year. _____

_____

13. Forbidden to see each other. _____

_____

14. Minding her own business. _____

_____

15. To graduate with honors. _____

_____

■ WRITING FIRST: Flashback

Look back at your response to the Writing First exercise on page 282. Underline any present or past participles. Are the sentences in which these words appear complete? Are any other phrases incorrectly punctuated as sentences? Correct each fragment by adding any words necessary to create complete sentences. (Hint: You may

(continued on the following page)

(continued from the previous page)
find these words in a sentence that comes before or after the fragment.) Write your edited sentences on the lines below.

_____

_____

_____

_____

C Correcting Dependent Clause Fragments

Every sentence must express a complete thought. A **dependent clause** is a group of words that includes a subject and a verb but does not express a complete thought. Therefore, it cannot stand alone as a sentence. To correct a dependent clause fragment, you must complete the thought.

Dependent Clauses Introduced by Subordinating Conjunctions

Some dependent clauses are introduced by **subordinating conjunctions**.

> FRAGMENT <u>Although</u> the sisters had dreamed for years of coming to America.

This sentence fragment includes a subject *(the sisters)* and a complete verb *(had dreamed),* but it is not a sentence; it is a dependent clause introduced by the subordinating conjunction *although.*

One way to correct this fragment is to add an **independent clause** (a complete sentence) to complete the idea and finish the sentence.

> SENTENCE Although the sisters had dreamed for years of coming to America, they did not have enough money for the trip until 1985.

Another way to correct the fragment is to delete the subordinating conjunction *Although,* the word that makes the idea incomplete.

> SENTENCE The sisters had dreamed for years of coming to America.

Dependent Clauses Introduced by Relative Pronouns

Other dependent clauses are introduced by **relative pronouns** *(who, which,* or *that).*

> FRAGMENT Novelist Richard Wright, <u>who</u> came to Paris in 1947.

> FRAGMENT A quinceañera, <u>which</u> celebrates a Latina's fifteenth birthday.

● **Writing Tip**
Subordinating conjunctions include *although, because, even, if,* and *though.* (See 17A.)

FRAGMENT   A key World War II battle <u>that</u> was fought on the Pacific island of Guadalcanal.

Although each sentence fragment listed above includes a subject *(Richard Wright, quinceañera, battle)* and a complete verb *(came, celebrates, was fought)*, they aren't sentences because they don't express complete thoughts. In each case, a relative pronoun creates a dependent clause.

One way to correct each fragment is to add the words needed to complete the idea.

SENTENCE   Novelist Richard Wright, who came to Paris in 1947, spent the rest of his life there.

SENTENCE   A quinceañera, which celebrates a Latina's fifteenth birthday, signifies her entrance into womanhood.

SENTENCE   A key World War II battle that was fought on the Pacific island of Guadalcanal took place in 1943.

Another way to correct the fragments is to delete the relative pronouns that make the ideas incomplete.

SENTENCE   Novelist Richard Wright came to Paris in 1947.

SENTENCE   A quinceañera celebrates a Latina's fifteenth birthday.

SENTENCE   A key World War II battle was fought on the Pacific island of Guadalcanal.

FOCUS   **Completing the Thought**

Every sentence must express a complete thought. A word group such as *Although the sisters had dreamed for years of coming to America* is incomplete because *Although* leads us to expect the idea to continue. We are puzzled when the fragment stops before telling us what happened to the sisters' dream. Similarly, a fragment such as *Richard Wright, who came to Paris in 1947* leaves us wondering what Richard Wright did. Adding words to complete the thought turns each fragment into a sentence.

◆ **PRACTICE 22-3**

Correct each of these dependent clause fragments in two ways. First, make the fragment a complete sentence by adding a group of words that completes the idea. Second, delete the subordinating conjunction or relative pronoun that makes the idea incomplete.

Example: Before it became a state.

Revised: *Before it became a state, West Virginia was part of Virginia.*

Revised: *It became a state.*

1. Because many homeless people are mentally ill.

   Revised: _____

   _____

   Revised: _____

   _____

2. The film that frightened me.

   Revised: _____

   _____

   Revised: _____

   _____

3. Although people disagree about the effects of violence in children's television shows.

   Revised: _____

   _____

   Revised: _____

   _____

Relative 4. People who drink and drive.

   Revised: _____

   _____

   Revised: _____

   _____

5. As competition among college students for athletic scholarships increased.

   Revised: _____

   _____

   Revised: _____

   _____

6. Whenever a new semester begins.

   Revised: _____

   _____

   Revised: _____

   _____

7. Pizza, which is high in fat.

Revised: _____

_____

Revised: _____

_____

8. Animals that are used in medical research.

Revised: _____

_____

Revised: _____

_____

9. Unless something is likely to change.

Revised: _____

_____

Revised: _____

_____

10. Although it is a very controversial issue.

Revised: _____

_____

Revised: _____

_____

◆ PRACTICE 22-4

All of the following are fragments. Turn each fragment into a complete sentence, and write the revised sentence on the line below the fragment. Whenever possible, try creating two different revisions.

Example: Waiting in the dugout.

Revised: *Waiting in the dugout, the players chewed tobacco.*

Revised: *The players were waiting in the dugout.*

1. Because three-year-olds are still very attached to their parents.

Revised: _____

_____

Revised: _____

_____

2. Going around in circles.

Revised: _____

_____

Revised: _____

_____

3. To win the prize for the most unusual costume.

Revised: _____

_____

Revised: _____

_____

4. Students who thought they couldn't afford to go to college.

Revised: _____

_____

Revised: _____

_____

5. On an important secret mission.

Revised: _____

_____

Revised: _____

_____

6. Although many instructors see cheating as a serious problem.

Revised: _____

_____

Revised: _____

_____

7. Hoping to get another helping of chocolate fudge cake.

Revised: _____

_____

Revised: _____

_____

8. The rule that I always felt was the most unfair.

Revised: _____

_____

Revised: _____

_____

9. A really exceptional worker.

Revised: _____

_____

Revised: _____

_____

10. Finished in record time.

Revised: _____

_____

Revised: _____

_____

■ WRITING FIRST: Flashback

Look back at your response to the Writing First exercise on page 282. Underline every subordinating conjunction you find (first consult the list on page 219), and underline *which, that,* and *who* wherever you find them. Do any of these words create a dependent clause that is punctuated as if it were a sentence? If so, either cross out the subordinating conjunction or relative pronoun, or attach the fragment to another word group to create a complete sentence. Write your edited sentences here.

_____

_____

_____

_____

_____

_____

■ WRITING FIRST: Revising and Editing

Look back at your response to the Writing First exercise on page 282. Is every sentence complete? Check every one to be sure that it has a subject and a verb, that the verb is complete, and that the sentence expresses a complete thought. If you find a fragment, revise it by adding whatever is necessary to complete it, or by attaching it to a nearby sentence. (Use your responses to the Flashback exercises on pages 284, 287, and 293 to help you revise.) If you don't find any fragments, work with a classmate to correct his or her writing, or edit the work you did in response to another assignment.

CHAPTER REVIEW

◆ EDITING PRACTICE

Read the following student essay, into which incomplete sentences have been introduced. Underline each fragment. Then, correct it by adding the words necessary to complete it or attaching it to a nearby sentence that completes the idea. The first fragment has been underlined and corrected for you.

                    My First Job

    Like many other teenagers, I got my first job when
                                                  in
I was in high school. I worked as a salesperson/ ~~In~~ a
                                              ^
retail clothing chain. At first, I was really excited.
Learning about pricing procedures and arranging displays,
and I got to see all the new styles. As they were introduced. I also got to use my employee discount. A benefit
that saved me a lot of money.

    People always coming into the store, asking for help
in finding things. They would have requests like "Could you
tell me where to find a blue and purple lambswool sweater?"
and "You're about the same size as my niece. Could you try
this on for me?" Sometimes, the customers were annoying.
Still, I felt useful and important. When I was able to
help them.

The job had its bad side, though. I always seemed to be running. To be constantly straightening the same racks over and over. Also rearranging displays several times every night. When the store was busy, it was very hectic. Not all the customers were patient or polite. Some lost their tempers. Because they couldn't find a particular size or color. Then, they took out their anger on me. On slow nights, when the store was almost empty. I was restless and bored. Eventually, I found a more stimulating position. At a preschool for developmentally delayed children.

◆ COLLABORATIVE ACTIVITIES

1. Exchange workbooks with another student and read each other's responses to the Writing First exercise on page 294. On a separate sheet of paper, make a list of five questions for the other student, asking more about his or her family's holiday celebration and why it is meaningful to the student. When your own workbook is returned, answer your partner's questions about your holiday celebration, and add this information to your Writing First exercise response. Be sure all the sentences you have added are complete.

2. Working in a group of three or four students, add different subordinating conjunctions to sentences *a* through *d* below to create several different fragments. (See 17A for a list of subordinating conjunctions.) Turn each of the resulting fragments into a complete sentence by adding a word group that completes the idea.

Example

SENTENCE	FRAGMENT	NEW SENTENCE
I left the party.	As I left the party	As I left the party, I fell.
	After I left the party	After I left the party, the fun stopped.
	Until I left the party	Until I left the party, I had no idea it was so late.

   a. My mind wanders.
   b. She caught the ball.
   c. He made a wish.
   d. Disaster struck.

3. Working in a group of three or four students, build as many sentences as you can around fragments *a* through *e* listed on page 296, each of which is introduced by a past or present participle. Use your imagination to create as many creative, comical, or even silly sentences as you can.

Example

FRAGMENT   Known for his incredible memory

SENTENCES   Zack, known for his incredible memory, has somehow managed to forget everything he learned about chemistry.

Known for his incredible memory, Monty the Magnificent mesmerized audiences.

a. wandering in the desert
b. stranded in the jungle
c. looking for his ideal mate
d. always using as much ketchup as possible
e. folded, stapled, and mutilated

☑ REVIEW CHECKLIST:
Sentence Fragments

▪ A sentence fragment is an incomplete sentence. Every sentence must include a subject and a verb and express a complete thought. (See 22A.)

▪ Phrases cannot stand alone as sentences. (See 22B.)

▪ Dependent clauses cannot stand alone as sentences. (See 22C.)

Subject-Verb Agreement

■ WRITING FIRST

Describe a place that has special significance to you—a room, a building, or an outdoor location. What does the place look like? Why does it appeal to you? Write your description in the present tense (for example, "A picture *hangs* on the wall").

PREVIEW

In this chapter, you will learn

■ to understand subject-verb agreement (23A)

■ to avoid agreement problems with *be, have,* and *do* (23B)

■ to avoid agreement problems when words come between the subject and the verb (23C)

■ to avoid agreement problems with indefinite pronouns as subjects (23D)

■ to avoid agreement problems when the verb comes before the subject (23E)

■ to avoid agreement problems with the relative pronouns *who, which,* and *that* (23F)

A Understanding Subject-Verb Agreement

A sentence's subject (a noun or pronoun) and its verb must **agree** in number. Singular subjects must have singular verbs, and plural subjects must have plural verbs.

Subject-Verb Agreement with Regular Verbs

	Singular	**Plural**
1st person	I play	Molly and I/we play
2nd person	you play	you play
3rd person	he/she/it/plays	they play
	the man plays	the men play
	Molly plays	Molly and Sam play

    s   v

The <u>museum</u> <u>opens</u> at ten o'clock. (singular noun subject *museum* takes singular verb *opens*)

    s   v

The <u>museums</u> <u>open</u> at ten o'clock. (plural noun subject *museums* takes plural verb *open*)

For information on identifying plural noun and pronoun subjects, see 28A and 28B.

S   V
She always <u>watches</u> the eleven o'clock news. (singular pronoun subject *she* takes singular verb *watches*)

S   V
They always <u>watch</u> the eleven o'clock news. (plural pronoun subject *they* takes plural verb *watch*)

Most subject-verb agreement problems occur in the present tense, where third-person singular subjects require special verb forms. Regular verbs form the *third-person singular* by adding *-s* or *-es* to the base form (the form of the verb used with *I*).

INCORRECT   He <u>go</u> to the store.

CORRECT   He <u>goes</u> to the store.

● **Writing Tip**
Subject-verb agreement presents special problems with the irregular verb *be*. (See 23B.)

● **Writing Tip**
The rules that govern compound subjects and *or* also govern compound subjects and *neither . . . nor.*

FOCUS   **Subject-Verb Agreement with Compound Subjects**

The subject of a sentence is not always a single word. It can also be a **compound subject**, consisting of two or more words.

■ When the parts of a compound subject are connected by *and*, the compound subject takes a plural verb.

S   V
<u>John and Marsha</u> <u>share</u> an office.

■ If both parts of a compound subject connected by *or* are singular, the compound subject takes a singular verb.

S   V
<u>John or Marsha</u> <u>locks</u> up at the end of the day.

■ If both parts of a compound subject connected by *or* are plural, the compound subject takes a plural verb.

S   V
<u>Buses or trains</u> <u>take</u> you to the center of the city.

■ If one part of a compound subject connected by *or* is singular and the other is plural, the verb agrees with the word that is closer to it.

S   V
<u>The mayor or the council members</u> <u>meet</u> with community groups.

S   V
<u>The council members or the mayor</u> <u>meets</u> with community groups.

◆ PRACTICE 23-1

Underline the correct form of the verb in each of the following sentences.
Make sure the verb agrees with its subject.

Example: Stray cats (is/<u>are</u>) a problem in many cities.

(1) Jean Toomey (care/cares) for 446 cats. (2) In fact, she (run/runs) a home for cats. (3) More than two hundred cats (come/comes) from owners who have left money to Ms. Toomey's home so she will take care of their cats. (4) The other cats (come/comes) from the streets.

(5) The cat home (stand/stands) on thirty-five acres of rural land in northwest Connecticut. (6) When you (walk/walks) into the home, you (see/sees) cats everywhere. (7) One cat (watch/watches) television. (8) Another cat (take/takes) a nap on the large wooden deck at the side of the house. (9) Resident cats (come/comes) and (go/goes) through the windows. (10) Cats (run/runs) through five acres of woods, having every adventure a cat could want. (11) Newcomers (stay/stays) in a special room until they get used to their new surroundings. (12) Older cats (live/ lives) in the north wing, where the music and food are softer.

(13) Every morning, workers (serve/serves) 125 cans of cat food. (14) Dry food (disappear/disappears) during afternoon snacks. (15) A local lumberyard (donate/donates) a monthly truckload of sawdust for cat boxes. (16) A veterinarian (provide/provides) discount health care. (17) Some cats (spend/spends) their entire lives at Ms. Toomey's home, while others are adopted.

◆ PRACTICE 23-2

Fill in the blank with the correct present tense form of the verb.

Example: Every day, she __*visits*__ the computer lab in the basement of Reinhold Hall. (visit)

(1) Lynn _____ with a computer. (write) (2) It _____ her work easier. (make) (3) I _____ one too. (use) (4) Our instructors _____ our work. (supervise) They _____ our computer disks.

(collect) (5) Each week, Ms. Keane and Mr. Marlowe _____ back the disks. (give) (6) The disks _____ our instructors' comments. (contain) (7) I _____ my disk into the computer (put) and _____ Mr. Marlowe's comments as I revise. (read) (8) We _____ this technique for marking papers. (like) (9) One student says he _____ the computer, however. (hate) (10) The screen _____ him headaches. (give)

■ WRITING FIRST: Flashback

Look back at your response to the Writing First exercise on page 297. Choose two sentences that contain present tense verbs, and rewrite them on the lines below. Underline the subject of each sentence once and the verb twice. If the subject and verb of each sentence do not agree, correct them here.

_____

_____

_____

_____

_____

B   Avoiding Agreement Problems with *Be*, *Have*, and *Do*

The irregular verbs *be*, *have*, and *do* often present problems with subject-verb agreement in the present tense. Memorizing their forms is the only sure way to avoid trouble.

For more on regular and irregular verbs, see 26A and 26B.

Subject-Verb Agreement with Be

	Singular	**Plural**
1st person	I am	we are
2nd person	you are	you are
3rd person	he/she/it is	they are
	Tran is	Tran and Ryan are
	the boy is	the boys are

Subject-Verb Agreement with Have

	Singular	**Plural**
1st person	I have	we have
2nd person	you have	you have
3rd person	he/she/it has	they have
	Shana has	Shana and Robert have
	the student has	the students have

Subject-Verb Agreement with Do

	Singular	**Plural**
1st person	I do	we do
2nd person	you do	you do
3rd person	he/she/it does	they do
	Ken does	Ken and Mia do
	the book does	the books do

◆ PRACTICE 23-3

Fill in the blank with the correct present tense form of the verb *be, have,* or *do.*

Example: Sometimes, people ___*do*___ damage without really meaning to. (do)

(1) Biologists _____ serious worries about the damage that exotic animals can cause when they move into places where native species have developed few defenses against them. (have) (2) The English sparrow _____ one example. (be) (3) It _____ a role in the decline in the number of bluebirds. (have) (4) On the Galapagos Islands, cats _____ another example. (be) (5) Introduced by early explorers, they currently _____ much damage to the eggs of the giant tortoises that live on the islands. (do) (6) Scientists today _____ worried about a new problem. (be) (7) This _____ a situation caused by fish and wildlife agencies that deliberately introduce exotic fish into lakes and streams. (be) (8) They _____ this to please those who enjoy fishing. (do) (9) Although popular with people who fish, this policy _____ major drawbacks. (have) (10) It _____ one drawback in particular: many species of fish have been pushed close to extinction. (have)

■ WRITING FIRST: Flashback

Look back at your response to the Writing First exercise on page 297. Have you used a form of *be, have,* or *do* in any of your sentences? Write these sentences on the lines below. Have you used the correct forms of *be, have,* and *do?* Correct any agreement errors here.

_____

_____

_____

_____

C **Avoiding Agreement Problems
When Words Come between the Subject and the Verb**

▼ **Student Voices**
*When I revise, I always look
for grammar mistakes, especially agreement errors.*
Hiro Nakamura

Words that come between the subject and the verb do not affect subject-verb agreement.

                   S   V

CORRECT High <u>levels</u> of mercury <u>occur</u> in some fish.

Sometimes, however, a subject-verb agreement problem occurs when a prepositional phrase comes between the subject and the verb. In such cases, the object of the preposition may appear to be the subject of the sentence when it really is not.

    By crossing out the prepositional phrase, you can easily see if there are any agreement errors.

*For more on prepositional
phrases, see 15B. For a list of
prepositions, see 30L.*

High levels ~~of mercury~~ occur in some fish.

FOCUS **Words That Come between Subject and Verb**

Words and phrases such as *in addition to, along with, together with, as well as, except,* and *including* also introduce prepositional phrases. A noun or pronoun that follows such phrases is an object of the preposition; therefore, it cannot be the subject of the sentence.

        S   V

St. Thomas, ~~along with St. Croix and St. John,~~ <u>is</u> part of the United States Virgin Islands.

● **Writing Tip**
An agreement error can
occur when a long group of
words comes between the
subject and the verb. To
check for agreement, find
the subject and the verb, and
then cross out the words
between them.

◆ **PRACTICE 23-4**

In each of the following sentences, cross out the prepositional phrase that separates the subject and the verb. Then, underline the subject of the sentence once and the verb that agrees with the subject twice.

Example: The stains ~~on the carpet~~ (suggest/suggests) that they had a party.

1. The cupids in the painting (symbolize/symbolizes) lost innocence.

2. Fans at a concert (get/gets) angry if a group is late.

3. The appliances in the kitchen (make/makes) strange noises.

4. The United States, along with Germany and Japan, (produce/produces) most of the world's cars.

5. A good set of skis and poles (cost/costs) a lot.

6. Unfortunately, one out of ten men (gets/get) prostate cancer.

7. Workers in the city (pays/pay) a high wage tax.

8. Each summer, fires from lightning (cause/causes) hundreds of millions of dollars in property damage.

9. Volunteers, including people like my father, (help/helps) paramedics in my community.

10. The starving children in Somalia (need/needs) food quickly.

■ WRITING FIRST: Flashback

Look back at your response to the Writing First exercise on page 297. Can you find any sentences in which words come between the subject and the verb? Write each subject and verb on the lines below.

Subject   *Verb*

_____   _____

_____   _____

_____   _____

_____   _____

Now, correct any errors in subject-verb agreement.

● **Writing Tip**
Many indefinite pronouns
end in *-one, -body,* or *-thing.*
These words are almost
always singular.

D **Avoiding Agreement Problems
with Indefinite Pronouns as Subjects**

An **indefinite pronoun** does not refer to a particular person, place, or idea. When an indefinite pronoun is the subject of a sentence, the verb must agree with it. Most indefinite pronouns, such as *no one* and *everyone,* are singular and take a singular verb.

        _S   _V
No one likes getting up early.

        _S   _V
Everyone likes to sleep late.

       _S   _V
Neither likes beets.

Singular Indefinite Pronouns			
anybody	either	neither	one
anyone	everybody	nobody	somebody
anything	everyone	no one	someone
each	everything	nothing	something

A few indefinite pronouns are plural *(many, several, few, both, some)* and take a plural verb.

      _S   _V
Many were left homeless by the storm.

FOCUS **Indefinite Pronouns as Subjects**

When an indefinite pronoun is a sentence's subject, the verb must agree with it. If a prepositional phrase comes between the indefinite pronoun and the verb, cross out the prepositional phrase to help you identify the sentence's subject.

   _S   _V
Each ~~of the boys~~ has a bike.

   _S   _V
Many ~~of the boys~~ have bikes.

◆ PRACTICE 23-5

Underline the correct verb in each sentence.

    Example: Each of the three streams in our area (<u>is</u>/are) polluted.

(1) Some of the streams no longer (have/has) any fish. (2) Another (contain, contains) a lot of algae. (3) Everybody (want/wants) to improve the situation. (4) No one (are/is) willing to do anything. (5) Somebody always (take/takes) control. (6) Everyone (know/knows) that pollution is difficult to control. (7) Neither of the candidates (seem/seems) willing to act. (8) Whenever anyone (ask/asks) them for suggestions, neither (have, has) any. (9) According to the candidates, everything (is/are) being done that can be done. (10) One of my friends (say/says) that she will not vote for either candidate.

■ WRITING FIRST: Flashback

Look back at your response to the Writing First exercise on page 297. Do any of the sentences contain indefinite pronouns that act as subjects? Do the verbs in these sentences agree with the indefinite pronoun subjects? If you find any that do not, rewrite the correct form of the verb below.

Indefinite pronoun subject   *Verb*

_____   _____

_____   _____

_____   _____

_____   _____

_____   _____

E   **Avoiding Agreement Problems When the Verb Comes before the Subject**

A verb always agrees with its subject, even if the subject comes *after* the verb. In questions, for example, word order is frequently reversed, with the subject coming after the verb or between two parts of the verb.

        V   S
Where is the telephone booth?

  V   S   V
Are you going to the party?

If you have trouble identifying the subject of a question, answer the question with a statement.

The <u>telephone booth</u> <u>is</u> outside.

<u>We</u> <u>are</u> <u>going</u> to the party.

● **Writing Tip**
To write more concise sentences, replace *there is* and *there are* with action verbs. (*Nine justices* sit *on the Supreme Court. One chief justice* presides.)

> **FOCUS** *There Is* and *There Are*
>
> In a sentence that begins with *there is* or *there are*, the subject comes after the form of the verb *be*. (*There* can never be the subject.)
>
> There <u>are</u> nine <u>justices</u> on the Supreme Court.
>
> There <u>is</u> one <u>chief justice</u> presiding over the Court.

◆ **PRACTICE 23-6**

Underline the subject of each sentence, and circle the correct form of the verb.

Example: Who (is/are) <u>the writer</u> who won the 1992 Nobel Prize in literature?

1. Where (is/are) the Bering Straits?

2. Why (do/does) the compound change color after being exposed to light?

3. (Is/Are) the twins identical or fraternal?

4. How (do/does) Congress override a presidential veto?

5. What (have/has) this to do with me?

6. There (is/are) ten computers in the writing center.

7. There (is/are) more than nine million people living in Mexico City.

8. There (is/are) several reference books in this library that can help you with your research.

9. There (is/are) four reasons that we should save the spotted owl from extinction.

10. There (is/are) more than one way to answer the question.

■ WRITING FIRST: Flashback

Look back at your response to the Writing First exercise on page 297. Do you have any sentences in which the subject comes after the verb? If so, write those sentences on the lines below. If the subject and verb of each sentence do not agree, correct them here.

_____

_____

_____

_____

F · Avoiding Agreement Problems with the Relative Pronouns *Who, Which,* and *That*

The relative pronouns *who, which,* and *that* are singular when they refer to a singular word and plural when they refer to a plural word. In the following sentences, the relative pronouns are singular.

For more on who, which, that, *and other relative pronouns, see 17B.*

The author, who <u>writes</u> about Chinese immigrants, spoke at our college.

Here, the verb *writes* is singular because the relative pronoun *who* refers to *author,* a singular word. In the next sentence, however, the relative pronoun is plural.

Computers that <u>have</u> color monitors are expensive.

Here, the verb *have* is plural because the relative pronoun *that* refers to *computers,* a plural word.

◆ PRACTICE 23-7

Draw an arrow from *who, which,* or *that* to the word that it refers to. Circle the correct form of the verb.

Example: Edgar Allan Poe, who (tell/tells) tales of horror, was born in 1809.

(1) Poe's "The Fall of the House of Usher" is a story that (have/has) entertained many readers. (2) The story, which (contain/contains) the poem "The Haunted Palace," was published in 1839. (3) The narrator, who (have/has) not seen Roderick Usher for many years, is summoned to the House of Usher. (4) The decaying mansion, which (is/are) dark

and dreary, stands at the edge of a swamp. (5) Roderick's twin sister
Madeline, who (live/lives) in the house, is very ill. (6) At one point in the
story, Roderick's sister, who (is/are) in a trance, is thought to be dead.
(7) Roderick buries her in the family vault that (is/are) beneath the
house. (8) Later, Madeline, who (is/are) dressed in her shroud, walks
into the room. (9) Roderick, who (is/are) terrified, falls down dead.
(10) Running outside, the narrator sees the house, which (have/has) split
apart, sink into the swamp.

■ WRITING FIRST: Flashback

Look back at your response to the Writing First exercise on page
297. Can you find any sentences that include the relative pronouns
who, which, or *that?* Be sure you have used a singular verb when
who, which, or *that* refers to a singular word, and a plural verb
when the reference is to a plural word.

■ WRITING FIRST: Revising and Editing

Look back at your response to the Writing First exercise on page
297. Make sure all your verbs agree with their subjects. Cross out
any incorrect verb forms, and write the correct forms above them.
Next, rewrite the entire paragraph, changing all the singular subjects to plural subjects and the plural subjects to singular ones.
(For example, *picture* would become *pictures,* and *I* would become
we.) Then, change the verbs so they agree with their new subjects.

CHAPTER REVIEW

◆ EDITING PRACTICE

Read the following student essay, into which errors of subject-verb agreement have been introduced. Decide whether each of the underlined verbs
agrees with its subject. If it does not, cross out the verb and write in the

correct form. If it does, write *C* above the verb. The first sentence has been done for you.

Cartoon Violence

~~know~~ [knows] cartoons are violent. There are many great old cartoons that illustrates this point. The Road-runner cartoons, which are staples of children's television, is very violent. The coyote with all his tricks suffer many setbacks as he attempt to catch the elusive bird. No matter how hard he tries, he never succeeds. Everything seem to backfire. The result is that the coyote, who looks pathetically at viewers, experience at least fifteen different episodes of violence per cartoon.

Another violent cartoon character is Bugs Bunny. Bugs Bunny, along with Elmer Fudd, Daffy Duck, and Yosemite Sam, are constantly fighting. A typical cartoon, which stars Bugs and Elmer Fudd, has Elmer trying to shoot Bugs. "Why do Elmer want to shoot Bugs?" you may ask. There is many reasons, but the main reason is that it is hunting season. Neither of the two characters seem to be able to resist a test of wits. Elmer, who is constantly outsmarted, walk away saying, "Gosh darn wabbit!"

Nothing in these cartoons are good for children. Perhaps the most dangerous idea for children are that they can shoot someone, set someone on fire, or hit someone with a hammer without actually harming that person.

◆ COLLABORATIVE ACTIVITIES

1. Working in a group of four students, list ten nouns (five singular and five plural)—people, places, or things—on the left-hand side of a sheet of paper. Beside each noun, write the present tense form of a verb that could logically go with the noun. Exchange papers with another group, and check to see that singular nouns have singular verbs and plural nouns have plural verbs.

2. Working with your group, expand each noun-and-verb combination you listed in Collaborative Activity 1 into a complete sentence. Next, write a sentence that could logically follow each of these sentences, using a pronoun as the subject of the new sentence. Make sure the pronoun you choose refers to the noun in the previous sentence, as in the

example *Alan watches three movies a week. He is addicted to films.*
Check to be certain the nouns and pronouns in the new sentences
agree with the verbs.

3. Exchange the final version of your edited Writing First exercise with
another student in your group. Answer the following questions about
each sentence in your partner's exercise.

■ Do any words come between the subject and the verb?
■ Does the sentence contain an indefinite pronoun used as a subject?
■ Does the subject come after the verb?
■ Does the sentence contain the relative pronoun *who, which,* or
that?

As you answer these questions, check to make sure all the verbs agree
with their subjects. When your own exercise is returned to you, make
any necessary corrections.

☑ **REVIEW CHECKLIST:**
Subject-Verb Agreement

Singular subjects (nouns and pronouns) take singular verbs,
and plural subjects take plural verbs. (See 23A.)

The irregular verbs *be, have,* and *do* often present problems
with subject-verb agreement in the present tense. (See 23B.)

Words that come between the subject and the verb do not affect
subject-verb agreement. (See 23C.)

Most indefinite pronouns, such as *no one* and *everyone,* are singular and take a singular verb when they serve as the subject of
a sentence. (See 23D.)

A verb agrees with its subject even if the subject comes after the
verb. (See 23E.)

The relative pronouns *who, which,* and *that* are singular when
they refer to a singular word and plural when they refer to a
plural word. (See 23F.)

Illogical Shifts

■ **WRITING FIRST**

Write about how you think parents can help their children learn how to succeed in life. How can parents increase their children's self-esteem? What can they say that will motivate their children to set realistic goals and work to achieve them? Be sure to give specific examples.

A **shift** occurs anytime a writer changes *tense, person, number, discourse,* or *voice.* As you write and revise, be sure that any shifts you make are logical—that is, that you make them for a good reason.

A   Avoiding Illogical Shifts in Tense

An **illogical shift in tense** occurs when a writer changes tenses for no apparent reason.

> ILLOGICAL SHIFT IN TENSE   The dog <u>walked</u> to the fireplace. Then, he <u>circles</u> twice and <u>lies</u> down in front of the fire. (past to present)
>
> REVISED   The dog <u>walked</u> to the fireplace. Then, he <u>circled</u> twice and <u>lay</u> down in front of the fire. (consistent past)
>
> REVISED   The dog <u>walks</u> to the fireplace. Then, he <u>circles</u> twice and <u>lies</u> down in front of the fire. (consistent present)

◆ **PRACTICE 24-1**

Edit the following sentences for illogical shifts in tense. If a sentence is correct, write *C* in the blank.

Examples

received
She was surprised when she ~~receives~~ the news. _____
                                          ^

Last year, she was a captain on the force. Now, she is chief of police.
  _C_

(1) When Beverly Harvard became the chief of the Atlanta police force in 1994, she is the first African-American woman ever to hold that title in a major U.S. city. _____ (2) She started on the police force when she was twenty-two, at a time when mostly white men work as Atlanta police. _____ (3) Now, more than half the department is African American, and women made up about a quarter of the force. _____ (4) Harvard first thought about joining the force because her husband and a male friend said they do not believe women are capable of doing police work. _____ (5) Her husband even agrees to pay her $100 if she made it on to the force. _____ (6) She accepted the challenge in 1973, and today she looks back on her first years of training with amazement at how little she knew then. _____ (7) In fact, when she entered the police academy, she did not really plan to be a police officer. She just wants to prove her husband wrong and to win the $100 bet. _____ (8) One thing that helped her to progress was her administrative ability. Another is her talent for effective management. _____ (9) When her promotion was announced, some veteran officers criticize her appointment as police chief, but most younger officers praised the choice. _____ (10) Now, most members of the force appreciate her accessibility and were happy about her willingness to listen to new ideas and approaches. _____

■ WRITING FIRST: Flashback

Look back at your response to the Writing First exercise on page 311. Check each sentence to make sure you have no illogical shifts from one tense to another. If you find an incorrect sentence, rewrite it below, correcting any illogical shifts in tense.

(continued on the following page)

(continued from the previous page)

_____

_____

_____

_____

B　Avoiding Illogical Shifts in Person

Person is the form a pronoun takes to indicate who is speaking, spoken about, or spoken to.

Person

	Singular	**Plural**
First person	I	we
Second person	you	you
Third person	he, she, it	they

An **illogical shift in person** occurs when a writer shifts from one person to another for no apparent reason.

ILLOGICAL SHIFT　The <u>hikers</u> were told that <u>you</u> had to stay on the trail. (from third to second person)

REVISED　The <u>hikers</u> were told that <u>they</u> had to stay on the trail. (consistent use of third person)

ILLOGICAL SHIFT　<u>Anyone</u> can learn to cook if <u>you</u> practice. (from third to second person)

REVISED　<u>People</u> can learn to cook if <u>they</u> practice. (consistent use of third person)

REVISED　<u>You</u> can learn to cook if <u>you</u> practice. (consistent use of second person)

◆ PRACTICE 24-2

The following sentences contain illogical shifts between the second person and the third person. Edit each sentence so that it uses third-person pronouns consistently. Be sure to change the verb if necessary to make it agree with the new subject.

For more on subject-verb agreement, see Chapter 32.

Example:　Before a person finds a job in the fashion industry, ~~you~~
he or she has
~~have~~ to have some experience.

(1) Young people who want a career in the fashion industry don't always realize how hard you will have to work. (2) They think that working in the world of fashion will be glamorous and that you will quickly make a fortune. (3) In reality, no matter how talented you are, a recent college graduate entering the industry is paid only about $18,000 a year. (4) The manufacturers and retailers who employ new graduates expect you to work for three years or more at this salary before you are promoted. (5) A young designer may receive a big raise if you are very talented, but this is unusual. (6) New employees have to pay their dues, and you soon realize that most of your duties are tedious. (7) Employees may be excited to land a job as an assistant designer but then find that you color in designs that have already been drawn. (8) Other beginners in fashion houses discover that you spend most of your time sewing or typing up orders. (9) If a person is serious about working in the fashion industry, you have to be realistic. (10) For most newcomers to the industry, the ability to do what you are told to do is more important than your artistic talent or fashion sense.

● **Writing Tip**
Be careful not to use the pronoun *he* to refer to a noun that could be either masculine or feminine. (See 20E.)

■ WRITING FIRST: Flashback

Look back at your response to the Writing First exercise on page 311. Check each sentence to make sure there are no illogical shifts in person. If you find an incorrect sentence, rewrite it on the lines below, correcting any illogical shifts in person.

_____

_____

_____

_____

C **Avoiding Illogical Shifts in Number**

Number is the form a noun, pronoun, or verb takes to indicate whether it is singular (one) or plural (more than one).

Number

Singular	Plural
I	we
he, she	they
Fred	Fred and Ethel
man	men
an encyclopedia	encyclopedias
his, her	their
am, is, was	are, were

An **illogical shift in number** occurs when a writer shifts from singular to plural (or the other way around) for no apparent reason.

ILLOGICAL SHIFT IN NUMBER Each <u>visitor</u> to the museum must check <u>their</u> cameras at the entrance. (from singular to plural)

REVISED Each <u>visitor</u> to the museum must check <u>his or her</u> camera at the entrance. (consistent singular)

REVISED <u>Visitors</u> to the museum must check <u>their</u> cameras at the entrance. (consistent plural)

● **Writing Tip**
A pronoun must agree in number with the word it refers to (its antecedent). (See 28D.)

◆ PRACTICE 24-3

Edit the following sentences for illogical shifts from singular to plural. You can either change the singular element to the plural or change the plural element to the singular. Be sure to change the verb so it agrees with the new subject. If the sentence is correct, write *C* in the blank.

Example

              his or her
Each attorney first makes ~~their~~ opening speech. _____
                  ^

Good jurors
~~A good juror~~ take$ their time in making their decision. _____

(1) According to recent studies, a juror may have their mind made up before the trial even begins. _____ (2) As attorneys offer their opening arguments, a juror may immediately decide whether they think the defendant is innocent or guilty. _____ (3) This unfounded conclusion often depends on which attorney makes their initial description of the case the most dramatic. _____ (4) During the trial, that juror will pay attention only to evidence that corresponds to the decision they have already made. _____ (5) A juror with poor decision-making skills is also not likely to listen to challenges to their opinions when the full jury comes together to deliberate. _____ (6) No matter how wrong they are,

such a juror argues their positions strongly and urges the strictest sentencing or the highest damage payments. _____ (7) These jurors feel their responsibility is to argue for their version of the truth rather than to weigh all the evidence and alternative possibilities. _____ (8) Such a juror will even make up their own evidence to support their case. _____ (9) For example, one juror argued that a man being tried for murder was acting in their own defense because the victim was probably carrying a knife, but no knife was mentioned during the trial. _____ (10) Studies suggest that a person who jumps to conclusions on a jury probably won't take their time when making other important decisions in life. _____

■ WRITING FIRST: Flashback

Look back at your response to the Writing First exercise on page 311. Find all the sentences in which you use the pronoun *they* or *their*. Check every sentence to make sure each of these pronouns refers to a plural noun or pronoun. If you find an incorrect sentence, rewrite it on the lines below, correcting any illogical shifts in number.

_____

_____

_____

_____

D   Avoiding Illogical Shifts in Discourse

Writers use **direct discourse** when they present someone's exact words. Direct discourse is always enclosed in quotation marks and is often accompanied by a phrase that identifies the speaker *(he says, she says, Natalie says)*. Writers use **indirect discourse** when they summarize someone's words. Indirect discourse is not enclosed in quotation marks, and the reported statement is often introduced with the word *that*.

> DIRECT DISCOURSE   Carla said, "I am going to drive to Phoenix." (first person, present tense)

> INDIRECT DISCOURSE   Carla said that she was going to drive to Phoenix. (third person, past tense)

● **Writing Tip**
When you shift from direct to indirect discourse, the verb in the summarized quotation moves one step back in tense.

Questions in direct discourse end with a question mark. When recorded as indirect discourse, a question includes a word like *who, if, why, whether, what,* or *how* and does not end with a question mark.

DIRECT
DISCOURSE   Demi looked at her brother and asked, "What do you think you're doing?"

INDIRECT
DISCOURSE   Demi looked at her brother and asked him what he thought he was doing.

An **illogical shift in discourse** occurs when a writer shifts from direct discourse to indirect discourse (or from indirect to direct discourse) for no apparent reason. The result is an awkward or ungrammatical sentence.

For more on punctuating indirect discourse, see 33B.

ILLOGICAL
SHIFT   Elena said that "all this studying is not worth the trouble."

REVISED   Elena said, "All this studying is not worth the trouble." (direct discourse)

REVISED   Elena said that all this studying was not worth the trouble. (indirect discourse)

ILLOGICAL
SHIFT   Molly asked could she help me plan my trip?

REVISED   Molly asked, "Can I help you plan your trip?" (direct discourse)

REVISED   Molly asked if she could help me plan my trip. (indirect discourse)

◆ PRACTICE 24-4

The following sentences contain illogical shifts in discourse. Edit each sentence so that it consistently uses either direct or indirect discourse. Be sure to punctuate correctly. If the sentence is correct, write *C* in the blank.

Examples

After three dates, my husband asked would *if I* ~~I~~ marry him. _____

After three dates, my husband asked, *"Will you* ~~would I~~ marry ~~him.~~ *me?"* _____

1. The coach finished his pep talk and then asked were we ready to win.

   _____

2. One student wondered was this information going to be on the test?

   _____

3. The union leaders announced that "the strike is over." _____

4. The attorney asked the witnesses if they had been near the scene of the

   crime. _____

5. Oprah Winfrey asked the audience did they sympathize more with the husband or the wife. _____

■ WRITING FIRST: Flashback

Look back at your response to the Writing First exercise on page 311. Check the sentences in which you have discussed what parents should say, and make sure you have not mixed direct and indirect discourse. If you find an incorrect sentence, rewrite it on the lines below, correcting any illogical shifts in discourse.

_____

_____

_____

_____

If you don't find any illogical shifts, rewrite one of your sentences so that you change direct discourse to indirect discourse or indirect discourse to direct discourse.

E Avoiding Illogical Shifts in Voice

When the subject of a sentence performs the action, the sentence is in the **active voice**. When the subject of a sentence receives the action, the sentence is in the **passive voice**. Compare these two sentences.

ACTIVE VOICE   Nat Turner <u>launched</u> a slave rebellion in August 1831. (Subject *Nat Turner* performs the action.)

PASSIVE VOICE   A slave rebellion <u>was launched</u> by Nat Turner in 1831. (Subject *slave rebellion* receives the action.)

An **illogical shift in voice** occurs when a writer changes from active to passive voice or from passive to active voice for no apparent reason.

ILLOGICAL SHIFT IN VOICE   J. D. Salinger <u>wrote</u> *The Catcher in the Rye,* and *Franny and Zooey* <u>was</u> also <u>written</u> by him. (active to passive)

REVISED   J. D. Salinger <u>wrote</u> *The Catcher in the Rye,* and he also <u>wrote</u> *Franny and Zooey.* (consistent voice)

ILLOGICAL SHIFT IN VOICE   Radium <u>was discovered</u> by Marie Curie, and Watson and Crick <u>described</u> the structure of DNA. (passive to active)

REVISED   Marie Curie <u>discovered</u> radium, and Watson and Crack <u>described</u> the structure of DNA. (consistent voice)

FOCUS Correcting Illogical Shifts in Voice

To change a sentence from the passive to the active voice, determine who or what performs the action, and make this noun the subject of a new active voice sentence.

PASSIVE VOICE   The campus escort service is used by some of my friends. (*Friends* performs the action.)

ACTIVE VOICE   Some of my friends use the campus escort service.

To change a sentence from the active to the passive voice, determine who or what receives the action, and make this noun the subject of a new passive voice sentence.

ACTIVE VOICE   César Ritz opened a hotel in Paris in 1898. (*Hotel* receives the action.)

PASSIVE VOICE   A hotel was opened by César Ritz in Paris in 1898.

Computer Tip
To see if your writing overuses the passive voice, use the Search or Find command to look for *is, are, was,* and *were,* which often appear as part of passive-voice verbs.

◆ PRACTICE 24-5

The following sentences contain illogical shifts in voice. Revise each sentence by changing the underlined passive voice verb to the active voice.

Example
Several researchers are interested in leadership qualities, and a study of decision making was conducted by them recently.

Several researchers are interested in leadership qualities, *and they recently conducted a study of decision making.*

1. A local university funded the study, and the research team was led by Dr. Alicia Flynn.

A local university funded the study,_____

_____

2. The researchers developed a series of questions about decision making, and then a hundred subjects were interviewed by them.

The researchers developed a series of questions about decision making,

_____

_____

3. Instinct alone <u>was relied on</u> by two-thirds of the subjects while only one-third used <u>logical analysis</u>.

_____while only one-third

used logical analysis.

4. After the researchers completed the study, a report <u>was written</u> about their findings.

After the researchers completed the study,_____

_____

5. The report <u>was read</u> by many experts, and most of them found the results surprising.

_____ , and most

of them found the results surprising.

■ WRITING FIRST: Flashback

Look back at your response to the Writing First exercise on page 311. Check each sentence to make sure there are no illogical shifts in voice. If you find an incorrect sentence, rewrite it on the lines below, correcting any illogical shifts in voice.

_____

_____

_____

_____

_____

_____

■ WRITING FIRST: Revising and Editing

Look back at your response to the Writing First exercise on page 311. Revise any illogical shifts in tense, person, number, discourse, or voice. When you have finished, do the same for another assignment you are currently working on.

CHAPTER REVIEW

◆ EDITING PRACTICE

Read the following student essay, into which illogical shifts in tense, person, number, discourse, and voice have been introduced. Edit the passage to eliminate the unnecessary shifts, making sure subjects and verbs agree. The first sentence has been edited for you.

The Mixing of Cultures

    Because the United States is the melting pot of the world, it ~~drew~~ *draws* thousands of immigrants from Europe, Asia, and Africa. Many of them come to the United States because they wanted to become Americans. At the same time, they also want to preserve parts of their original cultures. This conflict confuses many immigrants. Some immigrants think that in order to become American, you have to give up your ethnic identity. Others think it is possible to become an American without losing your ethnic identity. To me, this is the strength of the United States: Filipino Americans are able to be both Filipino and American. I know of no other country in the world where this was true.

    Many Filipino Americans try to maintain their Filipino culture in the United States. For example, they decorate their houses to remind them of traditional houses in the Philippines. Filipinos also try to preserve their native language. Although every Filipino speaks English, Tagalog is also spoken by them--usually at home. On holidays, Filipinos observe the traditions of the Philippines. They sing Filipino folk songs, do traditional dances, and cook Filipino foods. Everyone tries to visit their relatives in the Philippines as often as they can. In this way, a Filipino child can often experience their ethnic culture firsthand.

My father left the Philippines because of the political persecution he experienced. He was a teacher, and the government did not like some of the ideas he expresses. One day, his brother, who worked for the police, warned him that he would be arrested if you keep criticizing the government. The next day, my father and mother buy plane tickets for the United States. Today, he often talks about his life in the Philippines. He describes his village and his boyhood on his father's coffee plantation. He says that he cannot explain how beautiful his home was. As he talks, he got a faraway look in his eyes. I know that he loves his home and that he missed it. When I ask him if he would ever want to move back, he says that "the United States is his home now."

A Filipino family that wants to hold on to their ethnic background can learn to live in America. Here, cultures mix and enrich one another. Each culture has something to offer America--their food, language, and traditions. At the same time, America had something to offer each culture--economic opportunity, education, and freedom.

◆ COLLABORATIVE ACTIVITIES

1. On a separate sheet of paper, write five sentences that include shifts from present to past tense, some logical and some illogical. Exchange papers with another person in your group, and revise any incorrect sentences.

2. As a group, compose a test made up of five sentences containing illogical shifts in tense, person, number, discourse, and voice. Exchange tests with another group in the class. After you have taken their test, compare your answers with theirs.

3. As a group, choose five words from the list below, and use each as the subject of a sentence. Make sure each sentence includes a pronoun that refers to the subject.

   Example: Doctors must know their patients.

doctors	anything	a parent	everybody
someone	raccoons	anyone	a woman
workers	no one	children	everyone
something	a book	anybody	people

Make sure the sentences you have written do not include any illogical shifts in person or number.

> ☑ REVIEW CHECKLIST:
> ## Illogical Shifts
>
> - An illogical shift in tense occurs when tense changes for no apparent reason. (See 24A.)
>
> - An illogical shift in person occurs when person shifts for no apparent reason. (See 24B.)
>
> - An illogical shift in number occurs when number shifts from singular to plural (or the other way around) for no apparent reason. (See 24C.)
>
> - An illogical shift in discourse occurs when discourse changes from direct to indirect (or from indirect to direct) for no apparent reason. (See 24D.)
>
> - An illogical shift in voice occurs when voice changes from active to passive or from passive to active for no apparent reason. (See 24E.)

Dangling and Misplaced Modifiers

PREVIEW

In this chapter, you will learn

- to identify present participle modifiers (25A)

- to identify past participle modifiers (25B)

- to recognize and correct dangling modifiers (25C)

- to recognize and correct misplaced modifiers (25D)

■ WRITING FIRST

Write about an event in your life that helped make you the person you are today. The event can be a positive experience (for example, a graduation, the birth of a child, or a particularly good job) or a negative experience (for example, an encounter with prejudice). Use clear transitional words and phrases to link the events you discuss.

A **modifier** is a word or word group that functions as an adjective or an adverb. Thus, a modifier describes or limits another word or word group in a sentence. Many word groups that act as modifiers are introduced by present participles or past participles.

> ● **Writing Tip**
> An adjective modifies a noun or a pronoun. An adverb modifies a verb, an adjective, or another adverb. See Chapter 29.

For more on present participles, see 18C.

A   Identifying Present Participle Modifiers

A **present participle modifier** consists of the *-ing* form of the verb along with the words it introduces. This word group modifies (provides information about) a noun or pronoun that appears next to it in the sentence.

PRESENT PARTICIPLE MODIFIER

Using his garage as a workshop, Steve Jobs invented the personal computer.

PRESENT PARTICIPLE MODIFIER

Running through the streets, Archimedes could not wait to tell people what he had discovered.

FOCUS **Punctuating Sentences with Present Participle Modifiers**

Use commas to set off a present participle modifier from the rest of the sentence.

PRESENT PARTICIPLE MODIFIER

Remembering his working-class roots, Paul McCartney returned to Liverpool to give a concert.

PRESENT PARTICIPLE MODIFIER

Paul McCartney, remembering his working-class roots, returned to Liverpool to give a concert.

◆ PRACTICE 25-1

Underline the present participle modifier in each of the following sentences. Draw an arrow from the modifier to the word or word group it modifies.

Example: Possessing a simple beauty, Doo-Wop was sung by groups such as the Moonglows, the Flamingos, and the Cadillacs.

(1) Evolving out of street-corner singing, Doo-Wop was a popular form of rock and roll from about 1951 to 1956. (2) Becoming one of Doo-Wop's biggest stars, Frankie Lymon sang with the passion of his tenement streets. (3) Living in the Bronx, he made his first record with a group called the Teen Agers. (4) Echoing the yearning of all teenagers, "Why Do Fools Fall in Love?" shot to the top of the music charts. (5) Cutting one hit after another, Frankie Lymon and the Teen Agers became part of Doo-Wop history. (6) Beginning in the 1960s, the British invasion of rock music pushed Doo-Wop off the charts. (7) Returning to the streets they had left, many Doo-Wop artists were soon forgotten. (8) Following the path of many of rock's early stars, Lymon died penniless and addicted to heroin. (9) Lying for years in an unmarked grave in a Bronx cemetery, Lymon seemed forgotten. (10) Honoring his contribution to early rock and roll, fans of Doo-Wop voted in 1993 to induct Frankie Lymon and the Teen Agers into the Rock and Roll Hall of Fame.

■ WRITING FIRST: Flashback

Look back at your response to the Writing First exercise on page 324. Find any sentences that contain present participle modifiers, and write them on the lines below. (If you cannot find any, write two new sentences.) Check to make sure you have punctuated your sentences correctly.

_____

_____

_____

_____

B Identifying Past Participle Modifiers

For more on past participles, see 18C and 27A.

A **past participle modifier** consists of the past tense form of the verb (usually ending in *-ed*) along with the words it introduces. This word group provides information about a noun or a pronoun that is located next to it in the sentence.

PAST PARTICIPLE MODIFIER

Rejected by Hamlet, Ophelia goes mad and drowns herself.

For more on irregular past participles, see 27B.

Keep in mind that not all past participles end in *-ed*. Irregular verbs may have past tense forms that do not end in *-ed*—*known, cut,* and *written,* for example. In addition, some irregular verbs may have past participle forms that are different from their past tense forms—*bit/bitten, came/come,* and *did/done,* for example.

FOCUS **Punctuating Sentences with Past Participle Modifiers**

Use commas to set off a past participle modifier from the rest of the sentence.

PAST PARTICIPLE MODIFIER

Terrorized by soldiers, the inhabitants of the town fled into the desert.

PAST PARTICIPLE MODIFIER

The inhabitants of the town, terrorized by soldiers, fled into the desert.

◆ **PRACTICE 25-2**

Underline the past participle modifier in each of the following sentences. Draw an arrow from each past participle modifier to the word or word group it modifies.

Example: Seized last year by the F. B. I., a fossilized *Tyrannosaurus rex* caused a great deal of controversy.

(1) The best-preserved fossil ever found, it was claimed by a South Dakota dealer. (2) Uncovered in 1990, the fossil was found on government land. (3) The fossil hunters, excited by the find, paid the Indian owner of the land $5,000. (4) Known as "Sue," the fossil was stored at a private museum in Hill City, South Dakota. (5) Supported by previous rulings, a judge ordered the fossil turned over to the government. (6) Accompanied by federal agents, local law enforcement officials impounded the fossil. (7) Questioned by the press, some fossil hunters praised the verdict. (8) Others said commercial dealers, hindered by the verdict, would stop collecting fossils. (9) Shocked by the ruling, the dealer appealed. (10) Believed to be the first legal civil action involving a *Tyrannosaurus rex,* the case was settled in favor of the dealer.

■ WRITING FIRST: Flashback

Look back at your response to the Writing First exercise on page 324. Identify any sentences that contain past participle modifiers, and write them on the lines below. (If you cannot find any, write two new sentences.) Check to make sure you have punctuated your sentences correctly.

_____

_____

_____

_____

_____

_____

_____

C **Correcting Dangling Modifiers**

A **dangling modifier** is a modifier that cannot logically describe any word or word group in the sentence. Consider the following example.

Using my computer, the report was finished in two days.

The present participle modifier *Using my computer* appears to refer to *the report*, but this makes no sense. (How can the report use the computer?) Because the word to which the modifier should logically refer is not included in the sentence, this word must be supplied.

Using my computer, I finished the report in two days.

The easiest way to correct a dangling modifier is to supply a word or word group to which the dangling modifier can logically refer.

INCORRECT Moving the microscope's mirror, the light can be directed onto the slide. (dangling present participle modifier)

CORRECT Moving the microscope's mirror, you can direct the light onto the slide.

INCORRECT Paid in advance, the furniture was delivered. (dangling past participle modifier)

CORRECT Paid in advance, the movers delivered the furniture.

FOCUS **Placing Present and Past Participle Modifiers**

Present and past participle modifiers can often be placed either before or after the word or word group they describe.

Catching the pass, Charlie Garner ran into the end zone for a touchdown.

or

Charlie Garner, catching the pass, ran into the end zone for a touchdown.

Dressed to kill, Peggy Sue went to her class reunion.

or

Peggy Sue, dressed to kill, went to her class reunion.

◆ **PRACTICE 25-3**

Rewrite the following sentences, which contain dangling modifiers, so that each modifier refers to a word or word group it can logically modify.

Example
Waiting inside, my bus passed by.

Waiting inside, I missed my bus.

1. Paid by the school, the books were sorted in the library.

_____

_____

2. Pushing on the brakes, my car would not stop for the red light.

_____

_____

3. Short of money, the trip was canceled.

_____

_____

4. Working overtime, my salary almost doubled.

_____

_____

5. Angered by the noise, the concert was called off.

_____

_____

6. Using the proper formula, the problem is easy to solve.

_____

_____

7. Stacked high with notes, Matthew did not want to look at his desk.

_____

_____

8. Sitting in the park, the pigeons were fed.

_____

_____

9. Dressed professionally, the interview was something that Judith was not nervous about.

_____

_____

10. Driving for a long time, my leg began to hurt.

_____

_____

◆ **PRACTICE 25-4**

Complete the following sentences by supplying words to which the modifiers can logically refer.

Example: Dancing with the man of her dreams, _she decided that it_

was time to wake up.

1. Tired of studying, _____

_____

2. Sleeping late this morning, _____

_____

3. Seeing a strange light in the sky, _____

_____

4. Warned about driving in the snow, _____

_____

5. Alerted by a sound from outside, _____

_____

6. Sent to fight in a foreign land, _____

_____

7. Jumping over the rail and grabbing the chandelier, _____

_____

8. Told by her instructor to study more, _____

_____

9. Wanting desperately to go to the concert, _____

_____

10. Distrusting the advice he got from his friends, _____

_____

■ **WRITING FIRST: Flashback**

Look back at your response to the Writing First exercise on page 324. Do any of your sentences contain dangling modifiers? On the lines below, rewrite any sentence that contains a dangling modifier, and correct it by supplying a word or word group to which the modifier can logically refer.

1. _____

   _____

   _____

2. _____

   _____

   _____

D   **Correcting Misplaced Modifiers**

A **misplaced modifier** is a modifier that has no clear relationship to the word it modifies because it is too far from it. Frequently, the result is confusing, illogical, or even silly.

INCORRECT   Sarah fed the dog wearing her pajamas. (misplaced present participle modifier)

CORRECT   Wearing her pajamas, Sarah fed the dog.

INCORRECT   Kevin went into the exam scared to death. (misplaced past participle modifier)

CORRECT   Scared to death, Kevin went into the exam.

Not all modifiers are participles. Prepositional phrases, too, can modify other words in the sentence.

INCORRECT   At the wedding, she danced with the groom in her new dress. (misplaced modifier)

CORRECT   At the wedding, she danced in her new dress with the groom.

For more on prepositional phrases, see 15B.

When you write and revise, be sure to put modifiers as close as possible to the word or words they modify.

FOCUS **Misplaced Modifiers**

Be especially careful when placing **limiting modifiers** such as *almost, even, hardly, just, nearly, only,* and *simply*. Notice how the meaning of the following sentences changes when the modifier *only* is placed in different positions.

<u>Only</u> David could go to the movies yesterday.

David could <u>only</u> go to the movies yesterday.

David could go <u>only</u> to the movies yesterday.

David could go to the movies <u>only</u> yesterday.

◆ **PRACTICE 25-5**

Rewrite the following sentences, which contain misplaced modifiers, so that each modifier clearly refers to the word it logically modifies.

Example: Mark ate a pizza standing in front of the refrigerator.

Standing in front of the refrigerator, Mark ate a pizza.

1. The cat broke the vase frightened by a noise.

   _____

   _____

2. Running across my bathroom ceiling, I saw two large, hairy bugs.

   _____

   _____

3. Lori looked at the man sitting in the chair with red hair.

   _____

   _____

4. *Titanic* is a film about a love affair directed by James Cameron.

   _____

   _____

5. With their deadly venom, people are sometimes killed by snakes.

   _____

   _____

6. *Pudd'nhead Wilson* is a book about an exchange of identities by Mark Twain.

_____

_____

7. Jumping out of bed, I saw a sleigh and eight tiny reindeer in my bathrobe.

_____

_____

8. Barking all night, I listened to my neighbor's dog.

_____

_____

9. The exterminator sprayed the insect wearing a mask.

_____

_____

10. With a mysterious smile, Leonardo da Vinci painted the *Mona Lisa.*

_____

_____

■ WRITING FIRST: Flashback

Look back at your response to the Writing First exercise on page 324. Do any sentences contain misplaced modifiers? On the lines below, rewrite any such sentences by placing the modifiers as close as possible to a word or word group they can logically modify.

1. _____

_____

2. _____

_____

■ WRITING FIRST: Revising and Editing

Look back at your response to the Writing First exercise on page 324. Revise any dangling or misplaced modifiers. Make sure the modifiers refer to words they can logically describe.

CHAPTER REVIEW

◆ EDITING PRACTICE

Read the following student essay. Rewrite sentences to correct dangling and misplaced modifiers. In some cases, you may have to supply a word or word group to which the modifier can logically refer. The first incorrect sentence has been corrected for you.

> The ABCs of My Education
>
> I was born in New York and went to school in the South Bronx. Working hard, ~~the money~~ my parents earned ~~was~~ just *money* enough for us to get by. Raised in this environment there was a lot of violence. I saw my friends get involved with gangs and drugs and ruin their lives. To keep me out of trouble, my mother or father walked me to school every day. My parents thought that school was a safe place for me. Getting older, school was the place I stayed longer and longer. After a while, I started getting good grades, and my guidance counselor told me about the A Better Chance (A.B.C.) program.
>
> The A.B.C. program is nationally acclaimed. Participating in the program, classes help minority children get a better education. I was able to go to Strath Haven High School in Swarthmore, Pennsylvania. When I first got there, I had a hard time adjusting. Forcing me to work hard, a lot was demanded of me by my teachers. They encouraged everyone to go to college. With the help of my teachers, my friends, and most of all, my parents, I gradually got used to the workload. When I graduated in the top 20 percent of my class, anything seemed possible.
>
> The A.B.C. program helped me realize how important it is to have a good education. After I get out of college, I hope to return to the South Bronx as a teacher. Teaching in the Bronx, my students will be shown how important

```
learning is. I will also tell them that with hard work and
discipline, they too can make something of themselves.
```

◆ COLLABORATIVE ACTIVITIES

1. Working in a group of five or six students, make a list of five present participle modifiers and five past participle modifiers. Exchange your list with another group, and complete one another's sentences.

   Example
   Typing as fast as he could, _____

   Typing as fast as he could, <u>John could not wait to finish writing his screenplay</u>, *The Tomato That Ate Cleveland*.

2. Working in a team of three students, compete with other teams to compose sentences that contain outrageous and confusing dangling or misplaced modifiers. As a class, correct the sentences. Then, vote on which group developed the most challenging sentences.

3. In a group of four of five students, find examples of confusing dangling and misplaced modifiers in several magazines and newspapers. Rewrite the sentences, making sure each modifier is as close as possible to the word or word group it describes.

☑ REVIEW CHECKLIST:
Dangling and Misplaced Modifiers

  - A present participle modifier consists of the present participle (the *-ing* form of the verb) and the words it introduces. (See 25A.)

  - A past participle modifier consists of the past participle (usually the past tense form of the verb) and the words it introduces. (See 25B.)

  - Correct a dangling modifier by supplying a word or word group to which the dangling modifier can logically refer. (See 25C.)

  - Avoid misplaced modifiers by placing modifiers as close as possible to the word or word group they modify. (See 25D.)

UNIT SIX

Understanding Basic Grammar

26

Verbs: Past Tense

PREVIEW

In this chapter, you will learn

- to understand regular verbs in the past tense (26A)

- to understand irregular verbs in the past tense (26B)

- to deal with problem verbs in the past tense (26C and 26D)

■ WRITING FIRST

Write your own obituary. (Refer to yourself by name or by *he* or *she*.) Assume that you have led a long life and have achieved almost everything you hoped you would. Be sure to include the quality or qualities for which you would most like to be remembered, and use transitional words and phrases that clearly show the relationship of one event in your life to another.

Tense is the form a verb takes to show when an action or situation took place.

A Understanding Regular Verbs in the Past Tense

The **past tense** is the form a verb takes to show that an action has occurred in the past. **Regular verbs** form the past tense by adding either *-ed* or *-d* to the form of the verb that is used with the pronoun *I* in the present tense. This form is called the **base form** of the verb.

● **Writing Tip**
Not all verbs ending in *-ed* or *-d* are in the past tense. Some are past participles. (See 27A.)

FOCUS Regular Verbs in the Past Tense

- Most regular verbs form the past tense by adding *-ed*.

I registered for classes yesterday.

Juan walked to the concert.

(continued on the following page)

Writing Tip

All regular verbs use the
same form for singular and
plural in the past tense: *I
cheered. They cheered.*

> *(continued from the previous page)*
>
> ■ Regular verbs that end in *-e* form the past tense by adding *-d*.
>
> Walt Disney <u>produced</u> short cartoons in 1928.
>
> Tisha <u>liked</u> to read romance novels.
>
> ■ Regular verbs that end in *-y* form the past tense by changing the *y* to *i* and adding *-ed*.
>
> tr<u>y</u>   tr<u>ied</u>
>
> appl<u>y</u>   appl<u>ied</u>

◆ PRACTICE 26-1

Change the verbs in the following sentences to the past tense. Cross out the present tense form of each underlined verb, and write the past tense form above it.

Example: My grandparents ~~live~~ *lived* in a small town.

(1) My grandparents <u>own</u> a combination magazine stand and candy store in downtown Madison. (2) They <u>stock</u> about three hundred different magazines that <u>range</u> in subject matter from health and fitness to guns and ammo to angels and flying saucers. (3) Customers sometimes <u>browse</u> for an hour or more. (4) As they <u>look</u> through the magazines, they often <u>munch</u> on candy bars or <u>try</u> a soda. (5) When the candy bar or soda <u>turns</u> out to be a customer's only purchase, my grandfather <u>wants</u> to throw out the "library patron." (6) My grandmother, however, <u>recognizes</u> the importance of customer satisfaction. (7) She always <u>insists</u> that my grandfather be more patient. (8) My grandfather sometimes <u>refuses</u> to listen to her. (9) He never actually <u>kicks</u> out a customer. (10) Sometimes, though, he noisily <u>storms</u> out of the store, leaving my grandmother to deal with the startled customer.

■ WRITING FIRST: Flashback

Look back at your response to the Writing First exercise on page 339. Underline the past tense verbs that end in *-ed* and *-d*. Then write them here.

_____   _____   _____

_____   _____   _____

_____   _____   _____

_____   _____   _____

B   Understanding Irregular Verbs in the Past Tense

Unlike regular verbs, whose past tense forms end in *-ed* or *-d*, **irregular verbs** have irregular forms in the past tense.

Most irregular verbs use different forms for present tense and past tense.

Present	Past
come	came
teach	taught
know	knew

A few irregular verbs have the same form in both present tense and past tense.

Present	*Past*
Barbers <u>cut</u> hair.	I <u>cut</u> class and finished my homework.
Some gamblers <u>bet</u> compulsively.	I <u>bet</u> ten dollars on the Super Bowl last year.

The following chart lists the base form (the form used with *I* in the present tense) and past tense form of some of the most commonly used irregular verbs.

Irregular Verbs in the Past Tense

Base Form	Past	Base Form	Past
awake	awoke	begin	began
be	was, were	bet	bet
become	became	bite	bit

(continued on the following page)

▼ **Student Voices**
My spell checker doesn't pick up verb tenses used incorrectly, so I still have to proofread.

Doreen Queenan

■ **Computer Tip**
Use the Search or Find command to locate the irregular verbs that give you the most trouble.

(continued from the previous page)

Base Form	Past	Base Form	Past
blow	blew	lose	lost
break	broke	make	made
bring	brought	meet	met
build	built	pay	paid
buy	bought	quit	quit
catch	caught	read	read
choose	chose	ride	rode
come	came	ring	rang
cost	cost	rise	rose
cut	cut	run	ran
dive	dove (dived)	say	said
do	did	see	saw
draw	drew	sell	sold
drink	drank	send	sent
drive	drove	set	set
eat	ate	shake	shook
fall	fell	shine	shone (shined)
feed	fed	sing	sang
feel	felt	sit	sat
fight	fought	sleep	slept
find	found	speak	spoke
fly	flew	spend	spent
forgive	forgave	spring	sprang
freeze	froze	stand	stood
get	got	steal	stole
give	gave	stick	stuck
go (goes)	went	sting	stung
grow	grew	swear	swore
have	had	swim	swam
hear	heard	take	took
hide	hid	teach	taught
hold	held	tear	tore
hurt	hurt	tell	told
keep	kept	think	thought
know	knew	throw	threw
lay (to place)	laid	understand	understood
lead	led	wake	woke
leave	left	wear	wore
let	let	win	won
lie (to recline)	lay	write	wrote
light	lit		

◆ **PRACTICE 26-2**

In the following sentences, fill in the correct past tense form of the irregular verb in parentheses.

Example: They _____*said*_____ (say) it couldn't be done.

(1) In August 1991, long-jumper Mike Powell _____ (break) the longest-standing record in track and field. (2) His leap of twenty-nine feet four and one-half inches _____ (make) headlines around the world. (3) Mike Beaman had set the previous record of twenty-nine feet and two and one-half inches when he _____ (win) the Olympics in Mexico City in 1968. (4) Competing against his great rival Carl Lewis, Powell _____ (swear) to himself that this time he would prevail. (5) He _____ (feel) that if he _____ (lose) to Lewis again, his career might suffer. (6) He _____ (beat) Lewis in that contest, but the world _____ (see) a different story at the Olympics the following year. (7) Lewis _____ (let) it be known that he was out to break Powell's record. (8) Before his first jump, Powell _____ (draw) a mark in the sand at twenty-nine feet six and one-half inches, or nine meters. (9) His jump _____ (fall) far short of that goal. (10) Lewis then _____ (take) the gold medal by jumping twenty-eight feet five and one-half inches on his first jump. (11) Powell's best jump of twenty-eight feet four and one-half inches _____ (leave) him with the silver medal. (12) However, his August 1991 record still _____ (stand).

■ WRITING FIRST: Flashback

Look back at your response to the Writing First exercise on page 339. Circle each irregular past tense verb you find. Then, write each one in the column on the left. In the column on the right, write the verb's base form. (If necessary, consult the list of irregular verbs on pages 341–42.)

Past Tense	*Base Form*
_____	_____
_____	_____
_____	_____
_____	_____
_____	_____
_____	_____

● **Writing Tip**
Be is the only verb in English with more than one past tense form. For detailed information about subject-verb agreement with *be*, see 23B.

C   Problem Verbs in the Past Tense: *Be*

The irregular verb *be* can be especially troublesome because it has two different past tense forms—one for singular and one for plural.

> Carlo <u>was</u> interested in becoming a city planner. (singular)
> They <u>were</u> happy to help out at the school. (plural)

Past Tense Forms of the Verb *Be*

	Singular	**Plural**
1st person	I <u>was</u> tired.	We <u>were</u> tired.
2nd person	<u>You</u> <u>were</u> tired.	You <u>were</u> tired.
3rd person	He <u>was</u> tired.	
	She <u>was</u> tired.	They <u>were</u> tired.
	It <u>was</u> tired.	

◆ **PRACTICE 26-3**

Edit the following passage for errors in the use of the verb *be*. Cross out any underlined verbs that are incorrect, and write the correct forms above them. If a verb form is correct, label it *C*.

> **Example:**   Until recently, there ~~was~~ ^{were} no well-known Korean-American comics.

● **Writing Tip**
Watch for agreement errors with *wasn't* (= was not) and *weren't* (= were not).

(1) Korean-American comic Margaret Cho <u>was</u> born in 1969. (2) Her mother and father <u>was</u> from prominent families in Korea, but in the United States, they <u>wasn't</u> able to maintain their former standard of living. (3) Eventually, they <u>was</u> able to open a bookstore. (4) Cho <u>was</u> one of the first successful Asian-American comics in the country, beginning her career at the age of eighteen. (5) Her parents, however, <u>was</u> opposed to her career choice. (6) For years, they <u>wasn't</u> able to admit to friends that their daughter had a performing career. (7) Cho <u>weren't</u> to be stopped, though. (8) Even when an agent refused to sign her as a client because he said Asians <u>wasn't</u> going anywhere in the comedy business, Cho didn't back down. (9) Ultimately, her determination <u>was</u> rewarded when she was signed to star in her own television series, *All-American Girl*, which

ran during the 1994 to 1995 season. (10) In 1997, she <u>was</u> featured in the movie *Face/Off*, which starred John Travolta and Nicholas Cage.

■ **WRITING FIRST: Flashback**

Look back at your response to the Writing First exercise on page 339. Find all the sentences in which you use the past tense of *be*. Copy two or three of these sentences in the space below, and underline each subject of the verb *be*. Make sure you have used the correct form of the verb in each case.

1. _____

   _____

2. _____

   _____

3. _____

   _____

D | **Problem Verbs in the Past Tense: *Can/Could* and *Will/Would***

The helping verbs *can* and *could* express the ability to do something, and the helping verbs *will* and *would* refer to action in the future. These helping verbs present problems because their past tense forms are sometimes confused with their present tense forms.

Can/Could

Can, a present tense verb, means "is able to" or "are able to."

First-year students <u>can</u> apply for financial aid.

Could, the past tense of *can*, means "was able to" or "were able to."

Harry Houdini claimed that he <u>could</u> escape from any prison.

Will/Would

Will, a present tense verb, talks about the future from a point in the present.

A solar eclipse <u>will</u> occur in ten months.

Would, the past tense of *will,* talks about the future from a point in the past.

> I told him yesterday that I <u>would</u> think about it.

FOCUS *Will and Would*

Note that *will* is used with *can,* and *would* is used with *could.*

> I <u>will</u> feed the cats if I <u>can</u> find their food.
>
> I <u>would</u> feed the cats if I <u>could</u> find their food.

◆ **PRACTICE 26-4**

Circle the appropriate helping verb from the choices in parentheses.

Example: Years ago, travel took so long that my grandfather (will/ (would)) rarely drive more than ten miles from home.

(1) In years past, it (can/could) take hours to travel across the state. (2) With the new highway, the trip now (can/could) take as little as an hour. (3) As people make the drive, they (will/would) be surprised. (4) Before I made the trip, I (will/would) not have believed the difference. (5) On the old highway, I (can/could) get stuck behind a truck on those winding, two-lane roads. (6) With the new highway, I (can/could) zip along on four lanes each way. (7) Because they were so low, those old roads (will/would) often be flooded. (8) The new highway (will/would) never flood because it is elevated. (9) If they (can/could) go back to the old ways, some people would do so. (10) However, I (will/would) always try to adapt to progress and change if I can.

■ WRITING FIRST: Flashback

Look back at your response to the Writing First exercise on page 339. On the following lines, add a few sentences that describe what you would have accomplished if you had had the chance. Be sure to use *could* and *would* correctly.

(continued on the following page)

(continued from the previous page)

_____

_____

_____

_____

_____

_____

_____

_____

■ WRITING FIRST: Revising and Editing

Look back at your response to the Writing First exercise on page 339. Make sure you have used the correct past tense form for each of your verbs. If you haven't, cross out the incorrect form, and write the proper past tense form of the verb above the line. Then, try to add one or two of the sentences you wrote for the Flashback exercises above.

CHAPTER REVIEW

◆ EDITING PRACTICE

Read the following student essay, into which errors in past tense verb forms have been introduced. Decide whether each of the underlined past tense verbs is correct. If the verb is correct, write *C* above it. If it is not, cross out the verb, and write in the correct past tense form. The first sentence has been corrected for you. (If necessary, consult the list of irregular verbs on pages 341–42.)

Healing

The window seat ~~were~~ *was* our favorite place to sit. I piled comfortable pillows on the ledge and <u>spended</u> several minutes rearranging them. My friend and I <u>lied</u> on our backs and propped our feet on the wall. We <u>sat</u> with our arms around our legs and thinked about the mysteries of life. We also stared at the people on the street below and wonder who they was and where they was going. We imagined that they can be millionaires, foreign spies, or ruthless drug smugglers. We believed that everyone except us leaded wonderful and exciting lives.

I heard a voice call my name. Reluctantly, I standed up, tearing myself away from my imaginary world. My dearest and oldest friend--my teddy bear--and I reentered the real world. I grabbed Teddy and brung him close to my chest. Together we go into the cold sitting room, where twelve other girls sit around a table eating breakfast. None of them looked happy. In the unit for eating disorders, meals was always tense. Nobody wants to eat, but the nurses watched us until we eated every crumb. I set Teddy on the chair beside me and stared gloomily at the food on our plate. I closed my eyes and taked the first bite. I feeled the calories adding inches of ugly fat. Each swallow were like a nail being ripped from my finger. At last, it was over. I had survived breakfast.

Days passed slowly; each passing minute was a triumph. I learned how to eat properly. I learned about other people's problems. I also learned that people loved me. Eventually, even Teddy stopped feeling sorry for me. I begun to smile--and laugh. Sometimes, I even considered myself happy. My doctors challenged me--and, surprisingly, I rised to the occasion.

◆ COLLABORATIVE ACTIVITIES

1. Working in a group of three or four students, choose a famous living figure—an actor, a sports star, or a musician, for example—and brainstorm together to identify details about this person's life. Then, working on your own, use the details to write a profile of him or her.
2. Working in a group, list several contemporary problems that you think will be solved within ten or fifteen years. Each member of the group should then select a problem from the list, and write a paragraph or

two describing how the problem could be solved. As a group, use the paragraphs for the body of an essay. Develop a thesis statement, write an introduction and a conclusion, and then revise the body paragraphs of your essay.

3. Form a group with other students. What news events do you remember most vividly? Take ten minutes to list news events in the areas of sports, science, entertainment, or politics that you think have defined the last five years. On your own, write a short essay in which you discuss the significance of the three or four events that the members of your group agree were the most important.

☑ REVIEW CHECKLIST:
Verbs: Past Tense

- The past tense is the form a verb takes to show that an action has occurred in the past. (See 26A.)

- Regular verbs form the past tense by adding either -ed or -d to the present tense form of the verb. (See 26A.)

- Irregular verbs have irregular forms in the past tense. (See 26B.)

- *Be* is the only verb in English that has two different forms in the past tense—one for singular and one for plural. (See 26C.)

- *Could* is the past tense of *can*. *Would* is the past tense of *will*. (See 26D.)

27

Verbs: Past Participles

■ **WRITING FIRST**

Write about an activity—a hobby or a sport, for example—that you have been involved in for a relatively long time. Begin by identifying the activity and stating why it has been important to you. Then, describe the activity, paying particular attention to what you have gained over the years from this activity.

A Identifying Regular Past Participles

Verbs are sometimes combined with other verbs. In the following sentences, each verb has two parts: a **helping verb** (a form of the verb *have*) and a **past participle**.

> HV PP
> The band has changed its name from The Broken Melons to The Dead Cats.

> HV PP
> The major television networks have introduced their new programs.

> HV PP
> I had finished studying for the test by Tuesday.

The past participle of a regular verb is identical to its past tense form. Both are formed by adding *-ed* or *-d* to the base form of the verb.

For more on the base form of verbs, see 26A.

> PAST
> He earned.

350

> HV PP
> He has earned.

FOCUS **Past Participles**

The helping verb changes form to agree with its subject, but the past participle of a verb always has the same form.

    S   HV   PP

I <u>have earned</u> more than two thousand dollars this summer.

       S   HV   PP

Brad <u>has earned</u> more than two thousand dollars this summer.

◆ PRACTICE 27-1

Fill in the correct past participle form of each verb in parentheses.

Example: Coffee prices have ___*dropped*___ (drop) recently.

(1) Americans have _____ (start) a coffee craze in the last fifteen years. (2) Since the early 1980s, more than ten thousand coffee bars have _____ (open) in the United States. (3) Many of these bars have _____ (appear) in metropolitan areas. (4) However, they have _____ (sprout) in suburban malls and small college towns, too. (5) One chain alone has _____ (expand) to more than four hundred outlets. (6) Americans have always _____ (enjoy) coffee. (7) In fact, Americans have traditionally _____ (consume) one-third of the world's yearly coffee production. (8) One survey has _____ (estimate) that Americans drink 130 million cups a day. (9) Tastes have _____ (change), though. (10) Today's market has _____ (broaden) to include espresso and cappuccino.

■ WRITING FIRST: Flashback

Look back at your response to the Writing First exercise on page 350. Identify each helping verb (a form of the verb *have*) followed by a regular past participle (ending in *-ed* or *-d*). Write both the helping verb and the past participle on the following lines.

(continued on the following page)

(continued from the previous page)

Helping Verb	Regular Past Participle
_____	_____
_____	_____
_____	_____
_____	_____
_____	_____

B **Identifying Irregular Past Participles**

Irregular verbs nearly always have irregular past participles. They do not form the past participle by adding *-ed* or *-d* to the base form of the verb.

Base Form	Past	Past Participle
choose	chose	chosen
buy	bought	bought
ride	rode	ridden

The chart on pages 354–55 lists the base form, the past tense form, and the past participle of some commonly used irregular verbs.

◆ **PRACTICE 27-2**

Fill in the correct past participle of the verb in parentheses. Refer to the chart on pages 354–55 as needed.

Example: The network has _____*won*_____ (win) a loyal audience.

(1) Nick at Night has _____ (find) a receptive audience for old television programs. (2) The cable network Nickelodeon, which broadcasts children's programs during the day, has _____ (catch) on with adults at night. (3) It has _____ (draw) viewers away from current network sitcoms to ones from the 1970s and earlier. (4) Many viewers have _____ (know) and loved these shows since they were children themselves. (5) They feel this affection even if they haven't _____ (see) them for years. (6) They have _____ (run) the candy-making machine with Lucy, _____ (fall) in love with Mary, and _____ (keep) up with the jokes of

Rob and his pals. (7) As they have _____ (get) older, they

have _____ (grow) nostalgic for these familiar characters.

(8) Young viewers have _____ (have) a chance to discover

them for the first time. (9) Both older and younger viewers have

_____ (begin) to appreciate the shows for their corniness as

well as their real humor. (10) Nick has also _____ (make) a

name for itself with its clever commercials and station breaks, which

parody 1950s style.

◆ PRACTICE 27-3

Edit the following passage for errors in irregular past participles. Cross
out any underlined past participles that are incorrect, and write in the correct form above them. If the verb form is correct, label it *C*.

> *felt*
> **Example:** Some people have always ~~feeled~~ that killing animals for
> fur is immoral.

(1) The war against wearing fur has <u>became</u> a major campaign in

recent years. (2) Recently, activists have <u>took</u> a more visible role in the

struggle against fur. (3) Organizations have <u>fighted</u> to convince clothing

designers not to work with fur, and their efforts have <u>been</u> surprisingly

successful. (4) Designers like Calvin Klein and Giorgio Armani have

<u>sayed</u> they will no longer include fur in their collections. (5) Many

celebrities have <u>choosed</u> to take a public stand against furs, and several

well-known models have <u>gave</u> their time to pose for anti-fur ads. (6) They

have <u>send</u> the message that wearing furs is no longer the thing to do.

(7) Some critics complain that many of the more radical activists have

<u>went</u> too far. (8) It is true that some have <u>sat</u> chained to racks in depart-

ment stores and have even <u>tore</u> fur collars from women's coats. (9) Others

have <u>stole</u> furs as they were being shipped from warehouses. (10) Such

efforts have <u>costed</u> the fur industry a great deal, so now the fur manu-

facturers and retailers are fighting back with publicity campaigns of

their own.

Irregular Past Participles

Base Form	Past Tense	Past Participle
awake	awoke	awoken
be (am, are)	was (were)	been
beat	beat	beaten
become	became	become
begin	began	begun
bet	bet	bet
bite	bit	bitten
blow	blew	blown
break	broke	broken
bring	brought	brought
build	built	built
buy	bought	bought
catch	caught	caught
choose	chose	chosen
come	came	come
cost	cost	cost
cut	cut	cut
dive	dove, dived	dived
do	did	done
draw	drew	drawn
drink	drank	drunk
drive	drove	driven
eat	ate	eaten
fall	fell	fallen
feed	fed	fed
feel	felt	felt
fight	fought	fought
find	found	found
fly	flew	flown
forgive	forgave	forgiven
freeze	froze	frozen
get	got	got, gotten
give	gave	given
go	went	gone
grow	grew	grown
have	had	had
hear	heard	heard
hide	hid	hidden
hold	held	held
hurt	hurt	hurt
keep	kept	kept
know	knew	known
lay (to place)	laid	laid

(continued on the following page)

(continued from the previous page)

Base Form	Past Tense	Past Participle
lead	led	led
leave	left	left
let	let	let
lie (to recline)	lay	lain
light	lit	lit
lose	lost	lost
make	made	made
meet	met	met
pay	paid	paid
quit	quit	quit
read	read	read
ride	rode	ridden
ring	rang	rung
rise	rose	risen
run	ran	run
say	said	said
see	saw	seen
sell	sold	sold
send	sent	sent
set	set	set
shake	shook	shaken
shine	shone, shined	shone, shined
sing	sang	sung
sit	sat	sat
sleep	slept	slept
speak	spoke	spoken
spend	spent	spent
spring	sprang	sprung
stand	stood	stood
steal	stole	stolen
stick	stuck	stuck
sting	stung	stung
swear	swore	sworn
swim	swam	swum
take	took	taken
teach	taught	taught
tear	tore	torn
tell	told	told
think	thought	thought
throw	threw	thrown
understand	understood	understood
wake	woke, waked	woken, waked
wear	wore	worn
win	won	won
write	wrote	written

■ WRITING FIRST: Flashback

Look back at your response to the Writing First exercise on page 350, and identify each helping verb followed by an irregular past participle. Then, write both the helping verb and the irregular past participle below.

Helping Verb   *Irregular Past Participle*

_____   _____

_____   _____

_____   _____

_____   _____

_____   _____

C   Using the Present Perfect Tense

The **present perfect tense** consists of the present tense of *have* plus the past participle.

The Present Perfect Tense
(have *or* has + *past participle*)

Singular	**Plural**
I have gained.	We have gained.
You have gained.	You have gained.
He has gained.	They have gained.
She has gained.	
It has gained.	

The past tense *(I gained)* indicates an action that began and ended in the past. The present perfect tense *(I have gained)* shows a continuing action—generally one that began in the past and continues into the present.

PAST   The <u>nurse</u> <u>worked</u> at the Welsh Mountain clinic for two years.

PRESENT PERFECT   The <u>nurse</u> <u>has worked</u> at the Welsh Mountain clinic for two years.

In the first sentence above, the past tense verb *worked* indicates that the nurse worked at the clinic for two years but now no longer does. In the second sentence, the present perfect verb *has worked* indicates that the nurse worked at the clinic for two years and still works there today.

◆ PRACTICE 27-4

Circle the appropriate verb tense (past or present perfect) from the choices in parentheses.

Example: My new kitten (began/has begun) to dominate the house-hold.

(1) I (was/have been) a cat addict all my life. (2) I (got/have gotten) my first cat when I was seven years old. (3) I (named/have named) him Tweetie after the little bird in the cartoons. (4) Since then, I (owned/have owned) many more felines. (5) At one point, I (had/have had) five cats at once. (6) Last year, one (died/has died). (7) My sister (adopted/has adopted) another when she got married. (8) Since then, I (took/have taken) care of the other three cats. (9) Through the years, my cats (gave/have given) me much pleasure but also a lot of aggravation. (10) Anyone who (raised/has raised) cats will understand what I mean.

◆ PRACTICE 27-5

Fill in the appropriate verb tense (past or present perfect) of the verb in parentheses.

Example: In 1994, many polls ___predicted___ (predict) election results inaccurately.

(1) Newspapers and magazines in America _____ (present) the results of public opinion polls since the mid-1900s. (2) Until the early twentieth century, however, these polls _____ (be) unscientific and their results far from accurate. (3) In the 1930s, however, George Horace Gallup _____ (devise) original techniques for polling. (4) Over the last sixty years, these methods _____ (achieve) considerable success in predicting elections. (5) Since its development, the Gallup poll _____ (become) the most well known of all public opinion polls. (6) Such polls _____ (occupy) a larger and larger place in our public lives. (7) In recent years, however, some critics _____ (begin) to argue against the extensive use of polls to chart public opinion.

■ WRITING FIRST: Flashback

Look back at your response to the Writing First exercise on page 350. Choose three sentences with past tense verbs, and rewrite them below, changing past tense to present perfect tense. How does your revision change the meaning of each sentence? Do you have to make other changes when you change the verb tense?

1. _____

_____

_____

2. _____

_____

_____

3. _____

_____

_____

D **Using the Past Perfect Tense**

The **past perfect tense** consists of the past tense of *have* plus the past participle.

The Past Perfect Tense
(had + past participle)

Singular   **Plural**

I had returned.   We had returned.

You had returned.   You had returned.

He had returned.   They had returned.

She had returned.

It had returned.

The past perfect tense describes an action that occurred before another past tense action.

                    PAST PERFECT   PAST TENSE
Chief Sitting Bull had fought many battles before he defeated General Custer.

This sentence identifies two actions that happened in the past—the fighting done by Sitting Bull and his defeat of Custer. The action in the first part of the sentence is in the past perfect tense. This tense indicates that Sitting Bull's battles took place *before* the action in the second part of the sentence, which is expressed in the past tense.

◆ PRACTICE 27-6

Circle the appropriate verb tense (present perfect or past perfect) from the choices in parentheses.

Example: Although the children (have eaten/had eaten) dinner, they still had room for ice cream.

1. Ren wondered where he (has left/had left) his keys.

2. He believes he (has lost/had lost) them.

3. The receptionist told the interviewer that the applicant (has arrived/ had arrived).

4. The interviewer says that she (has waited/had waited) for an hour.

5. The jury decided that the defendant (has lied/had lied) on the witness stand.

6. The jury members are still deliberating; they (have been/had been) in the jury room for three days now.

7. By the time I reached the pizza parlor, I (have decided/had decided) to order a pepperoni pie.

8. By the time my pizza is ready, I usually (have finished/had finished) my pinball game.

9. The movie (has been/had been) on only ten minutes when I turned it off.

10. This movie is excellent; I (have seen/had seen) it at least five times.

■ WRITING FIRST: Flashback

Look back at your response to the Flashback on page 358. Rewrite the three present perfect tense sentences on the following lines, this time changing them to the past perfect tense. How do your revisions change the meaning of each sentence?

1. _____

_____

_____

(continued on the following page)

(continued from the previous page)

2. _____

_____

_____

3. _____

_____

_____

E Using Past Participles as Adjectives

● **Writing Tip**
A linking verb—such as
seemed or *looked*—connects
a subject to the word that
describes it. (See 15C.)

The past participle can function as an adjective after a **linking verb**, as it does in the following sentences, where the past participle describes the subject.

Jason seemed underline{surprised}.

He looked underline{shocked}.

The past participle can also function as an adjective before a noun.

I cleaned up the underline{broken} glass.

The underline{exhausted} runner crossed the line first.

◆ PRACTICE 27-7

Edit the following passage for errors in past participle forms used as adjectives. Cross out any underlined participles that are incorrect, and write the correct form above them. If the participle form is correct, label it *C*.

C

Example: College students are often underline{strapped} for cash.

(1) College students in their teens and twenties may be underline{surprise} when they find underline{preapprove} applications for credit cards turning up in their mail. (2) Credit-card companies also recruit underline{targeted} students through booths that are underline{locate} near student unions and libraries. (3) The booths are underline{design} to attract new customers with offers of underline{inscribe} coffee mugs and tote bags. (4) Why have companies gone to all this effort to attract underline{quali-fied} young people? (5) Most older Americans already have at least five credit cards that are underline{stuff} in their billfolds. (6) Banks and credit-card

companies see younger college students as their major <u>untapped</u> market.
(7) According to experts, students are also a good credit risk because
<u>concern</u> parents have often bailed them out when they haven't been able
to pay a bill. (8) Finally, people tend to feel <u>tie</u> to their first credit card.
(9) Companies want to be the first card that is <u>acquire</u> by a customer.

■ WRITING FIRST: Flashback

Look back at your response to the Writing First exercise on page
350. Choose three nouns you used in your paragraph, and list them
in the right-hand column below. Then, think of a past participle
that can modify each noun, and write the modifier in the left-hand
column.

Past Participle	*Noun*
1. _____	_____
2. _____	_____
3. _____	_____

    Now, use each of these nouns and its past participle modifier
in an original sentence.

1. _____

   _____

2. _____

   _____

3. _____

   _____

■ WRITING FIRST: Revising and Editing

Look back at your response to the Writing First exercise on page
350. Do you need to revise any sentences to add the correct present
perfect and past perfect tense verb forms? If so, cross out the incorrect verb forms and write your corrections above them. When you
have finished, check the past participles and perfect tenses in
another writing assignment on which you are currently working.

28

Nouns and Pronouns

PREVIEW

In this chapter, you will learn

- to identify nouns (28A)

- to form plural nouns (28B)

- to identify pronouns (28C)

- to understand pronoun-antecedent agreement (28D)

- to solve special problems with pronoun-antecedent agreement (28E)

- to understand pronoun case (28F)

- to identify reflexive and intensive pronouns (28G)

For information on capitalizing proper nouns, see 33A.

■ WRITING FIRST

Explain why you like a particular musician or group, television show, or movie. Assume your readers are not familiar with your subject.

A   Identifying Nouns

A **noun** is a word that names a person *(singer, Gloria Estefan),* an animal *(dolphin, Flipper),* a place *(downtown, Houston),* an object *(game, Tetris),* or an idea *(happiness, Darwinism).*

> ### FOCUS   Common and Proper Nouns
>
> Most nouns, called **common nouns**, begin with lowercase letters.
>
> character   holiday
>
> Some nouns, called **proper nouns**, name particular people, places, objects, or events. A proper noun always begins with a capital letter.
>
> Homer Simpson   Labor Day

A **singular noun** names one thing. A **plural noun** names more than one thing.

companies see younger college students as their major <u>untapped</u> market.
(7) According to experts, students are also a good credit risk because
<u>concern</u> parents have often bailed them out when they haven't been able
to pay a bill. (8) Finally, people tend to feel <u>tie</u> to their first credit card.
(9) Companies want to be the first card that is <u>acquire</u> by a customer.

■ WRITING FIRST: Flashback

Look back at your response to the Writing First exercise on page
350. Choose three nouns you used in your paragraph, and list them
in the right-hand column below. Then, think of a past participle
that can modify each noun, and write the modifier in the left-hand
column.

Past Participle	*Noun*
1. _____	_____
2. _____	_____
3. _____	_____

    Now, use each of these nouns and its past participle modifier
in an original sentence.

1. _____

  _____

2. _____

  _____

3. _____

  _____

■ WRITING FIRST: Revising and Editing

Look back at your response to the Writing First exercise on page
350. Do you need to revise any sentences to add the correct present
perfect and past perfect tense verb forms? If so, cross out the incorrect verb forms and write your corrections above them. When you
have finished, check the past participles and perfect tenses in
another writing assignment on which you are currently working.

CHAPTER REVIEW

◆ EDITING PRACTICE

Read the following student essay, into which errors in the use of past participles and the perfect tenses have been introduced. Decide whether each of the underlined verbs or participles is correct. If it is correct, write *C* above it. If it is not, write in the correct verb form. The first error has been corrected for you.

The U.S. War on Drugs

In our effort to halt the spread of a drug epidemic,
the United States has ~~took~~ *taken* extreme measures, some of which
had not been in its best interest. Using both internal and
external controls, the government has fighted the problem
on a number of fronts. It has rely on internal actions,
such as providing rehabilitation for substance abusers and
punishing drug traffickers and people found to possess
drugs. In addition, it has spended funds on external solutions, such as limiting the flow of drugs from other countries. Unfortunately, these efforts have not work.

Most internal strategies for dealing with the drug
trade have made hardly a dent in the problem. In fact, the
United States had discovered that some methods actually
create new problems. Stricter laws prohibiting the sale and
use of drugs have lead to longer jail sentences, and longer
jail sentences have force overcrowded prisons to release
dangerous prisoners before their sentences have expire. In
addition, lack of funding has keeped many approved applicants from receiving adequate rehabilitation services.

More frustrating is the failure of the external
strategies we had employed to protect our borders. By the
end of 1998, we have poured millions of dollars of military
aid into certain countries to encourage them to control
traffickers who shipped drugs into the United States. Much
of this money, however, was use to line the pockets of

corrupt government officials. Not only <u>have</u> the officials <u>receive</u> money from the United States to control drugs, but they <u>have</u> also <u>took</u> bribes from drug lords. By the time U.S. agents discovered that many corrupt officials <u>have</u> <u>funneled</u> millions of dollars into foreign bank accounts, the war was basically lost. It is unlikely that our policies did much at all to control the flow of drugs from other countries.

◆ COLLABORATIVE ACTIVITIES

1. Exchange Writing First exercises with another student. Read each other's work, making sure that present perfect and past perfect tenses are used correctly.

2. Assume that you are a restaurant employee who has been nominated for the prestigious Employee of the Year Award. To win this award (along with a thousand-dollar prize), you have to explain in writing what you have done during the past year to deserve this honor. When you have finished, trade papers with another student, and edit his or her work. Decide whose writing is more convincing, and read it to the class.

☑ REVIEW CHECKLIST:
Verbs: Past Participles

- The past participle of regular verbs is formed by adding -*ed* or -*d* to the base form. (See 27A.)

- Irregular verbs usually have irregular past participles. (See 27B.)

- The present perfect tense consists of the present tense of *have* plus the past participle. It shows a continuing action, usually one that began in the past and continues into the present. (See 27C.)

- The past perfect tense consists of the past tense of *have* plus the past participle. It describes an action that occurred before another past tense action. (See 27D.)

- The past participle can function as an adjective. (See 27E.)

For information on capitalizing proper nouns, see 33A.

CHAPTER

28

Nouns and Pronouns

■ WRITING FIRST

Explain why you like a particular musician or group, television show, or movie. Assume your readers are not familiar with your subject.

A Identifying Nouns

A **noun** is a word that names a person *(singer, Gloria Estefan)*, an animal *(dolphin, Flipper)*, a place *(downtown, Houston)*, an object *(game, Tetris)*, or an idea *(happiness, Darwinism)*.

FOCUS **Common and Proper Nouns**

Most nouns, called **common nouns**, begin with lowercase letters.

character   holiday

Some nouns, called **proper nouns**, name particular people, places, objects, or events. A proper noun always begins with a capital letter.

Homer Simpson   Labor Day

A **singular noun** names one thing. A **plural noun** names more than one thing.

B **Forming Plural Nouns**

Most nouns add -*s* to form plurals. Other nouns, whose singular forms end
in -*s*, -*ss*, -*sh*, -*ch*, -*x,* or -*z,* add -*es* to form plurals. Some nouns that end in
-*s* or -*z* double the *s* or *z* before adding -*es*.

Singular	*Plural*
street	streets
gas	gases
class	classes
bush	bushes
church	churches
fox	foxes
quiz	quizzes

Irregular Noun Plurals

Some nouns form plurals in unusual ways.

■ Nouns whose plural forms are the same as their singular forms

Singular	**Plural**
a deer	some deer
this species	these species
a television series	two television series

■ Nouns ending in -*f* or -*fe*

Singular	**Plural**
each half	both halves
my life	our lives
a lone thief	a gang of thieves
one loaf	two loaves
the third shelf	several shelves

Familiar exceptions: roof (plural *roofs*), proof (plural *proofs*),
belief (plural *beliefs*)

■ Nouns ending in -*y*

Singular	**Plural**
another baby	more babies
every worry	many worries

Note that when the *y* follows a vowel, the noun has a regular
plural form: monkey (plural *monkeys*), day (plural *days*).

(continued on the following page)

● **Writing Tip**
When a noun has an irregular plural, the dictionary lists
its plural form.

● **Writing Tip**
Sometimes you can tell
whether a word is singular
or plural by the word that
introduces it. For example,
each always introduces a
singular noun, and *many*
always introduces a plural
noun. (See 30E.)

28 B

(continued from the previous page)

■ Hyphenated compound nouns

Singular	Plural
Lucia's sister-in-law	Lucia's two favorite sisters-in-law
a mother-to-be	twin mothers-to-be
the first runner-up	all the runners-up

■ Miscellaneous irregular plurals

Singular	Plural
that child	all children
a good man	a few good men
the woman	lots of women
my left foot	both feet
a wisdom tooth	my two front teeth
this bacterium	some bacteria

◆ PRACTICE 28-1

Next to each of the following singular nouns, write the plural form of the noun. Then, circle the plural forms of irregular nouns.

Examples: bottle ___*bottles*___   child ___(*children*)___

1. headache _____

2. life _____

3. foot _____

4. chain _____

5. deer _____

6. honey _____

7. bride-to-be _____

8. woman _____

9. loaf _____

10. kiss _____

11. beach _____

12. duty _____

13. son-in-law _____

14. species _____

15. wife _____

16. city _____

17. elf _____

18. tooth _____

19. catalog _____

20. patty _____

◆ PRACTICE 28-2

Proofread the underlined nouns in the following paragraph, checking for correct singular or plural form. If a correction needs to be made, cross out the noun and write the correct form above it. If the noun is correct, write *C* above it.

Example: Many ~~studys~~ *studies* prove this.

(1) I recently talked to a group of my unmarried <u>friend</u> about what they look for in a person of the opposite sex. (2) Most of the <u>woman</u> said that their <u>standardes</u> were the same whether they just wanted to date a <u>men</u> for fun or to consider him as a potential mate. (3) Both just-for-fun <u>date</u> and potential <u>husband-to-bes</u> were considered real <u>catchs</u> if they had decent <u>job</u> or were working in that direction, if they were consider-ate and honest, and if they had good <u>sensess</u> of humor. (4) My male <u>buddies</u>, however, had different <u>ideaes</u>. (5) They wanted <u>dates</u> to be good-looking, to have outgoing <u>personalitys</u>, and to have independent <u>lifes</u> of their own. (6) Potential <u>wifes</u>, on the other hand, should not be too attractive to other <u>mens</u>, should be <u>homebodies</u>, and should see them-selves not as independent but as <u>halfes</u> of a whole. (7) Sometimes I think the two <u>sexs</u> are different <u>specieses</u>.

■ WRITING FIRST: Flashback

Look back at your response to the Writing First exercise on page 364. Circle each noun. Write any plural nouns on the lines below, and circle any irregular plurals.

_____   _____   _____   _____

_____   _____   _____   _____

C   Identifying Pronouns

A **pronoun** is a word that takes the place of a noun or another pronoun.

> Michelle was really excited. <u>She</u> had finally found a job.

Without pronouns, your sentences would be tedious because you would have to repeat the same nouns over and over again.

> Michelle was really excited. Michelle had finally found a job.

Pronouns, like nouns, can be singular or plural. The pronouns *I*, *he*, *she*, and *it* are always singular and take the place of singular nouns.

> Geoff left his jacket at work, so <u>he</u> went back to get <u>it</u>.

● **Writing Tip**
Too many pronouns can make a paragraph monoto-nous, especially when pro-nouns begin several sentences. Vary your sen-tence openings. (See 18B.)

For lists of pronouns, see 28E, 28F, and 28G.

The pronouns *we* and *they* are always plural and take the place of plural nouns.

> Jessie and Dan got up early, but <u>they</u> still missed the train.

The pronoun *you* can be either singular or plural.

> When the volunteers met the mayor, they said, "We really admire <u>you</u>." The mayor replied, "I admire <u>you</u>, too."

◆ PRACTICE 28-3

In the following sentences, fill in each blank with an appropriate pronoun.

Example: <u>*I*</u> like to be direct with my friends.

(1) _____ pride myself on always being honest. (2) My father used to tell me that honesty is the best policy, and _____ was right. (3) Sometimes my honesty hurts my friends' feelings, and _____ tell me that _____ am being rude to them. (4) _____ answer them by saying that _____ all need to hear the honest truth about ourselves sometimes. (5) My friend Linda understands my point, and _____ is always eager to let me hear the honest truth about myself whenever _____ have made a comment about her. (6) She tells me, "If _____ are going to dish _____ out, then _____ had better learn to take _____ yourself." (7) It's true that if her comment is really strong, _____ can upset me for a day or two. (8) But then _____ remember that it's only Linda's opinion, and _____ is never right about anything.

■ WRITING FIRST: Flashback

Look back at your response to the Writing First exercise on page 364. In the column on the left, list all the pronouns (*I, he, she, it, we, you, they*) you used. In the column on the right, list the noun each pronoun replaces.

Pronoun	*Noun*
_____	_____
_____	_____
_____	_____

(continued on the following page)

(continued from the previous page)

Pronoun	Noun
_____	_____
_____	_____
_____	_____
_____	_____
_____	_____

D Understanding Pronoun-Antecedent Agreement

As you learned in 28C, pronouns take the place of nouns or other pronouns. The word that a pronoun refers to is called the pronoun's **antecedent**. In the following sentence, the noun *leaf* is the antecedent of the pronoun *it*.

The leaf turned yellow, but <u>it</u> did not fall.

A pronoun must always agree in **number** with its antecedent. If an antecedent is singular, as it is in the sentence above, the pronoun must be singular. If the antecedent is plural, the pronoun must also be plural.

The leaves turned yellow, but <u>they</u> did not fall.

Pronouns must also agree with their antecedents in **gender**. If an antecedent is feminine, the pronoun that refers to it must also be feminine.

Melissa passed <u>her</u> driver's exam with flying colors.

If an antecedent is masculine, the pronoun that refers to it must be masculine.

Matt wondered what courses <u>he</u> should take.

If an antecedent is neuter (that is, neither masculine nor feminine), the pronoun that refers to it must also be neuter.

Lee's car broke down, but she refused to fix <u>it</u> again.

◆ PRACTICE 28-4

In the following sentences, circle the antecedent of each underlined pronoun. Then, draw an arrow from the pronoun to the antecedent.

Example: College (students) today often fear <u>they</u> will be the victims of crime on campus.

(1) Few campuses are as safe as <u>they</u> should be, experts say. (2) However, crime on most campuses is probably not really worse than <u>it</u> is in any other community. (3) Still, students have a right to know how safe <u>their</u> campuses are. (4) My friend Joyce never sets foot on campus without <u>her</u> can of Mace. (5) Joyce believes <u>she</u> must be prepared for the worst. (6) Joyce's boyfriend attended a self-defense program that <u>he</u> said was very helpful. (7) My friends won't let fear of crime keep <u>them</u> from enjoying the college experience. (8) Our school is doing what <u>it</u> can to provide a safe environment.

◆ PRACTICE 28-5

Fill in each blank in the following passage with an appropriate pronoun.

Example: Multiplexes are springing up everywhere; sometimes <u>*they*</u> are replacing drive-ins.

(1) Drive-in movie theaters used to be common in the United States, but now _____ are fairly rare. (2) In 1958, there were more than four thousand drive-ins across the country, but _____ have been reduced to fewer than nine hundred today. (3) One of the most amazing is the Thunderbird Drive-In in Ft. Lauderdale, Florida; _____ has twelve different screens. (4) Owner Preston Henn says _____ is the largest drive-in theater in the world. (5) _____ opened the theater with only one screen in 1963. (6) _____ also opened a flea market on the property. (7) _____ is now one of the largest flea markets in the state, with over two thousand vendors, a circus, and an amusement park. (8) The vendors think _____ are getting a good deal, and so do movie viewers.

■ WRITING FIRST: Flashback

Look back at your response to the Writing First exercise on page 364. Underline each pronoun in your paragraph, circle its antecedent, and draw an arrow from each pronoun to its antecedent. Do all your pronouns agree with their antecedents? If not, correct your pronouns.

E Solving Special Problems with Pronoun-Antecedent Agreement

Certain situations present special pronoun-antecedent problems.

Compound Antecedents

A **compound antecedent** consists of two or more words connected by *and* or *or*. Compound antecedents connected by *and* are plural, and they are used with plural pronouns.

During World War II, Belgium and France tried to protect their borders.

Compound antecedents connected by *or* may take a singular or a plural pronoun. When both elements of a compound antecedent connected by *or* are singular, use a singular pronoun.

Either a dog or a cat must have put its paw in the frosting.

When both elements are plural, use a plural pronoun.

Are dogs or cats more loyal to their owners?

For information on subject-verb agreement with compound subjects, see 23A.

FOCUS **Singular and Plural Antecedents Connected by *Or***

When one element of a compound antecedent connected by *or* is singular and one is plural, use the pronoun that agrees with the word closer to it.

Is it possible that European nations or Russia may send its (not *their*) troops?

Is it possible that Russia or European nations may send their (not *its*) troops?

◆ PRACTICE 28-6

In each of the following sentences, underline the compound antecedent and circle the connecting word *(and* or *or)*. Then, circle the appropriate pronoun in parentheses.

Example: Groucho (and) Harpo were younger than (his/their) brother Chico.

1. Larry (and) Curly were younger than (his/their) partner Moe.

2. Either Chip (or) Dale has a stripe down (his/their) back.

3. Most critics believe Stan (and) Ollie did (his/their) best work in silent comedies.

4. Lucy (and) Ethel never seem to learn (her/their) lesson.

5. Either *MASH* (or) *The Fugitive* had the highest ratings for any television show in (its/their) final episode.

6. Was it Mario Van Peebles (or) his father Melvin who made (his/their) directing debut with *New Jack City?*

7. Either film (or) videotapes lose (its/their) clarity over time.

8. Either Tower (or) Blockbuster is having (its/their) grand opening today.

9. The popcorn (and) soft drinks here are expensive for (its/their) size.

10. Do comedies (or) dramas have a greater impact on (its/their) audiences?

Indefinite Pronoun Antecedents

Some pronouns are called **indefinite pronouns** because they do not refer to any particular person or thing.

● **Writing Tip**
Some indefinite pronouns (such as *all, any, none, more, most,* and *some*) can be singular or plural. (*"All* the material is irrelevant." *"All* candidates were qualified.")

Indefinite Pronouns

Singular			**Plural**
another	everyone	nothing	both
anybody	everything	one	few
anyone	much	somebody	many
anything	neither	someone	others
each	nobody	something	several
either	none		
everybody	no one		

For information on subject-verb agreement with indefinite pronouns, see 23D.

Most indefinite pronouns are singular. They are used with singular pronouns, as in the following sentence.

Everything was in <u>its</u> place.

Some indefinite pronouns are plural and are used with plural pronouns.

ESL Tip
Remind students that singular indefinite pronouns don't have plural forms.

They all wanted to graduate early, but few received <u>their</u> diplomas in January.

FOCUS *His or Her* with Singular Indefinite Pronouns

Even though certain indefinite pronouns—such as *anybody, anyone, everybody, everyone, somebody,* and *someone*—are usually singular, many people use plural pronouns to refer to them.

Everyone must hand in their completed work before 2 P.M.

Because many people think of *everyone* as plural, sentences like the one above are widely used—and widely accepted—in spoken English. Nevertheless, *everyone* is singular, and written English requires a singular pronoun.

Although using the singular pronoun *his* to refer to *everyone* is technically correct, doing so assumes that *everyone* refers to an individual who is male. Using *his or her* allows for the possibility that the indefinite pronoun may refer to either a male or a female.

Everyone must hand in his or her completed work before 2 P.M.

When used repeatedly, however, *he or she, him or her,* and *his or her* can create wordy or awkward sentences. Whenever possible, use plural forms.

All students must hand in their completed work before 2 P.M.

FOCUS Indefinite Pronouns with *Of*

Sometimes indefinite pronouns are used in phrases with *of*—*each of, either of, neither of,* or *one of,* for example. Even in such phrases, these indefinite pronoun antecedents are always singular and take singular pronouns.

Each of the routes has its (not *their*) own special challenges.

◆ **PRACTICE 28-7**

In the following sentences, first circle the indefinite pronoun antecedent. Then, circle the appropriate pronoun in parentheses.

Example: (Each) of the artists will have (his or her/their) own exhibit.

1. (Either) of those paintings will be sold with (its/their) frame.

2. (Each) of the artist's brushes has (its/their) own use.

3. Everything in the room made (its/their) contribution to the whole design.

4. Everyone must remember to take (his or her/their) paint box.

5. Neither of my sisters wanted (her/their) picture displayed.

6. Many of the men brought (his/their) children to the exhibit.

7. Several of the colors must be mixed with (its/their) contrasting colors.

8. When someone compliments your work, be sure to tell (him or her/them) that it's for sale.

9. Anyone can improve (his or her/their) skills as an artist.

10. Both of these workrooms have (its/their) own advantages.

◆ PRACTICE 28-8

Edit the following sentences for errors in pronoun-antecedent agreement. In some sentences, substitute *his or her* for *their* when the antecedent is singular. In other sentences, replace the antecedent with a plural word.

Examples

Everyone will be responsible for ~~their~~ own transportation.
          his or her

All
~~Each of~~ the children took their books out of their bags and closed their desks.

1. Everyone has the right to their own opinion.

2. Everyone can eat their lunch in the cafeteria.

3. Somebody must have forgotten to take their shower this morning.

4. Each of the patients had their own rooms, with their own televisions and their own private baths.

5. Someone in the store has left their car's lights on.

6. Simone keeps everything in her kitchen in their own little container.

7. Each of the applicants must have their associate's degree.

8. Anybody who's ever juggled a job and children knows how valuable their free time can be.

9. Either of the coffeemakers comes with their own filter.

10. Almost everyone waits until the last minute to file their income tax returns.

Collective Noun Antecedents

Collective nouns are words (like *band* and *team*) that name a group of people or things but are singular. Because they are singular, collective noun antecedents are used with singular pronouns.

> The band played on, but <u>it</u> never played our song.

Frequently Used Collective Nouns

army	club	gang	mob
association	committee	government	posse
band	company	group	team
class	family	jury	union

FOCUS   **Vague Pronoun References**

A pronoun should always refer to a specific antecedent.

VAGUE   On the evening news, <u>they</u> said a baseball strike was inevitable.

REVISED   On the evening news, <u>the sportscaster</u> said a baseball strike was inevitable.

◆ PRACTICE 28-9

Circle the collective noun antecedent in the following sentences. Then, circle the correct pronoun in parentheses.

Example: The (jury) returned with (its/their) verdict.

1. The company provides (its/their) employees with very generous benefits.

2. Each study group is supposed to hand in (its/their) joint project by the end of the week.

3. Any government should be concerned for the welfare of (its/their) citizens.

4. The Black Students Union is sponsoring a party to celebrate (its/their) fifteenth anniversary.

5. Every family has (its/their) share of troubles.

6. An army is only as strong as the loyalty of (its/their) soldiers.

7. Even the best team has (its/their) off days.

8. The orchestra has just signed a contract to make (its/their) first record.

9. The gang is known for (its/their) violent initiation rites.

10. I wouldn't join any club that would have me as one of (its/their) members.

◆ **PRACTICE 28-10**

Edit the following passage for correct pronoun-antecedent agreement. First, determine the antecedent of each underlined pronoun. (Some antecedents will be compounds, some will be indefinite pronouns, and some will be collective nouns.) Then, cross out any pronoun that does not agree with its antecedent, and write the correct form above it. If the pronoun is correct, write *C* above it.

Example: Diversity is an important goal for the American corpora-

tion and ~~their~~ workers.
its

(1) Diversity has come to corporate America. (2) The average company counts among their employees many more women and members of minority groups today than at any other time in our history. (3) The U.S. government has established laws to protect its citizens from discrimination in employment. (4) Anyone who can prove discrimination can usually see their company punished. (5) This means that a corporation and their board will usually set diversity in the work force as one of its goals. (6) Having a diverse work force, however, doesn't mean that an organization has truly met the needs of its employees. (7) While a Hispanic employee or a female employee may now find that their opportunities are greater, issues remain to be resolved. (8) Employees and management must first understand its common goals. (9) Only then will a company be able to implement the kinds of policies that will make it possible for each of their employees to work at his or her best. (10) For example, a vice president or a mail-room clerk may need to take time off to see their family through a crisis. (11) Company policy should allow leave time to anyone in the company, regardless of their position. (12) In a truly diverse work force, workers must be treated fairly.

■ WRITING FIRST: Flashback

Look back at your response to the Writing First exercise on page 364.
Does your paragraph contain any antecedents that are compounds,
indefinite pronouns, or collective nouns? If so, list them below.

Compounds   *Indefinite Pronouns*   *Collective Nouns*

_____   _____   _____

_____   _____   _____

_____   _____   _____

_____   _____   _____

Have you used the correct pronoun with each of these words? If
not, correct your pronouns.

F   Understanding Pronoun Case

A **personal pronoun**—a pronoun that refers to a particular person or
thing—changes form according to the way it functions in a sentence. When
a pronoun functions as a sentence's subject, it is in the **subjective case**.

Finally, <u>she</u> realized that dreams could come true.

When a pronoun functions as an object, it is in the **objective case**.

If Joanna hurries, she can stop <u>him</u>. (The pronoun *him* is the direct
object of the verb *stop*.)

Professor Miller sent <u>us</u> information about his research. (The pronoun *us* is the indirect object of the verb *sent*.)

Marc threw the ball to <u>them</u>. (The pronoun *them* is the object of the
preposition *to*.)

FOCUS Objects

A **direct object** is a noun or pronoun that receives the action of the
verb.

DO
What did I send yesterday? I sent a <u>fax</u> yesterday.

DO
Whom will I call today? I'll call <u>him</u> today.

(continued on the following page)

(continued from the previous page)

An **indirect object** is the noun or pronoun that has received or benefited from the action of the verb.

IO
To whom did I send a fax? I sent <u>Adam</u> a fax.

IO
To whom did I give money? I gave <u>her</u> money.

A word or word group introduced by a preposition is called the **object of the preposition**. (See 15B.)

OP
From what did she run? She ran from the <u>fire</u>.

OP
For whom did Kelly work? Kelly worked for <u>them</u>.

When a pronoun shows ownership, it is in the **possessive case**.

Hieu took <u>his</u> lunch to the meeting

Debbie and Kim decided to take <u>their</u> lunches, too.

The following chart lists the various forms that personal pronouns take in subjective, objective, and possessive cases.

Personal Pronouns

Subjective Case	Objective Case	Possessive Case
I	me	my, mine
he	him	his
she	her	her, hers
it	it	its
we	us	our, ours
you	you	your, yours
they	them	their, theirs
who	whom	whose
whoever	whomever	

Three special situations can cause problems when you are trying to determine which pronoun case to use. One occurs with pronouns *in compounds,* another occurs with pronouns *in comparisons,* and the third occurs with the pronouns *who* and *whom.*

Pronouns in Compounds

Sometimes a pronoun is linked to a noun or to another pronoun with *and* or *or* to form a **compound**.

> The teacher and I met for an hour.

> She and I had a good meeting.

To determine whether to use the subjective or objective case for a pronoun in a compound, follow the same rules that apply for a pronoun that is not part of a compound.

If the compound in which the pronoun appears is the sentence's subject, use the subjective case.

> Toby and I [not *me*] like jazz.

> He and I [not *me*] went to the movies.

If the compound in which the pronoun appears is the object of the verb or the object of a preposition, use the objective case.

> The school sent my father and me [not *I*] the financial aid forms.

> This fight is between her and me [not *I*].

FOCUS   **Choosing Pronouns in Compounds**

To determine which pronoun case to use in a compound that joins a noun and a pronoun, drop the noun and rewrite the sentence with just the pronoun.

> Toby and *[I or me?]* like jazz.

> I like jazz. (not *Me like jazz*)

> Toby and I like jazz.

Pronouns in Comparisons

Sometimes a pronoun appears after the word *than* or *as* in a **comparison**.

> John is luckier than I.

> The inheritance changed Raymond as much as her.

If the pronoun is a subject, use the subjective case.

> John is luckier than I [am].

If the pronoun is an object, use the objective case.

> The inheritance changed Raymond as much as [it changed] her.

● **Writing Tip**
To decide whether to use the subjective or objective form of a pronoun, add in brackets the words needed to complete the comparison.

> **FOCUS** **Choosing Pronouns in Comparisons**
>
> Sometimes your choice of pronoun can change your sentence's meaning. For example, if you say, "I like Cheerios more than he," you mean that you like Cheerios more than the other person likes them.
>
> I like Cheerios more than he [does].
>
> If, however, you say, "I like Cheerios more than him," you mean that you like Cheerios more than you like the other person.
>
> I like Cheerios more than [I like] him.

The Pronouns *Who* and *Whom*

● **Writing Tip**
In conversation, people often use *who* for both subjective case *(Who wrote that song?)* and objective case *(Who are you going with?)*. In writing, always use *whom* for the objective case: *With whom are you going?*

To determine whether to use *who* or *whom,* you need to know how the pronoun functions within the clause in which it appears.

When the pronoun is the subject of the clause, use *who.*

I wonder <u>who</u> wrote that song. *(Who is the subject of the clause who wrote that song.)*

When the pronoun is the object, use *whom.*

I wonder <u>whom</u> the song is about. *(Whom is the object of the preposition about in the clause whom the song is about.)*

> **FOCUS** *Who* and *Whom*
>
> To determine whether to use *who* or *whom,* try substituting another pronoun for *who* or *whom* in the clause. If you can substitute *he* or *she,* use *who;* if you can substitute *him* or *her,* use *whom.*
>
> [Who/whom] wrote a love song? <u>He</u> wrote a love song.
>
> [Who/whom] was the song about? The song was about <u>her</u>.

◆ PRACTICE 28-11

In the following sentences, check the underlined pronouns, which are part of compound constructions, for correct subjective or objective case. If a correction needs to be made, cross out the pronoun, and write the correct form above it. If the pronoun is correct, write *C* above it.

Example: The reward was divided between my friend and <u>me</u>.   *c*

(1) The deejay at the wedding reception asked Dionne and <u>I</u> to do an encore. (2) <u>Her</u> and <u>I</u> enjoy singing together. (3) The first time we sang, we really played up to <u>he</u> and the crowd. (4) <u>We</u> talked with <u>he</u> for a few minutes about what we should sing for the encore. (5) Dionne and <u>me</u> couldn't agree. (6) <u>Us</u> two always have trouble deciding on a song. (7) Finally, the deejay made the decision for <u>her</u> and <u>I</u>. (8) After <u>she</u> and <u>I</u> finished, the guests went wild. (9) <u>Them</u> and the servers started chanting, "More, more, more." (10) It was too much for Dionne and <u>me</u> to believe.

◆ PRACTICE 28-12

Write in each blank the correct form (subjective or objective) of the pronouns in parentheses. In brackets, add the word or words needed to complete the comparison.

Example: He's a better poker player than ___*I [am]*___ (I/me).

1. Sharon Stone is a better actress than _____ (she/her).

2. They are such a mismatched couple. Everybody likes her so much more than _____ (he/him).

3. No one enjoys shopping more than _____ (she/her).

4. My brother and our Aunt Cecile were very close. Her death affected him more than _____ (I/me).

5. Could any two people have a better relationship than _____ (we/us)?

6. I'll admit my roommate drives better than _____ (I/me).

7. We at Steer Hut serve juicier steaks than _____ (they/them).

8. Even if you are as old as _____ (I/me), you're not as smart.

9. That jacket fits you better than _____ (I/me).

10. The Trumps may be richer than _____ (we/us), but I'll bet they don't have as much fun.

◆ PRACTICE 28-13

Circle the correct form of *who* or *whom* in parentheses in each sentence.

Example: With (who/whom) did Rob collaborate?

1. The defense team learned (who/whom) was going to testify for the prosecution.

2. (Who/Whom) does she think she can find to be a witness?

3. I think the runner (who/whom) crosses the finish line first will be the winner.

4. From (who/whom) did you get these tickets?

5. It will take time to decide (who/whom) the record holder is.

6. Take these forms to the clerk (who/whom) is at the front desk.

7. I wonder (who/whom) missed class yesterday.

8. (Who/Whom) did Kobe take to the prom?

9. We saw the man (who/whom) fired the shots.

10. To (who/whom) am I speaking?

■ WRITING FIRST: Flashback

Look back at your response to the Writing First exercise on page 364. Can you find any sentences that contain a pronoun used in a compound or a comparison? If so, write the sentences here, making sure to use the appropriate pronoun case.

_____

_____

Circle any uses of *who* and *whom*. Have you used these pronouns correctly?

G   Identifying Reflexive and Intensive Pronouns

Two special kinds of pronouns, *reflexive pronouns* and *intensive pronouns*, also always agree with their antecedents in person and number. Although the functions of the two kinds of pronouns are different, their forms are identical.

Reflexive Pronouns

Reflexive pronouns always end in *-self* (singular) or *-selves* (plural). They indicate that people or things did something to themselves or for themselves.

Rosanna lost <u>herself</u> in the novel.

You need to watch <u>yourself</u> when you mix those solutions.

Mehul and Paul made <u>themselves</u> cold drinks.

Intensive Pronouns

Intensive pronouns also end in *-self* or *-selves*. However, they always appear directly after their antecedents, and they are used for emphasis.

I <u>myself</u> have had some experience in sales and marketing.

The victim <u>himself</u> collected the reward.

They <u>themselves</u> were uncertain of the significance of their findings.

Reflexive and Intensive Pronouns

Singular Forms

Antecedent	Reflexive or Intensive Pronoun
I	myself
you	yourself
he	himself
she	herself
it	itself

Plural Forms

Antecedent	Reflexive or Intensive Pronoun
we	ourselves
you	yourselves
they	themselves

◆ PRACTICE 28-14

Fill in the correct reflexive or intensive pronoun in each of the following sentences.

Example: Sometimes I find _____*myself*_____ daydreaming in class.

1. The leaders gave _____ more credit than they deserved.

2. That woman takes _____ too seriously.

3. The president _____ visited the AIDS patients.

4. I don't see _____ as a particularly funny person.

5. Have you _____ ever actually seen an extraterrestrial?

6. We Americans pride _____ on our tolerance of diversity, but we can still be discriminatory and narrow-minded.

7. The bird settled _____ on my window ledge.

8. You should all give _____ a big pat on the back for a job well done.

9. Dorothy and the others hardly recognized _____ after the transformation.

10. I _____ am opposed to the legislation, but I don't condemn others who support it.

■ WRITING FIRST: Flashback

Look back at your response to the Writing First exercise on page 364. Have you used any reflexive or intensive pronouns? If so, list them here.

Reflexive pronouns: _____

Intensive pronouns: _____

■ WRITING FIRST: Revising and Editing

Look back at your response to the Writing First exercise on page 364. Change every singular noun to a plural noun and every plural noun to a singular noun. Then, edit your pronouns so singular pronouns refer to singular nouns and plural pronouns refer to plural nouns. You might also do this exercise with a piece of writing you did for another class.

CHAPTER REVIEW

◆ **EDITING PRACTICE**

Read the following student essay, into which noun and pronoun errors have been introduced. Check for errors in plural noun forms, pronoun case, and pronoun-antecedent agreement, as well as for any vague pronouns. Make any editing changes you think are necessary. The first sentence has been edited for you.

Going beyond Books

activities

Extracurricular ~~activitys~~ can be just as important for

a college student as their coursework. Two students I

myself have met illustrate the truth of this statement. For

each of them, their extracurricular activity made a real

difference.

Julia joined our school's rifle team. As the only

female on the team, she had some problems at first. Eventu-

ally, though, her teammates saw that she could shoot as

well as them, and she began to feel comfortable with the

group and their routine. In her first year, her team won

the state Junior Varsity championship, and judges ranked

them third in the region. In her second year, her and the

team placed sixth in the championship match held at the

United States Military Academy at West Point. Julia found

she enjoyed these triumphs. Like her teammates, she enjoyed

rifle shooting because the sport requires precision and

concentration in the midst of intense competition. It also

gave she and her teammates an occasional escape from their

studies. Most important, Julia had the opportunity to visit

other campuses when she competed in away matches and to

meet other competitors, some of whom were also woman. For

Julia, intercollegiate competition offered a lot of

benefits.

Chris, a chemistry major, received similar benefits

from his participation in the student affiliate of the

American Chemical Society (ACS). By the time he was a

sophomore, he was president of our school's chapter. Serv-

ing in this office taught him how to handle leadership and

responsibility. The organization was geared toward educat-

ing their members about chemistry through seminars and

visits to industry sites. They also encouraged members to

attend social functions with other chemistry majors and

faculty. Chris was active in organizing all these events. Through the school's ACS chapter, a student could increase their knowledge of chemistry beyond what their textbooks offered.

Many students believe courses are what school is all about, but Julia and Chris would disagree. For students like they, time spent on extracurricular activities can be as valuable as time spent in a classroom or library. Studying and extracurricular activities are two halfs of a whole educational experience.

◆ **COLLABORATIVE ACTIVITIES**

1. Working in a group, fill in the following chart, writing one noun on each line. If the noun is a proper noun, be sure to capitalize it.

Cars	Trees	Foods	Famous Couples	Cities
_____	_____	_____	_____	_____
_____	_____	_____	_____	_____
_____	_____	_____	_____	_____
_____	_____	_____	_____	_____

Now, use as many of the nouns listed above as possible to write a news article. Exchange your work with another group, and check the other group's article to be sure the correct pronoun form refers to each noun. Return the articles to their original groups for editing.

2. Working in a group, write a silly story that uses each of these nouns at least once: *Martians, eggplant, MTV, toupee, kangaroo, Iceland, bat, herd,* and *kayak*. Then, exchange stories with another group. After you have read the other group's story, edit it so that it includes all of the following pronouns: *it, its, itself, they, their, them, themselves.* Return the edited story to its authors. Finally, reread your group's story, and edit to make sure pronoun-antecedent agreement is clear and correct.

✓ REVIEW CHECKLIST:
Nouns and Pronouns

- A noun is a word that names something. A singular noun names one thing; a plural noun names more than one thing. (See 28A.)

- Most nouns add -s to form plurals. Some nouns have irregular plural forms. (See 28B.)

- A pronoun is a word that takes the place of a noun. (See 28C.)

- The word a pronoun refers to is called the pronoun's antecedent. (See 28D.)

- Compound antecedents connected by *and* are plural and are used with plural pronouns. Compound antecedents connected by *or* may take singular or plural pronouns. (See 28E.)

- Most indefinite pronoun antecedents are singular. Therefore, they are used with singular pronouns. (See 28E.)

- Collective noun antecedents are singular and must be used with singular pronouns. (See 28E.)

- A pronoun should always refer to a specific antecedent. (See 28E.)

- Personal pronouns can be in the subjective, objective, or possessive case. (See 28F.)

- Pronouns present special problems when they are used in compounds and comparisons. The pronouns *who* and *whom* also cause problems. (See 28F.)

- Reflexive and intensive pronouns must agree with their antecedents in person and number. (See 28G.)

Adjectives and Adverbs

> ■ **WRITING FIRST**
>
> Try to imagine events or circumstances that might make you decide to move from the United States to another country. Describe a specific situation that might force you to leave, and your reasons for leaving. Where would you go? Why?

A   Identifying Adjectives and Adverbs

Adjectives and adverbs are words that modify—that is, describe or identify—other words. They help make sentences more specific and more interesting.

An **adjective** answers the question *What kind? Which one?* or *How many?* Adjectives modify nouns or pronouns.

> The Turkish city of Istanbul spans two continents. (*Turkish* modifies the noun *city,* and *two* modifies the noun *continents.*)
>
> It is fascinating because of its location and history. (*Fascinating* modifies the pronoun *it.*)

● **Writing Tip**
Some adjectives, such as *Turkish,* are capitalized because they are formed from proper nouns. Proper nouns name particular people, animals, places, or things. For more on proper nouns, see 28A.

> **FOCUS** **Demonstrative Adjectives**
>
> Some adjectives—called **demonstrative adjectives**—do not describe other words. These adjectives—*this, that, these,* and *those*—simply identify particular nouns.
>
> *(continued on the following page)*

(continued from the previous page)

This and *that* identify singular nouns.

This encyclopedia is much more thorough and up-to-date than that one.

These and *those* identify plural nouns.

These words and phrases are French, but those expressions are Creole.

An **adverb** answers the question *How? Why? When? Where?* or *To what extent?* Adverbs modify verbs, adjectives, or other adverbs.

Traffic moved steadily. *(Steadily* modifies the verb *moved.)*

Still, we were quite impatient. *(Quite* modifies the adjective *impatient.)*

Very slowly, we inched into the center lane. *(Very* modifies the adverb *slowly.)*

FOCUS **Distinguishing Adjectives from Adverbs**

Many adverbs are formed when *-ly* is added to an adjective form.

Adjective	Adverb
slow	slowly
nice	nicely
quick	quickly
real	really

ADJECTIVE Let me give you one quick reminder. *(Quick* modifies the noun *reminder.)*

ADVERB He quickly changed the subject. *(Quickly* modifies the verb *changed.)*

ADJECTIVE Tell me your real name. *(Real* modifies the noun *name.)*

ADVERB It was really rude of her to ignore me. *(Really* modifies the adjective *rude.)*

> ● **Writing Tip**
> Some adjectives—*lovely, friendly,* and *lively,* for example—end in *-ly.* Don't mistake these words for adverbs.

◆ **PRACTICE 29-1**

In the following sentences, circle the correct adjective or adverb form from the choices in parentheses.

Example: Women who are (serious/seriously) walkers or runners need to wear athletic shoes that fit.

(1) Doctors have found that many athletic shoes are (poor/poorly) designed for women. (2) Women's athletic shoes are (usual/usually) just scaled-down versions of men's shoes. (3) Consequently, they cannot provide a (true/truly) comfortable fit. (4) Studies have shown that to get a shoe that fits (comfortable/comfortably) in the heel, most women must buy one that is too (tight/tightly) for the front of the foot. (5) This can have a (real/really) negative impact on athletic performance. (6) It can also cause (serious/seriously) pain and even physical deformity. (7) Some athletic shoe manufacturers have begun to market athletic shoes that are designed (specific/specifically) for women. (8) Experts say that women must become informed consumers and choose (careful/carefully) when they shop for athletic shoes. (9) One (important/importantly) piece of advice is to shop for shoes (immediate/immediately) after exercising or at the end of a work day, when the foot is at its largest. (10) Experts advise that athletic shoes should feel (comfortable/comfortably) from the moment they are tried on — or else be returned to the box.

FOCUS *Good and Well*

Be careful not to confuse *good* and *well*. Unlike regular adjectives, whose adverb form adds *-ly*, the adjective *good* is irregular. Its adverb form is *well*.

ADJECTIVE   Fred Astaire was a good dancer. *(Good* modifies the noun *dancer.)*

ADVERB   He danced especially well with Ginger Rogers. *(Well* modifies the verb *danced.)*

Always use *well* when you are describing a person's health.

He really didn't feel well [not *good*] after eating an entire pizza.

◆ **PRACTICE 29-2**

Choose the correct form *(good* or *well)* in the sentences below.

Example: Eating (good/well) is part of (good/well) living.

(1) A particular food can sometimes be (good/well) for you in ways you might not expect. (2) For example, if you're feeling down and just not doing (good/well) emotionally, you might need a carbohydrate pick-me-up. (3) Some doctors recommend pasta, rice cakes, or pretzels as (good/well) sources of carbohydrates. (4) If you need to perform (good/well) mentally—on a test, for example—protein-rich foods may be helpful. (5) Three to four ounces of fish or chicken can be especially (good/well) for helping you remain alert. (6) Carbohydrates can be eaten with the protein, but you would do (good/well) to avoid fats, which can make you drowsy. (7) Most people know that caffeine works (good/well) to help overcome drowsiness. (8) Caffeine can also be a (good/well) stimulant for helping one stay alert. (9) High-fat foods are also useful because they encourage the brain to produce endorphins, the same substances that make us feel so (good/well) when we are with someone we love. (10) However, the most endorphins are produced in people who exercise regularly and eat (good/well).

■ WRITING FIRST: Flashback

Look back at your response to the Writing First exercise on page 388. Underline each adjective and adverb, and draw an arrow from each to the word it describes or identifies. Do all adjectives modify nouns or pronouns? Do all adverbs modify verbs, adjectives, or other adverbs? Have you used *good* and *well* correctly? Revise any sentences that use modifiers incorrectly on the lines below.

_____

_____

_____

_____

29 B

Sometimes, an adjective or adverb describes something by comparing it to something else. The **comparative** form of an adjective or adverb compares two people or things. Adjectives and adverbs form the comparative with -*er* or *more*. The **superlative** form of an adjective or adverb compares more than two things. Adjectives and adverbs form the superlative with -*est* or *most*.

ADJECTIVES   This film is <u>dull</u> and <u>predictable</u>.

COMPARATIVE   The film I saw last week was even <u>duller</u> and <u>more predictable</u> than this one.

SUPERLATIVE   The film I saw last night was the <u>dullest</u> and <u>most predictable</u> one I've ever seen.

ADVERB   For a beginner, Jane did needlepoint <u>skillfully</u>.

COMPARATIVE   After she had watched the demonstration, Jane did needlepoint <u>more skillfully</u> than Rosie.

SUPERLATIVE   Of the twelve beginners, Jane did needlepoint the <u>most skillfully</u>.

Forming Comparatives and Superlatives

Adjectives

■ One-syllable adjectives generally form the comparative with -*er* and the superlative with -*est.*

great   greater   greatest

■ Adjectives with two or more syllables form the comparative with *more* and the superlative with *most.*

wonderful   more wonderful   most wonderful

Exception: Two-syllable adjectives ending in -*y* add -*er* or -*est* after changing the *y* to an *i.*

funny   funnier   funniest

Adverbs

■ All adverbs ending in -*ly* form the comparative with *more* and the superlative with *most.*

efficiently   more efficiently   most efficiently

■ Some other adverbs form the comparative with -*er* and the superlative with -*est.*

soon   sooner   soonest

> **FOCUS** **Special Problems with Comparatives and Superlatives**
>
> ■ Never use both *-er* and *more* to form the comparative or both *-est* and *most* to form the superlative.
>
> Nothing could have been <u>more awful</u>. (not *more awfuller*)
>
> Space Mountain is the <u>most frightening</u> (not *most frighteningest*) ride at Disney World.
>
> ■ Never use the superlative when you are comparing only two things.
>
> This is the <u>more serious</u> (not *most serious*) of the two problems.
>
> ■ Never use the comparative when you are comparing more than two things.
>
> This is the <u>worst</u> (not *worse*) day of my life.

◆ PRACTICE 29-3

Fill in the correct comparative form of the word supplied in parentheses.

Example: Children tend to be _____*noisier*_____ (noisy) than adults.

1. Traffic always moves _____ (slow) during rush hour than during the evening.

2. The weather report says temperatures will be _____ (cold) tomorrow.

3. Some elderly people are _____ (healthy) than younger people.

4. It has been proven that pigs are _____ (intelligent) than they look.

5. When someone asks you to repeat yourself, you usually answer _____ (loud).

6. The _____ (tall) the building, the more damage the earthquake caused.

7. They want to teach their son to be _____ (respectful) of women than many young men are.

8. Zsa Zsa Gabor is _____ (famous) for her husbands and her temper than for her acting.

9. The WaterDrop is _____ (wild) than any other ride in the park.

10. You must move _____ (quick) if you expect to catch the ball.

◆ PRACTICE 29-4

Fill in the correct superlative form of the word supplied in parentheses.

Example: Consumers now pay the _____*highest*_____ (high) surcharge ever when they buy tickets for arena events.

(1) Ticketmaster is the _____ (large) seller of sports and entertainment tickets in the country. (2) The company was the _____ (early) off the mark in selling concert and sporting event tickets both by phone and through retail outlets. (3) It has also been the _____ (successful) at making deals to keep rival ticket agencies from carrying tickets for large arenas and stadiums. (4) Its markup on tickets adds at least 20 percent to the cost of each ticket sold and is by far the _____ (great) in the business. (5) Because Ticketmaster is the _____ (powerful) ticket outlet in the country, however, fans have no choice but to pay the price. (6) Critics have argued that Ticketmaster's control of the market is the _____ (strong) monopoly in the country. (7) In 1994, the rock group Pearl Jam launched the _____ (serious) offensive to date against the ticket giant. (8) Wanting its fans to be able to buy the _____ (cheap) tickets possible, Pearl Jam proposed to lower its own profits as well as Ticketmaster's for its 1994 summer tour. Ticketmaster refused. (9) One of the _____ (popular) groups in the country, Pearl Jam then could not find enough suitable arenas that were not controlled by Ticketmaster. (10) Ticketmaster's president argues that it has succeeded not because of unfairness but because it has worked the

_____ (hard) and is the _____ (aggressive) com-

pany in the business.

| FOCUS | *Good/Well and Bad/Badly* |

Most adjectives and adverbs form the comparative with *-er* or *more*
and the superlative with *-est* or *most*. The adjectives *good* and *bad*
and their adverb forms *well* and *badly* are exceptions.

Adjective	Comparative Form	Superlative Form
good	better	best
bad	worse	worst

Adverb	Comparative Form	Superlative Form
well	better	best
badly	worse	worst

◆ PRACTICE 29-5

Fill in the correct comparative or superlative form of *good, well, bad,* or
badly.

Example: She is at her ____*best*____ (good) when she is under

pressure.

1. Today in track practice, Luisa performed _____ (well) than she

    has in weeks.

2. In fact, she ran her _____ (good) time ever in the fifty meter.

3. When things are bad, we wonder whether they will get _____

    (good) or _____ (bad).

4. I've had some bad pizza before, but this one is the _____ (bad).

5. The world always looks _____ (good) when you're in love than

    when you're not.

6. Athletes generally play _____ (badly) when their concentration

    is poorest.

7. The Sport Shop's prices may be good, but Athletic Attic's are the

    _____ (good) in town.

8. There are _____ (good) ways to solve conflicts than by fighting.

9. People seem to hear _____ (well) when they agree with what you're saying than when they don't agree with you.

10. Of all the children, Manda took the _____ (good) care of her parents.

■ WRITING FIRST: Flashback

Look back at your response to the Writing First exercise on page 388. Copy the adjectives and adverbs from your paragraph in the column on the left. Write the comparative and superlative forms for each adjective or adverb in the other columns.

Adjective or Adverb	Comparative Form	Superlative Form
_____	_____	_____
_____	_____	_____
_____	_____	_____
_____	_____	_____
_____	_____	_____

■ WRITING FIRST: Revising and Editing

Look back at your response to the Writing First exercise on page 388. Have you used adjectives and adverbs that effectively communicate the situation you describe? Have you used enough adjectives and adverbs to explain your ideas to readers? Add or substitute modifying words as needed to enrich and clarify your paragraph, deleting any unnecessary adjectives and adverbs.

CHAPTER REVIEW

◆ EDITING PRACTICE

Read the following student essay, into which errors in the use of adjectives and adverbs have been introduced. Make any changes necessary to correct adjectives incorrectly used for adverbs, adverbs incorrectly used for adjectives, and errors in the use of comparatives and superlatives, and in the use of demonstrative adjectives. You may also add adjectives and adverbs that you feel would make the writer's ideas clearer or more specific. The first sentence has been edited for you.

```
                       Starting Over
                     most joyful
        A wedding can be the j̶o̶y̶f̶u̶l̶l̶e̶s̶t̶ occasion in two
                          ^
people's lives, the beginning of a couple's most happiest

years. For some unlucky women, however, a wedding can be

the worse thing that ever happens; it is the beginning not

of their happiness but of their battered lives. As I went

through the joyful day of my wedding, I wanted bad to find

happiness for the rest of my life, but what I hoped and

wished for did not come true.

     I was married in the Savannah belt of the Sudan in

the western part of Africa, where I grew up. I was barely

twenty-two years old. The first two years of my marriage

progressed peaceful, but problems started as soon as our

first child was born.

     Many American women say, "If my husband gave me just

one beating, that would be it. I'd leave." But those atti-

tude does not work in cultures where tradition has over-

shadowed women's rights and divorce is not accepted. All

women can do is accept their sadly fate. Battered women

give many rationalizations for staying in their marriages,

but fear is the commonest. Fear immobilizes these women,

ruling their decisions, their actions, and their very

lives. This is how it was for me.

     Of course, I was real afraid whenever my husband hit

me. I would run to my mother's house and cry, but she

would always talk me into going back and being more

patiently with my husband. Our tradition discourages

divorce, and wife-beating is taken for granted. The

situation is really quite ironic: Islam, the religion I

practice, sets harsh punishments for abusive husbands, but

tradition has so overpowered religion that the laws do not

really work very good.
```

One night, after nine years of torture, I asked myself whether life had treated me fair. True, I had a high school diploma and two of the beautifullest children in the world, but all this was not enough. I realized that to stand up to the husband who treated me so bad, I would have to achieve a more better education than he had. That night, I decided to get a college education in the United States. My husband opposed my decision, but with the support of my father and mother, I was able to begin to change my life.

This period has been real difficult for me. I miss my children every day. But I hope that one day I will be able to fight our traditions intellectually and with dignity so that my little daughters will remember even when I am gone that their mother fought back and won.

◆ COLLABORATIVE ACTIVITIES

1. Working in a small group, write a plot summary for an imaginary film. Begin with one of the following three sentences.

   ▩ Dirk and Clive were sworn enemies, but that night on Boulder Ridge they vowed to work together just this once, for the good of their country.

   ▩ Genevieve entered the room in a cloud of perfume, and when she spoke, her voice was like velvet.

   ▩ The desert sun beat down on her head, but Susanna was determined to protect what was hers, no matter what the cost.

2. Trade summaries with another group. Add as many adjectives and adverbs as you can to the other group's summary. Make sure each modifier is appropriate.

3. Reread your group's plot summary and edit it carefully, paying special attention to the way adjectives and adverbs are used.

☑ REVIEW CHECKLIST:
Adjectives and Adverbs

  ☐ Adjectives modify nouns or pronouns. (See 29A.)

  ☐ Demonstrative adjectives—*this, that, these,* and *those*—identify particular nouns. (See 29A.)

(continued on the following page)

(continued from the previous page)

- Adverbs modify verbs, adjectives, or other adverbs. (See 29A.)

- To compare two people or things, use the comparative form of an adjective or adverb. To compare more than two people or things, use the superlative form of an adjective or adverb. Adjectives and adverbs form the comparative with *-er* or *more* and the superlative with *-est* or *most*. (See 29B.)

- The adjectives *good* and *bad* and their adverb forms *well* and *badly* have irregular comparative and superlative forms. (See 29B.)

30

Grammar and Usage Issues for ESL Writers

■ WRITING FIRST

Explain a process—for example, how to renew a driver's license or how to apply for financial aid. Begin with a sentence that tells readers what the process is and why it is necessary. Then, use the present tense to explain how to perform each step of this process.

Learning English as a second language involves more than just learning grammar. If you grew up speaking a language other than English, you will need to learn conventions of usage and ways of thinking that are second nature to native speakers. This chapter covers the grammar and usage issues that typically give nonnative speakers the most trouble.

A Including Subjects in Sentences

In almost all cases, English requires that every sentence state its subject. In fact, every dependent clause must also have a subject.

> INCORRECT My parents don't make much money although work hard.
>
> CORRECT My parents don't make much money although <u>they</u> work hard.

English even requires a false or "dummy" subject to fill the subject position in sentences like this one.

> <u>It</u> is hot here.

Do *not* write just "Hot here" or "Is hot here."

B Avoiding Special Problems with Subjects

Some languages commonly begin a sentence with a word or phrase that has no grammatical link to the sentence but that states clearly what the sentence is about. If you speak such a language, you might write a sentence like this one.

INCORRECT   Career plans I am studying to be a computer scientist.

● **Writing Tip**
Special dictionaries help nonnative speakers answer usage questions. Your college librarian or English instructor can help you find a dictionary that meets your needs.

A sentence like this cannot occur in English. The phrase *career plans* appears at the beginning of the sentence (a normal position for a subject). However, it cannot be a subject because the sentence already includes one, the pronoun *I*, which agrees with the verb *am studying*. In addition, *career plans* is not connected to the rest of the sentence in any other way, such as with a preposition. One way to revise this sentence is to rewrite it so that *career plans* is the subject.

For more on subjects, see 15A.

CORRECT   My career plans are to be a computer scientist.

Another way to revise is to make *career plans* the object of a preposition.

CORRECT   As for my career plans, I am studying to be a computer scientist.

Standard English also does not permit a two-part subject in which the second part is a pronoun referring to the same person or thing as the first part.

INCORRECT   My sister <u>she</u> is a cardiologist.
CORRECT   My sister is a cardiologist.

When the real subject follows the verb, and the normal subject position before the verb is empty, it must be filled by a "dummy" subject, such as *there*.

INCORRECT   Are tall mountains in my country.
CORRECT   <u>There</u> are tall mountains in my country.

■ WRITING FIRST: Flashback

Look back at your response to the Writing First exercise on page 400. Does every sentence state its subject? Underline the subject of each sentence. If a sentence doesn't have a subject, add one. If any sentence has a two-part subject, cross out the extra word.

*For more on singular and
plural nouns, see 28A and 28B.*

C   Identifying Plural Nouns

In English, most nouns add -*s* to form plurals. Every time you use a noun, ask yourself whether you are talking about one item or more than one, and choose a singular or plural form accordingly. Consider this sentence.

CORRECT   The <u>books</u> in both <u>branches</u> of the <u>library</u> are deteriorating.

The three nouns in this sentence are underlined: one is singular *(library)*, and the other two are plural *(books, branches)*. You might think that *both* is enough to indicate that *branch* is plural and that it is obvious that there would have to be more than one book in any branch of a library. It does not matter, however, whether the information is unimportant or obvious or whether it has already been supplied. You must always use a form that indicates explicitly that a noun is plural.

■ **WRITING FIRST: Flashback**

Look back at your response to the Writing First exercise on page 400. List all the plural nouns on the lines below.

_____   _____   _____   _____

_____   _____   _____   _____

Does each plural noun have a form that shows the noun is plural? Correct any errors you find.

D   Understanding Count and Noncount Nouns

A **count noun** names a distinct individual thing or a group of distinct individual things: *a teacher, a panther, a bed, an ocean, a cloud; teachers, panthers, beds, oceans, clouds.* A **noncount noun**, on the other hand, names things that cannot be counted: *gold, cream, sand, blood, smoke.* (The term *noncount* does not mean you cannot use numbers with words like *smoke* but only that English grammar requires you to apply numbers to these words indirectly: *one wisp of smoke* or *two columns of smoke,* not *one smoke, two smokes.*)

Count nouns usually have a singular form and a plural form: *cloud, clouds.* Noncount nouns usually have only a singular form: *smoke.* Note how the nouns *cloud* and *smoke* differ not only in meaning but also in the way they are used in sentences.

CORRECT   The sky is full of clouds.

CORRECT   The sky is full of smoke.

INCORRECT   The sky is full of smokes.

CORRECT   I can count ten clouds in the distance.

INCORRECT   I can count ten smokes in the distance.

Often, the same idea can be represented with either a count noun or a noncount noun.

Count	*Noncount*
people (plural of *person*)	humanity (not *humanities*)
tables, chairs, beds	furniture (not *furnitures*)
letters	mail (not *mails*)
tools	equipment (not *equipments*)
facts	information (not *informations*)
sofas	furniture (not *furnitures*)

Some words can be either count or noncount, depending on the meaning intended.

COUNT   Students in this course are expected to submit two papers.

NONCOUNT   These artificial flowers are made of paper.

● **Writing Tip**
Sometimes a noncount noun such as *smoke* appears to have a plural form *(smokes)*. Although these forms end in *-s,* they are verbs and not plural nouns: *He smokes two cigars a day.*

FOCUS   Count and Noncount Nouns

Here are some general guidelines for using count and noncount nouns.

■ Use a count noun to refer to a living animal, but use a noncount noun to refer to the food derived from that animal.

COUNT   There are several live lobsters in the tank.

NONCOUNT   This restaurant specializes in lobster.

■ If you use a noncount noun for a substance or class of things that can come in different varieties, you can often make that noun plural if you want to talk about those varieties.

NONCOUNT   Cheese is a rich source of calcium.

COUNT   Many different cheeses come from Italy.

■ If you want to shift attention from a concept in general to specific instances of it, you can often use a noncount noun as a count noun.

NONCOUNT   You have a great deal of talent.

COUNT   My talents don't include singing.

Determiners are adjectives that *identify* rather than describe the nouns they modify. Determiners may also *quantify* nouns (that is, indicate an amount or a number).

When a determiner is accompanied by one or more other adjectives, the determiner always comes first. For example, in the phrase *my expensive new digital watch, my* is a determiner; you cannot put *expensive, new, digital,* or any other adjective before *my.*

Determiners include the following words.

- Articles: *a, an, the*
- Demonstrative pronouns: *this, these, that, those*
- Possessive pronouns: *my, our, your, his, her, its, their*
- Possessive nouns: *Sheila's, my friend's*
- *Whose, which, what*
- *All, both, each, every, some, any, either, no, neither, many, much, a few, a little, few, little, several, enough*
- All numerals: *one, two,* and so on

A singular count noun must be accompanied by a determiner—for example, *my watch* or *the new digital watch,* not just *watch* or *new digital watch.* Noncount nouns and plural count nouns, on the other hand, sometimes have determiners but sometimes do not. *This honey is sweet* and *Honey is sweet* are both acceptable, as are *These berries are juicy* and *Berries are juicy.* (In each case, the meaning is different.) You cannot say *Berry is juicy,* however; say instead *This berry is juicy, Every berry is juicy,* or *A berry is juicy.*

FOCUS   **Determiners**

Some determiners can be used only with certain types of nouns.

- *This* and *that* can be used only with singular nouns (count or noncount): *this berry, that honey.*
- *These, those, a few, few, many, both,* and *several* can only be used with plural count nouns: *these berries, those apples, a few ideas, few people, many students, both sides, several directions.*
- *Much* and *a little* can be used only with noncount nouns: *a little honey, much affection.*
- *Some* and *enough* can be used only with noncount or plural count nouns: *some honey, some berries, enough trouble, enough problems.*
- *A, an, every,* and *each* can be used only with singular count nouns: *a berry, an elephant, every possibility, each citizen.*

■ **WRITING FIRST: Flashback**

Look back at your response to the Writing First exercise on page 400. List all the count nouns in the column on the left and all the noncount nouns in the column on the right. If a determiner comes before a noun, write it with the noun.

Count nouns   *Noncount nouns*

_____   _____

_____   _____

_____   _____

_____   _____

Have you used count and noncount nouns correctly? Correct any errors you find.

F   Understanding Articles

The definite article *the* and the indefinite articles *a* and *an* are determiners that tell readers whether the noun that follows is one they can identify *(the book)* or one they cannot yet identify *(a book)*.

Definite Articles

When the definite article *the* is used with a noun, the writer is saying to readers, "You can identify which particular thing or things I have in mind. The information you need to make that identification is available to you. Either you have it already, or I am about to supply it to you."

Readers can find the necessary information in the following ways.

■ By looking at other information in the sentence.

> Meet me at <u>the</u> corner of Main Street and Lafayette.

In this example, *the* is used with the noun *corner* because other words in the sentence tell readers which particular corner the writer has in mind: the one located at Main and Lafayette.

■ By looking at information in other sentences.

> Aisha ordered a slice of pie and a cup of coffee. <u>The</u> pie was delicious. She asked for a second slice.

Here, *the* is used before the word *pie* in the second sentence to indicate that it is the same pie identified in the first sentence. Notice, however, that the noun *slice* in the third sentence is preceded by an indefinite article *(a)* because it is not the same slice referred to in the first sentence. There is no information that identifies it specifically.

- By drawing on general knowledge

   The earth revolves around <u>the</u> sun.

   Here, *the* is used with the nouns *earth* and *sun* because readers are expected to know which particular things the writer is referring to.

   In the following cases, *the* is always used rather than *a* or *an*.

For information on the superlative forms of adjectives and adverbs, see 29B.

- Before the word *same: the same day*
- Before the superlative form of an adjective: *the youngest son*
- Before a number indicating order or sequence: *the third time*

Indefinite Articles

When an indefinite article is used with a noun, the writer is saying to readers, "I don't expect you to have enough information right now to identify a particular thing that I have in mind. I do expect you to recognize that I'm referring to only one item."

Consider the following sentences.

We need <u>a</u> table for our computer.

I have <u>a</u> folding table; maybe you can use that.

In the first sentence, the writer has a hypothetical table, but no actual one, in mind. Since the table is indefinite to the writer, it is clearly indefinite to the reader, so *a* is used, not *the*. The second sentence refers to an actual table, but because the writer does not expect the reader to be able to identify the table specifically, it is also used with *a* rather than *the*.

FOCUS **Indefinite Articles**

Unlike the definite article, the indefinite articles *a* and *an* occur only with singular count nouns. *A* is used when the next sound is a consonant, and *an* is used when the next sound is a vowel. In choosing *a* or *an*, pay attention to sounds rather than to spelling: *a house, a year, a union,* but *an hour, an uncle.*

No Article

For more on count and non-count nouns, see 30D.

Only noncount and plural count nouns can stand without articles: *butter, sweet chocolate, cookies, fresh strawberries,* but *a cookie* or *the fresh strawberry.*

Nouns without articles can be used to make generalizations.

<u>Infants</u> need <u>affection</u> as well as <u>food</u>.

Here, the absence of articles before the nouns *infants, affection,* and *food* indicates that the statement is not about particular infants, affection, or food but about infants, affection, and food in general. Remember not to use *the* in such sentences; in English, a sentence like *The infants need affection as well as food* can refer to only particular, identifiable infants, not infants in general.

Articles with Proper Nouns

Proper nouns split into two classes: names that take *the* and names that take no article.

For more on proper nouns, see 33A.

- Names of people usually take no article unless they are used in the plural to refer to members of a family, in which case they take *the: Napoleon, Mahatma Gandhi,* but *the Kennedys.*
- Names of places that are plural in form usually take *the: the Andes, the United States.*
- The names of most places on land (cities, states, provinces, and countries) take no article: *Salt Lake City, Mississippi, Alberta, Japan.* The names of most bodies of water (rivers, seas, and oceans, though not lakes or bays) take *the: the Mississippi, the Mediterranean, the Pacific,* but *Lake Erie* and *San Francisco Bay.*
- Names of streets take no article: *Main Street.* Names of highways take *the: the Belt Parkway.*

■ WRITING FIRST: Flashback

Look back at your response to the Writing First exercise on page 400. Circle each definite article *(the)* and indefinite article *(a* or *an)* you have used. Have you used articles correctly? Correct any errors you find.

G Forming Negative Statements and Questions

Negative Statements

To form a negative statement, add the word *not* directly after the first helping verb of the complete verb.

For more on helping verbs, see 15C.

Global warming has been getting worse.

Global warming has <u>not</u> been getting worse.

When there is no helping verb, a form of the verb *do* must be inserted before *not*.

> Automobile traffic contributes to pollution.

> Automobile traffic <u>does not</u> contribute to pollution.

Questions

To form a question, move the helping verb that follows the subject to the position directly before the subject.

> The governor <u>is</u> trying to compromise.

> <u>Is</u> the governor trying to compromise?

> The governor <u>is</u> working on the budget.

> What <u>is</u> the governor working on?

As with negatives, when the verb does not include a helping verb, you must supply a form of *do*. To form a question, put *do* directly before the subject.

> The governor <u>works</u> hard.

> <u>Does</u> the governor <u>work</u> hard?

For information on subject-verb agreement with the verb do, see 23B.

Remember that when *do* is used as a helping verb, no other helping verb is allowed. Furthermore, the form of *do* used must match the tense and number of the original main verb. Note that the main verb loses its tense and appears in the base form.

> INCORRECT Automobile traffic <u>does</u> not <u>contributes</u> to pollution.

> CORRECT Automobile traffic <u>does</u> not <u>contribute</u> to pollution.

A helping verb never comes before the subject if the subject is a question word or contains a question word.

> <u>Who</u> is talking to the governor?

> <u>Which</u> bills have been vetoed by the governor?

■ WRITING FIRST: Flashback

Look back at your response to the Writing First exercise on page 400. Do you see any negative statements? If so, check to make sure you have formed them correctly. Then, on the lines below, write a question that you could add to your Writing First exercise.

Question: _____

_____

Check carefully to make sure you have formed the question correctly.

H Indicating Verb Tense

In English, a verb's form must always indicate when the action referred to by the verb took place (for instance, in the past or in the present). Use the appropriate tense of the verb, even if the time is obvious or if the sentence includes other indications of time (such as *two years ago* or *at present*).

For more on verb tense, see Chapters 26 and 27.

CORRECT   Yesterday, I <u>got</u> a letter from my sister Yunpi.

INCORRECT   Yesterday, I <u>get</u> a letter from my sister Yunpi.

■ WRITING FIRST: Flashback

Look back at your response to the Writing First exercise on page 400. Are all your verbs in the present tense? Correct any errors you find.

I Recognizing Stative Verbs

Stative verbs usually tell us that someone or something is in a state that will not change, at least for a while.

Hiro <u>knows</u> American history backward and forward.

The **present progressive** tense consists of the present tense of *be* plus the present participle *(I am going)*. The **past progressive** tense consists of the past tense of *be* plus the present participle *(I was going)*. Most English verbs show action, and these action verbs can be used in the progressive tenses without restriction. Stative verbs, however, are rarely used in the progressive tenses.

INCORRECT   Hiro <u>is knowing</u> American history backward and forward.

FOCUS   **Stative Verbs**

Verbs that are stative, at least for some of their meanings, often refer to mental states like *know, understand, think, believe, want, like, love,* and *hate.* Other stative verbs include *be, have, need, own, belong, weigh, cost,* and *mean.* Certain verbs of sense perception, like *see* and *hear,* are also stative even though they can refer to momentary events rather than states.

Many verbs have more than one meaning, and some of these verbs are active with one meaning but stative with another. An example is the verb *weigh*.

ACTIVE   The butcher <u>is weighing</u> the meat.

STATIVE   The meat <u>weighs</u> three pounds.

In the first sentence above, the verb *weigh* means "to put on a scale"; it is active, not stative, as the use of the progressive shows. In the second sentence, however, the same verb means "to have weight," so it is stative, not active. It would be unacceptable to say, "The meat is weighing three pounds."

■ WRITING FIRST: Flashback

Look back at your response to the Writing First exercise on page 400. Can you identify any stative verbs? If so, list them here.

Stative verbs: _____ _____ _____

_____ _____ _____

Check carefully to be sure you have not used any of these verbs in a progressive tense. Correct any errors you find.

J   Placing Adjectives in Order

Adjectives and other modifiers that come before a noun usually follow a set order. In some cases, a specific position for a modifier is required; in others, a certain position may be preferred but is not required.

Required Order

For more on determiners, see 30E.

■ Determiners always come first in a series of adjectives: *these fragile glasses*. The determiners *all* or *both* always precede any other determiners: *all these glasses*.

■ If one of the modifiers is a noun, it must come directly before the noun it modifies: *these wine glasses*.

■ All other adjectives are placed between the determiners and the noun modifiers: *these fragile wine glasses*. If there are two or more of these adjectives, the following order is preferred.

Preferred Order

■ Adjectives that show the writer's attitude generally precede adjectives that merely describe: *these lovely fragile wine glasses*.

■ Adjectives that indicate size generally come early: *these lovely large fragile wine glasses.*

■ Most other adjectives are placed in the middle.

■ WRITING FIRST: Flashback

Look back at your response to the Writing First exercise on page 400. Have you used several adjectives before a single noun? If so, list here all the adjectives and the noun that follows them.

Adjectives: _____ _____ _____ Noun: _____

Adjectives: _____ _____ _____ Noun: _____

Have you arranged the adjectives in the correct order? Make any necessary corrections.

K Choosing Correct Prepositions

The prepositions *in, on,* and *at* sometimes cause problems for nonnative speakers of English. For example, to identify the location of a place or an event, you can use *in, on,* or *at.*

The preposition *at* specifies an exact point in space or time.

Please leave the package with the janitor <u>at</u> 150 South Street. I'll pick it up <u>at</u> 7:30 tonight.

Expanses of space or time are treated as containers and therefore require *in.*

Jean-Pierre went to school <u>in</u> the 1970s.

On must be used in two cases: with names of streets (but not with exact addresses) and with days of the week or month.

We'll move into our new office <u>on</u> 18th Street either <u>on</u> Monday or <u>on</u> March 12.

L Using Prepositions in Familiar Expressions

Many familiar expressions end with prepositions. Learning to write clearly and *idiomatically*—in keeping with the conventions of written English—means learning which preposition is used in each expression.

The sentences that follow illustrate idiomatic use of prepositions in various expressions. Note that sometimes different prepositions are used with the same word. For example, both *on* and *for* can be used with *wait* to form two different expressions with two different meanings (*He waited on their table; she waited for the bus).* **Which preposition you choose depends on your meaning. (Pairs of similar expressions that end with different prepositions are bracketed.)**

Expression with Preposition	*Sample Sentence*
acquainted with	It took the family several weeks to become <u>acquainted with</u> their new neighbors.
addicted to	I think Abby is becoming <u>addicted to</u> pretzels.
agree on (a plan or objective)	It is vital that all members of the school board <u>agree on</u> goals for the coming year.
agree to (a proposal)	Striking workers finally <u>agreed to</u> the terms of management's offer.
angry about or at (a situation)	Taxpayers are understandably <u>angry about</u> (or <u>at</u>) the deterioration of city recreation facilities.
angry with (a person)	When the mayor refused to hire more police officers, his constituents became <u>angry with</u> him.
approve of	Amy's adviser <u>approved of</u> her decision to study in Guatemala.
bored with	Just when Michael was getting <u>bored with</u> his life, he met Sharon.
capable of	Dogs may be able to fetch and roll over, but they certainly aren't <u>capable of</u> complex reasoning.
consist of	The deluxe fruit basket <u>consisted of</u> five pathetic pears, two tiny apples, a few limp bunches of grapes, and one lonely kiwi.
contrast with	Coach Headley's relaxed style <u>contrasts with</u> the previous coach's more formal approach.
convenient for	The proposed location of the new day-care center is <u>convenient for</u> many families.
deal with	Many parents and educators believe it is possible to <u>deal with</u> the special needs of autistic children in a regular classroom.
depend on	Children <u>depend on</u> their parents for emotional as well as financial support.
differ from (something else)	The music of Boyz II Men <u>differs from</u> the music of The Fugees.
differ with (someone else)	I strongly <u>differ with</u> your interpretation of my dream about *The Wizard of Oz.*
emigrate from	My grandfather and his brother <u>emigrated from</u> the part of Russia that is now Ukraine.

grateful for (a favor)	If you can arrange an interview next week, I will be very grateful for your time and trouble.
grateful to (someone)	Jerry Garcia was always grateful to his loyal fans.
immigrate to	Many Cubans want to leave their country and immigrate to the United States.
impatient with	Keshia often gets impatient with her four younger brothers.
interested in	Diana, who was not very interested in the discussion of the Treaty of Versailles, stared out the window.
interfere with	Sometimes it's hard to resist the temptation to interfere with a friend's life.
meet with	I hope I can meet with you soon to discuss my research paper.
object to	The defense attorney objected to the prosecutor's treatment of the witness.
pleased with	Marta was very pleased with Eric's favorable critique of her speech.
protect against	Nobel Prize winner Linus Pauling believed that large doses of vitamin C could protect people against the common cold.
reason with	When a two-year-old is having a tantrum, it's nearly impossible to reason with her.
reply to	If no one replies to our ad within two weeks, we will advertise again.
responsible for	Parents are not responsible for the debts of their adult children.
similar to	The blood sample found at the crime scene was remarkably similar to one found in the suspect's residence.
specialize in	Dr. Casullo is a dentist who specializes in periodontal surgery.
succeed in	Lisa hoped her M.B.A. would help her succeed in a business career.
take advantage of	Some consumer laws are designed to prevent door-to-door salespeople from taking advantage of gullible buyers.
wait for (something to happen)	Snow White sang while she waited for her prince to arrive.
wait on (in a restaurant)	We sat at the table for twenty minutes before someone waited on us.
worry about	Why worry about things you can't change?

■ WRITING FIRST: Flashback

Look back at your response to the Writing First exercise on page 400. Have you used any of the idiomatic expressions listed on pages 412–13? If so, bracket each expression. Have you used the correct prepositions? Make any necessary corrections.

M Using Prepositions in Two-Word Verbs

Some two-word verbs consist of a verb and a preposition. In such cases, the preposition comes immediately after the verb. In the following sentence, *at* functions as a preposition because it introduces the prepositional phrase *at the video monitor;* therefore, *at* must directly follow the verb.

> CORRECT Please <u>look at</u> the video monitor.
>
> INCORRECT Please <u>look</u> the video monitor <u>at</u>.

In other two-word verbs, however, the second word is not a preposition; it is part of the verb. In the following pair of sentences, *off,* the second word of the two-word verb, does not introduce a prepositional phrase. Because the object is a noun *(printer),* the second word of such a verb can come either before the object of that verb or after the object.

> CORRECT Please <u>turn off</u> the printer.
>
> CORRECT Please <u>turn</u> the printer <u>off</u>.

When the object is a pronoun, however, the two-word verb must be split, and the pronoun must come between the two parts.

> CORRECT Please <u>turn</u> it <u>off</u>.
>
> INCORRECT Please <u>turn off</u> it.

Other examples of two-word verbs in which the second word does not function as a preposition include *take (it) down, put (it) on, let (it) out,* and *make (it) up.*

■ WRITING FIRST: Flashback

Look back at your response to the Writing First exercise on page 400. Have you used any two-word verbs? If so, list them here.

_____

_____

Have you placed the second word correctly in each case? Make any necessary corrections.

■ WRITING FIRST: Revising and Editing

Look back at your response to the Writing First exercise on page
400. Then, review all your Flashback exercises, and be sure you
have made all necessary corrections in grammar and usage. When
you have finished, add any additional transitional words and
phrases you need to make the process you have explained clear to
your readers.

CHAPTER REVIEW

◆ EDITING PRACTICE

Read the following student essay, into which errors in use of articles and
errors in idiomatic expressions with prepositions have been introduced.
Check each underlined phrase. If an article or preposition is not used
idiomatically, cross it out, and write the correct word above the line. If it
is correct, write C above it. The first sentence has been edited for you.

                    History and Myth
                                        about C
    In 1935, the United States was worrying ~~with~~ a serious

economic depression. Rather than write an history that

dealt in the grim events around her, Laura Ingalls Wilder

chose to write *Little House on the Prairie*, a book about a

time in history similar with the tough days of the 1930s.

Written as an novel, the book consists in many historical

details of the Ingalls family's life. Like most history, it

is part fact and part myth.

    In the late nineteenth century, the Homestead Act

offered a adult 160 acres, provided that person would live

on the land for at least five years. Some, like Wilder's

father Charles Ingalls, took advantage for the offer and

emigrated from the East. The Ingalls family settled on land

that was Indian territory, hoping the government would dis-

place the Indians. However, the government interfered in

this plan, making farmers like Mr. Ingalls relocate. This

is fact.

At the beginning of Chapter 15 of *Little House*, Wilder casually mentions the presence of mosquitoes. Later in the chapter, she describes the Ingalls family as sick in bed. No one at the time knew why they were sick, but Wilder, looking back on their illness and acquainted to later medical research, notes that the fever was actually malaria, whose spread depended of mosquitoes. The mosquitoes Wilder discusses are also based in historical fact.

Other details also seem accurate. For example, the children are very grateful for their father when he gives them the penny; this makes sense because very little currency was actually in circulation in the 1870s. Mr. Ingalls seldom purchases goods for money. More often, he and a neighbor agree with a deal by which he trades his services as payment, helping to build a house or dig a well in exchange for something the family needs.

Despite its many facts, much of *Little House* differs with the reality of prairie life. In a book, everything always turns out for the best. Wilder omits many of her family's more negative experiences. The book contrasts to reality in that the family's life is never violent or tragic, and the settlers never seem to be in real danger. By omitting the bleakness and tragedy of her family's life, Laura Ingalls Wilder succeeded on turning history into myth.

◆ COLLABORATIVE ACTIVITIES

1. Working in a small group, make a list of ten prepositional phrases that include the prepositions *above, around, at, between, from, in, on, over, under,* and *with.* Use specific nouns as objects of these prepositions, and use as many modifying words as you wish. (Try, for example, to write something like *above their hideously unflattering wedding portrait,* not just *above the picture.*)

2. Exchange lists with another group. Still working collaboratively, compose a list of ten sentences—one that includes each of the other group's ten prepositional phrases. Give your list of ten sentences to another group.

3. Working with this new list of ten sentences, substitute a different prepositional phrase for each one that appears in a sentence. Make sure each sentence still makes sense.

✔ REVIEW CHECKLIST:
Grammar and Usage Issues for ESL Writers

- In almost all cases, English sentences must state their subjects. (See 30A and 30B.)

- In English, most nouns add -s to form plurals. Always use a form that indicates explicitly that a noun is plural. (See 30C.)

- English nouns may be count nouns or noncount nouns. A count noun names a distinct individual thing or a group of distinct individual things (a teacher, oceans). A noncount noun names something that cannot be counted (gold, sand). (See 30D.)

- Determiners are adjectives that identify rather than describe the nouns they modify. Determiners may also indicate amount or number. (See 30E.)

- The definite article the and the indefinite articles a and an are determiners that indicate whether the noun that follows is one readers can identify (the book) or one they cannot yet identify (a book). (See 30F.)

- To form a negative statement, add the word not directly after the first helping verb of the complete verb. To form a question, move the helping verb that follows the subject to the position directly before the subject. (See 30G.)

- A verb's form must indicate when the action referred to by the verb took place. (See 30H.)

- Stative verbs indicate that someone or something is in a state that will not change, at least for a while. Stative verbs are rarely used in the progressive tenses. (See 30I.)

- Adjectives and other modifiers that come before a noun usually follow a set order. (See 30J.)

- The prepositions in, on, and at sometimes cause problems for nonnative speakers of English. (See 30K.)

- Many familiar expressions end with prepositions. (See 30L.)

- When a preposition is part of a two-word verb, it comes immediately after the verb. (See 30M.)

UNIT SEVEN

Understanding Punctuation, Mechanics, and Spelling

Using Commas

■ WRITING FIRST

Describe an ideal public housing complex for low-income families. Where should it be located? What kinds of buildings should be constructed? What facilities and services should be offered to residents?

A **comma** is a punctuation mark that separates words or groups of words within sentences. In this way, commas keep ideas distinct from one another. In earlier chapters, you learned to use a comma between two independent clauses linked by a coordinating conjunction (16A) and to use a comma after a dependent clause that comes before an independent clause (17A). Commas have several other uses, as you will learn in this chapter.

A Using Commas in a Series

Use commas to separate elements in a **series** of three or more words or word groups.

<u>Leyla</u>, <u>Zack</u>, and <u>Kathleen</u> campaigned for Representative Fattah.

<u>Leyla</u>, <u>Zack</u>, or <u>Kathleen</u> will be elected president of Students for Fattah.

Leyla <u>made phone calls</u>, <u>licked envelopes</u>, and <u>ran errands</u> for the campaign.

<u>Leyla is president</u>, <u>Zack is vice-president</u>, and <u>Kathleen is treasurer</u>.

▼ **Student Voices**
I always feel as if I put too many commas in my writing.
Felicia May

421

> **FOCUS** **Using Commas in a Series**
>
> Although the comma before the coordinating conjunction in a series
> of three or more items is usually omitted in newspaper and maga-
> zine writing, your writing will be clearer if you use a comma before
> the coordinating conjunction.
>
> Leyla, Zack‚ and Kathleen worked on the campaign.
>
> Don't use *any* commas, however, if all the items in a series are sepa-
> rated by coordinating conjunctions.
>
> Leyla or Zack or Kathleen will be elected president of Stu-
> dents for Fattah.

◆ PRACTICE 31-1

Edit the following sentences for the use of commas in a series. If the sentence is correct, write *C* in the blank.

Examples

Costa Rica produces bananas, cocoa, and sugar cane. __C__

The pool rules state that there is no running/ or jumping/ or diving.

____

1. A triple-threat musician, he plays guitar bass and drums. ____

2. The organization's goals are feeding the hungry, housing the homeless
   and helping the unemployed find work. ____

3. *The Price Is Right, Let's Make a Deal,* and *Jeopardy!* are three of the
   longest-running game shows in television history. ____

4. In native Hawaiian culture, yellow was the color worn by the royalty
   red was worn by priests and a mixture of the two colors was worn by
   others of high rank. ____

5. The remarkable diary kept by young Anne Frank while her family was
   in hiding from the Nazis is insightful, touching and sometimes humorous. ____

6. A standard bookcase is sixty inches tall forty-eight inches wide and
   twelve inches deep.

7. Most coffins manufactured in the United States are lined with bronze, or copper, or lead. ____

8. Young handsome and sensitive, Leonardo DiCaprio was the 1990s answer to the 1950s actor James Dean. ____

9. California's capital is Sacramento, its largest city is Los Angeles and its oldest settlement is San Diego. ____

10. Watching television, playing video games, and riding his bicycle are the average ten-year-old boy's favorite pastimes. ____

■ WRITING FIRST: Flashback

Look back at your response to the Writing First exercise on page 421. If you have included a series of three or more words or word groups in any of your sentences, copy it here. Did you use commas correctly to separate elements in the series? If not, correct your punctuation.

_____

_____

B   **Using Commas to Set Off Introductory Phrases, Conjunctive Adverbs, and Transitional Expressions**

Use a comma to set off an introductory phrase from the rest of the sentence.

> <u>In the event of a fire</u>, proceed to the nearest exit.
>
> <u>Walking home</u>, Nelida decided to change her major.
>
> <u>To keep fit</u>, people should try to exercise regularly.

Also use commas to set off conjunctive adverbs or transitional expressions whether they appear at the beginning, in the middle, or at the end of a sentence.

> <u>In fact</u>, Thoreau spent only one night in jail.
>
> He was, <u>of course</u>, bailed out by a friend.
>
> He did spend more than two years at Walden Pond, <u>however</u>.

For lists of conjunctive adverbs and transitional expressions, see 16C.

● **Writing Tip**
A conjunctive adverb or transitional expression that joins two complete sentences requires a semicolon and a comma: *Thoreau spent only one night in jail; however, he spent more than two years at Walden Pond.*

◆ **PRACTICE 31-2**

Edit the following sentences for the use of commas with introductory phrases. If the sentence is correct, write *C* in the blank.

Examples

From professional athletes to teenagers, people have begun to find alternatives to steroids. _____

Regulated by the Drug Enforcement Administration, steroids are a controlled substance and can be obtained only illegally. __C__

(1) During the 1992 Summer Olympics in Barcelona two American athletes and several athletes from other countries were sent home because they tested positive for banned drugs. _____ (2) To the surprise of many fans these drugs were not steroids. _____ (3) For the first time, athletes were accused of taking a drug for animals called clenabutal. _____ (4) In addition to clenabutal the poison strychnine showed up in one athlete's bloodstream. _____ (5) Banned by the rules of the Olympics these drugs still appeal to athletes because they supposedly enhance performance. _____ (6) Because of the laws prohibiting steroids many athletes are now turning to these and other unregulated substances. _____ (7) Often called dietary supplements these alternative chemicals are claimed to enhance athletic performance in the same way steroids supposedly do. _____ (8) According to the *Journal of the American Medical Association* these dietary supplements do no such thing. _____ (9) Instead of enhancing performance they often cause considerable damage to the body. _____ (10) Over the course of the last few years investigators have collected more than three thousand samples of such products sold on the black market. _____

◆ PRACTICE 31-3

Edit the following sentences for the use of commas with conjunctive adverbs and transitional expressions. If the sentence is correct, write *C* in the blank.

Example: Some holidays, of course, are fairly new.

(1) For example the African-American celebration of Kwanzaa is less than forty years old. _____ (2) This holiday to remind us of important

African traditions has, however attracted many celebrants over its short life. _____ (3) By the way the word *Kwanzaa* means "first fruits" in Swahili. _____ (4) In other words, Kwanzaa stands for renewal. _____ (5) This can in fact be demonstrated in some of the seven principles of Kwanzaa. _____ (6) Kwanzaa is, after all celebrated over seven days to focus on each of these seven principles. _____ (7) The focus first of all is on unity *(umoja)*. _____ (8) Also Kwanzaa focuses on personal self-determination *(kujichagulia)*. _____ (9) In addition Kwanzaa celebrations emphasize three kinds of community responsibility *(ujima, ujamaa,* and *nia)*. _____ (10) The other principles of Kwanzaa are creativity *(kuumba)* and finally, faith *(imani)*. _____

■ WRITING FIRST: Flashback

Look back at your response to the Writing First exercise on page 421. Underline any introductory phrases, conjunctive adverbs, or transitional expressions. Have you set off each of these with commas when appropriate? Revise any incorrect sentences here, adding commas where needed.

_____

_____

_____

_____

C Using Commas with Appositives

Use commas to set off an **appositive**—a word or word group that identifies, describes, or renames a noun or pronoun.

I have visited only one country, <u>Canada</u>, outside the United States.
Carlos Santana, <u>leader of the group Santana</u>, played at Woodstock in 1969.

FOCUS **Using Commas with Appositives**

An appositive is always set off by commas, whether it falls at the beginning, in the middle, or at the end of a sentence.

A dreamer, he spent his life thinking about what he could not have.

He always wanted to build a house, a big white one, overlooking the ocean.

He finally built his dream house, a log cabin.

◆ **PRACTICE 31-4**

Edit the following sentences for the correct use of commas to set off appositives. If the sentence is correct, write *C* in the blank.

Examples

The Buccaneers haven't joined the Cheese League, the group of NFL teams that holds summer training in Wisconsin. _____

William Filene, the Boston merchant who founded Filene's department store, invented the "bargain basement." _____

1. Traditional Chinese medicine is based on meridians channels of energy believed to run in regular patterns through the body. _____

2. Acupuncture the insertion of thin needles at precise points in the body, stimulates these meridians. _____

3. Herbal medicine the basis of many Chinese healing techniques requires twelve years of study. _____

4. Gary Larson, creator of the popular *Far Side* cartoons ended the series in 1995. _____

5. A musician at heart, Larson has said he wants to spend more time practicing the guitar. _____

6. *Far Side* calendars and other product tie-ins have earned $500 million a lot of money for guitar lessons. _____

7. Nigeria the most populous country in Africa is also one of the fastest-growing nations in the world. _____

8. On the southwest coast of Nigeria lies Lagos a major port. _____

9. The Yoruban people the Nigerian settlers of Lagos, are unusual in Africa because they tend to form large urban communities. _____

10. A predominantly Christian people the Yoruba have incorporated many native religious rituals into their practice of Christianity. _____

■ WRITING FIRST: Flashback

Look back at your response to the Writing First exercise on page 421. Have you used any appositives? Underline each one. Have you set off appositives with commas? Revise any incorrect sentences here.

_____

_____

_____

_____

D   Using Commas to Set Off Nonrestrictive Clauses

Use commas to set off **nonrestrictive clauses**, clauses that do not add essential information to a sentence.

A **restrictive** clause is necessary to the meaning of the sentence; therefore, a restrictive clause is *not* set off from the rest of the sentence by commas.

Many rock stars who recorded hits in the 1950s made little money from their songs.

In the sentence above, the clause *who recorded hits in the 1950s* supplies specific information that is essential to the meaning of the sentence: it tells readers which group of rock stars made little money. Eliminating the clause changes the sentence's meaning.

Many rock stars made little money from their songs.

A **nonrestrictive** clause is *not* necessary to the meaning of the sentence; therefore, a nonrestrictive clause *is* set off from the rest of the sentence by commas.

Telephone calling-card fraud, which cost consumers and phone companies four billion dollars last year, is increasing.

Here, the underlined clause provides extra information to help readers understand the sentence, but the sentence communicates the same point without this information.

Telephone calling-card fraud is increasing.

FOCUS *Who, Which, and That*

- *Who* can introduce either a restrictive or a nonrestrictive clause.

  RESTRICTIVE Many parents <u>who work</u> feel a lot of stress. (no commas)

  NONRESTRICTIVE Both of my parents, <u>who have always wanted the best for their children</u>, have worked two jobs for years. (set off by commas)

- *Which* always introduces a nonrestrictive clause.

  The job, <u>which had excellent benefits</u>, did not pay well.

- *That* always introduces a restrictive clause.

  He accepted the job <u>that had the best benefits</u>.

◆ **PRACTICE 31-5**

Edit the following sentences so that commas set off all nonrestrictive clauses. (Remember, commas are *not* used to set off restrictive clauses.) If a sentence is correct, write *C* in the blank.

Example: An Alaska museum exhibition that celebrates the Alaska highway has rescued the story of its construction. __*C*__

(1) During the 1940s, a group of African-American soldiers who defied the forces of nature and human prejudice were shipped to Alaska. ____ (2) They built the Alaska highway which stretches twelve hundred miles across Alaska. ____ (3) The African-American troops who worked on the highway have received little attention in most historical accounts. ____ (4) Fifty years later, the men who worked on the road have been remembered. ____ (5) The highway which cut through some of the roughest terrain in the world was begun in 1942. ____ (6) The Japanese had just

landed in the Aleutian Islands which lay west of the tip of the Alaska Peninsula. _____ (7) Military officials, who oversaw the project, doubted the ability of African-American troops. _____ (8) As a result, they made the African-American troops work under conditions, that made construction difficult. _____ (9) The African-American troops who worked on the road proved their commanders wrong by finishing the highway months ahead of schedule. _____ (10) In one case, white engineers, who surveyed a river, said it would take two weeks to bridge. _____ (11) To the engineers' surprise, the African-American soldiers who worked on the project beat the estimate by half a day. _____ (12) A military report that was issued in 1945 praised them. _____ (13) It said the goals that the black regiments achieved would be remembered through the ages. _____

■ WRITING FIRST: Flashback

Look back at your response to the Writing First exercise on page 421. Make sure you have included commas to set off nonrestrictive clauses and have *not* set off restrictive elements with commas.

E　Using Commas in Dates and Addresses

Use commas in dates to separate the day of the week from the month and the day of the month from the year.

> The first Cinco de Mayo we celebrated in the United States was Tuesday, May 5, 1998.

When a date that includes commas falls in the middle of a sentence, place a comma after the date.

> Tuesday, May 5, 1998, was the first Cinco de Mayo we celebrated in the United States.

Use commas in addresses to separate the street address from the city and the city from the state or country.

> The office of the famous fictional detective Sherlock Holmes was located at 221b Baker Street, London, England.

● **Writing Tip**
Do not use commas between a month and the number of the day (*May 5*) or year (*May 1998*).

● **Writing Tip**
In addresses, don't use a comma between the building number and the street name.

When an address that includes commas falls in the middle of a sentence, place a comma after the state or country.

> The office at 221b Baker Street, London, England, belonged to the famous fictional detective Sherlock Holmes.

◆ PRACTICE 31-6

Edit the following sentences for the correct use of commas in dates and addresses. Add any missing commas, and cross out any unnecessary commas. If the sentence is correct, write *C* in the blank.

Examples

June 3, 1968, is the day my parents were married. _____

Their wedding took place in Santiago, Chile. _____

1. The American Declaration of Independence was approved on July 4 1776. _____

2. The Pelican Man's Bird Sanctuary is located at 1705 Ken Thompson Parkway, Sarasota Florida. _____

3. At 175 Carlton Avenue Brooklyn New York is the house where Richard Wright began writing *Native Son*. _____

4. I found this information in the February 12, 1994 issue of the *New York Times*. _____

5. The Mexican hero Father Miguel Hidalgo y Costilla was shot by a firing squad on June 30, 1811. _____

6. The Palacio de Gobierno at Plaza de Armas, Guadalajara, Mexico houses a mural of the famous revolutionary. _____

7. The Pueblo Grande Museum is located at 1469 East Washington Street Phoenix Arizona. _____

8. Brigham Young led the first settlers into the valley that is now Salt Lake City, Utah, in July, 1847. _____

9. St. Louis Missouri was the birthplace of writer Maya Angelou, but she spent most of her childhood in Stamps Arkansas. _____

10. Some records list the actress's birthday as May 19 1928 while others indicate she was born on May 20 1924. _____

FOCUS Unnecessary Commas

Do not use commas in the following situations.

■ Before the first item in a series

  INCORRECT *Duck Soup* starred, Groucho, Chico, and Harpo Marx.

  CORRECT *Duck Soup* starred Groucho, Chico, and Harpo Marx.

Writing Tip
Use commas between items in a series. (See 31A.)

■ After the last item in a series

  INCORRECT Groucho, Chico, and Harpo Marx, starred in *Duck Soup*.

  CORRECT Groucho, Chico, and Harpo Marx starred in *Duck Soup*.

■ Between a subject and a verb

  INCORRECT Students and their teachers, should try to respect one another.

  CORRECT Students and their teachers should try to respect one another.

■ Before the coordinating conjunction that separates the two parts of a compound verb

  INCORRECT The transit workers voted to strike, and walked off the job.

  CORRECT The transit workers voted to strike and walked off the job.

Writing Tip
Use a comma before a coordinating conjunction that links independent clauses in a compound sentence. (See 16A.)

■ Before the coordinating conjunction that separates the two parts of a compound subject

  INCORRECT The transit workers, and the sanitation workers voted to strike.

  CORRECT The transit workers and the sanitation workers voted to strike.

■ To set off a restrictive clause

  INCORRECT People, who live in glass houses, shouldn't throw stones.

  CORRECT People who live in glass houses shouldn't throw stones.

Writing Tip
Use commas to set off a non-restrictive clause. (See 31D.)

■ Before a dependent clause that follows an independent clause

  INCORRECT He was exhausted, because he had driven all night.

  CORRECT He was exhausted because he had driven all night.

Writing Tip
Use a comma after a dependent clause that precedes an independent clause.

■ WRITING FIRST: Revising and Editing

Look back at your response to the Writing First exercise on page 421.
Then, revise your paragraph by making the following additions.

1. Add a sentence that includes a series of three or more words or
   word groups.
2. Add introductory phrases to two of your sentences.
3. Add an appositive to one of your sentences.
4. Add a transitional word or expression to one of your sentences.
5. Add a nonrestrictive clause to one of your sentences.

When you have made all the additions, reread your paragraph to
check your use of commas with the new material.

CHAPTER REVIEW

◆ EDITING PRACTICE

Read the following student essay, from which some commas have been
intentionally deleted. Add commas where necessary between items in a
series and with introductory phrases, conjunctive adverbs or transitional
expressions, appositives, and nonrestrictive clauses. Cross out any unnecessary commas. The first sentence has been edited for you.

Brave Orchid

One of the most important characters in The Woman

Warrior, Maxine Hong Kingston's autobiographical work, is

Brave Orchid, Kingston's mother. Brave Orchid, a complex

character is an imaginative storyteller, who tells vivid

tales of China. A quiet woman she still impresses her

medical school classmates with her intelligence. She is

also a traditional woman. However she will stop at nothing

to make her family exactly what she wants it to be. Brave

Orchid strongly believes in herself; even so, she sees

herself as a failure.

In her native China Brave Orchid trains to be a doc-

tor. The other women in her class envy her independence

brilliance and courage. One day Brave Orchid proves her courageousness by confronting the Fox Spirit, and telling him he will not win. First of all she tells him she can endure any pain that he inflicts on her. Next she gathers together the women in the dormitory to burn the ghost away. After this event the other women admire her even more.

Working hard Brave Orchid becomes a successful doctor in China. After coming to America however she cannot work as a doctor because she does not speak English. Instead she works in a Chinese laundry, and picks tomatoes. None of her medical school classmates could have imagined this outcome. During her later years in America Brave Orchid becomes a woman, who is overbearing and domineering. We see another side of her at this point in the book. She bosses her children around, she tries to ruin her sister's life and she criticizes everyone and everything around her. Her daughter, a straight-A student is the object of her worst criticism.

Brave Orchid's intentions are good. Nevertheless she devotes her energy to the wrong things. She wants the people, around her, to be as strong as she is. Because she bullies them however she eventually loses them. In addition she is too busy noticing her daughter's faults to see all her accomplishments. Brave Orchid an independent woman and a brilliant student never reaches her goals. She is hard on the people around her because she is in fact disappointed in herself.

◆ COLLABORATIVE ACTIVITIES

1. Bring a homemaking, sports, or fashion magazine to class. Working in a small group, look at the people pictured in the ads. In what roles are men most often depicted? In what roles are women most often presented? Identify the three or four most common roles for each sex, and give each kind of character a descriptive name—*jock* or *mother,* for example.

2. Working on your own, choose one type of character from the list your group made in the preceding activity. Write a paragraph in which you

describe this character's typical appearance and habits. Refer to the appropriate magazine pictures to support your characterization.

3. Collaborating with other members of your group, write two paragraphs, one discussing how men are portrayed in ads and one discussing how women are portrayed.

4. Circle every comma in the paragraph you wrote for Collaborative Activity 2. Work with your group to explain why each comma is used. If no one in your group can justify a particular comma's use, cross it out.

☑ **REVIEW CHECKLIST:**
Using Commas

- Use commas to separate elements in a series of three or more words or word groups. (See 31A.)

- Use commas to set off introductory phrases, conjunctive adverbs, and transitional expressions from the rest of the sentence. (See 31B.)

- Use commas to set off an appositive from the rest of the sentence. (See 31C.)

- Use commas to set off nonrestrictive clauses. (See 31D.)

- Use commas to separate parts of dates and addresses. (See 31E.)

- Avoid unnecessary commas. (See 31E.)

Using Apostrophes

PREVIEW

In this chapter, you will learn

■ to use apostrophes to form contractions (32A)

■ to use apostrophes to form possessives (32B)

■ to revise incorrect use of apostrophes (32C)

■ **WRITING FIRST**

Certain household tasks have traditionally been considered "men's work," and others have been considered "women's work." Although the family, like the workplace, has changed considerably in recent years, some habits and behavior patterns have remained the same. Discuss any tasks that are considered "men's work" and "women's work" in your household. Be sure to give examples of the responsibilities of different family members.

An **apostrophe** is a punctuation mark that is used in contractions and in possessive forms of nouns and indefinite pronouns.

A   Using Apostrophes to Form Contractions

A **contraction** uses an apostrophe to combine two words. The apostrophe takes the place of the omitted letters.

I <u>didn't</u> *(did not)* realize how late it was.

<u>It's</u> *(it is)* not right for cheaters to go unpunished.

Frequently Used Contractions

I + am = I'm	are + not = aren't
we + are = we're	can + not = can't
you + are = you're	do + not = don't
it + is = it's	will + not = won't
I + have = I've	should + not = shouldn't

(continued on the following page)

● **Writing Tip**
Even though contractions are used in speech and informal writing, they are not acceptable in most business or college writing situations.

435

(continued from the previous page)

I + will = I'll	let + us = let's
there + is = there's	that + is = that's
is + not = isn't	who + is = who's

◆ **PRACTICE 32-1**

In the following sentences, add apostrophes to contractions if needed. If the sentence is correct, write *C* in the blank.

Example: If you ~~dont~~ *don't* eat healthy foods, you ~~are'nt~~ *aren't* going to feel your best. _____

(1) Were all trying hard to watch our diets, but its not easy. _____
(2) Have you ever noticed how wer'e bombarded by images of high-calorie, high-fat foods? _____ (3) Maybe we shouldnt be so tempted, but it's hard to resist the lure of the fast-food chains and their commercials. _____ (4) Of course, the actual sandwich doesnt look much like the one on television, but that isnt the point. _____ (5) When wer'e away from home and hungry, its the picture of that burger that pops into our minds. _____ (6) Well be likely to rush to a fast-food place for lunch instead of looking for a meal thats healthier. _____ (7) It should'nt be so hard to find a fast, healthy meal. _____ (8) For example, a grilled chicken sandwich doesn't have nearly as much fat or calories as a burger has. _____ (9) Its still not the perfect meal for a dieter, but it isnt too bad. _____ (10) When we dont have many options, wev'e got to make the best of the situation. _____

■ WRITING FIRST: Flashback

Look back at your response to the Writing First exercise on page 435, and underline any contractions. Have you used apostrophes correctly to replace the missing letters? If not, rewrite the contractions correctly on the lines below. If you have not used any contractions, look for any words that could be combined into contractions, and write those contractions here.

_____ _____ _____ _____

_____ _____ _____ _____

B Using Apostrophes to Form Possessives

Possessive forms indicate ownership. Nouns and indefinite pronouns do not have special possessive forms. Instead, they use apostrophes to indicate ownership.

Singular Nouns and Indefinite Pronouns

To form the possessive of singular nouns (including names) and indefinite pronouns, add an apostrophe plus an -*s*.

> Cesar Chavez's goal (*the goal of Cesar Chavez*) was justice for American farm workers.
>
> The strike's outcome (*the outcome of the strike*) was uncertain.
>
> Whether it would succeed was anyone's guess (*the guess of anyone*).

> **FOCUS Singular Nouns Ending in -s**
>
> Even if a singular noun already ends in -*s*, add an apostrophe plus an -*s* to form the possessive.
>
> > The class's next assignment was a research paper.
> >
> > Dr. Ramos's patients are participating in a double-blind study.

Plural Nouns

To form the possessive of most plural nouns (including names), add just an apostrophe (not an apostrophe plus -*s*).

> The two drugs' side effects (*the side effects of the two drugs*) were quite different.
>
> The Johnsons' front door (*the front door of the Johnsons*) is painted red.

◆ PRACTICE 32-2

Rewrite the following phrases, changing the noun or indefinite pronoun that follows *of* to the possessive form. Be sure to distinguish between singular and plural nouns.

Examples

the mayor of the city _*the city's mayor*_____

the uniforms of the players _*the players' uniforms*_____

● **Writing Tip**
Possessive pronouns have special forms, such as *its* and *his*, and these forms never include apostrophes. For information on possessive pronouns, see 28F.

▼ **Student Voices**
I never know where to put the apostrophe to form the possessive of a word that ends in -s.
Krishna Mahajan

● **Writing Tip**
Most nouns form the plural by adding -*s*. For a list of frequently used irregular noun plurals, see 28B.

1. the video of the singer _____

2. the scores of the students _____

3. the first novel of the writer _____

4. the office of the boss _____

5. the union of the players _____

6. the specialty of the restaurant _____

7. the bedroom of the children _____

8. the high cost of the tickets _____

9. the dreams of everyone _____

10. the owner of the dogs _____

◆ **PRACTICE 32-3**

Edit the underlined possessive nouns and indefinite pronouns in the following sentences for correct use of apostrophes. If a correction needs to be made, cross out the noun or pronoun, and write the correct form above it. If the possessive form is correct, write *C* above it.

Example: The ~~boss'~~ ^{boss's} desk is bigger than the <u>managers'</u> ^C desks.

1. My boss at Defend Systems believes it is <u>everyones'</u> responsibility to keep up with other <u>businesses's</u> marketing strategies.

2. Therefore, her <u>offices'</u> back wall is covered with various <u>competitors'</u> ads.

3. At the same time, she requires that our <u>firms'</u> strategy and all <u>departments'</u> goals be kept as confidential as possible.

4. The <u>company's</u> policy on confidentiality is explained in detail during every single <u>employees'</u> initial orientation session.

5. Defend Systems has thirty <u>year's</u> experience in the home security business and has installed systems in thousands of <u>people's</u> houses.

6. The company <u>founders'</u> name actually is Clarence Defend, much to many of our <u>customer's</u> surprise.

7. <u>Mr. Defend's</u> daughter now runs the <u>familys'</u> business.

8. I started at the company three years ago as the <u>bookkeepers'</u> assistant, and now I work as the fifteen <u>installer's</u> administrative coordinator.

9. My <u>job's</u> big advantage is that the hours are flexible, which allows me to attend college part-time and still take care of my <u>childrens'</u> needs.

10. I don't want to be on <u>Defend Systems's</u> payroll forever, but so far the company has provided this working <u>persons'</u> "security."

■ WRITING FIRST: Flashback

Look back at your response to the Writing First exercise on page 435. Circle any possessive forms of nouns or indefinite pronouns. Have you used apostrophes correctly to form these possessives? If not, rewrite them correctly in the appropriate columns.

Singular Nouns	Indefinite Pronouns	Plural Nouns
_____	_____	_____
_____	_____	_____

C Revising Incorrect Use of Apostrophes

Be careful not to confuse a plural noun *(boys)* with the singular possessive form of the noun *(boy's)*.

> Termites can be dangerous <u>pests</u> [not *pest's*].
>
> The <u>Velezes</u> [not *Velez's*] live on Maple Drive.

Also, be careful not to use apostrophes with possessive pronouns that end in *-s: theirs* (not *their's*), *hers* (not *her's*), *its* (not *it's*), *ours* (not *our's*), and *yours* (not *your's*).

FOCUS Possessive Pronouns

Be especially careful not to confuse possessive pronouns with sound-alike contractions. Possessive pronouns never include apostrophes.

Possessive Pronoun	*Contraction*
The dog bit <u>its</u> master.	<u>It's</u> *(it is)* time for breakfast.
The choice is <u>theirs</u>.	<u>There's</u> *(there is)* no place like home.
<u>Whose</u> house is this?	<u>Who's</u> *(who is)* on first?
Is this <u>your</u> house?	<u>You're</u> *(you are)* late again.

◆ **PRACTICE 32-4**

Check the underlined words in the following sentences for correct use of apostrophes. If a correction needs to be made, cross out the word, and write the correct version above it. If the noun or pronoun is correct, write *C* above it.

                                       C

    Example: The <u>president's</u> views were presented after several other

speakers

~~<u>speaker's</u>~~ first presented ~~<u>their's.</u>~~ *theirs.*

1. <u>Parent's</u> should realize that when it comes to disciplining children, the responsibility is <u>their's</u>.

2. <u>It's</u> also important that parents offer praise for a <u>child's</u> good behavior.

3. In <u>it's</u> first few <u>week's</u> of life, a child is already developing a personality.

4. His and <u>her's</u> towels used to be popular with <u>couple's</u>, but <u>it's</u> not so common to see them today.

5. The <u>Reagan's</u> lived in the White House for eight <u>year's</u>, and then they stayed for a while at a <u>friend's</u> home in California.

6. From the radio came the lyrics "<u>You're</u> the one <u>who's</u> love I've been waiting for."

7. If you expect to miss any <u>classes'</u>, you will have to make arrangements with someone <u>who's</u> willing to tell you <u>you're</u> assignment.

8. No other <u>school's</u> cheerleading squad ever tried as many tricky stunts as <u>our's</u> did.

9. Surprise <u>test's</u> are a regular feature of my economics <u>teacher's</u> class.

10. <u>Jazz's</u> influence on many mainstream <u>musician's</u> is one of the <u>book's</u> main <u>subject's</u>.

■ WRITING FIRST: Flashback

Look back at your response to the Writing First exercise on page 435. Circle each plural noun. Then, circle each possessive pronoun that ends in *-s*. Have you incorrectly used an apostrophe with any of the circled words? If so, revise your work.

■ WRITING FIRST: Revising and Editing

Look back at your response to the Writing First exercise on page 435. Because this is an informal exercise, contractions are acceptable; in fact, they may be preferable because they give your writing a conversational tone. Edit your writing so that you have used contractions in all possible situations.

Now add two sentences—one that includes a singular possessive noun and one that includes a plural possessive noun. Make sure these two new sentences fit smoothly into your writing and that they, too, use contractions wherever possible.

CHAPTER REVIEW

◆ EDITING PRACTICE

Read the following student essay, into which errors in the use of apostrophes have been introduced. Edit it to eliminate errors by crossing out incorrect words and writing corrections above them. (Note that this is an informal response paper, so contractions are acceptable.) The first sentence has been edited for you.

For more on informal response writing, see 35E.

The Women of Messina

In William ~~Shakespeares'~~ *Shakespeare's* play <u>Much Ado about Nothing,</u> the women of Messina, whether they are seen as love objects or shrew's, have very few options. A womans role is to please a man. She can try to resist, but she will probably wind up giving in. The plays two women, Hero and Beatrice, are very different. Hero is the obedient one. Heros' cousin, Beatrice, tries to oppose the mans world in which she lives. However, in a place like Messina, even women like Beatrice find it hard to get the respect that should be their's.

Right from the start, we are drawn to Beatrice. Shes funny, she has a clever comment for most situation's, and she always speaks her mind about other peoples behavior.

Unlike Hero, she tries to stand up to the men in her life, as we see in her and Benedicks conversations. But even though Beatrice's intelligence is obvious, she often mocks herself. Its obvious that she doesn't have much self-esteem. In fact, Beatrice is'nt the strong woman she seems to be.

Ultimately, Beatrice does get her man, and she will be happy--but at what expense? Benedicks' last words to her are "Peace! I will stop your mouth" (5.4.97). Then, he kisses her. The kiss is a symbolic end to their bickering. It is also the mark of Beatrices' defeat. She has lost. Benedick has shut her up. Now, she will be Benedick's wife and do what he wants her to do. Granted, she will have more say in her marriage than Hero will have in her's, but she is still defeated. Even Beatrice, the most rebellious of Messinas women, finds it impossible to achieve anything of importance in Messinas' male-dominated society.

◆ COLLABORATIVE ACTIVITIES

1. Working in a group of four and building on your individual responses to the Writing First exercise at the beginning of the chapter, consider which specific occupational and professional roles are still associated largely with men and which are associated primarily with women. Make two lists, heading one "women's jobs" and one "men's jobs."

2. Now, work in pairs, with one pair of students in each group concentrating on men and the other pair on women. Write a paragraph that attempts to justify why the particular jobs you listed should or should not be restricted to one gender. In your discussion, list the various qualities men or women possess that qualify (or disqualify) them for particular jobs. Use possessive forms whenever possible—for example, *women's energy* and not *women have energy*.

3. Bring to class a book, magazine, or newspaper whose style is informal—for example, a romance novel, *TV Guide,* your school newspaper, or even a comic book. Working in a group, circle every contraction you can find on one page of each publication, and substitute for each contraction the words it combines. Are your substitutions an improvement? (You may want to read a few paragraphs aloud before you reach a conclusion.)

☑ REVIEW CHECKLIST:
Using Apostrophes

- Use apostrophes to form contractions. (See 32A.)

- Use an apostrophe plus an -*s* to form the possessive of singular nouns and indefinite pronouns, even when a noun ends in -*s*. (See 32B.)

- Use an apostrophe alone to form the possessive of most plural nouns, including names. (See 32B.)

- Do not use apostrophes with plural nouns unless they are possessive. Do not use apostrophes with possessive pronouns. (See 32C.)

33

Understanding Mechanics

PREVIEW

In this chapter, you will learn

- to capitalize proper nouns (33A)

- to punctuate direct quotations (33B)

- to set off titles of books, stories, and other works (33C)

- to use minor punctuation marks (33D)

● **Writing Tip**
The words *black* and *white* are generally not capitalized when they name racial groups. However, *African American* and *Caucasian* are always capitalized.

■ WRITING FIRST

What makes a television commercial effective? Give examples of particularly effective commercials, and mention the names of the television shows in which you see them. Be sure to identify the product each commercial advertises and to use actual words and phrases from each commercial. Finally, explain the qualities that contribute to making these commercials memorable.

A Capitalizing Proper Nouns

A **proper noun** names a particular person, animal, place, or thing. Proper nouns are always capitalized. The list that follows explains and illustrates specific rules for capitalizing proper nouns and also includes some important exceptions.

1. Always capitalize names of races, ethnic groups, tribes, nationalities, languages, and religions.

   The census data revealed a diverse community of Caucasians, African Americans, and Asian Americans, with a few Latino and Navajo residents. Native languages include English, Korean, and Spanish. Most people identified themselves as Catholic, Protestant, or Muslim.

2. Capitalize names of specific people and the titles that accompany them. In general, do not capitalize titles used without a name.

   In 1994, President Nelson Mandela was elected to lead South Africa.

   The newly elected fraternity president addressed the crowd.

3. Capitalize names of specific family members and their titles. Do not capitalize words that identify family relationships, including those introduced by possessive pronouns.

> The twins, Aunt Edna and Aunt Evelyn, are Dad's sisters.
>
> My aunts, my father's sisters, are twins.

4. Capitalize names of specific countries, cities, towns, bodies of water, streets, and so forth. Do not capitalize words that identify nonspecific places.

> The Seine runs through Paris, France.
>
> The river runs through the city.

5. Capitalize names of specific geographical regions. Do not capitalize such words when they specify direction.

> William Faulkner's novels are set in the American South.
>
> Turn right at the golf course, and go south for about a mile.

6. Capitalize names of specific buildings and monuments. Do not capitalize general references to buildings and monuments.

> He drove past the Liberty Bell and looked for a parking space near City Hall.
>
> He drove past the monument and looked for a parking space near the building.

7. Capitalize names of specific groups, clubs, teams, and associations. Do not capitalize general references to groups of individuals.

> The Teamsters Union represents workers who were at the stadium for the Republican Party convention, the Rolling Stones concert, and the Phillies-Astros game.
>
> The union represents workers who were at the stadium for the political party's convention, the rock group's concert, and the baseball teams' game.

8. Capitalize names of specific historical periods, events, and documents. Do not capitalize nonspecific references to periods, events, or documents.

> The Emancipation Proclamation was signed during the Civil War, not during Reconstruction.
>
> The document was signed during the war, not during the postwar period.

9. Capitalize names of businesses, government agencies, schools, and other institutions. Do not capitalize nonspecific references to such institutions.

> The Department of Education and Apple Computer have launched a partnership project with Central High School.
>
> A government agency and a computer company have launched a partnership project with a high school.

● **Writing Tip**
Trade names that have
become part of the language
—*nylon*, for example—are
no longer capitalized.

10. Capitalize brand names. Do not capitalize general references to kinds of products.

   While Jeff waited for his turn at the <u>X</u>erox machine, he drank a can of <u>C</u>oke.

   While Jeff waited for his turn at the <u>c</u>opier, he drank a can of <u>s</u>oda.

11. Capitalize titles of specific academic courses. Do not capitalize names of general academic subject areas, except for proper nouns—for example, a language or a country.

   Are <u>I</u>ntroduction to <u>A</u>merican <u>G</u>overnment and <u>B</u>iology 200 closed yet?

   Are the <u>i</u>ntroductory American <u>g</u>overnment course and the <u>b</u>iology course closed yet?

12. Capitalize days of the week, months of the year, and holidays. Do not capitalize the names of seasons.

   The Jewish holiday of <u>P</u>assover usually falls in <u>A</u>pril.

   The Jewish holiday of <u>P</u>assover falls in the <u>s</u>pring.

◆ **PRACTICE 33-1**

Edit the following sentences, capitalizing letters or changing capitals to lowercase where necessary.

Example: The third largest <s>C</s>ity in the <s>u</s>nited <s>s</s>tates is <s>c</s>hicago, <s>I</s>llinois.

(1) Located in the midwest on lake Michigan, chicago is an important port city, a rail and highway hub, and the site of o'hare international airport, the Nation's busiest. (2) The financial center of the city is Lasalle street, and the lakefront is home to Grant park, where there are many Museums and monuments. (3) To the North of the city, soldier field is home to the chicago bears, the city's football team, and wrigley field is home to the chicago cubs, an american league Baseball Team. (4) In the mid-1600s, the site of what is now Chicago was visited by father jacques marquette, a catholic missionary to the ottawa and huron tribes, who were native to the area. (5) By the 1700s, the city was a trading post run by john kinzie. (6) The city grew rapidly in the 1800s, and immigrants included germans, irish, italians, poles, greeks, and chinese, along with african americans, who migrated from the south. (7) In 1871, much of the city was destroyed in one of the worst fires in united states history,

when, according to legend, mrs. O'Leary's Cow kicked over a burning

lantern. (8) Today, Chicago's skyline is marked by many Skyscrapers,

built by businesses like the john hancock company, sears, and amoco.

(9) I know Chicago well because my Mother grew up there and my aunt

jean and uncle amos still live there. (10) I also got information from the

Chicago Chamber of Commerce when I wrote a paper for introductory

research writing, a course I took at Graystone high school.

■ WRITING FIRST: Flashback

Look back at your response to the Writing First exercise on page
444. Underline every proper noun, including brand names of products. Does each begin with a capital letter? On the lines below, correct any that do not.

_____   _____   _____

_____   _____   _____

B   Punctuating Direct Quotations

A **direct quotation** reproduces the *exact* words of a speaker or of a printed source. Direct quotations are always placed within quotation marks.

> Lauren said, "My brother and Tina have gotten engaged."

> A famous advertiser wrote, "Don't sell the steak; sell the sizzle."

When a quotation is a complete sentence, it begins with a capital letter. When a quotation falls at the end of a sentence, as in the two examples above, the period is placed inside the quotation marks. If the quotation is a question or exclamation, the question mark or exclamation point is also placed inside the quotation marks.

> The instructor asked, "Has anyone read *Sula*?"

> Officer Warren shouted, "Hold it right there!"

For information on indirect
quotations, see 24D.

▼ **Student Voices**
*I'm good at punctuation, but
sometimes I have trouble
using quotation marks and
commas together.*
                    Sutapa Das

FOCUS   Identifying Tags

A direct quotation is usually accompanied by an **identifying tag**, a phrase that names the person or work being quoted.

(continued on the following page)

(continued from the previous page)

Identifying Tag at the Beginning

When the identifying tag comes *before* the quotation, it is followed by a comma.

> Alexandre Dumas wrote, "Nothing succeeds like success."

Identifying Tag at the End

When the identifying tag comes at the *end* of the sentence, it is followed by a period. A comma inside the closing quotation marks separates the quotation from the identifying tag.

> "Life is like a box of chocolates," stated Forrest Gump.

Identifying Tag in the Middle

When the identifying tag comes in the *middle* of the quoted sentence, it is followed by a comma. The first part of the quotation is also followed by a comma, placed inside the quotation marks. Because the part of the quotation that follows the tag is not a new sentence, it does not begin with a capital letter.

> "This is my life," Bette insisted, "and I'll live it as I please."

Identifying Tag between Two Sentences

When the identifying tag comes between two quoted sentences, it is followed by a period, and the second quoted sentence begins with a capital letter.

> "Producer Berry Gordy is an important figure in the history of music," Tony claimed. "He was the creative force behind Motown records."

◆ PRACTICE 33-2

In the following sentences containing direct quotations, first underline the identifying tag. Then, punctuate the quotation correctly, adding capital letters as necessary.

Example: "Why, Darryl asked, "are teachers so out of it?"

1. We who are about to die salute you said the gladiators to the emperor.

2. When we turned on the television, the newscaster was saying ladies and gentlemen, President Reagan has been shot.

3. The bigger they are said boxer John L. Sullivan the harder they fall.

4. Do you take Michael to be your lawfully wedded husband asked the minister.

5. Lisa Marie replied I do.

6. If you believe the *National Enquirer* my friend always says then I've got a bridge I'd like to sell you.

7. When asked for the jury's verdict, the foreman replied we find the defendant not guilty.

8. I had felt for a long time that if I was ever told to get up so a white person could sit Rosa Parks recalled I would refuse to do so.

9. Yabba dabba doo Fred exclaimed when the brontoburger arrived.

10. Where's my money Addie Pray asked you give me my money.

◆ **PRACTICE 33-3**

These quotations are followed in parentheses by the names of the people who wrote or spoke them. On the blank lines, write a sentence that includes the quotation and places the identifying tag in the position that the directions specify. Be sure to punctuate and capitalize correctly.

Example: Nothing endures but change. (written by the Greek philosopher Heraclitus)

Identifying tag in the middle *"Nothing endures," wrote the Greek philosopher Heraclitus, "but change."*

1. One is not born a woman; one becomes one. (written by essayist Simone de Beauvoir)

   Identifying tag at the beginning _____

   _____

2. I want a kinder, gentler nation. (spoken by President George Bush)

   Identifying tag at the end _____

   _____

3. Tribe follows tribe, and nation follows nation. (spoken by Suquamish Chief Seattle in 1854)

   Identifying tag in the middle _____

   _____

4. When I'm good, I'm very good. When I'm bad, I'm better. (spoken by Mae West in *I'm No Angel*)

Identifying tag in the middle _____

_____

5. The rich rob the poor, and the poor rob one another. (spoken by Sojourner Truth)

Identifying tag at the beginning_____

_____

6. Heaven is like an egg, and the earth is like the yolk of the egg. (written by Chinese philosopher Chang Heng)

Identifying tag in the middle_____

_____

7. When I found I had crossed that line, I looked at my hands to see if I was the same person. (spoken by Harriet Tubman)

Identifying tag at the beginning _____

_____

8. If a man hasn't discovered something he will die for, then he isn't fit to live. (spoken by Martin Luther King Jr.)

Identifying tag at the end _____

_____

9. No man chooses evil because it is evil. He only mistakes it for happiness. (written in 1790 by Mary Wollstonecraft)

Identifying tag in the middle _____

_____

10. Marriage is an evil, but a necessary evil. (written by the ancient Greek poet Menander)

Identifying tag at the beginning _____

_____

■ **WRITING FIRST: Flashback**

Look back at your response to the Writing First exercise on page 444. Make sure you have enclosed any direct quotations in quotation marks and placed other punctuation correctly. Revise any incorrectly punctuated quotations on the following lines.

(continued on the following page)

(continued from the previous page)

_____

_____

_____

C   Setting Off Titles of Books, Stories, and Other Works

Some titles are set in *italic* type (or <u>underlined</u> to indicate italics). Others are set within quotation marks. The following box shows how to set off different kinds of titles.

Italicized Titles	**Titles in Quotation Marks**
Books: *How the Garcia Girls Lost Their Accents*	Book chapters: "Reading Critically"
Newspapers: the *Miami Herald*	Short stories: "The Tell-Tale Heart"
Magazines: *People*	Essays and articles: "The Old Block"
Long poems: *John Brown's Body*	Short poems: "Richard Cory"
Plays: *Death of a Salesman*	Songs: "Lift Every Voice and Sing"
Films: *The Rocky Horror Picture Show*	Individual episodes of television or radio series: "The Montgomery Bus Boycott," an episode of the PBS series *Eyes on the Prize*
Television or radio series: *Star Trek: The Next Generation*	

The first letters of all important words in a title are capitalized. Do not capitalize an article *(a, an, the)*, a preposition *(to, of, around)*, or a coordinating conjunction *(and, but)* unless it is the first or last word of the title or subtitle *(<u>On</u> the Road;* "<u>To</u> an Athlete Dying Young"; *No Way <u>Out</u>; <u>And</u> Quiet Flows <u>the</u> Don).*

FOCUS   **Titles of Papers**

When you type one of your own papers, capitalize the first letter of each word in your title — except for articles, prepositions, and coordinating conjunctions. Don't underline your title or enclose it in quotation marks. (Only *published* works are set off this way.)

◆ **PRACTICE 33-4**

Edit the following sentences, capitalizing letters as necessary in titles.

> **Example:** Eudora Welty's "*a worn path*" is a very moving short story.

1. Directed by the wacky Ed Wood, the 1959 movie *plan nine from outer space* has been called the worst picture of all time.

2. Gary Larson's cartoon collections include the books *in search of the far side*, *it came from the far side*, and *valley of the far side*.

3. En Vogue's first hit album, *born to sing*, included the songs "you don't have to worry," "time goes on," and "just can't stay away."

4. Everyone should read Martin Luther King Jr.'s "i have a dream" and "letter from birmingham jail."

5. The Fox Network has had hits with shows like *the simpsons*, *beverly hills 90210*, *party of five*, and *in living color*.

◆ **PRACTICE 33-5**

In the following sentences, underline or insert quotation marks around titles. (Remember that titles of books and other long works are underlined, and titles of stories, essays, and other shorter works are enclosed in quotation marks.)

> **Example:** An article in the <u>New York Times</u> called "It's Not Easy Being Green" is a profile of former Chicago Bulls player Dennis Rodman, who once had green hair.

1. Sui Sin Far's short story The Wisdom of the New, from her book Mrs. Spring Fragrance, is about the clash between Chinese and American cultures in the early twentieth century.

2. The rock band Judybats released its single Sorry Counts in 1995.

3. Interesting information about fighting skin cancer can be found in the article Putting Sunscreens to the Test that appeared in the magazine Consumer Reports.

4. One of the best-known poems of the twentieth century is Robert Frost's The Road Not Taken.

5. Wayne Wang has directed several well-received films, including The Joy Luck Club and Smoke.

6. It is surprising how many people enjoy reruns of the 1960s television series Bewitched and I Dream of Jeannie.

7. The title of Lorraine Hansberry's play A Raisin in the Sun comes from Langston Hughes's poem Harlem.

8. In his 1994 autobiography Breaking the Surface, Olympic diving champion Greg Louganis writes about his struggle with AIDS.

■ WRITING FIRST: Flashback

Look back at your response to the Writing First exercise on page 444. Circle the titles of the television shows you have mentioned. Have you underlined each one? Are capital letters used where necessary? Make any corrections on the lines below.

_____   _____

_____   _____

D Using Minor Punctuation Marks

For information on sentence types, see 18A.

A statement ends with a **period**, a question ends with a **question mark**, and an exclamation ends with an **exclamation point**. Other important punctuation marks are the **comma** (Chapter 31), the **apostrophe** (Chapter 32), and the **semicolon** (16B). Three additional punctuation marks—*colons, dashes,* and *parentheses*—are used to set off material from the rest of the sentence.

● **Writing Tip**
When a colon introduces a quotation, example, or list, it must follow a complete sentence.

The Colon

A **colon** can be used to introduce a quotation.

> Our family motto is a simple one: "Accept no substitutes."

A colon can be used to introduce an explanation, a clarification, or an example.

● **Writing Tip**
All items in a list should be parallel. See Chapter 19.

> Only one thing kept him from climbing Mt. Everest: fear of heights.

A colon is also used to introduce a list.

● **Writing Tip**
Use a colon to separate hours from minutes: *The train arrived at 4:02.*

> I left my job for four reasons: a terrible supervisor, boring work, poor working conditions, and low pay.

● **Writing Tip**
Dashes give writing an informal tone; use them sparingly in college and professional writing.

The Dash

Dashes focus attention on information by setting it off from the rest of the sentence.

> I parked my car—a red Firebird—in a towaway zone.

Parentheses

Parentheses deemphasize material that is not an essential part of the sentence.

> The weather in Portland (a city in Oregon) was overcast.

◆ **PRACTICE 33-6**

Add colons, dashes, and parentheses to the following sentences where necessary.

> **Example:** Three long-running soap operas have retained their popularity over the years: *All My Children, Days of Our Lives,* and *General Hospital.*

(1) In its earliest years, *General Hospital* featured three main characters Audrey March, Steve Hardy, and Jessie Brewer. (2) The characters worked at a hospital in Port Charles a city in New York State and had complicated personal lives. (3) Tom Beradino a former major-league baseball player played Steve Hardy, a doctor. (4) Audrey a nurse had a serious problem infertility. (5) When she finally managed to adopt a child, he was kidnapped by her first husband the evil Tom Baldwin. (6) Jessie also had many problems, including her husband Phil Brewer who kept disappearing .(7) Now, more than thirty years after the soap's debut, newer characters Monica, Alan, Bobbi, and Lucky have very different problems. (8) New themes such as rape, AIDS, and organized crime have been introduced. (9) New tragedies and also new triumphs have been experienced by the characters. (10) Still, the formula is the same Friday's crisis is resolved on Monday.

■ WRITING FIRST: Flashback

Look back at your response to the Writing First exercise on page
444. Do you see places where you might add a quotation, an example, or a list that could be introduced by a colon? Write your
possible additions here.

Quotation _____

Example _____

List _____

■ WRITING FIRST: Revising and Editing

Look back at your response to the Writing First exercise on page
444. If you have quoted specific lines from commercials, try varying the placement of the identifying tags you have used. If you
didn't include quotations, try adding one or two. Then, add the
quotation, example, or list from the Flashback above to your Writing First exercise, introducing it with a colon. Finally, edit for
proper use of capital letters, quotation marks, and underlining.

CHAPTER REVIEW

◆ EDITING PRACTICE

Read the following student essay, into which errors in capitalization and
punctuation and in the use of direct quotations and titles have been introduced. Edit the passage to correct any such errors. The first sentence has
been edited for you.

The Big Sleep

"The Big Sleep," released in 1946, is a classic movie
mystery set in Los Angeles, in which Humphrey Bogart plays
a private detective named Philip Marlowe. In an early

scene, Marlowe learns from his client, general Sternwood, that Sternwood is being blackmailed about his daughter Carmen's gambling habits. Sternwood wants Marlowe to find the Blackmailers and get rid of them.

The movie was produced by warner brothers a studio that made many mysteries, and it is set up in classic hollywood style. It includes elements found in many mysteries murder, suspicion, and betrayal. It also has a romantic subplot involving the General's other daughter, Vivian, and Marlowe. By the end of the movie, all the questions about murder and blackmail have been answered. The only questions that remain are: about the romance between Marlowe and Vivian.

The movie is full of classic lines. When Vivian learns that Marlowe is a private detective, she says "I didn't know they existed, except in books--or else they were greasy little men sneaking around Hotel corridors." When a character criticizes his manners, Marlowe has a quick comeback: "I don't mind if you don't like my manners," he answers. "I don't like them myself."

The only major criticism of the movie is that (unlike most Classic mysteries) it is often very confusing. In fact, one reviewer wrote: The plot is so fast and complicated that you can hardly catch it. Despite their confusion, however, audiences identify strongly with Marlowe, who is clearly a Good Guy trying to make an honest living. We root for him and want everything to turn out all right for him. So even though the plot of the Big Sleep is hard to follow, the audience sticks with it--as Marlowe does-- until the end.

◆ COLLABORATIVE ACTIVITIES

1. Imagine that you and the other members of your group are the nominations committee for this year's Emmy, Oscar, or Grammy Awards. Work together to compile a list of categories and several nominees for each category.

Trade lists with another group. From each category, select the individual artist or work you believe deserves to win the award. Write a sentence about each winner, explaining why it is the best in its category.

When you have finished, exchange papers with another group. Check one another's papers for correct use of capitals, quotation marks, and underlining.

2. Using a separate sheet of paper, work in groups to list as many items in each of the following five categories as you can: planets, islands, musicians or bands, automobile models, sports teams. Be sure all your items are proper nouns.

Write five original sentences on the lines below, using one proper noun from each category in each sentence.

■ _____

_____

■ _____

_____

■ _____

_____

■ _____

_____

■ _____

_____

3. Working in pairs, write a conversation between two characters, real or fictional, who have very different positions on a particular issue. Place all direct quotations within quotation marks, and include identifying tags that clearly indicate which character is speaking. (Begin a new paragraph each time a new person speaks.)

Exchange your conversations with another pair of students, and check their work to see that all directly quoted speech is set within quotation marks and that all other punctuation is used correctly.

☑ REVIEW CHECKLIST:
Understanding Mechanics

▢ Capitalize proper nouns. (See 33A.)

▢ Always place direct quotations within quotation marks. (See 33B.)

▢ In titles, capitalize all important words, as well as the first and the last words. Use italics or quotation marks to set off titles. (See 33C.)

▢ Use colons, dashes, and parentheses to set off material from the rest of the sentence. (See 33D.)

CHAPTER

34

Understanding Spelling

PREVIEW

In this chapter, you will learn

■ to become a better speller (34A)

■ to know when to use *ie* and *ei* (34B)

■ to understand prefixes (34C)

■ to understand suffixes (34D)

■ to identify commonly confused words (34E)

● **Writing Tip**
The best place to check spelling is a good college dictionary. It will also tell you how to pronounce a word and which syllables to stress.

▼ **Student Voices**
Thank heaven for spell checkers.
          Jason Walsh

■ WRITING FIRST

Summarize the plot of one of your favorite books or movies or an episode of a favorite television show. Present events in the order in which they occurred. Include as many specific details as possible, and use transitional words and phrases to help readers follow your summary. Do *not* include your own opinions.

A   Becoming a Better Speller

Even though computers come equipped with spell checkers, you still need to be able to recognize and correct misspelled words. For one thing, you may not always write on a computer. For another, spell checkers have their limitations. Improving your spelling may take time, but the following steps can make this task a lot easier.

1. *Use a dictionary.* As you write, circle words whose spellings you are unsure of. After you have finished your draft, look up these words in the dictionary to make sure they are spelled correctly.
2. *Use a spell checker.* If you write on a computer, use your spell checker. It will correct most misspelled words and also identify many typos, such as transposed or omitted letters.
3. *Proofread carefully.* Always proofread your papers for spelling before you hand them in, even if you have used a spell checker. A spell checker points out words that are *spelled* incorrectly. It does not locate words you have *used* incorrectly—*to* for *too*, for example.
4. *Keep a personal spelling list.* Write down all the words you misspell. If you keep a writing journal, set aside a few pages in the back for your personal spelling list. As you find new words, add them to your list.

458

5. *Look over corrected papers for misspelled words.* Whenever your instructor hands back one of your papers, look for misspelled words— usually circled and marked *sp.* Add these to your spelling list.

6. *Look for patterns in your misspelling.* Do you consistently misspell words with *ei* combinations? Do you have trouble forming plurals? Once you figure out which errors you make frequently, you can take steps to eliminate them.

7. *Learn the basic spelling rules.* Study the spelling rules in this chapter, especially those that apply to areas in which you are weak. Remember that one rule can help you spell many words correctly.

8. *Review the list of commonly confused words on pages 466 to 475.* If you have problems with any of these word pairs, add them to your personal spelling list.

9. *Make flash cards.* If you consistently have trouble with spelling, put individual words on 3 × 5 cards. You can use them to test yourself periodically.

10. *Use memory cues.* Memory cues help you remember how to spell certain words. For example, thinking of the word *finite* helps you remember that *definite* is spelled with an *i*, not an *a.* Also, the sentence "The principal is your pal" helps you remember that the *principal* of a school ends with *pal*, not *ple.*

11. *Learn to spell some of the most commonly misspelled words.* Identify those on the list below that give you trouble, and add them to your personal spelling list.

Commonly Misspelled Words

across	disappoint	loneliness	reference
all right	early	medicine	restaurant
a lot	embarrass	minute	roommate
already	entrance	necessary	secretary
argument	environment	noticeable	sentence
beautiful	everything	occasion	separate
becoming	exercise	occur	speech
beginning	experience	occurred	studying
believe	finally	occurrences	surprise
benefit	forty	occurring	tomato
calendar	fulfill	occurs	tomatoes
cannot	generally	personnel	truly
careful	government	possible	until
careless	grammar	potato	usually
cemetery	harass	potatoes	Wednesday
certain	height	prejudice	weird
conscience	holiday	prescription	window
definite	integration	privilege	withhold
definitely	intelligence	probably	woman
dependent	interest	professor	women
describe	interfere	receive	writing
develop	judgment	recognize	written

FOCUS **Vowels and Consonants**

Knowing which letters are vowels and which are consonants will
help you understand the spelling rules presented in this chapter.

> ***Vowels:*** *a, e, i, o, u*
>
> ***Consonants:*** *b, c, d, f, g, h, j, k, l, m, n, p, q, r, s, t, v, w, x, z*

The letter *y* is considered either a vowel or a consonant, depending
on how it is pronounced. In *young, y* acts as a consonant because it
has the sound of *y;* in *truly,* it acts as a vowel because it has the
sound of *ee.*

Because English pronunciation is not always a reliable guide for spelling,
most people find it useful to memorize some spelling rules.

B **Deciding between *ie* and *ei***

Many people have memorized the rule that *i* comes before *e*. This rule
holds true except when *i* comes after *c* or when the *ei* sound is pronounced
ay (as in *neighbor*).

i before *e*	except after *c*	or when *ei* is pronounced *ay*
achieve	ceiling	eight
believe	conceive	freight
friend	deceive	neighbor

FOCUS **Exceptions to the "*i before e*" Rule**

There are some exceptions to the "*i before e*" rule. The exceptions
follow no pattern, so you must memorize them.

ancient	either	leisure	seize
caffeine	foreign	neither	species
conscience	height	science	weird

◆ PRACTICE 34-1

Proofread the underlined words in the following sentences for correct spelling. If a correction needs to be made, cross out the incorrect word, and write the correct spelling above it. If the word is spelled correctly, write *C* above it.

                           C   *receive*

Example: It was a <u>relief</u> to ~~recieve~~ the good news.

1. Be sure to <u>wiegh</u> the pros and cons before making an important decision, particularly those involving <u>friends</u>.

2. When your <u>beliefs</u> are tested, you may be able to <u>acheive</u> a better understanding of yourself.

3. In our <u>society</u>, many people <u>decieve</u> themselves into <u>beleiving</u> that they are better than everyone else.

4. <u>Cheifly</u> because they have been lucky, they have reached a certain <u>height</u> in the world.

5. They think that the blood running through <u>their</u> <u>viens</u> makes them a higher <u>species</u> than the average person.

6. In fact, they are probably <u>niether</u> smarter nor more talented than others, but they are certainly <u>deficient</u> in humility.

7. <u>Thier</u> <u>impatient</u> attitude can cause others a lot of <u>greif</u>.

8. I have always <u>percieved</u> myself as thoughtful of others, and my <u>conscience</u> leads me to treat everyone with respect.

9. There are a <u>vareity</u> of ways to learn a <u>foriegn</u> language.

10. *Waterworld* was a really <u>weird</u> movie, even for <u>science</u> fiction.

■ WRITING FIRST: Flashback

Look back at your response to the Writing First exercise on page 458. Underline any words that have *ie* or *ei* combinations, and check a dictionary to make sure they are spelled correctly. Correct any spelling errors on the lines below.

_____

_____

_____

C Understanding Prefixes

A **prefix** is a group of letters added at the beginning of a word to change its meaning. Adding a prefix to a word never affects the spelling of the original word.

dis + service = disservice   pre + heat = preheat
un + able = unable   un + natural = unnatural
co + operate = cooperate   over + rate = overrate

◆ PRACTICE 34-2

Write in the blank the new word that results when the specified prefix is added to each of the following words.

Example: dis + respect = ____*disrespect*____

1. un + happy = _____   6. non + negotiable = _____

2. tele + vision = _____   7. im + patient = _____

3. pre + existing = _____ 8. out + think = _____

4. dis + satisfied = _____ 9. over + react = _____

5. un + necessary = _____ 10. dis + solve = _____

■ WRITING FIRST: Flashback

FLASHBACK

Look back at your response to the Writing First exercise on page 458. Underline words that have prefixes, and check a dictionary to make sure each word is spelled correctly. Correct any spelling errors on the lines below.

_____   _____

_____   _____

D Understanding Suffixes

A **suffix** is a group of letters attached to the end of a word to change the word's meaning or its part of speech. Unlike prefixes, suffixes can affect the spelling of words to which they are added.

Words Ending in Silent *-e*

If a word ends with a silent (unpronounced) *-e*, drop the *e* if the suffix
begins with a vowel.

DROP THE *E*

hope + <u>i</u>ng = hoping   dance + <u>e</u>r = dancer

continue + <u>o</u>us = continuous   insure + <u>a</u>ble = insurable

EXCEPTIONS

change + able = changeable   courage + ous = courageous

notice + able = noticeable   replace + able = replaceable

Keep the *e* if the suffix begins with a consonant.

KEEP THE *E*

hope + <u>f</u>ul = hopeful   bore + <u>d</u>om = boredom

excite + <u>m</u>ent = excitement   same + <u>n</u>ess = sameness

EXCEPTIONS

argue + ment = argument   true + ly = truly

judge + ment = judgment   nine + th = ninth

◆ **PRACTICE 34-3**

Write in the blank the new word that results from adding the specified suffix to each of the following words.

Examples

insure + ance = _____*insurance*_____

love + ly = _____*lovely*_____

1. lone + ly = _____   11. effective + ness = _____

2. use + ful = _____   12. arrange + ment = _____

3. revise + ing = _____   13. fortune + ate = _____

4. base + ment = _____   14. taste + ful = _____

5. desire + able = _____   15. argue + ment = _____

6. true + ly = _____   16. disable + ed = _____

7. microscope + ic = _____ 17. advertise + ment = _____

8. prepare + ation = _____ 18. notice + able = _____

9. nine + th = _____   19. care + less = _____

10. indicate + ion = _____ 20. judge + ment = _____

Words Ending in -y

When you add a suffix to a word that ends in -y, change the y to an i if the letter before the y is a consonant.

CHANGE Y TO I

beauty + ful = beautiful   busy + ly = busily

try + ed = tried   friendly + er = friendlier

EXCEPTIONS

■ Keep the y if the suffix starts with an i.

cry + ing = crying   baby + ish = babyish

■ Keep the y when you add a suffix to some one-syllable words.

shy + er = shyer   dry + ness = dryness

Keep the y if the letter before the y is a vowel.

KEEP THE Y

annoy + ance = annoyance   enjoy + ment = enjoyment
play + ful = playful   display + ed = displayed

EXCEPTIONS

day + ly = daily   say + ed = said
gay + ly = gaily   pay + ed = paid

◆ PRACTICE 34-4

Write in the blank the new word that results from adding the specified suffix to each of the following words.

Examples

study + ed = _____studied_____

employ + ment = _____employment_____

1. happy + ness = _____   9. forty + ish = _____

2. convey + or = _____   10. day + ly = _____

3. deny + ing = _____   11. cry + ed = _____

4. carry + ed = _____   12. delay + ed = _____

5. ready + ness = _____   13. busy + ness = _____

6. annoy + ing = _____   14. lonely + ness = _____

7. destroy + er = _____   15. spy + ing = _____

8. twenty + eth = _____   16. prepay + ed = _____

17. lively + hood = _____   19. joy + ful = _____

18. ally + ance = _____   20. marry + ing = _____

Doubling the Final Consonant

When you add a suffix that begins with a vowel—for example, *-ed, -er,* or
-ing—double the final consonant in the original word if (1) the last three
letters of the word have a consonant-vowel-consonant pattern (cvc), and
(2) the word has one syllable, or the last syllable is stressed.

FINAL CONSONANT DOUBLED

cut	+ ing	=	cutting (cvc—one syllable)
bat	+ er	=	batter (cvc—one syllable)
pet	+ ed	=	petted (cvc—one syllable)
commit	+ ed	=	committed (cvc—stress is on last syllable)
occur	+ ing	=	occurring (cvc—stress is on last syllable)

FINAL CONSONANT NOT DOUBLED

answer	+ ed	=	answered (cvc—stress is not on last syllable)
happen	+ ing	=	happening (cvc—stress is not on last syllable)
act	+ ing	=	acting (no cvc)

◆ PRACTICE 34-5

Write in the blank the new word that results from adding the specified suffix to each of the following words.

Examples

rot + ing = _____rotting_____

narrow + er = _____narrower_____

1. hope + ed = _____   11. appeal + ing = _____

2. shop + er = _____   12. resist + ed = _____

3. rest + ing = _____   13. refer + ing = _____

4. combat + ed = _____   14. skip + er = _____

5. reveal + ing = _____   15. omit + ed = _____

6. open + er = _____   16. want + ing = _____

7. unzip + ed = _____   17. fat + er = _____

8. trap + ed = _____   18. fast + er = _____

9. cram + ing = _____   19. repel + ed = _____

10. star + ing = _____   20. repeal + ed = _____

> ■ **WRITING FIRST: Flashback**
>
> Look back at your response to the Writing First exercise on page 458. Underline words that have suffixes, and check a dictionary to make sure each word is spelled correctly. Correct any spelling errors on the lines below.
>
> _____   _____
>
> _____   _____

E Learning Commonly Confused Words

Accept/Except   *Accept* means "to receive something." *Except* means "with the exception of" or "to leave out or exclude."

"I accept your challenge," said Alexander Hamilton to Aaron Burr.

Everyone except Darryl visited the museum.

Affect/Effect   *Affect* is a verb meaning "to influence." *Effect* is a noun meaning "result" and sometimes a verb meaning "to bring about."

Carmen's job could affect her grades.

Overexposure to sun can have a long-term effect on skin.

Commissioner Williams tried to effect changes in police procedure.

All ready/Already   *All ready* means "completely prepared." *Already* means "previously, before."

Serge was all ready to take the history test.

Gina had already been to Italy.

Brake/Break   *Brake* means "a device to slow or stop a vehicle." *Break* means "to smash" or "to detach."

Peter got into an accident because his foot slipped off the brake.

Babe Ruth bragged that no one would ever break his home run record.

Buy/By   *Buy* means "to purchase." *By* is a preposition meaning "close to" or "next to" or "by means of."

The Stamp Act forced colonists to buy stamps for many public documents.

He drove by but didn't stop.

He stayed by her side all the way to the hospital.

Malcolm X wanted "freedom by any means necessary."

◆ **PRACTICE 34-6**

Proofread the underlined words in the following sentences for correct spelling. If a correction needs to be made, cross out the incorrect word, and write the correct spelling above it. If the word is spelled correctly, write *C* above it.

                                 accept   *C*

Example: We must ~~except~~ the fact that the human heart can break.

1. The affects of several new AIDS drugs have all ready been reported.

2. *Consumer Reports* gave high ratings to the breaks on all new cars tested accept one.

3. Advertisements urge us to by a new product even if we already own a comparable item.

4. If you except the charges for a collect telephone call through the ITC network, you'll probably have to brake your piggy bank to pay their bill.

5. Cigarette smoking affects the lungs by creating deposits of tar that inhibit breathing.

6. The show was already to begin except that the star had not arrived.

7. People who live buy the landfill have complained for years about its affects on the neighborhood.

8. The physical therapy program has all ready excepted 20 percent more applicants than it admitted last year.

9. Even a hairline break in a bone can strongly effect an athlete's performance.

10. When they by their textbooks, most students accept the fact that they'll lose a lot when they resell them.

Conscience/Conscious *Conscience* refers to the part of the mind that urges a person to choose right over wrong. *Conscious* means "aware" or "deliberate."

    After he cheated at cards, his conscience started to bother him.

    As she walked through the woods, she became conscious of the hum of insects.

    Elliott made a conscious decision to stop smoking.

Everyday/Every day *Everyday* is a single word that means "ordinary" or "common." *Every day* is two words that mean "occurring daily."

I Love Lucy was a successful comedy show because it appealed to everyday people.

Every day, Lucy and Ethel would find a new way to get into trouble.

Fine/Find   *Fine* means "superior quality" or "a sum of money paid as a penalty." *Find* means "to locate."

He sang a fine solo at church last Sunday.

Demi had to pay a fine for speeding.

Some people still use a willow rod to find water.

Hear/Here   *Hear* means "to perceive sound by ear." *Here* means "at or in this place."

I moved to the front so I could hear the speaker.

My great-grandfather came here in 1883.

Its/It's   *Its* is the possessive form of *it*. *It's* is the contraction of *it is* or *it has*.

The airline canceled its flights because of the snow.

It's twelve o'clock, and we're late.

Ever since it's been in the accident, the car has rattled.

◆ PRACTICE 34-7

Proofread the underlined words in the following sentences for correct spelling. If a correction needs to be made, cross out the incorrect word, and write the correct spelling above it. If the word is spelled correctly, write *C* above it.

Example: It's often difficult for celebrities to adjust to ~~every day~~ *everyday* life.

1. Hear at Simonson's Fashions, we try to make our customers feel that everyday is a sale day.

2. The minister was a find person, and its a shame that he died so young.

3. That inner voice you hear is your conscious telling you how you should behave.

4. In the every day world of work and school, it can be hard to fine the time to relax and appreciate life.

5. By the time I became conscience of the leaking pipe, it's damage ran to more than a hundred dollars.

6. The judge slapped the major corporation with a thousand-dollar fine for everyday that it was not in compliance with the county's safety codes.

7. When immigrants first arrive <u>hear</u> in the United States, they may <u>find</u> that <u>its</u> difficult at first to adjust to their new home.

8. In <u>every day</u> decision making, let your <u>conscience</u> be your guide when it comes to moral issues.

9. Even though they <u>here</u> over and over about the dangers of drinking and driving, young people always think, "<u>It's</u> not going to happen to us."

10. The college is holding <u>it's</u> fourth annual contest to <u>fine</u> the most popular teacher on campus.

Know/Knew/New/No   *Know* means "to have an understanding of" or "to have fixed in the mind." *Knew* is the past tense form of the verb *know. New* means "recent or never used." *No* expresses a negative response.

I <u>know</u> there will be a lunar eclipse tonight.

He <u>knew</u> how to install a <u>new</u> light switch.

Yes, we have <u>no</u> bananas.

Lie/Lay   *Lie* means "to rest or recline." The past tense of *lie* is *lay. Lay* means "to put or place something down." The past tense of *lay* is *laid.*

Every Sunday I <u>lie</u> in bed until noon.

They <u>lay</u> on the grass until it began to rain.

Tammy told Carl to <u>lay</u> his cards on the table.

Brooke and Cassia finally <u>laid</u> down their hockey sticks.

Loose/Lose   *Loose* means "not fastened" or "not attached securely." *Lose* means "to mislay" or "to misplace."

In the 1940s, many women wore <u>loose</u>-fitting pants.

I don't gamble because I hate to <u>lose</u>.

Mine/Mind   *Mine* is a possessive pronoun that indicates ownership. *Mind* can be a noun meaning "human consciousness" or "intelligence" or a verb meaning "to obey" or "to attend to."

That red mountain bike is <u>mine</u>.

A <u>mind</u> is a terrible thing to waste.

"<u>Mind</u> your manners when you visit your grandmother," Dad said.

Passed/Past   *Passed* is the past tense of the verb *pass.* It means "moved by" or "succeeded in." *Past* is a noun meaning "earlier than the present time."

The car that <u>passed</u> me must have been doing more than eighty miles an hour.

David finally <u>passed</u> his driving test.

The novel was set in the <u>past</u>.

Peace/Piece   *Peace* means "the absence of war" or "calm." *Piece* means "a part of something."

> The British prime minister thought he had achieved <u>peace</u> with honor.
>
> My <u>peace</u> of mind was destroyed when the flying saucer landed.
>
> "Have a <u>piece</u> of cake," said Marie.

◆ PRACTICE 34-8

Proofread the underlined words in the following sentences for correct spelling. If a correction needs to be made, cross out the incorrect word, and write the correct spelling above it. If the word is spelled correctly, write *C* above it.

Example: I thought I would ~~loose~~ *lose* my <u>mind</u>. *C*

1. In the <u>passed</u>, many people <u>new</u> their neighbors well.

2. Today, however, we often <u>loose</u> touch with our neighbors or do not <u>know</u> them at all.

3. In a search for inner <u>piece</u> and serenity, we may use relaxation techniques to reach our unconscious <u>minds</u>.

4. We may want to <u>loose</u> ourselves in a place where <u>no</u> other person can reach us.

5. She <u>lay</u> in bed reading for an hour and then <u>lay</u> the book on the table.

6. I don't <u>mind</u> if I <u>loose</u> occasionally; <u>know</u> person can be a winner every time.

7. Once they have <u>past</u> a test, some students put everything they have learned for it out of their <u>minds</u>.

8. In the <u>past</u>, dress codes in schools were not nearly as <u>lose</u> as they are today, and most parents <u>lay</u> down the law about curfews.

9. A musician may <u>no</u> a <u>piece</u> of music by heart and still not <u>mine</u> listening to it over and over again.

10. You may <u>loose</u> your way if you wander <u>passed</u> the warning signs.

Plain/Plane   *Plain* means "simple, not elaborate." *Plane* is the shortened form of *airplane*.

> Sometimes the Amish are referred to as the <u>plain</u> people.
>
> Chuck Yeager was the first person to fly a <u>plane</u> faster than sound.

Principal/Principle   *Principal* means "first" or "highest" or "the head of a school." *Principle* means "a law or basic assumption."

She had the <u>principal</u> role in the movie.

I'll never forget the day the <u>principal</u> called me into his office.

It was against his <u>principles</u> to lie.

Quiet/Quit/Quite   *Quiet* means "free of noise" or "still." *Quit* means "to leave a job" or "to give up." *Quite* means "actually" or "very."

Jane looked forward to the <u>quiet</u> evenings at the lake.

Sammy <u>quit</u> his job and followed the girls into the parking lot.

"You haven't <u>quite</u> got the hang of it yet," she said.

After practicing all summer, Tamika got <u>quite</u> good at handball.

Raise/Rise   *Raise* means "to elevate" or "to increase in size, quantity, or worth." The past tense of *raise* is *raised*. *Rise* means "to stand up" or "to move from a lower position to a higher position." The past tense of *rise* is *rose*.

Carlos <u>raises</u> his hand when the teacher asks for volunteers.

They <u>raised</u> the money for the down payment.

The crowd <u>rises</u> every time their team scores a touchdown.

Sarah <u>rose</u> before dawn so she could see the eclipse.

Right/Write   *Right* means "correct" or "the opposite of left." *Write* means "to form letters with a writing instrument."

If you turn <u>right</u> at the corner, you will be going in the <u>right</u> direction.

All students are required to <u>write</u> three short papers.

Sit/Set   *Sit* means "to assume a sitting position." The past tense of *sit* is *sat*. *Set* means "to put down or place" or "to adjust something to a desired position." The past tense of *set* is *set*.

I usually <u>sit</u> in the front row at the movies.

They <u>sat</u> at the clinic waiting for their names to be called.

Every semester I <u>set</u> goals for myself.

Elizabeth <u>set</u> the mail on the kitchen table and left for work.

Suppose/Supposed   *Suppose* means "to assume" or "to guess." *Supposed* is both the past tense and the past participle of *suppose*. *Supposed* also means "expected" or "required." (Note that when *supposed* has this meaning, it is followed by *to*.)

<u>Suppose</u> researchers found a cure for AIDS tomorrow.

We <u>supposed</u> the movie would be over by ten o'clock.

You were <u>supposed</u> to finish a draft of the report by today.

◆ **PRACTICE 34-9**

Proofread the underlined words in the following sentences for correct spelling. If a correction needs to be made, cross out the incorrect word, and write the correct spelling above it. If the word is spelled correctly, write *C* above it.

                 C   *supposed*

Example: A <u>principal</u> is ~~suppose~~ to care about his or her students' welfare.

1. After a <u>plain</u> crash is reported in the news, many people vow to <u>quit</u> flying forever.

2. It is not <u>write</u> to expect everyone to agree with your personal <u>principals</u> of morality in every case.

3. In earlier times, children were always <u>suppose</u> to be <u>quite</u> and not speak when their elders were talking.

4. My favorite teacher never <u>raised</u> his voice in anger, which <u>set</u> a good example for students.

5. Surveys have shown that many college students' <u>principle</u> goal in life is to become <u>quite</u> wealthy.

6. <u>Suppose</u> for a moment that the defense is <u>write</u> and the district attorney is wrong.

7. It takes <u>quit</u> a few years of training to learn to fly a <u>plain</u>.

8. All test-takers are <u>supposed</u> to <u>sit</u> their books on the table at the front of the room.

9. Even the strictest high school <u>principals</u> cannot always keep students <u>quite</u> and orderly in the hallways.

10. Some passengers insist when they fly on a <u>plain</u> that they have to <u>set</u> on the <u>right</u> side of the aisle, while others insist on sitting on the left.

Their/There/They're *Their* is the possessive form of *they. There* means "at or in that place." *There* is also used in the phrases *there is* and *there are. They're* is a contraction meaning "they are."

Jane Addams wanted poor people to improve <u>their</u> living conditions.

I put the book over <u>there</u>.

<u>There</u> are three reasons I will not eat meat.

<u>They're</u> the best volunteer firefighters I've ever seen.

Then/Than *Then* means "at that time" or "next in time." *Than* is used to introduce the second element in a comparison.

> He was young and naive <u>then</u>.
>
> I went to the job interview and <u>then</u> stopped off for a double chocolate shake.
>
> My dog is smarter <u>than</u> your dog.

Threw/Through *Threw* is the past tense of *throw*. *Through* means "in one side and out the opposite side" or "finished."

> Satchel Paige <u>threw</u> a baseball more than ninety-five miles an hour.
>
> It takes almost thirty minutes to go <u>through</u> the tunnel.
>
> "I'm <u>through</u>," said Clark Kent, storming out of Perry White's office.

To/Too/Two *To* means "in the direction of." *Too* means "also" or "more than enough." *Two* denotes the numeral 2.

> During spring break, I am going <u>to</u> Disney World.
>
> My roommates are coming <u>too</u>.
>
> The microwave popcorn is <u>too</u> hot to eat.
>
> "If we get rid of the tin man and the lion, the <u>two</u> of us can go to Oz," said the scarecrow to Dorothy.

Use/Used *Use* means "to put into service" or "to consume." *Used* is both the past tense and past participle of *use*. *Used* also means "accustomed." (Note that when *used* has this meaning, it is followed by *to*.)

> I <u>use</u> a soft cloth to clean my glasses.
>
> "Hey! Who <u>used</u> all the hot water?" he yelled from the shower.
>
> Mary had <u>used</u> all the firewood during the storm.
>
> After living in Alaska for a year, they got <u>used</u> to the short winter days.

● **Writing Tip**
Don't use the informal spelling *thru* for *through*.

◆ **PRACTICE 34-10**

Proofread the underlined words in the following sentences for correct spelling. If a correction needs to be made, cross out the incorrect word, and write the correct spelling above it. If the word is spelled correctly, write *C* above it.

> **Example:**   Most chemicals aren't dangerous when ~~their~~ *they're* <u>used</u> *C* properly.

1. <u>Their</u> is more <u>than</u> one way to get ahead in this world.

2. Critics charge that in preventing crime our country's criminal justice system often does <u>two</u> little <u>to</u> late.

3. An appeals judge <u>through</u> out the evidence that the jury had <u>used</u>.

4. When they think of <u>there</u> past, people often wonder whether they were better off earlier <u>then</u> they are now.

5. Eighty percent of the students who responded <u>too</u> the survey said that <u>their</u> in favor of a moment of silence but they aren't in favor of school prayer.

6. It <u>use</u> to take more <u>then</u> thirty hours to drive from New York to Miami.

7. Before the interstate highway was opened, drivers had to maneuver <u>their</u> cars <u>threw</u> many small towns.

8. Fewer people <u>use</u> to make the trip in the past because it was just <u>to</u> much trouble <u>then</u>.

9. When the President <u>threw</u> out the first ball of the baseball season this afternoon, he <u>use</u> his left hand.

10. When <u>too</u> people are in love, <u>their</u> often unable to see any fault in each other.

Weather/Whether   *Weather* refers to the state of the atmosphere with respect to temperature, humidity, precipitation, and so on. *Whether* is used in indirect questions.

> The *Farmer's Almanac* says that the <u>weather</u> this winter will be severe.

> <u>Whether</u> or not this prediction will be correct is anyone's guess.

Where/Were/We're   *Where* means "at or in what place." *Were* is the past tense of *are*. *We're* is a contraction meaning "we are."

> <u>Where</u> are you going, and <u>where</u> have you been?

> Charlie Chaplin and Mary Pickford <u>were</u> popular stars of silent movies.

> <u>We're</u> doing our back-to-school shopping early this year.

Whose/Who's   *Whose* is the possessive form of *who*. *Who's* is a contraction meaning "who is" or "who has."

> My roommate asked, "<u>Whose</u> book is this?"

> "<u>Who's</u> there?" squealed the second little pig as he leaned against the door.

> <u>Who's</u> left a yellow 1957 Chevrolet blocking the driveway?

Your/You're   *Your* is the possessive form of *you*. *You're* is a contraction meaning "you are."

"You should have worn your running shoes," said the hare as he passed the tortoise.

"You're too kind," said the tortoise sarcastically.

◆ **PRACTICE 34-11**

Proofread the underlined words in the following sentences for correct spelling. If a correction needs to be made, cross out the incorrect word, and write the correct spelling above it. If the word is spelled correctly, write *C* above it.

 we're   *C*
Example: As citizens, ~~were~~ all concerned with where our country is going.

1. Authorities are attempting to discover who's fingerprints were left at the scene of the crime.

2. Cancer doesn't care weather your rich or poor, young or old, black or white; it can strike anyone.

3. Santa Fe, were I lived for many years, has better weather than New Jersey has.

4. Whenever we listen to politicians debate, were likely to be wondering whose telling the truth.

5. You should take your time before deciding weather to focus your energy on school or on work.

6. The people who's lives influenced me most were my grandmother and grandfather.

7. You can't just sit around wondering whose going to make you're dreams come true.

8. Even when the weather report advises us that it's going to be sunny, were always careful to carry an umbrella.

9. By the time your in high school, people expect you to have decided were you want to be ten years down the road.

10. Only someone who's experienced combat understands the difficulty of deciding weather to face the enemy or retreat.

■ WRITING FIRST: Flashback

Look back at your response to the Writing First exercise on page 458. Identify any words that appear on the lists of commonly confused words (pages 466–475), and check to make sure you have spelled them correctly. Correct any misspelled words and write them here.

_____   _____

_____   _____

■ WRITING FIRST: Revising and Editing

Type your response to the Writing First exercise on page 458 if you haven't already done so. (You can also use a longer writing assignment you are currently working on.) Now, run a spell check. Did the computer pick up all the errors? Which did it identify? Which did it miss? Correct the spelling errors the computer identified.

CHAPTER REVIEW

◆ EDITING PRACTICE

Read the following student essay, into which spelling errors have been introduced. Identify the words you think are misspelled; then, look them up in a dictionary. Finally, cross out each incorrectly spelled word, and write the correct spelling above the line. The first sentence has been edited for you.

Fudging

The origin of the word <u>fudge</u> is ~~unnown.~~ *unknown.* It's meaning seems to have been adopted from many diffrent sources. At present, it has too meanings. The first is "a rich candy made of sugar, butter, milk, and chocolate." The second-- and more intresting--definition is "to fake or falsify."

Everone can remember fudging on an essay test during his or her academic career. A good freind of mine, for example, couldn't answer a question on a history test because he didn't know all the causes of World War II. What did he do? He made some causes up and got a B. Some people, like my friend, have had great success and become expert fudgers. Those students who were able to get away with fudging in high school continue to fudge in college and beyond. Many politicians, for example, feel comfortible fudging there campain speeches to attract voters. They promise to fight corruption, find homes for the homeless, and put an end to crime. Of course, these are empty promises. How are voters suppose to judge a canidate if he or she does not tell them the truth?

Fudging takes place not only in politics but also in many other professions. In sceince, people fudge to save time and money. Many products on the market are the result of sceintific fudging. Some researchers manufacture data so that there research projects can be finished quickly and cheaply. For example, in the 1980s, a firm fudged data to get the Food and Drug Aministration to approve one of it's products: a pill to help people loose wieght. When con-sumers complained they were getting sick, the FDA puled the pill off the market. Of course, weather the researcher was fired makes no difference. The damage was all ready done.

◆ COLLABORATIVE ACTIVITIES

1. Working in pairs, compare responses to the Writing First exercise on page 458. How many of the same misspelled words did both you and your partner find?
2. What patterns of misspelling do you see in each Writing First exercise? What types of spelling errors seem most common?
3. Collaborate with your partner to make a spelling list for the two of you, and then work with other groups to create a spelling list for the whole class. When you have finished, determine which types of errors are most common.

☑ REVIEW CHECKLIST:
Understanding Spelling

- ☐ Follow the steps to becoming a better speller. (See 34A.)

- ☐ *I* comes before *e*, except after *c* or in any *ay* sound, as in *neighbor*. (See 34B.)

- ☐ Adding a prefix to a word never affects the word's spelling. (See 34C.)

- ☐ Adding a suffix to a word may change the word's spelling. (See 34D.)

- ☐ When a word ends with -*e*, drop the *e* if the suffix begins with a vowel. Keep the *e* if the suffix begins with a consonant. (See 34D.)

- ☐ When you add a suffix to a word that ends with a -*y*, change the *y* to an *i* if the letter before the *y* is a consonant. Keep the *y* if the letter before the *y* is a vowel. (See 34D.)

- ☐ When you add a suffix that begins in a vowel, double the final consonant in the original word if (1) the last three letters of the word have a consonant-vowel-consonant pattern (cvc), and (2) the word has one syllable, or the last syllable is stressed. (See 34D.)

- ☐ Memorize the most commonly confused words. (See 34E.)

UNIT EIGHT

Reading Essays

35

Reading Critically

Reading is essential to all your college courses. To get the most out of your reading, approach the books and articles you read in a practical way, asking yourself what these works can offer you. Be willing to read and reread. Finally, approach assigned readings critically—just as you approach your own writing when you reread and revise.

Reading critically does not mean finding fault with every point and challenging or arguing with every idea, but it does mean wondering, commenting, questioning, and judging. Most of all, it means being an active rather than a passive reader. To benefit from what you read, you need to participate actively in the reading process. Being an **active reader** involves approaching a reading assignment with a clear understanding of your purpose, highlighting the selection, annotating it, and perhaps outlining it—all *before* you begin to respond in writing to what you have read.

A Approaching a Reading Assignment

The first step in the process of reading critically—a step that begins even before you start reading—is to ask yourself questions about your purpose for reading. The answers to these questions can help you understand what you hope to get out of what you are reading and how you will use what you get.

PREVIEW

In this chapter, you will learn

- how to approach a reading assignment (35A)

- how to highlight a reading assignment (35B)

- how to annotate a reading assignment (35C)

- how to outline a reading assignment (35D)

- how to write a response paragraph (35E)

Questions about Purpose

- Why are you reading?
- How thoroughly must you understand the reading selection?
- Will you be expected to discuss the reading selection in class or with your instructor in a conference?
- Will you have to write about the reading selection? If so, will you be expected to respond informally (for example, in a journal entry) or more formally (for example, in an essay)?
- Will you be tested on the material?

Keeping these questions in mind, **preview** the reading selection. As you preview, your goal is to get a sense of the writer's main point and key supporting ideas. You do this by looking at the title, at *italicized* and **boldfaced** words, at headings, and at illustrations (graphs, charts, photographs, and so on). Read at least the first sentence or two of every paragraph, and skim the complete opening and closing paragraphs.

◆ PRACTICE 35-1

"No Comprendo" ("I Don't Understand") is an article arguing against bilingual education by Barbara Mujica, a professor of Spanish at Georgetown University in Washington, D.C. Suppose that your assignment has two parts—to discuss this article in class and later to express your own views on the issue of bilingual education in a response paragraph.

Preview the article, keeping in mind the Questions about Purpose on page 481. As you read, try to identify the author's main point and key supporting ideas.

No Comprendo

Last spring, my niece phoned me in tears. She was graduating from high school and had to make a decision. An outstanding soccer player, she was offered athletic scholarships by several colleges. So why was she crying? 1

My niece came to the United States from South America as a child. Although she had received good grades in her schools in Miami, she spoke English with a heavy accent, and her comprehension and writing skills were deficient. She was afraid that once she left the Miami environment, she would feel uncomfortable and, worse still, have difficulty keeping up with class work. 2

Programs that keep foreign-born children in Spanish-language classrooms for years are only part of the problem. During a visit to my niece's former school, I observed that all business, not just teaching, was conducted in Spanish. In the office, secretaries spoke to the administrators and the children in Spanish. Announcements over the public-address system were made in an English so fractured that it was almost incomprehensible. 3

I asked my niece's mother why, after years in public schools, her daughter had poor English skills. "It's the whole environment," she 4 replied. "All kinds of services are available in Spanish or Spanglish. Sports and after-school activities are conducted in Spanglish. That's what the kids hear on the radio and in the street."

Until recently, immigrants made learning English a priority. But even when they didn't learn English themselves, their children grew up speaking it. Thousands of first-generation Americans still strive to learn English, but others face reduced educational and career opportunities because they have not mastered this basic skill they need to get ahead.

According to the 1990 census, 40 percent of the Hispanics born in the United States do not graduate from high school, and the Department of Education says that a lack of proficiency in English is an important factor in the drop-out rate.

People and agencies that favor providing services only in foreign languages want to help people who do not speak English, but they may be doing these people a disservice by condemning them to a linguistic ghetto from which they cannot easily escape.

And my niece? She turned down all of her scholarship opportunities, deciding instead to attend a small college in Miami, where she will never have to put her English to the test.

Author's main point

_____

_____

Key supporting ideas

1. _____

2. _____

3. _____

4. _____

B Highlighting a Reading Assignment

As you read, **highlight** the selection, using underlining and symbols to identify key ideas. This active reading strategy will help you understand the writer's main ideas and make connections among these ideas when you reread. Since your time is limited, your highlighting should be selective. Remember, you will eventually be rereading every highlighted word, phrase, and sentence—so highlight only the most important, most useful information.

The most effective highlighting uses different symbols for different purposes. When you reread—for example, in preparing to take an exam or write a paper—these symbols will convey specific information to you. The number and kinds of highlighting symbols you use when reading are up to you. All that matters is that your symbols are clear and easy to remember.

Highlighting Symbols

- ■ <u>Underline</u> key ideas—for example, topic sentences.
- ■ Box or circle words or phrases you want to remember.
- ■ Place a check mark (✔) or star (⋆) next to an important idea.
- ■ Place a double check mark (✔✔) or double star (⋆⋆) next to an especially significant idea.
- ■ Draw lines or arrows to connect related ideas.
- ■ Put a question mark (?) beside a word or idea that you don't understand.
- ■ Number the writer's key supporting points or examples.

Here is how a student highlighted an excerpt from the newspaper column "Barbie at Thirty-Five" by Anna Quindlen.

Consider the recent study at the University of Arizona investigating the <u>attitudes of white and black teenage girls toward body image</u>. The ⋆ attitudes of the white girls were a nightmare. Ninety percent expressed ✔ <u>dissatisfaction with their own bodies</u>, and many said they saw dieting as a kind of all-purpose panacea? "I think the reason I would diet would be to gain self-confidence," said one. "I'd feel like it was a way of getting control," said another. And they were curiously united in their description of the perfect girl. She's 5 feet 7 inches, weighs just over 100 pounds, has long legs and flowing hair. The researchers concluded, "The ideal girl was a living manifestation of the Barbie doll."

While white girls described an impossible ideal, black teenagers talked about appearance in terms of style, attitude, pride, and personality. White respondents talked "thin," black ones "shapely." Seventy percent of the black teenagers said they were <u>satisfied with their</u> ✔ <u>weight</u>, and there was little emphasis on dieting. "We're all brought up and taught to be realistic about life," said one, "and we don't look at things the way you want them to be. You look at them the way they are."

The student who highlighted this passage was preparing to write an essay about eating disorders. She began by underlining and starring Quindlen's main idea. She then boxed the two key groups the passage compares—*white girls* and *black teenagers*—and underlined two phrases that illustrate how the attitudes of the two groups differ (*dissatisfaction with their own bodies* and *satisfied with their weight*). Check marks in the margin emphasize the importance of these two phrases, and arrows connect each phrase to the appropriate group of girls.

The student also circled three related terms that characterize white girls' attitudes—*perfect girl, Barbie doll,* and *impossible ideal*—drawing lines to connect them to one another. Finally, she circled the unfamiliar word *panacea,* which she planned to look up in a dictionary, and put a question mark above it.

◆ PRACTICE 35-2

Review the highlighted passage by Anna Quindlen (page 484). How would your own highlighting of this passage be similar to or different from the sample student highlighting?

◆ PRACTICE 35-3

Reread "No Comprendo" (page 482). As you reread, highlight the article by underlining and starring main ideas, boxing and circling key words, checkmarking important points, and, if you wish, drawing lines and arrows to connect related ideas. Also, circle each unfamiliar word, and put a question mark in the margin beside it.

C Annotating a Reading Assignment

To be most effective, highlighting should be accompanied by another active reading strategy: annotating. **Annotating** a passage involves making notes—of questions, reactions, reminders, ideas for writing or discussion—in the margins or between the lines. Keeping this kind of informal record of ideas as they occur to you can help prepare you for class discussion and provide a useful source of material for writing.

As you read a passage, asking yourself the following questions will help you write effective annotations.

Questions for Reading Critically

■ What is the writer saying? What do you think the writer is suggesting or implying? What makes you think so?

■ What is the writer's purpose?

(continued on the following page)

(continued from the previous page)

- What audience is the writer addressing?
- Is the writer responding to another writer's ideas?
- What is the writer's main point?
- How does the writer support his or her points? Does the writer use facts, opinions, or a combination of the two?
- Does the writer include enough supporting details and examples?
- What pattern of development does the writer use to arrange his or her ideas? Is this pattern the best choice?
- Does the writer seem well informed? Reasonable? Fair?
- What kind of language does the writer use?
- Do you understand the writer's vocabulary?
- Do you understand the writer's ideas?
- Do you agree with the points the writer is making?
- How are the ideas presented in this reading selection like (or unlike) those presented in other selections you've read?

The following passage reproduces the student's highlighting from page 484 and also illustrates her annotations.

Consider the recent study at the University of Arizona investigating the attitudes of white and black teenage girls toward body image. The attitudes of the white girls were a nightmare. Ninety percent expressed dissatisfaction with their own bodies, and many said they saw dieting as a kind of all-purpose panacea. "I think the reason I would diet would be to gain self-confidence," said one. "I'd feel like it was a way of getting control," said another. And they were curiously united in their description of the perfect girl. She's 5 feet 7 inches, weighs just over 100 pounds, has long legs and flowing hair. The researchers concluded, "The ideal girl was a living manifestation of the Barbie doll."

While white girls described an impossible ideal, black teenagers talked about appearance in terms of style, attitude, pride, and personality. White respondents talked "thin," black ones "shapely." Seventy percent of the black teenagers said they were satisfied with their weight, and there was little emphasis on dieting. "We're all brought up and taught to be realistic about life," said one, "and we don't look at things the way you want them to be. You look at them the way they are."

= cure-all

Need for control, perfection. Why? Media? Parents?

Barbie Doll = plastic, unreal, superficial

"Thin" vs. "shapely"

Only 30% dissatisfied — vs. 90% of white girls

vs. Barbie doll (=unrealistic)

overgeneralization?

With her annotations, this student noted the meaning of the word *panacea*, translated the Barbie doll reference and the contrasting statistics into her own words, and recorded questions she intended to explore further.

◆ PRACTICE 35-4

Reread "No Comprendo" (page 482). As you reread, refer to the Questions for Reading Critically (page 485), and use them to help you annotate the article by writing down your own thoughts and questions in the margins. Note where you agree or disagree with the writer, and briefly explain why. Quickly summarize any points you think are particularly important. Take time to look up any unfamiliar words you have circled, and write brief definitions. Think of these annotations as your preparation for discussing the article in class and eventually writing about your response to it.

◆ PRACTICE 35-5

Trade workbooks with another student, and read over his or her highlighting and annotating of "No Comprendo." How are your written responses similar to the other student's? How are they different? Do your classmate's responses help you see anything new about the article?

D Outlining a Reading Assignment

Yet another technique you can use to help you better understand a passage you are reading is **outlining**. Unlike a **formal outline**, which must follow fairly rigid conventions, an **informal outline** is easy to make, and it can be a valuable reading tool. In fact, after you have finished your informal outline, you should be able to see at a glance what the writer's emphasis is—which ideas are more important than others—and how ideas are related.

To make an informal outline of a reading selection, follow the guidelines in the box below.

● **Writing Tip**
Formal outlines can help you keep track of ideas in long essays or research papers. See Appendix B for an example of a formal outline.

FOCUS Making an Informal Outline

1. Write or type the passage's main idea across the top of a sheet of paper. (This will remind you of the passage's focus and help keep your outline on track.)
2. At the left margin, write down the most important idea of the first paragraph or section of the passage.
3. Indent the next line a few spaces, and list the examples or details that support this idea.
4. As ideas become more specific, indent further. (Ideas that have the same degree of importance are indented the same distance from the left margin.)
5. Repeat the process with each paragraph or section of the passage.

The student who highlighted and annotated the passage from "Barbie at Thirty-Five" by Anna Quindlen (page 484) made the following informal outline to help her understand the ideas in the passage.

```
Main idea: Black and white teenage girls have very dif-
ferent attitudes about their body images.
     White girls dissatisfied
          90% dissatisfied with appearance
          Dieting = cure-all
               —self-confidence
               —control
          Ideal = unrealistic
               —tall and thin
               —Barbie doll
     Black girls satisfied
          70% satisfied with weight
          Dieting not important
          Ideal = realistic
               —shapely
               —not thin
```

◆ PRACTICE 35-6

Working on your own or in a small group, make an informal outline of "No Comprendo" (page 482). Refer to your highlighting and annotations as you construct your outline. When you have finished, check to make certain your outline indicates the writer's emphasis and the relationships among her ideas.

E Writing a Response Paragraph

Once you really understand a passage, you are ready to write about it. Sometimes you will be asked to write an essay analyzing a writer's ideas or comparing them with another writer's position. At other times, you will be asked to write a **response paragraph** in which you record your informal reactions to a passage.

For more on writing a paragraph, see Chapters 1 and 2.

Because a response paragraph is informal, no special guidelines or rules govern its format or structure. Your goal is simply to think on paper, letting your mind react to the writer's ideas. As in any paragraph, however, you should include a topic sentence, write in complete sentences, and link sentences with appropriate transitions. Informal style and personal opinions are perfectly acceptable.

The student who highlighted, annotated, and outlined the Quindlen passage wrote this response paragraph.

```
     Why are white and black girls' body images so differ-
ent? Why do black girls think it's okay to be "shapely"
while white girls are obsessed with being thin? Maybe
```

it's because music videos and movies and fashion magazines show so many more white models, all half-starved,
with perfect hair and legs. Or maybe white girls get
different messages from their parents or the people they
date. Do white and black girls' attitudes about their
bodies stay the same when they get older? And what about
<u>male</u> teenagers' self-images? Do white and black <u>guys</u>
have different body images too?

The process of writing this paragraph was very helpful to the student. The questions she asked raised a number of interesting ideas that she could explore in class discussion or in a longer, more formal, and more fully developed piece of writing.

◆ PRACTICE 35-7

On a separate sheet of paper, write an informal response paragraph expressing your reactions to "No Comprendo" (page 482) and the issue of bilingual education.

☑ REVIEW CHECKLIST:
Reading Critically

▢ Understand your purpose before you begin to read. (See 35A.)

▢ Highlight your reading assignment. (See 35B.)

▢ Annotate your reading assignment. (See 35C.)

▢ Outline your reading assignment. (See 35D.)

▢ Write a response paragraph. (See 35E.)

36

Readings for Writers

See Chapters 3–11 for information on using various patterns for developing paragraphs; see Chapter 14 for information on writing essays that use these patterns of development.

The following nineteen essays by professional writers give you interesting material to read, react to, think critically about, discuss, and write about. In addition, these essays illustrate some of the ways you can organize ideas in your own writing.

The essays in this chapter use the nine patterns of development you learned about in Units 1 to 3 of this book: exemplification, narration, description, process, cause and effect, comparison and contrast, classification, definition, and argument. These patterns are not your only options for arranging ideas in essays; in fact, many essays combine several patterns of development. Still, the nine patterns illustrated here suggest useful strategies for organizing material in your own writing. Understanding how each pattern works will help you use the most effective organization strategy when you are writing for a particular purpose and audience.

In this chapter, two essays by professional writers illustrate each pattern of development. (For argument, three model essays are included.) Each essay is preceded by a short introduction that tells you something about the writer and suggests what to look for as you read. Following each selection are four sets of questions. (Questions you can do in collaboration with other students are marked with an asterisk.)

For more on highlighting and annotating, see Chapter 35.

- **Reacting to the Reading** questions suggest guidelines for highlighting and annotating the essay.
- **Reacting to Words** questions focus on the writer's word choice.
- **Reacting to Ideas** questions encourage you to respond critically to the writer's ideas and perhaps to consider his or her audience or purpose.
- **Reacting to the Pattern** questions ask you to consider how ideas are arranged within the essay and how they are connected to one another.

Each section ends with **Writing Practice** suggestions that give you the opportunity to work either on your own or in collaboration with other students.

A   Exemplification

An **exemplification** essay uses one or more specific examples to support a thesis statement. The two selections that follow, "Don't Call Me a Hot Tamale" by Judith Ortiz Cofer and "The Suspected Shopper" by Ellen Goodman, are exemplification essays. The first uses a series of short examples to support a thesis; the second uses a single extended example.

For more on how to write an exemplification essay, see 14A.

DON'T CALL ME A HOT TAMALE

Judith Ortiz Cofer

Award-winning poet, novelist, and essayist Judith Ortiz Cofer often writes about her experiences as a Latina—a Hispanic woman—living in a non-Hispanic culture. In "Don't Call Me a Hot Tamale" (1993), she discusses how being Puerto Rican has affected her in the world beyond Puerto Rico. Note that all her examples illustrate the stereotypes she encounters not simply in reaction to her heritage but also in reaction to her gender.

1   On a bus to London from Oxford University, where I was earning some graduate credits one summer, a young man, obviously fresh from a pub, approached my seat. With both hands over his heart, he went down on his knees in the aisle and broke into an Irish tenor's rendition of "Maria" from *West Side Story*. I was not amused. "Maria" had followed me to London, reminding me of a prime fact of my life: You can leave the island of Puerto Rico, master the English language, and travel as far as you can, but if you're a Latina, especially one who so clearly belongs to Rita Moreno's[1] gene pool, the island travels with you.

2   Growing up in New Jersey and wanting most of all to belong, I lived in two completely different worlds. My parents designed our life as a microcosm of their *casas* on the island—we spoke in Spanish, ate Puerto Rican food bought at the *bodega*, and practiced strict Catholicism complete with Sunday mass in Spanish.

3   I was kept under tight surveillance by my parents, since my virtue and modesty were, by their cultural equation, the same as their honor. As teenagers, my friends and I were lectured constantly on how to behave as proper *señoritas*. But it was a conflicting message we received, since our Puerto Rican mothers also encouraged us to look and act like women by dressing us in clothes our Anglo schoolmates and their mothers found too "mature" and flashy. I often felt humiliated when I appeared at an American friend's birthday party wearing a dress more suitable for a semiformal. At Puerto Rican festivities, neither the music nor the colors we wore could be too loud.

4   I remember Career Day in high school, when our teachers told us to come dressed as if for a job interview. That morning, I agonized in front of

---

1. A Puerto Rican actress, dancer, and singer. She is well known for her role in the movie musical *West Side Story*, a version of Shakespeare's *Romeo and Juliet* set among Anglos and Puerto Ricans in New York City.

my closet, trying to figure out what a "career girl" would wear, because the only model I had was Marlo Thomas[2] on TV. To me and my Puerto Rican girlfriends, dressing up meant wearing our mother's ornate jewelry and clothing.

At school that day, the teachers assailed us for wearing "everything at once"—meaning too much jewelry and too many accessories. And it was painfully obvious that the other students in their tailored skirts and silk blouses thought we were hopeless and vulgar. The way they looked at us was a taste of the cultural clash that awaited us in the real world, where prospective employers and men on the street would often misinterpret our tight skirts and bright colors as a come-on. 5

It is custom, not chromosomes, that leads us to choose scarlet over pale pink. Our mothers had grown up on a tropical island where the natural environment was a riot of primary colors, where showing your skin was one way to keep cool as well as to look sexy. On the island, women felt freer to dress and move provocatively since they were protected by the traditions and laws of a Spanish/Catholic system of morality and machismo, the main rule of which was: *You may look at my sister, but if you touch her I will kill you.* The extended family and church structure provided them with a circle of safety on the island; if a man "wronged" a girl, everyone would close in to save her family honor. 6

Off-island, signals often get mixed. When a Puerto Rican girl who is dressed in her idea of what is attractive meets a man from the mainstream culture who has been trained to react to certain types of clothing as a sexual signal, a clash is likely to take place. She is seen as a Hot Tamale, a sexual firebrand. I learned this lesson at my first formal dance when my date leaned over and painfully planted a sloppy, overeager kiss on my mouth. When I didn't respond with sufficient passion, he said in a resentful tone: "I thought you Latin girls were supposed to mature early." It was only the first time I would feel like a fruit or vegetable—I was supposed to *ripen,* not just grow into womanhood like other girls. 7

These stereotypes, though rarer, still surface in my life. I recently stayed at a classy metropolitan hotel. After having dinner with a friend, I was returning to my room when a middle-aged man in a tuxedo stepped directly into my path. With his champagne glass extended toward me, he exclaimed, "Evita!"[3] 8

Blocking my way, he bellowed the song "Don't Cry for Me, Argentina." Playing to the gathering crowd, he began to sing loudly a ditty to the tune of "La Bamba"[4]—except the lyrics were about a girl named Maria whose exploits all rhymed with her name and gonorrhea. 9

I knew that this same man—probably a corporate executive, even worldly by most standards—would never have regaled a white woman with a dirty song in public. But to him, I was just a character in his universe of "others," all cartoons. 10

Still, I am one of the lucky ones. There are thousands of Latinas without the privilege of the education that my parents gave me. For them every day is a struggle against the misconceptions perpetuated by the myth of the Latina as whore, domestic worker or criminal. 11

---

2. Star of a popular 1970s television comedy about a young woman living in New York City.

3. Eva Peron, wife of Juan Peron, president of Argentina in the 1940s and 1950s. She is the subject of the musical *Evita.*

4. A song with Spanish lyrics popular in the late 1950s.

Rather than fight these pervasive stereotypes, I try to replace them   12
with a more interesting set of realities. I travel around the U.S. reading
from my books of poetry and my novel. With the stories I tell, the dreams
and fears I examine in my work, I try to get my audience past the particu-
lars of my skin color, my accent or my clothes.

I once wrote a poem in which I called Latinas "God's brown daugh-   13
ters." It is really a prayer, of sorts, for communication and respect. In it,
Latin women pray "in Spanish to an Anglo God/with a Jewish heritage,"
and they are "fervently hoping/that if not omnipotent,/at least He be
bilingual."

Reacting to the Reading

1. Preview the essay. As you read it more carefully, highlight and annotate
   as needed to help you understand the writer's ideas.

2. Underline the essay's thesis statement. In the margins of the essay,
   number the examples Cofer uses to support this thesis.

Reacting to Words

*1. Define these words: *rendition* (paragraph 1), *microcosm* (2), *ornate* (4),
   assailed (5), *riot* (6), *machismo* (6), *firebrand* (7), *regaled* (10), *perpetu-*
   ated (11), *pervasive* (12), *omnipotent* (13). Can you suggest a synonym
   for each word that will work in the essay?

2. What connotations does the phrase *hot tamale* have for you? What do
   you think Cofer intends it to convey? Can you think of a word or
   phrase that might be more effective?

Reacting to Ideas

*1. Cofer states her thesis in paragraph 1: "You can leave the island of
   Puerto Rico, master the English language, and travel as far as you can,
   but if you're a Latina, . . . the island travels with you." Restate this
   thesis in your own words. Do you think this statement applies only to
   Latinas or to other ethnic groups as well? Explain.

2. How, according to Cofer, are the signals sent by dress and appearance
   interpreted differently in Puerto Rico and "off-island" (paragraph 7)?
   How does this difference create problems for Cofer? Do you think
   there is anything she can do to avoid these problems?

Reacting to the Pattern

1. What examples does Cofer use to support her thesis? Do you think
   she uses enough examples to convince readers that her thesis is
   reasonable?

2. Like the body paragraphs, the essay's introductory paragraph includes
   an example. Do you think this is an effective opening strategy? Why or
   why not? How else might Cofer have begun her essay?

3. All of Cofer's examples are personal experiences. Are they as convincing as statistics or examples from current news articles would be? Are
   they more convincing? Explain.

Writing Practice

1. What kinds of examples can you think of to counteract the stereotype of the Latina as "whore, domestic worker or criminal" (paragraph 11)? Write a letter to a television network in which you propose the addition of several different Latina characters to actual programs in which they might appear.

2. What do you think Cofer can do to avoid being stereotyped? Write an essay that gives examples of specific things she could do to change the way others see her.

3. Do you think others stereotype you because of your heritage—or because of your age, your gender, or where you live? Discuss some specific instances of such stereotyping.

THE SUSPECTED SHOPPER

Ellen Goodman

Journalist Ellen Goodman wrote "The Suspected Shopper" in 1981 for her syndicated newspaper column. Note that although Goodman develops a single extended example of a "suspected shopper"—herself—throughout her essay, she supports her thesis with specific examples of incidents in which she was suspected. As you read, consider whether the essay is still relevant to readers today—or whether it is perhaps even more relevant.

1 It is Saturday, Shopping Saturday, as it's called by the merchants who spread their wares like plush welcome mats across the pages of my newspaper.

2 But the real market I discover is a different, less eager place than the one I read about. On this Shopping Saturday I don't find welcomes, I find warnings and wariness.

3 At the first store, a bold sign of the times confronts me: SHOPLIFTERS WILL BE PROSECUTED TO THE FULL EXTENT OF THE LAW.

4 At the second store, instead of a greeter, I find a doorkeeper. It is his job, his duty, to bar my entrance. To pass, I must give up the shopping bag on my arm. I check it in and check it out.

5 At the third store, I venture as far as the dressing room. Here I meet another worker paid to protect the merchandise rather than to sell it. The guard of this dressing room counts the number of items I carry in and will count the number of items I carry out.

6 In the mirror, a long, white, plastic security tag juts out from the blouse tucked into the skirt. I try futilely to pat it down along my left hip, try futilely to zip the skirt.

7 Finally, during these strange gyrations, a thought seeps through years of dulled consciousness, layers of denial. Something has happened to the relationship between shops and shoppers. I no longer feel like a woman in search of a shirt. I feel like an enemy at Checkpoint Charlie.[1]

8 I finally, belatedly, realize that I am treated less like a customer these days and more like a criminal. And I hate it. This change happened grad-

---

1. A military security checkpoint.

ually, and understandably. Security rose in tandem with theft. The defenses of the shopkeepers went up, step by step, with the offenses of the thieves.

But now as the weapons escalate, it's the average consumer, the innocent bystander, who is hit by friendly fire.   9

I don't remember the first time an errant security tag buzzed at the doorway, the first time I saw a camera eye in a dress department. I accepted it as part of the price of living in a tight honesty market.   10

In the supermarket, they began to insist on a mug shot before they would cash my check. I tried not to take it personally. At the drugstore, the cashier began to staple my bags closed. And I tried not to take it personally.   11

Now, these experiences have accumulated until I feel routinely treated like a suspect. At the jewelry store, the door is unlocked only for those who pass judgment. In the junior department, the suede pants are permanently attached to the hangers. In the gift shop, the cases are only opened with a key.   12

I am not surprised anymore, but I am finally aware of just how unpleasant it is to be dealt with as guilty until we prove our innocence. Anyplace we are not known, we are not trusted. The old slogan, "Let the Consumer Beware," has been replaced with a new slogan: "Beware of the Consumer."   13

It is no fun to be Belgium[2] in the war between sales and security. Thievery has changed the atmosphere of the marketplace. Merchant distrust has spread through the ventilation system of a whole business, a whole city, and it infects all of us.   14

At the cashier counter today, with my shirt in hand, I the Accused stand quietly while the saleswoman takes my credit card. I watch her round up the usual suspicions. In front of my face, without a hint of embarrassment, she checks my charge number against the list of stolen credit vehicles. While I stand there, she calls the clearinghouse of bad debtors.   15

Having passed both tests, I am instructed to add my name, address, serial number to the bottom of the charge. She checks one signature against another, the picture against the person. Only then does she release the shirt into my custody.   16

And so this Shopping Saturday I take home six ounces of silk and a load of resentment.   17

Reacting to the Reading

1. Preview the essay. As you read it more carefully, highlight and annotate as needed to help you understand the writer's ideas.

2. Reread the essay, and review your highlighting and annotations. In the margins of the essay, supplement Goodman's examples with one or two examples from your personal experience (or from the experiences of your friends) that support her thesis.

Reacting to Words

*1. Define these words: *futilely* (paragraph 6), *gyrations* (7), *belatedly* (8), *tandem* (8), *errant* (10). Can you suggest a synonym for each word that will work in the essay?

2. Country located between France and Germany, which were enemies in several wars.

2. What is Goodman's purpose in choosing words like *enemy* (paragraph 7) and *mug shot* (11)? How do they help to support her thesis? Can you find additional words or expressions that serve the same purpose?

Reacting to Ideas

*1. Goodman, a middle-class white woman, uses *we* in the sentence "Anyplace we are not known, we are not trusted" (13). Who is this *we?* Do you think Goodman is really part of the group with which she identifies?

2. In paragraph 8, Goodman says the change in attitude she observes is understandable. Do you think she is right?

3. Do you think shoplifting is more or less of a problem today than it was in 1981 when Goodman wrote her essay? What makes you think so?

Reacting to the Pattern

1. In paragraph 8, Goodman states her thesis: "I finally, belatedly, realize that I am treated less like a customer these days and more like a criminal." However, she introduces a number of her examples even before she states this thesis. Why do you think she does this?

2. List the specific examples of times when Goodman was "treated less like a customer . . . and more like a criminal" (8).

3. How does Goodman arrange the specific examples that support her thesis? Is each discussed in an individual paragraph, or are examples grouped together?

Writing Practice

*1. Why do you think people shoplift? Write an exemplification essay in which you discuss a different reason in each body paragraph.

2. Have you ever wavered between giving in to peer pressure and maintaining your own sense of right and wrong? Develop an extended example that illustrates what it was like to be caught in the middle and explains how you resolved the problem.

3. What do you think merchants can do to reduce shoplifting without making shoppers feel like criminals? Using exemplification to organize your ideas, write a letter to a store you patronize regularly.

B   Narration

For more on how to write a narrative essay, see 14B.

A **narrative** essay tells a story by presenting a series of events in chronological order. In the first of the two essays that follow, "The Sanctuary of School," Lynda Barry tells a story about home and family. In the second, "Thirty-Eight Who Saw Murder Didn't Call the Police," Martin Gansberg reports the story of a tragic murder.

THE SANCTUARY OF SCHOOL

Lynda Barry

In her cartoon strip "Ernie Pook's Comeek," which appears in a number of newspapers and magazines, Lynda Barry looks at the world through the eyes of children. Her characters remind adult readers of the tumultuous world of young people and of the clarity with which they see social situations. In "The Sanctuary of School," Barry tells a story from her own childhood. As you read this 1992 essay, note how Barry relates her personal experience to a broader issue involving childhood.

1   I was 7 years old the first time I snuck out of the house in the dark. It was winter and my parents had been fighting all night. They were short on money and long on relatives who kept "temporarily" moving into our house because they had nowhere else to go.

2   My brother and I were used to giving up our bedroom. We slept on the couch, something we actually liked because it put us that much closer to the light of our lives, our television.

3   At night when everyone was asleep, we lay on our pillows watching it with the sound off. We watched Steve Allen's mouth moving. We watched Johnny Carson's mouth moving.[1] We watched movies filled with gangsters shooting machine guns into packed rooms, dying soldiers hurling a last grenade and beautiful women crying at windows. Then the sign-off finally came and we tried to sleep.

4   The morning I snuck out, I woke up filled with a panic about needing to get to school. The sun wasn't quite up yet but my anxiety was so fierce that I just got dressed, walked quietly across the kitchen and let myself out the back door.

5   It was quiet outside. Stars were still out. Nothing moved and no one was in the street. It was as if someone had turned the sound off on the world.

6   I walked the alley, breaking thin ice over the puddles with my shoes. I didn't know why I was walking to school in the dark. I didn't think about it. All I knew was a feeling of panic, like the panic that strikes kids when they realize they are lost.

7   That feeling eased the moment I turned the corner and saw the dark outline of my school at the top of the hill. My school was made up of about 15 nondescript portable classrooms set down on a fenced concrete lot in a rundown Seattle neighborhood, but it had the most beautiful view of the Cascade Mountains. You could see them from anywhere on the playfield and you could see them from the windows of my classroom—Room 2.

8   I walked over to the monkey bars and hooked my arms around the cold metal. I stood for a long time just looking across Rainier Valley. The sky was beginning to whiten and I could hear a few birds.

9   In a perfect world my absence at home would not have gone unnoticed. I would have had two parents in a panic to locate me, instead of two parents in a panic to locate an answer to the hard question of survival during a deep financial and emotional crisis.

---

1. Steve Allen and Johnny Carson were late-night television hosts.

But in an overcrowded and unhappy home, it's incredibly easy for any   10
child to slip away. The high levels of frustration, depression and anger in
my house made my brother and me invisible. We were children with the
sound turned off. And for us, as for the steadily increasing number of
neglected children in this country, the only place where we could count on
being noticed was at school.

"Hey there, young lady. Did you forget to go home last night?" It was   11
Mr. Gunderson, our janitor, whom we all loved. He was nice and he was
funny and he was old with white hair, thick glasses and an unbelievable
number of keys. I could hear them jingling as he walked across the playfield. I felt incredibly happy to see him.

He let me push his wheeled garbage can between the different por-   12
tables as he unlocked each room. He let me turn on the lights and raise
the window shades and I saw my school slowly come to life. I saw Mrs.
Holman, our school secretary, walk into the office without her orange lip-
stick on yet. She waved.

I saw the fifth-grade teacher Mr. Cunningham, walking under the   13
breezeway eating a hard roll. He waved.

And I saw my teacher, Mrs. Claire LeSane, walking toward us in a red   14
coat and calling my name in a very happy and surprised way, and suddenly
my throat got tight and my eyes stung and I ran toward her crying. It was
something that surprised us both.

It's only thinking about it now, 28 years later, that I realize I was cry-   15
ing from relief. I was with my teacher, and in a while I was going to sit at
my desk, with my crayons and pencils and books and classmates all
around me, and for the next six hours I was going to enjoy a thoroughly
secure, warm and stable world. It was a world I absolutely relied on. Without it, I don't know where I would have gone that morning.

Mrs. LeSane asked me what was wrong and when I said "Nothing," she   16
seemingly left it at that. But she asked me if I would carry her purse for
her, an honor above all honors, and she asked if I wanted to come into
Room 2 early and paint.

She believed in the natural healing power of painting and drawing for   17
troubled children. In the back of her room there was always a drawing
table and an easel with plenty of supplies, and sometimes during the day
she would come up to you for what seemed like no good reason and quietly ask if you wanted to go to the back table and "make some pictures for
Mrs. LeSane." We all had a chance at it—to sit apart from the class for a
while to paint, draw and silently work out impossible problems on 11 × 17
sheets of newsprint.

Drawing came to mean everything to me. At the back table in Room 2,   18
I learned to build myself a life preserver that I could carry into my home.

We all know that a good education system saves lives, but the people   19
of this country are still told that cutting the budget for public schools is
necessary, that poor salaries for teachers are all we can manage and that
art, music and all creative activities must be the first to go when times
are lean.

Before- and after-school programs are cut and we are told that public   20
schools are not made for baby-sitting children. If parents are neglectful
temporarily or permanently, for whatever reason, it's certainly sad, but
their unlucky children must fend for themselves. Or slip through the
cracks. Or wander in a dark night alone.

We are told in a thousand ways that not only are public schools not important, but that the children who attend them, the children who need them most, are not important either. We leave them to learn from the blind eye of a television, or to the mercy of "a thousand points of light"[2] that can be as far away as stars. 21

I was lucky. I had Mrs. LeSane. I had Mr. Gunderson. I had an abundance of art supplies. And I had a particular brand of neglect in my home that allowed me to slip away and get to them. But what about the rest of the kids who weren't as lucky? What happened to them? 22

By the time the bell rang that morning I had finished my drawing and Mrs. LeSane pinned it up on the special bulletin board she reserved for drawings from the back table. It was the same picture I always drew—a sun in the corner of a blue sky over a nice house with flowers all around it. 23

Mrs. LeSane asked us to please stand, face the flag, place our right hands over our hearts and say the Pledge of Allegiance. Children across the country do it faithfully. I wonder now when the country will face its children and say a pledge right back. 24

Reacting to the Reading

1. Preview the essay. As you read it more carefully, highlight and annotate as needed to help you understand the writer's ideas.
2. Underline passages that describe Barry's home life in negative terms and her school life in positive terms. What specific features of the two places are contrasted?

Reacting to Words

*1. Define these words: *nondescript* (paragraph 7), *fend* (20). Can you suggest a synonym for each word that will work in the essay?
2. Look up the word *sanctuary* in a dictionary. Which of the listed definitions do you think comes closest to Barry's meaning?

Reacting to Ideas

1. In paragraph 10, Barry characterizes herself and her brother as "children with the sound turned off." What do you think she means?
2. List the ways in which Barry's home and school worlds are different.
*3. What is the main point of Barry's essay—the idea that she wants to convince readers to accept? Is this idea actually stated in her essay? If so, where? If not, should it be?

Reacting to the Pattern

1. Paragraphs 9–10 and 19–22 interrupt Barry's story. What purpose do these paragraphs serve in her essay? Do you think the essay would be more effective if paragraphs 9 and 10 came earlier? If paragraphs 19–22 came after paragraph 24? Explain.
2. What transitional words and phrases does Barry use to move readers from one event to the next? Do you think her essay needs more transitions? If so, where should they be added?

---

2. Phrase used by President George Bush to promote volunteerism rather than government programs.

Writing Practice

1. Did you see elementary school as a sanctuary or as something quite different? Write a narrative essay that conveys to readers what school meant to you when you were a child.

2. In addition to school, television was a sanctuary for Barry and her brother. Did television watching (or some other activity) serve this function for you when you were younger? Is there some activity that fills this role now? In a narrative essay, tell about your own "sanctuary."

3. What role does college play in your life? Write an article for your school newspaper in which you use narrative to illustrate what school means to you now that you are an adult.

THIRTY-EIGHT WHO SAW MURDER DIDN'T CALL THE POLICE

Martin Gansberg

This newspaper story uses objective language to tell about an incident that occurred in New York in 1964. As Gansberg reconstructs a crime two weeks after it happened, he gives readers a detailed picture of the sequence of events that led up to a young woman's murder—in full view of thirty-eight of her "respectable, law-abiding" neighbors. As you read, consider how you might have acted if you had been a witness to this tragedy.

For more than half an hour 38 respectable, law-abiding citizens in Queens 1 watched a killer stalk and stab a woman in three separate attacks in Kew Gardens.

Twice their chatter and the sudden glow of their bedroom lights inter- 2 rupted him and frightened him off. Each time he returned, sought her out, and stabbed her again. Not one person telephoned the police during the assault; one witness called after the woman was dead.

That was two weeks ago today. 3

Still shocked is Assistant Chief Inspector Frederick M. Lussen, in 4 charge of the borough's detectives and a veteran of 25 years of homicide investigations. He can give a matter-of-fact recitation on many murders. But the Kew Gardens slaying baffles him—not because it is a murder, but because the "good people" failed to call the police.

"As we have reconstructed the crime," he said, "the assailant had three 5 chances to kill this woman during a 35-minute period. He returned twice to complete the job. If we had been called when he first attacked, the woman might not be dead now."

This is what the police say happened beginning at 3:20 a.m. in the 6 staid, middle-class, tree-lined Austin Street area:

Twenty-eight-year-old Catherine Genovese, who was called Kitty by 7 almost everyone in the neighborhood, was returning home from her job as manager of a bar in Hollis. She parked her red Fiat in a lot adjacent to the Kew Gardens Long Island Rail Road Station, facing Mowbray Place. Like many residents of the neighborhood, she had parked there day after day since her arrival from Connecticut a year ago, although the railroad frowns on the practice.

She turned off the lights of her car, locked the door, and started to walk   8
the 100 feet to the entrance of her apartment at 82-70 Austin Street, which is in a Tudor building, with stores on the first floor and apartments on the second.

The entrance to the apartment is in the rear of the building because the   9
front is rented to retail stores. At night the quiet neighborhood is shrouded in the slumbering darkness that marks most residential areas.

Miss Genovese noticed a man at the far end of the lot, near a seven-   10
story apartment house at 82-40 Austin Street, She halted. Then, nervously, she headed up Austin Street toward Lefferts Boulevard, where there is a call box to the 102nd Police Precinct in nearby Richmond Hill.

She got as far as a street light in front of a bookstore before the man   11
grabbed her. She screamed. Lights went on in the 10-story apartment house at 82-67 Austin Street, which faces the bookstore. Windows slid open and voices punctuated the early-morning stillness.

Miss Genovese screamed: "Oh, my God, he stabbed me! Please help   12
me! Please help me!"

From one of the upper windows in the apartment house, a man called   13
down: "Let that girl alone!"

The assailant looked up at him, shrugged, and walked down Austin   14
Street toward a white sedan parked a short distance away. Miss Genovese struggled to her feet.

Lights went out. The killer returned to Miss Genovese, now trying to   15
make her way around the side of the building by the parking lot to get to her apartment. The assailant stabbed her again.

"I'm dying!" she shrieked. "I'm dying!"   16

Windows were opened again, and lights went on in many apartments.   17
The assailant got into his car and drove away. Miss Genovese staggered to her feet. A city bus, O-10, the Lefferts Boulevard line to Kennedy International Airport, passed. It was 3:35 a.m.

The assailant returned. By then, Miss Genovese had crawled to the   18
back of the building, where the freshly painted brown doors to the apartment house held out hope for safety. The killer tried the first door; she wasn't there. At the second door, 82-62 Austin Street, he saw her slumped on the floor at the foot of the stairs. He stabbed her a third time —fatally.

It was 3:50 by the time the police received their first call, from a man   19
who was a neighbor of Miss Genovese. In two minutes they were at the scene. The neighbor, a 70-year-old woman, and another woman were the only persons on the street. Nobody else came forward.

The man explained that he had called the police after much delibera-   20
tion. He had phoned a friend in Nassau County for advice and then he had crossed the roof of the building to the apartment of the elderly woman to get her to make the call.

"I didn't want to get involved," he sheepishly told police.   21

Six days later, the police arrested Winston Moseley, a 29-year-old busi-   22
ness machine operator, and charged him with homicide. Moseley had no previous record. He is married, has two children and owns a home at 133-19 Sutter Avenue, South Ozone Park, Queens. On Wednesday, a court committed him to Kings County Hospital for psychiatric observation.

When questioned by the police, Moseley also said that he had slain 23 Mrs. Annie May Johnson, 24, of 146-12 133d Avenue, Jamaica, on Feb. 29 and Barbara Kralik, 15, of 174-17 140th Avenue, Springfield Gardens, last July. In the Kralik case, the police are holding Alvin L. Mitchell, who is said to have confessed to that slaying.

The police stressed how simple it would have been to have gotten in 24 touch with them. "A phone call," said one of the detectives, "would have done it." The police may be reached by dialing "O" for operator or SPring 7-3100.

Today witnesses from the neighborhood, which is made up of one-family homes in the $35,000 to $60,000 range with the exception of the two apartment houses near the railroad station, find it difficult to explain why they didn't call the police.

A housewife, knowingly if quite casually, said, "We thought it was a 26 lovers' quarrel." A husband and wife both said, "Frankly, we were afraid." They seemed aware of the fact that events might have been different. A distraught woman, wiping her hands in her apron, said, "I didn't want my husband to get involved."

One couple, now willing to talk about that night, said they heard the 27 first screams. The husband looked thoughtfully at the bookstore where the killer first grabbed Miss Genovese.

"We went to the window to see what was happening," he said, "but the 28 light from our bedroom made it difficult to see the street." The wife, still apprehensive, added: "I put out the light and we were able to see better."

Asked why they hadn't called the police, she shrugged and replied: "I 29 don't know."

A man peeked out from a slight opening in the doorway to his apartment and rattled off an account of the killer's second attack. Why hadn't he called the police at the time? "I was tired," he said without emotion. "I went back to bed."

It was 4:25 a.m. when the ambulance arrived to take the body of Miss 31 Genovese. It drove off. "Then," a solemn police detective said, "the people came out."

Reacting to the Reading

1. Preview the essay. As you read it more carefully, highlight and annotate as needed to help you understand the writer's ideas.
2. Place a check mark beside each passage of dialogue Gansberg uses. Then, add brief marginal annotations next to three of these passages.

Reacting to Words

*1. Define these words: *staid* (paragraph 6), *shrouded* (9). Can you suggest a synonym for each word that will work in the essay?
2. What is Gansberg's purpose in using terms like *respectable* (paragraph 1), *law-abiding* (1), and *good people* (4)? What is your reaction to these words?

Reacting to Ideas

1. What reasons do the witnesses give for not coming to Kitty Genovese's aid? Why do *you* think no one helped her? Do you think the witnesses should be held accountable for their lack of action?

*2. Suppose Genovese's attack were to occur today. How do you think her neighbors would react? What might be different about the situation?

Reacting to the Pattern

1. What other patterns could Gansberg have used to develop his essay? For instance, could he have used comparison and contrast or exemplification? Given the alternatives, do you think narration is the best choice? Why or why not?

*2. Gansberg uses many transitional words and phrases, including references to specific times, to move readers from one event to the next. List as many of these transitions as you can, and note any you believe should be added.

Writing Practice

1. Write a narrative essay about a time when you were a witness who chose not to become involved in events you were observing.

2. Find a brief newspaper article that tells a story about a similar incident in which bystanders witnessed a crime. Expand the article into a longer essay, inventing characters, dialogue, and additional details.

3. Retell Kitty Genovese's story—but this time, have a witness come to her rescue.

C   Description

A **descriptive** essay tells what something looks, sounds, smells, tastes, or feels like. It uses details to give readers a clear, vivid picture of a person, place, or object. In "Graduation," Maya Angelou describes her school and her fellow students. In "The Grandfather," Gary Soto describes a beloved family member.

For more on how to write a descriptive essay, see 14C.

GRADUATION

Maya Angelou

Maya Angelou is a poet, historian, actress, playwright, civil-rights activist, producer, and director. At the request of President Clinton, she wrote and delivered a poem at his 1993 inauguration. "Graduation," from her autobiographical *I Know Why the Caged Bird Sings* (1969), presents a vivid picture of a specific time (the 1930s) and place (the rural Arkansas town of Stamps). Against this backdrop, the young African-American students at Lafayette County Training School prepare for their high school graduation. As you read, notice how Angelou moves from a general description of the school and its inhabitants, to a more specific physical description of the school's exterior, and finally to a description of the students eager for graduation.

The children in Stamps trembled visibly with anticipation. Some adults were excited too, but to be certain the whole young population had come   1 down with graduation epidemic. Large classes were graduating from both the grammar school and the high school. Even those who were years removed from their own day of glorious release were anxious to help with preparations as a kind of dry run. The junior students who were moving into the vacating classes' chairs were tradition-bound to show their talents for leadership and management. They strutted through the school and around the campus exerting pressure on the lower grades. Their authority was so new that occasionally if they pressed a little too hard it had to be overlooked. After all, next term was coming, and it never hurt a sixth grader to have a play sister in the eighth grade, or a tenth-year student to be able to call a twelfth grader Bubba. So all was endured in a spirit of shared understanding. But the graduating classes themselves were the nobility. Like travelers with exotic destinations on their minds, the graduates were remarkably forgetful. They came to school without their books, or tablets or even pencils. Volunteers fell over themselves to secure replacements for the missing equipment. When accepted, the willing workers might or might not be thanked, and it was of no importance to the pregraduation rites. Even teachers were respectful of the now quiet and aging seniors, and tended to speak to them, if not as equals, as beings only slightly lower than themselves. After tests were returned and grades given, the student body, which acted like an extended family, knew who did well, who excelled, and what piteous ones had failed.

Unlike the white high school, Lafayette County Training School distin- 2
guished itself by having neither lawn, nor hedges, nor tennis court, nor climbing ivy. Its two buildings (main classrooms, the grade school and home economics) were set on a dirt hill with no fence to limit either its boundaries or those of bordering farms. There was a large expanse to the left of the school which was used alternately as a baseball diamond or basketball court. Rusty hoops on swaying poles represented the permanent recreational equipment, although bats and balls could be borrowed from the P.E. teacher if the borrower was qualified and if the diamond wasn't occupied.

Over this rocky area relieved by a few shady tall persimmon trees the 3
graduating class walked. The girls often held hands and no longer bothered to speak to the lower students. There was a sadness about them, as if this old world was not their home and they were bound for higher ground. The boys, on the other hand, had become more friendly, more outgoing. A decided change from the closed attitude they projected while studying for finals. Now they seemed not ready to give up the old school, the familiar paths and classrooms. Only a small percentage would be continuing on to college—one of the South's A&M (agricultural and mechanical) schools, which trained Negro youths to be carpenters, farmers, handymen, masons, maids, cooks and baby nurses. Their future rode heavily on their shoulders, and blinded them to the collective joy that had pervaded the lives of the boys and girls in the grammar school graduating class.

Parents who could afford it had ordered new shoes and ready-made 4
clothes for themselves from Sears and Roebuck or Montgomery Ward. They also engaged the best seamstresses to make the floating graduating dresses and to cut down secondhand pants which would be pressed to a military slickness for the important event.

Oh, it was important, all right. Whitefolks would attend the ceremony, 5
and two or three would speak of God and home, and the Southern way of life, and Mrs. Parsons, the principal's wife, would play the graduation

march while the lower-grade graduates paraded down the aisles and took their seats below the platform. The high school seniors would wait in empty classrooms to make their dramatic entrance.

Reacting to the Reading

1. Preview the essay. As you read it more carefully, highlight and annotate as needed to help you understand the writer's ideas.
2. Throughout her essay, Angelou implies that the African-American students of Stamps have fewer privileges and opportunities than their white counterparts. Underline phrases that reveal what the black students lack. In marginal notes, speculate about what the white students might have access to that Angelou and her classmates do not.

Reacting to Words

*1. Define these words: *piteous* (paragraph 1), *expanse* (2), *collective* (3), *pervaded* (3). Can you suggest a synonym for each word that will work in the essay?
2. Angelou uses the word *Negro* in her essay (paragraph 3); she also uses the word *whitefolks* (paragraph 5). What is your reaction to her use of these words? What different connotations do they have?

Reacting to Ideas

1. The selection begins with a sense of anticipation, comparing the students to "travelers with exotic destinations on their minds" (paragraph 1), and ends with the students about "to make their dramatic entrance" (paragraph 5) into the world. What details suggest that their future may not be quite as bright as they expect?
2. How is Lafayette County Training School different from the white high school?

Reacting to the Pattern

1. Paragraph 2 focuses on physical description of the school's exterior. What main idea does this paragraph convey? In what ways is it an appropriate lead-in to paragraph 3, which describes the students?
*2. "Graduation" conveys a mixture of anxiety about and eager anticipation of the future. List the details that help to convey each of these moods.

Writing Practice

1. Describe the mood at your school in the days preceding your own high school graduation. Move from your fellow students, to the teachers, to your family, and then focus on your own feelings.
2. Describe your high school. Begin with its setting, move to the exterior of the building, and finally focus on one particular room. (If you prefer, describe your workplace, your home, or some other place that holds special meaning for you.)
3. Write the valedictory address you would give if you were graduating from your high school this year. Include detailed descriptions of people and places important to your classmates.

THE GRANDFATHER

Gary Soto

Poet and essayist Gary Soto often writes about family members and about his childhood. In this 1990 essay, he remembers his grandfather with affection, conveying his habits and attitudes by describing the trees in his backyard. As you read, notice how Soto blends objective and subjective descriptions of his grandfather.

Grandfather believed a well-rooted tree was the color of money. His money he kept hidden behind portraits of sons and daughters or taped behind the calendar of an Aztec warrior. He tucked it into the sofa, his shoes and slippers, and into the tight-lipped pockets of his suits. He kept it in his soft brown wallet that was machine tooled with "MEXICO" and a campesino and donkey climbing a hill. He had climbed, too, out of Mexico, settled in Fresno and worked thirty years at Sun Maid Raisin, first as a packer and later, when he was old, as a watchman with a large clock on his belt.

After work, he sat in the backyard under the arbor, watching the water gurgle in the rose bushes that ran along the fence. A lemon tree hovered over the clothesline. Two orange trees stood near the alley. His favorite tree, the avocado, which had started in a jam jar from a seed and three toothpicks lanced in its sides, rarely bore fruit. He said it was the wind's fault, and the mayor's, who allowed office buildings so high that the haze of pollen from the countryside could never find its way into the city. He sulked about this. He said that in Mexico buildings only grew so tall. You could see the moon at night, and the stars were clear points all the way to the horizon. And wind reached all the way from the sea, which was blue and clean, unlike the oily water sloshing against a San Francisco pier.

During its early years, I could leap over that tree, kick my bicycling legs over the top branch and scream my fool head off because I thought for sure I was flying. I ate fruit to keep my strength up, fuzzy peaches and branch-scuffed plums cooled in the refrigerator. From the kitchen chair he brought out in the evening, Grandpa would scold, "Hijo, what's the matta with you? You gonna break it."

By the third year, the tree was as tall as I, its branches casting a meager shadow on the ground. I sat beneath the shade, scratching words in the hard dirt with a stick. I had learned "Nile" in summer school and a dirty word from my brother who wore granny sunglasses. The red ants tumbled into my letters, and I buried them, knowing that they would dig themselves back into fresh air.

A tree was money. If a lemon cost seven cents at Hanoian's Market, then Grandfather saved fistfuls of change and more because in winter the branches of his lemon tree hung heavy yellow fruit. And winter brought oranges, juicy and large as softballs. Apricots he got by the bagfuls from a son, who himself was wise for planting young. Peaches he got from a neighbor, who worked the night shift at Sun Maid Raisin. The chile plants, which also saved him from giving up his hot, sweaty quarters, were propped up with sticks to support an abundance of red fruit.

But his favorite tree was the avocado because it offered hope and the promise of more years. After work, Grandpa sat in the back yard, shirtless, tired of flagging trucks loaded with crates of raisins, and sipped glasses of ice water. His yard was neat: five trees, seven rose bushes, whose fruit were the red and white flowers he floated in bowls, and a statue of St. Francis that stood in a circle of crushed rocks, arms spread out to welcome hungry sparrows.

After ten years, the first avocado hung on a branch, but the meat was flecked with black, an omen, Grandfather thought, a warning to keep an eye on the living. Five years later, another avocado hung on a branch, larger than the first and edible when crushed with a fork into a heated tortilla. Grandfather sprinkled it with salt and laced it with a river of chile.

"It's good," he said, and let me taste.

I took a big bite, waved a hand over my tongue, and ran for the garden hose gurgling in the rose bushes. I drank long and deep, and later ate the smile from an ice cold watermelon.

Birds nested in the tree, quarreling jays with liquid eyes and cool, pulsating throats. Wasps wove a horn-shaped hive one year, but we smoked them away with swords of rolled up newspapers lit with matches. By then, the tree was tall enough for me to climb to look into the neighbor's yard. But by then I was too old for that kind of thing and went about with my brother, hair slicked back and our shades dark as oil.

After twenty years, the tree began to bear. Although Grandfather complained about how much he lost because pollen never reached the poor part of town, because at the market he had to haggle over the price of avocados, he loved that tree. It grew, as did his family, and when he died, all his sons standing on each other's shoulders, oldest to youngest, could not reach the highest branches. The wind could move the branches, but the trunk, thicker than any waist, hugged the ground.

Reacting to the Reading

1. Preview the essay. As you read it more carefully, highlight and annotate as needed to help you understand the writer's ideas.

2. Circle all the words in the essay that designate colors. Then, write a brief marginal note in which you consider what these words contribute to the essay.

Reacting to Words

*1. Define these words: *campesino* (paragraph 1), *lanced* (2), *hijo* (3), *meager* (4), *laced* (7), *haggle* (11). Can you suggest a synonym for each word that will work in the essay?

*2. What **figure of speech** is each of these expressions?
   - "the tight-lipped pockets of his suits" (paragraph 1)
   - "large as softballs" (5)
   - "a river of chile" (7)

   Can you identify any other figures of speech in the essay?

For more on figures of speech, see 14C.

Reacting to Ideas

1. In the first sentence of his essay, Soto says, "Grandfather believed a well-rooted tree was the color of money." Where does Soto refer to this idea again? What do you think he means?

2. Soto calls his essay "The Grandfather." Could you argue that it is not really about the man but about the trees in his backyard—or about one tree in particular? Could you make the point that the essay is really about Soto himself?

Reacting to the Pattern

*1. Soto's grandfather is introduced in paragraph 1. In paragraph 2, we see him sitting in his yard, and then the essay focuses on the avocado tree. Continue tracing the essay's movement from paragraph to paragraph. What is the central focus of each paragraph's description? Is the essay's progression from one paragraph to the next logical?

2. Does Soto use any phrases that convey senses other than sight? Give examples of any phrases that describe sound, smell, taste, or touch.

Writing Practice

1. Write a description of a grandparent or other close relative, focusing on your family member's physical appearance. Move from head to toe or from the least to the most striking feature (or in some other logical order).

2. Write an essay about a grandparent or other relative in which you characterize your subject by describing his or her favorite possessions.

3. Write an essay about a grandparent or other relative in which you characterize your subject by describing a setting with which you associate him or her—a room, an office, or a garden, for example.

D   Process

For more on how to write a process essay, see 14D.

A **process** essay explains the steps in a procedure, telling how something is (or was) done. In "Slice of Life," Russell Baker gives a set of instructions for carving a turkey. In "Indelible Marks," Joyce Howe explains the routine of her family's laundry business.

SLICE OF LIFE

Russell Baker

Pulitzer Prize–winning columnist and author Russell Baker is known for his keen political insight and sharp social commentary. He is also known for being funny. The source of much of Baker's humor is his deadpan approach, in which he pretends to be completely serious. In the following essay, written in 1974, note how he uses this approach to turn what seems to be a straightforward set of instructions into a humorous discussion of a holiday ritual.

How to carve a turkey: 1

Assemble the following tools—carving knife, stone for sharpening 2
carving knife, hot water, soap, wash cloth, two bath towels, barbells, meat cleaver. If the house lacks a meat cleaver, an ax may be substituted. If it is, add bandages, sutures, and iodine to above list.

Begin by moving the turkey from the roasting pan to a suitable carv- 3
ing area. This is done by inserting the carving knife into the posterior

stuffed area of the turkey and the knife-sharpening stone into the stuffed area under the neck.

Thus skewered, the turkey may be lifted out of the hot grease with relative safety. Should the turkey drop to the floor, however, remove the knife and stone, roll the turkey gingerly into the two bath towels, wrap them several times around it and lift the encased fowl to the carving place. 4

You are now ready to begin carving. Sharpen the knife on the stone and insert it where the thigh joins the torso. If you do this correctly, which is improbable, the knife will almost immediately encounter a barrier of bone and gristle. This may very well be the joint. It could, however, be your thumb. If not, execute a vigorous sawing motion until satisfied that the knife has been defeated. Withdraw the knife and ask someone nearby, in as testy a manner as possible, why the knives at your house are not kept in better carving condition. 5

Exercise the biceps and forearms by lifting barbells until they are strong enough for you to tackle the leg joint with bare hands. Wrapping one hand firmly around the thigh, seize the turkey's torso in the other hand and scream. Run cold water over hands to relieve pain of burns. 6

Now, take a bath towel in each hand and repeat the above maneuver. The entire leg should snap away from the chassis with a distinct crack, and the rest of the turkey, obedient to Newton's law[1] about equal and opposite reactions, should roll in the opposite direction, which means that if you are carving at the table the turkey will probably come to rest in someone's lap. 7

Get the turkey out of the lap with as little fuss as possible, and concentrate on the leg. Use the meat cleaver to sever the sinewy leather which binds the thigh to the drumstick. 8

If using the alternate, ax method, this operation should be performed on a cement walk outside the house in order to preserve the table. 9

Repeat the above operation on the turkey's uncarved side. You now have two thighs and two drumsticks. Using the wash cloth, soap and hot water, bathe thoroughly and, if possible, go to a movie. Otherwise, look each person in the eye and say, "I don't suppose anyone wants white meat." 10

If compelled to carve the breast anyhow, sharpen the knife on the stone again with sufficient awkwardness to tip over the gravy bowl on the person who started the stampede for white meat. 11

While everyone is rushing about to mop the gravy off her slacks, hack at the turkey breast until it starts crumbling off the carcass in ugly chunks. 12

The alternative method for carving white meat is to visit around the neighborhood until you find someone who has a good carving knife and borrow it, if you find one, which is unlikely. 13

This method enables you to watch the football game on neighbors' television sets and also creates the possibility that somebody back at your table will grow tired of waiting and do the carving herself. 14

In this case, upon returning home, cast a pained stare upon the mound of chopped white meat that has been hacked out by the family carving knife and refuse to do any more carving that day. No one who cares about the artistry of carving can be expected to work upon the mutilations of amateurs, and it would be a betrayal of the carver's art to do so. 15

---

1. Sir Isaac Newton, seventeenth-century physicist and mathematician known for formulating the laws of gravity and light, and for inventing calculus.

Reacting to the Reading

1. Preview the essay. As you read it more carefully, highlight and annotate as needed to help you understand the writer's ideas.
2. Underline or star the cautions and warnings Baker provides for readers.

Reacting to Words

*1. Define these words: *sutures* (paragraph 2), *gingerly* (4), *encased* (4), *torso* (5), *execute* (5), *testy* (5), *chassis* (7). Can you suggest a synonym for each word that will work in the essay?
2. In paragraph 12, Baker uses the pronoun *her* to refer to the antecedent *everyone;* in paragraph 14, he uses *herself* to refer to *somebody.* What is your reaction to this pronoun use? What other options did Baker have? Why do you think he chose to use *her* and *herself?*

Reacting to Ideas

1. This process is not intended to be taken seriously or followed exactly. How can you tell?
*2. List the steps in Baker's process of carving a turkey. Then, cross out all nonessential or humorous material. Are the instructions that remain logically ordered? Clear? Accurate?

Reacting to the Pattern

1. How can you tell that this essay is a set of instructions and not an explanation of a process?
*2. Do you think the phrase "How to carve a turkey" is an adequate introduction for this essay? What other kind of introduction might Baker have written?
3. Review the various cautions and warnings that you identified in Reacting to the Reading question 2. Are they all necessary? Explain.

Writing Practice

*1. Write a paragraph that introduces this essay. Then, turn Baker's instructions into a straightforward process explanation, deleting any material you consider irrelevant to your purpose. Be sure to include all necessary articles and transitions.
2. List the steps in a recipe for preparing one of your favorite dishes. Then, expand your recipe into an essay, adding transitions and cautions and reminders. Finally, add opening and closing paragraphs that describe the finished product and tell readers why the dish is worth preparing.
3. Write an essay that explains to your fellow students how you juggle the demands of family, work, and school in a typical day. Organize your essay either as a process explanation or as a set of instructions.

INDELIBLE MARKS

Joyce Howe

Joyce Howe grew up in Queens, New York, in a neighborhood where
everyone knew her father as "the man who ran the Chinese laundry."
As his daughter, she had mixed feelings about his occupation and felt
ashamed that she lived with her parents and sisters behind the store
and helped in the laundry business. In this passage from a 1983 essay,
she explains the process by which laundry was sorted, washed, dried,
starched, ironed, folded, and wrapped. As you read, try to get a sense
of what the process meant to Howe.

1   In Queens, on the block where we moved, my father was known as the
man who ran the Chinese laundry, like Ernie who ran the deli, Benny the
upholsterer, and the butcher a few doors down. To all of his customers he
was Joe. And they—middle-aged housewives, young bachelors and students, mainly white—were known to him by a first name or by the unique
indelible "mark" on their collars and hems. (This "mark," consisting of one
or more characters, was written on each item for the duration of a customer's patronage; if he switched laundries, the new establishment usually
did not bother changing it.) With all of them, as tickets, laundry bills, and
change passed from hand to hand over the wide counter, my father
exchanged comments: "Too much of this rain, huh?", "Yeah, the Mets
looked lousy last night," or "How's the wife and the kids?"

2   Saturday was his busiest day. It was not only the day more customers
came in and out, but it was also one of the three days on which the long
and tedious job of laundry-sorting was done. The entire floor of the store
became a dumping ground for soiled clothes. My father divided the laundry into piles: 10 to 15 sheets and pillowcases were bundled up into one
sheet and the ticket stubs of the customers whose laundry made up the
bundle were then stapled together and put aside for later identification.
"Wet items," such as towels, underwear, and socks, were separated into
two categories—light and dark; shirts were separated into four categories
—colored, white, starch, and no starch. Each pile of "wet items" and shirts
was then placed in a laundry bag with its respective tag.

3   The bags and bundles were picked up Sunday morning by the truck
drivers, who had names like Rocky and Louie, from the wholesale laundry
or "wet wash" contracted by my father. ("Hand laundry" has been a
misnomer since the late 1930s and '40s, when a whole new industry of
Chinese-operated wholesale laundries and pressing concerns sprang up
and contracted to do the actual washing and pressing for laundrymen.)
Every Sunday, we were awakened from our sleep by the sound of the
drivers' keys turning in the front door's locks.

4   When the "wet wash" drivers returned Monday with the previous day's
load, the sheets and pillowcases, or "flat pieces," were wrapped in a heavy
brown paper which my mother later would use for tablecloths. The shirts
returned in the same bags they went out in. My father pulled out the bag
of shirts to be starched and hand-ironed, leaving the rest for the shirt-press
truck to pick up that night. On Tuesday night, they returned—clean,
pressed, folded—in large square cardboard boxes, each shirt ringed in its
own pale blue paper band.

For a short time, we had our own automatic dryer to take care of the damp "wet items" when they returned. After it broke down, irreparably, the dryer retired, and was left to hold stacks of comic books and board games. My sisters and I took turns making pilgrimages to the local laundromat, our metal shopping cart bent from the weight of the load. We wheeled those three blocks three times a week. On my turn, I always hoped that no one I knew would see me as I struggled with two hands to keep laundry and cart intact when maneuvering the high curbs. Even then, the irony of going from the laundry to the laundromat was not lost.

5

Of course, there were days when the system was off, when the shirt press might return its load late, or when my father didn't feel well enough to wrap every package. On those days, we were all expected to help. We made sure that the promise my father had made to customers on Saturday that their shirts would be ready by Wednesday was kept. Behind the tan curtain drawn across our plate-glass window every evening at seven and the door's pulled venetian blind, we settled into a tableau. My family formed a late-night assembly line, each member taking his place amid the shelves, boxes, white cones of string, rolls of wrapping paper, and the familiar fragrance of newly laundered cloth.

6

Reacting to the Reading

1. Preview the essay. As you read it more carefully, highlight and annotate as needed to help you understand the writer's ideas.
2. In the margins of the essay, number the steps in the process that is presented in paragraphs 2 through 6.

Reacting to Words

*1. Define these words: *indelible* (paragraph 1), *duration* (1), *patronage* (1), *tedious* (2), *irreparably* (5), *pilgrimages* (5), *tableau* (6). Can you suggest a synonym for each word that will work in the essay?
2. Howe's father makes a "unique indelible 'mark'" (paragraph 1) on the collars of each customer's shirts. Where else does he make an indelible mark?

Reacting to Ideas

1. What does Howe achieve by describing this process?
2. Do you think Howe's memories of her childhood as the laundryman's daughter are largely positive or negative? Support your position with specific examples.

Reacting to the Pattern

1. Is this essay a set of instructions or an explanation of how a process is performed? How can you tell?
*2. Using the numbers you wrote in the margins for Reacting to the Reading question 2 as a guide, list the individual steps in the process Howe describes. Does the process vary at all, or is it always the same?

Writing Practice

1. Write a process essay explaining the daily routine you followed in a job you hold (or held). Include a thesis statement that tells readers how you feel about the job.

*2. Write a process essay in which you tell how to perform a particular task at a job—for example, how to keep a potential customer on the phone during a sales call, how to clean a deep-fat fryer, or how to set up the housekeeping corner at a day-care center.

3. Write a process essay in which you take readers through the stages of a successful job search. In your conclusion, identify the job you found.

E   Cause and Effect

A **cause-and-effect** essay identifies causes or predicts effects; sometimes it does both. In "The 'Black Table' Is Still There," Lawrence Otis Graham focuses on a troubling situation from his junior high school days. In "The Old Block," Anna Quindlen returns to the neighborhood she grew up in and confronts an upsetting reality.

For more on how to write a cause-and-effect essay, see 14E.

THE "BLACK TABLE" IS STILL THERE

Lawrence Otis Graham

A corporate lawyer and best-selling author, Graham is best known for "Invisible Man," an article he wrote about the racism he encountered while working as a busboy at an exclusive country club during a leave from his job as a lawyer. In the following 1991 essay, Graham reflects on the "black table," a situation that has continued in the school cafeteria since his junior high days. As you read, note how his conclusions about what motivates people to sit where they sit have changed over the years.

During a recent visit to my old junior high school in Westchester County, I came upon something that I never expected to see again, something that was a source of fear and dread for three hours each school morning of my early adolescence: the all-black lunch table in the cafeteria of my predominantly white suburban junior high school.

As I look back on 27 years of often being the first and only black person integrating such activities and institutions as the college newspaper, the high school tennis team, summer music camps, our all-white suburban neighborhood, my eating club at Princeton or my private social club at Harvard Law School, the one scenario that puzzled me the most then and now is the all-black lunch table.

Why was it there? Why did the black kids separate themselves? What did the table say about the integration that was supposedly going on in home rooms and gym classes? What did it say about the black kids? The white kids? What did it say about me when I refused to sit there, day after day, for three years?

Each afternoon, at 12:03 p.m., after the fourth period ended, I found myself among 600 12-, 13- and 14-year-olds who marched into the brightly-lit cafeteria and dashed for a seat at one of the 27 blue formica lunch tables.

No matter who I walked in with—usually a white friend—no matter what mood I was in, there was one thing that was certain: I would not sit at the black table.

I would never consider sitting at the black table.

What was wrong with me? What was I afraid of?

I would like to think that my decision was a heroic one, made in order to express my solidarity with the theories of integration that my community was espousing. But I was just 12 at the time, and there was nothing heroic in my actions.

I avoided the black table for a very simple reason: I was afraid that by sitting at the black table I'd lose all my white friends. I thought that by sitting there I'd be making a racist, anti-white statement.

Is that what the all-black table means? Is it a rejection of white people? I no longer think so.

At the time, I was angry that there was a black lunch table. I believed that the black kids were the reason why other kids didn't mix more. I was ready to believe that their self-segregation was the cause of white bigotry.

Ironically, I even believed this after my best friend (who was white) told me I probably shouldn't come to his bar mitzvah because I'd be the only black and people would feel uncomfortable. I even believed this after my Saturday afternoon visit, at age 10, to a private country club pool prompted incensed white parents to pull their kids from the pool in terror.

In the face of this blatantly racist (anti-black) behavior, I still somehow managed to blame only the black kids for being the barrier to integration in my school and my little world. What was I thinking?

I realize now how wrong I was. During that same time, there were at least two tables of athletes, an Italian table, a Jewish girls' table, a Jewish boys' table (where I usually sat), a table of kids who were into heavy metal music and smoking pot, a table of middle class Irish kids. Weren't these tables just as segregationist as the black table? At the time, no one thought so. At the time, no one even acknowledged the segregated nature of these other tables.

Maybe it's the color difference that makes all-black tables or all-black groups attract the scrutiny and wrath of so many people. It scares and angers people; it exasperates. It did those things to me, and I'm black.

As an integrating black person, I know that my decision *not* to join the black lunch table attracted its own kind of scrutiny and wrath from my classmates. At the same time that I heard angry words like "Oreo" and "white boy" being hurled at me from the black table, I was also dodging impatient questions from white classmates: "Why do all those black kids sit together?" or "Why don't you ever sit with the other blacks?"

The black lunch table, like those other segregated tables, is a comment on the superficial inroads that integration has made in society. Perhaps I should be happy that even this is a long way from where we started. Yet, I can't get over the fact that the 27th table in my junior high school cafeteria is still known as the "black table"—14 years after my adolescence.

Reacting to the Reading

1. Preview the essay. As you read it more carefully, highlight and annotate as needed to help you understand the writer's ideas.

2. Graham asks a number of questions in this essay—for example, in paragraph 3 and in paragraph 7. In marginal annotations, answer two or three of these questions.

Reacting to Words

*1. Define these words: *scenario* (paragraph 2), *espousing* (8), *bar mitzvah* (12), *incensed* (12), *blatantly* (13), *scrutiny* (15), *wrath* (15), *inroads* (17). Can you suggest a synonym for each word that will work in the essay?

2. What images does the phrase *black table* bring to mind? Does it have positive or negative connotations to you? Can you think of another term Graham might use to identify the black table?

Reacting to Ideas

*1. Why didn't Graham sit at the black table? Do you understand the forces that motivated him? Do you think he should have sat with the other African-American students?

2. When he was in junior high school, who did Graham think was at fault for the existence of the black table? Who does he now think was at fault? Do you agree with him?

3. In paragraph 14, Graham considers other lunch tables and asks, "Weren't these tables just as segregationist as the black table?" Answer his question.

Reacting to the Pattern

1. Is Graham's essay primarily about causes or about effects? Explain your answer.

*2. Graham focuses largely on his own experiences and actions. Where, if anywhere, does he consider other forces that could have created segregated lunch tables? Do you think he should have considered other causes? For example, should he have discussed the school administration's role? Housing patterns in his community? Explain your position.

Writing Practice

1. Graham's essay, written in 1991, describes his adolescence fourteen years earlier (1977). Try to recall the lunch tables in the cafeteria of your own junior high school or middle school. Were they segregated as they were in Graham's school? What factors do you believe led students to sit where they did? Write a cause-and-effect essay that discusses the possible causes of the seating patterns you remember.

2. What do you see as the *effects* of segregated lunch tables? Do you think they are necessarily a bad thing, or do they have advantages? Write a cause-and-effect essay that explores the possible results of such seating patterns.

3. What kinds of self-segregation (by race, gender, class, and so on) do you observe in your school, workplace, or community? In an essay, discuss both causes and effects.

THE OLD BLOCK

Anna Quindlen

A former columnist for the *New York Times* op-ed page, Anna Quindlen resigned her position at the end of 1994 to devote herself to a career as a novelist. She has since published *One True Thing* and *Black and Blue*. As a columnist, she focused mainly on social and political issues related to women's roles and family life. As you read "The Old Block," a 1992 column, notice how Quindlen moves from an examination of a troubling effect (the poverty of her family's old neighborhood) to the cause of the neighborhood's decline.

The block on which my father grew up half a century ago is a truncated little street that leads nowhere. If it were a foot or two narrower, the map makers might have called it an alley. The houses are identical two-story attached brick buildings with bay windows on the top floor, an over-obvious attempt at grandeur. 1

In this quiet backwater in the southwestern part of the city the children of Irish-Catholic families played in the late afternoons after they had changed from their parochial school uniforms. A police officer walked by twice a day, talking to the people he knew so well. 2

My father remembers that in one fifteen-minute span when he was eight years old he was hit by four people to whom he was not related: the cop; the neighbor whose window he drew upon with spit; the priest who saw him messing with a statue; and the nun who saw the priest whack him and wanted to second the emotion. So he grew. 3

Today the kids on the block are black. The house where the seven Quindlen children were raised, the boys packed two to a bed, has long been empty. The small setback porch is still covered with debris from the fire that gutted the building several years ago. There is plywood nailed over the glassless windows and the doorless doorway. 4

This was a prosperous neighborhood, a way station to something better. Today it is a poor one, a dead end. Charred interiors are common. So are crime, drugs, and a sense of going nowhere. 5

Since L.A. burst into flames[1] we have cast a net of blame in our search for those who abandoned America's cities. 6

The answer is simple. We did. Over my lifetime prosperity in America has been measured in moving vans, backyards and the self-congratulatory remark "I can't remember the last time I went to the city." America became a circle of suburbs surrounding an increasingly grim urban core. 7

In the beginning there was a synergy between the two; we took the train to the city to work and shop, then fled as the sun went down. But by the 1970s we no longer needed to shop there because of the malls. And by the 1980s we no longer had to work there because of the now-you-see-it 8

---

1. Riots that broke out in Los Angeles in 1993 in response to the acquittal of the policemen who were videotaped beating Rodney King, an African-American motorist.

rise of industrial parks and office complexes. Pseudo-cities grew up, built of chrome, glass, and homogeneity. Half of America now lives in the 'burbs.

We abandoned America's cities.   9

Ronald Reagan and George Bush did, too, and so did many Democrats,   10
truth be told. And they're going to have to ante up now. But it's not enough anymore to let those boys take all the responsibility. They don't carry it well enough.

I understand how Eugene Lang[2] felt when he gave a speech at his old   11
grade school and, overwhelmed by the emptiness of words, offered all the students in the class a chance to go to college. I've heard the argument that Mr. Lang's largesse takes government off the hook. But I bet it's not compelling for kids who might have gone down the drain if one man hadn't remembered where he came from, before he moved on to someplace greener, richer, better.

Over the years I've heard about sister-city programs between places   12
here and places abroad, places like Minsk or Vienna. Pen pals. Cultural exchange. Volunteer philanthropy. And all the while, twenty minutes away from the suburbs are cultures and lives and problems about which we are shamefully ignorant. I like the sister-city concept. Short Hills and Newark. South-central L.A. and Simi Valley. Both sides benefit.

The pols will lose interest in the cities again soon enough, because so   13
many city residents are poor and powerless and not white. It would be nice to think of Congress as the home of idealists, but thinking like that makes you feel awfully foolish. America's cities will prosper when America's prosperous citizens demand it. When they remember their roots.

I've walked many times down blocks like the one on which my father   14
grew up. I've been a poverty tourist with a notebook, but I never felt ashamed of it until now.

On that little street were the ghosts of the people who brought me into   15
being and the flesh-and-blood kids who will be my children's companions in the twenty-first century. You could tell by their eyes that they couldn't figure out why I was there. They were accustomed to being ignored, even by the people who had once populated their rooms. And as long as that continues, our cities will burst and burn, burst and burn, over and over again.

Reacting to the Reading

1. Preview the essay. As you read it more carefully, highlight and annotate as needed to help you understand the writer's ideas.

2. Circle all the descriptive words and phrases—for example, *glassless windows* (paragraph 4)—that convey the neighborhood's decline to readers.

Reacting to Words

*1. Define these words: *truncated* (paragraph 1), *grandeur* (1), *backwater* (2), *debris* (4), *charred* (5), *synergy* (8), *homogeneity* (8), *ante* (10), *largesse* (11), *philanthropy* (12). Can you suggest a synonym for each word that will work in the essay?

2. Founder of the I Have a Dream Foundation, which provides counseling and financial support for students in poor urban communities to help them stay in school and get through college.

2. Quindlen uses *we* throughout her essay—for example, "We abandoned America's cities" (paragraph 9). Why do you think she does this?

3. In paragraph 14, Quindlen refers to herself as a "poverty tourist." What do you think she means by this phrase? Do you see it as a positive or negative characterization?

Reacting to Ideas

*1. List the differences between the neighborhood Quindlen sees today and "the old block."

2. Do you think Quindlen feels guilty? Do you think she should?

Reacting to the Pattern

1. According to Quindlen, what three things caused her block to decline? Which cause do you see as most important? Why? What other factors do you think might have played a role in the neighborhood's deterioration?

2. What further effects does Quindlen predict? Do you think her predictions are accurate?

Writing Practice

1. Do you still live in your old neighborhood, or have you or your family moved? Write a cause-and-effect essay explaining why you or your family decided to remain—or to leave.

*2. Why do people leave cities and move to the suburbs? Write a cause-and-effect essay that answers this question.

3. Consider Quindlen's suggestion in paragraph 12. Pair your city or town with a "sister city," and write an essay discussing the possible beneficial effects of a sister-city program.

F | **Comparison and Contrast**

For more on how to write a comparison-and-contrast essay, see 14F.

A **comparison-and-contrast** essay explains how two things are alike or how they are different; sometimes it discusses both similarities and differences. In "How the Lawyers Stole Winter," Christopher B. Daly compares his own boyhood to the childhood of his children. In "Men Are from Mars, Women Are from Venus," John Gray compares men and women.

HOW THE LAWYERS STOLE WINTER

Christopher B. Daly

A veteran journalist who has worked for the Associated Press and the *Washington Post*, Christopher B. Daly now divides his time between teaching and freelance writing. In the following 1995 essay, Daly returns to the New England of his boyhood and compares his childhood to that of his children. As you read, pay attention to the way Daly, writing about the same place during two different times, observes both differences and similarities.

When I was a boy, my friends and I would come home from school each day, change our clothes (because we were not allowed to wear "play clothes" to school), and go outside until dinnertime. In the early 1960s in Medford, a city on the outskirts of Boston, that was pretty much what everybody did. Sometimes there might be flute lessons, or an organized Little League game, but usually not. Usually we kids went out and played.

In winter, on our way home from the Gleason School, we would go past Brooks Pond to check the ice. By throwing heavy stones on it, hammering it with downed branches, and, finally, jumping on it, we could figure out if the ice was ready for skating. If it was, we would hurry home to grab our skates, our sticks, and whatever other gear we had, and then return to play hockey for the rest of the day. When the streetlights came on, we knew it was time to jam our cold, stiff feet back into our green rubber snow boots and get home for dinner.

I had these memories in mind recently when I moved, with my wife and two young boys, into a house near a lake even closer to Boston, in the city of Newton. As soon as Crystal Lake froze over, I grabbed my skates and headed out. I was not the first one there, though: the lawyers had beaten me to the lake. They had warned the town recreation department to put it off limits. So I found a sign that said DANGER, THIN ICE. NO SKATING.

Knowing a thing or two about words myself, I put my own gloss on the sign. I took it to mean *When the ice is thin, there is danger and there should be no skating*. Fair enough, I thought, but I knew that the obverse was also true: *When the ice is thick, it is safe and there should be skating*. Finding the ice plenty thick, I laced up my skates and glided out onto the miraculous glassy surface of the frozen lake. My wife, a native of Manhattan, would not let me take our two boys with me. But for as long as I could, I enjoyed the free, open-air delight of skating as it should be. After a few days others joined me, and we became an outlaw band of skaters.

What we were doing was once the heart of winter in New England—and a lot of other places, too. It was clean, free exercise that needed no StairMasters, no health clubs, no appointments, and hardly any gear. Sadly, it is in danger of passing away. Nowadays it seems that every city and town and almost all property holders are so worried about liability and lawsuits that they simply throw up a sign or a fence and declare that henceforth there shall be no skating, and that's the end of it.

As a result, kids today live in a world of leagues, rinks, rules, uniforms, adults, and rides—rides here, rides there, rides everywhere. It is not clear that they are better off; in some ways they are clearly *not* better off.

When I was a boy skating on Brooks Pond, there were no grown-ups around. Once or twice a year, on a weekend day or a holiday, some parents might come by with a thermos of hot cocoa. Maybe they would build a fire (which we were forbidden to do), and we would gather round.

But for the most part the pond was the domain of children. In the absence of adults, we made and enforced our own rules. We had hardly any gear—just some borrowed hockey gloves, some hand-me-down skates, maybe an elbow pad or two—so we played a clean form of hockey, with no high-sticking, no punching, and almost no checking. A single fight could ruin the whole afternoon. Indeed, as I remember it, thirty years later, it was the purest form of hockey I ever saw—until I got to see the Russian national team play the game.

But before we could play, we had to check the ice. We became serious junior meteorologists, true connoisseurs of cold. We learned that the best weather for pond skating is plain, clear cold, with starry nights and no snow. (Snow not only mucks up the skating surface but also insulates the ice from the colder air above.) And we learned that moving water, even the gently flowing Mystic River, is a lot less likely to freeze than standing water. So we skated only on the pond. We learned all the weird whooping and cracking sounds that ice makes as it expands and contracts, and thus when to leave the ice.

Do kids learn these things today? I don't know. How would they? We don't let them. Instead we post signs. Ruled by lawyers, cities and towns everywhere try to eliminate their legal liability. But try as they might, they cannot eliminate the underlying risk. Liability is a social construct; risk is a natural fact. When it is cold enough, ponds freeze. No sign or fence or ordinance can change that.

In fact, by focusing on liability and not teaching our kids how to take risks, we are making their world more dangerous. When we were children, we had to learn to evaluate risks and handle them on our own. We had to learn, quite literally, to test the waters. As a result, we grew up to be savvier about ice and ponds than any kid could be who has skated only under adult supervision on a rink.

When I was a boy, despite the risks we took on the ice no one I knew ever drowned. The only people I heard about who drowned were graduate students at Harvard or MIT who came from the tropics and were living through their first winters. Not knowing (after all, how could they?) about ice on moving water, they would innocently venture out onto the half-frozen Charles River, fall through, and die. They were literally out of their element.

Are we raising a generation of children who will be out of their element? And if so, what can we do about it? We cannot just roll back the calendar. I cannot tell my six-year-old to head down to the lake by himself to play all afternoon—if for no other reason than that he would not find twenty or thirty other kids there, full of the collective wisdom about cold and ice that they had inherited, along with hockey equipment, from their older brothers and sisters. Somewhere along the line that link got broken.

The whole setting of childhood has changed. We cannot change it again overnight. I cannot send my children out by themselves yet, but at least some of the time I can go out there with them. Maybe that is a start.

As for us, last winter was a very unusual one. We had ferocious cold (near-zero temperatures on many nights) and tremendous snows (about a hundred inches in all). Eventually a strange thing happened. The town gave in—sort of. Sometime in January the recreation department "opened" a section of the lake, and even dispatched a snowplow truck to clear a good-sized patch of ice. The boys and I skated during the rest of winter. Ever vigilant, the town officials kept the THIN ICE signs up, even though their own truck could safely drive on the frozen surface. And they brought in "lifeguards" and all sorts of rules about the hours during which we could skate and where we had to stay.

But at least we were able to skate in the open air, on real ice.   16
And it was still free.   17

Reacting to the Reading

1. Preview the essay. As you read it more carefully, highlight and annotate as needed to help you understand the writer's ideas.
2. In the margin beside each paragraph, label the paragraphs of Daly's essay "Then" or "Now" to distinguish discussions of the past from discussions of the present.

Reacting to Words

*1. Define these words: *gloss* (paragraph 4), *obverse* (4), *domain* (8), *connoisseurs* (9), *mucks* (9), *construct* (10), *ordinance* (10), *savvier* (11). Can you suggest a synonym for each word that will work in the essay?
2. In paragraph 5, Daly uses the expression "clean, free"; in paragraph 4, he uses the word "free"; and in paragraph 8, he uses the word "clean." He ends the essay with the word "free." What do these words contribute to the essay?

Reacting to Ideas

1. Daly is comparing his own childhood with the childhood of his children. How are they different? *Why* are they different?
2. In paragraph 6, Daly says, "kids today live in a world of leagues, rinks, rules, uniforms, adults, and rides." What does he mean? Do you agree with him? Do you see this as a good thing or a bad thing?
3. Whose childhood is more like your own—Daly's or his children's?
*4. Exactly how have the lawyers stolen winter?

Reacting to the Pattern

*1. Does this essay develop a point-by-point or a subject-by-subject comparison? Explain.

For more on point-by-point and subject-by-subject comparisons, see 14F.

2. What transitional words and phrases does Daly use to move readers from one subject to another?
3. What transitional words and phrases does Daly use to move readers from one point to the next?

Writing Practice

1. Write a comparison-and-contrast essay that explores the differences between an urban childhood and a suburban or a rural one.
2. How do you expect your own children's childhood to differ from yours? Write a comparison-and-contrast essay in which you explore possible differences and try to account for the differences you identify.
3. As you have grown older, have you become more or less likely to take risks? Compare your younger self with the person you are today in terms of your willingness to take risks in social situations, financial decision making, or matters of personal safety.

MEN ARE FROM MARS,
WOMEN ARE FROM VENUS

John Gray

Marriage counselor, seminar leader, and author John Gray has written a number of books that examine relationships between men and women. His best-known book, *Men Are from Mars, Women Are from Venus* (1992), uses a two-planet model to show how, in his view, men and women are at times so different that they might as well come from different planets. In the following excerpt from this book, Gray contrasts the different communication styles that he believes are characteristic of men and women. As you read, consider whether Gray's comparison oversimplifies the gender differences he discusses.

The most frequently expressed complaint women have about men is that men don't listen. Either a man completely ignores [a woman] when she speaks to him, or he listens for a few beats, assesses what is bothering her, and then proudly puts on his Mr. Fix-It cap and offers her a solution to make her feel better. He is confused when she doesn't appreciate this gesture of love. No matter how many times she tells him that he's not listening, he doesn't get it and keeps doing the same thing. She wants empathy, but he thinks she wants solutions. 1

The most frequently expressed complaint men have about women is that women are always trying to change them. When a woman loves a man she feels responsible to assist him in growing and tries to help him improve the way he does things. She forms a home-improvement committee, and he becomes her primary focus. No matter how much he resists her help, she persists—waiting for any opportunity to help him or tell him what to do. She thinks she's nurturing him, while he feels he's being controlled. Instead, he wants her acceptance. 2

These two problems can finally be solved by first understanding why men offer solutions and why women seek to improve. Let's pretend to go back in time, where by observing life on Mars and Venus—before the planets discovered one another or came to Earth—we can gain some insights into men and women. 3

Martians value power, competency, efficiency, and achievement. They are always doing things to prove themselves and develop their power and skills. Their sense of self is defined through their ability to achieve results. They experience fulfillment primarily through success and accomplishment. 4

Everything on Mars is a reflection of these values. Even their dress is designed to reflect their skills and competence. Police officers, soldiers, businessmen, scientists, cab drivers, technicians, and chefs all wear uniforms or at least hats to reflect their competence and power. 5

They don't read magazines like *Psychology Today, Self,* or *People.* They are more concerned with outdoor activities, like hunting, fishing, and racing cars. They are interested in the news, weather, and sports and couldn't care less about romance novels and self-help books. 6

They are more interested in "objects" and "things" rather than people and feelings. Even today on Earth, while women fantasize about romance, men fantasize about powerful cars, faster computers, gadgets, gizmos, and new more powerful technology. Men are preoccupied with the "things" that can help them express power by creating results and achieving their goals. 7

Achieving goals is very important to a Martian because it is a way for 8
him to prove his competence and thus feel good about himself. And for
him to feel good about himself he must achieve these goals by himself.
Someone else can't achieve them for him. Martians pride themselves in
doing things all by themselves. Autonomy is a symbol of efficiency, power,
and competence.

Understanding this Martian characteristic can help women under- 9
stand why men resist so much being corrected or being told what to do. To
offer a man unsolicited advice is to presume that he doesn't know what to
do or that he can't do it on his own. Men are very touchy about this,
because the issue of competence is so very important to them.

Because he is handling his problems on his own, a Martian rarely talks 10
about his problems unless he needs expert advice. He reasons: "Why
involve someone else when I can do it by myself?" He keeps his problems
to himself unless he requires help from another to find a solution. Asking
for help when you can do it yourself is perceived as a sign of weakness.

However, if he truly does need help, then it is a sign of wisdom to get 11
it. In this case, he will find someone he respects and then talk about his
problem. Talking about a problem on Mars is an invitation for advice.
Another Martian feels honored by the opportunity. Automatically he puts
on his Mr. Fix-It hat, listens for a while, and then offers some jewels of
advice.

This Martian custom is one of the reasons men instinctively offer solu- 12
tions when women talk about problems. When a woman innocently shares
upset feelings or explores out loud the problems of her day, a man mistakenly assumes she is looking for some expert advice. He puts on his Mr.
Fix-It hat and begins giving advice; this is his way of showing love and of
trying to help.

He wants to help her feel better by solving her problems. He wants to 13
be useful to her. He feels he can be valued and thus worthy of her love
when his abilities are used to solve her problems.

Once he has offered a solution, however, and she continues to be upset 14
it becomes increasingly difficult for him to listen because his solution is
being rejected and he feels increasingly useless.

He has no idea that by just listening with empathy and interest he can 15
be supportive. He does not know that on Venus talking about problems is
not an invitation to offer a solution.

Venusians have different values. They value love, communication, 16
beauty, and relationships. They spend a lot of time supporting, helping,
and nurturing one another. Their sense of self is defined through their feelings and the quality of their relationships. They experience fulfillment
through sharing and relating.

Everything on Venus reflects these values. Rather than building high- 17
ways and tall buildings, the Venusians are more concerned with living
together in harmony, community, and loving cooperation. Relationships
are more important than work and technology. In most ways their world
is the opposite of Mars.

They do not wear uniforms like the Martians (to reveal their compe- 18
tence). On the contrary, they enjoy wearing a different outfit every day,
according to how they are feeling. Personal expression, especially of their
feelings, is very important. They may even change outfits several times a
day as their mood changes.

Communication is of primary importance. To share their personal feel- 19
ings is much more important than achieving goals and success. Talking
and relating to one another is a source of tremendous fulfillment.

This is hard for a man to comprehend. He can come close to under- 20
standing a woman's experience of sharing and relating by comparing it to
the satisfaction he feels when he wins a race, achieves a goal, or solves a
problem.

Instead of being goal oriented, women are relationship oriented; they 21
are more concerned with expressing their goodness, love, and caring. Two
Martians go to lunch to discuss a project or business goal; they have a
problem to solve. In addition, Martians view going to a restaurant as an
efficient way to approach food: no shopping, no cooking, and no washing
dishes. For Venusians, going to lunch is an opportunity to nurture a relationship, for both giving support to and receiving support from a friend.
Women's restaurant talk can be very open and intimate, almost like the
dialogue that occurs between therapist and patient.

On Venus, everyone studies psychology and has at least a master's 22
degree in counseling. They are very involved in personal growth, spiritual-
ity, and everything that can nurture life, healing, and growth. Venus is covered with parks, organic gardens, shopping centers, and restaurants.

Venusians are very intuitive. They have developed this ability through 23
centuries of anticipating the needs of others. They pride themselves in
being considerate of the needs and feelings of others. A sign of great love
is to offer help and assistance to another Venusian without being asked.

Because proving one's competence is not as important to a Venusian, 24
offering help is not offensive, and needing help is not a sign of weakness.
A man, however, may feel offended because when a woman offers advice
he doesn't feel she trusts his ability to do it himself.

A woman has no conception of this male sensitivity because for her it 25
is another feather in her hat if someone offers to help her. It makes her feel
loved and cherished. But offering help to a man can make him feel incom-
petent, weak, and even unloved.

On Venus it is a sign of caring to give advice and suggestions. Venu- 26
sians firmly believe that when something is working it can always work
better. Their nature is to want to improve things. When they care about
someone, they freely point out what can be improved and suggest how to
do it. Offering advice and constructive criticism is an act of love.

Mars is very different. Martians are more solution oriented. If some- 27
thing is working, their motto is don't change it. Their instinct is to leave
it alone if it is working. "Don't fix it unless it is broken" is a common
expression.

When a woman tries to improve a man, he feels she is trying to fix him. 28
He receives the message that he is broken. She doesn't realize her caring
attempts to help him may humiliate him. She mistakenly thinks she is just
helping him to grow.

Reacting to the Reading

1. Preview the essay. As you read it more carefully, highlight and annotate
   as needed to help you understand the writer's ideas.
2. In marginal annotations, number the specific characteristics of men
   and women that Gray identifies. Then, make an outline for a point-by-
   point comparison.

Reacting to Words

*1. Define these words: *empathy* (paragraph 1), *nurturing* (2), *autonomy* (8), *unsolicited* (9). Can you suggest a synonym for each word that will work in the essay?

2. Do you think referring to men as Martians and women as Venusians is an effective strategy? What other contrasting labels could work?

Reacting to Ideas

*1. Do you think Gray is serious? What makes you think so?

*2. Do you think Gray's specific observations about men and women are accurate? Is he stereotyping men and women? Explain.

*3. Do you agree with Gray's general point that men and women seem to be from two different planets? Why or why not?

Reacting to the Pattern

1. This essay is a subject-by-subject comparison. How does Gray signal the movement from the first subject to the second subject? Why do you suppose he chose to write a subject-by-subject rather than a point-by-point comparison?

*2. If you were going to add a more complete conclusion to sum up this essay's points, what closing strategy would you use? Do you think the essay needs such a conclusion?

Writing Practice

1. Are young (or adolescent) boys and girls also from two different planets? Take a position on this issue, and support it in a subject-by-subject comparison. In your thesis statement, try to account for the differences you identify between boys and girls.

2. Identify one general area in which you believe men's and women's attitudes, behavior, or expectations are very different — for example, dating, careers, food and diet, sports, housekeeping, or driving. Write a comparison-and-contrast essay (serious or humorous) that explores the differences you identify.

3. Are men and women portrayed differently in television dramas (including soap operas) and comedies? Choose a program that has several well-developed male and female characters, and contrast the men and the women in terms of their actions and their conversations.

G   Classification

A **classification** essay divides a whole into parts and sorts various items into categories. Tom Bodett's "Wait Divisions" considers the different kinds of waiting we do. Scott Russell Sanders's "The Men We Carry in Our Minds" classifies the working men he has known.

For more on how to write a classification essay, see 14G.

WAIT DIVISIONS

Tom Bodett

Public radio commentator, author, and motel-chain spokesperson Tom Bodett's down-home, no-nonsense style lends itself well to examinations of the everyday. In the following excerpt from his 1987 book *Small Comforts,* Bodett considers an easily overlooked part of life: the times when we are not doing anything but waiting. Note how his precise classification of different kinds of waiting is both humorous and revealing.

1 I read somewhere that we spend a full third of our lives waiting. I've also read where we spend a third of our lives sleeping, a third working, and a third at our leisure. Now either somebody's lying, or we're spending all our leisure time waiting to go to work or sleep. That can't be true or league softball and Winnebagos[1] never would have caught on.

2 So where are we doing all of this waiting and what does it mean to an impatient society like ours? Could this unseen waiting be the source of all our problems? A shrinking economy? The staggering deficit? Declining mental health and moral apathy? Probably not, but let's take a look at some of the more classic "waits" anyway.

3 The very purest form of waiting is what we'll call the *Watched-Pot Wait.* This type of wait is without a doubt the most annoying of all. Take filling up the kitchen sink. There is absolutely nothing you can do while this is going on but keep both eyes glued to the sink until it's full. If you try to cram in some extracurricular activity, you're asking for it. So you stand there, your hands on the faucets, and wait. A temporary suspension of duties. During these waits it's common for your eyes to lapse out of focus. The brain disengages from the body and wanders around the imagination in search of distraction. It finds none and springs back into action only when the water runs over the edge of the counter and onto your socks.

4 The phrase "A watched pot never boils" comes of this experience. Pots don't care whether they are watched or not; the problem is that nobody has ever seen a pot actually come to a boil. While they are waiting, their brains turn off.

5 Other forms of the Watched-Pot Wait would include waiting for your drier to quit at the laundromat, waiting for your toast to pop out of the toaster, or waiting for a decent idea to come to mind at a typewriter. What they all have in common is that they render the waiter helpless and mindless.

6 A cousin to the Watched-Pot Wait is the *Forced Wait.* Not for the weak of will, this one requires a bit of discipline. The classic Forced Wait is starting your car in the winter and letting it slowly idle up to temperature before engaging the clutch. This is every bit as uninteresting as watching a pot, but with one big difference. You have a choice. There is nothing keeping you from racing to work behind a stone-cold engine save the thought of the early demise of several thousand dollars' worth of equipment you haven't paid for yet. Thoughts like that will help you get through a Forced Wait.

7 Properly preparing packaged soup mixes also requires a Forced Wait. Directions are very specific on these mixes. "Bring three cups water to boil,

---

1. A kind of recreational vehicle with sleeping accommodations.

add mix, simmer three minutes, remove from heat, let stand five minutes."
I have my doubts that anyone has ever actually done this. I'm fairly
spineless when it comes to instant soups and usually just boil the bejeezus
out of them until the noodles sink. Some things just aren't worth a Forced
Wait.

All in all Forced Waiting requires a lot of a thing called *patience*, which   8
is a virtue. Once we get into virtues I'm out of my element, and can't
expound on the virtues of virtue, or even lie about them. So let's move on
to some of the more far-reaching varieties of waiting.

The *Payday Wait* is certainly a leader in the long-term anticipation   9
field. The problem with waits that last more than a few minutes is that you
have to actually do other things in the meantime. Like go to work. By far
the most aggravating feature of the Payday Wait is that even though you
must keep functioning in the interludes, there is less and less you are able
to do as the big day draws near. For some of us the last few days are best
spent alone in a dark room for fear we'll accidentally do something that
costs money. With the Payday Wait comes a certain amount of hope that
we'll make it, and faith that everything will be all right once we do.

With the introduction of faith and hope, I've ushered in the most   10
potent wait class of all, the *Lucky-Break Wait*, or the *Wait for One's Ship to
Come In*. This type of wait is unusual in that it is for the most part voluntary. Unlike the Forced Wait, which is also voluntary, waiting for your
lucky break does not necessarily mean that it will happen.

Turning one's life into a waiting game of these proportions requires   11
gobs of the aforementioned faith and hope, and is strictly for the optimists
among us. For these people life is the thing that happens to them while
they're waiting for something to happen to them. On the surface it seems
as ridiculous as following the directions on soup mixes, but the Lucky-
Break Wait performs an outstanding service to those who take it upon
themselves to do it. As long as one doesn't come to rely on it, wishing for
a few good things to happen never hurt anybody.

In the end it is obvious that we certainly do spend a good deal of our   12
time waiting. The person who said we do it a third of the time may have
been going easy on us. It makes a guy wonder how anything at all gets
done around here. But things do get done, people grow old, and time boils
on whether you watch it or not.

The next time you're standing at the sink waiting for it to fill while   13
cooking soup mix that you'll have to eat until payday or until a large bag
of cash falls out of the sky, don't despair. You're probably just as busy as
the next guy.

Reacting to the Reading

1. Preview the essay. As you read it more carefully, highlight and annotate
   as needed to help you understand the writer's ideas.

2. In the margins of Bodett's essay, number the categories he identifies,
   and write a brief definition of each category in your own words.

Reacting to Words

*1. Define these words: *suspension* (paragraph 3), *lapse* (3), *disengages* (3),
   render (5), *demise* (6), *expound* (8), *potent* (10). Can you suggest a synonym for each word that will work in the essay?

2. Bodett repeats the words *wait* and *waiting* throughout his essay. Do you think he should have tried to use other words with similar meanings? If so, give some suggestions. If not, defend his choices.

*3. Bodett uses contractions as well as informal words—for example, *bejeezus* (paragraph 7) and *gobs* (paragraph 11)—in his essay. Identify as many informal words and expressions as you can. Does this informal style strengthen or weaken his essay? Explain your conclusion.

Reacting to Ideas

1. Is there a serious message beneath the humorous surface of Bodett's essay, or is it just a lighthearted discussion? Explain.

*2. Do Bodett's categories cover all the situations in which people find themselves waiting? Can you think of any kinds of waiting that do not fit into his categories? If so, create as many new categories as necessary. Why do you suppose Bodett did not include these categories?

Reacting to the Pattern

1. List the categories Bodett identifies. Is his treatment of each category similar, or does he develop some in greater depth than others? Do you think he should devote more space to any particular category? If so, why?

2. Do you think Bodett gives enough examples of each kind of waiting? Suggest some examples he does not include.

3. What, if anything, seems to determine the order in which Bodett presents his categories? Is this the most effective possible order? Why does he introduce the "Lucky-Break Wait" last?

Writing Practice

1. Write a classification essay in which you discuss the same categories Bodett presents, substituting examples from your own experience.

2. Write a serious essay about the kinds of waiting Bodett discusses. Try to respond to the question he poses in the first sentence of paragraph 2.

3. Write a humorous (or serious) essay called "Worry Divisions." Identify three or four kinds of worries you have, arrange them in order of importance, and discuss the most serious worry last. Be sure to provide specific examples in each category.

THE MEN WE CARRY IN OUR MINDS

Scott Russell Sanders

Scott Russell Sanders is a professor of English and an essayist. His essays are personal reflections that contain social commentary and philosophical reflection and are often set in the Midwest, where he was born and raised. In "The Men We Carry in Our Minds," Sanders reflects on the working lives of the men he knew when he was a boy and classifies them according to their work. His essay discusses not only his boyhood impressions of the work these men did but also the

direction his own professional life has taken. As you read, notice how
Sanders moves from classifying men's work to comparing men's lives
to women's lives.

The first men, besides my father, I remember seeing were black convicts   1
and white guards, in the cottonfield across the road from our farm on the
outskirts of Memphis. I must have been three or four. The prisoners wore
dingy gray-and-black zebra suits, heavy as canvas, sodden with sweat. Hat-
less, stooped, they chopped weeds in the fierce heat, row after row, breathing the acrid dust of boll-weevil poison. The overseers wore dazzling white
shirts and broad shadowy hats. The oiled barrels of their shotguns flashed
in the sunlight. Their faces in memory are utterly blank. Of course those
men, white and black, have become for me an emblem of racial hatred.
But they have also come to stand for the twin poles of my early vision of
manhood—the brute toiling animal and the boss.

When I was a boy, the men I knew labored with their bodies. They were   2
marginal farmers, just scraping by, or welders, steelworkers, carpenters;
they swept floors, dug ditches, mined coal, or drove trucks, their forearms
ropy with muscle; they trained horses, stoked furnaces, built tires, stood
on assembly lines wrestling parts onto cars and refrigerators. They got up
before light, worked all day long whatever the weather, and when they
came home at night they looked as though somebody had been whipping
them. In the evenings and on weekends they worked on their own places,
tilling gardens that were lumpy with clay, fixing broken-down cars, hammering on houses that were always too drafty, too leaky, too small.

The bodies of the men I knew were twisted and maimed in ways visible   3
and invisible. The nails of their hands were black and split, the hands tat-
tooed with scars. Some had lost fingers. Heavy lifting had given many of
them finicky backs and guts weak from hernias. Racing against conveyor
belts had given them ulcers. Their ankles and knees ached from years of
standing on concrete. Anyone who had worked for long around machines
was hard of hearing. They squinted, and the skin of their faces was creased
like the leather of old work gloves. There were times, studying them, when
I dreaded growing up. Most of them coughed, from dust or cigarettes, and
most of them drank cheap wine or whiskey, so their eyes looked bloodshot
and bruised. The fathers of my friends always seemed older than the mothers. Men wore out sooner. Only women lived into old age.

As a boy I also knew another sort of men, who did not sweat and break   4
down like mules. They were soldiers, and so far as I could tell they scarcely
worked at all. During my early school years we lived on a military base, an
arsenal in Ohio, and every day I saw GIs in the guardshacks, on the stoops
of barracks, at the wheels of olive drab Chevrolets. The chief fact of their
lives was boredom. Long after I left the Arsenal I came to recognize the
sour smell the soldiers gave off as that of souls in limbo. They were all
waiting—for wars, for transfers, for leaves, for promotions, for the end of
their hitch—like so many braves waiting for the hunt to begin. Unlike the
warriors of older tribes, however, they would have no say about when the
battle would start or how it would be waged. Their waiting was broken
only when they practiced for war. They fired guns at targets, drove tanks
across the churned-up fields of the military reservation, set off bombs in
the wrecks of old fighter planes. I knew this was all play. But I also felt certain that when the hour for killing arrived, they would kill. When the real

shooting started, many of them would die. This was what soldiers were *for*, just as a hammer was for driving nails.

Warriors and toilers: those seemed, in my boyhood vision, to be the chief destinies for men. They weren't the only destinies, as I learned from having a few male teachers, from reading books, and from watching television. But the men on television — the politicians, the astronauts, the generals, the savvy lawyers, the philosophical doctors, the bosses who gave orders to both soldiers and laborers — seemed as removed and unreal to me as the figures in tapestries. I could no more imagine growing up to become one of these cool, potent creatures than I could imagine becoming a prince.

A nearer and more hopeful example was that of my father, who had escaped from a red-dirt farm to a tire factory, and from the assembly line to the front office. Eventually he dressed in a white shirt and tie. He carried himself as if he had been born to work with his mind. But his body, remembering the earlier years of slogging work, began to give out on him in his fifties, and it quit on him entirely before he turned sixty-five. Even such a partial escape from man's fate as he had accomplished did not seem possible for most of the boys I knew. They joined the Army, stood in line for jobs in the smoky plants, helped build highways. They were bound to work as their fathers had worked, killing themselves or preparing to kill others.

A scholarship enabled me not only to attend college, a rare enough feat in my circle, but even to study in a university meant for the children of the rich. Here I met for the first time young men who had assumed from birth that they would lead lives of comfort and power. And for the first time I met women who told me that men were guilty of having kept all the joys and privileges of the earth for themselves. I was baffled. What privileges? What joys? I thought about the maimed, dismal lives of most of the men back home. What had they stolen from their wives and daughters? The right to go five days a week, twelve months a year, for thirty or forty years to a steel mill or a coal mine? The right to drop bombs and die in war? The right to feel every leak in the roof, every gap in the fence, every cough in the engine, as a wound they must mend? The right to feel, when the layoff comes or the plant shuts down, not only afraid but ashamed?

I was slow to understand the deep grievances of women. This was because, as a boy, I had envied them. Before college, the only people I had ever known who were interested in art or music or literature, the only ones who read books, the only ones who ever seemed to enjoy a sense of ease and grace were the mothers and daughters. Like the menfolk, they fretted about money, they scrimped and made-do. But, when the pay stopped coming in, they were not the ones who had failed. Nor did they have to go to war, and that seemed to me a blessed fact. By comparison with the narrow, ironclad days of fathers, there was an expansiveness, I thought, in the days of mothers. They went to see neighbors, to shop in town, to run errands at school, at the library, at church. No doubt, had I looked harder at their lives, I would have envied them less. It was not my fate to become a woman, so it was easier for me to see the graces. Few of them held jobs outside the home, and those who did filled thankless roles as clerks and waitresses. I didn't see, then, what a prison a house could be, since houses seemed to me brighter, handsomer places than any factory. I did not realize — because such things were never spoken of — how often women suffered from men's bullying. I did learn about the wretchedness of abandoned wives, single mothers, widows; but I also learned about the wretchedness of lone men. Even then I could see how exhausting it was for a mother to cater all day to the needs of young children. But if I had been asked, as a boy, to choose between tending a baby and tending a machine, I think I would have chosen the baby. (Having now tended both, I know I would choose the baby.)

So I was baffled when the women at college accused me and my sex of having cornered the world's pleasures. I think something like my bafflement has been felt by other boys (and by girls as well) who grew up in dirt-poor farm country, in mining country, in black ghettos, in Hispanic barrios, in the shadows of factories, in Third World nations—any place where the fate of men is as grim and bleak as the fate of women. Toilers and warriors. I realize now how ancient these identities are, how deep the tug they exert on men, the undertow of a thousand generations. The miseries I saw, as a boy, in the lives of nearly all men I continue to see in the lives of many—the body-breaking toil, the tedium, the call to be tough, the humiliating powerlessness, the battle for a living and for territory.

When the women I met at college thought about the joys and privileges of men, they did not carry in their minds the sort of men I had known in my childhood. They thought of their fathers, who were bankers, physicians, architects, stockbrokers, the big wheels of the big cities. These fathers rode the train to work or drove cars that cost more than any of my childhood houses. They were attended from morning to night by female helpers, wives and nurses and secretaries. They were never laid off, never short of cash at month's end, never lined up for welfare. These fathers made decisions that mattered. They ran the world.

The daughters of such men wanted to share in this power, this glory. So did I. They yearned for a say over their future, for jobs worthy of their abilities, for the right to live at peace, unmolested, whole. Yes, I thought, yes yes. The difference between me and these daughters was that they saw me, because of my sex, as destined from birth to become like their fathers, and therefore as an enemy to their desires. But I knew better. I wasn't an enemy, in fact or in feeling. I was an ally. If I had known, then, how to tell them so, would they have believed me? Would they now?

Reacting to the Reading

1. Preview the essay. As you read it more carefully, highlight and annotate as needed to help you understand the writer's ideas.
2. In the margins of the essay, name and number the categories Sanders identifies. If he does not name a particular category, supply a suitable name.

Reacting to Words

*1. Define these words: *sodden* (paragraph 1), *acrid* (1), *overseers* (1), *tilling* (2), *finicky* (3), *toilers* (5), *savvy* (5), *expansiveness* (8), *undertow* (9), *yearned* (11). Can you suggest a synonym for each word that will work in the essay?
2. Suggest two or three alternative names for the categories *warriors* and *toilers* (paragraph 5). Do you think any of your suggestions are better than Sanders's choices?

Reacting to Ideas

1. When Sanders was young, what did he see as his destiny? How did he escape his fate? How else might he have escaped?
2. What were the grievances of the women Sanders met at college? Why did Sanders have trouble understanding these grievances?
*3. Who do you believe has an easier life—men or women? Explain.

Reacting to the Pattern

1. What two types of men did Sanders know when he was young? How are they different? What do they have in common?
2. What kinds of men discussed in the essay do not fit into the two categories Sanders identifies in paragraphs 2–4? Why don't they fit?
*3. Sanders does not categorize the women he discusses. Can you think of a few categories into which these women can fit?

Writing Practice

1. Write a classification essay in which you identify and discuss three or four categories of workers (females as well as males) you observed in your community when you were growing up. In your thesis, draw a conclusion about the relative status and rewards of these workers' jobs.
2. Consider your own work history as well as your future career. Write a classification essay in which you discuss your experience in several different categories of employment in the past, present, and future. Give each category a descriptive title, and include a thesis statement that sums up your progress.
3. Categorize the workers in your current place of employment or on your college campus.

 H **Definition**

For more on how to write a definition essay, see 14H.

A **definition** essay presents an extended definition, using other patterns of development to move beyond a simple dictionary definition. In "Tortillas," José Antonio Burciaga defines a food. In "Dyslexia," Eileen Simpson defines a reading disorder.

TORTILLAS

José Antonio Burciaga

Bilingual essayist and poet José Antonio Burciaga included this essay in his 1988 collection *Weedee Peepo,* an affectionate look at his family and culture. Here he defines the tortilla, remembering its important role in his childhood. As you read, notice how he combines various patterns of development to shape his definition.

My earliest memory of *tortillas* is my *Mamá* telling me not to play with them. I had bitten eyeholes in one and was wearing it as a mask at the dinner table.

As a child, I also used *tortillas* as hand warmers on cold days, and my family claims that I owe my career as an artist to my early experiments with *tortillas*. According to them, my clowning around helped me develop a strong artistic foundation. I'm not so sure, though. Sometimes I wore a *tortilla* on my head, like a *yarmulke*, and yet I never had any great urge to convert from Catholicism to Judaism. But who knows? They may be right.

For Mexicans over the centuries, the *tortilla* has served as the spoon and the fork, the plate and the napkin. *Tortillas* originated before the Mayan civilizations, perhaps predating Europe's wheat bread. According to Mayan mythology, the great god Quetzalcoatl, realizing that the red ants knew the secret of using maize as food, transformed himself into a black ant, infiltrated the colony of red ants, and absconded with a grain of corn. (Is it any wonder that to this day, black ants and red ants do not get along?) Quetzalcoatl then put maize on the lips of the first man and woman, Oxomoco and Cipactonal, so that they would become strong. Maize festivals are still celebrated by many Indian cultures of the Americas.

When I was growing up in El Paso, *tortillas* were part of my daily life. I used to visit a *tortilla* factory in an ancient adobe building near the open *mercado* in Ciudad Juárez. As I approached, I could hear the rhythmic slapping of the *masa* as the skilled vendors outside the factory formed it into balls and patted them into perfectly round corn cakes between the palms of their hands. The wonderful aroma and the speed with which the women counted so many dozens of *tortillas* out of warm wicker baskets still linger in my mind. Watching them at work convinced me that the most handsome and *deliciosas tortillas* are handmade. Although machines are faster, they can never adequately replace generation-to-generation experience. There's no place in the factory assembly line for the tender slaps that give each *tortilla* character. The best thing that can be said about mass-producing *tortillas* is that it makes it possible for many people to enjoy them.

In the *mercado* where my mother shopped, we frequently bought *taquitos de nopalitos*, small tacos filled with diced cactus, onions, tomatoes, and *jalapeños*. Our friend Don Toribio showed us how to make delicious, crunchy *taquitos* with dried, salted pumpkin seeds. When you had no money for the filling, a poor man's *taco* could be made by placing a warm *tortilla* on the left palm, applying a sprinkle of salt, then rolling the *tortilla* up quickly with the fingertips of the right hand. My own kids put peanut butter and jelly on *tortillas*, which I think is truly bicultural. And speaking of fast foods for kids, nothing beats a *quesadilla*, a *tortilla* grilled-cheese sandwich.

Depending on what you intend to use them for, *tortillas* may be made in various ways. Even a run-of-the-mill *tortilla* is more than a flat corn cake. A skillfully cooked homemade *tortilla* has a bottom and a top; the top skin forms a pocket in which you put the filling that folds your *tortilla* into a taco. Paper-thin *tortillas* are used specifically for *flautas*, a type of taco that is filled, rolled, and then fried until crisp. The name *flauta* means *flute*, which probably refers to the Mayan bamboo flute; however, the only sound that comes from an edible *flauta* is a delicious crunch that is music to the palate. In México *flautas* are sometimes made as long as two feet and then cut into manageable segments. The opposite of *flautas* is *gorditas*, meaning *little fat ones*. These are very thick small *tortillas*.

The versatility of *tortillas* and corn does not end here. Besides being 7 tasty and nourishing, they have spiritual and artistic qualities as well. The Tarahumara Indians of Chihuahua, for example, concocted a corn-based beer called *tesgüino,* which their descendants still make today. And everyone has read about the woman in New Mexico who was cooking her husband a *tortilla* one morning when the image of Jesus Christ miraculously appeared on it. Before they knew what was happening, the man's breakfast had become a local shrine.

Then there is *tortilla* art. Various Chicano artists throughout the South- 8 west have, when short of materials or just in a whimsical mood, used a dry *tortilla* as a small, round canvas. And a few years back, at the height of the Chicano movement, a priest in Arizona got into trouble with the Church after he was discovered celebrating mass using a *tortilla* as the host. All of which only goes to show that while the *tortilla* may be a lowly corn cake, when the necessity arises, it can reach unexpected distinction.

Reacting to the Reading

1. Preview the essay. As you read it more carefully, highlight and annotate as needed to help you understand the writer's ideas.
2. Circle all the Spanish words Burciaga uses in his essay.

Reacting to Words

*1. Define these words: *yarmulke* (paragraph 2), *maize* (3), *infiltrated* (3), *adobe* (4), *edible* (6), *concocted* (7), *whimsical* (8). Can you suggest a synonym for each word that will work in the essay?
2. Review the Spanish words you circled in Reacting to the Reading question 2. Do you think most people who don't know Spanish could determine the meanings of these words from their context? Can you?

Reacting to Ideas

*1. List all the uses of the tortilla Burciaga identifies. Then, divide your list into two categories—*practical* uses and *impractical* uses. Can you suggest any other uses to add to either category?
2. What information does this essay give you about Burciaga and his family? What kind of person do you think he is? What makes you think so?
3. What is Burciaga's thesis? Where in the essay does he state it? Do you think it should be stated earlier?

Reacting to the Pattern

*1. Identify sections of his essay where Burciaga develops his definition with examples, description, and narration. Can you identify any other patterns of development?
2. Burciaga does not include a formal dictionary definition of *tortilla* in his essay. Try writing a one- or two-sentence definition that begins, "Tortillas are . . ."

Writing Practice

1. Is there an ethnic food that you feel as much affection for as Burciaga feels for the tortilla? Write an essay in which you use narration, exemplification, and description to define this food.

*2. Write a definition of one of these food items for an audience that has never seen or heard of the food before: a hot dog, pizza, chili, nachos, grits, or a Big Mac. Begin by defining the food in a single sentence, and go on to describe it and show how it is like and unlike other foods with which your readers may be familiar.

DYSLEXIA

Eileen Simpson

In *Reversals: A Personal Account of Victory over Dyslexia* (1979), psychotherapist and author Eileen Simpson tells the story of her own struggle with dyslexia. In her account, she describes how she was able to overcome dyslexia only when she understood what it was and how it made reading difficult. As you read the following excerpt from *Reversals*, watch for the various ways in which Simpson develops her definition, and note especially her use of exemplification.

Dyslexia (from the Greek, *dys*, faulty, + *lexis*, speech, cognate with the Latin *legere*, to read), developmental or specific dyslexia as it's technically called, the disorder I suffered from, is the inability of otherwise normal children to read. Children whose intelligence is below average, whose vision or hearing is defective, who have not had proper schooling, or who are too emotionally disturbed or brain-damaged to profit from it belong in other diagnostic categories. They, too, may be unable to learn to read, but they cannot properly be called dyslexics.   1

For more than seventy years the essential nature of the affliction has been hotly disputed by psychologists, neurologists, and educators. It is generally agreed, however, that it is the result of a neurophysiological flaw in the brain's ability to process language. It is probably inherited, although some experts are reluctant to say this because they fear people will equate "inherited" with "untreatable." Treatable it certainly is: not a disease to be cured, but a malfunction that requires retraining.   2

Reading is the most complex skill a child entering school is asked to develop. What makes it complex, in part, is that letters are less constant than objects. A car seen from a distance, close to, from above, or below, or in a mirror still looks like a car even though the optical image changes. The letters of the alphabet are more whimsical. Take the letter *b*. Turned upside down it becomes a *p*. Looked at in a mirror, it becomes a *d*. Capitalized, it becomes something quite different, a *B*. The *M* upside down is a *W*. The *E* flipped over becomes Ǝ. This reversed *E* is familiar to mothers of normal children who have just begun to go to school. The earliest examples of art work they bring home often have I LOVƎ YOU written on them.   3

Dyslexics differ from other children in that they read, spell, and write letters upside down and turned around far more frequently and for a much longer time. In what seems like a capricious manner, they also add letters,   4 syllables, and words, or, just as capriciously, delete them. With palindromic words (was-saw, on-no), it is the order of the letters rather than the orientation they change. The new word makes sense, but not the sense intended. Then there are other words where the changed order—"sorty" for story—does not make sense at all.

The inability to recognize that g, g, and G are the same letter, the inability to maintain the orientation of the letters, to retain the order in which they appear, and to follow a line of text without jumping above or below it—all the results of the flaw—can make of an orderly page of words a dish of alphabet soup.

5

Also essential for reading is the ability to store words in memory and to retrieve them. This very particular kind of memory dyslexics lack. So, too, do they lack the ability to hear what the eye sees, and to see what they hear. If the eye sees "off," the ear must hear "off" and not "of," or "for." If the ear hears "saw," the eye must see that it looks like "saw" on the page and not "was." Lacking these skills, a sentence or paragraph becomes a coded message to which the dyslexic can't find the key.

6

It is only a slight exaggeration to say that those who learned to read without difficulty can best understand the labor reading is for a dyslexic by turning a page of text upside down and trying to decipher it.

7

While the literature is replete with illustrations of the way these children write and spell, there are surprisingly few examples of how they read. One, used for propaganda purposes to alert the public to the vulnerability of dyslexics in a literate society, is a sign warning that behind it are guard dogs trained to kill. The dyslexic reads:

8

> Wurring
> Guard God
> Patoly

for

> Warning
> Guard Dog
> Patrol

and, of course, remains ignorant of the danger.

Looking for a more commonplace example, and hoping to recapture the way I must have read in fourth grade, I recently observed dyslexic children at the Educational Therapy Clinic in Princeton, through the courtesy of Elizabeth Travers, the director. The first child I saw, eight-year-old Anna (whose red hair and brown eyes reminded me of myself at that age), had just come to the Clinic and was learning the alphabet. Given the story of "Little Red Riding Hood," which is at the second grade level, she began confidently enough, repeating the title from memory, then came to a dead stop. With much coaxing throughout, she read as follows:

9

> Grandma you a top. Grandma [looks over at picture of Red Riding Hood]. Red Riding Hood [long pause, presses index finger into the paper. Looks at me for help. I urge: Go ahead] the a [puts head close to the page, nose almost touching] on Grandma

for

Once upon a time there was a little girl who had a red coat with a red hood. Etc.

"Grandma" was obviously a memory from having heard the story read aloud. Had I needed a reminder of how maddening my silences must have been to Miss Henderson, and how much patience is required to teach these children, Anna, who took almost ten minutes to read these few lines, furnished it. The main difference between Anna and me at that age is that Anna clearly felt no need to invent. She was perplexed, but not anxious, and seemed to have infinite tolerance for her long silences. 10

Toby, a nine-year old boy with superior intelligence, had a year of tutoring behind him and could have managed "Little Red Riding Hood" with ease. His text was taken from the *Reader's Digest's Reading Skill Builder,* Grade IV. He read: 11

A kangaroo likes as if he had but truck together warm. His saw neck and head do not . . . [Here Toby sighed with fatigue] seem to feel happy back. They and tried and so every a tiger Moses and shoots from lonesome day and shouts and long shore animals. And each farm play with five friends . . .

He broke off with the complaint, "This is too hard. Do I have to read any more?" 12

His text was: 13

A kangaroo looks as if he had been put together wrong. His small neck and head do not seem to fit with his heavy back legs and thick tail. Soft eyes, a twinkly little nose and short front legs seem strange on such a large strong animal. And each front paw has five fingers, like a man's hand.

An English expert gives the following bizarre example of an adult dyslexic's performance: 14

An the bee-what in the tel mother of the biothodoodoo to the majo- ram or that emidrate eni eni Krastrei, mestriet to Ketra lotombreidi to ra from treido as that.

His text, taken from a college catalogue the examiner happened to have close at hand, was: 15

It shall be in the power of the college to examine or not every licen- tiate, previous to his admission to the fellowship, as they shall think fit.

That evening when I read aloud to Auntie for the first time, I probably began as Toby did, my memory of the classroom lesson keeping me close to the text. When memory ran out, and Auntie did not correct my errors, I began to invent. When she still didn't stop me, I may well have begun to improvise in the manner of this patient—anything to keep going and keep up the myth that I was reading—until Auntie brought the "gibberish" to a halt. 16

Reacting to the Reading

1. Preview the essay. As you read it more carefully, highlight and annotate as needed to help you understand the writer's ideas.
2. Underline the definition of *dyslexia* in the essay; in a marginal annotation, paraphrase the definition.

Reacting to Words

*1. Define these words: *process* (paragraph 2), *whimsical* (3), *capricious* (4), *orientation* (5), *replete* (8), *commonplace* (9), *perplexed* (10), *gibberish* (16). Can you suggest a synonym for each word that will work in the essay?
2. Can you think of a synonym or near-synonym for *dyslexia*? If not, try to coin a suitable word to describe the disorder.

Reacting to Ideas

1. What is dyslexia? How are children with dyslexia different from their peers?
2. What central point or idea do you think Simpson wishes to communicate to her readers? Does she ever actually state this idea? If so, where? If not, do you think she should?
*3. If you were dyslexic, how would your life be different?

Reacting to the Pattern

1. Simpson develops her definition of dyslexia with examples. Identify some of these examples. Do you find the material drawn from her own childhood struggle with dyslexia more or less effective than the examples of cases she observes as an adult? Explain.
*2. What other patterns does Simpson use to develop her definition?

Writing Practice

1. Choose a problem—physical, economic, or behavioral—that handicaps you as a student. Identify the problem, define it, and give examples to expand your definition.
2. Consider the tasks you do each day at home, at school, and at work. How would you manage these tasks differently if you were dyslexic? Write an essay in which you define *dyslexia* in terms of the things you, as a dyslexic adult, would not be able to do.

▮ Argument

For more on how to write an argument essay, see 14I.

An **argument** essay takes a stand on one side of a debatable issue, using facts, examples, and expert opinion to persuade readers to accept a position. The writers of the three essays that follow—Barbara Ehrenreich in "In Defense of Talk Shows," Charles Krauthammer in "The New Prohibitionism," and Martin Luther King Jr. in "I Have a Dream"—attempt to convince readers to accept their positions—or at least to acknowledge that they are reasonable.

IN DEFENSE OF TALK SHOWS

Barbara Ehrenreich

Sociologist, feminist, and author of books and articles on subjects such as the family, women, social class, and violence, Barbara Ehrenreich often asks us to look beneath the surface of her subjects to examine underlying social truths. In "In Defense of Talk Shows," she argues that criticisms of talk shows overlook their more serious problems. As you read her 1995 essay, notice how she develops her argument.

Up until now, the targets of Bill (*The Book of Virtues*) Bennett's[1] crusades have at least been plausible sources of evil. But the latest victim of his wrath—TV talk shows of the *Sally Jessy Raphael* variety—are in a whole different category from drugs and gangsta rap. As anyone who actually watches them knows, the talk shows are one of the most excruciatingly moralistic forums the culture has to offer. Disturbing and sometimes disgusting, yes, but their very business is to preach the middle-class virtues of responsibility, reason and self-control.

Take the case of Susan, recently featured on *Montel Williams* as an example of a women being stalked by her ex-boyfriend. Turns out Susan is also stalking the boyfriend and—here's the sexual frisson—has slept with him only days ago. In fact Susan is neck deep in trouble without any help from the boyfriend: she's serving a yearlong stretch of home incarceration for assaulting another woman, and home is the tiny trailer she shares with her nine-year-old daughter.

But no one is applauding this life spun out of control. Montel scolds Susan roundly for neglecting her daughter and failing to confront her role in the mutual stalking. A therapist lectures her about this unhealthy "obsessive kind of love." The studio audience jeers at her every evasion. By the end Susan has lost her cocky charm and dissolved into tears of shame.

The plot is always the same. People with problems—"husband says she looks like a cow," "pressured to lose her virginity or else," "mate wants more sex than I do"—are introduced to rational methods of problem solving. People with moral failings—"boy crazy," "dresses like a tramp," "a hundred sex partners"—are introduced to external standards of morality. The preaching—delivered alternately by the studio audience, the host and the ever present guest therapist—is relentless. "This is wrong to do this," Sally Jessy tells a cheating husband. "Feel bad?" Geraldo asks the girl who stole her best friend's boyfriend, "Any sense of remorse?" The expectation is that the sinner, so hectored, will see her way to reform. And indeed, a Sally Jessy update found "boy crazy," who'd been a guest only weeks ago, now dressed in schoolgirlish plaid and claiming her "attitude [had] changed"—thanks to the rough-and-ready therapy dispensed on the show.

All right, the subjects are often lurid and even bizarre. But there's no part of the entertainment spectacle, from *Hard Copy* to *Jade*, that doesn't trade in the lurid and bizarre. At least in the talk shows, the moral is always loud and clear: Respect yourself, listen to others, stop beating on your wife. In fact it's hard to see how *The Bill Bennett Show*, if there were

---

1. Former chairman of the National Endowment for the Humanities and secretary of education. More recently he has written books and articles that promote conservative values.

to be such a thing, could deliver a more pointed sermon. Or would he prefer to see the feckless Susan, for example, tarred and feathered by the studio audience instead of being merely booed and shamed?

There *is* something morally repulsive about the talks, but it's not anything Bennett or his co-crusader Senator Joseph Lieberman has seen fit to mention. Watch for a few hours, and you get the claustrophobic sense of lives that have never seen the light of some external judgment, of people who have never before been listened to, and certainly never been taken seriously if they were. "What kind of people would let themselves be humiliated like this?" is often asked, sniffily, by the shows' detractors. And the answer, for the most part, is people who are so needy—of social support, of education, of material resources and self-esteem—that they mistake being the center of attention for being actually loved and respected.

What the talks are about, in large part, is poverty and the distortions it visits on the human spirit. You'll never find investment bankers bickering on *Rolonda*, or the host of *Gabrielle* recommending therapy to sobbing professors. With few exceptions the guests are drawn from trailer parks and tenements, from bleak streets and narrow, crowded rooms. Listen long enough, and you hear references to unpaid bills, to welfare, to 12-hour workdays and double shifts. And this is the real shame of the talks: that they take lives bent out of shape by poverty and hold them up as entertaining exhibits. An announcement appearing between segments of *Montel* says it all: the show is looking for "pregnant women who sell their bodies to make ends meet."

This is class exploitation, pure and simple. What next—"homeless people so hungry they eat their own scabs"? Or would the next step be to pay people outright to submit to public humiliation? For $50 would you confess to adultery in your wife's presence? For $500 would you reveal your thirteen-year-old's girlish secrets on *Ricki Lake*? If you were poor enough, you might.

It is easy enough for those who can afford spacious homes and private therapy to sneer at their financial inferiors and label their pathetic moments of stardom vulgar. But if I had a talk show, it would feature a whole different cast of characters and category of crimes than you'll ever find on the talks: "CEOs who rake in millions while their employees get downsized" would be an obvious theme, along with "Senators who voted for welfare and Medicaid cuts"—and, if he'll agree to appear, "well-fed Republicans who dithered about talk shows while trailer-park residents slipped into madness and despair."

Reacting to the Reading

1. Preview the essay. As you read it more carefully, highlight and annotate as needed to help you understand the writer's ideas.

2. Circle all the labels that Ehrenreich uses—for example, "people with problems" and "cheating husband" (paragraph 4)—to characterize the people who appear on talk shows.

Reacting to Words

*1. Define these words: *excruciatingly* (paragraph 1), *frisson* (2), *incarceration* (2), *evasion* (3), *hectored* (4), *feckless* (5), *detractors* (6), *bleak* (7). Can you suggest a synonym for each word that will work in the essay?

2. What does Ehrenreich mean when she says talk shows are "moralistic forums" (paragraph 1)? Do you see this characterization as positive or negative?

Reacting to Ideas

1. Do you agree with Ehrenreich's point that television talk shows "preach the middle-class virtues of responsibility, reason and self-control" (paragraph 1)? Do you see this as a problem?
2. According to Ehrenreich, in what way is the plot of talk shows "always the same" (paragraph 4)?
*3. What is Ehrenreich's major objection to talk shows? Do you agree with her analysis?

Reacting to the Pattern

*1. Ehrenreich presents examples to support her argument. List several of these examples. Are there enough? Would additional examples have made her argument more convincing?
2. Ehrenreich begins her essay by comparing talk shows to "drugs and gangsta rap." Can you think of another introduction that would have been more effective?
3. Ehrenreich develops her argument inductively—that is, by moving from specific examples to a general conclusion. What are the advantages and disadvantages of this organization strategy?

For more on inductive arguments, see 14I.

Writing Practice

*1. Watch several television talk shows. Then, write an essay that argues for or against Ehrenreich's assertion that talk shows are largely about "poverty and the distortions it visits on the human spirit" (paragraph 7). Do you think she is being fair, or does she oversimplify the situation?
2. Write a response to Ehrenreich in which you argue that in spite of her objections, television talk shows serve some useful functions.
3. Write a letter to the producers of a popular television talk show, trying to convince them to let you appear. Be persuasive.

THE NEW PROHIBITIONISM

Charles Krauthammer

Charles Krauthammer is the author of a Pulitzer Prize–winning column for the *Washington Post* and a frequent contributor to various magazines. His work often discusses current political and social issues. In the following 1997 column, Krauthammer constructs an argument about the antismoking movement. Krauthammer's medical training (he was a practicing psychiatrist) and experience as a political and social commentator are evident in the way he develops his argument. As you read, note the ways in which he builds support for his thesis.

The oddest thing about the current national crusade against tobacco is not its frenzy—our culture lives from one frenzy to the next—but its selectivity. Of course tobacco is a great national killer. It deserves all the pummeling it gets. But alcohol is a great national killer too, and it has enjoyed an amazingly free ride amid the fury of the New Prohibitionism.

Joe Camel[1] has been banished forever, but those beloved Budweiser frogs—succeeded by even cuter Budweiser lizards—keep marching along, right into the consciousness of every TV-watching kid in the country.

For 26 years television has been free of cigarette ads. Why? Because TV persuades as nothing else, and we don't want young people—inveterate TV watchers—persuaded. Yet television is bursting with exhortations to drink. TV sports in particular, a staple of adolescents, is one long hymn to the glories of beer.

And the sports-worshipping years are precisely the time that kids learn to drink. The median age at which they start drinking is just over 13. A 1990 survey found that 56% of students in Grades 5 through 12 say alcohol advertising encourages them to drink. Surprise!

Am I for Prohibition? No. But I am for a little perspective. We tend to think of the turn-of-the-century temperance movement as little blue-haired ladies trying to prevent people from having a good time on Saturday night. In fact, the temperance movement was part of a much larger progressive movement seeking to improve the appalling conditions of the urban working class. These were greatly exacerbated by rampant alcoholism that contributed to extraordinary levels of spousal and child abuse, abandonment and destitution.

Alcohol is still a cause of staggering devastation. It kills 100,000 Americans a year—not only from disease but also from accidents. In 1996, 41% of all U.S. traffic fatalities were alcohol related. It causes huge economic losses and untold suffering. Why, then, do the Bud frogs get to play the Super Bowl while Joe Camel goes the way of the Marlboro Man?

The most plausible answer is that tobacco is worse because it kills more people. Indeed it does. But 100,000 people a year is still a fair carnage. Moreover, the really compelling comparison is this: alcohol is far more deadly than tobacco *to innocent bystanders*. In a free society, should we not consider behavior that injures others more worthy of regulation than behavior that merely injures oneself? The primary motive for gun control, after all, is concern about homicide, not suicide.

The antitobacco folk, aware of this bedrock belief, try to play up the harm smokers cause others. Thus the attorneys general seeking billions of dollars in damages from the tobacco companies are claiming that taxpayers have been unfairly made to pay for the treatment of smoking-related illnesses.

A clever ploy. But the hardheaded truth is that premature death from smoking, which generally affects people in their late-middle and early retirement years, is an economic boon to society. The money saved on pensions and on the truly expensive health care that comes with old age—something these smokers never achieve—surely balances, if it does not exceed, the cost of treating tobacco-related diseases.

---

1. Retired cartoon image used to advertise Camel cigarettes; withdrawn by industry following complaints that it was aimed at underage smokers.

The alternative and more dramatic antitobacco tactic is to portray   10
smoking as an assault on nonsmokers via secondhand smoke. Now, secondhand smoke is certainly a nuisance. But the claim that it is a killer is
highly dubious. "The statistical evidence," reported the nonpartisan Congressional Research Service in 1994, "does not appear to support a conclusion that there are substantive health effects of passive smoking."

Unlike secondhand smoke, secondhand booze is a world-class killer.   11
Drunk driving alone kills 17,000 people a year. And alcohol's influence
extends far beyond driving: it contributes to everything from bar fights to
domestic violence. One study found that 44% of assailants in cases of
marital abuse had been drinking. Another study found that 60% of wife
batterers had been under the influence. Whatever claims you make against
tobacco, you'd have quite a time looking for cases of the nicotine-crazed
turning on their wives with a butcher knife.

Moreover, look at the *kinds* of people alcohol kills. Drunk drivers kill   12
toddlers. They kill teens. They kill whole families. Tobacco does not kill
toddlers and teens. Tobacco strikes late. It kills, but at a very long remove
in time. Its victims generally have already had their chance at life. Tobacco
merely shortens life; alcohol can deprive people of it.

Still undecided which of the two poisons is more deserving of social   13
disapprobation? Here's the ultimate test. Ask yourself this: If you knew
your child was going to become addicted to either alcohol or tobacco,
which would you choose?

Reacting to the Reading

1. Preview the essay. As you read it more carefully, highlight and annotate
   as needed to help you understand the writer's ideas.
2. Underline the transitional words and phrases that signal the movement from one part of the argument to another or that connect specific
   points to other points or to the thesis statement.

Reacting to Words

*1. Define these words: *selectivity* (paragraph 1), *pummeling* (1), *inveterate*
    (3), *median* (4), *temperance* (5), *devastation* (6), *plausible* (7), *dubious*
    (10). Can you suggest a synonym for each word that will work in the
    essay?
2. Krauthammer uses the word *kill* in many of the sentences of paragraph 12. Why does he do this? Would the paragraph have been more
   effective if he had used a different word in some sentences?

Reacting to Ideas

*1. Do you agree with Krauthammer when he says, "TV persuades as noth-
    ing else" (paragraph 3)? Do you believe that television advertising
    images like the Budweiser frogs can encourage children to drink?
2. How convincing is Krauthammer's argument that premature death
   from smoking "is an economic boon to society" (paragraph 9)? Can
   you think of another point that might be more effective?
3. Krauthammer argues against the current "national crusade against
   tobacco" (paragraph 1) by maintaining that alcohol is far more deadly
   than tobacco. Is this line of reasoning valid? Does the fact that alcohol

may be more dangerous than tobacco eliminate the need for legislation against tobacco?

Reacting to the Pattern

*1. Throughout his essay, Krauthammer asks a series of questions. What function do these questions serve? Is this technique effective?

2. Krauthammer makes his point by contrasting alcohol and tobacco. What points does he make about each? What other points could he have made?

3. Krauthammer concludes by asking readers whether they would rather have their children addicted to tobacco or to alcohol. Is this question fair? Are there other alternatives?

Writing Practice

1. Do you think government prohibition of smoking would work? Write an essay in which you argue for or against the banning of all tobacco products. Be sure to consider the problems that such a policy would create.

*2. Can you think of a product—firearms or over-the-counter medications, for example—whose sale should be controlled more strictly than it is now? Write an essay in which you present an argument for controlling this product's sale, discussing the problems that this product causes and suggesting ways that controls could improve the situation. Make sure your essay has a clearly stated thesis.

3. Instead of banning tobacco products, what can local and state governments do to discourage people from smoking? Write an essay in which you argue for a particular course of action—for example, charging smokers higher health-insurance premiums.

I HAVE A DREAM

Martin Luther King Jr.

On August 28, 1963, Martin Luther King Jr. delivered the following speech on the steps in front of the Lincoln Memorial in Washington, D.C. King used the occasion of this speech—the March on Washington, in which more than two hundred thousand people participated—to reinforce his ideas about racial equality and nonviolent protest. The speech itself is a deductive argument that makes a compelling case for racial justice in the United States. As you read, notice King's effective use of repetition.

Five score years ago, a great American, in whose symbolic shadow we stand, signed the Emancipation Proclamation. This momentous decree came as a great beacon light of hope to millions of Negro slaves who had been seared in the flames of withering injustice. It came as a joyous daybreak to end the long night of captivity.

But one hundred years later, we must face the tragic fact that the Negro is still not free. One hundred years later, the life of the Negro is still sadly crippled by the manacles of segregation and the chains of discrimination. One hundred years later, the Negro lives on a lonely island of poverty in the midst of a vast ocean of material prosperity. One hundred years later, the Negro is still languishing in the corners of American society and finds himself an exile in his own land. So we have come here today to dramatize an appalling condition.

In a sense we have come to our nation's capital to cash a check. When the architects of our republic wrote the magnificent words of the Constitution and the Declaration of Independence, they were signing a promissory note to which every American was to fall heir. This note was a promise that all men—yes, black men as well as white men—would be guaranteed the unalienable rights of life, liberty, and the pursuit of happiness.

It is obvious today that America has defaulted on this promissory note insofar as her citizens of color are concerned. Instead of honoring this sacred obligation, America has given the Negro people a bad check, a check which has come back marked "insufficient funds." But we refuse to believe that there are insufficient funds in the great vaults of opportunity of this nation. So we have come to cash this check—a check that will give us upon demand the riches of freedom and the security of justice. We have also come to this hallowed spot to remind America of the fierce urgency of *now*. This is no time to engage in the luxury of cooling off or to take the tranquilizing drugs of gradualism. *Now* is the time to make real the promises of Democracy. *Now* is the time to rise from the dark and desolate valley of segregation to the sunlit path of racial justice. *Now* is the time to open the doors of opportunity to all of God's children. *Now* is the time to lift our nation from the quicksands of racial injustice to the solid rock of brotherhood.

It would be fatal for the nation to overlook the urgency of the moment and to underestimate the determination of the Negro. This sweltering summer of the Negro's legitimate discontent will not pass until there is an invigorating autumn of freedom and equality; 1963 is not an end, but a beginning. Those who hope that the Negro needed to blow off steam and will now be content will have a rude awakening if the nation returns to business as usual. There will be neither rest nor tranquility in America until the Negro is granted his citizenship rights. The whirlwinds of revolt will continue to shake the foundations of our nation until the bright day of justice emerges.

But there is something that I must say to my people who stand on the warm threshold which leads into the palace of justice. In the process of gaining our rightful place we must not be guilty of wrongful deeds. Let us not seek to satisfy our thirst for freedom by drinking from the cup of bitterness and hatred. We must forever conduct our struggle on the high plane of dignity and discipline. We must not allow our creative protest to degenerate into physical violence. Again and again we must rise to the majestic heights of meeting physical force with soul force. The marvelous new militancy which has engulfed the Negro community must not lead us to a distrust of all white people, for many of our white brothers, as evidenced by their presence here today, have come to realize that their destiny is tied up with our destiny and their freedom is inextricably bound to our freedom. We cannot walk alone.

And as we walk, we must make the pledge that we shall march ahead. We cannot turn back. There are those who are asking the devotees of civil rights, "When will you be satisfied?" We can never be satisfied as long as the Negro is the victim of the unspeakable horrors of police brutality. We can never be satisfied as long as our bodies, heavy with the fatigue of travel, cannot gain lodging in the motels of the highways and the hotels of the cities. We cannot be satisfied as long as the Negro's basic mobility is from a smaller ghetto to a larger one. We can never be satisfied as long as a Negro in Mississippi cannot vote and a Negro in New York believes he has nothing for which to vote. No, no, we are not satisfied, and we will not be satisfied until justice rolls down like waters and righteousness like a mighty stream.

I am not unmindful that some of you have come here out of great trials and tribulations. Some of you have come fresh from narrow jail cells. Some of you have come from areas where your quest for freedom left you battered by the storms of persecution and staggered by the winds of police brutality. You have been the veterans of creative suffering. Continue to work with the faith that unearned suffering is redemptive.

Go back to Mississippi, go back to Alabama, go back to South Carolina, go back to Georgia, go back to Louisiana, go back to the slums and ghettos of our northern cities, knowing that somehow this situation can and will be changed. Let us not wallow in the valley of despair.

I say to you today, my friends, that in spite of the difficulties and frustrations of the moment I still have a dream. It is a dream deeply rooted in the American dream.

I have a dream that one day this nation will rise up and live out the true meaning of its creed: "We hold these truths to be self-evident, that all men are created equal."

I have a dream that one day on the red hills of Georgia the sons of former slaves and the sons of former slaveowners will be able to sit down together at the table of brotherhood.

I have a dream that one day even the state of Mississippi, a desert state sweltering with the heat of injustice and oppression, will be transformed into an oasis of freedom and justice.

I have a dream that my four little children will one day live in a nation where they will not be judged by the color of their skin but by the content of their character.

I have a dream today.

I have a dream that one day the state of Alabama, whose governor's lips are presently dripping with the words of interposition and nullification, will be transformed into a situation where little black boys and black girls will be able to join hands with little white boys and white girls and walk together as sisters and brothers.

I have a dream today.

I have a dream that one day every valley shall be exalted, every hill and mountain shall be made low, the rough places will be made plain, and the crooked places will be made straight, and the glory of the Lord shall be revealed, and all flesh shall see it together.

This is our hope. This is the faith with which I return to the South. With this faith we will be able to hew out of the mountain of despair a stone of hope. With this faith we will be able to transform the jangling discords of our nation into a beautiful symphony of brotherhood. With this faith we will be able to work together, to pray together, to struggle together, to go to jail together, to stand up for freedom together, knowing that we will be free one day.

This will be the day when all of God's children will be able to sing with new meaning

My country, 'tis of thee,
Sweet land of liberty,
   Of thee I sing:
Land where my fathers died,
Land of the pilgrim's pride,
From every mountainside,
   Let freedom ring.

So let freedom ring from the prodigious hilltops of New Hampshire. 21
Let freedom ring from the mighty mountains of New York. Let freedom
ring from the heightening Alleghenies of Pennsylvania. Let freedom ring
from the snowcapped Rockies of Colorado. Let freedom ring from the curvaceous peaks of California.

But not only that. Let freedom ring from Stone Mountain of Georgia. 22
Let freedom ring from Lookout Mountain of Tennessee. Let freedom ring
from every hill and molehill of Mississippi. From every mountainside, let
freedom ring.

When we let freedom ring, when we let it ring from every village and 23
every hamlet, from every state and every city, we will be able to speed up
that day when all of God's children, black men and white men, Jews and
Gentiles, Protestants and Catholics, will be able to join hands and sing in
the words of the old Negro spiritual, "Free at last! Free at last! Thank God
almighty, we are free at last!"

Reacting to the Reading

1. Preview the essay. As you read it more carefully, highlight and annotate
   as needed to help you understand the writer's ideas.

2. Highlight the passage in which King outlines his dream for the United
   States. In a marginal annotation, explain what he means when he says
   his dream is "deeply rooted in the American dream" (paragraph 10).

Reacting to Words

*1. Define these words: *score* (paragraph 1), *beacon* (1), *withering* (1), *languishing* (2), *appalling* (2), *promissory* (3), *unalienable* (3), *hallowed* (4),
   gradualism (4), *invigorating* (5), *inextricably* (6), *redemptive* (8), *wallow*
   (9), *prodigious* (21), *curvaceous* (21). Can you suggest a synonym for
   each word that will work in the essay?

2. King uses a number of words again and again in his speech. Identify
   some of these words. Why do you think he repeats them? Would the
   speech have been more or less effective without this repetition?

Reacting to Ideas

1. In paragraph 3, King says that he and the other marchers have come
   to Washington "to cash a check." How does this image represent what
   he and the other protesters want to achieve? Can you think of another
   image that might also work in the speech?

2. In his speech, King addresses the marchers who have come to Washington. Whom else do you think he is addressing?

3. Do you think the current racial climate in the United States still warrants King's criticism? Are we any closer today than we were in 1963 to realizing his dream?

Reacting to the Pattern

For more on deductive arguments, see 14I.

*1. King uses a deductive argument to present his ideas about racial justice. Do you think an inductive argument would have been more effective?

2. King's argument reaches its conclusion in paragraph 4. What does he do in the rest of his speech?

3. Why do you think King chose to include only a few specific examples to illustrate his points? Should he have used more evidence?

Writing Practice

1. In paragraph 4, King says, "America has defaulted on this promissory note. . . ." Can you think of some person or organization that has defaulted on its promissory note to you? Write an argument essay in which you make your case. If you wish, you may use King's image of a bad check.

*2. Write an essay in which you argue that if King were alive today, he would (or would not) think his dream of racial justice has been realized.

3. Choose an issue you feel strongly about. Write a letter to the editor of your local paper in which you argue your position.

Writing Paragraphs and Essays for Exams

Knowing how to plan, write, and revise paragraphs and essays is a skill you can apply throughout your college years and beyond. One situation in which you will need this skill as a student is during an examination.

Many exam questions call for just a short answer—*yes* or *no, true* or *false*. Others ask you to fill in a blank with a few words. Still others require you to select the one correct answer from among several choices. In these situations, reading and study skills are more important than writing skills.

In many cases, however, an exam question will specifically tell you to write a paragraph or an essay, and then your writing skills will be important. Knowing in advance exactly what you are expected to do (and how to do it) will give you the confidence you need to perform at your best.

1 Before the Exam

Exams are usually announced in advance, so you should have time to study. Not making good use of this study time deprives you of an important advantage. However, preparation for an exam should begin well before it is announced. In a sense, you begin this preparation on the first day of the semester.

Attend Every Class

Regular attendance in class—where you can listen, ask questions, and take notes—lays the best possible groundwork for academic success. If you do have to miss a class, make arrangements to copy (and read) another student's notes before the next class so you will be able to follow the discussion.

Read Every Assignment

Doing the assigned reading on time is very important. If you don't keep up with the reading, it will be extremely difficult for you to understand what is being said in class. This means you will not be able to ask intelligent questions or take useful notes.

Take Careful Notes

Take careful, thorough notes, but be selective. Don't write down everything your instructor says: first listen; then write. Some students find it helpful to reread their notes as soon as possible after taking them; others outline or even recopy their notes. Try different strategies, and do whatever works for you. If you can, try to compare notes on a regular basis with other students in your class; working together, you can fill in omissions or correct misinterpretations. Establishing a buddy system will also ensure that you review your notes regularly instead of only on the night before the exam.

Study on Your Own

When an exam is announced, make a study schedule so you will have time to cover everything. Making a schedule—and sticking to it—is especially important if you have more than one exam in a short period of time. Review all your material (class notes, readings, and so on) slowly and carefully, and then review it again. Make a note of anything you don't understand, and keep track of points you need to review. Try to anticipate the most likely questions, and—if you have time—practice drafting paragraphs or brief essays that answer these questions.

Study with a Group

If you can arrange to study with one or more classmates, you should certainly do so. Studying with others can often alert you to material you have overlooked or help you to see new interpretations or perspectives.

Make an Appointment with Your Instructor

If your schedule (and your instructor's) permits, try to arrange regular conferences throughout the semester. In addition, always try to set up an appointment to meet with your instructor or with the course's teaching assistant a few days before an exam. Bring to this meeting any specific questions you have about course content and about the format of the upcoming exam. (Review all your material at least once before the meeting.)

Review the Material One Last Time

The night before the exam is not the time to begin your studying; it is the time to review, in a leisurely way, all the material you have studied. When you have finished this review, get a good night's sleep.

2 At the Exam

By the time you walk into an exam room, you will already have done all you could do to get ready for the test. Your goal now is to keep the momentum going and not do anything to undermine all your hard work.

Read Through the Entire Examination

Be sure you understand how much time you have, how much each question is worth, and exactly what each question is asking you to do. For example, are you supposed to write a paragraph? An essay? Should you summarize the assigned readings? Interpret them? Evaluate their ideas? Present your own ideas? If you are not absolutely certain what kind of answer a particular question calls for, ask your instructor or the proctor *before* you begin to write.

Budget Your Time

Once you understand how much each section of the exam and each individual question is worth, plan your time, devoting the most time to the most important questions.

▼ **Student Voices**
I've learned to watch the clock so I don't spend too much time on one point or paragraph.

Jason Varghese

Reread Each Question

Carefully reread each question on the exam *before* you start to answer it. Underline the **key words**, the words that give you information about the required *content, emphasis,* and *organization* of your answer. In the following essay question, the key words have been underlined.

> <u>What is mob psychology?</u> Give some <u>specific recent examples</u> of this phenomenon, and explain in each case both the <u>origins</u> and the <u>outcomes</u> of the situations that occurred.

The wording of this question supplies a good deal of useful information. The initial "What is . . . ?" question tells you that you are being asked to *define* a term. The rest of the question asks you to focus on a few *examples* and to discuss both *causes* (origins) and *effects* (outcomes) of each. Thus, in this question, the key words reveal the expected content and emphasis as well as the patterns of development you are to use.

For more on using different patterns of development, see Chapters 3–11 and Chapter 14.

FOCUS Key Words

Here are some other helpful key words to look for on exams and in other situations.

(continued on the following page)

● **Writing Tip**
Key words can help you decide how to organize and develop writing you do on the job or on community projects.

A 2

> *(continued from the previous page)*
>
> | | | |
> |---|---|---|
> | analyze | give examples | suggest results, effects, |
> | argue | identify | outcomes |
> | compare | illustrate | summarize |
> | contrast | recount | support |
> | define | suggest causes, | take a stand |
> | describe | origins, | trace |
> | evaluate | contributing | |
> | explain | factors | |

Remember, even if everything you say is correct, your response is not acceptable if you don't answer the question. For example, a list of nineteenth-century examples of mob psychology (rather than the required *recent examples*) is not an appropriate response to the question; neither is a discussion of *only* causes or *only* effects.

Brainstorm to Help Yourself Recall Your Material

For more on brainstorming, see 1B.

Looking frequently at the exam question, **brainstorm** on the inside cover of your exam book. Jot down all the relevant points you can think of— what your textbook had to say about the nature of mob psychology, any specific examples mentioned in assigned newspaper articles, your instructor's comments (recorded in your class notes) about causes and results of these specific incidents, and so on. The more you can think of now, the more you will have to choose from when you outline your essay.

Write Down the Main Idea

For more on topic sentences, see 2A. For more on thesis statements, see 12D.

Looking closely at the wording of the exam question as well as at the material on your brainstorming list, write down the main idea of your answer in a single sentence. If your response is in the form of a paragraph, this idea will be your topic sentence; if the answer is a full-length essay, this idea will be your thesis statement.

List Your Main Points

It makes little sense for you to use your limited (and valuable) time to construct a detailed, multilevel outline; however, a quick outline that lists your main points is well worth the small amount of time it takes. With such an outline as a guide, you will be able to plan a clear direction for your paragraph or essay.

Draft Your Answer

You will spend the greatest percentage of your time actually writing the answer to the question (or questions) on the exam. Follow your outline, keep track of time, consult your brainstorming notes when you need to—but stay focused on the task at hand.

Reread, Revise, and Edit

When you have finished a draft of your paragraph or essay, reread it carefully, making sure you have answered the question. Now is the time to add any supporting details, delete unasked-for information or irrelevant material, and clarify the topic sentences and transitions that will help your instructor follow your reasoning.

3   Writing a Paragraph

Some exam questions call for paragraph-length responses. Typically, these questions are **identifications**, questions that ask you to explain the significance of a person or event and place it in context, or to define a key term or concept.

What was the local color movement? (literature)

Who was José Martí? (history)

What is a conditioned response? (psychology)

The following is a paragraph written in response to an examination question.

For more on writing paragraphs, see Chapter 2.

Question: Identify the term *triangular trade*.

Answer:

> Triangular trade is the name for a pattern of trade with three destination points. Triangular trade routes were often used in colonial times by ships involved in the slave trade. For example, a ship could take rum from a New England port to Africa. There it would trade the rum for a cargo of slaves, which it would bring to the West Indies. Then, the slaves would be traded for sugar, molasses, or spices, which would be brought back to New England, where it would be distilled into rum. Then, the cycle would begin again, with the African slaves treated as just another commodity in a commercial transaction.

Topic sentence identifies term to be defined

Definition developed with an extended example

4   Writing an Essay

Sometimes, an exam question calls for an essay-length response. Remember to leave time to brainstorm and outline before you start to write, and to leave time to reread, revise, and edit your draft when you have finished writing.

For guidelines for writing essays, see Chapter 12.

A 4

> When you take an exam, the amount of time you have is always limited. Therefore, you should devote the bulk of your writing time to developing the body paragraphs of your essay—the paragraphs that actually answer the exam question. In your introduction, just indicate which question you are answering (using the words of the question itself) and state your thesis; in your conclusion, *briefly* summarize the key points you have made. (Note that the introduction and conclusion of the essay below are relatively brief and straightforward.)

The following essay was written in response to a question on a midterm exam for a first-year composition course.

Question: Several of the essays we have read so far this semester deal with personal and social responsibility. Choose three or four reading selections we have discussed in class, and give examples from each to explain the author's concept of personal and social responsibility.

Answer:

Being Responsible

Opening sentence echoes wording of question; next sentence lists essays to be discussed

    Although several of the essays we have read this semester deal with personal and social responsibility, each author means something different when he or she considers what it means to be responsible. Martin Gansberg's "Thirty-Eight Who Saw Murder Didn't Call the Police," Anna Quindlen's "The Old Block," and Martin Luther King Jr.'s "I Have a Dream" all suggest how important it is to be a responsible citizen, but responsibility means something different for each writer.

Thesis statement

Topic sentence identifies Gansberg's concept of responsibility

    Gansberg believes that <u>responsibility</u> means being responsible for others as well as for ourselves. Maybe Kitty Genovese should have been considered responsible for her own actions; maybe she had a responsibility to protect herself by not exposing herself to the dangers of a dark, deserted street. But this is not the focus of Gansberg's article. He believes that the thirty-eight neighbors who watched her murder and did nothing were the ones who were most guilty of acting irresponsibly. For the people in Gansberg's essay, being responsible would have meant taking action to save Kitty Genovese's life, even if it might have put their own lives at risk (which it apparently would not have). When Gansberg sarcastically criticizes the "respectable" people and exposes their flimsy excuses for not helping, he is criticizing them for their failure to be responsible for another human being.

Quindlen's essay seems to suggest that <u>responsi-bility</u> means being responsible not just for oneself or for other individuals but for the community as a whole. When Quindlen tours the old neighborhood and sees its crime, drugs, and burned-out, abandoned buildings, she does not blame politicians for neglecting the cities. She does not even blame her own family for moving away. Instead, she blames the decline of city neighborhoods on all the people who abandoned the cities and moved to the suburbs. Now, she believes, it is the responsibility of those same people to remember where they came from and begin working to save those dying cities. If they do not, she says, the situation will get worse.

More than Gansberg or Quindlen, King sees <u>responsi-bility</u> as something that is collective rather than individual or personal. King believes all men and women in society share an obligation to act as responsible citizens. He believes it is our responsibility not just to change society gradually, through the choices we make and the behavior we engage in, but sometimes to take specific, immediate action to bring about needed change. Although he is addressing African Americans, his dream goes beyond his hopes for them to his hopes for "all of God's children."

Crime, drugs, decaying cities, and racial discrimi-nation are all problems that confront people in our society. As Gansberg, Quindlen, and King show, all of us are responsible, individually and collectively, for working to solve these problems.

Topic sentence identifies Quindlen's concept of responsibility

Topic sentence identifies King's concept of responsibility

Brief conclusion summarizes essay's main points

B

Writing a Research Paper

When you write a research paper, you find material—from books, articles, television programs, the Internet, and other sources—to support your ideas. You will have an easier time writing a research paper if you follow these steps:

1. Choose a topic.
2. Look for sources.
3. Zero in on your topic.
4. Do research.
5. Take notes.
6. Watch out for plagiarism.
7. Draft a thesis statement.
8. Make an outline.
9. Write your paper.
10. Document your sources.

1 Choosing a Topic

The first step in writing a research paper is finding a topic to write about. Before you choose a topic, ask yourself the following questions.

- What is your page limit?
- When is your paper due?
- How many sources are you expected to use?

The answers to these questions will help you tell if your topic is too broad or too narrow.

When Allison Rogers, a student in a college composition course, was asked to write a three- to five-page research paper that was due in five weeks, she knew she wanted to write about the violence she saw in society. She knew, however, that the general topic "violence" would be too broad for a short paper—and that "one example of violence in the movie *Natural Born Killers*" would be too narrow. "The effect of the media on violent behavior," however, might work well because Allison could discuss it in the required number of pages, and she would be able to finish her paper within her five-week time limit.

2   Looking for Sources

To get an overview of your topic and see whether you will be able to find enough material, quickly survey the resources of your library. (First, arrange a meeting with your college librarian, who can answer questions, give suggestions, and point you toward helpful resources.)

Begin by looking at your library's *subject catalog* to see what books it lists on your topic. For example, under the general topic of "violence," Allison found the related headings "movie violence" and "media violence." Under each of these headings were a variety of books and government studies on the topic. In addition to books, you can look for articles. To do this, consult an index such as *Readers' Guide to Periodical Literature*, which lists articles in newspapers and magazines, or *InfoTrac*, a computer database that contains the texts of many articles. (Your librarian can show you how to use these resources). A quick look at *Readers' Guide* showed Allison that many articles had been written about violence in the media.

> ● **Writing Tip**
> For each source you find, record full publication information (for books, the title, author, publisher, and call number; for articles, the title, author, periodical name, date, and page numbers). Then you can find the source again later.

3   Zeroing In on Your Topic

As you skim the library's resources, the subject headings as well as the titles of books and articles should help you zero in on your topic. For example, Allison discovered that several of the books and a number of the articles she located focused on the effect of media violence on society. A few focused specifically on children, examining the effect of violent movies and television on their behavior. Because she had always been interested in children and because she was an education major, Allison decided to concentrate on this aspect of her topic. Following her instructor's guidelines, she knew the purpose of her paper would be either to *present information* about media violence and children or *make a point* about it. She could present information by discussing some of the current research into the relationship between media violence and violent behavior in children, or she could make the point that media violence can have a negative effect on the behavior of children.

> ■ **Computer Tip**
> An Internet search can help you narrow your topic. Ask your college librarian to show you effective searching techniques.

4   Doing Research

Once you have zeroed in on a topic, you need to gather information. Begin by going back to the library and checking out any books you think will be useful. Next, photocopy any relevant magazine articles, and make copies of material stored on microfilm or microfiche. If you use a computer

> ● **Writing Tip**
> Don't forget to record the page numbers of all material you copy.

> ● **Writing Tip**
> Record full publication information for all material you photocopy or download; you will need this information when you document your sources.

> ● **Writing Tip**
> If you're not sure whether a source is reliable, check with your instructor or college librarian.

database such as *InfoTrac*, print out the full text of any articles you plan to use. Finally, if you have access to the Internet, browse the World Wide Web for possible sources. Remember, the quality and reliability of material found on the Web can vary, so use only information from reliable sources —a Web site sponsored by a well-known national publication or organization, for example.

When Allison searched the Web using the key term *media violence*, she found the Web site produced by ERIC Counseling and Student Services Clearinghouse. This site contained "Children and Television Violence," an article posted by the American Psychological Association, a nationally recognized professional organization.

5 Taking Notes

Once you have gathered the material you will need, read it carefully, writing down any information you think you can use in your paper. As you take notes, keep your topic in mind; it will help you decide what material is useful. Record your notes on three-by-five-inch cards, on separate sheets of paper, or in a computer file you have created for this purpose.

When you use information from a source in your writing, you do not always *quote* the exact words of your source. Most often, you *paraphrase* or *summarize* a source, putting its ideas into your own words.

When you **paraphrase**, you present the ideas of a source in your own words, following the order and emphasis of the original. You paraphrase when you want to make a discussion easier to understand while still conveying a clear sense of the original. Here is a passage from the article "Children and Television Violence" followed by Allison's paraphrase.

Original

> Children often behave differently after they've been watching violent programs on television. In one study done at Pennsylvania State University, about 100 preschool children were observed both before and after watching television; some watched cartoons that had many aggressive and violent acts; others watched shows that didn't have any kind of violence. The researchers noticed real differences between the kids who watched the violent shows and those who watched nonviolent ones.

Paraphrase

> At Pennsylvania State University, researchers did a study. They divided 100 young children into two groups. One group watched television programs that contained a lot of violence. The other group watched programs that contained very little violence. Researchers found that the two groups of children behaved very differently.

When you write a **summary**, you also put the ideas of a source into your own words. But unlike a paraphrase, a summary condenses a passage, giving only the general meaning of the original. Here is Allison's summary of the original passage on page 558.

Summary

> According to a study conducted at Pennsylvania State University, young children who watched violent television shows behaved differently from those who watched nonviolent shows.

● **Writing Tip**
In a paraphrase or a summary, you present only the source's ideas, not your own ideas or opinions about the source.

When you **quote**, you restate the exact words of a source, enclosing them in quotation marks. Because using too many quotations can distract readers, quote only when an author's words are memorable or when you want to give readers the flavor of the original source.

To show readers that you are using a source and to integrate a quotation smoothly into your essay, introduce paraphrases, summaries, and quotations with a phrase that identifies the source or its author. You can position this identifying phrase at various places in a sentence. You can also use different words to introduce source material—for example, *points out, observes, comments, notes, remarks,* and *concludes.*

> According to the article "Children and Television Violence," "Children often behave differently after they've been watching violent programs on television."

> "Children often behave differently after they've been watching violent programs on television," observes one Pennsylvania State University study.

> "Children often behave differently," claim researchers in a study reported by the American Psychological Association, "after they've been watching violent programs on television."

For information on documentation, see section 10 of this appendix.

6 Watching Out for Plagiarism

As a rule, you must document any words or ideas from an outside source that are not **common knowledge**, factual information widely available in reference works. When you present information from another source as if it were your own (whether you do it intentionally or unintentionally), you commit **plagiarism**—and plagiarism is theft. You can avoid plagiarism by understanding what you must document and what you do not have to document.

FOCUS **Avoiding Plagiarism**

You should document

- Word-for-word quotations from a source
- Ideas from a source that you put in your own words
- Tables, charts, graphs, or statistics from a source

You do not need to document

- Your own ideas
- Common knowledge
- Familiar quotations

Whenever you consult a source to get ideas for your writing, you must be careful to avoid the errors that commonly lead to plagiarism. The following paragraph from Brian Siano's essay "Frankenstein Must Be Destroyed: Chasing the Monster of TV Violence" and the four rules outlined below will help you understand and correct these common errors.

ORIGINAL

Of course, there are a few crazies out there who will be unfavorably influenced by what they see on TV. But even assuming that somehow the TV show (or movie or record) shares some of the blame, how does one predict what future crazies will take for inspiration? What guidelines would ensure that people write, act, or produce something that *will not upset a psychotic?* Not only is this a ridiculous demand, it's insulting to the public as well. We would all be treated as potential murderers in order to gain a hypothetical 5 percent reduction in violence.

Document Ideas from Your Sources

PLAGIARISM

```
Even if we were to control the programs that are shown
on television, we would only decrease violence in soci-
ety by perhaps 5 percent.
```

Even though the writer does not quote Siano directly, she must still identify him as the source of the paraphrased material.

CORRECT

```
According to Brian Siano, even if we were to control
the programs that are shown on television, we would only
decrease violence in society by perhaps 5 percent (24).
```

Place Borrowed Words in Quotation Marks

PLAGIARISM

```
According to Brian Siano, there will always be a few
crazies out there who will be unfavorably influenced by
what they see on television (24).
```

Although the writer cites Siano as the source, the passage incorrectly uses Siano's exact words without quoting them. The writer must either quote the borrowed words or rephrase the material.

CORRECT (BORROWED WORDS IN QUOTATION MARKS)

```
According to Brian Siano, there will always be "a few
crazies out there who will be unfavorably influenced by
what they see on TV" (24).
```

CORRECT (BORROWED WORDS REPHRASED)

```
According to Brian Siano, some unstable people will
commit crimes because of the violence they see in the
media (24).
```

Use Your Own Phrasing

PLAGIARISM

```
Naturally, there will always be people who are affected
by what they view on television. But even if we agree
that television programs can influence people, how can
we really know what will make people commit crimes? How
can we be absolutely sure that a show will not disturb
someone who is insane? The answer is that we can't. To
pretend that we can is insulting to law-abiding citi-
zens. We can't treat everyone as if they were criminals
just to reduce violence by a small number of people
(Siano 24).
```

Even though the writer acknowledges Siano as her source, and even though she does not use Siano's exact words, her passage closely follows the order, emphasis, syntax, and phrasing of the original. In the following passage, the writer uses her own wording, quoting one distinctive phrase from her source.

CORRECT

```
According to Brian Siano, we should not censor a televi-
sion program just because "a few crazies" may be incited
to violence (24). Not only would such censorship deprive
the majority of people of the right to watch what they
want, but it would not significantly lessen the violence
in society (24).
```

B 8

Distinguish Your Ideas from the Source's Ideas

PLAGIARISM

> Any attempt to control television violence will quickly reach the point of diminishing returns. There is no way to make absolutely certain that a particular television program will not cause a disturbed person to commit a crime. It seems silly, then, to treat the majority of people as "potential murderers" just to control the behavior of a few (Siano 24).

In the preceding passage, it appears that only the quotation in the last sentence is borrowed from Siano's article. In fact, the ideas in the second sentence are also Siano's. The writer should use an identifying phrase (such as "According to Siano") to acknowledge the borrowed material in this sentence and to show where it begins.

CORRECT

> Any attempt to control television violence will quickly reach the point of diminishing returns. According to Brian Siano, there is no way to make absolutely certain that a particular television program will not cause a disturbed person to commit a crime (24). It seems silly, then, to treat the majority of people as "potential murderers" just to control the behavior of a few (24).

● **Writing Tip**
Each quotation requires its own separate parenthetical documentation.

---

7 | **Drafting a Thesis Statement**

For more on thesis statements, see 12A.

After you have taken notes, review the information you have gathered, and draft a thesis statement. Your **thesis statement** is a single sentence that states the main idea of your paper and tells readers what to expect. After reviewing her notes, Allison Rogers came up with the following thesis statement for her paper on media violence.

Thesis Statement

● **Writing Tip**
At this stage, your thesis statement is tentative; you will probably change it as you write your paper.

> Although the media can affect us in many ways, no amount of media violence can eliminate our responsibility for our actions.

---

8 | **Making an Outline**

Once you have drafted a thesis statement, you are ready to make an outline. Your outline, which covers just the body paragraphs of your paper, can be either a *topic outline* (in which each idea is expressed in a word or a short phrase) or a *sentence outline* (in which each idea is expressed in a complete sentence). After reviewing her notes, Allison Rogers wrote the following sentence outline for her paper.

    I. Teenagers claim the movie <u>Natural Born Killers</u> made
       them commit murder.
       A. According to John Grisham, the movie inspired
          the teenagers to commit their crimes.
       B. Grisham says that several murders have been com-
          mitted by teenagers who say they were influenced
          by the movie.
   II. The idea that movie violence causes violent behav-
       ior is not supported.
       A. Other factors could have influenced the
          teenagers.
       B. No clear link between media violence and aggres-
          sive behavior has been discovered.
  III. Anecdotal evidence supporting the link between
       "copycat crimes" and media violence has two prob-
       lems.
       A. Movies are seldom definitively linked to crimes.
       B. Anecdotal evidence is not representative.
   IV. The right of the majority to watch television shows
       should not be limited because some unbalanced
       people may commit crimes.
    V. Still, young children should be protected from
       media violence.
       A. Parents should protect young children.
          1. Parents should monitor what children watch.
          2. Parents should watch with children and discuss
             program content.
          3. Parents should block violent shows.
       B. The media should do more to protect young
          children.
          1. Movie theaters should enforce rating systems.
          2. Violent programs should not be shown on sta-
             tions whose audience is primarily children.

Allison's outline uses roman numerals for first-level headings, capital letters for second-level headings, and numbers for third-level headings. All the outline's points are expressed in parallel terms.

For more on parallelism, see Chapter 19.

 Writing Your Paper

Once you have decided on a thesis and written an outline, you are ready to write a draft of your paper. Begin with an introduction that includes your thesis statement. Usually, your introduction will be a single paragraph; sometimes, it will be longer.

 Writing Tip
Use a thesis-and-support structure to organize your research paper. (See 12A.)

In the body of your research paper, you support your thesis statement, with each body paragraph developing a single idea. These paragraphs should have clear topic sentences so that your readers will know exactly what points you are making. Use transitional words and phrases to help readers follow the progression of your ideas.

Finally, your conclusion should give readers a sense of completion. Like your introduction, your conclusion will usually be a single paragraph, but it could be longer. It should reinforce your thesis statement and your paper's main ideas, and it should end with a memorable sentence.

Remember that you will probably write several drafts of your paper before you submit it. You can use the Self-Assessment Checklists on page 118 to revise and edit your paper.

Allison Rogers's completed paper on media violence appears on page 571.

For more on introductions and conclusions, see 13A and 13B.

● **Writing Tip**
Check to make sure you have not committed plagiarism. (See section 6 of this appendix.)

10 Documenting Your Sources

When you **document** your sources, you tell readers where you found the ideas that you have used in your paper. The Modern Language Association (MLA) recommends the following documentation style for research papers. This format consists of *parenthetical references* within a paper that refer to a *Works Cited* list at the end of the paper.

Parenthetical References in the Text

A parenthetical reference should include just enough information to guide readers to a specific entry in your Works Cited list. A typical parenthetical reference consists of the author's last name and the page number: (Grisham 2). If you use more than one work by the same author, include a shortened form of the title in the parenthetical reference: (Grisham, "Killers" 4). Notice that there is no *p* or *p.* before the page number.

Whenever possible, introduce information from a source with a phrase that includes the author's name. (If you do this, include only the page number in parentheses.)

```
As John Grisham observes in "Unnatural Killers," Oliver
Stone celebrates gratuitous violence (4).
```

Place documentation so that it doesn't interrupt the flow of your ideas, preferably at the end of a sentence.

The format for parenthetical references departs from these guidelines in three special situations.

● **Writing Tip**
For more on MLA documentation style, see the *MLA Handbook for Writers of Research Papers*, 5th ed. (New York: MLA, 1995). For guidelines for documenting Internet sources, see the *MLA Guide to Scholarly Publications*, 2nd ed. (New York: MLA, 1998) or the MLA Web site (http://www.mla.org).

When You Are Citing a Work by Two Authors

```
Film violence has been increasing during the past ten
years (Williams and Yorst 34).
```

FOCUS Formatting Quotations

■ **Short quotations** Quotations of no more than four typed lines are run in with the text of your paper. End punctuation comes after the parenthetical reference (which follows the quotation marks).

> According to Grisham, there are "only two ways to curb the excessive violence of a film like Natural Born Killers" (5).

■ **Long quotations** Quotations of more than four lines are set off from the text of your paper. Indent a long quotation ten spaces (or one inch) from the left-hand margin, and do not enclose it in quotation marks. The first line of a long quotation is not indented even if it is the beginning of a paragraph. If a quoted passage has more than one paragraph, indent the first line of each subsequent paragraph three additional spaces (or one-quarter inch). Introduce a long quotation with a complete sentence followed by a colon, and place the parenthetical reference one space *after* the end punctuation.

> Grisham believes that eventually the courts will act to force studio executives to accept responsibility for the effects of their products:
>
>> But the laughing will soon stop. It will take only one large verdict against the likes of Oliver Stone, and his production company, and perhaps the screenwriter, and the studio itself, and then the party will be over. The verdict will come from the heartland, far away from Southern California, in some small courtroom with no cameras. (5)

When You Are Citing a Work without a Listed Author

> Ever since cable television came on the scene, shows with graphically violent content have been common ("Cable Wars" 76).

When You Are Citing an Indirect Source

If you use a statement by one author that is quoted in the work of another author, show this by including the abbreviation *qtd. in* ("quoted in").

> When speaking of television drama, Leonard Eron, of the University of Illinois, says "perpetrators of violence should not be rewarded for violent acts" (qtd. in Siano 23).

| FOCUS | Preparing the Works Cited List |

- Begin the Works Cited list on a new page after the last page of your paper.
- Number the Works Cited page as the next page of your paper.
- Center the heading *Works Cited* one inch from the top of the page; don't underline the heading or put it in quotation marks.
- Double-space the list.
- List entries alphabetically according to the author's last name.
- Alphabetize unsigned articles according to the first major word of the title.
- Begin typing each entry at the left-hand margin.
- Indent second and subsequent lines five spaces (or one-half inch).
- Separate each division of the entry—author, title, and publication information—by a period and one space.

The Works Cited List

The Works Cited list includes all the works you cite (refer to) in your paper. Use the guidelines in the box above to prepare your list.

The following sample Works Cited entries cover the situations you will encounter most often. Follow the formats exactly as they appear here.

Books

Book by One Author

List the author, last name first. Underline the title. Include the city of publication and a shortened form of the publisher's name—for example, *Prentice* for *Prentice Hall* or *Random* for *Random House, Inc.* Use the abbreviation *UP* for *University Press,* as in *Princeton UP* and *U of Chicago P.* End with the date of publication.

```
Brown, Charles T. The Rock and Roll Story. Englewood
    Cliffs: Prentice, 1983.
```

Book by Two or Three Authors

List second and subsequent authors, first name first, in the order in which they are listed on the book's title page.

```
Coe, Sophie D., and Michael D. Coe. The True History of
    Chocolate. New York: Thames, 1996.
```

Book by More Than Three Authors

List only the first author, followed by the abbreviation *et al.* ("and others").

```
Sklar, Robert E., et al. Movie-Made America: A Cultural
    History of American Movies. New York: Random, 1994.
```

Two or More Books by the Same Author

List two or more books by the same author in alphabetical order according to title. In each entry after the first, use three unspaced hyphens (followed by a period) instead of the author's name.

> Angelou, Maya. Getting Together in My Name. New York:
> Bantam, 1980.
>
> ---. I Know Why the Caged Bird Sings. New York: Bantam,
> 1985.

Edited Book

> Dickinson, Emily. The Complete Poems of Emily Dickinson.
> Ed. Thomas H. Johnson. New York: Little, 1990.

Translation

> García Márquez, Gabriel. Love in the Time of Cholera.
> Trans. Edith Grossman. New York: Knopf, 1988.

Revised Edition

> Gans, Herbert J. The Urban Villagers. 2nd ed. New York:
> Free, 1982.

Anthology

> Kirszner, Laurie G., and Stephen R. Mandell, eds.
> Patterns for College Writing. 7th ed. New York:
> St. Martin's, 1998.

Essay in an Anthology

> Grisham, John. "Unnatural Killers." Patterns for College
> Writing. 7th ed. Ed. Laurie G. Kirszner and Stephen
> R. Mandell. New York: St. Martin's, 1998. 570-77.

More Than One Essay in the Same Anthology

List each essay separately with a cross-reference to the entire anthology.

> Grisham, John. "Unnatural Killers." Kirszner and Mandell
> 570-77.
> Kirszner, Laurie G., and Stephen R. Mandell, eds.
> Patterns for College Writing. 7th ed. New York:
> St. Martin's, 1998.
> Stone, Oliver. "Memo to John Grisham: What's Next--
> 'A Movie Made Me Do It'?" Kirszner and Mandell
> 580-82.

Section or Chapter of a Book

> Gordimer, Nadine. "Once upon a Time." Jump and Other
> Stories. New York: Farrar, 1991.

Periodicals

Article in a Journal with Continuous Pagination throughout an Annual Volume

Some scholarly journals have continuous pagination; that is, one issue might end on page 234, and the next would then begin with page 235. In

> ● **Writing Tip**
> When the abbreviation *ed(s).*
> follows a name, it means
> "editor(s)"; when the abbreviation *Ed.* comes before a
> name, it means "edited by."

● **Writing Tip**
When one title enclosed in quotation marks falls within another, use single quotation marks for the inside title.

this case, the volume number is followed by the date of publication in parentheses.

> Allen, Dennis W. "Horror and Perverse Delight: Faulkner's 'A Rose for Emily.'" <u>Modern Fiction Studies</u> 30 (1984): 685-96.

Article in a Journal with Separate Pagination in Each Issue

For a journal in which each issue begins with page 1, the volume number is followed by a period and the issue number and then by the date. Leave no space after the period.

> Lindemann, Erika. "Teaching as a Rhetorical Art." <u>CEA Forum</u> 15.2 (1985): 9-12.

Article in a Monthly or Bimonthly Magazine

If an article doesn't appear on consecutive pages—for example, if it begins on page 43, skips to page 47, and continues on page 49—include only the first page, followed by a plus sign.

> O'Brien, Conor Cruise. "Thomas Jefferson: Radical and Racist." <u>Atlantic Monthly</u> Oct. 1996: 43+.

Article in a Weekly or Biweekly Magazine (Signed or Unsigned)

> "The Dead Don't Tell Lies." <u>Time</u> 28 Oct. 1996: 37.

> Miller, Arthur. "Why I Wrote <u>The Crucible</u>." <u>New Yorker</u> 21 Oct. 1996: 158-63.

Article in a Newspaper

> Haberman, Clyde. "Is Graffiti 'Art'?" <u>New York Times</u> 22 Oct. 1996, late ed.: B1.

Editorial or Letter to the Editor

> "High Taxes Kill Cities." Editorial. <u>Philadelphia Inquirer</u> 8 Aug. 1995, late ed., sec. 1: 17.

Internet Sources

When citing Internet sources appearing on the World Wide Web, include both the date of electronic publication (if available) and the date you accessed the source. (Some of the following examples include only the date of access; this indicates that the date of publication was not available.)

Professional Site

> <u>Words of the Year</u>. American Dialect Society. 30 Dec. 1998 <http://www.americandialect.org/woty.shtml>.

Personal Site

> Lynch, Jack. Home page. 11 Nov. 1998 <http://dept.english.upenn.edu/~jlynch>.

Article in an Online Reference Book or Encyclopedia

> "Croatia." <u>The 1997 World Factbook</u>. 30 Mar. 1998. Central Intelligence Agency. 30 Dec. 1998 <http://www.odci.gov/cia/publications/factbook/country-frame.html>.

"Empire State Building." <u>Britannica Online</u>. Vers.
      98.1.1. Nov. 1997. Encyclopaedia Britannica. 8 Mar.
      1999 <http://www.eb.com>.

Article in a Newspaper

Lohr, Steve. "Microsoft Goes to Court." <u>New York
      Times on the Web</u> 19 Oct. 1998. 9 Apr. 1999
      <http://archives.nytimes.com/archives/search/
      fastweb?search>.

Editorial

"Be Serious." Editorial. <u>Washington Post</u> 25 Mar. 1999.
      9 Apr. 1999 <http://newslibrary.Krmediastream.com/
      cgi-bin/search/wp>.

Article in a Magazine

Webb, Michael. "Playing at Work." <u>Metropolis Online</u> Nov.
      1997. 11 Nov. 1997 <http://www.metropolismag.com/
      nov97/eames/eames.html>.

Posting to a Discussion List

Be sure to include the phrase "Online posting."

Thune, W. Scott. "Emotion and Rationality in Argument."
      Online posting. 23 Mar. 1997. CCCC/97 Online. 11
      Nov. 1997 <http://www.missouri.edu/HyperNews/get/
      cccc98/proplink/12.html>.

Other Nonprint Sources

Television or Radio Program

"Prime Suspect 3." Writ. Lynda La Plante. With Helen
      Mirren. <u>Mystery</u>! WNET, New York. 28 Apr. 1994.

Videotape, Movie, Record, or Slide Program

Murray, Donald. <u>Interview with John Updike</u>. Dir. Bruce
      Schwartz. Videocassette. Harcourt, 1997.

Personal Interview

Garcetti, Gilbert. Personal interview. 7 May 1994.

Material Accessed through a Computer Service

When citing information from a commercial computer service such as
CompuServe, America Online, or Prodigy, include the name of the computer service (America Online, for example), the date you accessed the
material, and the keyword.

Glicken, Natalie. "Brady Defends Gun Law in Court."
      <u>Congressional Quarterly</u>. America Online. 10 Oct.
      1996. Keyword: CQ.

If instead of entering a keyword, you followed a series of topic labels, indicate the path you used.

"Cloning." <u>BioTech's Life and Science Dictionary</u>. 30
      June 1998. Indiana U. America Online. 4 July 1998.

```
Path: Research and Learning; Science; Biology;
Biotechnology Dictionary.
```

If the material you are citing has appeared in print, include the print publication information before the electronic information. Use the abbreviation *n. pag.* ("no pagination") if no pages are given.

Material Accessed on a CD-ROM

In addition to the publication information, include the medium (CD-ROM), the vendor (UMI-Proquest, for example), and the date you accessed the information.

```
Braunmiller, A. R., ed. Macbeth. By William Shakespeare.
        CD-ROM. New York: Voyager, 1994.
```

Sample Research Paper in MLA Style

Following is Allison Rogers's final essay on the topic of media violence. The essay follows the conventions of MLA documentation style. It has been reproduced in a narrower format than you will have on a standard (8½" × 11") sheet of paper.

Rogers 1

Allison Rogers
English ~~122-83~~ O21.17
Essay 3
8 April 1999

Violence in the Media

Mickey and Mallory, two characters in
Oliver Stone's film <u>Natural Born Killers</u>,
travel across the Southwest, killing a total of
fifty-two people. After watching this movie,
two teenagers went on a crime spree of their
own and killed one person and wounded another,
paralyzing her for the rest of her life. At
their trial, their defense was that watching
<u>Natural Born Killers</u> had made them commit their
crimes and that Hollywood, along with the
director of the movie, Oliver Stone, was to
blame. As creative as this defense is, it is
hard to accept. The power of the media to
shape lives may be great, but no amount of
violence on the screen can eliminate a person's
responsibility for his or her actions, especially when it comes to murder.

According to John Grisham, Oliver Stone's
<u>Natural Born Killers</u> "inspired" two teenagers
"to commit murder" (5). Grisham goes on to say
that since the movie was released, several
murders have been committed by troubled young
people who claimed they were "under the influence" of Mickey and Mallory (5). This type of
defense keeps reappearing as the violence in
our everyday lives increases: "I am not to
blame," says the perpetrator. "That movie (or
television show) made me do it."

The idea that violence in the media causes
violent behavior is not supported by the facts.
When we look at Ben and Sarah, the two
teenagers who supposedly imitated Mickey and
Mallory, it is clear that factors other than

Introduction

Thesis statement

Paragraph combines quotation and
paraphrase from Grisham article with
Allison's own observations

Paragraph combines clearly documented paraphrases of Stone and Siano
articles with Allison's own conclusions

Natural Born Killers could have influenced their decision to commit murder. Both young adults had long histories of drug and alcohol abuse as well as psychiatric treatment (Stone 39). In addition, no clear experimental link between violent movies and television shows and aggressive behavior has been discovered. Many studies have shown that after watching violent television shows, children tend to act aggressively, but after about a week they return to their normal pattern of behavior (Siano 22).

What, then, are we supposed to make of crimes that seem to be inspired by the media? As Siano points out, a body of anecdotal evidence supports the link between these "copycat crimes" and media violence (24). Two problems exist with this type of "evidence," however. The first problem is that in most cases, the movie or television show is never definitely linked to the crime. For example, after the movie The Money Train was released, a clerk in a New York City subway token booth was set on fire in much the same way a subway token clerk was in the movie. Naturally, it appeared as if the movie had inspired the crime. But at the time of the crime, several newspapers reported that the violent act shown in the movie was not unusual and had in fact occurred at least twice in the year before the movie's release. So the question remains: Did the movie cause the violence, or did it simply reflect a kind of violent behavior that was already present in society? The truth is that we cannot answer this question.

The second problem with anecdotal evidence is that it is not representative. Crimes that are inspired by the media--killers imitating Freddy Krueger, for example--are unusual. As

Phrase "As Siano points out" introduces Allison's summary of source's ideas

No documentation necessary for common knowledge

Rogers 3

Siano says, most people who watch violent movies do not go out and commit crimes (24). Only a few people will have extreme reactions, and because they are mentally unbalanced, we cannot predict what will set them off. It could be a movie like Natural Born Killers, but it could also be a Bugs Bunny cartoon or a Three Stooges movie. The point is that society should not limit the right of the majority to watch the movies and television shows they want to see just because a few unbalanced individuals may go out and commit crimes.

Even if the link between media violence and violent behavior is not clear, most people agree that young children are easily influenced by what they see. One study has shown that young children who watch violent television shows behave differently from those who watch nonviolent television shows (American Psychological Association). For this reason, young children should be protected. First, parents need to understand their responsibility for monitoring what their children watch on television. This monitoring needs to begin at home, where it is the parents' job to give their children a sense of what is real and what is not. Second, as the American Psychological Association suggests, parents should take the time to watch shows along with their children and discuss the content with them. Finally, if parents cannot watch television with their children, they can at least buy devices that will prevent children from watching violent programs.

The media have already taken steps to protect children. For example, rating systems now in place can help. These give parents the ability to judge the content of movies before chil-

The two paragraphs on this page combine paraphrases from an article with Allison's own observations

Rogers 4

dren go to see them and to evaluate television shows before they are turned on. Clearly, however, more needs to be done to protect young children. For one thing, these rating systems must be enforced. If an R movie is being shown at a theater, for example, the management must require proof of age. In addition, any movie or television show containing violence should not be shown on stations whose audience is primarily children, such as Nickelodeon or the Disney Channel, even at night. The time of day should not matter. When you think of Nickelodeon or Disney, The Brady Bunch and Mickey Mouse should come to mind, not Dirty Harry (American Psychological Association).

There is no doubt that violence is learned and that violent media images encourage violent behavior. It is not clear, however, that violent movies and television shows will actually cause a person to commit a crime. Placing the blame on the media is just an easy way to sidestep the hard questions, such as what is causing so much violence in our society and what can we do about it. If we prohibit violent programs, we will only deprive many people of their right to view the programs of their choice, and we will prevent artists from expressing themselves freely. In the process, these restrictions will also deprive society of a good deal of worthwhile entertainment.

Conclusion

This paragraph needs no documentation because it represents Allison's own ideas

Rogers 5

Works Cited

American Psychological Association. "Children
    and Television Violence." School Violence
    Virtual Library 6 June 1997. 19 Oct. 1998
    <http://www.uncg.edu/edu/ericcass/violence/
    index.htm>.

Grisham, John. "Unnatural Killers." The Oxford
    American Spring 1996: 2-5.

Siano, Brian. "Frankenstein Must Be Destroyed:
    Chasing the Monster of TV Violence." The
    Humanist Jan.-Feb. 1994: 20-25.

Stone, Oliver. "Memo to John Grisham: What's
    Next--'A Movie Made Me Do It'?" LA Weekly
    29 Mar.-4 Apr. 1996: 39.

Answers to Odd-Numbered Exercises

Chapter 15

◆ **PRACTICE 15-1, page 198**

Answers: **(1)** Derek Walcott **(3)** years **(5)** poems **(7)** Walcott **(9)** poet **(11)** poet

◆ **PRACTICE 15-2, page 199**

Answers: **(1)** Prepositional phrases: With more than 27 percent of the vote, in history; subject: Theodore Roosevelt **(3)** Prepositional phrases: on the ballot, of the Prohibition Party; subject: Other candidates **(5)** Prepositional phrases: of other parties, after 1912; subject: some candidates **(7)** Prepositional phrases: In 1968, with more than 13 percent of the popular vote, behind Republican Richard M. Nixon and Democrat Hubert H. Humphrey; subject: George C. Wallace **(9)** Prepositional phrases: With nearly 19 percent of the popular vote, against Democrat Bill Clinton and Republican George Bush in 1992; subject: Ross Perot

◆ **PRACTICE 15-3, page 201**

Answers: **(1)** wrote **(3)** is **(5)** feels **(7)** lives **(9)** progresses, frightens

◆ **PRACTICE 15-4, page 203**

Answers: **(1)** Helping verb: had; rest of verb: become **(3)** Helping verb: had; rest of verb: become **(5)** Helping verb: would; rest of verb: get **(7)** Helping verb: did; rest of verb: cause **(9)** Helping verb: would; rest of verb: remain

Chapter 16

◆ **PRACTICE 16-1, page 207**

Answers: **(1)** and **(3)** and **(5)** and **(7)** so/and **(9)** for

◆ **PRACTICE 16-4, page 212**

Answers: **(1)** The United States has a long history of disastrous fires; in addition, it has a long history of innovations in fire safety. **(3)** City governments became more concerned about fires; therefore, volunteer fire companies were started in the eighteenth century. **(5)** Other innovations were clearly needed; consequently, fire alarm boxes and steam-powered fire engines were developed.

◆ **PRACTICE 16-5, page 213**

Possible edits: **(1)** *Time* selects the Man of the Year to honor the person who has most influenced the previous year's events; consequently, the choice is often a prominent politician. **(3)** In 1936, the Man of the Year was not a head of state; in fact, it was Wallis Warfield Simpson, the woman for whom King Edward VIII of England abdicated the throne. **(5)** Occasionally, the Man of the Year was not an individual; for instance, in 1950, it was The American Fighting Man. **(7)** Only a few individual women have been selected; for example, Queen Elizabeth II was featured in 1952 and Corazon Aquino in 1986.

Chapter 17

◆ **PRACTICE 17-1, page 220**

Possible edits: **(1)** After **(5)** Although **(7)** until **(9)** When

◆ **PRACTICE 17-2, page 221**

Possible edits: **1.** Although professional midwives are used widely in Europe, in the United States, they usually practice independently only in areas where there are few doctors. **3.** Stephen Crane powerfully describes battles in *The Red Badge of Courage* even though he never experienced a war. **5.** After Jonas Salk developed the first polio vaccine in the 1950s, the incidence of polio began to decline rapidly in the United States. **7.** Before the gunpowder manufacturers the Du Ponts arrived in Rhode

Island from France in 1800, American gunpowder was expensive and inferior to the kind manufactured by the French.   **9.** Because Thaddeus Stevens thought plantation land should be distributed to freed slaves, he disagreed with Lincoln's peace terms for the South.

◆ PRACTICE 17-3, page 223

Answers: **1.** This image is reinforced by a television show that started several years ago.   **3.** One Sunday, Hyota was wandering through the streets, which were full of people, looking for someone to help him.   **5.** This television program, which teaches American street expressions to Japanese viewers, is very popular.   **7.** The English they learn, which is of little use in the real world, is not enough to protect them from street hustlers.   **9.** For example, a sixteen-year-old Japanese exchange student who did not understand the command *freeze* was shot.

Chapter 18

◆ PRACTICE 18-1, page 230

Possible edits: **(3)** What is responsible for this trend?   **(9)** What a dilemma!

◆ PRACTICE 18-2, page 232

Possible edits: **(1)** In 1981, a disaster struck Kansas City, tragically killing more than one hundred people.   **(3)** Suddenly, the dancers heard a very loud cracking sound.   **(5)** As the walkways began to crash into the lobby, the dancers watched in horror.   **(7)** Then, with a loud roar, both concrete walkways collapsed into the hotel's crowded lobby bar.   **(9)** Certainly, it was a scene the survivors would not soon forget.

◆ PRACTICE 18-3, page 233

Possible edits: **(7)** In fact, one coach is rumored to have placed bounties on rival players.   **(9)** Of course, the fans also share the blame for the violence of football.

◆ PRACTICE 18-4, page 235

Answers: **1.** *Growing* up in the slums of London, Charlie Chaplin held various jobs and played small parts in vaudeville shows.   **3.** *Turning* to writing and directing, Chaplin made his first famous film, *The Tramp.*   **5.** *Moving* from silent to talking pictures, Chaplin made *City Lights* and *Modern Times.*   **7.** *Criticizing* him for his politics and his personal behavior, anticommunist crusaders attacked Chaplin in the 1950s.

◆ PRACTICE 18-5, page 236

Answers: **1.** *Interested* in writing since his high school days, Hughes published his first poem in 1921.   **3.** *Convinced* that African-American music could be translated into poetry, Hughes wrote his first book of poems, *The Weary Blues.*   **5.** *Known* primarily as a poet, Hughes also

collaborated on several plays and published a novel and a collection of stories.   **7.** *Determined* to convey his ideas to a wide audience, Hughes wrote columns for several newspapers.

◆ PRACTICE 18-6, page 238

Answers: **(1)** These college presidents and their supporters want to improve the academic performance of college athletes.   **(3)** A second proposal requires athletes to earn a certain number of credits every year and mandates a similar advancement in an athlete's grade point average.   **(5)** Many Big East coaches believe standardized test scores are biased and want their use in screening student athletes banned.   **(7)** According to supporters, however, many athletes under the current system fail to advance academically and often finish their eligibility fifty or more hours short of graduation.   **(9)** In the supporters' view, poor supervision by athletic directors and lack of support for academic excellence are to be blamed for the poor performance of student athletes.

◆ PRACTICE 18-7, page 239

Possible edits: **(1)** Alfred Hitchcock's first big success came in 1935 with *The Thirty-Nine Steps,* a thriller about an innocent man mistaken for a criminal.   **(3)** His first Hollywood film was the suspense classic *Rebecca,* a 1940 film version of a popular novel by Daphne du Maurier.   **(5)** His most controversial film, *Psycho,* stars Anthony Perkins as the mentally unstable proprietor of the Bates Motel, as well as his own "mother."   **(7)** A well-known television personality as well as a film director, Hitchcock hosted two successful series in the late 1950s and the early 1960s.   **(9)** One of the great masters of film technique, Hitchcock made movies admired by both popular audiences and academic critics.

◆ PRACTICE 18-8, page 241

Possible edits: Kente cloth is made in western Africa and produced primarily by the Ashanti people. It has been worn for hundreds of years by African royalty, who consider it a sign of power and status. Many African Americans wear kente cloth because they see it as a link to their heritage. Each motif or pattern on the cloth has a name, and each color has a special significance. For example, red and yellow suggest a long and healthy life, while green and white suggest a good harvest. Although African women may wear kente cloth as a dress or head wrap, African-American women, like men, usually wear strips of cloth around their shoulders. Men and women of African descent wear kente cloth as a sign of black pride.

Chapter 19

◆ PRACTICE 19-1, page 249

Answers: **1.** Parallel   **3.** They also admit that cigarettes are expensive, smelly, and dangerous.   **5.** Being happy in life is more important to me than making a lot of money.   **7.** Judges must care about justice, uphold the laws, and treat defendants fairly.   **9.** Love is blind, but hate is blinder.

◆ **PRACTICE 19-3, page 249**

Answers: **1.** Pasadena, Claremont, and Pomona are major cities in the valley. **3.** Watching the big Tournament of Roses Parade is more exciting than viewing the Macy's Thanksgiving parade. **5.** Judges rate the rose-covered floats on their originality, artistic merit, and overall impact. **7.** The Rose Bowl game is not only America's oldest collegiate championship but also the country's most popular bowl game. **9.** Visitors come to play challenging skill games and enjoy various ethnic foods.

Chapter 20

◆ **PRACTICE 20-1, page 256**

Answers: **(1)** three fifty-watt bulbs; coal oil; baking bread **(3)** wooden table; unfinished game of checkers; apple-tree stump

◆ **PRACTICE 20-4, page 259**

Possible edits: **(1)** Adult children can become frustrated because their parents seem to treat them as if they were not capable of making their own decisions. **(3)** When this happens, the children may begin to whine childishly or even throw a temper tantrum although such behavior only reinforces their parents' attitude. **(5)** To get parents to stop being critical, an adult child might turn the tables and encourage his or her parents to talk about their own childhoods. **(7)** Adult children might also explain that while they value their parents' opinion, they are still going to make their own decisions. **(9)** Although parents may have been telling these stories the same way for years, the child may have a very different perspective on the event.

◆ **PRACTICE 20-5, page 260**

Possible edits: **(1)** Marcia Morris believes that in all species the female makes the original choice of mate. **(3)** After this, she begins to send signals to show that he may approach. **(5)** She and her assistants visited singles bars to observe and to record their observations. **(7)** After they turn away, they may toss their heads, flip their hair, or laugh. **(9)** Ultimately, Morris's studies show that a woman's ability to get a man to talk to her depends less on her looks than on her flirting skills.

◆ **PRACTICE 20-6, page 261**

Possible edits: **(1)** Clichés: working like a dog; living high on the hog. Many people think that a million-dollar lottery jackpot allows the winner to stop working long hours and start living a comfortable life. **(3)** Cliché: hit the jackpot. For one thing, lottery winners who win big prizes do not receive their winnings all at once; instead, payments—$50,000—are usually spread out over twenty years. **(5)** Clichés: with their hands out; between a rock and a hard place. Next come relatives and friends who ask for money, leaving winners with difficult choices to make. **(7)** Cliché: adding insult to injury. Even worse, many lottery winners have lost their jobs because employers thought that once they were "millionaires," they no longer needed to draw a salary. **(9)** Cliché: in their hour of need. Faced with financial difficulties, many would like to sell their future earnings to companies that offer lump-sum payments of forty to forty-five cents on the dollar.

◆ **PRACTICE 20-7, page 263**

Answers: **1.** Simile: as a newly laid egg. **3.** Simile: like the inside of a jellyfish. **5.** Simile: like a lopsided wedding cake.

◆ **PRACTICE 20-10, page 266**

Answers: **1.** Many people today would like to see more police officers patrolling the streets. **3.** The attorneys representing the plaintiff are Geraldo Diaz and Barbara Wilkerson. **5.** Travel to other planets will be a significant step for humanity.

Chapter 21

◆ **PRACTICE 21-1, page 273**

Answers: **(1)** Run-on **(3)** Run-on **(5)** Run-on **(7)** Correct **(9)** Correct **(11)** Correct

◆ **PRACTICE 21-2, page 276**

Possible edits: **1.** Nursing offers job security and high pay; therefore, many people are choosing nursing as a career. **3.** The Democratic Republic of the Congo was previously known as Zaire; before that, it was the Belgian Congo. **5.** Millions of Jews were killed during the Holocaust; in addition, Catholics, Gypsies, homosexuals, and other "undesirables" were killed. **7.** First-generation Japanese Americans are called nisei; second-generation Japanese Americans are called sansei. **9.** Père Noel is another name for Santa Claus; he is also known as Father Christmas and St. Nicholas.

◆ **PRACTICE 21-3, page 277**

Possible edits: **(1)** Harlem, which was populated mostly by European immigrants at the turn of the century, saw an influx of African Americans beginning in 1910. **(3)** Many African-American artists and writers settled in Harlem during the 1920s, which led to a flowering of African-American art. **(5)** When scholars of the era recognize the great works produced then, they point to writers such as Langston Hughes and Countee Cullen and sculptors such as Henry Tanner and Sargent Johnson. **(7)** Because Harlem was an exciting place in the 1920s, people from all over the city went there to hear jazz and to dance. **(9)** While contemporary African-American artists know about the Harlem Renaissance, it is still not so familiar to others.

◆ **PRACTICE 21-4, page 278**

Possible edits: In the late nineteenth century, Coney Island was famous; in fact, it was legendary. Every summer, it was crowded, and people mailed hundreds of

ANSWERS TO
ODD-NUMBERED EXERCISES

◆ **PRACTICE 21-4, page 278** *(continued)*

thousands of postcards from the resort on some days. Coney Island, which was considered exotic and exciting, even boasted a hotel shaped like an elephant. Although some saw Coney Island as seedy, others thought it was a wonderful, magical place. It had beaches, hotels, racetracks, and a stadium; however, by the turn of the century, it was best known for three amusement parks. These parks were Luna Park, Steeplechase, and Dreamland. Even though gaslight was still the norm in New York, a million electric lights lit Luna Park. While Steeplechase offered many rides, its main attraction was a two-mile ride on mechanical horses. At Dreamland, people could see a submarine; in addition, they could travel through an Eskimo village or visit Lilliputia, with its three hundred midgets. Today, the old Coney Island no longer exists. Fire destroyed Dreamland in 1911, and Luna Park burned down in 1946. In 1964, Steeplechase closed. The once-grand Coney Island is gone. Still, its beach and its boardwalk endure. Its famous roller coaster, the Cyclone, still exists, and its giant Ferris wheel, the Wonder Wheel, keeps on turning. Maybe someday the old Coney Island will be reborn.

Chapter 22

◆ **PRACTICE 22-1, page 283**

Rewrite: Sara Paretsky writes detective novels such as *Burn Marks* and *Guardian Angel*. The novels are about V.I. Warshawski, a private detective. V.I. lives and works in Chicago, the Windy City. Every day as a detective, V.I. takes risks. V.I. is tough. She is also a woman.

◆ **PRACTICE 22-3, page 289**

Possible edits: **(1)** Many homeless people are mentally ill. **(3)** People disagree about the effects of violence in children's television shows. **(5)** Competition among college students for athletic scholarships increased. **(7)** Pizza is high in fat. **(9)** Something is likely to change.

Chapter 23

◆ **PRACTICE 23-1, page 298**

Answers: **(1)** cares **(3)** come **(5)** stands **(7)** watches **(9)** come; go **(11)** stay **(13)** serve **(15)** donates **(17)** spend

◆ **PRACTICE 23-2, page 299**

Answers: **(1)** Lynn writes with a computer. **(3)** I use one too. **(5)** Each week, Ms. Keane and Mr. Marlowe give back the disks. **(7)** I put my disk into the computer and read Mr. Marlowe's comments as I revise. **(9)** One student says he hates the computer, however.

◆ **PRACTICE 23-3, page 301**

Answers: **(1)** Biologists have serious worries about the damage that exotic animals can cause when they move into places where native species have developed few defenses against them. **(3)** It has a role in the decline in the number of bluebirds. **(5)** Introduced by early explorers, they currently do much damage to the eggs of giant tortoises that live on the islands. **(7)** This is a situation caused by fish and wildlife agencies that deliberately introduce exotic fish into lakes and streams. **(9)** Although popular with people who fish, this policy has major drawbacks.

◆ **PRACTICE 23-4, page 303**

Answers: **1.** Subject: cupids; verb: symbolize **3.** Subject: appliances; verb: make **5.** Subject: set; verb: costs **7.** Subject: Workers; verb: pay **9.** Subject: Volunteers; verb: help

◆ **PRACTICE 23-5, page 304**

Answers: **(1)** Some of the streams no longer have any fish. **(3)** Everybody wants to improve the situation. **(5)** Somebody always takes control. **(7)** Neither of the candidates seems willing to act. **(9)** According to the candidates, everything is being done that can be done.

◆ **PRACTICE 23-6, page 306**

Answers: **1.** Subject: Bering Straits; verb: are **3.** Subject: twins; verb: Are **5.** Subject: this; verb: has **7.** Subject: people; verb: are **9.** Subject: reasons; verb: are

◆ **PRACTICE 23-7, page 307**

Answers: **(1)** Subject: story; verb: has **(3)** Subject: narrator; verb: has **(5)** Subject: Madeline; verb: lives **(7)** Subject: vault; verb: is **(9)** Subject: Roderick; verb: is

Chapter 24

◆ **PRACTICE 24-1, page 311**

Answers: **(1)** When Beverly Harvard became the chief of the Atlanta police force in 1994, she was the first African-American woman ever to hold that title in a major U.S. city. **(3)** Now, more than half the department is African American, and women make up about a quarter of the force. **(5)** Her husband even agreed to pay her $100 if she made it on to the force. **(7)** In fact, when she entered the police academy, she did not really plan to be a police officer. She just wanted to prove her husband wrong and to win the $100 bet. **(9)** When her promotion was announced, some veteran officers criticized her appointment as police chief, but most younger officers praised the choice.

◆ **PRACTICE 24-2, page 313**

Answers: **(1)** Young people who want a career in the fashion industry don't always realize how hard they will have to work. **(3)** In reality, no matter how talented he or she is, a recent college graduate entering the industry is paid only about $18,000 a year. **(5)** A young designer may receive a big raise if he or she is very talented, but this is unusual. **(7)** Employees may be excited to land a job as an assistant designer but then find that they color in designs that have already been drawn. **(9)** If a person is serious about working in the fashion industry, he or she has to be realistic.

◆ **PRACTICE 24-3, page 315**
Possible edits: **(1)** According to recent studies, a juror may have his or her mind made up before the trial even begins. **(3)** This unfounded conclusion often depends on which attorney makes his or her initial description of the case the most dramatic. **(5)** Jurors with poor decision-making skills are also not likely to listen to challenges to their opinions when the full jury comes together to deliberate. **(7)** Correct **(9)** For example, one juror argued that a man being tried for murder was acting in his own defense because the victim was probably carrying a knife, but no knife was mentioned during the trial.

◆ **PRACTICE 24-4, page 317**
Possible edits: **1.** The coach finished his pep talk and then asked if we were ready to win. **3.** The union leaders announced, "The strike is over." **5.** Oprah Winfrey asked the audience whether they sympathized more with the husband or the wife.

◆ **PRACTICE 24-5, page 319**
Answers: **1.** A local university funded the study, and Dr. Alicia Flynn led the research team. **3.** Two-thirds of the subjects relied on instinct alone while only one-third used logical analysis. **5.** Many experts read the report, and most of them found the results surprising.

Chapter 25

◆ **PRACTICE 25-1, page 325**
Answers: **(1)** Present participle modifier: Evolving out of street-corner singing; modifies: Doo Wop **(3)** Present participle modifier: Living in the Bronx; modifies: he **(5)** Present participle modifier: Cutting one hit after another; modifies: Frankie Lymon and the Teen Agers **(7)** Present participle modifier: Returning to the streets they had left; modifies: Doo Wop artists **(9)** Present participle modifier: Lying for years in an unmarked grave in a Bronx cemetery; modifies: Lymon

◆ **PRACTICE 25-2, page 327**
Answers: **(1)** Past participle modifier: The best-preserved fossil ever found; modifies: it **(3)** Past participle modifier: excited by the find; modifies: hunters **(5)** Past participle modifier: Supported by previous rulings; modifies: judge **(7)** Past participle modifier: Questioned by the press; modifies: hunters **(9)** Past participle modifier: Shocked by the ruling; modifies: dealer

◆ **PRACTICE 25-5, page 332**
Answers: **1.** Frightened by a noise, the cat broke the vase. **3.** Lori looked at the man with red hair sitting in the chair. **5.** With their deadly venom, snakes sometimes kill people. **7.** Jumping out of bed in my bathrobe, I saw a sleigh and eight tiny reindeer. **9.** Wearing a mask, the exterminator sprayed the bug.

Chapter 26

◆ **PRACTICE 26-1, page 340**
Answers: **(1)** owned **(3)** browsed **(5)** turned; wanted **(7)** insisted **(9)** kicked

◆ **PRACTICE 26-2, page 342**
Answers: **(1)** broke **(3)** won **(5)** felt; lost **(7)** let **(9)** fell **(11)** left

◆ **PRACTICE 26-3, page 344**
Answers: **(1)** Correct **(3)** were **(5)** were **(7)** wasn't **(9)** Correct

◆ **PRACTICE 26-4, page 346**
Answers: **(1)** could **(3)** will **(5)** could **(7)** would **(9)** could

Chapter 27

◆ **PRACTICE 27-1, page 351**
Answers: **(1)** started **(3)** appeared **(5)** expanded **(7)** consumed **(9)** changed

◆ **PRACTICE 27-2, page 354**
Answers: **1.** found **3.** drawn **5.** seen **7.** gotten; grown **9.** begun

◆ **PRACTICE 27-3, page 355**
Answers: **(1)** The war against wearing fur has become a major campaign in recent years. **(3)** Organizations have fought to convince clothing designers not to work with fur, and their efforts have been surprisingly successful. **(5)** Many celebrities have chosen to take a public stand against furs, and several well-known models have given their time to pose for anti-fur ads. **(7)** Some critics complain that many of the more radical activists have gone too far. **(9)** Others have stolen furs as they were being shipped from warehouses.

◆ **PRACTICE 27-4, page 357**
Answers: **(1)** have been **(3)** named **(5)** had **(7)** adopted **(9)** have given

◆ **PRACTICE 27-5, page 357**
Answers: **(1)** have presented **(3)** devised **(5)** has become **(7)** have begun

◆ **PRACTICE 27-6, page 359**

Answers: **1.** had left **3.** had arrived **5.** had lied
7. had decided **9.** had been

◆ **PRACTICE 27-7, page 360**

Answers: **(1)** surprised; preapproved **(3)** designed;
inscribed **(5)** stuffed **(7)** concerned; haven't been able
to **(9)** acquired

Chapter 28

◆ **PRACTICE 28-1, page 366**

Answers: **1.** headaches (regular) **3.** feet (irregular)
5. deer (irregular) **7.** brides-to-be (irregular) **9.** loaves
(irregular) **11.** beaches (regular) **13.** sons-in-law
(irregular) **15.** wives (irregular) **17.** elves (irregular)
19. catalogs (regular)

◆ **PRACTICE 28-2, page 366**

Answers: **(1)** I recently talked to a group of unmarried
friends about what they look for in a person of the opposite sex. **(3)** Both just-for-fun dates and potential hus-
bands-to-be were considered real catches if they had
decent jobs or were working in that direction, if they were
considerate and honest, and if they had good senses of
humor. **(5)** They wanted dates to be good-looking, to
have outgoing personalities, and to have independent
lives of their own. **(7)** Sometimes I think the two sexes
are different species.

◆ **PRACTICE 28-3, page 368**

Answers: **(1)** I **(3)** they; I **(5)** we; I **(7) it**

◆ **PRACTICE 28-4, page 369**

Answers: **(1)** Antecedent: campuses; pronoun: they
(3) Antecedent: students; pronoun: their **(5)** Antecedent: Joyce; pronoun: she **(7)** Antecedent: friends;
pronoun: them

◆ **PRACTICE 28-5, page 370**

Answers: **(1)** they **(3)** it **(5)** He **(7)** It

◆ **PRACTICE 28-6, page 371**

Answers: **1.** Compound antecedent: Larry and Curly;
connecting word: and; pronoun: their **3.** Compound
antecedent: Stan and Ollie; connecting word: and; pronoun: their **5.** Compound antecedent: *MASH* or *The
Fugitive*; connecting word: or; pronoun: its **7.** Compound antecedent: film and videotape; connecting word:
and; pronoun: their **9.** Compound antecedent: popcorn
and soft drinks; connecting word: and; pronoun: their

◆ **PRACTICE 28-7, page 373**

Answers: **1.** Indefinite pronoun antecedent: Either; pronoun: its **3.** Indefinite pronoun antecedent: Everything;
pronoun: its **5.** Indefinite pronoun antecedent: Neither;

pronoun: their **7.** Indefinite pronoun antecedent: Several; pronoun: their **9.** Indefinite pronoun antecedent:
Anyone; pronoun: his or her

◆ **PRACTICE 28-8, page 374**

Possible edits: **1.** Everyone has the right to his or her
own opinion. **3.** Somebody must have forgotten to take
his or her shower this morning. **5.** Someone in the store
has left his or her car's lights on. **7.** Each of the applicants must have his or her associate's degree. **9.** Either
of the coffeemakers comes with its own filter.

◆ **PRACTICE 28-9, page 375**

Answers: **1.** Collective noun antecedent: company; pronoun: its **3.** Collective noun antecedent: government;
pronoun: its **5.** Collective noun antecedent: family; pronoun: its **7.** Collective noun antecedent: team; pronoun:
its **9.** Collective noun antecedent: gang; pronoun: its

◆ **PRACTICE 28-10, page 376**

Answers: **(3)** Correct **(5)** its; their **(7)** his or her
(9) its; correct **(11)** his or her

◆ **PRACTICE 28-11, page 380**

Answers: **(1)** me **(3)** him **(5)** I **(7)** Correct; me
(9) They

◆ **PRACTICE 28-12, page 381**

Answers: **1.** she [is] **3.** she [does] **5.** we [have]
7. they [serve] **9.** [it fits] me

◆ **PRACTICE 28-13, page 381**

Answers: **1.** who **3.** who **5.** who **7.** who **9.** who

◆ **PRACTICE 28-14, page 383**

Answers: **1.** themselves **3.** himself **5.** yourself **7.**
itself **9.** themselves

Chapter 29

◆ **PRACTICE 29-1, page 389**

Answers: **(1)** poorly **(3)** truly **(5)** really **(7)** specifically **(9)** important; immediately

◆ **PRACTICE 29-2, page 391**

Answers: **(1)** good **(3)** good **(5)** good **(7)** well
(9) good

◆ **PRACTICE 29-3, page 393**

Answers: **1.** more slowly **3.** healthier **5.** more loudly
7. more respectful **9.** wilder

◆ **PRACTICE 29-4, page 394**

Answers: **(1)** largest **(3)** most successful **(5)** most
powerful **(7)** most serious **(9)** most popular

◆ **PRACTICE 29-5, page 395**

Answers: **1.** better **3.** better; worse **5.** better **7.** best
9. better

Chapter 31

◆ PRACTICE 31-1, page 422

Possible edits: **1.** A triple-threat musician, he plays guitar, bass, and drums. **3.** *The Price Is Right, Let's Make a Deal,* and *Jeopardy!* are three of the longest-running game shows in television history. **5.** The remarkable diary kept by a young Anne Frank while her family was in hiding from the Nazis is insightful, touching, and sometimes humorous. **7.** Most coffins manufactured in the United States are lined with bronze, copper, or lead. **9.** California's capital is Sacramento, its largest city is Los Angeles, and its oldest settlement is San Diego.

◆ PRACTICE 31-2, page 423

Answers: **(1)** During the 1992 Summer Olympics in Barcelona, two American athletes and several athletes from other countries were sent home because they tested positive for banned drugs. **(3)** Correct **(5)** Banned by the rules of the Olympics, these drugs still appeal to athletes because they supposedly enhance performance. **(7)** Often called dietary supplements, these alternative chemicals are claimed to enhance athletic performance in the same way steroids supposedly do. **(9)** Instead of enhancing performance, they often cause considerable damage to the body.

◆ PRACTICE 31-3, page 424

Answers: **(1)** For example, the African-American celebration of Kwanzaa is less than forty years old. **(3)** By the way, the word *Kwanzaa* means "first fruits" in Swahili. **(5)** This can, in fact, be demonstrated in some of the seven principles of Kwanzaa. **(7)** The focus, first of all, is on unity (*umoja*). **(9)** In addition, Kwanzaa celebrations emphasize three kinds of community responsibility (*ujima, ujamaa,* and *nia*).

◆ PRACTICE 31-4, page 426

Answers: **1.** Traditional Chinese medicine is based on meridians, channels of energy believed to run in regular patterns through the body. **3.** Herbal medicine, the basis of many Chinese healing techniques, requires twelve years of study. **5.** Correct **7.** Nigeria, the most populous country in Africa, is also one of the fastest-growing nations in the world. **9.** The Yoruban people, the Nigerian settlers of Lagos, are unusual in Africa because they tend to form large urban communities.

◆ PRACTICE 31-5, page 428

Answers: **(1)** Correct **(3)** Correct **(5)** The highway, which cut through some of the roughest terrain in the world, was begun in 1942. **(7)** Military officials who oversaw the project doubted the ability of African-American troops. **(9)** Correct **(11)** Correct **(13)** Correct

◆ PRACTICE 31-6, page 430

Answers: **1.** The American Declaration of Independence was approved on July 4, 1776. **3.** At 175 Carlton Avenue, Brooklyn, New York, is the house where Richard Wright began writing *Native Son*. **5.** Correct **7.** The Pueblo Grande Museum is located at 1469 East Washington Street, Phoenix, Arizona. **9.** St. Louis, Missouri, was the birthplace of writer Maya Angelou, but she spent most of her childhood in Stamps, Arkansas.

Chapter 32

◆ PRACTICE 32-1, page 436

Answers: **(1)** We're all trying hard to watch our diets, but it's not easy. **(3)** Maybe we shouldn't be so tempted, but it's hard to resist the lure of the fast-food chains and their commercials. **(5)** When we're away from home and hungry, it's the picture of that burger that pops into our minds. **(7)** It shouldn't be so hard to find a fast, healthy meal. **(9)** It's still not the perfect meal for a dieter, but it isn't too bad.

◆ PRACTICE 32-2, page 437

Answers: **1.** the singer's video **3.** the writer's first novel **5.** the players' union **7.** the children's bedroom **9.** everyone's dream

◆ PRACTICE 32-3, page 438

Answers: **1.** everyone's; businesses' **3.** firm's; correct **5.** years'; correct **7.** Correct; family's **9.** Correct; children's

◆ PRACTICE 32-4, page 440

Answers: **1.** Parents; theirs **3.** its; weeks **5.** Reagans; years; correct **7.** classes; correct; your **9.** tests; correct

Chapter 33

◆ PRACTICE 33-1, page 446

Answers: **(1)** Midwest; Lake Michigan; Chicago; O'Hare International Airport; nation's **(3)** north; Soldier's Field; Chicago Bears; Wrigley Field; Chicago Cubs; American League; baseball team **(5)** John Kinzie **(7)** United States; Mrs.; cow **(9)** mother; Aunt Jean; Uncle Amos

◆ PRACTICE 33-2, page 448

Answers: **1.** "We who are about to die salute you," said the gladiators to the emperor. **3.** "The bigger they are," said boxer John L. Sullivan, "the harder they fall." **5.** Lisa Marie replied, "I do." **7.** When asked for the jury's verdict, the foreman replied, "Not guilty." **9.** "Yabba dabba doo," exclaimed Fred when the brontoburger arrived.

◆ PRACTICE 33-3, page 449

Answers: **1.** Essayist Simone de Beauvoir wrote, "One is not born a woman; one becomes one." **3.** "Tribe follows tribe," said Suquamish Chief Seattle in 1854, "and nation follows nation." **5.** Sojourner Truth said, "The rich rob

584

ANSWERS TO
ODD-NUMBERED EXERCISES

◆ **PRACTICE 33-3, page 449** *(continued)*

the poor, and the poor rob one another." **7.** Harriet Tubman said, "When I found I had crossed that line, I looked at my hands to see if I was the same person." **9.** "No man chooses evil because it is evil," wrote Mary Wollstonecraft in 1790. "He only mistakes it for happiness."

◆ **PRACTICE 33-4, page 452**

Answers: **1.** *Plan Nine from Outer Space* **3.** *Born to Sing;* "You Don't Have to Worry"; "Time Goes On"; "Just Can't Stay Away" **5.** *The Simpsons; Beverly Hills 90210; Melrose Place; Party of Five; In Living Color*

◆ **PRACTICE 33-5, page 452**

Answers: **1.** Sui Sin Far's short story "The Wisdom of the New," from her book *Mrs. Spring Fragrance,* is about the clash between Chinese and American cultures in the early twentieth century. **3.** Interesting information about fighting skin cancer can be found in the article "Putting Sunscreens to the Test" that appeared in the magazine *Consumer Reports.* **5.** Wayne Wang has directed several well-received films, including *The Joy Luck Club* and *Smoke.* **7.** The title of Lorraine Hansberry's play *A Raisin in the Sun* comes from Langston Hughes's poem "Harlem."

◆ **PRACTICE 33-6, page 454**

Answers: **(1)** In its earliest years, *General Hospital* featured three main characters: Audrey March, Steve Hardy, and Jessie Brewer. **(3)** Tom Beradino—a former major league baseball player—played Steve Hardy, a doctor. **(5)** When she finally managed to adopt a child, he was kidnapped by her first husband (the evil Tom Baldwin). **(7)** Now, more than thirty years after the soap's debut, newer characters—Monica, Alan, Bobbi, and Lucky—have very different problems. **(9)** New tragedies—and also new triumphs—have been experienced by the characters.

Chapter 34

◆ **PRACTICE 34-1, page 461**

Answers: **1.** weigh; correct **3.** Correct; deceive; believing **5.** Correct; veins; correct **7.** Their; correct; grief **9.** variety; foreign

◆ **PRACTICE 34-2, page 462**

Answers: **1.** unhappy **3.** preexisting **5.** unnecessary **7.** impatient **9.** overreact

◆ **PRACTICE 34-3, page 463**

Answers: **1.** lonely **3.** revising **5.** desirable **7.** microscopic **9.** ninth **11.** effectiveness **13.** fortunate **15.** argument **17.** advertisement **19.** careless

◆ **PRACTICE 34-4, page 464**

Answers: **1.** happiness **3.** denying **5.** readiness **7.** destroyer **9.** fortyish **11.** cried **13.** business **15.** spying **17.** livelihood **19.** joyful

◆ **PRACTICE 34-5, page 465**

Answers: **1.** hoped **3.** resting **5.** revealing **7.** unzipped **9.** cramming **11.** appealing **13.** referring **15.** omitted **17.** fatter **19.** repelled

◆ **PRACTICE 34-6, page 467**

Answers: **1.** effects; already **3.** buy; correct **5.** Correct; correct **7.** by; effects **9.** Correct; affect

◆ **PRACTICE 34-7, page 468**

Answers: **1.** Here; every day **3.** Correct; conscience **5.** conscious; its **7.** here; correct; it's **9.** hear; correct

◆ **PRACTICE 34-8, page 470**

Answers: **1.** past; knew **3.** peace; correct **5.** Correct; laid **7.** passed; correct **9.** know; correct; mind

◆ **PRACTICE 34-9, page 472**

Answers: **1.** plane; correct **3.** supposed; quiet **5.** principal; correct **7.** quite; plane **9.** correct; quiet

◆ **PRACTICE 34-10, page 473**

Answers: **1.** there; correct **3.** threw; correct **5.** to; they're **7.** Correct; through **9.** Correct; used

◆ **PRACTICE 34-11, page 475**

Answers: **1.** whose; correct **3.** where; correct **5.** Correct; whether; correct **7.** who's; your **9.** you're; where

Acknowledgments (continued from copyright page)

Chapter 14 exercises: *Practice 14-3:* Rick Berkowitz/Index Stock Imagery; *Practice 14-6:* Culver Pictures; *Practice 14-9:* Frank Siteman/Monkmeyer; *Practice 14-12:* Rube Goldberg. 2 cartoons: "Professor Butts' Moth Exterminator" and "An Automatic Back Scratcher." All rights reserved by Rube Goldberg Incorporated, 40 Central Park South 7E, New York, NY 10019-1633, telephone: (212) 371-3760, fax: (212) 371-3761. Reprinted by permission of United Media; *Practice 14-15:* Bob Daemmrich/Stock, Boston; *Practice 14-18:* (top) Dennis Macdonald/Index Stock Imagery, (bottom) Adam Tanner/The Image Works; *Practice 14-21:* Todd Phillips/Index Stock Imagery; *Practice 14-24:* (top left) Ken Cavanagh/Photo Researchers, (top right) Sybil Shackman/Monkmeyer, (bottom left) Bob Daemmrich/Stock, Boston, (bottom right) James Wilson/Woodfin Camp & Associates; *Practice 14-27:* UPI/Corbis.

Text acknowledgments

Maya Angelou, "Graduation." Excerpt taken from I Know Why the Caged Bird Sings. Copyright © 1969 by Maya Angelou. Reprinted with the permission of Random House, Inc.

Russell Baker. "Slice of Life." From the *New York Times*, November 24, 1974. Copyright © 1974 by The New York Times Company. Reprinted by permission.

Lynda Barry, "The Sanctuary of School." From the *New York Times*, January 5, 1992. Copyright © 1992 by the *New York Times* Company. Reprinted by permission.

Tom Bodett, "Wait Divisions." Taken from *Small Comforts: More Comments and Comic Pieces* by Tom Bodett. Copyright © 1987 by Tom Bodett. Reprinted by permission of Perseus Books Publishers, a member of Perseus Books, L.L.C.

Jose Antonio Burciaga, "Tortillas." Originally titled "I Remember Mama" from *Weedee Peepo* by Jose Antonio Burciaga. Copyright © 1988 by Jose Antonio Burciaga. Reprinted with the permission of the author.

Judith Ortiz Cofer, "Don't Call Me a Hot Tamale." Originally titled "The Myth of the Latin Woman: I Just Met a Girl Named Maria" from *Latin Deli: Prose and Poetry* by Judith Ortiz Cofer. Copyright © 1993 by Judith Ortiz Cofer. Reprinted by permission of University of Georgia Press.

Christopher B. Daly, "How the Lawyers Stole Winter." Copyright © 1995 Christopher B. Daly, as first appeared in the *Atlantic Monthly*. Reprinted by permission of the author.

Barbara Ehrenreich, "In Defense of Talk Shows." From *Time*, December 4, 1995. Copyright © 1995 Time, Inc. Reprinted by permission.

Martin Gansberg, "Thirty-Eight Who Saw Murder Didn't Call the Police." From the *New York Times*, March 27, 1964. Copyright © 1964 by the New York Times Company, Inc. Reprinted by permission.

Ellen Goodman, "The Suspected Shopper." From *Keeping in Touch* by Ellen Goodman. Copyright © 1985 by Ellen Goodman. Reprinted with the permission of Simon & Schuster, Inc.

John Gray, excerpt taken from *Men Are from Mars, Women Are from Venus* by John Gray. Copyright © 1992 by John Gray. Reprinted by permission of HarperCollins, Inc.

Lawrence Otis Graham, "The Black Table Is Still There." From the *New York Times*, February 3, 1991. Copyright © 1991 by The New York Times Company, Inc. Reprinted by permission.

Joyce Howe, "Indelible Marks." From the *Village Voice*, February 1983. Reprinted by permission.

Martin Luther King Jr., "I Have a Dream." Copyright © 1963 by Martin Luther King Jr., copyright renewed 1991 Coretta Scott King. Reprinted by arrangement with The Heirs to the Estate of Martin Luther King, Jr., c/o Writers House, Inc. as agent for the proprietor.

Charles Krauthammer, "The New Prohibitionism." From *Time*, October 6, 1997. Copyright © 1997 Time, Inc. Reprinted by permission.

Barbara Mujica, "No Comprendo." From the *New York Times*, February 21, 1962. Copyright © 1962 by The New York Times Company. Reprinted by permission.

Anna Quindlen, "The Old Block." Excerpt from *Thinking Out Loud* by Anna Quindlen. Copyright © 1993 by Anna Quindlen. Reprinted by permission of Random House, Inc.

Anna Quindlen, "Barbie at 35." From the *New York Times*, August 10, 1994. Copyright © 1994 by The New York Times Company. Reprinted by permission.

Index

*Note: Numbers in **bold** type indicate pages where terms are defined.*